KOREAN CHALLENGES AND AMERICAN POLICY

The Washington Institute for Values in Public Policy
The Washington Institute sponsors research that helps provide
the information and fresh insights necessary for formulating policy
in a democratic society. Founded in 1982, the Institute is an
independent, non-profit educational and research organization
which examines current and upcoming issues with particular
attention to ethical implications.

ADDITIONAL TITLES

Building Sino-American Relations: An Analysis for the 1990s
Edited by William T. Tow (1991)

Reform and Transformation in Communist Systems: Comparative Perspectives
Edited by Ilpyong J. Kim and Jane Shapiro Zacek (1991)

The Carter Years: Toward a New Global Order
By Richard C. Thornton (1991)

Asian-Pacific Regional Security
Edited by June Teufel Dreyer (1990)

Confucianism and Economic Development: An Oriental Alternative
Edited by Hung-chao Tai (1989)

Vietnam: Strategy for a Stalemate
By F. Charles Parker (1989)

The Politics of Latin American Liberation Theology:
Challenges to U.S. Public Policy
Edited by Richard L. Rubenstein and John K. Roth (1988)

The East Wind Subsides: Chinese Foriegn Policy
and the Origins of the Cultural Revolution
By Andrew Hall Wedeman (1987)

Rebuilding a Nation: Philippine Challenges and American Policy
Edited by Carl H. Landé (1987)

Strategic Defenses and Arms Control
Edited by Alvin M. Weinberg and Jack N. Barkenbus (1987)

KOREAN CHALLENGES AND AMERICAN POLICY

Edited by
Ilpyong J. Kim

A Washington Institute Book

PARAGON HOUSE
New York

Published in the United States by

Paragon House Publishers
90 Fifth Avenue
New York, New York 10011

© 1991 by The Washington Institute for Values in Public Policy
First printing, June 1991

A Washington Institute Book

Cover design by Evangeline P. Josephides

Library of Congress Cataloging-in-Publication Data

Korean Challenges and American Policy / edited by Ilpyong J. Kim

608 p.
"A Washington Institute Book"
Includes bibliographical references and index.
ISBN 0-88702-056-9 (pbk.)
1. United States—Relations—Korea (South) 2. Korea
(South)—Relations—United States. 3. Korea (South)—Politics and
government—1960- I. Kim, Ilpyong J., 1930.
E183.8.K6K68 1990

327.7305195—dc20   90-20958
                                    CIP

Manufactured in the United States of America

Table of Contents

List of Tables

Preface

Ilpyong J. Kim

A MAJOR CONFERENCE ON THE THEME "Korean Challenges and American Policy" was held in Washington on December 7 and 8, 1988, under the sponsorship of the Washington Institute for Values in Public Policy. The primary objective of the conference was to assess and evaluate the development of United States-Korea relations since World War II, with special emphasis on the rise of anti-Americanism and the recent political changes in South Korea. In the atmosphere of transition from an authoritarian system to a democratic one, and with regard to what may be expected in the future, what should United States policy be toward Korea?

A planning committee consisting of Selig Harrison, Donald Macdonald, Robert Smith, and myself met in Washington on February 2 and 4, 1988 to discuss the general theme of the conference and identify the scholars to do research papers and present them to the conference. More than fifty scholars were contacted, and a total of three dozen Korea specialists took part in the conference as paper writers, commentators of the papers, moderators of the panels, and rapporteurs.

As the chairman of the conference and editor of this volume, I would like to express my gratitude to all the participants for their invaluable contributions. Neil Albert Salonen, Director of the Washington Institute, conceived the idea of the conference, generously funded it, and was an inspired and imaginative coordinator. Robert Sullivan worked tirelessly to expedite the conference and the travel of the participants, making their stay in Washington both convenient and pleasant.

I would like to take this opportunity to acknowledge the special contributions of Dr. Ramon H. Myers, scholar-curator of East Asian Collection of the Hoover Institution on War, Revolution and Peace at Stanford University, and Professor John P. Lovel of Indiana University at Bloomington, who served as reviewers of the conference papers and made constructive criticisms as well as invaluable suggestions for the improvement of the quality of this volume. I am most grateful for the copyediting efforts of Rebecca Salonen, who undertook the task of producing a uniform and readable text. However, any omissions and errors that may appear in this volume are the responsibility of the editor, not those who took part in the production of this volume.

Ilpyong J. Kim

Introduction

The Future of
United States-Korea Relations

Ilpyong J. Kim

FOUR DECADES AND A HALF HAVE ELAPSED since the United States participated in August 1945 in the division of the Korean peninsula at the 38th parallel. The occupation and military government of Korea ensued, with the United States in the southern part and the Soviet Union in the north. The United States helped to establish the Republic of Korea in 1948, sustained its security, and assisted in its growth and development in the years following. Almost a half-century of United States involvement in Korean affairs has produced a love-hate relationship between the two nations. Though the alliance was maintained during the crucial decades of the 1950s and 1960s, the emergence of critical issues including the presence of American troops and nuclear weapons in Korea, along with the growing tensions produced by trade frictions and protectionist economic policies, brought about the rise of anti-American sentiments in Korea in the 1970s and 1980s. As a result, a general reassessment of United States-Korea relations has been occurring, contributing to the emergence of "new thinking" about bilateral ties in the future.

The great challenges that the United States and the Republic of Korea face in their relations in the 1990s are in the areas of military and security arrangements, economic and political policy, and the reunification of North and South Korea. The object of this book is to explore these challenges.

As the conference on "Korean Challenges and American Policy" was convened on December 7, 1988, in Washington, the cold war was beginning to wind down. The 1988 Seoul Olympics had just successfully concluded, having had the active participation of the People's Republic of China (PRC), the Soviet Union, and East European nations but without representation from the Democratic People's Republic of Korea (DPRK). The U.S. Department of State had made it clear prior to the opening of the Olympics that it could begin discussions on the future of United States-North Korea relations if North Korea did not disrupt the Seoul games. A series of conferences between United States government officials and North Korean representatives has thus been held in Beijing during the past two years. United States contacts with the representatives of the DPRK were aimed at agreement on issues such as the reduction of tension in the Korean peninsula, the opening of cultural and humanitarian exchanges, and the ultimate establishment of economic and diplomatic relations in the context of cross-recognition (that is, the United States and Japan could recognize the DPRK, while the Soviet Union and China would recognize the Republic of Korea). The cold war in Europe ended in 1989, but the cold war in Korea and Asia as a whole will not end until the United States and North Korea conclude a peace treaty ending the Korean War and take steps toward the reunification of Korea. This is the major challenge for the powers involved in the peninsula in the 1990s.

Political and Security Issues

A centennial of United States-Korea relations was celebrated in Seoul and Washington in 1982, commemorating the signing of a treaty of "peace, amity, commerce and navigation" between the Kingdom of Choson (Korea) and the United States in 1882. Thus, United States relations with Korea opened with commercial and cultural interchange at the beginning of the twentieth century. The ties formed with the treaty, signed by an American negotiator, Commodore Robert W. Schufeldt, and therefore commonly known as the Schufeldt Treaty, lasted only a little over two decades before Japan seized Korea in 1905.

During the Japanese domination of Korea, American policy toward Korea was conducted in the context of United States-Japanese relations, since Korea had lost her status as a sovereign state. The United States victory over Japan at the end of World War II in 1945, however, brought about a new relationship between Korea and the United States. The American armed forces under the command of Lt. Gen. John R. Hodge landed in Korea to accept the Japanese surrender there and help to establish an independent nation-state. The American military government during the 1945–1948 period carried out a program of restructuring the economic, political, and social systems of Korea and eradicating the legacy of Japanese colonial administration. However, the United States failed to come to grips with the needs and aspirations of the Korean people and reverted to the Japanese style of government, retaining Japanese-trained bureaucrats and police to maintain law and order in liberated Korea. For this and other reasons, there has been continuing debate among Korean scholars on the question of whether or not the United States occupation of 1945–1948 was a success or a failure.

Evaluating the performance of the American military government in Korea during the 1945–1948 period, some critics argue that the United States policy failed because the Americans were ignorant of Korean culture, history, and politics and had developed no plan to govern the Korean people and society. Thus they failed to consider the hopes and needs of the Korean people. Other scholars, however, emphasize the contribution of the United States in freeing Korea from the Japanese and the achievement of the American military government in maintaining law and order in the immediate postwar period, even if Japanese-trained police had to be utilized, and in assisting pro-American politicians led by Dr. Syngman Rhee to establish the Republic of Korea in 1948.

The creation of the Republic of Korea in the south on August 15, 1948, with the election by the National Assembly of Syngman Rhee as the country's first president, was counterbalanced by the establishment of the Democratic People's Republic of

Korea in the north on September 9, 1948, with the election of Kim Il Sung as head of state (then the premier but since 1972, the president). Thus two competing Korean regimes emerged with different ideologies, economic structures, and political systems.

After the establishment of the two independent states in the south and north, the United States military forces withdrew from Korea, leaving only 500 military advisers to help build the ROK army in the south; the Soviet Union likewise withdrew its armed forces from the north. In January 1950, in an address at the National Press Club in Washington, Secretary of State Dean Acheson defined the United States defense perimeter in Asia. It excluded the Korean peninsula. North Korean decision makers were thus led to misperceive United States intentions. They launched an attack on South Korea on June 25, 1950, seeking to unify the two Koreas by military means. The American troops sent to counter the aggression from the north helped to preserve the Republic of Korea as a nation. During the three-year Korean War, the United States suffered more than 150,000 casualties (38,000 killed in action and 120,000 wounded) and spent more than $75 billion. More than three million Koreans lost their lives, and over ten million people suffered forced separation from family members on the opposite side of the 38th parallel, as there has been no free communication or travel between north and south. The Korean War itself produced enormous human suffering in both north and south as a result of bombing and the general destruction throughout the country.

An armistice was signed on July 23, 1953, by the United States, the People's Republic of China, and the Democratic People's Republic of Korea. The Korean War was halted, but no peace treaty was signed. The Republic of Korea was not a signatory even to the armistice; Syngman Rhee rejected the agreement as neither signifying victory nor producing reunification. After the conclusion of the war, the United States and the South Korean governments also signed a mutual defense treaty (October 1, 1953), in which the two sides agreed to mutual consultation and assistance if either was threatened by external armed attack.

During his official visit to the United States in 1954, President Rhee appealed for aid as his country was totally devastated as a result of the war and its economy was shattered. In response, the United States began a massive economic assistance program and also built up the ROK armed forces. However, between 1948 and 1960, South Korea continued to be under the firm control of Syngman Rhee, who came to be considered a dictator by Korean students and intellectuals. Despite the deterioration of democracy and the increasing authoritarianism in South Korea, the United States was obliged to support the Rhee government and continued to provide assistance to rehabilitate the Korean economy and strengthen the defense capabilities of the South Korean army to counter the North Korean buildup in the 1950s. The security interest of the United States took precedence over fostering democracy in Korea. Nevertheless, the United States position was decisive in the fall of the Rhee government in April 1960, when students and intellectuals led a popular uprising against his authoritarian rule.

During the genuine democratic experiment with a cabinet system of government under Chang Myon (John M. Chang) in 1960–1961, the United States gave unswerving support; but the fragile government was overthrown by a military coup on May 16, 1961. The military rebels under the leadership of Park Chung Hee and Kim Jong Pil replaced the democratically elected government of Chang Myon by an authoritarian military regime. American relations with the military government were greatly strained, but the United States compromised with Park Chung Hee, again for security reasons at the expense of democracy, and continued to render economic and military assistance throughout the eighteen-year rule of Park, who was finally assassinated by his own security chief in October 1979. However, it was during the 1960s and 1970s that great stresses and strains developed in American-South Korean relations in general, and specifically in the security and political arenas.

During this time the Park Chung Hee government became increasingly repressive, declaring martial law and emergency measures under what many believed was only a pretext that the threat from North Korea was imminent. Suppression of human rights and curtailment of civil liberties during the 1960s and 1970s because of the purported threat from the North produced growing opinion in the United States that South Korea should no longer receive economic and military aid. Criticism of Park's authoritarian rule mounted in the U.S. Congress, in the press, and among the Korean community in the United States. Students, intellectuals, and church leaders in South Korea formed a strong pro-democracy protest movement aimed at replacing authoritarian rule. However, the United States had no alternative but to support the Park Chung Hee government because of security considerations.

In 1969 the Nixon Doctrine was announced, and the Nixon administration began to withdraw the U.S. Army's Seventh Division from Korea in 1971. This induced the Korean government to intensify its lobbying activities in Washington, with the "Koreagate" scandal as a result. To compensate for the withdrawal of the Seventh Division and to balance the continuing buildup in the North, the Nixon administration provided South Korea with a $1.25 billion military modernization program, including F-4 Phantom aircraft, M-48 Patton tanks, armored personnel carriers, heavy artillery, and Honest John surface-to-surface missiles.

In response to the Nixon Doctrine and the American defeat in Vietnam, the Park Chung Hee government began to develop an indigenous arms industry under the "Force Improvement Plan," and the Korean government increased its military expenditures from 4 to 7 percent of GNP. Special defense taxes were levied on sales of goods in Korea. President Carter's decision to remove further ground troops from Korea generated a series of debates in Congress and among the academic community. In anticipation of the planned withdrawal in 1977, more military aid was provided by the Carter administration to the ROK, including $275 million in Foreign Military Sales (FMS) credits, $800 million worth of selected equipment from the withdrawing troops on a cost-free basis, and roughly $2.5 billion worth of technical training for the ROK armed forces for the operation of the newly acquired equipment. Besides increased FMS credits from $390 million to $900 million from 1978 to 1979, the South Korean government also received such additional weapons as TOW, Sidewinder, and Sparrow missiles; F-4 and F-5 fighters; C-130 transports; armored personnel carriers; and sophisticated radar communications equipment. When the Carter administration suspended its withdrawal of American troops in 1979, the United States also sold F-16s to Korea and sent AWACs and a flotilla to the ROK army. The Reagan administration decided to eliminate the troop withdrawal plan when it took office.

With Ronald Reagan's inauguration in 1981, great emphasis was placed on the East-West conflict, and United States alliance relations were strengthened to enhance the position of the United States vis-à-vis the Soviet Union. President Reagan began to improve relations with South Korea by inviting President Chun Doo Hwan to meet with him in the White House in January 1981. Under the Reagan administration, the status of the Republic of Korea was upgraded from an important strategic interest of the United States to a vital one; Korea was assured that it was under the United States' nuclear umbrella. South Korea was now seen as a defense shield for Japan, a cornerstone of the United States military infrastructure in the Western Pacific. The Bush administration, however, had a new perspective toward United States-Korea relations. In 1989 Secretary of Defense Richard Cheney announced the phased reduction and eventual withdrawal of all United States troops from South Korea amid increasing debate on the strategic value of Korea to the United States at the end of the cold war.

Economic and Trade Issues

Today the Republic of Korea is the United States' seventh-largest trade partner. The United States played a pivotal role in the economic development of South Korea, providing a total of $3.84 billion in economic aid in the 1945–1978 period. From the American involvement in liberated Korea in 1945 to the end of the Korean War in 1953, the United States gave relief assistance and economic and military aid to rebuild the Korean economy and defense forces. From the end of the war until 1960, the United States and the United Nations relief organizations provided $2 billion in economic aid. From 12 percent of United States aid in 1953 to almost 100 percent in 1960 was channeled through the Agency for International Development (AID).

In the early 1960s, President Park announced a drastic

change in Korea's economic policy from the laissez-faire style
of the Syngman Rhee government, which had produced only
slow economic growth. Under the new policy, planning was
initiated by the government to enhance the country's economic
growth and development. The first five-year economic development plan concentrated on import substitution and the
mobilization of domestic capital, while the second five-year plan
(1966–1971) placed emphasis on export-oriented industrialization using foreign capital. South Korea began to rely more on
foreign loans and borrowed heavily in the 1965–1972 period,
raising the ROK's debt to $36 billion in the 1970s. The United
States had also begun to decrease its economic aid, from $245
million in 1960 to $165 million in 1964, and finally phased out
aid grants in 1972. However, normalization of relations with
Japan brought an influx of Japanese capital—$200 million as
grants-in-aid and $300 million in commercial credit. Thus the Re-
public of Korea's dependence on American assistance declined.

The Vietnam War further increased the capital needs of the
South Korean economy. The ROK government sent 50,000
troops to South Vietnam to help with the American war effort
from 1965 to 1975. South Korea earned $546 million in the
1965–1969 period, and the earnings resulting from the Vietnam War doubled in the 1970s. This money came largely from
the United States government, which paid the salaries and
expenses of the South Korean troops occupying Vietnam. The
Americans also contracted a number of South Korean construction companies to build the bridges, roads, and port
facilities needed for the infrastructure of United States military
Vietnam bases. Through capital investment from abroad and
its planned economic policy, the ROK was able to achieve a
growth rate of 10 to 12 percent in the 1970s. The South Korean
economy continued its growth in the 1980s, so that by 1988
there were refrigerators in three-quarters of Korean homes
and telephones and television sets in almost every household.
South Korea has become the seventeenth-largest economy in
the non-communist world and the twelfth-largest trading nation in the world. The ROK conducts 40 percent of its trade
with the United States (its primary trade partner) and had
achieved a $10 billion annual trade surplus by the late 1980s.
Unfortunately, this also brought about trade frictions and

protectionism in the United States' relations with the Republic of Korea.

Although the ROK's $10 billion trade surplus was achieved in 1987, that level was not met in subsequent years. In 1988, the surplus decreased to $8.64 billion and dropped further, to $4.72 billion, in 1989. A trade deficit was registered in 1990 against the background of pressure from the United States to open the Korean market to American products. After a series of negotiations between the United States trade representative and ROK government officials, South Korea agreed to open its market in the areas of communications facilities, intellectual properties, and the financial market, among others, and the opening of the market for United States agricultural products is being negotiated despite the fact that Korean farmers are protesting the government's concessions.

Trade frictions appeared as early as the 1970s, when the United States put restrictions on importing of Korean textile goods and took measures to curtail dumping of color television sets, record albums, and other electronic items. In 1982, when the Korean trade surplus had begun to increase, the United States demanded that Korea open its market by the mid-1980s to American industrial goods and agricultural products, and secure protection of the service sector, including copyrights, patents, and intellectual property rights. In the late 1980s, the United States demanded that Korea open its market further in the service sector, and to more items of agricultural produce, and lower the exchange rate of the Korean *won.* By 1989 the United States had cancelled the Generalized System of Preferences (GSP) for Korea. Many specific trade disputes and the issue of protectionism remain unresolved and will become challenges for United States-Korea relations in the 1990s.

The Rise of Anti-Americanism

The American press reported in the 1960s and 1970s that South Korea was the only place on the globe where you would not find such slogans as "Yankee Go Home," and that Koreans loved Americans and continued to express their gratitude for United States aid and security protection, even when anti-American sentiment was rising in Europe and Latin America. However, in the 1980s Korean students also began to shout anti-American slogans. They burned the American Cultural Center in Kwangju in 1980 and took control of the U.S. Information Service building in 1988. There have been anti-American protests and demonstrations throughout the 1980s in Korea. More than a dozen books and numerous articles have been published in Seoul attacking United States policy toward Korea and demanding the withdrawal of American troops and nuclear weapons from Korea. Anti-Americanism in Korea will be another critical challenge for United States policy in the 1990s.

In explaining the reasons for the rise of anti-Americanism, some analysts point to the failures of United States policy toward Korea since World War II and to the influence in Korea of certain currents of Western political thought such as dependency theory, liberation theology, and revisionist interpretations of United States foreign policy. There is also a widening gap between the older generation of Koreans, who remember and appreciate American assistance during and after the Korean War, and the younger generation who have no memory of the war. These younger people account for more than 60 percent of the Korean population today, and they are more critical of the American role in Korea. Those born after the war tend to interpret American motivations and intentions in Korea from more radical political perspectives than their elders do.

An alarming account of the new Korean views on United States policy in Korea has been presented by *New York Times* reporter Harrison E. Salisbury. He visited North Korea and reported his experiences in *To Peking and Beyond: A Report on the New Asia* (Quadrangle Books, New York, 1973), in which he describes the North Korean explanation of the origins and causes of anti-Americanism, from the invasion of Korea by the American ship, *General Sherman*, on August 15, 1866, to atrocities perpetrated on civilians stemming from American bombing and devastation during the Korean War. The antipathy toward American policy and economic activities seemed to enhance the chauvinism and ultra-nationalism in North Korea, which in turn made an impact on the postwar generation of students and intellectuals in the South. The radical students hold the United States responsible for the division of Korea in 1945 and for perpetuating it by maintaining troops and nuclear weapons in Korea in order to serve the security interests of the United States. Thus, Korea has become the victim of American "imperialism," according to the students' argument, replacing Japanese colonialism and militarism in the post-World War II period.

Further, the pursuit of democratic ideals has been greatly frustrated by the United States' emphasis on its security interests rather than on promoting a democratic system of government in Korea. The critics charge that the United States acquiesced in the military coup of Park Chung Hee in May 1961 at the expense of the democratically elected government and supported his undemocratic and authoritarian rule for eighteen years. The United States has been criticized for also supporting the military coup led by Chun Doo Hwan in December 1979 following the assassination of President Park and for not objecting to the establishment of the military-controlled fifth republic under Chun in the 1980s. What emerges out of the charges made by the Korean students is that American policy since 1945 has failed to serve the aspirations and interests of the Korean people, who sought reunification of their country but served instead the interests of the United States in containing the expansion of communist China and the Soviet Union.

The United States is thus seen to have supported Korean leaders who were willing to serve the interests of the United States rather than those leaders committed to serving the national interest of the Korean people. Pro-American regimes in Korea have been perpetuated, and this has alienated the people. In a recent public opinion survey conducted by a group of college professors in Seoul, it has been reported that only 19 percent of the population are pro-American, while 30 percent are anti-American and 50 percent maintained neutrality, that is, were neither pro- nor anti-American. When asked about the causes of anti-Americanism in Korea, 47 percent of the population believed that trade frictions were the primary cause, 27 percent of them considered political relations to be the cause, while 8 percent of them thought cultural differences were responsible. Only 4 percent considered the defense question to be the cause of anti-Americanism. (This survey was conducted in November 1990 with a random sample of 1,200 in the age group of seventeen and older.)

No matter how harsh and mistaken the accusations may be, they have succeeded in generating a force of anti-Americanism in South Korea in the 1990s, and they accentuate the challenges of the 1990s for United States policy.

December 7, 1990
Storrs, Connecticut

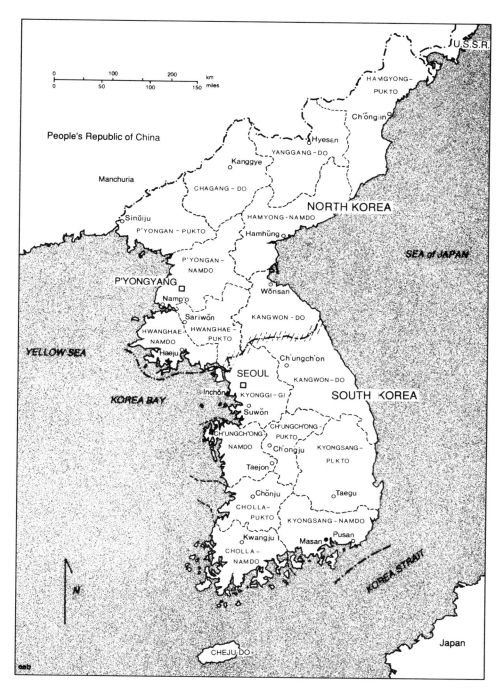

The Korean Peninsula, 1991

Korea and the World 1860–1945

Gari Ledyard

Korea and the World: The Cultural Background

THE CONCEPT "WORLD" must always be a relative one. In Korea during the first half of the nineteenth century, for millions of peasants who toiled in their fields, it would scarcely have extended beyond the neighboring counties: Seoul, a place of power, lay someplace far away, if not in geography at least in imagination. Other Koreans, better informed, would have known of China and Japan, Korea's two powerful neighbors, with whom the less one had to do the better. Some few who were Christians of very recent conversion probably had an awareness that "Yesu" had lived in lands very far away from even China; but still they identified their religion as having come into Korea from China, and it is doubtful that their curiosity led their thoughts any further afield. Merchants and politicians in Seoul and a few commercial and frontier towns would have had a more sophisticated understanding of the East Asian area, and beyond that they would have known something of Europe and of Catholicism through notices in books and the conversation of their knowledgeable friends. A very few intellectuals and diplomatic travelers had actually met Europeans

3

in Beijing, carried on conversations with them (in written Chinese), taken tours of their churches and wine-making facilities, and questioned them on Western religion and science. If one can judge from the attention given various foreign countries in the Korean books of the day, Korean intellectuals in the 1800s indeed knew much more about Europe than they did about other parts of Asia, such as the relatively close Philippines (then known as "Ryosong," a Koreanization of the Chinese name for Luzon) or the kingdoms of Vietnam and Thailand, or even India, the source of the Buddhism that had come to Korea countless centuries earlier.

Knowledge of the West went back at least to 1521, when Korean court historians noted in the official annals that a people known as "Pullangi" (from *feringhi*, an Islamic term for "Franks"—not limited to Frenchmen but comprising all Western Europeans of Roman Catholic faith) had arrived in China. Western military technology, in the form of muskets in the hands of hundreds of thousands of Japanese soldiers, had become all too familiar during the Japanese invasions of the 1590s, although few if any Koreans then were aware of their ultimate origin. Two Jesuit missionaries actually spent a few months in Korea in Japanese military camps, although there is no evidence that Koreans noticed their presence. In 1620, a classified compendium of miscellaneous information on natural and human affairs presented Korean readers with the first garbled description of Catholicism. In 1653, a Dutch ship was wrecked on the southern coast of Cheju Island: 36 crew members who survived the disaster were interned, but by 1668 the fifteen who had lived through their captivity had either escaped or been repatriated through Japan. Although interesting descriptions of the strange Dutchmen found their way into Korean writings, the more significant fact is that Koreans forgot about them almost immediately.

In the early years of the eighteenth century, Korean diplomats began to visit the Jesuit churches in Beijing: by 1784, a young man whose father was attached to the Korean embassy there had taken religious instruction, been baptized and returned home to baptize many of his friends and acquaintances. It is estimated that by 1801, in addition to an ordained Chinese Catholic priest, there were about ten thousand people in Korea involved with Catholicism to some degree. But that year also saw the execution of the priest and a vigorous persecution of the budding Christian community. It did not disappear, however. One of the most amazing stories in the history of religious proselytization is how a few Catholics maintained their religious community underground between 1784 and 1836, when a pair of Western missionaries finally managed to smuggle themselves into their midst. Between 1836 and 1866, about twenty courageous French fathers of the Paris-based Société des Missions Étrangères worked in this community, and all but three of them were martyred.

In addition to the missionaries, Western ships began to visit Korean shores. In 1799, an English ship sought water and supplies near Pusan. In 1816, English ships surveyed and mapped some of Korea's western coast and islands. As English trading companies became more and more involved in attempts to force China to open to Western commerce from the 1830s on, it was inevitable that more of their ships would come into Korean waters from time to time, and they did. Koreans who witnessed these visits, fearing the worst, usually stayed out of sight; county magistrates and military officials who dealt with the foreigners were concerned only they go away as soon as possible.

It is not easy to give a simple explanation for this isolationist sentiment. After all, Korea shared with China, Japan, and its more distant neighbor, Vietnam, the principal elements of East Asian culture: the classical Chinese language, used for official records and most formal literature; Buddhism, with its incomparably rich religious tradition and its enduring art and architecture; and a deeply rooted Confucianism which informed every aspect of national life. These cornerstones made Korea in every sense a member of the broader community that we call East Asian civilization. From the very beginning, however, there had been within this civilization a strong tendency to separateness and insularity. It was quite different from Western European civilization, in which young aristocrats would go on their "grand tours," visiting the courts and countrysides of the neighboring nations, learning their spoken languages, and returning after a year or two having lost their cultural as well as—most likely—their individual virginity. In East Asia, it would have been unthinkable for someone of elite status to simply "travel" in a neighboring country, much less to learn its vernacular language and mix socially with its population. East Asia had nothing similar to the integrating institutions of Europe: a Catholic church with its universalist reach and papal power; the Holy Roman Empire, which, even if it had been neither holy, Roman, nor an empire, had integrated Western Europe in the minds of its people; a network of royalty, internationalized through centuries of dynastic intermarriage; or finally and fundamentally, the Indo-European family of languages that implied a shared approach to life in the deeper levels of the subconscious. In East Asia, apart from a possible relationship between Koreans and Japanese in ancient times that has been hypothesized by many but proven by no one, the early cultural foundations of the four member nations were, as far as we can tell, fundamentally separate and distinct from the very beginning. Even today Koreans, Japanese, and Chinese may be generally aware of the shared values of their civilization, but their fundamental instinct is to consider themselves separate and unique.

For Koreans, the normal insularity of East Asian life had been strengthened by the circumstances of their more recent history. The Japanese invasions of the 1590s had convinced them that intercourse with Japan had to be restricted to the very minimum levels of trade and diplomatic access, and this was matched by a generally parallel attitude on the part of the Tokugawa shogunate. Looking northward, Koreans had, in 1637, seen the Manchus sweep into Seoul and force a total separation between the Choson court and the Ming dynasty. To guarantee the separation from Beijing the enemy had taken away a number of royal and aristocratic Korean hostages who were not returned until 1644, when the Manchus seized Beijing and brought the Ming dynasty to an end. There had then followed an uncomfortable period during which the more regular and ritual diplomatic exchanges of the Ming-oriented past was replaced by intrusive and predatory Manchu imperial commissioners (the dreaded *ch'iksa*), who tended to have an unquenchable thirst for bribes and payoffs. In spite of a regularization of the diplomatic relationship by the early years of the eighteenth century, and an informed appreciation on the part of many Korean intellectuals for the virtues of Manchu rule in China, most Koreans never lost the idea of an essential Manchu barbarity, which simply could not measure up to their own exalted level of Confucian civilization.

Thus, China, Japan, and Korea had to a significant degree sealed themselves off against each other. *A fortiori* they had sealed themselves off against the less familiar Westerners. In Korea, one senses not merely a wish to insulate the nation from foreign influences, but that the value of insulation itself had become a national obsession. If Westerners, in their shameless propensity to exoticize the East, had taken to calling Korea the "hermit kingdom," there was still something to it. It took a considerable period of time, a series of formidable domestic crises, and ultimately irresistible foreign pressures before Koreans were led to reconsider their isolation and open up to the outside world. Even then there was no consensus on doing so; many were willing to die, and many ultimately did die, in defending their unique Korean way of life against foreign intrusion. These two basic dispositions—to be open to the world or closed to it—persist in Korea to this day in the contrasting faces that are projected by the Republic of Korea in the South and the Democratic People's Republic of Korea in the North. And even in the relatively cosmopolitan South, a deep sense of Korean uniqueness and separateness inheres in the souls of many.

The Crises of the 1860s

Before 1860, the Korean attitude toward the Western countries was marked more by contempt than by fear. If Westerners intruded, as by the unwelcome visits of English ships between 1799 and 1855, the basic Korean response was annoyance, and all efforts were concentrated on getting rid of the ships quickly. If the ships' masters asked for trade, the Koreans responded along the lines of "we have nothing and need nothing, please go away." Catholicism, though recognized to be of Western origin, was essentially seen as a bizarre religious cult which had entered the country from China. It was a domestic problem to be controlled by strict border surveillance and suppressive measures on the local level. At no point in the years before 1860 does one sense that Korean officials felt themselves at a loss to deal with these foreign intrusions or that they lacked confidence in the virtues and capabilities of their own way of life. Although disquieting noises came from China from time to time, few Koreans imagined any Western threat that they could not handle.

But in 1860, an event occurred which decisively changed this complacent attitude. The British and French had sent a military expedition to the capital city of China, Beijing, had burned down the summer palace and were carrying out all manner of other operations intended to intimidate the Chinese authorities. This was a retaliatory measure designed to punish the Chinese for not following through on promises they had made in 1857 and 1858 to permit foreign missionaries in China and resident European diplomats in its capital. In the same year, in one of the many unequal nineteenth-century treaties which the Chinese protest to this day, China was forced to cede a large part of Manchuria—the very homeland of the Qing rulers—to the Russian empire.

Koreans viewed these developments with great alarm. If the great and mighty Chinese empire could not keep the Europeans at bay, Korea suddenly looked very vulnerable. If the Korean government were compelled to accept the missionaries they had hitherto executed with impunity, how could Catholicism be controlled? Moreover, in centuries of relations with the Chinese and Japanese the institution of resident foreign diplomats had been unknown: if there were diplomatic business, you sent an embassy to the country involved, settled things and returned home as soon as possible. As for the Russians, the new Maritime Province, with its growing port of Vladivostok, now directly abutted Korea on its northeastern frontier. Russian traders were demanding commercial relations, and Koreans were already beginning to move across the border.

An atmosphere of crisis permeated the country at all levels. Many feared that the British and French would arrive in Korea at any moment to force the concessions they had exacted in China. The country's defenses were weak or nonexistent. The condition of the common people was bad; peasant rebellions had already broken out in several counties, and by 1862 they would be pandemic. The government itself was in a deplorable state; revenues had plummeted since about 1800, and royal authority had withered away as kings who were only children came to be manipulated by in-law families who controlled everything. Official corruption seemed beyond control. The government was at a loss over how to respond to such overwhelming problems. Fortunately, it had overestimated the foreign lust to send predators to Korea, and that did give the country some extra time; but even the internal difficulties were staggering. On the lower levels of national life the situation was incomparably worse, because it was accompanied by poverty and suffering to a degree that seemed unprecedented. The ruling class had alienated itself from the people by its depredations and cruelties.

The initial responses to this crisis, not surprisingly, were in the direction of arming the nation against the foreign threat. By way of emphasizing the social variety of these responses, I will outline briefly the details of two of them. The first presented a spiritual answer to the crisis in the religious career of an innovative martyr named Ch'oe Cheu, and the second was the political response directed by one of the most remarkable personalities in Korean history, the Taewon'gun.

Ch'oe Cheu, more respectfully known by his public and religious name of Suun, was a native of Kyongju, the old Silla capital. A fallen country teacher and part-time peddler of a type all too common in the rural areas of Korea in those days, Suun had taken to an itinerant life, which opened up his vision both outwardly to the situation of his country and inwardly to the suffering of his own soul. He was disturbed by the Catholicism that by then had reached most areas of the country and alarmed over the possibility that Western powers might actually invade Korea. Although he himself had the Confucian training normal for the literate in those days, it would appear that he had lost confidence in the ability of Confucian teaching to stand up against the foreign danger or redeem the corruption of contemporary Korean life. He began to see visions and hear voices which pointed out a new way. In the spring of 1860, as news of Western depredations up and down the Chinese coast flowed into Korea, he experienced a fundamental revelation and began his career as a religious teacher. His creed was a syncretic mix of the religious life available in Korean experience. A direct identification with Heaven, achieved through study, enlightenment, and good works, was necessary to salvation. While the core beliefs and practice reflected the ingrained habits of country Confucianism, there were also Buddhist and shamanic elements, including direct and equal participation by women, which sharply diverged from Confucianism. Magical practices, secret medicines, and faith-healing played major roles in rituals. Important elements of the faith even came from Catholicism: congregational assembly, hymn-singing, and the name of God as "Ch'onju" (Sino-Korean "Lord of Heaven," semantically identical with the later Protestant Christian—and pure Korean—term "Hananim," which may be based on it). The name which became attached to Suun's religion, Tonghak ("Eastern learning") was an antonym of Sohak ("Western learning"), one of the terms by which Catholicism was known at that time, and highlights the role of Tonghak as a defense against and an alternative to the West.

As far as Korean officialdom was concerned, however, Tonghak was a superstitious cult subversive of Confucian orthodoxy and a threat to authority and social order. Far from perceiving it as opposed to Catholicism, many officials made no distinction between the two religions; both were contemptuously referred to as "heterodox creeds" (sagyo). As the cult grew in popularity and organization, particularly in Kyongsang province, the government persecuted it more and more aggressively. Along with Catholicism it was made a scapegoat for the peasant uprisings that wracked the country. Suun was arrested late in 1863 and executed on March 19, 1864.

So often in religious history, short-run reverse betokens long-run success. Christ gives way to St. Paul; Joseph Smith yields to Brigham Young. Suun's successor was Ch'oe Sihyong, or Haewol. He revitalized the religion, brought some of its more superstitious elements under control, established its texts, strengthened its organization, and encouraged the people in their faith. Within thirty years, the Tonghak religion would set the stage for one of the pivotal turns of Korean history in its relationship with the outside world. By 1919, under the new name Ch'ondogyo, its leaders would be among the principal organizers of the March First Movement. And still today it plays a major role in Korean religious life.

If Tonghak was a early failure and a final success, the

Taewon'gun was an early success and a final failure. But from the day he came to power in 1864 until the day he died in 1898, he was a force in Korean politics. His career collided with everybody: the kingdom's ruling Confucian elite, the French, the Americans, the Russians, the fundamentalist Confucians of the countryside, the Chinese, the Japanese, his own son the king, and above all his daughter-in-law, Queen Min. For the remainder of the nineteenth-century, he was at or near the nodal point of many of the key events of Korea's internal politics and external relations.

When the young king Ch'olchong died without an heir in January 1864, ancient custom dictated that the most senior female member of the royal family choose his successor. The duty fell to the aged dowager, Queen Cho, whose husband had been posthumously designated king in 1835. The royal family at that time mirrored the fate of the country: it was severely depleted. Given the ritual requirement that the successor be of the succeeding generation to the deceased king, and the general practice at this time of favoring boys just on the threshold of puberty, there were very few candidates, perhaps only one. That was the second son of Prince Hungson, a boy of eleven. Prince Hungson, as one who was the father of the king but who had not himself reigned, was given the special title of Taewon'gun in accordance with venerable dynastic practice.

The Taewon'gun is often described as a regent, but to do so is to misunderstand the situation fundamentally. The regent in this case was the dowager queen, Lady Cho, whose authority was largely ritualistic and symbolic. The Taewon'gun indeed governed the country, but his power derived simply from the force of his personality and the circumstance that he was unchallenged. The only formal authority he had was as the king's father. Although the king (whom we will call, according to the posthumous name given him in 1919, Kojong), perhaps out of filial piety, and the dowager, for whatever reason, accepted the Taewon'gun's authority, nothing bound them to do so. Two earlier kings had come to the throne in similar circumstances, yet their fathers, both honored as Taewon'gun, had exercised no governing functions. The essence of the Taewon'gun's authority, in fact, was that he was *not* a regent. If he had been, he could not have ruled for much more than a few years at the most (the Dowager Cho in fact yielded her position after two); had he tried to prolong that power, he would almost certainly have provoked a legally well-founded movement against him. Only two things made his authority possible: the very anomaly of his position and his willingness to command when the country sorely needed a commander.

We cannot here give much attention to the domestic politics of the Taewon'gun, some of which were either ineffectual or disastrous. He did take immediate and drastic steps against corruption, righted outrageous wrongs, abolished factional affiliation as a criterion for public office, and in general sought and found talented people to carry out his order. But it was to protect the nation that the nation looked to him, and he did not let the nation down. Two things were necessary: the rebuilding of Korea's military defenses, which had been neglected for over a century, and the control and elimination of Catholicism. The first priority went to the military. Military administration and financing, long a notorious scandal, were regularized. Army units which had existed only on paper were filled, and the soldiers trained. Coastal defenses were reorganized and reinforced. The coastal and riparian approaches to Seoul were fortified. The people's consciousness of national peril was strengthened, the soldiers' morale nourished. Within two years the nation's confidence in itself had been restored.

Next came Catholicism. At the beginning of 1866, Russian pressures to force commercial agreements with Korea had led some Christians to believe that foreign pressure to legitimize missionary activity might be in the offing, and indeed that the underground French missionaries might even serve the nation in helping to normalize relations with foreign countries, or possibly even in enlisting French military support against the Russians. This was foolishly dangerous and unrealistic thinking, given the hostility of the Korean government to Catholicism; but it stirred up Korean Christians just enough to get the renewed attention of the government, and the Taewon'gun decided that the moment had come to strike. Wholesale arrests were ordered and a general persecution launched. No one knows how many Catholics were killed at this time, but they surely numbered in the thousands. The bloodiness of the persecution was unprecedented. Christians died in every imaginable way; they were beheaded, they were crucified, they were drawn and quartered. Large numbers apostasized to save their lives. By the end of 1866, the Catholic church was virtually extinct in Korea.

Perhaps by coincidence, perhaps because Korea's time with the West had come, 1866 was also the year in which Korea's determination to defend itself would be decisively tested. The events of this year clearly mark it as a turning point in Korea's relations with the outside world. In February and March, the anti-Catholic persecution unfolded. In March, the Prussian merchant and adventurer Ernst Oppert came seeking trade; he was refused and sent away by coastal officials. In June the American merchant ship *Surprise* was shipwrecked on the country's northwestern coast; in a gesture of civilized restraint, Korea gave humane relief to the crew and repatriated them through Beijing. In August, Oppert returned seeking trade; again he was sent away. In September, the American merchant ship *General Sherman*, bound from Tientsin seeking trade, ignored Korean warnings and wandered up the estuary of the Taedong River close to the city of Pyongyang, where it stuck in the mud of a tidal flat. Panicking, the crew kidnapped a Korean military officer, enraged the local population by indiscriminate firing of weapons, and was wiped out to the last man when the local people burned the ship. In October, a fleet of eight French ships, under the command of Contre-Admiral Pierre Gustave Roze, came to seek reparations for the death of nine French missionaries. French marines captured the town of Kanghwa on October 15, but a few days later 160 marines on a patrol-in-force were badly mauled by a group of Korean "tiger-hunters," and on the 22nd Admiral Roze decided on a precipitous evacuation, taking with him about 3,000 books (today in the Bibliothèque Nationale) and what was then valued at 197,000 francs in silver. A Buddhist bronze bell, in the process of being stolen when the evacuation was ordered, was abandoned on a path and later taken back by the Koreans as a victory trophy.

At the end of 1866, Koreans could understandably feel that they had met every threat or attack sent against them by Western countries. The Catholic church was for all practical purposes finished in Korea, and the Taewon'gun was at the height of his popularity. Koreans had no way of knowing the essentially unconnected character of some of these events; as far as they were concerned, they had repelled a Western invasion. In 1868, the American ship *Shenandoah* came to inquire after the *General Sherman*, but no Korean official would talk with its commander. A few months later the determined Oppert once again appeared, this time with a mysterious American, a Lieutenant Jenkins, on a ghoulish mission to kidnap and hold for ransom the *corpse* of the Taewon'gun's father; but they could not get the tomb open and had to withdraw in the face of a Korean militia. Finally in 1871, a naval force of American ships and marines arrived at Kanghwa to again investigate the *General Sherman* affair and to negotiate a treaty. Like the French, they too engaged in combat with Korean defenders. They occupied part of Kanghwa Island but were unable to enter into communication with any acceptably senior Korean official, and in the end they in turn found themselves in a risky position from which it was prudent to withdraw. After five years, in terms of international encounters the score was Korea 9, the West 0. The Taewon'gun had mobilized the people, showed them they could hold their own against foreigners, and done much to redress the intolerable domestic conditions current at the time he began his rule.

But of course the bill had to be paid. Upper and lower class alike were taxed, driven, and fleeced to raise money for fortifications, weapons, and palace construction. If the Taewon'gun's economic policies had not been disastrously misguided, and if he had not bought the hostility of much of the Yangban class by closing a large number of their favorite Confucian academies (many of them notorious tax shelters), raising their taxes, and forcing them to bear defense costs (which had never in Korean history been a Yangban obligation), he might have held on politically. But already in 1868, a voice from the countryside—the voice of a single-minded, feisty, and determined Confucian scholar named Ch'oe Ikhyon, a voice the country would still be hearing nearly forty years later—was using the rhetoric of moral impeachment to call the Taewon'gun to account for the burdens of the people. By 1873, the Taewon'gun's position was untenable, he was forced into retirement, and his son King Kojong assumed personal rule. Alas, Kojong was not made of the stuff his father was.

Difficulties with Japan

With hindsight, it is easy to smile a little at the Korean feeling of self-satisfaction over the Taewon'gun's success in rebuffing the Western attempts to open the country. Clearly, he had not seen the real power of the West; his victories were surely pyrrhic. It was hopeless for Koreans to think they could remain isolated. But such an assessment reflects as much Western as Korean hubris. The fact is, the Taewon'gun had stymied France and the United States. Admiral Roze had steamed away from Kanghwa determined to return and get the job done; but the French government (which had not given advance approval to the operation anyway) never launched another initiative against Korea, and reparations were never received for the murdered French missionaries. And when Minister Frederick Low and his American marines sailed away having likewise failed in 1871, neither he nor other American officials had any idea what to do next. The *General Sherman* affair remained unresolved. It would be eleven years before another American naval vessel would venture toward Korean shores. For the time being, Korea appeared to be a hornets' nest from which it was advisable to keep a safe distance. The Americans constantly sought Chinese assistance in the *General Sherman* matter, but the Chinese, understanding from long experience the complexities of Korea and with plenty of difficulties of their own in dealing with the West, preferred at the time to remain uninvolved. Korea remained closed.

It was Japan that found a way to force its opening. After the Meiji Restoration Japan proceeded to reorganize its foreign relations along Western lines. Among its more anomalous foreign relationships was that with Korea. Since 1609, when the Tokugawa shogunate had reestablished a Japan-Korea relationship in the wake of the Hideyoshi debacle, there had been regular but always very delicate ties with Korea. Indeed, the relationship was by far the oldest continuous one that Japan had with any country. But in a formal sense, the Japanese did not really have relations with Korea. The daimyo of Tsushima had official standing with the Korean Board of Rites (traditionally responsible for foreign affairs) and was empowered to trade in Pusan by an official seal conferred upon him by the Korean court. Likewise, he was the sole authority permitted by the shogunate to deal with Korea. On the one hand, he was technically an intermediary between two national governments; on the other hand, he was both a sworn retainer of the Tokugawa shogun and a tributary of the king of Korea. The Meiji government's new Foreign Office did not like this arrangement at all.

But it was not a simple matter to restructure the relationship along Western lines. Take for instance Korea's relationship with China, in 1868 unchanged from its traditional form. Korea was a tributary of China. Japan naturally intended to open equal relations with China. But if Japan were equal to China and Korea was subordinate to China, how could Japan be equal to Korea? Moreover, there was no dearth of Meiji oligarchs for whom the restoration of imperial rule meant the restoration of the emperor's historical prerogatives, and these included, in their deep belief, suzerain rights over Korea. At the very least, the Koreans would have to recognize Japan's new political system—that is, the emperor—but that presented tremendous difficulties for both Korea and Japan. The radicals in the Meiji leadership were in no doubt over what had to be done: they had to "conquer Korea" (*seikan*). But the moderate pragmatist knew that in that direction lay troubles that Japan did not need.

The Meiji government's first approach to Korea was in February 1869. An official of the Foreign Office was escorted to Pusan by the Tsushima authorities to inform Korea that the emperor had been restored and that the form of Japanese-Korean relations must be renegotiated. The Koreans refused to accept his documents on the grounds that they did not conform to traditional protocol and used terminology that was proper only to Korea's relations with China. Thus was framed the stalemate that would last for seven years.

In 1873, this issue moved to the forefront in both countries. Korea's continued refusal to negotiate a new relationship had put the Japanese moderates under increasing pressure from the militants, who took it as an insult to the emperor and to Japan's national face. Pressure rose to launch the "conquest of Korea." The militants were defeated on this issue and suffered a permanent loss of power, but the outcome of the debate put even more pressure on the moderates to find a way out of the dilemma. Meanwhile, in Korea, the fall of the Taewon'gun also brought more moderate politics into the open. Kojong had assumed his royal role and agreed with the pragmatic views of two of his senior advisers, Yi Yuwon and Pak Kyusu, that it was neither necessary nor prudent to leave the Japanese matter unresolved. However, their attempt to break the diplomatic impasse by accepting the Japanese communication ran into heavy political opposition and had to be abandoned. Unfortunately, the nation as a whole still analyzed the problem along the lines of the Taewon'gun's isolationist policies, and neither the king nor his moderates were able to figure out how to overcome this opposition. For more than two years the stalemate between Japan and Korea continued.

By this time, however, Japan had worked out a bolder approach to the problem. In 1875 the Japanese ship *Unyo* was sent close to the west coast of Korea, drew fire from Korean shore batteries, and thereby provoked an incident which quickly and inexorably led to the Kanghwa Treaty of 1876. (The incident was not dissimilar to the American scenario for opening up Japan.) When a strong Japanese naval force with a fully accredited plenipotentiary appeared and demanded to speak with a similarly empowered Korean official, the Korean reaction was consternation. But as the court analyzed the situation and considered the power of the ships and that they were not at Pusan but at Seoul's door, an attitude of sobriety quickly took hold. Sin Hon, a high military officer, was appointed plenipotentiary, and the negotiations for a treaty began. But as the news spread around the country, conservative opposition again strengthened; Ch'oe Ikhyon, the perennial gadfly of the radical Confucian opposition, joined others in protesting any negotiations. But this time the king and others who wanted to end the uncertainty with Japan prevailed, and the isolationist opposition was blunted. In a relatively short time the treaty was negotiated and signed.

Korean court opinion had it that with the treaty signed the Japan problem would go away. Korea in fact had had no earlier experience of signing a treaty structured on Western principles of international relations, and had not fully analyzed the consequences of what they had signed. The Japanese, on the other hand, had considerable experience in this area and knew that once nations signed a treaty it had the force of law in international opinion. The treaty had provisions for trade between the two countries, the opening of some ports to foreign commerce with the right of Japanese residence, coastal survey rights, and others. But its most important provision established that Korea was an autonomous (*chaju*) state and fully capable of contracting for itself on an equal basis with foreign countries. By this provision, Japan considered that they had nullified forever Korea's tributary status vis-à-vis China. From that time on Japan insisted on that interpretation and gained international approval for it. Although Korea itself did not believe that the treaty involved its traditional relationship with China—in its interpretation, Korea had always been an "autonomous" state—the international community in general approached Korea as an independent country with uncompromised sovereignty from that time on. It would not be until 1895 and the defeat of China by Japan in the Sino-Japanese War that Korea accepted the severance of its tributary status with China. But by that time the country was anxious to be done with it.

A Survey of United States-Korean Relations: 1880–1905

William J. Brinker

THE HISTORY OF THE FIRST 25 YEARS of diplomatic relations between the United States and Korea includes elements which are both predictable and unique. The existence of certain constants in United States foreign policy practices and attitudes toward other nations during the nineteenth century accounts for the predictability. Throughout this period the United States followed a tradition of avoiding treaties which promised or required either political or military support. Except during wartime, the United States maintained a low level of military force, although the navy was gaining in size and capability toward the end of the century. In part, the lack of military strength dictated limited American involvement outside the Western Hemisphere. In addition, European and Asian problems were far from the immediate concerns of a population keenly interested in internal problems and development. These factors should be kept in mind when discussing United States foreign relations in general and those with Korea specifically.

In 1882 the United States carelessly and casually entered into a relationship with Korea, a nation peripheral to our interests. Although the political status of Korea was disputed, the United States declared that it considered Korea independent and established formal relations with it. For two years the United States had the opportunity to exert considerable influence, but then, faced with the reality of a less than sovereign Korea, the United States failed to pursue policies satisfactory to either Korea or the United States. America's ambiguous and contradictory policies frustrated both sides. Despite official statements which implied American support of Korean independence and development, and despite the presence of Americans in Korea who had a genuine desire to help, American accomplishments were meager. Having little real interest in Korea, United States officials in Washington established nonintervention and neutrality as American policy toward Korea, and this desire to avoid involvement explains nearly every American response to the sometimes bewildering but ever changing Korean scene. After 1895, neutrality and nonintervention continued to be American policy, albeit for slightly altered reasons.

Sadly, some Koreans had expected the American relationship to benefit their nation-strengthening aspirations. American failure to act in their behalf repeatedly disappointed hopeful Koreans, and the indifference of American leaders in Washington especially disturbed them.

The United States-Korea relationship really begins in the 1870s. The United States half-heartedly attempted to establish relations with Korea, which had avoided foreign ties with all nations except China and Japan. Admiral Perry's success in "opening" Japan a decade earlier had showed the benefits that commercial exchanges with Korea might bring, as well as the practical advantage of being able to communicate officially with the government of a country where shipwrecked seamen were sometimes stranded. These reasons led the United States to open relations, but they proved insufficient to overcome the existing obstacles to a mutually beneficial relationship.

The Korea which attracted this limited American interest was a curious nation in many respects. It was an agricultural nation with only limited manufacturing and small-scale localized economies. It was a Confucian society that often seemed a mockery of what a Confucian society might be. Corruption, inefficiency, and factionalism inhibited the government from operating successfully. The Confucian bureaucracy resisted change and exercised numerous checks on royal authority. Making matters worse, in 1864 a twelve-year-old had ascended the throne as King Kojong. Although the dowager queen served as regent, the young king's father, known as the Tae-won'gun, dominated the boy and the government.[1] In time, however, the young king's wife and her relatives began to exert themselves as rivals to the Taewon'gun, and other factions at the court also grouped and regrouped to their momentary advantage. Since they were a small nation located on China's borders, the Koreans were schooled in Confucian concepts of international relations—a system at variance with Western practices and ideas. Korea accepted a subordinate relationship with China that was often stated in Confucian terms as one of younger to elder brother. (To a Westerner such a definition often did more to confuse than to clarify.)

During the 1870s Korea's relationship with China had been challenged by Japan. Hoping to move Korea out of China's orbit and into a new relationship whereby they would benefit through trade and greater security, the Japanese had convinced Korea to negotiate the Treaty of Kanghwa in 1876.

Among its several provisions the treaty stated that Korea "being an independent state enjoys the same sovereign rights as does Japan."[2] There is evidence that the Chinese read "autonomous" rather than "independent" and raised no objections.[3] The Chinese came to regret their error and attempted to rectify the situation, thereby causing the question of Korea's status to become unsettled, troublesome, and dangerous—as the United States would learn.

In the years immediately following the Treaty of Kanghwa, Japan moved slowly and made a few gains. Li Hung-chang, the Chinese official most responsible for Chinese-Korean relations, became concerned lest Japan become a serious rival in Korea. Li favored establishing treaty relations between Korea and the Western powers as an antidote to the perceived threat.

Looking back, one does not envy the Koreans. Chinese power was waning while Japanese power was growing. The Confucian relationship with China could not long endure, and the thought of independence was disturbing. Korean leaders knew enough of the outside world to know that changes were needed in education, in economics, and in politics. But how far should they go, and in what direction? What leaders could take the nation forward? (For the moment, the faction loyal to the queen's family seemed to be obedient to the Chinese, the Taewon'gun appeared thoroughly anti-foreign, and the so-called "progressive" faction was small and inexperienced.) Would modernization mean the sacrifice of Korean identity? Had the Japanese sacrificed too much to modernize? What other models were available? Difficult choices faced the nation.

In 1881, the Taewon'gun was in semiretirement and the young king, with Chinese blessing and support from the Korean "progressive" faction, opted for treaty relations with the West. The United States was acceptable and even favored because it posed no threats. Americans did not appear to have nineteenth-century imperialist aspirations; and an American, Commodore Robert Wilson Schufeldt, had stopped recently in Japan and China to inquire about prospects for establishing relations with Korea. The Koreans, operating through Chinese officials, informed Schufeldt that conditions had changed and a new American effort might be successful.

The various interested countries and factions saw the projected negotiations from their own perspectives. The Chinese hoped to strengthen their hand by playing off the United States against Japan, while the Japanese wanted to weaken further Korea's dependency upon China. The Korean king and his supporters hoped the United States would offer aid and encouragement to them as a nation hesitantly entering the modern world, while many other Koreans feared change of any sort. Having almost accidentally wandered into an extremely complicated situation, the United States was most unlikely to play a significant role in Korean affairs.

American officials opted to seize the opportunity presented and sent Schufeldt again to East Asia, where he subsequently negotiated the terms of a Korean treaty in China and with Chinese officials: only the final, largely ceremonial exchanges in Korea involved Koreans directly. The circumstances wherein one nation conducted negotiations in the name of another suggested that an abnormal relationship existed and that caution was in order. The evidence suggests that the American State Department understood the potential difficulties of the situation but nonetheless opened relations with this not-fully-independent nation.

In the 1880s the United States foreign service employed men such as John Russell Young and Chester Holcombe in China and John Bingham in Tokyo. They were sensitive to the ambiguities of the Chinese-Korean relationship and had informed Washington officials accordingly. John Russell Young, United States minister to China, had advised Secretary of State Frederick Frelinghuysen regarding Korea's status to the effect that

> if Korea is an independent kingdom then we can treat with its sovereign without regard to China. If Korea is a province of the Chinese empire then we should treat directly with the Pekin foreign office. If the question is in doubt, as is most probably the case, then we should consider the wisdom of the United States endeavoring to settle it by the indirect method of a commercial treaty.[4]

Whether one likes or dislikes Young's somewhat cavalier approach, it deserves our attention. His advice was to establish commercial relations with a people whose political status was in doubt and then to work toward resolution of the problems.

The Schufeldt treaty, or Treaty of Chemulpo, which was signed in May 1882, contained fourteen articles which defined commercial and diplomatic rights, forbade traffic in opium, allowed for student exchanges, contained a most-favored-nation clause, and included a controversial "good offices" clause. Article 1 read: "If other Powers deal unjustly or oppressively with either Government, the other will exert their good offices, on being informed of the case, to bring about an amicable arrangement, thus showing their friendly feelings."[5] As to what this meant, one might turn again to Minister Young:

> I should also be disposed to think that as far as our good offices could be gracefully and efficiently given they should be used to protect Corea either in the "independence" which China will recognize, or in the tributary position which the Pekin government is indisposed to surrender.[6]

Whatever might be said later, the good offices clause initially was not thought to promise much to Korea. Most assuredly, the treaty contained no guarantee to preserve the independence of Korea.

During the negotiations Li Hung-chang, the powerful Chinese official who had orchestrated this Korean-Chinese-American encounter, had wanted the treaty to include an explicit statement that Korea was dependent upon China; but Schufeldt had raised objections and the resulting treaty made no mention of dependency. A letter to the United States president accompanying the treaty explained that "Korea was a state dependent upon China, although it was self-governing in matters of internal government and foreign intercourse."[7] Secretary of State Frelinghuysen, informed as to the nature of the Chinese-Korean relationship and of its possible implications for the United States, chose to interpret the treaty and the seemingly contradictory letter to mean that Korea was independent.

Complications in the relationship had only just begun. While the Schufeldt treaty was awaiting ratification in Washington, an uprising occurred in Seoul. A minor military disturbance escalated quickly into an anti-Japanese movement, which then obtained the support of the Taewon'gun and his supporters. Japan sent a small military force to protect its interests; China sent a superior force. The Chinese seized the Taewon'gun and sent him into exile in China, restored authority in Seoul, and established a sizable Chinese armed force in Korea. For some years there remained no question as to who was in charge.

Into this volatile scene stepped Lucius A. Foote, American envoy extraordinary and minister plenipotentary. Secretary of State Frelinghuysen instructed this first American minister not to interfere in Korean-Chinese relations "unless action be taken prejudicial to the rights of the United States."[8] Given Chinese determination and the lack of any significant American interests in Korea, Frelinghuysen had no alternative.

As a sign of their enthusiasm the Korean government dispatched a mission to tour the United States. While in Washington, the Koreans secured promises of United States civil and military advisers. The Koreans asked also that Ensign George C. Foulk, one of their escorts, be sent to Seoul as a naval attaché. Furthermore, the junketing Koreans understood that none other than Commodore Schufeldt would arrive in Korea as adviser to the king. The Koreans were anxious for American assistance.

Ensign Foulk served in Seoul from 1883 until 1887 and was a worthy companion and successor to Lucius Foote. The king and the progressive faction came to trust the two Americans and asked their advice on various political and economic matters. The first two years of the American presence in Seoul was the period of greatest potential for American influence, and both Foote and Foulk were anxious to contribute.

However, not all went according to plan. Commodore Schufeldt did not accept the proffered appointment as the king's adviser, causing the king great disappointment. Various legal issues complicated the appointment but there were other factors such as Schufeldt's indecision, political opposition, and a lack of interest from Washington. After approving the formal opening of relations with Korea, Secretary Frelinghuysen failed to deliver continued support. He realized the limits of his options, and those limits were not only political.

One of the purposes of an American presence in Korea was commercial, but expanding American trade opportunities proved most difficult during the early years of United States-Korea relations. China enjoyed a special status in economic matters, a status delineated during 1882, the very year in which the Schufeldt treaty was signed. Faced with China's position, Frelinghuysen instructed Foote to take no action regarding China's prerogatives "as the participation of Western nations in Corean trade is looked upon with jealousy by a large party."9 China, of course, was the large party.

Certain practical considerations further explain the paucity of United States trading activity. In 1884 Foote noted, "There is one notable cause for this, viz, there being no money other than copper cash, the traffic must necessarily be done by bartering one product for another; and our people either cannot successfully compete with the Japanese and Chinese, or they do not care to engage in this small business." Foote continued and gives us food for thought: "It takes time to educate these people to their own necessities and to the superiority of foreign wares, and that pioneer work necessarily involves loss."10

Although various officials commented favorably over time regarding the benefits of trade with Korea and Minister Foote himself made profitable investments while there, one should not misunderstand the official United States trade position. In the mid-1880s the State Department lectured Ensign Foulk to the effect that the government could not "show an interest in the success of any particular project. All this government asks is fair and equal treatment of its citizens."[11] This attitude expresses nineteenth-century American values and was a cornerstone of United States goals throughout East Asia. Off to such weak beginnings, it is little wonder that American commercial activity in and with Korea remained minimal even at century's end, and beyond.

If commercial development did not meet expectations and hopes, the ability of American missionaries to gain influence in Korea was surprisingly successful. Missionaries from the United States first arrived in Korea in 1884, and although officially prohibited from proselytizing, became involved in medical and educational enterprises. Subsequently, missionaries gained acceptance from some prominent Koreans and came to be in a position to offer advice on issues of the day. In general, the missionaries supported Korean strivings for political independence against Chinese actions during the 1880s and encouraged resistance to Japanese and Russian threats during the 1890s.

The overt encouragement given to Korean nationalists displeased the State Department, which tried to keep missionaries out of political matters. In 1897 Washington ordered American Minister John M.B. Sill, who sympathized with Korea's plight, to inform the American community in Korea as to their proper role:

> I am required to make publicly known to every citizen of the United States sojourning or being temporarily or permanently in Korea, the repeatedly expressed view of the Government of the United States that it behooves loyal citizens...to observe the same scrupulous abstention from participating in the domestic concerns thereof which is internationally incumbent upon his government. They should strictly refrain from any expression of opinion or from giving advice concerning the international management of the country, or from any intermeddling in its political questions.[12]

Washington expected support for noninvolvement and neutrality to extend beyond government officials.

In 1885 Yuan Shih-k'ai, a lieutenant of Li Hung-chang's, arrived in Seoul and for the next nine years served as a Chinese viceroy. Thereafter, American activities in Korea occurred with his sufferance. This situation prevailed until 1894, when the power struggle over Korea assumed new dimensions.

Continuity rather than change characterized the United States response to events of the nineties. Two incidents illustrated the constancy of the American position. In 1894, on the eve of the Sino-Japanese War, Secretary of State Walter Q. Gresham, responding to a Korean request to exercise "good offices" in their behalf, instructed the United States minister in Seoul to make every possible effort "for the preservation of peaceful conditions." However, when further requests for aid reached his desk, Gresham stated that the United States would maintain "impartial neutrality" and "in no event intervene jointly with other powers." After the outbreak of hostililties, Gresham allowed Americans to serve as "channels of communication between China and Japan" but no more.[13]

A second incident occurred in 1895—the year of the Treaty of Shimonoseki—when the three European powers (Russia, France, and Germany) forced Japan to decline possession of the Liaotung Peninsula and when coups and countercoups took place in Seoul. In November, American Minister Sill took a few cautious steps to stabilize the situation in Seoul. In response, Secretary of State Richard Olney telegraphed, "Intervention in political concerns of Korea is not among your functions, and is forbidden by diplomatic instruction."[14] Several months later Olney wrote, "Your course in continued intermeddling with Korean political affairs in violation of repeated instructions noted with astonishment and emphatic disapproval. Cable briefly any explanation you have to make; also answer whether you intend to comply with instructions given."[15] A more forceful reprimand is hard to imagine. Minister Sill complied, but Olney's outburst illustrates the United States policy of noninterference with a vengeance.

Japan's victory over the Chinese led to dramatic changes in Korea. For all practical purposes Chinese political influence disappeared. Japan and Russia, the new power in the area, entered into ten years of diplomatic competition where first one and then the other seemed to have the upper hand. However, the basic dilemma remained for the United States. Korea, under either a Japanese or a Russian thumb, was not a nation whose interests the United States would support. The United States still favored nonintervention and neutrality.

During the next few years events in Cuba and the war with Spain distracted the United States. In the Far East, the Boxer Rebellion, the Open Door Notes, the Anglo-Japanese alliance, Russian expansion, and the growing power of Japan all demanded attention. In the midst of all this, when yet another crisis leading to the Russo-Japanese war unfolded, the United States showed little concern for Korean national interests.

The first years of the new century witnessed a Russo-Japanese rivalry that was building to dangerous levels. Korea figured prominently in that tense situation. Beginning in 1903, the Japanese and Russians searched for solutions, but their failure led to the Russo-Japanese War of 1904. The administration of Theodore Roosevelt became increasingly interested in the course of the war and in a settlement which would further American interests. Sounding remarkably like his nineteenth-century predecessors, Secretary of State John Hay, during the fighting stage, instructed United States Minister Horace Allen, "Presume you will do all possible for the protection of American interests consistent with absolute neutrality."[16] As Americans watched, Japan secured control quickly in Korea, and the war moved on toward its conclusion.

As the fighting progressed, President Roosevelt's interest quickened. His concern, heightened by Japan's apparent dominance, led Roosevelt to secure Russian and Japanese agreements to hold treaty negotiations in the United States. Those talks resulted in the Treaty of Portsmouth, in which Russia recognized Japan's paramount political, military, and economic interests in Korea, terms which seemed to settle the Korean question except for the details of its implementation.

An additional development which contributed to the status of Korea occurred at this time. In the summer of 1905, after the conclusion of fighting but before negotiations began in Portsmouth, Secretary of War William Howard Taft visited Tokyo while en route to the Philippines. In the Japanese capital, Taft conducted controversial discussions with Japan's Prime Minister Katsura Taro which touched on matters of interest to both nations. Not to be minimized was American concern for the Philippine Islands, and Japanese assurances of disinterest were most welcome. On the topic of Korea, Japan's leaders, based upon their encounter with Taft, had good reason to believe that the United States would not object to a Japanese takeover of the peninsula. In a memorandum to Secretary of State Elihu Root summarizing the content of the Tokyo talks, Taft wrote that, in his personal opinion, "the establishment by Japanese troops of a suzerainty over Korea to the extent of requiring that Korea enter into no foreign treaties without the consent of Japan was the logical result of the present war and would directly contribute to permanent peace in the East."[17] Theodore Roosevelt concurred with this view.

Soon after, the Japanese forced the Koreans to renounce control over their own foreign policy and to place it in Japanese hands. Abruptly, the United States closed its legation for diplomatic exchanges, and further questions regarding American interests in Korea were referred to Tokyo. United States-Korean diplomatic relations, begun with the Schufeldt treaty, now ceased. When Koreans representing their beleaguered government attempted to secure United States "good offices," Roosevelt explained that the requests did not arrive through proper and legal channels.[18] He obviously had scant interest in representing Korean interests. The Roosevelt administration's concurrence in Japanese control over Korea was but one more application of America's policy of neutrality and noninvolvement regarding the Korean peninsula.

Roosevelt's lack of sympathy for Korea's predicament and his willingness to continue the traditional stance of neutrality and noninvolvement there can be traced to several factors. The belief that American interests would be well served if Japan controlled Korea was not new. Alfred Thayer Mahan's magazine series, published in book form in 1900 as *The Problems of Asia and its Effect upon International Polities,* recommended an Anglo-American-Japanese understanding to counter Russia's expansive thrust. Roosevelt, in that same year, carried the idea of a tripartite understanding further and wrote that "it would be best if Japan held Korea so that it might be a check upon

Russia." Russian activities in the years immediately following could only have strengthened such attitudes, as did the conclusion of the Anglo-Japanese alliance, which implied Japanese dominance in Korea.

Roosevelt was most likely influenced by men in the State Department who were familiar with power realities of East Asia. John Hay, William Rockhill, and even Horace Allen accepted a Korea under Japanese control. Security for the Philippines, regional political stability, and American commercial interests were linked to the belief that Korea could not manage on its own. The cause of Korean independence had little support.

Perhaps a most telling commentary on American attitudes came in 1907, two years after Korea became a Japanese protectorate. William Howard Taft quoted an American Methodist bishop who praised Japan for furthering civilization and good government in Korea. The bishop believed that critical reports about Japan's actions in Korea were "prejudiced and grew out either of a lack of understanding or of enmity of those who fattened on the abuses of [the] old Korean government."[19] With voices of authority such as this cleric's endorsing Korea's disappearance as an independent entity, Roosevelt must have felt more confident that he had pursued the correct course for both Korea and the United States.

United States-Korean relations first had begun with optimism in 1882 but ended with cynicism and abandonment in 1905. This was perhaps inevitable because the United States and Korea had entered into a relationship under conditions that were unsettled and goals that were unclear. Many Koreans had naively believed that the United States would offer them substantial aid and direction. The Koreans, unfortunately, were not sufficiently masters in their own house to establish policy; and the United States, in turn, had only peripheral interests in Korea. If advantages could be secured which involved no risk for the United States, that was all to the good. Otherwise, nonintervention and neutrality determined American practices.

Notes

1. I am indebted to Gari Ledyard of Columbia University, whose paper "Korea and the World 1860–1945" clarified and corrected my understanding regarding the actual position or status of the Taewon'gun.
2. Charles I. Bevans, ed., *Treaties and Other International Agreements of the United States of America: 1776–1949*, vol. 9 (Washington, DC: Government Printing Office, 1972), 470–76.
3. C.I. Eugene Kim and Han Kyo Kim, *Korea and the Politics of Imperialism 1876–1910*, (Berkeley: University of California Press, 1967), 18.
4. John Russell Young to Frederick Frelinghuysen (Memorandum), May 1, 1882, National Archives, Records of the Department of State, Despatches: China. Hereafter cited as Despatches: China.
5. Bevans, *Treaties and Other International Agreements*, 471.
6. Young to Frelinghuysen, May 1, 1882, Despatches: China.
7. Cited in Tyler Dennett, *Americans in Eastern Asia: A Critical Study of United States' Policy in the Far East* (New York: Macmillan, 1922, reprint 1963), 460.
8. Cited in John Chay, "The First Three Decades of American-Korean Relations, 1882–1910: Reassessments and Reflections," in *U.S.-Korean Relations 1882–1982*, Tai-Hwan Kwak, John Chay, Soon Sung Cho and Shannon McCune, eds. (Seoul: Kyungnam University Press, 1982), 25.
9. Cited in Yur-Bok Lee, *Diplomatic Relations between the United States and Korea, 1866–1887* (New York: Humanities Press, 1970), 54.
10. U.S. Department of State, *Foreign Relations of the United States*, Lucius Foote to Frederick Frelinghuysen, April 1884, #74, 126. Hereafter cited as *FRUS*.
11. Cited in Lee, *Diplomatic Relations between the United States and Korea*, 113.
12. Cited in Dennett, *Americans in Eastern Asia*, 571–72.
13. Charles Calhoun, *Gilded Age Cato: The Life of Walter Q. Gresham* (Lexington: University of Kentucky Press, 1988) 172–74.
14. *FRUS* 1895, Richard Olney to John M.B. Sill, telegram, November 11, 1895, 972.
15. *Ibid*, January 10, 1896.
16. Cited in Chay, "The First Three Decades of American-Korean Relations," 28.
17. The Taft-Katsura Memorandum of 1905. Extract published in William A. Williams, ed., *The Shaping of American Diplomacy: Readings and Documents in American Foreign Relations*, vol. I (Chicago: Rand McNally & Co. 1970), 429.
18. Chay, "The First Three Decades of American-Korean Relations," 29.
19. Cited in Ralph E. Minger, *Willliam Howard Taft and United States Foreign Policy: The Apprenticeship Years 1900–1908*, (Urbana: University of Illinois Press, 1975), 154.

3

The American Occupation of Korea

John Merrill

EVEN BEFORE THE END OF WORLD WAR II, the idea of containment had begun to eclipse President Franklin D. Roosevelt's internationalist vision of cooperation among the great powers to manage the tensions of the postwar world. Roosevelt had thought that conflict in former colonial regions could be avoided by placing them under multilateral trusteeships and institutionalizing mechanisms, like the United Nations, for great power cooperation. After affirming the right of self-determination for all peoples in the Atlantic Charter, the President sketched out his ideas on trusteeship in wartime conferences at Cairo and Tehran. The Cairo Declaration pledged that "in due course Korea shall become free and independent," although Roosevelt suggested—with the American experience in the Philippines in mind—that trusteeship might last as long as forty years.[1]

The question of Korea came up again at Yalta in brief snatches of conversation. There it was agreed that foreign troops should not be permanently stationed in Korea and that the period of trusteeship should be fixed at twenty to thirty years. American policy makers avoided discussion of Korea after this, apparently fearing that it might encourage the Soviets to insist on a share in MacArthur's occupation of Japan. With the development of the atomic bomb, moreover, Russian participation in the war against Japan no longer seemed essential. The United States hoped to be in a position to define by itself the shape of postwar Asia.

The Soviet entry into the war on August 8, 1945, galvanized Washington into action. In a crushing offensive with a million and a half men, the Red Army swept across Manchuria and occupied the northern half of Korea in five days. Fearing that the Soviets might take all of the peninsula, the United States decided at an all-night meeting of the State-War-Navy Coordinating Committee on August 10–11 to divide Korea into separate occupation zones at the 38th parallel, ostensibly "to facilitate the surrender of Japanese troops."

MacArthur issued a general order to that effect the next day. Washington's decision to divide Korea into separate occupation zones was designed to prevent Moscow from gaining sole possession of it before a diplomatic settlement could be worked out. Surprisingly, "preemptive seizure by general orders," as Okonogi Masao has called it, worked. It took weeks for American troops to arrive, but the Red Army stopped at the 38th parallel. Stalin apparently regarded the line as tacit United States acknowledgment of a Soviet sphere of influence north of it—a traditional Russian foreign policy goal, and an arrangement that accorded well enough with Stalin's objective of ringing the Soviet Union with buffer states.

The occupation was cobbled together hastily. The end of the war came suddenly and before any preparations had been made for the occupation of Korea. The Tenth Army under General Joseph W. Stilwell had originally been slated to occupy Japan and Korea; but because Chiang Kai-shek protested "Vinegar Joe's" appointment, Lieutenant General John R. Hodge was tapped instead. Hodge's XXIV Corps was closest to Korea, and shipping was scarce. Hodge's command was detached from the Tenth Army and placed directly under MacArthur. Hodge, a hardbitten, up-from-the-ranks soldier with a distinguished combat record, was without Asian experience or "the slightest pretense" to the political demands of the job.[2]

Washington gave him little help. The military government

specialists sent with the XXIV Corps had been trained for the occupation of Japan and knew next to nothing about Korea. The chain of command was tangled, with responsibility for setting occupation policy divided among Washington, Tokyo, and Seoul. Hodge received virtually no policy guidance and had to improvise during the occupation's critical first months. His political adviser was a "third rate" State Department expert with extremely conservative political views. The surrender led to a period of unprecedented political turmoil, as the tensions of decades of Japanese colonial rule burst forth overnight. Hodge was in the midst of a social revolution—and completely at sea.

American forces arrived in Korea in early September to find a Korean government of sorts already in place. As the end of the Pacific war had drawn near, Japanese authorities sought to come to terms with Asian nationalism by encouraging formation of transitional governments to protect Japanese lives and property after the surrender. In Korea, the Japanese made their initial approaches to rightist leaders; when these were spurned, they reluctantly approached Yo Un Hyong, a leader of the democratic left. Yo's nationalist credentials were solid enough to enable him to work with the Japanese without being branded a collaborator. Yo agreed to form an interim administration in return for the release of political prisoners, guarantees of food supplies, and the promise of a free hand in organizing students, veterans, workers, and peasants. People's committees sprang up throughout the peninsula overnight, representing a broad spectrum of political opinion—at least at first—and giving expression to Koreans' desire for political participation. The committees were effective in keeping order and preventing any serious attacks on Japanese.

Two days before the arrival of American forces, the people's committees attempted to turn themselves into a full-fledged government by proclaiming a People's Republic of Korea. The cabinet lineup included prominent Korean nationalists of all political stripes—Syngman Rhee was even named president. But the people's committees drifted further to the left, and a split soon developed between them and the exiled Korean Provisional Government led by Kim Ku and Syngman Rhee. Representatives of the People's Republic were turned away when they tried to present themselves to General Hodge at

Inchon. Unfortunately, the way in which the military government dealt with the people's committees was to play a large role in determining its character. Alarmed by what he saw as a revolutionary tide, Hodge made a major *faux pas* by announcing that he would keep on Japanese administrators. The announcement created an uproar, and Hodge was forced to repatriate all of them immediately. With the Japanese out of the picture, Hodge turned over nearly the entire administrative structure to a "translators' government" staffed by members of the conservative Korean Democratic party (KDP).

The occupation bore down on the population nearly as heavily as had its predecessor. There was no reform or purge of collaborators until just before the 1948 elections. Koreans who had served under the Japanese were retained in many positions, especially in the police. Reform was also hamstrung by United States State Department objections to any measures that could complicate talks with the Soviet Union on Korean reunification. The military government's only major initiative was a plan to covertly fund a right-wing youth movement as the nucleus of a future Korean army.

The Korean economy was a shambles. Industry was paralyzed by shortages of raw materials, disruption of markets, and the loss of Japanese managers and technicians. Japanese-owned industrial facilities were abandoned and became vested in the military government, which lacked the skills necessary to run them. The lifting of Japanese agricultural controls created big food shortages, despite a bumper harvest. And an influx of two million Korean repatriates from Japan and Manchuria and refugees from the North threatened to swamp the economy.

The return of Syngman Rhee from the United States and the members of the Korean Provisional Government from China provided Hodge with an opportunity to broaden the occupation's political support. Although the State Department had opposed his quick return, Rhee's friends in Washington prevailed. Rhee got a grand homecoming, meeting with MacArthur in Tokyo and flying back to Seoul with Hodge aboard MacArthur's personal plane, *The Spirit of Bataan.* Later, the members of the Korean Provisional Government were allowed back in, its more right-wing leaders first.

The dilemmas of postwar United States policy posed themselves most starkly in Korea. Blunt and politically unsophisticated, Hodge often anticipated the policies Washington was later to adopt. MacArthur and his staff saw Korea as a "bastion" against communism, and from early November 1945 occupation leaders believed that Roosevelt's internationalist vision of trusteeship should be scrapped. A cable by William Langdon, Hodge's State Department adviser, outlined a strategy by which a Korean governing commission would be formed, gradually be given administrative control, and then put forward as the de facto government of Korea.

These plans nearly fell apart over the trusteeship controversy. Meeting in Moscow in December, the foreign ministers of the Soviet Union, the United States, and Great Britain reaffirmed a four-power trusteeship (including China) in Korea for five years. The agreement created a furor in Korea, with Koreans in both zones opposing it as a betrayal. Kept in the dark by Washington, Hodge tried to deflect criticism of trusteeship by painting it a Soviet scheme. The ground was cut out from under him, however, when the Soviet Union clarified its position—reaffirming its support of the Moscow agreement, but revealing that trusteeship was Washington's idea. Rhee exploited the trusteeship controversy for all it was worth, using it to consolidate his hold on the Korean right. South Korean communists led by Pak Hon Yong at first jumped on the anti-trusteeship bandwagon, but they made a *volte-face* when the Soviets issued their clarification. The Korean communists were thoroughly discredited for their last-minute switch in position, and even today many Koreans can forgive Pak everything but this.

The Moscow agreement provided for two sets of talks. Talks between the two commands to coordinate administrative and economic matters were held in January. The United States saw the negotiations as a way to integrate the two zones economically, while the Soviets seemed primarily interested in a barter deal. Agreements were reached on supplying North Korean electricity to the South and on some minor matters, but rejection of a Soviet request to buy rice created an atmosphere of hostility between the two commands, the Soviets suspecting that Washington was trying to destabilize the economy of the northern zone.

A joint United States-Soviet commission to deal with broader political questions convened in March but immediately hit a snag over the consultation issue. As the furor over trusteeship abated, the military government scrambled to put together a Korean coalition to provide it with political backing in the joint commission talks. At first, this effort included only the far right; later, moderates were approached; and towards the end, even "responsible" leftists were included. But the joint commission came to nothing. The Soviets insisted that Korean leaders who had opposed the Moscow agreement be ineligible for consult-ation—a formula that would have excluded all but communists. Thus the commission ended its first round of talks in June 1946.

Discontent over the policies of the occupation soon burst into violence in the "October People's Resistance." The protests began when the killing of a railroad striker precipitated large-scale riots in the port city of Pusan. These protests quickly coalesced with rural disturbances over forced grain collections by the police, and unrest completely engulfed Korea's south-eastern provinces. The violence was directed primarily at the Japanese-trained police, 400 of whom were killed. American troops had to be called out in some areas to assist in restoring order. Hodge blamed outside agitators for the violence—ignor-ing recommendations to reform the police, whose abuses, one ex-officer in the military government noted, "had done more to ruin the American reputation in Korea than any other factor."[3]

In this tense atmosphere elections were held for the Interim Legislative Assembly, the culmination of Hodge's governing commission plan. Half of the members of the legislative body were to be elected by community elders and half appointed. Not surprisingly, rightists captured nearly all of the elected seats. Trying to salvage the election, Hodge appointed moder-ates to the remaining slots to secure a more representative assembly. Kim Kyu Sik was elected chairman of the assembly; Hodge subsequently named another moderate, An Chae Hong, as chief civil administrator.

Furious over the packing of the assembly, Rhee flew to Washington to lobby for sacking Hodge and ending the occu-pation. Rhee gave orders to stoke up the anti-trusteeship campaign again while he was away. Kim Ku was volunteered by Rhee as a sacrificial goat: Kim was to stage an uprising on the anniversary of the March First Independence Movement against Japan and get himself arrested. But he backed out of the plot at the last minute. Unaware of this, Rhee went ahead as planned with a statement that events in Korea had "again called [him] to the presidency." The affair was hushed up by the military government as an embarrassment to all concerned. Rhee tarried abroad a few weeks longer on the excuse of lobbying for a Korean aid bill (a futile effort after Truman's aid commitment to Greece and Turkey dried up all available funds). Hodge wanted to keep Rhee from returning after the abortive plot, but was overruled by MacArthur.

The chill in United States-Soviet relations began to deepen early in 1947. As the United States shifted from seeking negotiated settlements of postwar issues to creating "situations of strength" around the periphery of the communist world, initiatives poured forth: the Truman Doctrine in March, the Marshall Plan in June, and Kennan's "Mr. X" article in July. Indian summer lingered for a few months longer. As the Soviets searched for appropriate policy responses, talks on Korea and other divided countries reopened. At Molotov's suggestion, the joint commission reconvened in May. But as it had a year earlier, the commission deadlocked over the issue of "free speech" and consultation of Korean political groups opposed to the Moscow agreements. Washington and Moscow instructed the joint commission to report on where negotiations stood so they could each consider "next steps." But the commission failed to agree even on this.

As the joint commission neared its final impasse, Washington began a major reevaluation of policy towards Korea. Over the summer of 1947, the Truman administration gradually came around to the military's view that Korea was of limited importance strategically and that continuing the occupation was likely to lead to major civil disturbances. Worried that Korea might blow up in its face, Washington decided to withdraw as quickly and gracefully as possible.[4] Talks were resumed with the Soviets, and as one last try Washington proposed elections for zonal representative bodies that would subsequently convene as a national legislature and set up a provisional government. When Moscow rejected the proposal, the United States

introduced a resolution in the UN General Assembly in November calling for establishment of the United Nations Temporary Commission on Korea (UNTCOK) to supervise elections for a unified Korean government. Refusing to accept the UN's competence to deal with Korea, the Soviet Union came back with a proposal for simultaneous withdrawal of all occupation forces by the end of the year.

The failure of the joint commission talks had an immediate effect on South Korean politics. The moderate coalition the United States had tried for a year to put together to provide it with political backing in the talks collapsed with the assassination in July of Yo Un Hyong, "the only hope for forceful moderate leadership" in Korea.[5] Rhee now confidently predicted that the United States would have to turn to him to form a separate government in the South. Polarization between left and right was virtually complete.

The South Korean Labor party (SKLP) also began to show signs of an alarming new militancy. The party began secretly to organize guerrilla units and to step up attempts to infiltrate the constabulary and police. It also reportedly opened talks with Kim Ku aimed at a single Korean government (an effort that was to cost Kim his life two years later). Rumors of a Soviet "master plan" to take over the South after the withdrawal of United States troops were rampant—possibly deliberately spread by the SKLP to unsettle the already jittery South Korean public.[6]

The arrival of UNTCOK brought the issue of separate elections to the fore. Although controlled by United States allies, the commission was determined to establish its own independence. Beyond a mandate to observe elections for a national assembly, UNTOK members had little guidance. In the face of Soviet opposition, moreover, many members of the commission doubted they would be able to accomplish much of anything. They were impressed by the arguments of Kim Kyu Sik and other moderates that elections in the United States zone would only harden the division of the peninsula and push the North more tightly into the Soviet orbit. The Australian and Canadian members, in particular, were loath to take any action in Korea that might exacerbate superpower tensions.[7]

The communist propaganda offensive against the commission opened in mid-December. Taking its cue from Pyongyang, the SKLP flayed the members of UNTCOK as American "stooges" and demanded the immediate implementation of the Moscow agreements. The SKLP was divided over strategy. Many of its leaders were deeply pessimistic over the direction of events, feeling they were "powerless to take physical means of opposing the elections."[8] A different assessment of the situation, however, was apparently reached by party head Pak Hon Yong. Pak had fled to the North after the Taegu riots, but he continued to direct operations in the South. In the end, Pak overrode all objections within the SKLP leadership and ordered a general strike. Although it is uncertain why he did so, the divisions within UNTCOK were widely known, and Pak may have felt he could influence it by a show of popular opposition to the elections.[9]

The strike itself lasted for only four days in early February. It was not particularly successful as a work stoppage, but the campaign of sabotage, mass demonstrations, and attacks on police that accompanied it posed a serious challenge to the authority of the military government. More than forty people were killed and 1500 arrested. North Korean party historians have severely criticized the strike, accusing Pak of calling an "adventurist charge" that needlessly exposed the SKLP organization to counterattack and nearly destroyed it.[10] But Pak almost succeeded.

Most members of UNTCOK were convinced that even if a vote were held, it should be only to form a consultative assembly. The commission voted to refer the question of whether to hold elections in the South to the Interim Committee of the UN General Assembly. It received with dismay the Interim Committee's February 26 decision to proceed with separate elections in that part of Korea that was accessible to UNTCOK. The majority of the commission felt the decision was a virtual "coup" that ran counter to their "nearly unanimous opinion." After considerable debate, UNTCOK decided to go ahead with a plan to supervise the elections in an effort to ensure that a free atmosphere prevailed.[11]

The North Korean response came a month later in a radio broadcast inviting southern political leaders to a unification conference in Pyongyang. The invitation to the conference, which was to open in mid-April, was attractive enough to draw many moderate, and even some rightist, opponents of Rhee. But while Pyongyang was getting ready for the big event, a rebellion broke out on Cheju-do that threatened to upset these united front tactics and to push the SKLP into a premature struggle it could not win. Before it was over, the rebellion was to claim as many as 60,000 victims, or 20 percent of the population of Cheju-do. Whole villages in the interior of the island were laid waste, their inhabitants massacred or forcibly relocated to refugee camps along the coast.[12]

In the early morning hours of April 3, SKLP guerrilla units descended from their bases on Halla-san, a 6000-foot-high cone dominating the island, to assault towns and police boxes along the shore. The 500 guerrillas, half of whom were armed with rifles, gathered thousands of additional supporters in coastal villages. The guerrillas killed scores of police and rightists, but did not attack the under-strength constabulary regiment or the United States military government company on the island.

There is still much about the rebellion that remains unclear, but it appears to have been touched off by local factors: the island's separatist tradition, the long-standing grievances of its people, and the politicized atmosphere on the island in the run-up to the May 10 elections. Cheju-do had a tradition of loose governmental control and periodic rebellion; a series of peasant uprisings had shaken it the last years of the Yi dynasty. During the colonial period, tens of thousands of islanders emigrated to Japan, where they found low-wage jobs in fishing, mining, and textile shops. There they were also exposed to contemporary currents of Marxism and socialist thought. The life of the islanders was disrupted by the stationing of a large Japanese garrison there during World War II. The Japanese turned Halla-san into a labyrinth of fortifications to prevent the allies from using Cheju-do as a jumping-off point for an invasion of the home islands.

The end of the war brought tremendous dislocation on Cheju-do. United States tactical forces supervised the repatriation of Japanese troops on the island and the destruction of their weapons. But it was months before a military government company arrived. Meanwhile, the people's committee had established itself as the island's de facto government. The local United States military authorities initially adopted a friendly attitude towards the committee and used it as a convenient way to administer the island. But in the aftermath of the October People's Resistance, the relationship soured. The committee found itself turned out of office and under attack.

The first serious violence occurred in 1947 during ceremonies to commemorate the March First Movement. Several onlookers were killed when United States troops fired warning shots over the heads of a crowd marching on the administration building in Cheju City. The military government responded by rushing in reinforcements. These police and right-wing youth group members came to the "red island" only months after the bloody Taegu incident; they had many scores to settle. A cycle of terror and counterterror quickly developed, with the island's SKLP branch organizing a "People's Liberation Army," headed by Kim Tal Sam, an ex-schoolteacher and "student draftee" in the Japanese army.

The military government moved swiftly to control the rebellion. Major General William F. Dean, the United States military governor, flew to the island in early May to personally inspect the situation. Dean tried to improve the image of the police by appointing a chief who was a native of the island; he also ordered the new constabulary commander to settle the rebellion with "minimal force." The two sides tried to negotiate in secret talks, but with no success. As the situation on the island deteriorated, Seoul newspapers speculated that United States troops might have to be sent in.

The rebellion on Cheju-do apparently was not planned by the SKLP's central leadership. The party's campaign of sabotage and low-level violence during the February general strike was primarily an attempt to influence the UN commission and to discredit the military government. It was not until the following spring that the SKLP switched to armed struggle. In fact, the Cheju-do uprising enormously complicated the party's task—it threatened to drive away the very leaders in the South whom the North was trying to attract to the Pyongyang conference.

The Cheju-do rebellion was one of a number of insurgencies that broke out in Asian countries in the aftermath of World War

II as communist-led nationalist movements resisted attempts to reimpose colonial structures. Its issues were explicitly political—opposition to the separate elections and support for a single Korean government controlled by the left. The uprising was directed by a leadership educated in Japan. It was sustained by an organizational network that encompassed all social groups on the island and by solidarity with the rest of the Korean left. Completely missing was the nativistic cast of the late-Yi dynasty uprisings.

Such violent popular opposition to a postwar United States occupation occurred nowhere else. The military government allowed a campaign of right-wing terror to develop on the island. The Cheju-do rebellion must stand as testimony to the occupation's failure to develop viable policies and establish the foundations of democracy in Korea.

The outbreak of the rebellion put Kim Ku and Kim Kyu Sik in a bind. The Pyongyang conference was to open in mid-April, only two weeks later. The two Kims were already hesitant about attending. If they went, they would be legitimizing the draft constitution the North had slated for discussion. They also had been angered by Kim Il Sung's threat to cut off electricity to the South for nonpayment of its electric bill. Even so, it was hard for them to flatly reject the invitation, since they had originally proposed the conference and had put their political futures on the line by coming out in opposition to separate elections. The two Kims half-wanted to avoid going, and the rebellion nearly gave them a convenient excuse. In the end, it may have been a campaign by the military government to discredit them as "communist dupes" that tipped the scales in favor of their attending the conference.[13]

As Kim Kyu Sik had expected, the Pyongyang conference turned out to be a stage-managed affair. Kim Kyu Sik refused to attend public sessions, but the more naive Kim Ku delivered a short speech opposing separate elections. Little genuine discussion was permitted.

> The content of [the] speeches was all the same. "Rhee is bad," "Oppose the separate elections." This was called discussion. It was more like a rally.[14]

In addition to adopting a statement on the South Korean political situation and issuing a call for a national salvation struggle, the conference sent a message to the commanders of the two zones requesting simultaneous withdrawal of United States and Soviet troops so that Koreans could "solve their own national problems" by holding countrywide elections. Informal discussions continued for a week after the conference, keeping the two Kims in Pyongyang just long enough to participate in May Day celebrations.

Almost totally ignored in Western accounts, the Pyongyang conference had a major impact on Korean politics. It not only failed to block separate elections but also paved the way for Rhee's accession to power in the South.

> According to General Dean, Kim Kyu-sik alone among the seven leaders opposing the conference had greater influence than Rhee at the time of the establishment of the South Korean government. Also, the fame of Kim Ku and his government in exile [during the Japanese colonial period] was no less than Rhee's. Thus, Rhee and his insistence on the separate election represented only a minority of Koreans, and was not greatly supported by the general public. On the whole, it is reasonable to think that Koreans hoped for North-South elections before any elections. If either Kim Ku or Kim Kyu-sik had participated in the elections to check Rhee, instead of staying committed to the South-North conference, they certainly could have beaten Rhee.[15]

In a move that seemed deliberately designed to punish the two Kims for not playing a more active role in opposing the southern elections, the North, within days of their return, renewed its threat to cut off electric power to the South. The two Kims' public image was a shambles.

The military government employed massive security precautions to prevent trouble at the polls. While American troops adopted a low profile, keeping to their bases on the May 10 election day, the Korean security forces were very much in evidence.

> Members of the newly formed Community Protective Associations accoutered with clubs and axes...patrolled the villages, proud of the government's "favor" to them and anxious to display their new status by interfering in the lives of ordinary citizens. Cases of police

or youth groups beating, threatening, robbing, blackmailing, and removing the ration cards of those who would not vote were reported to UNTCOK.[16]

In most areas, the voting went smoothly. Except in the traditional "communist strongholds" of Cholla Namdo, Taegu, and Cheju-do, there was little election-day violence. The SKLP leadership may have told its members not to make an all-out effort against the elections, hoping to place the blame for dividing the country on Rhee and preferring a southern regime dominated by rightist rather than moderate leaders.

The figures on voter turnout were certainly impressive—80 percent of eligible voters registered, and 95 percent of these cast their votes. The high level of participation was taken as a triumph for Rhee, but the results were actually much more ambiguous. Rhee's National Association for the Rapid Realization of Korean Independence did win 55 out of the 200 contested seats (another hundred were left vacant for North Korea). But independents—some of them followers of the two Kims running on their own—did almost as well. Candidates too closely associated with the military government generally did poorly. Indeed, it was mainly because the vote represented a step towards ending the occupation that the SKLP had a hard time convincing voters to support the boycott.

Not without some misgivings, UNTCOK eventually endorsed the election results. Although the balloting itself was secret, the names of those entering the polls were checked off against a list of eligible voters, and nonvoting was a matter of public record that could lead to retaliation by rightist groups and the police. The commission observed just a small sample of the polls, and its staff members were only able to "show themselves and hope to attract complaints and significant information." The military government's willingness to accommodate its procedural concerns, as well as the Pyongyang conference's failure to produce a political breakthrough, left UNTCOK with no other alternative.[17]

Political violence subsided over the summer as political leaders in the two occupation zones busied themselves with preparations for establishing rival governments. Rhee and the Korean Democratic party were less interested in bashing the heads of communists than in jockeying for control of the new assembly. Anxious to get through the summer without any last-minute hitch in transferring power to a Korean government, the military government was not eager to press cleanup operations against the insurgency on Cheju-do. The SKLP, meanwhile, was preoccupied with a signature-gathering campaign, the "August underground elections," to select delegates to a conference to choose southern representatives to the Supreme People's Assembly. The party also began to establish base areas in remote mountainous areas of the South and to train guerrillas for dispatch to the South.

At the end of May, the newly elected southern assemblymen formed themselves into a constituent assembly to draw up a constitution. Rhee was elected chairman but immediately fell out with his erstwhile KDP allies over whether to adopt a presidential or a cabinet system. The Korean Democratic Party was composed of a group of Cholla landowners and businessmen who had done well under the Japanese and needed the support of an influential nationalist of Rhee's stature. Certain to be elected the country's first president, Rhee was growing increasingly aloof and saw the push for a parliamentary system as a direct challenge to his authority. On the verge of assuming power, the once-solid rightist coalition split.

Pyongyang, too, was preoccupied during the summer with trying to legitimize itself as the sole government on the peninsula. Forty percent of the representatives in its legislature were to come from the northern zone, and elections for these seats were held on August 25. The remaining seats were set aside for the South. They were to be elected at a conference in Haeju by "representatives of the South Korean people" chosen in a massive signature-gathering campaign. The North's contention that these "underground elections" were conducted in the South has always been viewed with extreme skepticism, if not dismissed as an outright lie. Nevertheless, United States intelligence reports suggest that nearly a quarter of the rural population in the South may have signed the petitions—whether "knowingly," believing them for land reform or unification, or just out of fear. The Haeju conference, which opened on August 21, seemed devoted mainly to glorifying SKLP leader Pak Hon Yong, apparently to boost his influence in the new northern government. After the Supreme People's Assembly ratified a constitution, the Democratic People's Republic of Korea was formally established on September 9, 1948.

As the summer drew to a close, two hostile Korean regimes came into being, each claiming to be the sole government on the peninsula.

> Thus Mao's "two regimes in one country" became an actuality in Korea. Each government tried to prove that its own way represented genuine nationalism and attacked the other as a foreign puppet. South Korea called the North Korean government a "puppet of international communism"; the North Koreans responded that the Republic of Korea was a "stooge of American imperialism."[18]

The post-regime period was fundamentally different from the occupation years. Interestingly, this is also the North Korean position. A recent DPRK history of the war characterizes the post-regime period as a "grave" stage that was qualitatively different from the occupation years because of what it termed "stepped-up provocations against the North."[19] With the establishment of separate regimes, the superpower presence that had stabilized the potentially explosive situation on the peninsula began to erode. It was only a matter of time before the two hostile Korean governments, established by the United States and the Soviet Union, flew at each other's throats.

The Republic of Korea was established on August 15, 1948, the third anniversary of liberation from Japan. The assembly was filled with talk about a constitutional amendment to switch back to a parliamentary system. There was so much disgruntlement over Rhee's initial cabinet lineup and it drew so much criticism that the KDP introduced a "national traitor law" to go after his supporters as Japanese collaborators. Rhee came in for more criticism over the slowness of the transfer of government functions from the military government to the new South Korean government; a quarter of the assembly signed a resolution urging the speedy withdrawal of United States troops.

By most standards, the American occupation of Korea was a failure. It led to the tragic and artificial division of a country just liberated from decades of Japanese colonial rule, stifled the outpouring of popular participation that had found expression in the people's committees, and left entrenched in power rightist elements commanding powerful instruments of police repression and bureaucratic control. Many regard it as America's "original sin" from which the rest of Korea's ills flow. But from the standpoint of American policy, the case against the occupation is not quite so clear. For it was not only a series of blunders, misunderstandings, and failures but also an exercise in strategic denial that at least kept the southern half of the peninsula from falling under the control of the Soviet Union.

The occupation years still remain controversial. History took a tragically wrong turning—towards division, hostility, and war. But not everything was predetermined in 1945 with division of the country and the suppression of the people's committees. And the fault was not that of the United States alone, however great its responsibility. The Soviet Union was more interested in securing its position in the North than in cooperating with the United States to unify the country. Koreans played an important role in shaping the history of their country even then. We need to explore the roles of both popular movements and political leadership. Syngman Rhee, Kim Ku, and Kim Kyu Sik and, in the North, Kim Il Sung and Pak Hon Yong were their own men—they were far from being just puppets of the superpowers.

Until recently, a succession of authoritarian Korean regimes kept post-liberation history largely in darkness. With democratization, however, there have been a lifting of former constraints on scholarly research and a surge of interest in rediscovering the history of the American occupation period. Amid these changes, there have been many attempts to find contemporary relevance in the history of the popular struggles that took place under the United States military government. There is nothing intrinsically wrong with efforts to find "friends in the past." But we must be careful to avoid simply projecting present attitudes onto history.

History does not present us with a single line of development along which events can be strung like so many beads on a string. Obviously, useful trends can be identified by focusing on one factor or another, such as participation in popular resistance movements. But these events were not all of a kind—there were many qualitative differences. By highlighting one dimension of a situation, we also necessarily neglect others and introduce some bias into our interpretation. To overcome this, we should try to approach the problem from many different angles—what systems theorists term "perspective thinking." With this in mind, what is needed today is not more "verdicts"—these are obvious enough—but more work to rediscover the "hidden history" of the occupation years from as many aspects as possible.

Notes

1. The best published accounts of the American occupation are Bruce Cumings' *The Origins of the Korean War: Liberation and the Emergence of Separate Regimes, 1945–1947* (Princeton: Princeton University Press, 1981) and Gregory Henderson's *Korea: Politics of the Vortex* (Cambridge, MA: Harvard University Press, 1968). Richard D. Robinson's unpublished manuscript *Betrayal of a Nation*, 1960, remains the single most important source for the first two years of the occupation. Mark Paul argues that the United States delayed discussing Korea with the Soviet Union to use the atomic bomb as political leverage in redrawing the political map of postwar Asia. See "Diplomacy Delayed: The Atomic Bomb and the Division of Korea, 1945," in *Child of Conflict: The Korean-American Relationship, 1945–1953*, ed. Bruce Cumings (Seattle: University of Washington Press, 1983), 67–91. I have relied on Cumings, Henderson, and Robinson for much of the discussion that follows.
2. Henderson, *Politics of the Vortex.*
3. Robinson, *Betrayal,* 143-69.
4. Ibid., 148–150.
5. Henderson, *Politics of the Vortex,* 134.
6. Robert A. Scalapino and Chong-sik Lee, *Communism in Korea, Part 1: The Movement* (Berkeley and Los Angeles: University of California Press, 1971), 306–07.
7. Far East Command, *Intelligence Summary,* 5, 11 February and 15 March 1948. Also, Leon Gordendenker, *The United Nations and the Peaceful Unification of Korea: The Politics of Field Operations, 1947–1950* (The Hague: Martinus Nijoff, 1959) for background on the UN role.
8. Far East Command, *Intelligence Summary,* February 6, 1948.
9. Ibid., February 18, 1948.
10. See Glenn D. Paige, "Korea," in *Communism and Revolution: The Strategic Uses of Political Violence,* Cyril E. Black and Thomas P. Thornton, eds. (Princeton: Princeton University Press, 1964), 222, for a translation of the North Korean criticism of Pak in *Choson t'ong-sa* [general history of Korea].
11. Far East Command, *Intelligence Summary,* March 15, 1948.

12. Despite its importance, the Cheju-do rebellion has been little studied. Apart from my article, "The Cheju-do Rebellion," *Journal of Korean Studies* 2 (1980): 139–97, no more than a few paragraphs have been published on it in English. There is a great deal of new scholarship that is now starting to come out in Korean on the events of this period, including the Cheju-do rebellion. See, for example, the newspaper series "Sasam Ui Chungon" [Testimony on April 3]; and "Youn Sasan Ui Chinsil" [Posthumous Testimony on the Truth of the April 3 Incident] by Kim Ik Yol, ex-constabulary commander on the island; in Cheju Shimnum, April 3–December 9, and August 15–September 23, 1989, respectively. For an overview of the years just before the Korean War, see my *Korea: The Peninsular Origins of the War* (Newark and London: University of Delaware Press, 1989).
13. Far East Command, *Intelligence Summary*, April 23, 1948.
14. Kim Nam Sik, *Sillok namnodang* [authentic record of the South Korean Labor party] (Seoul: Sinhyonsil-sa, 1975), 379.
15. Yi Ho-jae, *Han'quk oeqyo chongch'aek ui isang kwa hyonsil: Yi Sung-man oegyo wa Miquk* [Ideal and reality of Korean diplomatic policy: Syngman Rhee's diplomacy and America] (Seoul: Pommun-sa, 1975), 243.
16. Henderson, *Politics of the Vortex,* 156.
17. James I. Matray, *The Reluctant Crusade: American Foreign Policy in Korea, 1941–1950* (Honolulu: University of Hawaii Press, 1985), 364.
18. Kim Young-jeh, "The Purpose of North Korea's Guerrilla Warfare and the Reactions of South Korea," *Issues and Studies*, August 1970, 18.
19. *The U.S. Imperialist Started the Korean War* (Pyongyang: Foreign Languages Publishing House, 1977), 62.

A History of Korean Presidential Elections

Donald S. Macdonald

Introduction and Summary

ON DECEMBER 16, 1987, four-fifths of the eligible citizens of South Korea cast their votes in the country's fourteenth presidential election. The return to direct popular election, the first since 1971, resulted from two years of mounting protest by the political opposition and intellectuals against authoritarian political controls, with growing popular support. The government party's candidate, ex-General Roh Tae Woo, won the election; but he gained a plurality of only 36.6 percent—the smallest of any presidential election in South Korea's history. His victory was due more to divisions among the opposition than to support for the government. In the legislative election of April 26, 1988, the government's plurality in the popular vote was even less; and for the first time since 1954 the government did not have a clear Assembly majority. Yet the great majority of the Korean people appear to have acquiesced in the choice of Roh as president. As he served out his term and won re-election, South Korea demonstrated that the electoral process has been effectively institutionalized as a significant part of Korea's political culture.

Direct popular election of the president in South Korea has in recent years become a symbol of political freedom. However, the election process has not played the same central role in Korean politics as it does in the United States and other mature democracies. Its meaning may be made clear by a brief examination of the historical background of Korean elections. In this paper, primary attention will be paid to presidential elections; but they cannot be totally separated from the other kinds of votes that Koreans have cast since 1945 (for members of the national legislature, for local executives and councils between 1952 and 1961, and in referenda on constitutional revision).

Eight basic points can be made about Korean elections:

1. They have no indigenous roots.
2. They are nonetheless valued by the Koreans as a symbol of modernity and international respectability, and may have become something of a latter-day substitute for the Mandate of Heaven.
3. They have become a standard feature of Korean political life, but have not yet been firmly established as a means of popular control over government, or as an acceptable communicator of public sentiment.
4. Traditionally, voters in rural areas have supported the incumbent regime and have gone to the polls in greater percentages, while most city voters have supported the opposition and turned out in lower proportions (although still high by American standards). As Korea has become more urbanized, the vote has been harder for the government to control.
5. Most elections have involved at least some irregularities and vote-rigging, and all but one of them have been influenced by official pressures on the electorate.
6. In general, personalities, family and regional identification, and individual ambitions have been determining factors in election campaigns, although issues have played some role.
7. Elections have several times conveyed a clear message of popular disapproval of government leaders or policies. Until now, however, the end result in each case has been to execute the messenger.

8. Given the history of the election process and the increasing sophistication of the Korean public, there is reason to believe that elections and an elected legislature are becoming a more significant part of South Korean politics.

The Tradition

To appreciate the place of elections in the Korean political process, it is important to recognize first of all that there was virtually no comparable political institution in Korea throughout its history until 1921, and the local elections held by the Japanese from then until 1945 had very limited impact. In Japan, elections began around 1890; in France, in the eighteenth century; in England, at least in rudimentary form, in the thirteenth century. The Korean public, except for a very small Western-trained elite, have been learning about elections only since 1945.

In the Confucian cultural tradition shared by Korea, the legitimacy of government was determined by the Mandate of Heaven, under which the ruler had responsibility to maintain order, harmony, and well-being in the national society. Possession of the Mandate was demonstrated by the ruler's performance of this responsibility. If he failed to carry it out, he lost the Mandate, usually because someone else took it from him by force.[1]

In such a polity, the ruler and his officials were supposed to be endowed with wisdom and benevolence. They alone controlled affairs of state, and they referred to the classics for guidance. Officials were selected largely through competitive examinations of their knowledge of the classics. The general public was never involved in the selection of officials, although the views of the people were supposed to be taken into account.[2] In Korea, more than in China, eligibility to take the examinations was limited in practice to families of those already qualified. Other individuals could occasionally pass the examinations through diligent study; they could petition (even directly to the king) for redress of grievances; but the only means of expressing mass discontent was through peasant revolts, of which there were a growing number at the end of each dynasty.[3]

Although rival factions of aristocrats plagued the Korean court, factions were viewed as illegitimate and had no mass base of support. The losers in factional struggles were exiled or disgraced. Ordinary people, as obedient subjects, had no voice in the selection process, nor could they question the officials' policies or performance, except by petition to the ruler or by revolt. There is only one recorded example in Korean history before 1921 in which the people's opinion was consulted: a referendum held by the great King Sejong in the fifteenth century on tax policy.[4]

The political history of traditional Korea also reveals among the elite an enormous ambition for power and status, which repeatedly took precedence over morality or the good of the polity. Although this is not peculiar to Korea, it must be borne in mind along with the fact that in the Korean tradition high government position is the supreme goal; other institutions have had little or no social importance. The competition for high office has been, and still is, a high-risk, high-stakes game.[5]

One of the greatest differences between the East Asian political tradition and that of the West is in the conception of law and constitutional order. In East Asia, the Confucian classics were the source of all wisdom, although they were subject to interpretation. Laws were issued by the ruler as a convenient means of expressing his will; they did not constrain his behavior. Accordingly, a principal means of obliging fair elections and of enforcing compliance with their result—the concept of the overarching rule of law, enforced by an independent judiciary—has no Korean cultural roots. As President Syngman Rhee once told a critical session of his National Assembly, "Laws are made for men, not men for laws."[6]

Repeatedly amending the constitution under these conditions is not necessarily an indication of political instability, because the constitution has not, either in theory or in pracice, been the foundation of the political system, in contrast to the United States. On the contrary, the Republic of Korea's six republics (1948–1960 under Syngman Rhee, 1960–1961 under Chang Myon as prime minister, 1963–1972 and 1972–1979 under Park Chung Hee, 1981–1988 under Chun Doo Hwan, and 1988 to the present under Roh Tae Woo) and ten constitutional amendments can be viewed as political experimentation by the South Koreans in search of a polity that suits their character and aspirations.[7]

The collapse of the traditional Confucian order in both China and Korea before the onslaught of Western industrial and military power had compelled the Koreans to look elsewhere for guidance in constructing a modern political system. Since elections are a leading element of all major Western polities, and of modern Japan's as well, the Koreans accepted that principle. (Even communist North Korea has elections.) The problem was one of practice. The people, long accustomed to a ruling class making decisions, never understood electoral voting and were easily manipulated by those viewed as their betters. The rulers, smug and superior, viewed elections as a ritual rather than a serious means of selection of new leaders. They manipulated, disregarded, or overruled election results rather than abiding by them.[8]

The Formative Period, 1876–1948

Western concepts of popular sovereignty and the concomitant idea of elections were brought to Korea in the late nineteenth century by Korean travellers to the West and by Western officials and missionaries. The example of Japan, where the modernizing process had begun a generation earlier, impressed some young Korean aristocrats. However, the conservative court prevented basic political change. An attempt by young reformers to seize control of the government in 1884, with Japanese encouragement and support, was put down by conservatives aligned with the Chinese.[9]

The Japanese victory over China in 1894–1995 not only severed Korea's long-standing subordinate political relationship to China, it also encouraged would-be political modernizers. While the Independence Club movement of 1897 did not challenge the institution of the monarchy, it did call for a legislature, among other reforms. Japan by this time already had a partially elective legislature under its 1889 constitution. However, the same conservative forces at court that had (with Chinese help) suppressed the modernizers' attempted 1884 coup d'état again triumphed. Their dominance in Korean national policy continued until the Russo-Japanese War brought Japanese hegemony and then annexation in 1910.

The Japanese were concerned during the early years of their rule with the subduing of their new subjects, not with soliciting their opinions. Adverse international reaction to the harsh Japanese suppression of the 1919 Korean independence movement forced an amelioration of Japanese colonial policy, including the introduction of elections for local councils in 1921.

These elections were the first ever held in Korea for public office. Held at intervals thereafter, they were of limited meaning for Koreans because property requirements gave the advantage to Japanese candidates and voters resident in Korea. Nevertheless, they are sometimes cited—along with elections for officers of churches and rural cooperatives—as a learning experience for Koreans. In 1942, elections were held for two representatives of the colony in the Japanese Diet. Additionally, elections of officers were held in such organizations as churches and rural cooperatives.[10]

Meanwhile, a Korean Provisional Government was established in Shanghai from among exiled leaders of the independence movement. Its constitution provided a parliamentary form of government responsible to a nominally elected legislature, which also elected a president as head of state.[11]

Before the Japanese surrender to the Allies in 1945, Koreans began to organize themselves into local people's committees to take over administration and security. In September 1945, a national congress of these committees (from both North and South Korea) convened in Seoul to declare a Korean People's Republic and confirm a slate of government leaders selected from among prominent nationalists. Representatives to the congress were claimed to have been chosen by the local committees through some sort of election process. However, the United States occupation authorities refused to recognize the People's Republic as a government and over the next several months disbanded the people's committees.[12]

To ameliorate growing public discontent with foreign military rule, the U.S. Army Military Government in Korea (USA MGIK) in July 1946 announced that elections would be held for a South Korean Interim Legislative Assembly (KILA). Elections were held in September and October 1946 for 45 assembly members in single-member districts, generally under the old Japanese rules. In consequence, all but two were conservatives far from representative of the political and social views of the poverty-stricken population (the other two never took their seats). In an attempt to balance the conservative bias, the military governor appointed 45 moderate notables. The result was deadlock, compounded by the United States refusal to permit the assembly to enact basic laws. The important legislation for the United States occupation zone originated by decree of the military governor. KILA ceased to meet after about a year; its record did little to improve Korean understanding of or respect for the election process.[13]

In the fall of 1947, following the failure of United States-Soviet negotiations for a transitional Korean administration, the United Nations General Assembly on American initiative passed a resolution calling for establishment of an independent Korean state through general elections under United Nations observation. Since the UN Temporary Commission on Korea was refused admission to North Korea, another American-drafted resolution called for elections to a constituent assembly in South Korea only. These were held in May 1948.

The election, administered by the United States military government, was observed by both UN and United States officials. Although conservative elements dominated a volunteer security force that was set up to help maintain order, and although two noted Korean nationalist leaders called for a boycott because they feared perpetuation of Korea's division, the election was reasonably free and fair according to the UN Temporary Commission on Korea and United States observers, despite a number of specific cases of abuse. About 80 percent of the eligible population voted; they chose 197 representatives by plurality in single-member districts from over 2,000 candidates representing hundreds of political and social groups (many of them organized by individual candidates for the occasion). The representatives from Cheju Island, then in revolt, were never seated.[14]

Elections in the First Republic, 1948–1960

The constituent assembly was elected in South Korea for the purpose of establishing a government.[15] One of its first acts was to set up a constitution drafting committee. An eminent Korean lawyer, Yu Chin O, prepared a draft which provided for a European-type parliamentary system. This had been the form of the Korean Provisional Government in exile, and was also the form of the postwar Japanese constitution adopted in 1947. Under this system, the president, elected by the legislature, would have a largely ceremonial role as chief of state while a prime minister actually headed the government. The conservative Han'guk Democratic party could then have dominated the government by putting Syngman Rhee, then popularly regarded as the preeminent nationalist hero, on a shelf in a relatively powerless presidency.

Dr. Rhee strongly opposed the plan. He believed that he should lead the country under a governmental structure similar to the American and refused to cooperate unless he got it. In the end, a compromise was reached: the president would be elected to a four-year term by a one-house legislature, but he would name his cabinet, subject to legislative approval of his choice of prime minister. The new constitution, adopted in July 1948, also provided that the constituent assembly chosen in May 1948 would become the national legislature (National Assembly) with an initial two-year term. Subsequent elections would be at four-year intervals. Rhee was elected president by a large Assembly majority and took office on August 15, 1948, when the Republic of Korea was proclaimed an independent and sovereign state.

In North Korea, under Soviet occupation, an election was held in August 1948. It was not observed by representatives of the United Nations (who had been refused access) or those of noncommunist governments. The North Korean authorities maintained that large numbers of South Koreans had participated in the election, as well as almost 100 percent of those in the North, voting unanimously for the single slate of candidates for a constituent assembly. This body adopted the constitution of the Democratic People's Republic of Korea, modeled after that of the Soviet Union. The DPRK was proclaimed in September.[16]

United States officials had no direct role in drafting the 1948 constitution of the Republic of Korea (South Korea), but General John R. Hodge, the United States commander, had insisted on an initial two-year term (rather than four) for the president in order to assure freedom from foreign influence. Rhee, foreseeing that his popularity among legislators would decline, tried to postpone the 1950 elections; but the United States forced him to hold them on schedule. The result (with unforeseen consequences) was that presidential elections came in the middle of the legislative term.

The first National Assembly was by no means a rubber stamp. It refused to confirm President Rhee's first nominee for prime minister. It enacted a number of laws that Rhee either vetoed or refused to implement. Rhee set out to dominate the Assembly first by arresting a leftist vice-speaker and fifteen other members whose views he suspected, and then by beating down a second attempt in 1949 by his conservative opponents to install a parliamentary regime by constitutional amendment, which would have made him a figurehead.

The Korean War briefly overshadowed domestic political differences; but by 1952, it was clear that the Assembly would not reelect Rhee for a second four-year term. A constitutional crisis ensued, in which the conservative opposition again sought a parliamentary system reducing the president to a figurehead, but Rhee—by strong-arm tactics including the detention of Assembly members on a bus during a vote and the arrest of key legislative leaders—forced enactment of provisions for direct popular election of the president, conceding to the opposition only a two-term limit on reelection. Rhee's popularity was high at the time, so he won easily in the general election that followed.

The 1952 crisis also inspired Rhee to implement local autonomy provisions of the constitution so that local councils could help in his reelection, and caused him to descend from his previous suprapartisan stand to head the pro-government Liberal party. Through a combination of force and guile, this party won a majority in the 1954 parliamentary election. Rhee then narrowly won a new constitutional amendment allowing him to succeed himself indefinitely.[17] This act unified the opposition, which gained such wide popular support in the 1956 presidential election that its vice-presidential candidate, Chang Myon, narrowly won over Rhee's running mate, although Rhee himself gained a respectable majority vote (the opposition presidential candidate, respected senior statesman Sin Ik Hui, died during the campaign).

In the mid-1950s, the influence of Rhee's open-minded lieutenant, Lee Ki Poong, and of the United States, kept politics reasonably free (at least for anticommunist conservatives), and something like a two-party system emerged, although left-of-center forces were suppressed. The conservative opposition increased its representation in the legislative election of 1958— a clear signal of mounting popular disapproval. The opposition also increased its representation in local council elections. In response, hard-line supporters of Rhee clamped down on the opposition with an intensifying series of laws and actions, negating the power of the Assembly, executing the left-liberal Cho Bong Am (who had challenged Rhee in the 1956 election), closing the principal opposition newspaper, and abolishing local councils. At the same time a lot of money was spent to win public support for the government party, despite a stagnant economy.

In the presidential election of March 1960, the pro-government Liberal party candidates for president and vice-president were the rapidly aging Rhee and his seriously ailing lieutenant, Liberal party chairman Lee Ki Poong. To ensure their victory in an increasingly hostile atmosphere, Rhee's supporters resorted to widespread coercion and ballot-stuffing, giving Rhee a 92 percent vote. The opposition Democratic party candidate, Chough Pyong Ok, had died in Walter Reed Hospital in Washington too close to the election to be replaced, but the lack of any vote for him was nonetheless suspicious. Rhee's running mate and probable anointed successor, Lee Ki Poong, won an incredible 8,221,000 votes to 1,844,000 for Chang Myon, notwithstanding the fact that Lee was so sick that he could barely stand up in campaign appearances. The irregularities were so blatant that the United States protested them in an *aide-mémoire*.

A month later, latent public resentment erupted into protest when the body of a student victim of a post-election riot in Masan (near Pusan in South Kyongsang Province) was found in the bay with tear-gas fragments in his eye. The resulting demonstrations, riots, and police brutality led to the Student Revolution of April 19 and to Rhee's resignation and exile. The armed forces stood aloof from the controversy and thus earned the respect of the citizens. The United States, in publicly acknowledging the "justifiable grievances" of the Korean people, gave its blessing to the change of regime.[18]

The Second and Third Republics, 1960–1972

The conservative opposition now came into its own in South Korea; it won its long-desired parliamentary form of government, and the elections of July 1960—equitably conducted by the interim government of Huh Chung—swept an overwhelming opposition majority into office. (Although the Democratic party candidates got only 39.9 percent of the vote, 49.3 percent was won by independent candidates, most of them with similar views and some of them Democrats without party endorsement.) However, the two main Democratic party factions, which had been united only by adversity, promptly split—first over which leader was to be figurehead president and which prime minister. After much infighting, Chang Myon, a prominent Catholic layman and statesman with the backing of the "new faction," was elected prime minister by vote of the National Assembly, while Yun Po Son, the candidate of the "old faction" that included the former Han'guk Democratic party leaders, became president through legislative election. The factional struggles over leadership and policy, combined with inexperienced administration and economic stagnation, led to near anarchy and to military *coup d'état* in May 1961.[19]

General Park Chung Hee, leader of the coup, had no legitimacy in Western constitutional terms. However, like his historical counterpart, General Yi Song Gye (founder of the Choson dynasty, 1392–1910), he could claim the Mandate of Heaven (although he never overtly did so) on the basis of his success in seizing and consolidating power. For two years, he and his military associates ran Korea through a 32-member Supreme Commitee for National Reconstruction; the 1960 constitution was suspended, the legislature dismissed, political parties were dissolved, and several hundred leaders were denied all political rights in the name of political purification.

Nevertheless—in part because of United States pressure—General Park accepted the idea of civilianizing his regime under a new constitution and submitted to a direct popular election in December 1963. Separate legislative elections were held the same month. The former president, Yun Po Son, ran Park a close race and might have won if the opposition had been united and if the military regime had been willing to accept that result. Park was nonetheless elected by a slim majority. The government's Democratic Republican party, which had been organized by Park's lieutenant, Kim Jong Pil, won a majority of the legislative seats; opposition forces were divided both by their own quarrels and by government manipulation.[20]

The legislature was again reduced to little more than a sounding board; one-third of its members were chosen from national slates by proportional representation, increasing the government's capacity for control. A lower turnout for elections from 1963 on, although partly due to growing urbanization (rural people in Korea, as in Japan, have a higher propensity to vote), can also be attributed to popular recognition of the Assembly's lessened importance.

In the elections of 1967, South Korea's burgeoning economic success and some relaxation of political controls had increased President Park's popularity, so that he won a second term easily, with a much greater majority than in 1963. The opposition was again divided. The separate legislative elections, heavily tainted with corruption, gave the government's party an increased working majority—enabling Park, like Rhee before him, to amend the constitution so he could have a third term. However, opposition forces again began to gain support, at the same time that Korea's national security was being called into question by the Vietnam War, the Guam Doctrine, and the United States opening to China.[21]

In the 1971 presidential election, the opposition managed to present a more or less united front, despite a struggle between Kim Young Sam and Kim Dae Jung for the New Democratic party candidacy. Kim Dae Jung, who emerged as the party's candidate, won 45 percent of the popular vote (which in a totally fair election might have been a majority), while the government's Democratic Republican party received only a plurality of the vote and a bare majority of seats in the National Assembly.[22]

The Fourth (Yushin) Republic, 1972–1980

In 1971, President Park thus faced both a domestic political challenge and, as he apparently perceived it, a threat to national security. The United States, Korea's traditional protector, was bogged down in Vietnam; it had proclaimed the Guam

Doctrine and had unilaterally pulled one of its two army divisions out of Korea; it had reversed its twenty-year hostility toward China. Secret contacts by the South Korean government with North Korea led to a brief thaw in North-South relations but also apparently gave the president a new sense of the extraordinary military preparedness of the North.

Park's response to the domestic and international situation was his 1972 "coup from within," establishing the draconian Yushin regime. Direct election of the president was replaced by a 2,500-person electoral college, the National Council for Unification, which also elected one-third of the legislature upon presidential nomination. Members of the council, popularly elected in small single-member districts, were forbidden to have political party affiliation. Terms of office (including those of council members) were extended to six years from the four that had prevailed since 1950, except that Assembly members elected by the council now had three-year terms. Election districts for popularly elected National Assembly members were enlarged, each returning two representatives. The government was thus assured of legislative support, and the legislature was reduced to virtual impotence.[23]

Further to ensure political control, operatives of the Korean Central Intelligence Agency abducted Kim Dae Jung, the opposition standard-bearer who had nearly won the 1971 presidential election, from his Tokyo hotel room in 1973. They probably intended to "deep-six" him in the Korea Strait; however, they brought him back to Korea instead, where he spent most of the ensuing seven years in prison or under house arrest. In 1980, Kim was sentenced to death but was eventually allowed to go to the United States for medical treatment.

In 1978, President Park was reelected by virtually unanimous vote of the electoral college. The opposition again enlarged its legislative representation, although it had no voice in the choice of president. This and other manifestations of growing opposition—such as student demonstrations and strikes—were due to economic difficulties resulting from government policies and the world oil crisis, as well because of popular resentment of the restrictive Yushin regime. The government's response was more repression, including the expulsion of the opposition leader Kim Young Sam from the National

Assembly. President Park's assassination in October 1979 brought the renewed cycle of discontent and repression to a halt. The civilian prime minister, Choi Kyu Hah, was duly elected Park's successor by the electoral college.

The ensuing "Seoul spring" of early 1980 saw some cautious liberalization of Korean politics, notwithstanding a growing military involvement after General Chun Doo Hwan's seizure of control within the armed forces in December 1979. As discussions of constitutional revision made it seem that the presidency might be filled through popular election, three leading contenders appeared—Kim Dae Jung, Park's 1971 opponent; Kim's rival, opposition leader Kim Young Sam; and Park's former lieutenant, Kim Jong Pil. Their rivalry began to dominate and destabilize the fragile political order, until it was closed off by General Chun Doo Hwan's declaration of martial law and assertion of political control in May 1980. The ensuing Kwangju uprising challenged this renewed assertion of authoritarian control; the uprising was brutally suppressed, leaving a residue of bitterness and anger that has overshadowed South Korean politics ever since. Choi Kyu Hah resigned as president in August; Chun was elected president by the electoral college to succeed him.[24]

The Fifth Republic, 1980–1988

A new constitution, approved by popular referendum in October 1980, established South Korea's fifth version of government,[25] somewhat similar to that of the 1960s except that an enlarged electoral college (now over 5,000 members) was retained for the presidential election. The members of the new college, however, were allowed to affiliate with political parties and endorse candidates, and the college was to be disbanded as soon as the election was completed. As in 1963, one-third of the 276 legislative seats were to be filled by proportional representation; the party receiving the largest popular vote was to have two-thirds of the one-third (a more sophisticated method of guaranteeing a government majority).

In the 1981 elections, Chun Doo Hwan gained a near-unanimous electoral college vote; the government's Democratic Justice party won 35 percent of the popular vote and 107 Assembly seats, while the rest were divided among two larger and some smaller opposition or quasi-opposition parties. As in previous legislatures, the opposition had power only to obstruct, but it could occasionally provoke attention-getting confrontations.

However, capitalizing upon a slowly liberalizing political climate, in early 1985 the opposition unexpectedly grouped itself into a new party that won fifty electoral district seats and seventeen proportional seats in the legislative election three weeks later. The voter turnout was one of the largest in the republic's history. By absorption of defectors from other parties, the new opposition group (the New Korea Democratic party) reached a total of 102 seats—more than a "blocking third." This success manifested the wide popular discontent with continued authoritarian controls and resentment over the suppression of the 1980 Kwangju uprising. The 1985 results laid the basis for a vigorous opposition campaign for greater political freedom, centering on amendment of the constitution.

The campaign was carried on despite constant government opposition and harassment but won growing public support and was accompanied by widespread student demonstrations against the regime. The opposition and government positions regarding the system of government were now reversed: the opposition, which had until recently advocated a parliamentary system, now saw the possibility of winning a powerful presidency, while the government now wanted a parliamentary system as a means of better controlling the election outcome. Both positions were cloaked in rhetoric—though not without validity—regarding their respective suitability to the Korean situation. Although the main opposition party split into two nearly equal groups—the Reunification Democratic party, headed by long-time opposition leader Kim Young Sam from the southeastern Kyongsang Province, and the Peace and Democracy party, headed by the newly liberated Kim Dae Jung from southwestern Cholla Province—the two parties nevertheless agreed on eight demands for reform, including release of political prisoners and constitutional revision, repeal, or amendment of oppressive laws. Government attempts to stop discussion of constitutional amendments and the government party's supine endorsement of President Chun's choice of fellow ex-General Roh Tae Woo to succeed him, lent added impetus to the campaign, which saw thousands of ordinary citizens in the streets in sympathy with demonstrating students and political activists.

The Sixth Republic and Direct Presidential Election

On June 29, 1987, despite rumors of martial law and military intervention to put down the mass demonstrations, Roh Tae Woo, government party leader and President Chun's choice as candidate to succeed him, surprised all observers by accepting virtually all the opposition demands for reform of the political system. President Chun endorsed this position. Subsequently, confounding the skeptics, the constitution was revamped to provide for Korea's sixth attempt at democracy, including direct popular election of the president and a strengthened National Assembly of 299 members, three-quarters of them elected from single-member districts (the remainder from national party slates in proportion to popular vote, with half going to the party with the largest number of popular votes).

Thus, for the first time since 1960 the opposition had won its campaign. It is possible to conclude, then, that for the first time in the history of the South Korean election process, the administration had responded to the signal of popular discontent, registered through the 1985 vote and subsequent demonstrations, instead of resorting to suppression and coercion (although the latter elements are still not absent).

In accordance with the revised constitution of October 1987, preparations were made for a presidential election by popular vote. During the brief campaign, in which the government party's candidate, Roh Tae Woo, was given as much government support as possible, the principal question was whether the two leading opposition figures, Kim Young Sam and Kim Dae Jung, could agree on a single candidate. In the end, they ran separately, as did the former prime minister, Kim Jong Pil. With the opposition vote thus split, Roh won the election with 36.7 percent of the vote against 28 percent for Kim Young Sam and 27 for Kim Dae Jung (a combined opposition majority of 55 percent) and about 10 percent for Kim Jong Pil, whose supporters tended to be partisans of the late President Park's regime. Although all opposition candidates charged massive election fraud, the Korean public blamed the outcome primarily on divisions among the opposition—a view supported by outside observers on the scene.[26]

President Roh assumed office in February, and the new constitution entered into force. On April 26, the legislative election was held under the new system. To the surprise of most observers, the government party lost its Assembly majority for the first time since the constitutional crisis of 1952, winning about 34 percent of the popular vote. Of the 299 legislative seats, the government's Democratic Justice party had 125 seats, Kim Dae Jung's Party for Peace and Democracy had 70 seats, Kim Young Sam's Reunification Democratic party held 59, and Kim Jong Pil's New Democratic Republican party had a surprising 35. There were 10 independents.[27]

It is difficult to predict what the effect of the two elections will be on Korean politics. Clearly, the situation is unprecedented. The government lacks a majority in the greatly strengthened legislature, but the opposition seems unable to unite. The opposition division during the two election campaigns had aggravated tendencies toward regional animosities already latent in Korean politics and exacerbated by the suppression of the 1980 Kwangju uprising. The new president has less than a majority mandate to rule, and has thus far demonstrated unwillingness to make a total break with the previous regime. Practically everyone in South Korea, except for a few radical students, wanted the 1988 Summer Olympics in Seoul to succeed, so that political contention was largely buried until mid-October, and there are still encouraging indications of willingness to compromise among political leaders. Nevertheless, the willingness of political forces in South Korea to abide by and make workable the most recent political system and election results will be sorely tested in the months and years ahead.

General Observations

The history of Korean elections shows a trend toward fewer competing candidates, fewer and better organized political groups, and a tendency—seldom completely realized—toward two-party politics. (If Japan can be said to have a one-and-a-half party system, then Korea's has been perhaps one-and-a-quarter party.) The record also shows that elections have become institutionalized, although they are still not central to the Korean political process. Korea has only once in its postwar history (from 1972 to 1978, during the autocratic Yushin regime of President Park) gone more than four years without a general election, although elections at provincial and local levels have not been reinstated since local assemblies were disbanded by the military government in 1961.[28]

There have been fourteen presidential elections—seven by direct popular vote, in 1952, 1956, 1960, 1963, 1967, 1971, and 1987; five by electoral college, in 1972, 1978, 1980 (twice), and 1981; and two by the legislature, in 1948 and 1960—fourteen legislative elections, in 1946, 1948, 1950, 1954, 1958, 1961, 1963, 1967, 1971, 1972, 1978, 1981, 1985, and 1988 (not counting the indirect legislative election of 1975); and three rounds of local elections, in 1952, 1955, and 1960. Additionally, referenda have become a part of the constitutional amendment process since 1963.

Election turnout in South Korea has generally been much higher than in the United States or Europe, resembling Japan in this respect and ranging from 60 to 85 percent of the eligible voters. Turnout is highest when public attention is most aroused: the turnout of 84.2 percent in the 1985 legislative elections was the highest since 1958, another year of widespread discontent; and the turnout in the presidential election of 1987 was even higher. In general, turnout is higher in rural areas, which generally support the regime in power and are most responsive to government officials' encouragement to vote. However, industrialization has diminished the proportion of rural voters.[29]

All Korean elections have elicited charges of corruption and irregularity, usually attributed to government pressures and schemes such as payoffs of voters with small gifts, police coercion, official threats to cut off government funds to opposition districts, official viewing of ballot marking, harassment of opposition candidates and campaign staffs, selective arrests for minor offenses or for violations of the national security law, and secret funding of splinter political groups to divide the opposition vote. The election process is subject to rigid limits on candidates' activities and the length of the campaign, and the limits can be selectively enforced.

However, the majority of elections have been fair enough, by international standards, to reflect popular sentiment—if the sentiment to avoid trouble from an authoritarian regime is included. Proof of this proposition is the number of votes cast for opposition and independent candidates. (Conspicuous exceptions were the presidential election of 1960, leading to the overthrow of the Rhee administration, and the legislative elections of 1967, which President Park acknowledged to have brought disgrace on his party.) Since 1963, the moderately prestigious Central Election Management Commission has overseen elections. Until 1973, Korean elections were routinely, if perfunctorily, observed by the United Nations Commission for the Unification and Rehabilitation of Korea, which reported annually to the UN General Assembly. Up to now, however, no election has returned an opposition president; and although the 1988 elections gave the majority of the legislative seats to nongovernment party members for the first time since 1950, unity among the opposition parties is fragile and at this writing has not been really tested. (The former opposition Democratic party overwhelmingly won the 1960 election, but by then it had become the government party.)

Individual personalities and interpersonal and regional ties continue to outweigh all but the most basic issues (such as general popular discontent) in determining campaign outcomes; and individual ambitions outweigh rational calculations of the prospects of success (how else to explain the internecine rivalry of Kim Dae Jung and Kim Young Sam in both 1980 and 1987?). The cynic would say that what matters to an ambitious Korean is not what he or she can do with power, but the possession of power for its own sake. This intense competitiveness together with the traditional lack of compromise or acceptance of opposition views and the intensity of personal loyalty among followers of individual politicians, have made Korean political progress difficult. The same factors have repeatedly divided the opposition forces and thus played into the government's hands in elections.

Moreover, the Korean public is only beginning to regard itself as the source of government legitimacy or as monitor of government performance. The tradition of subservience to the bureaucracy, even though mingled with cynicism and distrust, is still strong. The spirit of service to the ruler is strong among bureaucrats and security men, for whom the tradition is to get out a favorable vote by whatever means. As a result, the election process itself and the political systems of which it has been a part have been viewed with growing distrust, which is only now beginning to abate. At the same time, the voters' perception of their efficacy seems to have grown.[30]

The young radicals' position that the present Korean political system needs reform has some validity; the problem for them, as for others who wish Korea well, is that there is no substitute for a modern political culture, and it takes time and trial for the culture to develop. Moreover, the simplistic and idealistic concepts embraced by some of the radicals, such as the ill-defined "mass democracy" and the condemnation of past Korean elections as illegitimate (as indeed some of them were, in varying degrees), reflect a naive utopianism and desire for the fruits of democracy without recognizing the network of understanding and responsibility, on the part of both leaders and people, that is required to make democracy work. There is also the problem that the new and unaccustomed freedom may lead enthusiasts (or political saboteurs) to tear down rather than rebuild the underlying political stability that has characterized South Korea since 1945—as some people feared in 1960 and again in the 1980 "Seoul spring." There is also the opposite danger, that needed reforms and the confusion that inevitably accompanies them will lead law-and-order advocates to suppress progress.

Nevertheless, despite the problems and the risks, the trend of political evolution in South Korea is encouraging. It is useful to recall that South Korea was once considered unable to fight, and yet it proved itself; that South Korea was once adjudged a perpetual economic "basket case," and yet it has produced one of the world's most remarkable records of economic development. Political development is harder; but now there is good reason to expect that it will come and that elections will be a permanent and ever more significant part of the Korean political process.

Notes

1. Benjamin Schwartz, *The World of Thought in Ancient China* (Cambridge, MA: Belknap Press of Harvard University Press, 1985), 53, 110, 284, 346.
2. *Hankook Ilbo*, in an editorial on June 12, 1977, commented: "In the [Korean] nation's political history, what is most conspicuous is the tradition of managing state affairs through conferences and right arguments. For example, 'hwabaek' in the Silla Dynasty 'dodang' in the Koryo Dynasty, and 'myodang' in the Yi Dynasty...were...political systems . . . based upon the principle that state affairs were managed through people's consensus and arguments." (Press Translations, Korea, June 14, 1977, 12-13.) However, "people" here may well refer to the aristocracy rather than the masses.
3. Ki Baik Lee, *A New History of Korea*, trans. Edward W. Wagner (Cambridge, MA: Belknap Press of Harvard University Press, 1984), 142–44, 252–55; Joungwon A. Kim, *Divided Korea: The Politics of Development, 1945–1972* (Cambridge, MA: Belknap Press of Harvard University Press, 1975), 12–13.
4. I am indebted to Mr. Kwak So Jin, a former associate at the U.S. Embassy in Seoul, for this reference; I was given the exact citation at the time, but cannot now locate it in my files.
5. An American lawyer commissioned to make a study of education for the Korean judicial system commented in his report of 1965: "The sense of competition among all peoples in the struggle for life is starkly felt in Korea." Jay Murphy, "Legal Education in a Developing Nation: The Case of Korea" (Seoul: Graduate School of Law, Seoul National University, 1965), mimeographed typescript, 51.
6. Hahm Pyung Choon, *The Korean Political Tradition and The Law; Essays in Korean Law and Legal History*, Royal Asiatic Society, Korea Branch, Monograph Series No. 1 (Seoul: Hollym Corp.,) 5–6, 15ff.
7. Ahn Byong Man, Kil Soong Hoom, and Kim Kwang Woong, *Elections in Korea* (Seoul: Seoul Computer Press, 1988), 105: "The form of government [rather than specific issues] has repeatedly emerged as the most important political issue in the history of political development in Korea, and it is believed that the emergence of the issue at incessant intervals results from the fact that the variety of system alternatives have lacked such quality of orthodoxy and legitimacy as to be acceptable to the people."
8. "Elections [in Korea] were never designed to disperse power among the masses, but to concentrate it in the hands of the rulers. Election fraud and abuse has done more than preserve the power of the state however, it has also eroded the faith of the Koreans in elections and generated deep and abiding cynicism in the whole process." Ahn, Kil, and Kim, *Elections in Korea*, 41. See also Donald S. Macdonald, "Korea

and the Ballot: The International Dimension in Korean Political Development as Seen in Elections," unpublished Ph.D. dissertation, George Washington University, 1978, 8–12, 31–34, and the sources therein cited. See also Gregory Henderson, *Korea: The Politics of the Vortex* (Cambridge, MA: Harvard University Press, 1967), 285–86.

9. Lee, *A New History of Korea*, 275–78, 297–99.
10. Hahn Bae-ho, "The Authority Structure of Korean Politics," in *Korea Politics in Transition*, ed. Edwin R. Wright (Seattle: University of Washington Press, 1975), 297-300; Macdonald, "Korea and the Ballot," 11–14, 18–25.
11. Chong-sik Lee, *The Politics of Korean Nationalism* (Berkeley: University of California Press, 1963), 129–55.
12. Bruce Cumings, *The Origins of the Korean War* (Princeton: Princeton University Press, 1981), 81–100, 135–51.
13. The material in this paragraph is taken from Donald S. Macdonald, "The 1946 Elections and Legislative Assembly in South Korea: America's Bumbling Tutelage," *Journal of Northeast Asian Studies* 1 (No. 3, September 1982): 53–71.
14. For details of the 1948 election, see John E. McMahon, "Antecedents, Character, and Outcome of the Korean Election of 1948," unpublished M.A. thesis, University of California, Berkeley, 1954; and Macdonald, "Korea and The Ballot," 174–85.
15. Material in this section, unless otherwise noted, is drawn from Macdonald, "Korea and The Ballot," 208–403.
16. Joungwon A. Kim, *Divided Korea: The Politics of Development, 1945–1972* (Cambridge, MA: Harvard University Press, 1975), 166–68.
17. This amendment was initially declared by Ch'oe Son-ju, the presiding Liberal party vice-speaker, to have failed because it fell one-third vote short of the required two-thirds majority. An elderly mathematics professor was enlisted to argue for rounding off fractions (*sa-sa o-ip*, or "drop four [tenths], add five"), and the amendment was subsequently declared to have passed. Vice-Speaker Ch'oe resigned in disgrace and died not long afterward.
18. John Kie-chiang Oh, *Korea: Democracy on Trial* (Ithaca, NY: Cornell University Press, 1968), 51–71.
19. Joungwon Kim, *Divided Korea*, 202-23. See also Sungjoo Han, *The Failure of Democracy in South Korea* (Berkeley: University of California Press, 1974).
20. Kim, *Divided Korea*, 224–56.
21. Ibid., 268–72.
22. Ibid., 273–86.
23. Ahn, Kil, and Kim, *Elections in Korea*, 33–34.
24. See Han Sung-joo, "The Emerging Political Process in Korea," and Donald S. Macdonald, "Recent Political Change in Korea," in *Asian Affairs* (New York) 8 (No. 2, November–December 1980): 76–88 and 63–75, respectively.

25. Material in this section is based largely on materials in *Far Eastern Economic Review*, especially the issues of May 23, August 5, September 5, and October 31, 1980; February 27, March 6, and April 3, 1981; and February 28, 1985; and Ahn, Kil, and Kim, *Elections in Korea*, 37–40.

26. *Far Eastern Economic Review*, December 24, 1987, 8-9; *Korea Newsreview*, December 26, 1987, 4. The commonly reported vote percentage of 36.6 for Roh Tae Woo represents an adjustment upward from the "official" figures in the above two sources, which show slightly less than 36 percent for Roh.

27. *Far Eastern Economic Review*, April 30, 1988.

28. It is likely that the lack of local elections since 1960 has not until recently been a focus of popular concern, because all money and power were generally recognized to be concentrated at the national level. For example, voter turnout under the free conditions of the Chang Myon administration in the election for provincial governors in December 1960 was only about 35 percent. However, opposition parties have consistently called for local elections, which were provided for in the constitutions of both the Fifth and Sixth Republics. So far, they have not been carried out, but the question is under discussion in the National Assembly.

29. For a more sophisticated and detailed analysis of election turnout and other aspects of elections, see Ahn, Kil, and Kim, *Elections in Korea*, 231–93.

30. Ahn, Kil, and Kim, *Elections in Korea*, 298–300 and *passim*.

5

Political Change in South Korea

And Its Impact on United States-Korean Relations

Larry A. Niksch

IT IS NO SECRET TO OBSERVERS that the United States-Republic of Korea relationship is undergoing a transition. That transition is taking the relationship from one dominated by the issues of military integration and coordination solely within the context of the North Korean military threat to South Korea. Relations in the near term will contain a multiple set of more diverse issues. Defense against North Korea no doubt will remain a key component; but it will share importance with economic, financial, regional security, political, and diplomatic issues and challenges.

Two new factors have emerged that are creating a more complex relationship as the United States and South Korea move into the 1990s:

- The transition of South Korea from an authoritarian political system to a democratic and increasingly pluralistic one in the space of less than one year—a transition potentially as important as the economic change that South Korea has undergone in the last two decades.

- Changes in United States policy, especially the increased dominance of economic issues in American relations with East Asian countries and the emergence of a period of relative austerity in American defense spending.

Both of these factors are creating new expectations from each partner concerning the policies and conduct of the other. Conversely, they also provide the domestic political contexts in each country and potential political limitations to each government's reaction to the expectations arising from the other side.

South Korea's New Political Pluralism

The dramatic political developments in South Korea from June 1987 through April 1988 produced far more than just a more democratic system featuring expanded political and civil liberties for individual Koreans. Those events also have resulted in a redistribution of power among government institutions, between government and the nongovernment sectors, and even within the nongovernment sector. Pluralism now is a key and increasingly important factor in setting the agenda of issues and in decisionmaking. This will affect the United States-South Korea relationship nearly as much as it will influence day-to-day domestic matters.

Relations no longer will be determined solely by a relatively small group of South Korean civilian and military officials, many of whom have had education or other experiences in the United States and have personal friendships with their counterparts in the United States government. These South Korean officials still will have the lead role in policy formulation; however, they will now have to take into account views and proposals put forth by other individuals and groups and will have to have dialogue with and seek the support of some of these elements.

Within the South Korean government, the National Assembly has become a center of power, holding new checks on the powers of the executive. The National Assembly already is a forum for the public airing and debating of national issues.

Outside of government, important sectors of the society ai creating national organizations to promote their interests: new or revamped labor unions, a national farmers' federation, business conglomerates and associations, religious organizations, and national student bodies. These groups already are operating to an unprecedented degree in the political-governmental arena. Their participation will continue to grow as they evolve and as the democratic system is firmly established. They can be expected to promote their interests publicly, lobby government officials and legislators, and form links to political parties and candidates.

A new South Korean press also is emerging as another independent source of power and influence. Journalists whom the Chun Doo Hwan government ousted are back in business. Newspapers are expanding their coverage, and new ones are being formed. Although this process has only begun, the press has demonstrated several new roles: expressing editorial opinion and analysis independent of and even contrary to that of the government; providing a forum through which private sector groups can enunciate their views and promote their causes; and investigating the workings of government, business, and other institutions.[1]

Democratization and political pluralism are producing an expanded enunciation of Korean nationalism. Korean nationalism has reemerged as a potent political force after decades of suppression and dormancy caused by harsh Japanese colonial rule, the division of Korea after 1945, the devastation of the Korean War, and the preoccupation of most South Koreans with the struggle against poverty.

There are at least three strains of nationalism in South Korea which are important to South Korean attitudes towards the United States. They overlap, but they are distinct and to a degree mutually contradictory. One is the nationalism of success: the sense of pride that has surfaced as a result of South Korea's economic accomplishments, its strides in education, and the international recognition resulting from the 1988 Olympics. Many South Koreans viewed the Olympics as marking South Korea's "coming of age" in the international community and opening the way for South Korea to join the ranks of the developed countries.

This strain of nationalism is positive rather than anti-foreign. It recognizes for the most part the international context of South Korea's accomplishments and the relationship of other countries to them. It seeks to expand on the successful formula of international trade, investment, and technology. A nationalism based on achievement, its future influence will depend on continued economic success.

The second strain of nationalism is the demand for greater independence from the United States. Generational change in South Korea underlies this brand of nationalism and its impact on United States-South Korean relations. South Korea's population is dominated by a generation under forty years of age that has little or no memory of the Korean War, Korea's poverty of the 1950s and 1960s, and American aid to South Korea during this period. Younger Koreans are better educated than their forebears. They have political views formed against the historical background not of the 1950s but, instead, the period of Park Chung Hee's Yushin system (1972–1979) and the brief political liberalization after Park's assassination, which ended with a military takeover in May 1980. United States-South Korean relations were marred by controversy during this period, including the Korean influence-buying scandal in the U.S. Congress, the Carter administration's attempt to withdraw American ground forces from Korea, and the United States role in the military takeover in 1980.

The image of the United States has suffered from these events.[2] This is especially true with regard to the American role in the events of 1980. Antigovernment groups in South Korea have charged persistently that the United States military commander in Korea allowed South Korean troops under his command to suppress the antigovernment rebellion in Kwangju. Aside from the details of the Kwangju incident (United States officials have disputed the charges of American complicity), the resentment has grown out of a broader perception of a weak response by the Carter administration to the military takeover and the Reagan administration's policy of strengthening relations with the Chun government.[3]

The most virulent form of this type of nationalism is the anti-Americanism of radical students. The radicals base their views on Marxist ideology, including the so-called dependency theory, and a xenophobic defense of Korean cultural traditions against Western influence. The radicals demand a total removal of United States influence—military, political, economic, and cultural. They mix anti-United States views with demands for immediate reunification on terms similar to those proposed by North Korea and rejection of Western-style democratic institutions.[4]

This kind of nationalism, however, includes a milder and probably majority view—even among college students—that criticizes individual aspects of United States policy toward Korea but stops short of demanding an abrogation of the Korea-United States relationship. This school of thought also supports reunification, but it appears to view reunification as an extended process. It is critical of United States pressure on South Korea to open its markets further to American products but does not reject South Korea's participation in the liberal international trading system. In contrast to the radicals, this more moderate view supports democratic norms and institutions, despite frequent rejection of the older politicians.[5]

A third strain of nationalism is the desire for acceptance from the rest of the world and recognition of South Korea's accomplishments and new status. South Korean perceptions of the Seoul Olympics are based partially on this attitude. This view holds American approval and recognition as especially important, given the United States' traditional role as patron and protector. South Korean sensitivity toward NBC's coverage of their country during the Olympics pointed up this expectation of acceptance from the United States. The outburst of criticism toward NBC showed that, although this kind of nationalism is not inherently anti-United States or anti-foreign, it has the potential to turn in that direction. The most difficult kind of nationalism for the United States to deal with is this mixture of desire for greater independence from the United States and expectation that the United States will put substance into the "special relationship."

How will nationalism affect the future roles of the expanding South Korean body politic, especially affecting relations with the United States? One effect will likely be the amalgamation of nationalist and leftist views into a loose coalition of groups that could be called the urban left. This is a phenomenon that is occurring in several East Asian countries undergoing democratization. Major players in this coalition probably will be segments of academia and the press, mainline Protestant churches, and the Korean Council of Churches. The council issued in February 1988 a declaration on reunification that called for conversion of the armistice agreement into a peace accord and the withdrawal of all (that is, United States) nuclear weapons from the Korean peninsula.[6]

Of course, certain elements of the politicized university students will be involved. The strength and effectiveness of the student role, however, will probably depend on whether the radical leftists, usually estimated at about 5 percent of South Korea's one million college students (some estimates place the percentage lower), will abandon violent tactics, adopt a more conventional political role, and move away from hard-line Marxist-Leninist ideology.

It should be noted that leftist views stem from sources in addition to anti-United States attitudes—the traditional Korean cultural animosity toward merchants and open displays of wealth, the role of socially activist Christian churches in work with the urban poor, and political opposition to authoritarian governments of the right. Thus, the urban left could be expected to press for policies that would emphasize income redistribution, more government controls over business and industry, and more power to labor unions. This group undoubtedly would press for policy changes that would force the removal of United States nuclear weapons from South Korea, reduce or end the American military presence, and restrict South Korea's market for United States imports and investment. It probably would advocate policies on reunification that would accept at least some elements of the proposals put forward by North Korea, such as confederation, an end to anticommunist policies, mutual arms reduction, and unified delegations to international organizations and events. Groups on the political left would likely receive support and even material assistance from similar groups in Western countries.

Nationalism and some of the grievances associated with the urban left exist also within the broader, majority segments of South Korean society, but they so far have not grown into the driving force of political opinion. Businessmen, white collar professionals, service-sector workers, industrial workers, and farmers generally express nationalism as pride in material accomplishment for themselves and the country; and they view South Korea's relationship with the United States in that context. Attempts by radical students and church activists to woo workers and farmers have proven unsuccessful so far. The radicals received little support even from the majority of students who attempted in August and September 1988 to march to the demilitarized zone and disrupt the Olympics.

Nevertheless, criticisms of certain aspects of Korea-United States relations exist within these more representative groups. Businessmen, industrial workers, and farmers have voiced opposition to United States trade policy toward South Korea. Journalists often cover the trade issue with an accusatory tone toward the United States. These groups show more openness toward reconsideration of some aspects of the American security role. They displayed the greatest irritation with NBC's coverage of the Olympics, as indicated by newspaper editorials and letters to the editor.

These groups and the urban middle class will be increasingly sensitive and negative towards symbols or displays of a South Korean subordinate status in relation to the United States. Thus, there exists some potential for coalition building between the left and the majority center, at least on specific issues affecting Korea's relations with the United States.

Among the opposition political parties, the leadership appears to support the fundamentals of the Korea-United States security relationship. The rank-and-file membership seem generally to share this view, although there are more critical elements among backers of Kim Dae Jung. Opposition leaders, however, often do not have the same close personal association with Americans that government officials have. They give less priority to security issues and more to trade problems. Because they seek greater public backing, the parties likely will identify with public discontent toward United States policies. They already have sensed the public's interest in the reunification question and adopted positions slightly different from that of the government with regard to the attempted student march to the demilitarized zone. Kim Dae Jung has demonstrated repeatedly that he is willing to criticize the United States strongly and publicly.[7] That no doubt will continue.

Changing American Perceptions
of Western Pacific Security Issues

The impact of South Korea's changing political dynamics on relations with the United States will be influenced by the reactions and initiatives of the United States in an atmosphere of shifting American perceptions of its role in the western Pacific. Simply stated, the United States' twin deficits, budget and trade, are raising new doubts in American minds about the United States' security role in the western Pacific and Korea. Members of the U.S. Congress have been at the forefront in articulating these concerns; but congressional views do represent broader, though less specific, strains in American opinion. If voiced long enough, they often filter into the executive branch and into official United States policy. If congressional opinion merges into general agreement, Congress will attempt to legislate policy. A consensus already has developed to a degree with regard to South Korea.

Trade issues, especially the United States trade deficit with South Korea, stands as the number-one problem in the day-to-day conduct of United States policy towards South Korea. American policy, influenced by congressional pressure, places the highest priority on opening the South Korean market to a range of American products and reducing the trade deficit with the United States. This approach has resulted in three years of protracted trade negotiations, threats by the United States to restrict the import of Korean goods if Seoul does not agree to United States market-opening demands, and attempts by Congress to enact protectionist legislation that would severely restrict imports of South Korean textiles.

Thus, in the eyes of many Americans a financial dimension has been added to the security relationship. Although South Korea was not mentioned in a recent poll of American opinion by Marttila and Kiley, the expressed sentiment no doubt applied; 84 percent agreed with the statement, "While we spend billions to defend Japan and Europe, they are winning the economic competition and taking away American jobs."[8]

The American force structure in the western Pacific faces uncertainty in the diminishing public and congressional support for the Reagan defense buildup. The predominant view now stresses the need to cut the defense budget, or at least keep it at present levels. At this juncture, the outlook is that the basic force structure of the United States armed forces in and around Korea will not be affected. However, the controversy does reinforce the sentiment that American allies should contribute more financially to the common defense. Within the Congress, the issue of defense burden-sharing with South Korea—an idea nonexistent a few years ago—is viewed increasingly as an opportunity to achieve a financial offset to the trade deficit with South Korea.

More austere defense spending may create greater sentiment in favor of reducing United States forces overseas. Such views no doubt would focus on Europe, but American forces in South Korea and the western Pacific would not be exempt. Already, proposals have arisen in the United States to withdraw the Second Division from South Korea and demobilize it in order to save money.[9]

Challenges of a Revised Security Agenda

The Republic of Korea and United States governments will have to give more emphasis than previously to two ingredients—(1) flexibility and (2) equality and mutual benefit—if they are to meet successfully the challenges of a revised security agenda in the 1990s. The challenges will arise in at least four areas:

1. Building a stronger political consensus for the alliance, especially for the United States defense commitment, in both countries
2. Burden-sharing
3. The American military presence
4. Trade

The visible aspects of United States-South Korean relations currently are dominated by United States demands on South Korea covering a host of trade issues; more recently, regarding burden-sharing; and by anti-American protests by South Korean students. This has produced an impression among both Koreans and Americans of contentiousness in their relations and, for many Koreans, of American heavy-handedness.

South Korean and American policy makers will have to

become adept at balancing the increasingly diverse and numerous issues in their decisionmaking and not allowing excessive concentration on any single issue to dilute their ability to deal with the others in a way that will strengthen the bilateral relationship. United States and South Korean officials will have to give more consideration to adjustments in the component parts of the security relationship that will serve to strengthen the political position of supporters of the alliance and soften the criticisms of moderate critics.

It will not be easy for civilian and military bureaucracies in the two governments to adopt attitudes that seek greater flexibility and adaptability in policy decisions. They also will not accept easily the need for greater equality between the two countries within the alliance framework. Old habits die hard. Both bureaucracies are more nearly satisfied with the status quo in the security relationship than are the political constituencies in their countries. Both have concentrated on ad hoc damage limitation exercises at the expense of anticipating future problems and formulating measures to head off crises arising out of them. Components of the bureaucracies have narrowly defined their respective roles and responsibilities and are reluctant to take into account the bigger picture. Officials on both sides, but especially on the United States side, have been until recently slow to engage in outreach to Korean nongovernmental groups with interests in the security and economic relationships. For example, after nearly a decade of minimal outreach efforts, the United States embassy, the U.S. Information Agency, and the U.S. Military Command have no substantive dialogue or means of communicating with the huge Korean university population, the main source of criticism of United States polices and the American military presence.[10]

Democratization in South Korea contributes to this awareness, and the successful transition also has bought time for the two governments to consider options. The political challenge of building and strengthening political consensus for the alliance will require a firm and sustained commitment by South Korea to democracy even though the Republic of Korea government and armed forces may find democratic processes cumbersome in dealing with other issues in the security relationship. Increasingly, American views of East Asia acknowledge the democratization that is the main political trend in the region. A politically conservative administration in Washington has claimed Asian democratization as one of its chief accomplishments. The American political constituencies that would support authoritarian government unquestionably have shrunk as a result of the Reagan administration's position and record on democratization. The forging of common political values through democratization is the one new bond among the strains in other parts of the relationship. In American eyes, return to authoritarian rule would isolate South Korea even within the regional East Asian political context. It would place much greater strains on American political support for the defense commitment than has been the case before.

Shared democratic values will have to constitute an important component of a revised United States rationale for the defense commitment to South Korea in the 1990s. The United States could strengthen this further by finding new means of more substantive political identification with the new political system in South Korea. Possibilities certainly exist for greater contacts between American and South Korean institutions such as the legislature and the press and among academics. The United States government would strengthen further the principle of shared political values by cooperating with the South Korean National Assembly, the press, and academics as they analyze aspects of the relationship. The National Assembly's current plans to investigate the Kwangju uprising may prove an important first test for the United States in the post-Olympics period. The National Assembly may invite Ambassador William Glesteen and General John Wickham, United States officials in South Korea in 1980, to give testimony on the American role in the suppression of the rebellion. The State Department has said that it will not allow the officials to testify in Korea but that they can respond to written questions from the Korean National Assembly. If this restriction is followed, it is doubly important that answers to written questions be detailed and revealing and not vague and "canned." Information should not be held back even if it damages the reputation of American and Korean officials who were involved. Officials in Washington may be reluctant to allow such testimony, but failure to do so would damage the fragile American credibility on the democratization issue, which the Reagan administration's actions in June 1987 established after a long period of support for the Chun Doo Hwan government. United States cooperation would help South Koreans manage the difficult period after the Olympics when the government and opposition likely will tangle over Kwangju and several other issues. The investigation also may show that the United States role in suppression of the rebellion was less direct than many of the critics charge.

The isolation of the U.S. Military Command from the political aspects of United States policy implementation has acted against the achievement of policy goals in recent years. The many public statements made by American commanders concerning the North Korean threat are valid; but some observers believe that the Chun government followed a policy of soliciting statements from them at particular times in order to help justify restrictions on political and civil liberties.[11] This has contributed to the criticism of the United States military presence. The American military leadership, moreover, has been isolated from nongovernment sectors of South Korean society. South Korean university campuses have been as much off-limits to American commanders as Kim Il Sung University in Pyongyang.

This unquestionably needs to change. United States commanders should give high priority to communicating with the South Korean nongovernmental sector. The universities may not receive them immediately, but business and professional organizations no doubt would be receptive. In time, the students will open the door. Coordination between the U.S. Military Command and the American embassy needs to be tighter in the future to insure a unified implementation of *political policy* toward the Koreans. Top American officers in the future will have to possess a sharp sensitivity to the political currents in South Korea and a desire to deal frontally with those that potentially would affect the alliance.

Diplomacy towards North Korea also will be necessary to strengthen Korean support for the new political order and the alliance with the United States. Democratization has produced a more volatile public debate on the reunification question than anything seen in South Korea since the late 1940s. The reemergence of Korean nationalism contributes to this considerably;

but it is partly a public reaction to the perceived use of the North Korean threat by the Chun government to justify restrictions on political and civil liberties and repression of the domestic opposition. This reduced the credibility of the North Korean threat among some elements of South Korea's population, especially among younger Koreans. Students quoted in the American press often express the belief that North Korea does not constitute a threat to South Korea. Now democratization and a change of administrations has raised hopes that new initiatives toward North Korea will achieve success.

South Korea's politicians have sensed this public sentiment since Roh Tae Woo and Kim Dae Jung proposed new diplomatic initiatives toward North Korea. President Roh now has come forward with a broad-ranging offer of exchanges and negotiations with Pyongyang. Even if the immediate chances of success are small, South Korea's new pluralism will produce continuing public debate and scrutiny of the reunification question.

The United States has every reason to support President Roh's proposals and similar offers which he will likely make in the near future. United States backing will strengthen the government's position against any internal threats mounted by opponents of such initiatives, especially disgruntled elements of the Korean Army.

Burden-Sharing

The visit of U.S. Deputy Secretary of Defense William H. Taft to Seoul in May 1988 demonstrated that the burden-sharing issue will be on the agenda of future discussions and negotiations over security relations. During Taft's visit and at the annual United States-Republic of Korea security conference in June, the American side reportedly called on South Korea to provide $20 million for support of United States naval operations in the Persian Gulf, increase its direct financial support of United States forces by $45 million, and begin an economic aid program to the Philippines.[12]

South Korea is economically able to provide an increased direct financial contribution to the maintenance of American forces in South Korea. The United States no doubt will escalate pressure on Seoul to raise such expenditures beyond the present level of $287 million in 1987.[13] The outlook is that South Korea will comply to some degree, but negotiations may be difficult and politically volatile. Political resistance in South Korea could spark criticism of such attitudes in the United States.

South Koreans will have to view their financial capabilities pragmatically rather than through critical nationalist eyes. Americans will have to keep their financial requests more modest than similar requests of Japan and the NATO countries. South Korea already is spending heavily on defense (5.5 percent of GNP and about 30 percent of the national budget), and its present contribution to the maintenance of American forces already equals those of Japan and the Western European countries on a per capita United States-soldier basis, despite a much smaller economy and budget.[14] The South Korean government may face its own public and legislative pressure to reduce the growth of defense spending. Washington may have to shift its focus to this more fundamental issue if such pressure does arise.

The burden-sharing issue presents certain dangers in terms of public reactions. A strict concentration on the financial aspects of burden-sharing could lead the public in both countries to judge the security relationship increasingly in terms of monetary values and see it as a contest for financial advantage. It could create the perception that United States troops in South Korea are mercenaries in the pay of South Korea. Public support in the United States for the defense commitment could wane in the face of such attitudes. Criticisms of the security relationship could expand in South Korea. The two governments will have to find the proper balance between justifiable increases in the South Korean financial contribution and a commitment of American resources that corresponds with United States interests in Korea and Northeast Asia.

These possible pitfalls emphasize the importance of "strategic burden-sharing" as a suitable balance to financial burden-sharing. Strategic burden-sharing is defined here as the direct assumption by South Korea of regional defense and security responsibilities. It undoubtedly would be done in cooperation with the United States, but the South Korean role would be individual and distinct rather than one of financial support or subordination to the United States. Strategic burden-sharing would strengthen the United States-Korean alliance in several ways. Politically, it would demonstrate to the American public and Congress that the alliance is increasingly mutually beneficial. It also would highlight to both countries' people the political and security rationale for the alliance in a broader context than just defense against North Korea. A direct South Korean role probably would be more congenial to South Korean nationalist sentiment than monetary payments to the United States for United States regional military operations. (The reported United States call for financial support of Persian Gulf operations suggests the possibility of future requests related to American forces in the western Pacific. This would be especially likely if the United States lost the Philippines bases and faced the prospect of large expenditures for new bases.)

The Command Structure

Proposals in South Korea for changes in the United States-Republic of Korea military command structure draw surprising interest from civilians.[15] President Roh called for a change in command arrangements in the 1987 presidential election campaign.[16] The Reagan and Roh administrations agreed to undertake a study of the question.

Behind this issue lies two apparent South Korean motives which will have to be balanced:

1. To achieve equality with the United States in the command relationship: this is the sentiment within segments of the Korean public.
2. To avoid upsetting the United States position in the Combined Forces Command (CFC) to such an extent that the United States government would reevaluate its commitment of forces to South Korea: this is the concern of many government and military officials.

The United States Military Presence

The issue of the American military presence goes to the heart of the security relationship. President Carter's plan to withdraw American ground forces resulted in the most far-reaching crisis in the two countries' relationship since Syngman Rhee refused to sign the armistice agreement in 1953. In the United States, there is renewed discussion over the future of the United States military presence. Some congressmen have begun to call for a withdrawal of some of the 40,000 troops in South Korea. A resolution for the withdrawal of United States ground forces received 64 votes in the 435-member House of Representatives in 1987. Some individual members of the executive branch of the United States government believe that a change in the American force structure should occur in the early 1990s. A review of the ground force presence seemed possible after the United States presidential changeover in 1989 but it is doubtful that the Bush administration will now take a drastic step in its first term.

Antinuclear sentiment and calls for a United States troop withdrawal have arisen in South Korea in the wake of democratization and student protests.[17] Such sentiment is confined largely to segments of the university student population— probably not a majority of students—and to Christian church groups on the political left. Though important, it does not appear to represent the views of mainstream middle-class South Koreans. No opposition leaders, not even Kim Dae Jung, favor a United States troop withdrawal in the immediate future. Even in the alienated Cholla region of southwestern South Korea (the location of Kwangju), sentiment reportedly does not favor a withdrawal.[18] The great majority of South Koreans appear to support the government's opposition that United States troops should remain until North Korea ends its hostility and military threat towards South Korea.

Proposals for withdrawal likely would not be acted upon before 1992 or 1993 at the earliest. A political consensus for withdrawals is absent in both countries. In the longer term, a withdrawal of some United States ground forces at least appears quite possible.

If any withdrawal of United States troops appears several years away (barring a dramatic North Korean shift to a non-hostile policy), the issue of United States nuclear weapons in South Korea could become a major issue and possibly an emotional one in the very near future. The combination of United States secretiveness and public antinuclear sentiment has inflamed the issue in several western and south Pacific

countries, and these are emerging in South Korea.[19] Groups
on the political left in a number of western Pacific countries
have given high priority to the nuclear issue. Organized anti-
nuclear groups in the United States can be expected to support
their South Korean counterparts; this has already begun
among United States and South Korean church organizations.
The Soviet Union may try to exploit this issue in the future, as
it already has in the south Pacific and the Philippines.

The nuclear issue can produce strong reactions among the
citizens of countries where free debate is possible. In South
Korea, the emotional potential of the issue is magnified by the
presumption that nuclear weapons would be used against other
(i.e., North) Koreans and would be used very near the city of
Seoul, with its more than ten million people.

The United States' "neither confirm nor deny" policy is
defined differently in Korea than in Western Europe, with the
result that the South Korean public has had far less information
available to it than has the public in the NATO countries. With
regard to Europe, the United States and Western European
governments generally acknowledge that the United States
deploys nuclear weapons there, and they have stated publicly
a rationale for their deployment. The specific types of nuclear
weapons are not disclosed (although the general kinds of
weapons are known) and their locations are kept secret. For
South Korea, the United States and Republic of Korea governments have never stated officially that nuclear weapons are in
Korea, and they have provided no rationale. It is a policy of
total secrecy.

As this becomes a public issue, the United States and South
Korean governments undoubtedly will have to drop their
secretiveness and provide a public rationale for the deployment
of nuclear weapons in South Korea. The extensive discussion
of the issue at the CSIS-KIDA conference in Seoul in September
1988 is a harbinger of things to come. Both governments will
have to let their respective publics and legislative bodies judge
the validity of the rationale. One thing is certain: in contrast to
its heretofore exclusion from any role in this issue, the South
Korean public and its representatives in the National Assembly
will have a major say in the early 1990s as to whether nuclear
weapons remain.

"U.S. Army Golf Course Sparks Wrath of Korean Radicals" ran the headline in the *Washington Times* of August 24, 1988. This pointed up another emerging problem, that of the visibility of United States forces. Whether it be the golf course and bowling establishments of Yongsan, the shopping and entertainment area of Itaewon, or the American Forces Korea Network (AFKN), the American presence is under attack for visibly taking land from Koreans, subverting Korean culture and morals, and symbolizing the patron-client relationship between the two countries. Many of the accusations are exaggerated, but the sentiment goes well beyond the radical students. Irritants and disputes between the American military and South Korean civilians likely will increase in the future.

This issue may present opportunities as well as a new headache. The United States and South Korean governments probably can deal effectively with this through measures to remove some nonessentials at United States military facilities, programming changes at AFKN, and, if necessary, a relocation of some installations, including Yongsan, away from Seoul. The United States and Japanese governments successfully orchestrated base closures, consolidations, and relocations in the 1960s, which reduced irritants to local civilian communities and took the steam out of protests against American forces and the United States-Japan Security Treaty.

There is one difference, however, between the issue then and now. The United States would expect South Korea to bear much of the expense for construction of new facilities and other costs associated with these kinds of measures. Under these conditions, it would be a test of whether the alliance is evolving toward greater mutual responsibilities and benefits.

Trade

Resolving some of the issues of burden-sharing and American military visibility will be necessary to soften the edges of the trade issue. Trade disputes are a running sore in the relationship. The leveling off of the United States trade deficit with South Korea at about $10 billion in 1988 is a hopeful sign. It contrasts, however, with the Taiwan-American success in reducing the United States trade deficit by over $5 billion in 1988. It is uncertain whether the leveling off is the beginning of real reductions in 1989 and beyond or just a pause before further growth. For a contraction to occur, there will have to be a combination of more extensive *won*-dollar realignment, increased market openings by the South Koreans, and more intense efforts by American business to sell in the Korean market.

Some attitude changes on both sides will be required to soften the political impact of the trade controversy. Koreans have reacted in a more antagonistic and emotional manner to trade pressure from Washington than have the Japanese or Taiwanese. The contrast between Korean and Taiwanese responses is most noticeable. Substantive government measures are similar to a degree in both countries, although Taipei appears to have adopted broader market opening measures than has Seoul. South Koreans, moreover, complain vociferously that the United States is treating Korea unfairly. They argue frequently that Washington should not treat South Korea as a "second Japan." Leftists accuse the United States of "economic imperialism."

United States officials give the South Korean government little credit for the market opening measures that it has undertaken. The United States risks an even stronger anti-American reaction in the future if the United States trade deficit with South Korea begins to drop while the American negotiating approach remains one of demands and criticism accompanied by a similar tone in the American public and Congress. If the trade deficit is brought down to a point lower that $5 billion, political relations could suffer further if the United States does not mix its market opening demands with *quid pro quo* offers to ease key United States restrictions on imports from South Korea. The most combustible mix in United States-Korea relations over the next three or four years would be an American refusal to compromise substantially on these military issues while wringing concessions from South Korea on trade primarily through a combination of threats and suits filed under the "Super 301" section of the 1988 U.S. Trade Act.

Conclusions

Two issues, cooperation in the Kwangju investigation and the status of the Yongsan golf course, may require decisions by the United States government soon. Americans may not consider them important, and indeed they are not in material terms. The foundation of the United States-Republic of Korea relationship, however, is political—a truth becoming more obvious in the new Korean political environment. The two issues have a paramount importance in this context—especially after an Olympics that produced a score of negative symbols of the relationship and in the setting of continued American demands on South Korea on trade and burden-sharing.

United States decision makers, military and civilian, will have to deal with these two issues in terms of their political significance if they are to be settled in ways that will turn the symbols positive and set a constructive tone for managing issues of nuclear weapons, bases, burden-sharing, and status of American ground forces. That means concessions to South Korean sentiments. The danger for Washington is that it will adopt a no-concessions position similar to its initial position in the Philippine bases negotiations, which guaranteed the response of bitterness among Filipinos.

Americans will have to revise their view of South Korea as an ally that receives only benefits from the United States. A little humility in Washington would go a long way towards smoothing out the relationship.

South Koreans in the future will have to mix pragmatism and greater maturity into their new pride and nationalism in dealing with and reacting to the United States. Koreans need to reduce the level of emotionalism in their reactions to trade issues with the United States. The government, the politicians, the press, and business and civic leaders should openly condemn violent acts committed by radical students against Americans. If they do not, the American public will conclude that South Korea is rejecting a close association with the United States. The National Assembly ought to become soon a focal point of reasoned discussion and public education concerning the United States military presence; this would help remove the near monopoly over the issue presently enjoyed by the students and the newspapers.

The fundamentals of the relationship are changing. The strengths of the alliance bode well for a successful management of this change, but a neglect of the more symbolic issues in the near future could put more uncertainty into the longer term.

Hopefully, the two governments will conduct themselves so that irritants in boxing, petty theft, and TV coverage of the Olympics will not be forerunners to deadlock and acrimony over the basic issues of the relationship.

Notes

1. Charles Lee, "Watchdog with a Bite," *Far Eastern Economic Review*, April 28, 1988, 27–28.
2. *Kyonghyang Sinmun*, June 24, 1983. A Gallup poll taken in 1982 revealed that 68 percent of South Koreans over the age of fifty rated the United States as the country they "like most," but only 28 percent of those eighteen to 24 rated the United States the same. *Chungang Ilbo*, June 6, 1988. A nationwide survey found 25.6 of respondents under thirty to be anti-American versus 18.1 percent pro-American.
3. *Washington Times*, November 8, 1984. An illustration of the importance of the Kwangju incident in the perceptions of younger South Koreans was a poll of 800 students of the 20,000-member student body at Seoul National University. The poll found that 50 percent listed the Kwangju uprising as the most tragic event to befall Korea since World War II. Only 25 percent listed the Korean War.
4. For a Korean student's assessment of the radicals, see Pyon Chung Sop, "Student Dissent Drifts towards Extremism," *Far Eastern Economic Review*, July 9, 1987, 36–38; also Ian Buruma, "The Quarrelsome Koreans," *New York Times Magazine*, March 27, 1988, 42–94
5. *Korea Times*, July 14, 1988. A poll of Seoul National University students revealed some of the differences between the hard-core radicals and other students on the issue of democratization, but it also showed that the desire for early reunification was widespread. Thirty-four percent voted for "free democracy"; 41 percent supported democracy "seasoned with socialism"; 9 percent voted for "socialism seasoned with free democracy"; and 4 percent voted for "pure socialism." Forty-seven percent supported immediate reunification, while 45 percent viewed reunification as a task for the future. Another poll of 12,000 college students nationwide published in the *Korea Times*, May 11, 1988, found that 38 percent described differences in ideology and social systems as the chief obstacle to reunification, while 34 percent cited the dictatorial nature of the South Korean government and United States policies as the major barriers.
6. *Korea Times*, March 3, 1988.
7. *Washington Post*, April 29, 1988. At an April 28 news conference, Kim Dae Jung criticized the United States for "inconsiderate, imprudent interference in the internal politics" of South Korea, support for the

Roh Tae Woo "military regime," and pressure on South Korea to open its markets to American beef.

8. *Asian Wall Street Journal,* May 17, 1988.
9. For examples, see Gregory Henderson, "Time to Change the US-South Korea Military Relationship," *Far Eastern Economic Review,* September 24, 1987, 36–38; Doug Bandow, "Korea: The Case for Disengagement," Cato Institute Policy Analysis, December 8, 1987; *Business Week* (editorial), September 5, 1988.
10. During my U.S. Information Agency-sponsored speaking tour in South Korea in September 1987, USIA officials acknowledged that USIA programs attracted few college students and that USIA had practically no contacts with student bodies. Korean professors have described the situation in similar terms to me.
11. *New York Times,* October 26, 1986. The opposition-led Council for the Promotion of Democracy released a list of alleged government directives, including several instructing newspapers to give prominence to United States statements expressing concern for South Korea's security.
12. *Washington Post,* May 12, 1988; *Yonhap* (Seoul), June 9, 1988.
13. *Korea Herald,* May 12, 1988. Besides these direct expenditures, South Korea provides subsidies such as free utilities and other services and exemptions from rent and taxes on land, which totaled $1.9 billion in 1987.
14. Oh, Kwan-chi, "Some Thoughts on ROK-US Alliance and Burden Sharing." Paper Presented at the CSIS-KIDA International Conference, "The Future of ROK-US Security Relations," September 12–13, 1988, 14–16.
15. At every function during my USIA speaking tour in 1987, South Koreans raised the issue of the command structure and the possibilities of changes in it.
16. *Washington Post,* September 25, 1987.
17. For a recent analysis of the issue, see: "Little Buddy Grows Up," *Far Eastern Economic Review,* May 12, 1988, 16–19.
18. Charles Lee, "Living Bitter Memories," *Far Eastern Economic Review,* March 17, 1988, 26.
19. *Hangyore Sinmun,* July 22, 1988. An editorial in this recently founded newspaper criticized the United States position of neither confirming nor denying the presence of nuclear weapons.

6

The 1988 National Assembly Election in South Korea

Hong Nack Kim

I

THE RESULTS OF THE KOREAN NATIONAL ASSEMBLY ELECTION held on April 26, 1988, stunned political observers both in Korea and abroad, for many had expected the ruling Democratic Justice party (DJP) would win a comfortable majority in the unicameral legislature because the two major opposition parties, the Reunification and Democracy party (RDP) and the Party for Peace and Democracy (PPD), were hopelessly divided even after their bitter defeat in the presidential election of December 16, 1987, while newly elected Roh Tae Woo was gaining popular support after the earlier presidential election.[1] Contrary to the predictions made by many, when the ballots were tallied, for the first time since 1950 the government party had failed to capture a majority of seats in the National Assembly.

Compared to many parliamentary elections held under the regimes of Park Chung Hee (1961–1979) and Chun Doo Hwan (1980–February 1988), which were largely ritualistic affairs, the thirteenth National Assembly election was different in that it was not only a free election but also a meaningful contest for the control of a full-fledged democratic parliament. The National Assembly under the new constitution enjoys substantial powers as one of the three separate but equal branches of government. It is no longer relegated to the position of being simply a ratifier of government policy but is empowered to check the executive branch of government, as do many other democratic legislatures. The National Assembly now has the power to legislate, to approve the budget, to investigate the wrongdoings of government officials, to audit the expenditures of government agencies, to adopt a vote of no confidence against the premier and cabinet members, and to impeach executive and judicial officials by a majority vote and the president of the republic by a two-thirds vote. Furthermore, the National Assembly can by majority vote suspend martial law which has been proclaimed by the president of the republic. Moreover, unlike that under the Fourth and Fifth Republics, the new Constitution gives the president of the republic no power to dissolve the National Assembly. Thus, the constitutional power and status of the National Assembly have been substantially enhanced under the Sixth Republic, inaugurated in February 1988.

Because of the changed constitutional status and power of the parliament, winning the majority of seats in the thirteenth National Assembly election was newly important for both the government party and the opposition. Without controlling the National Assembly, the government party would have difficulty in pushing key legislative programs through the parliament; and the opposition parties needed to control the majority in the National Assembly in order to offset the DJP government headed by President Roh Tae Woo. They were particularly concerned about the prospect that control of the majority in the National Assembly by the Democratic Justice Party would impede, if not endanger, the process of democratization in South Korea, a process begun in earnest after the bloody constitutional crisis in the spring and summer of 1987. Thus, the stakes were high for both the government party and its opposition in the thirteenth National Assembly election.

The purpose of this study is to examine some important factors which have contributed to bringing about the so-called *yadae yoso* ("the large opposition and small government") phenomenon in the 1988 parliamentary election in South Korea. In addition to analyzing major variables which have shaped the outcome of the election, this paper will also evaluate the implications of the election results for the future of the South Korean party system.

II

In drafting the constitution of the Sixth Republic in the fall of 1987, the ruling DJP and its opposition were generally in agreement on the necessity of strengthening the power of the National Assembly, which was disproportionately weak vis-à-vis the executive branch of government under the constitution of the Fifth Republic. Under the new constitution, the National Assembly regained all of the powers it had lost under the Park and Chun regimes. However, there was not enough time to revise the existing parliamentary election law. Both the government and its opposition were willing to postpone the revision of the law governing election of the National Assembly until after the presidential election. The only other agreement reached between the DJP and the main opposition party, the Reunification and Democratic party (RDP), was to schedule the National Assembly election for no later than April 28, 1988.

Following the bitterly contested presidential election in December 1987, preliminary negotiations were conducted between the government party and the opposition to revise the parliamentary election law and to set the date for the National Assembly election. Initially, the DJP had wanted to hold the parliamentary election in February 1988[2] in order to benefit from the bandwagon effect of its victory in the presidential election as well as from the disarray of the opposition resulting from continuing discord between the two major opposition parties, the RDP (led by Kim Young Sam) and the Party for Peace and Democracy (PPD) led by Kim Dae Jung. Opposition parties favored setting the election forward to April 1988 because they needed more time to regroup and to prepare for it. Eventually, the ruling DJP agreed to an April date because of an unexpected delay caused by difficulty in revising the election law. Besides, scheduling the election for February would have enabled the incumbent President Chun to handpick many parliamentary candidates for the government party at the expense of incoming President Roh. Thus, the parliamentary election was scheduled for April 26, 1988.

A more difficult problem for the parties was overhauling the parliamentary electoral system. Under the Fifth Republic, beginning in 1980) two-thirds of 276 National Assembly members were elected from 92 two-member districts. The remaining one-third (92 seats) was filled through a proportional representation system.[3] Two-thirds of these 92 seats were allotted to the party winning the largest number of district seats, while the remainder was divided among the remaining parties in proportion to the seats won. The system as a whole favored the government party, assuring it a comfortable majority in the National Assembly. In the 1985 parliamentary election, for example, the DJP won 46 percent of district seats with 35.4 percent of the popular votes, but the seats available through the proportional representation formula boosted the party's share to a 54 percent majority in the National Assembly.[4] The electoral system was not only regarded as undemocratic by the opposition parties but was also unpopular with the voters.

In approaching the problem of overhauling the electoral system, the DJP initially favored a combination of single-member districts in rural areas and two- to four-member districts in urban areas, while reducing the number of at-large seats available under proportional representation.[5] When protracted negotiations failed to produce the necessary compromise, on March 8 the DJP rammed a bill through the National Assembly to amend the election law according to the single-member district (SMD) system. The DJP's strategy was based on shrewd calculations that the SMD system would be best for the party in view of strong popular support for such a system and especially in view of the continuing rivalry between the two major opposition parties, the RDP and the PPD, that was sure to split the opposition vote. Among the opposition parties, the PPD supported the SMD system, expecting to capitalize on the party's highly concentrated vote in the Cholla provinces and part of Seoul. The RDP, on the other hand, initially favored a multi-member district system because its vote was more evenly scattered and not concentrated in any particular region. However, it, too, eventually leaned toward the SMD system.[6] The only party which maintained uncompromising opposition to the SMD system was the New Democratic Republican party (NDRP) headed by former Premier Kim Jong Pil.

Under the new DJP-sponsored electoral system, the National Assembly consists of 299 seats: 224 seats are to be filled through the SMD system, while the remaining 75 at-large seats are to be allocated by a proportional representation scheme. If a party wins a majority of 224 district seats, the 75 at-large seats must be allocated in proportion to the share of the district seats won by each party. If no party wins a majority of the district seats, the party with the largest number of district seats is entitled to 38 of the 75 at-large seats. The remaining 37 seats are then allocated to the other parties winning at least 5 or more district seats in proportion to each party's share of seats.[7]

III

Following the decision to hold the National Assembly election on April 26, 1988, the DJP nominated its candidate for each of the 224 electoral districts. Many influential lawmakers including former DJP Chairman Kwon Ik Hyun; and former Secretary-general, Kwon Jung Dal and Kim Sang Koo, former President Chun's brother-in-law, were denied renomination as candidates. The DJP dismissed 28 of the 86 incumbent local chapter chairmen, or 32.6 percent, while nominating 125 new candidates. Denying the renomination of the key figures of the Fifth Republic power group was apparently designed to consolidate the power of the party's new president, Roh Tae Woo.[8] In addition, the DJP also named 62 candidates for the at-large seats available under the proportional representation.

Opposition parties also announced their lists of candidates for the thirteenth National Assembly election. The RDP fielded 202 candidates, including 41 incumbents. It denied renomination to 12 incumbents. The PPD nominated 168 candidates, including 20 incumbents but did not support candidates for many constituencies in Kyongsang and Chungchong provinces, where the party was weak and not popular. Five incumbent law makers were denied renomination by the PPD, but most of the former dissident figures aspiring to run in the election were named. The New Democratic Republican Party

(NDRP), led by former Premier Kim Jong Pil, fielded 181 candidates. By April 9, some 1,045 candidates had registered in 224 electoral districts.[9] The average competition rate per seat was 4.7 to 1. In terms of the number of candidates, it was the largest field since 1961. Most ran under the auspices of the fourteen different political parties, but 111 of them ran as independents.

With the start of the eighteen-day official campaign period on April 9, 1988, both government and opposition launched massive efforts, articulating their views on a number of important issues. In an attempt to win popular support, the ruling and opposition parties intensified their political offensives against each other, trading charges and countercharges over the Kwangju incident of 1980 in which nearly 200 people had been killed, the Saemaul (New Community) Movement Headquarters incident involving embezzlement of millions of dollars by former President Chun's brother, Chun Kyong Hwan, and other major scandals involving powerful elements of the Fifth Republic, including former President Chun and his family. Opposition parties also raised questions about the legitimacy of the Roh government, which they regarded as an extension of the illegitimate Fifth Republic.[10]

"The three Kims," namely Kim Young Sam, Kim Dae Jung, and Kim Jong Pil, all unsuccessful candidates in the 1987 presidential election, spearheaded the opposition parties' campaigns to expose the "corrupt nature of the ruling party,"[11] while President Roh appealed to voters to support the government party, aiding him in his efforts to carry out his election pledges of continued economic and political developments in an atmosphere of stability. Thus, the National Assembly election became another showdown between Roh Tae Woo and the three Kims.

The opposition's attack on the ruling party for the scandals of the Fifth Republic heated up as the election day drew closer. Contending that the DJP had been responsible for widespread corruption and had abused its political power, Kim Young Sam declared, "The Saemaul scandal is just the tip of the iceberg. All its corruption of the past should be brought to light, and those responsible to trial."[12] Kim called for popular support of his party, saying that the massive irregularities committed by

Chun's regime could have been avoided had there been a powerful opposition party.

Meanwhile, Kim Dae Jung denounced the DJP for the 1980 Kwangju incident.[13] Speaking at a rally in Kwangju, Kim demanded that the government reveal the truth of the event and restore the honor of the victims as well as that of all the citizens of Kwangju. He called for a fact-finding investigation to be conducted by a parliamentary task force after the election. Kim also urged that the property holdings of former President Chun Doo Hwan and his relatives be made public "to clear mounting public suspicion."[14] In a similar vein, Kim Jong Pil also declared at a party rally in Seoul that the next National Assembly should invoke its investigative power to look into financial scandals involving former President Chun and his family. He criticized measures previously announced by the government to heal the wounds of the Kwangju incident as "well short of public expectation."[15]

To counter the opposition's criticisms, the DJP chairman, Chae Mun Shik, announced on April 6 that the major scandals of the Fifth Republic would be thoroughly re-investigated after the parliamentary election. He made the remarks in response to mounting demands from the opposition that the truth of all major past charges against President Chun Doo Hwan's family be brought to light. At the same time, Chae accused the opposition of trying to agitate the people by exaggerating the facts.[16] As for the opposition's charge that the ruling party was resorting to "money power," buying votes in the election, Chae promised that the DJP would do its best to make it the "cleanest election" in the nation's political history.[17] Meanwhile, the DJP's chief spokesman, You Kyung Hyun, dismissed as "baseless" Kim Dae Jung's accusation in Kwangju on April 5 that the 1987 presidential election had been rigged with the use of computers.[18]

As the campaign entered its final stage, the ruling and opposition parties stepped up their efforts to win still-undecided voters. The DJP focused on "floating votes" by stressing the need for a DJP majority in the coming National Assembly to ensure political stability.[19] The opposition parties lashed out in chorus at alleged illegal campaign activities by the ruling party, the Saemaul scandal, and at other serious corruption and wrongdoing committed while Chun Doo Hwan was still in power. In fact, several opposition parties and other groups launched a nationwide campaign in April to collect a million signatures to petition for the investigation of former President Chun and his wife.[20]

Against the backdrop of the opposition's intensifying attack against the government party, Chae Mun Shik appealed to the voters to produce victory for the government party in the parliamentary election, stressing that without the DJP's winning a majority in the National Assembly, it might be difficult to "fully achieve the democratic reforms, initiated by President Roh Tae Woo's June 29 [1987] declaration."[21]

Contending that the government party was attempting to illegally utilize the local government infrastructure to mobilize voters for DJP candidates, RDP's Kim Young Sam called for the immediate termination of such activities. In a press conference held in Taegu, he demanded that President Roh and DJP chairman Chae Mun Shik "openly withdraw" instructions they had allegedly handed down to the heads of administrative organs and agencies soliciting their support in the elections.[22] He also demanded that President Roh investigate former President Chun Doo Hwan, his wife, Lee Soon-Ja, and their relatives in connection with their alleged wrongdoings.

At the same time, Kim Dae Jung also declared to the voters in the Cholla provinces that President Roh was conspiring to secure more than two-thirds of the total parliamentary seats in order to renege on his earlier pledge to hold a referendum after the Seoul Olympics on his performance as president. Kim went on to say that if President Roh won an overwhelming victory in the upcoming parliamentary elections, he would not hold a referendum and would use the parliamentary election as an excuse.[23] Kim Young Sam, for his part, warned that the ruling party was attempting to capture more than a two-thirds majority in the National Assembly and intended to revise the constitution and introduce a parliamentary cabinet system of government for the perpetuation of its power.[24] In the meantime, Kim Jong Pil declared that the NDRP would abolish the controversial Advisory Council of Elder Statesmen headed by former President Chun and the monthly neighborhood meetings called *pansang-hoe*.[25] In a press conference held at Puyo, Kim also pledged that his party would strive for the repeal of all "un-democratic" laws and for improvement in the protection of human rights. Similar pledges had also been made earlier by the other two Kims.[26]

Parliamentary candidates of the major opposition parties generally echoed their leaders' views on the major campaign issues in seeking popular support, while the government party's candidates took defensive postures on many campaign issues to blunt the opposition's criticisms. On the eve of the election, numerous irregularities, such as the use of violence, vote buying, and spreading of false rumors to defame opponents, were reported by numerous candidates in both government and opposition parties. It was not a clean election, but at least it was the freest election ever held in South Korea.

IV

On election day, 19,853,890 of 26,198,205 eligible voters, or 75.8 percent, went to the polls. When the ballots were tallied, the election results stunned many who had predicted the government party's victory by an overwhelming margin. The DJP had won only 87 of the nation's 224 constituencies, against 54 for the PPD, 46 for the RDP, and 27 for the NDRP.[27] Independents won 9 seats, and a candidate of the Hangyore Democratic Party was elected in South Cholla province though he quickly switched to the PDP. In terms of popular votes, the DJP garnered 34.0 percent, while the RDP received 23.8 percent, the PPD 19.3 percent, and the NDRP 15.6 percent. In a major upset, Kim Dae Jung's PPD emerged as the largest opposition party, displacing archrival Kim Young Sam's RDP. The PPD swept all but one of the 37 districts in Kim Dae Jung's home region and won 17 of the 42 seats in Seoul. The RDP was relegated to third place largely because of its lackluster performance in Seoul and in the provinces, except for Pusan, Kim Young Sam's political bastion. The NDRP chalked up a strong showing in Kim Jong Pil's home province, South Chungchong. The three Kims were thus elected to the National Assembly after a long absence. As the DJP failed to win a majority of the 224 electoral districts, it was awarded 38 of the 75 at-large seats under the proportional representation system. Sixteen of the remaining 37 seats were allocated to the PPD, 13 to the RDP, and

TABLE 6-1
Final National Assembly Election Returns Seats Won
in Special Cities and Provinces (1988)

	DJP	PPD	RDP	NDRP	Other	Total
Seoul	10	17	10	3	2	42
Pusan	1	—	14	—	—	15
Taegu	8	—	—	—	—	8
Inchon	6	—	1	—	—	7
Kwangju	—	5	—	—	—	5
Kyonggi-do	16	1	4	6	1	28
Kangwon-do	8	—	3	1	2	14
Chungchongbuk-do	7	—	—	2	—	9
Chungchongnam-do	2	—	2	13	1	18
Chollabuk-do	—	14	—	—	—	14
Chollanam-do	—	17	—	—	1	18
Kyongsangbuk-do	17	—	2	2	—	21
Kyongsangnam-do	12	—	9	—	1	22
Cheju-do	—	—	1	—	2	3
Subtotal	87	54	46	27	10	224
Proportional representation	38	16	13	8	75	
Total	125	70	59	35	10	299

Source: *Korea Newsreview*, 30 April 1988, p. 7.

8 to the NDRP. As a result, the DJP now holds 125 of the 299 seats in the National Assembly, while the PPD has 71, the RDP 59 and the NDRP 35. Nine seats are held by the independents.

There were more newcomers than incumbents among the winners—167 of 299 Assembly members, or 55.9 percent of the membership. Only 73 incumbents were reelected from 224 electoral districts, while 28 former lawmakers made comebacks.[28] In addition, 64 of 224 winners of district seats were party bureaucrats. Thus, professional politicians accounted for 165 of 224 winners (or 73.7 percent) of the district seats. In terms of educational background, most had attended institutions of higher learning, including eight who held doctorates. Thirteen lawyers also won district sets. In terms of age, 102 were in their 50s, 94 in their 40s, 15 in their 60s and 13 in their 30s. Although none of the 26 female candidates was successful in winning a district seat, 6 were elected as at-large members under the proportional representation formula.[29]

The voter turnout rate (75.8 percent), relatively low compared to previous elections, was generally higher in rural districts than in urban ones. The voting rate was lowest in Seoul and other metropolitan areas, while it was substantially higher in the semirural and rural districts (see Table 6-2). This means that there was an inverse correlation between urban residence and voter turnout, as had been the case for several previous elections from 1963 to 1985.[30] For 25 years, then, the more urbanized a district, the lower the voter turnout.

So far as partisan support is concerned, the so-called *yochon yado* (villages for the government, and cities for the opposition

TABLE 6-2
Percentage of Voter Participation in National Assembly Elections

Types of districts	1963 (N)	1967 (N)	1971 (N)	1973 (N)	1978 (N)	1988 (N)
Metropolitan districts	62.0% (15)	62.5% (15)	64.9% (15)	66.0% (11)	70.9% (11)	72.4% (77)
Urban districts	66.7 (9)	70.4 (9)	74.7 (10)	69.4 (4)	75.3 (4)	76.9 (44)
Semirural districts	76.2 (21)	80.6 (21)	78.2 (20)	77.8 (23)	80.7 (25)	79.3 (23)
Rural districts	76.2 (75)	82.7 (75)	78.4 (88)	71.8 (31)	83.3 (31)	81.4 (80)
Urban districts (Metropolitan + urban)	68.8 (24)	65.5 (24)	68.8 (25)	66.9 (15)	72.0 (15)	74.5 (121)
Rural (semirural + rural)	76.2 (96)	82.3 (96)	78.3 (108)	77.4 (54)	82.1 (56)	80.7 (103)
Total	73.7 (120)	78.9 (120)	76.5 (133)	75.1 (69)	80.0 (71)	75.8 (224)

Definitions: Metropolitan Districts: Districts in special cities of Seoul, Pusan, Taegu, Inchon, and Kwangju; Urban Districts: Districts in cities; Semirural Districts: Districts composed of a minor city and a county (or counties); Rural Districts: Districts composed of one or more counties

Sources: Hong N. Kim and Sunki Choe, "Urbanization and Changing Voting Patterns in South Korean Parliamentary Election," *Journal of Northeast Asian Studies*, Fall 1987, p. 37; and calculated from the data in Central Election Management Committee (ROK), *Chae 13 dae Kukhoe Uiwon Sonko Chiyokku Hubocha-pyol Tukpyo Sanghwang* (Seoul: Central Election Management Committee, 1988).

TABLE 6-3
Percentage of Votes Polled by Government Party
in National Assembly Elections

Party district types* (N)	1963**	1967**	1971**	1973**	1978**	1988**
A	52.0 (15)	42.7 (15)	41.1 (15)	44.6 (11)	38.4 (11)	30.03 (77)
B	57.4 (9)	54.9 (9)	47.4 (10)	64.3 (4)	50.5 (4)	30.63 (44)
C	70.8 (21)	63.0 (21)	53.5 (20)	64.3 (23)	55.4 (25)	40.49 (23)
D	66.2 (75)	68.2 (75)	59.2 (88)	56.3 (31)	58.0 (31)	40.37 (80)
Urban	54.0 (24)	47.2 (24)	43.6 (25)	49.8 (15)	41.6 (15)	30.35 (121)
Rural	67.2 (96)	67.1 (96)	58.2 (108)	58.8 (54)	56.8 (56)	40.43 (103)

*A - Metropolitan; B - Urban; C - Semirural; D - Rural
**The Democratic Republican Party (DRP)
***The Democratic Justice Party (DJP)
See Table 6-3 for definitions.
Sources: Kim and Choe, "Urbanization and Changing Voting Patterns," p. 41; and Central Election Management Committee, Statistics, 1988.

parties) pattern was clearly in effect. This was also the case with all but one (in 1981) of the parliamentary elections held from 1963 to 1985.[31] Politically conscious urban voters gave greater support to opposition parties, while the less sophisticated rural voters usually favored the government party in parliamentary elections. Compared to the rural electorate, urban voters were generally younger, better educated,[32] and more critical in matters of politics; thus they were less vulnerable to government pressures and provided more support to the opposition. The degree of support for the government party was inversely related to the degree of urbanization: the more urbanized a district, the less support for the government party (see Table 6-4). More specifically, support for the ruling DJP was 30.1 percent in the metropolitan and urban districts, while the DJP's share of the vote in the semirural and rural districts was 40.7 percent. The only exception to this general pattern was in Taegu, Roh Tae Woo's hometown, where the DJP garnered 48.4 percent of the vote and won all eight seats. The opposition

TABLE 6-4
Representation Rates in the 13th National Assembly Election*

Number of Seats Won Party	% Vote (A)	District (B)	At-large (C)	Total (B+ C)	% of Seats Won District Total (D)	Representation Rate (E) D/A, E/A
DJP	34.0	87	38	125	38.8	41.8 1.1, 1.2
PDP	19.3	54	16	70	24.1	23.4 1.3, 1.2
RDP	23.8	46	13	59	20.5	19.7 0.9, 0.8
NDRP	15.6	27	8	35	12.1	11.7 0.8, 0.8
Minor*	2.5	1	0	1	0.5	0.3 0.2, 0.1
Independent	4.8	9	0	9	4.0	3.0 0.8, 0.6
Total	100.0	224	75	229	100.0	99.9**

Sources: Compiled and calculated from the election data reported in *Dong-a Ilbo*, 28 through 30 April 1988.
*Percentage of seats divided by percentage of popular votes won by each party
**The total does not amount to 100 due to rounding errors.

parties as a whole did much better in urban and metropolitan districts than in rural or semirural districts. Since there were more metropolitan and urban districts (54 percent) than rural and semirural districts, the DJP's relatively good performance in rural and semirural districts was not sufficient to overcome the party's poor showing in more urbanized districts.

The 1988 election results nevertheless deviated sharply from those of previous parliamentary elections, where regionalism or regional voting (that is, voters' support of candidates from their regions) had become a significant factor in shaping the outcomes of elections. In contrast to presidential elections, regionalism was not a significant factor in the parliamentary elections in South Korea from 1948 to 1985. In the first place, the electoral district for the National Assembly is incomparably small compared to the national constituency used for presidential elections. Furthermore, most parliamentary candidates are

TABLE 6-5
Percentage of Votes Received by Major Parties in 1988
National Assembly Election

District Type	DJP	RDP	PDP	NDRP
Metropolitan (77)	30.03	29.61	20.99	14.75
Urban (44)	30.63	18.54	19.81	21.86
Semi-rural (23)	40.49	26.55	16.42	9.82
Rural (80)	40.37	18.05	17.13	17.51
Nation (224)	33.97	23.91	19.27	16.49

Source: Calculated from Central Election Management Committee (ROK), *Chae 13 dae Kukhoeuiwon Sonko Hubocha-pyol Tukpyo Sanghwang* (Seoul: Central Election Management Committee, 1988).

TABLE 6-6
Performance of Democratic Justice Party in the 1988
National Assembly Election

District Type (N)	% DJP Vote	Number of Seats Won	% of DJP Seats
Metropolitan (77)	30.03%	25	32.5
Urban (44)	30.63%	11	27.3
Semirural (23)	40.49%	11	43.5
Rural (80)	40.37%	40	50.0
Total (224)	34.00%	87	38.8

Source: Calculated from Central Election Management Committee (ROK), *Chae 13 dae Kukhoeuiwon Sonko Hubocha-pyol Tukpyo Sanghwang* (Seoul: Central Election Management Committee, 1988).

closely tied to districts by birth or other factors. Any favorite son phenomenon in the parliamentary election was usually confined to rivalry among subdistricts (counties) within an electoral district.

The region-party alliance was most conspicuous in the Cholla region, Kim Dae Jung's home area, where his PPD swept all but one of the 37 districts.[33] Indeed, the PPD captured all five seats in the city of Kwangju with an incredible 88.6 percent of the popular vote. It also won 17 of 18 district seats in South Cholla Province, with 67.9 percent of the popular vote, and 14 of 14 seats in North Cholla Province, with 61.5 percent of the popular vote. Since a seat-winner belonging to a minor opposition party decided to join the PPD immediately after the election, the PPD had in effect a clean sweep of the Cholla region: it won 37 of 37 seats contested.

A somewhat similar situation developed for Kim Jong Pil's NDRP, which won 13 of 18 seats in South Chungchong Province, with 46.5 percent of the popular votes cast in the province. The 13 seats accounted for roughly half of the 27 seats the party won in the parliamentary election. Kim Young Sam's RDP won 14 of 15 seats in Pusan, Kim's hometown, with 54.1 percent of the popular vote. His party did not, however, fare quite as well in South Kyongsang Province as a whole, where it won only 9 of 22 seats, with 36.9 percent of the popular vote. Apparently, the voters in the province were not as alienated from the government party as were the voters of the Cholla region and South Chungchong Province because the province had received quite favorable treatment under both the Park and Chun regimes.[34] Nevertheless, the 23 seats the RDP won in Pusan and South Kyongsang Province represented exactly half (50 percent) of the 46 seats the party obtained in the election.

Roh Tae Woo's DJP had a clean sweep in Taegu city, Roh's hometown, where it captured all 8 seats contested in the city, with 48.8 percent of the popular vote. In North Kyongsang Province, Roh's home province, the DJP again did exceptionally well, winning 17 of 21 seats (or 81 percent) of the total seats contested, with 51 percent of the popular vote. As a result of this region-party alliance phenomenon, the ruling DJP was unable to win a single seat in the Cholla region (37 electoral districts). Moreover, it captured only 2 of 18 seats in South Chungchong Province and failed to win any in Pusan.

Thus, regionalism was again a significant factor in shaping the outcome of the 1988 parliamentary election. The lopsided regional support for a party led by a former presidential candidate in his home region largely shaped the electoral fortunes of each major party.

V

The DJP's failure to dominate the thirteenth National Assembly election not only surprised the nation but has also aroused much speculation regarding the causes of their weak showing.

Some observers maintain that the DJP did poorly in the general elections because of the introduction of the single-member district (SMD) system.[35] Such a contention is untenable, however, when we analyze the representation rate of popular votes into seats (that is, the ratio between the popular votes and the seats won) of each party in the election. As table 6-5 indicates, the DJP's representation rate is 1.1; it obtained 38.8 percent of district seats with 34.0 percent of the popular votes garnered. When the at-large seats available under the proportional representation system are added, the DJP's total share of the Assembly seats constitutes 41.8 percent. Expressed another way, the ratio between its share of popular votes (34 percent) and the Assembly seats won by the party (41.8 percent) is 1.2. The only opposition party which fared better than the DJP in the representation rate is the PPD, which secured 24.1 percent of the district seats with 19.3 percent of popular votes, for a representation rate of 1.3. However, when the at-large seats are added, the PPD's share of the total Assembly seats is 23.4 percent, thus making the party's overall representation rate again 1.2. The other two major opposition parties, the RDP and the NDRP, did not fare well according to representation rate. The RDP received 20.5 percent of the district seats with 23.8 percent of the popular vote, or 0.9 percent in representation rate. When its share of the total seats won in the Assembly (19.7 percent) is divided by its share of popular votes (23.8 percent), its representation rate is 0.8. The NDRP's representation rate also stood at 0.8. In case of the minor parties, only one of which elected its single candidate, the rate was 0.1. It is clear that the SMD system favored the government party and permitted it to win more seats than its share of popular votes in the Assembly. Thus, it is clear the DJP's failure to control the election cannot be attributed to the introduction of the SMD system and another explanation must be found.

Among several other factors, it should first of all be pointed out that the DJP's defeat in the 1988 parliamentary election should be in part credited to the voters' desire to check the ruling party by strengthening its opposition in the National Assembly.[36] The government party failed to convince the voters that it was imperative for it to win a solid majority in the National Assembly. Although DJP's Roh Tae Woo won the 1987 presidential election with 36.7 percent of the popular vote, it is considered a victory by default resulting from the disunity

TABLE 6-7
Percentage of Vote and Seats Won by Party Leaders

Party & Leader	Leader's home city or province	% Vote (home region)	% Seats (home region)	Nation (% Vote)	Nation (% Seats)
DJP: Roh Tae Woo	*Taegu*, North Kyongsang	48.4 51.0	100.0	34.0	38.8 81.0
PDP: Kim Dae Jung	*Kwangju*, North Cholla	88.6	61.5	100.0	19.3
	South Cholla	67.9	24.1	100.0	94.4
RDP: Kim Young Sam	*Pusan*, South Kyongsang	54.1 36.9	93.3	23.8	20.5 40.9
NDRP: Kim Jong Pil	South Chungchong	46.5	72.2	15.6	12.1

Source: Calculated from the election data reported in Central Election Management Committee (ROK), *Chae 13 dae Kukhoeuiwon Sonko Hubocha-pyol Tukpyo Sanghwang* (Seoul: Central Election Management Committee, 1988).

between Kim Young Sam and Kim Dae Jung. Their combined share of popular votes (55 percent) was far greater than Roh's 36.7 percent. Although many were disappointed by the opposition's inability to close ranks both during and after the 1987 presidential election, the popular desire for the democratization of the South Korean political system remained strong. To many voters, President Roh's announcement of his new cabinet in February 1988 was a disappointment, for it retained seven holdovers from the discredited Chun government. Cynical journalists quickly coined the phrase "the 5.5th Republic" to characterize the newly established Roh government under the constitution of the Sixth Republic.[37] Under such circumstances, the voters' desire to restrain the power of the Roh government was stronger than their willingness to give a free hand to the new government.

Second, several major scandals and much corruption in the Fifth Republic implicating former President Chun and his family not only alienated voters from the ruling DJP but also increasingly aroused public pressures to investigate corruption of the former government. Popular demand for an investigation became stronger especially in the wake of the arrest of

Chun's younger brother, "Little Chun," in March 1988.[38] In order to look into such scandals and irregularities effectively, it was generally believed that the National Assembly would have to be controlled by the opposition rather than by the government, which still retained many powerful figures from the Fifth Republic.

Third, the DJP's weakness in the 1988 parliamentary election can be attributed to the party's inability to enlist the support of young and well-educated urban voters. According to a study by Kap Yun Lee based on an opinion survey conducted by a team of researchers from Sogang University in April 1988, there was an inverse relationship between the age of voters and their support for the DJP: the younger the voter, the less likely he supported the DJP. Furthermore, there was also an inverse relationship between the voter's degree of education and support for the DJP: the more educated he was, the less likely he was to support the government party.[39] Since 64.1 percent of voters in the urban districts are in their twenties and thirties with relatively more formal education (52.4 percent had more than nine years schooling) than their peers in rural areas (25.1 percent had more than nine years schooling), who constitute about 47 percent of the rural electorate,[40] it is not difficult to understand why the DJP has lagged behind the opposition in garnering votes in metropolitan and urban districts. The DJP's dull performance in urban areas as a whole undoubtedly affected its overall electoral fortunes in 1988.

Fourth, the DJP's prospects were adversely affected by a number of blunders committed by its candidates and supporters. One incident that dealt a serious blow to the DJP took place a day before the election in Andong, North Kyongsang Province, where a DJP candidate was caught attempting to mail over 3,700 envelopes, each containing 20,000 *won* (about $28.00), to constituents.[41] The occurrence not only shocked voters, it also tarnished the government party's image. Furthermore, it seriously undermined the voters' confidence in the DJP's assurances of an honest election. Another serious event damaging the DJP involved a government-controlled television station on Cheju Island which announced on the eve of the election that the DJP candidate was the winner in a local district. Apparently, this report had been taped during a rehearsal to acquaint anchormen with the use of new computers in preparation for the live broadcast of election returns on election day. It was not produced for actual use that day but it was inadvertently shown, giving credence to the opposition's charge that the government party was attempting to rig the elections by manipulating computers.[42] Undoubtedly, these episodes seriously damaged the DJP. Virtually all observers had predicted that the DJP would win the election, but it ended up winning only 87 of 224 electoral districts.[43]

Last but not least, the DJP's electoral fortunes were affected by growing regionalism. Historically a significant factor in South Korean politics, especially in direct presidential elections, regionalism was never an important element in parliamentary elections until 1988. The regional nature of Korean voting (voters' support of candidates from their regions) was quite strong in the 1987 presidential election. The three mahor candidates, Roh Tae Woo, Kim Young Sam and Kim Dae Jung, as favorite sons derive much support from their home provinces. Particularly strong was the tendency shown by the voters of the Cholla provinces for Kim Dae Jung, who received nearly 90 percent of the popular vote in that region in the 1987 presidential election. It is generally believed, however, that the voters in the Cholla region also were quite resentful of perceived discriminatory treatment in regional economic development and government personnel recruitment they had received under the Park and Chun regimes,[44] both of which had favored the Kyongsang region. The victory of Roh Tae Woo in the 1987 presidential election aggravated the situation further, for Roh, like his predecessors, Park and Chun, was a native of Kyongsang Province. Apparently, regional feeling spilled over to the 1988 parliamentary election, as the four major candidates who had run for president came to control four major parties. As the National Assembly campaigns heated up, nominees tried to utilize the coattail effects of their party's leader, who was particularly popular in a certain region, by linking their victory with a particular leader's political fortunes.

As a result of the regional voting alignment, the DJP was not able to win a single seat (out of 37) in the Cholla region. It captured only 2 of 18 seats contested in South Chungchong Province, and failed to win any of the 8 seats in Pusan. It did considerably better in South Kyongsang Province, where it won 12 out of 22 seats contested. In short, the DJP won only 14 of 78 seats in the three major opposition leaders' home regions. If such strong regionalism had not manifested itself in the 1988 parliamentary election, the DJP could have won substantially more seats in the National Assembly. In other words, the lopsided support given by voters to native son-led opposition parties in the Cholla region, Pusan, and South Chungchong Province nullified many of the advantages the DJP was supposed to enjoy under the single-member district system.[45]

VI

A few basic conclusions can be drawn with regard to the 1988 parliamentary election in South Korea.

First, this election has ushered in a new era of legislative politics in South Korea. Not only is the National Assembly significantly strengthened in performing its constitutional functions as a legislature, but it is also free from the domination of the government party for the first time since the establishment of the republic in 1948. As a result of the so-called *yoso yade* (weak government party, strong opposition) in the National Assembly, the government can no longer ram bills through the National Assembly disregarding the opposition. Without the support of at least one of the three major opposition parties, the DJP will be unable to pass any bill or resolution in the Assembly. On the other hand, the opposition parties cannot push their legislative programs at will either. In the first place, there is no consensus or unity among them. Futhermore, even if they unite on a particular bill, there is no guarantee that it will be enacted into law, because President Roh can veto that legislation. To override a presidential veto, it is necessary for the opposition party to muster a two-thirds majority in the National Assembly. However, that is virtually impossible, for the ruling DJP controls more than a third (41.8 percent) of the 299 seats in the Assembly. Thus, neither the government party nor the opposition party can enact any law unilaterally.

Under such circumstances, unless the government and its opponents are willing to compromise and work together, political stalemate will result in the National Assembly. Although such a situation is not ideal for either the government party or the opposition, it may provide good training in the art of negotiation and compromise for South Korean politicians. Viewed from such a perspective, the election results may be regarded as positive for the political development of South Korea. The emergence of a powerful opposition in the Assembly has brought about livelier, more active discussions and debates in the legislature over policy issues, ending its embarrassing reputation as a servant of the government.

Second, the election outcome came as a political setback for Roh Tae Woo, who won the presidential election with only a 36.7 percent plurality in December 1987. The general elections had been regarded as a popularity test for Roh's new government, inaugurated February 25, 1988. Without a stable majority in the National Assembly, Roh would face difficulty in having his programs enacted. The emergence of Kim Dae Jung's PPD as the major opposition party augurs rough sailing for the Roh government, for Kim has repeatedly vowed to bring to light all "irregularities" of the Fifth Republic, including the financial scandals involving President Chun and the Kwangju incident of 1980. The one-sided support that Kim's party received from the Kwangju voters in the election put even more pressure on Kim to pursue the incident.

Third, the strong regionalism displayed by voters in support of the opposition parties led by the three Kims neutralized whatever advantages the government party had sought to ensure under the single-member district system. Under the SMD plan, it is quite possible for the DJP to win the majority of the National Assembly seats with 34 percent of popular votes. In fact, in the 1963 parliamentary election, which had used the SMD system, the then-government party (the Democratic Republican party) won a two-thirds majority of the National Assembly seats with 33.5 percent of the popular vote. The DJP's failure to dominate the 1988 parliamentary election should be attributed primarily to region-party alliances which adversely affected the DJP's fortunes in important regions (that is, the Cholla region, South Chungchong Province, and Pusan). The DJP's inability to win its normal share of seats in these regions made it impossible for the party to win a majority in the National Assembly.

Fourth, in terms of electoral participation and partisan support, the 1988 National Assembly election did not deviate from traditional patterns. The voter turnout rate was inversely related to urbanization: the less urbanized a district, the higher the voter turnout rate. In terms of partisan support, again, there was an inverse correlation between urban residence and the votes for the government party: the more urbanized a district, the lower the vote for the government party. Thus, the patterns of *yochon yado* affected the thirteenth National Assembly election as they had most of the parliamentary elections in South Korea since 1963.

Finally, in terms of the implications of the 1988 parliamentary election for the future of the South Korean political party system, one can say that it has politically resurrected the three Kims, who have emerged as the leaders of three major opposition parties in the National Assembly. As a result, they are planning to run again for the presidency in 1992. To a great extent, therefore, party politics in South Korea both within and outside the National Assembly will be shaped by "one Roh and three Kims" in the next four years.

Notes

1. According to the opinion survey conducted jointly by *Hankuk Ilbo* and a research team from the Sogang University on March 3–April 1, 1988, 55 percent of the respondents indicated their satisfaction with the performance of the Roh government. See *Hankuk Ilbo,* April 5, 1988.
2. John McBeth, "Hats in Their Hands," *Far Eastern Economic Review,* January 7, 1988, 16. (Cited hereafter *FEER.*) See also John McBeth, "Electoral Expectations," *FEER,* January 21, 1988, 35.
3. C.I. Eugene Kim, "The Meaning of Korea's 12th National Assembly Election," *Korea Observer* 16 (Winter 1985): 367.
4. B.C. Koh, "The 1985 Parliamentary Election in South Korea," *Asian Survey* 25 (September 1985): 888–90.
5. McBeth, "Hats in Their Hands," 16. See also McBeth, "Electoral Expectations," 36.
6. McBeth, "Electoral Expectations," 36.
7. *Korea Newsreview,* 17 (April 30, 1988): 4. See also, *Hankuk Ilbo,* March 9, 1988.
8. *Dong-A Ilbo,* March 22, 1988. See also, *Korea Newsreview* 17 (March 26, 1988): 4–5.
9. Chang Hee Kim, "13-dae Chongson Kyolkwa, Cholmyo han Sontaek, Cholmyo han Kudo," *Shindong-A,* June 1988, 171. See also, *Korea Newsreview* 17: 5.
10. For a detailed analysis of the major campaign issues, see *Dong-A Ilbo,* April 8, 1988.
11. *Korea Newsreview* 17 (April 9, 1988): 4.
12. *Ibid.* See also, John McBeth, "'Little' Chun's Comedown," *FEER,* March 31, 1988, 32–33.
13. *Korea Newsreview* 17 (April 9, 1988): 5. See also, John McBeth, "Past But Not Forgotten," *FEER,* March 17, 1988, 25–26; and Charles Lee, "Living Bitter Memories," in *ibid.,* 26.
14. *Korea Newsreview,* 17 (April 9, 1988): 5.
15. Ibid.
16. Ibid.
17. Ibid.
18. Ibid.
19. *Korea Newsreview* 17 (April 23, 1988): 8.
20. Ibid.
21. Ibid.
22. Ibid.
23. Ibid.
24. *Korea Newsreview* 17 (April 9, 1988): 4.
25. *Korea Newsreview* 17 (April 23, 1988): 9.
26. Ibid.
27. *Korea Newsreview,* 17 (April 30, 1988): 4–7. See also, *Dong-A Ilbo,* 28,

29, and April 30, 1988; and Central Election Management Committee (ROK), *Chae 13 dae Kukhoe Uiwon Sonko Chiyukku Hubocha pyol Tukpyo Sanghwang* (Seoul: Central Election Management Committee, 1988).

28. Kim, "Meaning of Korea's 12th National Assembly Election," 167–69 and 172.

29. Ibid., 172–73.

30. For a detailed analysis, see Hong Nack Kim and Sunki Choe, "Urbanization and Changing Voting Patterns in South Korean Parliamentary Elections," *Journal of Northeast Asian Studies* 4 (Fall 1987): 31–50, esp. 35–40.

31. Ibid., 40–46.

32. Kap Yun Lee, "Chae 13-dae Kukhoe Uiwon Sonko ae so ui Tupyo Hyongtae wa Minjuhwa," a paper presented at the first workshop on "Democratization in Korea: Problems and Prospects," sponsored by the Institute for Far Eastern Studies, Kyongnam University, Seoul, Korea, on July 22, 1988, 8–9.

33. For a detailed analysis, see Wonmo Dong, "Regionalism and Electoral Politics in South Korea: A Comparative Analysis of the Direct Presidential Elections of 1971 and 1987," a paper presented at the 1988 annual meeting of the American Political Science Association, Washington, D.C., on September 1–4, 1988, 25–31.

34. Lee, "Chae 13-dae Kukhoe Uiwon Sonko ae so ui Tupyo Hyongtae wa Minjuhwa," 6–7.

35. *Yomiuri Shimbun,* April 28, 1988.

36. Kim, "Meaning of Korea's 12th National Assembly Election," 175–76. See also, *Washington Post,* April 27, 1988.

37. Kim, "Meaning of Korea's 12th National Assembly Election," 175–76. See also, *New York Times,* March 27, 1988; John McBeth, "Rough Road Ahead," *FEER,* March 3, 1988, 30; and John McBeth, "Problems of Power," *FEER,* March 10, 1988, 12.

38. For a detailed analysis, see "Chun K.H. Arrested on Embezzlement, Influence-Peddling, Tax Evasion Charges," *Korea Newsreview,* 17 (April 2, 1988): 4–5. See also McBeth, "'Little' Chun's Comedown," 32–33. See also, *Dong-A Ilbo,* April 1 and 2, 1988.

39. Lee, "Chae 13-dae Kukhoe Uiwon Sonko ae so ui Tupyo Hyongtae wa Minjuhwa," 9.

40. Ibid.

41. *Dong-A Ilbo,* April 25, 1988. See also, *Washington Post,* April 26, 1988.

42. *Washington Post,* April 27, 1988. See also, *Wall Street Journal,* April 27, 1988; and *Hankuk Ilbo,* April 27, 1988.

43. As of April 18, 1988, the DJP was projected to win 120–128 out of 224 district seats. See *Hankuk Ilbo,* April 19, 1988.

44. For a detailed analysis of the background, see Dong, "Regionalism and Electoral Politics," 6–12.

45. Lee, "Chae 13-dae Kukhoe Uiwon Sonko ae so ui Tupyo Hyongtae wa Minjuhwa," 4–5.

7

Economic Development in South Korea

Paul W. Kuznets

Introduction

THE REPUBLIC OF KOREA IS ONE OF THE FOUR East Asian "miracle economies" (the others are Taiwan, Singapore, and Hong Kong) whose speed and quality of economic development distinguish the group from the rest of the developing world.[1] Korea's gross national product increased at an average annual rate of almost ten percent from the mid-1960s to 1973 and, despite oil shocks and worldwide economic recession, rose by eight percent a year during the 1973–1987 period. One result of this rapid growth or development (the terms are used synonymously here) is that the average person's real income has more than tripled so that the typical Korean is now much better off than he was 25 years ago. Standard welfare surrogates for food and housing consumption, access to medical services, and so forth, all confirm the increase in individual economic wellbeing during the period. Also, the averages do not conceal wide disparities, as is often the case. Income inequality has increased somewhat since the mid-1960s, but it is still low by international standards. Though Korea's "miracle" status is not unique—it is shared with three other East Asian economies—it is nonetheless particularly impressive because Korea is much larger than the others and consequently has had to overcome larger problems, including the devastation of the Korean War.

Rapid output growth, relatively even income distribution, and widespread welfare gains are perhaps the main characteristics of Korea's recent development, but there are others also worth mentioning. In particular, development has altered the country's industrial structure and, with it, people's working lives. Growth has centered in the industrial sector, especially in manufacturing for export; and because manufacturing has been concentrated in urban areas, not only to benefit from agglomeration but also to make use of access to ports and to the government, new employment has also been concentrated in the cities. What was mainly a rural and agrarian economy only two decades ago is therefore now a predominantly urban and services-oriented industrial economy. The speed of the transformation is noteworthy because the same changes in structure (and urbanization) took place over much longer periods when they occurred in today's developed countries. The rapidity of Korea's growth has probably contributed to crowding, to pollution, and to inefficiency (this last since supply is less elastic in the short run than in the long run). Even if slower growth had not reduced the diseconomies or negative byproducts of development, it might have lessened their impact. On the other hand, the rapidity of Korea's growth has created an expansionary psychology, inspired business confidence, and induced receptivity to change. Without these, the alternative to rapid growth might not have been moderate growth but possibly little or no growth.

Though the welfare consequences of Korea's rapid development are necessarily a matter for speculation, the dimensions of this development are well documented. In particular, we know that development was slow and unsatisfactory from the end of the Korean War until the mid-1960s, when growth accelerated. It has remained unusually rapid during most of the period since then. This acceleration raises the question of why development was slow before the mid-1960s and fast afterward. Possible reasons for the acceleration are examined in the following section, which suggests that, although policy changes were needed for more rapid growth, acceleration could not have occurred without favorable external conditions and the previous accumulation of (unexploited) productive potential.

Reasons for acceleration are significant because they account for Korea's economic success. Success, in turn, has aroused interest in Korea as a development model. However, it is not at all clear that Korea's experience is transferable, and it is quite possible that the model may prove misleading. One reason for skepticism is that economic results have social, cultural, political, and institutional as well as economic causes. Some of Korea's non-economic attributes, such as the Confucian tradition, may be found elsewhere (most notably among the other East Asian miracle economies), but many are not. This does not necessarily mean that Korea's success is *sui generis*, but that the Korean model may be more or less applicable according to local circumstances and the particular characteristic being considered.[2] For instance, two characteristics that appear to be especially significant in Korea's development are examined in subsequent sections. One of these is the active role played by the government in economic affairs. Since the government's activism has cultural and political as well as economic causes, this is one instance where the Korean model may not be generally applicable. The second significant characteristic discussed here is the government's heavy emphasis on export expansion. This is an aspect of the Korean model that should be applicable elsewhere.

Though the public sector's share of economic activity is masked in Korea by accounting difficulties, it is probably smaller—and certainly not larger—than public-sector shares in other developing countries. It is therefore not so much the size of government output or expenditure as the government's influence on the private sector that makes the economic role of government significant. Korean governments have typically not hesitated to intervene in markets or to guide the invisible hand as policy has dictated. Possible reasons for activism are assessed and several features of the policy-implementation process—planning and credit allocation—are discussed in "The Government and the Economy." Reasons for choosing an export expansion strategy and the economic effects of expansion are examined in "Exports: Key to Korea's High-Growth

Strategy." Recent changes and possible future developments in the economic roles of government and exports are considered in "Recent, Current, and Future Developments."

The Record

Though Korea has a long and distinguished history, South Korea's development experience dates back only to 1948. Even during the relatively short period since then, development was interrupted by the Korean War (1950–1953). Development was of course seen in Korea's earlier years as a colony in the Japanese empire (1905–1945) or during the Yi dynasty (1392–1905), but in the first instance Korea was an economic and political satellite, not an independent country, and in both cases South Korea was only part of a unified Korea. These differences in circumstances, I believe, make comparison of South Korea's economic experience before 1948 with what followed of questionable value in explaining subsequent development, particularly as the South Koreans were unable to control their own economic and political fate.[3] This was also true of the years 1945–1948 when, though occupying the same territory as South Korea now does, the southern part of the Korean peninsula was ruled by a United States military government. Only with the establishment of the Republic of Korea under President Syngman Rhee in 1948 did South Korea (hereafter simply "Korea") acquire the independence needed to control its own development experience.

Political independence may cloak economic and military (strategic) dependence, and this was true of Korea before the mid-1960s. The modest economic progress achieved after 1945 with the help of United States emergency relief and economic assistance was wiped out in the Korean War, while the war itself confirmed United States responsibility to assist Korean reconstruction and subsequent development. Korea was clearly a client state during the reconstruction era (reconstruction was pretty much complete by 1958) and as late as the mid-1960s, when assistance was still sufficiently large to permit United States aid officials to influence Korea's economic policies, most notably the decision to adopt a liberalization program that would free the economy of restrictions, or what has been termed "the second postwar restructuring."[4] Since the mid-1960s grants have been replaced by loans, surplus agricultural (PL 480) commodity shipments have been phased out, and total economic assistance has been greatly reduced.[5] Military assistance has dropped too, particularly since the establishment of a domestic armaments industry. The decline in assistance, combined with Korea's own economic successes, means that Korea is no longer the American client state that it once was.[6]

The consistent statistics needed to explain Korea's economic growth or development are available only for the period since 1953. They show a quite unimpressive performance from the end of the Korean War through the student uprising in 1960 which unseated the Rhee regime, the short-lived successor government of Chang Myon, the military coup led by Park Chung Hee, and the ill-considered currency reform adopted in 1962 by the new military government under General Park. GNP rose at an average annual rate of 3.7 percent. From 1962 to 1973, however, GNP increased at an annual rate of 9.6 percent and has continued to grow only somewhat less rapidly since then (8.0 percent a year from 1973 to 1987) despite the oil shocks of the 1970s and the world recession and domestic political turmoil of the early 1980s.

Basic indicators of Korea's economic development and those for Korea's World Bank reference group of 24 upper middle-income countries are given in Table 7-1. These indicators and the acceleration in the pace of Korea's development raise questions of why development was so slow before the mid-1960s, and of what happened to raise the pace since then so that growth has been unusually rapid, either when compared with Korea's earlier experience or with the contemporary experience of other middle-income countries.

There are a number of possible reasons why development was slow from 1953 to 1963. One was the prior division of the peninsula, which separated two complementary parts of a single economy: rice production and light industry in the South; heavy industry, electric power generation, and wheat growing in the North. This was in addition to the breakup of the Japanese empire where Korea's specialized role no longer existed. (Korea supplied rice to Japan, for example, and imported finished consumer goods.) Also, there were immediate problems after liberation, including a shortage of administrators

TABLE 7-1

Basic Economic Indicators for Korea and for an Average of 24 Upper Middle-Income Countries, 1965 and 1986

	Korea		Upper Middle-Income Countries	
Per capita GNP (in dollars) 1986	2,370		1,890	
GDP growth rate (annual average) 1965–1980	9.5		6.7	
1980–1986	8.2		2.5	
	1965	1986	1965	1986
Distribution of GDP (%)				
Agriculture	17	13	18	10
Industry	42	44	37	40
Services	42	44	46	50
Expenditure of GDP (%)				
Public consumption	9	10	11	13
Private consumption	83	55	65	61
Gross domestic investment	15	29	23	24
Gross domestic saving	8	35	23	26
Exports [a]	9	41	18	22
Resource balance[b]	- 7	6	1	2

[a] Goods plus non-factor services
[b] Difference between exports and imports of goods and non-factor services
Source: World Bank, *World Development Report, 1988* (New York: Oxford University Press, 1988), Indicator Tables 1, 2, 3 and 5.

and professionals (high-level personnel had been Japanese), hyperinflation as the Japanese monetized their assets on departure, and a misoriented transport system. Coal was plentiful in the Northeast, for example, but there were no rail connections to bring it to Seoul. The process of transforming a fragmented economy into a functioning whole and of rebuilding after the Korean War was necessarily time consuming.

Another reason for slow growth was the Rhee government's preoccupation with political problems at the expense of the country's economic needs. There was no overall economic strategy, possibly because such a strategy would have been inconsistent with the political goal of reuniting the two Koreas.

Also, the economy was hampered by inflation, the overvalued exchange rates used to maximize American aid receipts, heavy trade deficits, unrealistically low bank interest rates, and inadequate tax collection. In short, Korea displayed all the characteristics of inept policy and weak implementation found in many developing countries. In addition, exports lagged while emphasis on import substitution created the usual web of controls that perverted entrepreneurial incentives by making avoidance of controls rather than increased productivity the main source of profit. Furthermore, substitution was becoming increasingly difficult as the opportunities were exhausted for the sort of easy substitution that suited domestic factor proportions (abundant labor, scarce capital) and employed simple technology. It is hardly surprising that growth slowed during the mid-1950s and then came to a halt in 1959–1962, when political upheaval and the new military government's initial fumbling upset everyday economic activities.

Development accelerated during the mid-1960s, and the economy expanded very rapidly during most of the period until 1979. One reason was a policy shift under the new government (Park was elected president in 1963) from emphasis on import substitution to promotion of exports. This shift was probably as much a result of the evident failure of import substitution and widespread public demand for better economic performance as it was due to pressure from American advisors and the imminent decline in United States assistance. Whatever the reason, the new strategy included a series of liberalization measures during the mid-1960s that encouraged entrepreneurs to expand output for export. The result was a spectacular increase in exports to the United States from $100 million in 1964 to $1 billion in 1971 and $21 billion by 1981. Rapid industrialization followed since these exports have included an increasingly varied range of manufactures. Table 7-1 documents this process during the 1965–1986 period: Korea's industrial share has been above average while its export share rose from less than to more than the upper middle-income country average. It shows, in short, that Korea is a good example of what is meant by "export-led" growth.

The shift in strategy may have been a necessary condition for acceleration in the pace of development, but it was not sufficient in itself. Korea's exports have soared since the mid-1960s because world markets were expanding rapidly, particularly those in the United States and Japan, Korea's main trading partners. On the supply side, Korea, the epitome of a labor-surplus economy, had unexploited comparative advantage in its hardworking and relatively well-educated workers. There was also an ample stock of entrepreneurial talent, no significant opposition to the new export strategy, and a regime in power with sufficient control of the bureaucratic process to implement its economic policies. A number of these elements, such as the well-educated labor force and the absence of opposition, can be traced to land reform and the generalization of education that predate the strategy shift by many years. The new strategy was therefore only one of many elements responsible for the acceleration of the mid-1960s.

Although exploitation of favorable export opportunities can explain rapid development through 1973, it does not explain the rapid development after 1973, when the first oil shock and subsequent worldwide inflation and contraction limited export opportunities. Development after 1973 was rapid because the Koreans employed a risky strategy to maintain growth. Instead of adopting restrictive policies to offset the inflationary impact of the oil shock, as did most countries, the Korean government increased foreign borrowing, and used the proceeds to expand industrial capacity and the new industrial capacity to generate more exports.[8] This strategy might have succeeded if it had not been combined with an obsessive drive to expand the heavy and chemical industries. This drive contributed to inflation; and the inflation, when combined with the second oil shock, the political unrest following President Park's assassination, and a disastrous harvest, led in 1980 to the first downturn in Korea's GNP growth since 1956.[9] Inflation was subsequently curbed by the new government of General (later President) Chun Doo Hwan, but the economy suffered from excess capacity and underemployment in 1981–1982 before recovery began in 1983 and growth accelerated to double-digit levels in 1986–1988.

The Government and the Economy

The influence of the political leadership on Korea's (or any other country's) economic development should depend on the size of the public sector, the capacity of the regime to implement policy, the priority attached to economic goals, the ease or difficulty of governing, and so forth.[10] These are all difficult to specify and depend, in turn, on such disparate factors as Korea's geopolitical position and the Confucian ethic as well as on the regime's characteristics and economic institutions— which, in Korea's case, are mainly the market mechanism and private property rights rather than central planning and state ownership. Economic response to regime stimulus is likely to differ among countries or between different regimes in the same country because of these intervening factors. We know, for example, that a change in required reserves alters the money supply and eventually affects prices. We know little about the size and speed of response, however, because these depend among other things upon how the bureaucracy responds to political directives. It is hardly surprising, therefore, that given the complexity of relationships and the obvious influence of institutional and cultural factors, economists treat "government" as exogenous, and that neither economists nor political scientists have a paradigm that can satisfactorily explain how a regime or government influences economic development.

One factor that ought to determine the impact of government actions on the economy is the relative size of the public sector, on the grounds that the larger a public sector's share of the economic activity the more ways the regime can affect the economy.[11] Possible measures of the size or relative importance of the public sector include the government's share in total expenditures (budget+ GNP), the proportion of gross domestic product that originates in the public sector, or the revenue ratio (government revenues+ GNP), the government's share of total claims on resources. In 1980, for instance, the revenue ratio was 22 percent, the government's share of total expenditures (the public consumption shown in Table 7-1 plus public investment) was 20 percent. There are no meaningful statistics on the proportion of GDP originating in the public sector. Any of these measures is misleading, however, because they understate the size of Korea's public sector. One reason is that accounts of public and quasi-public enterprises such as the tobacco monopoly and the Korea Electric Power Company are included with the private sector and not, as is the practice elsewhere, with the public sector. Also, United States military assistance to Korea is omitted from government budgets, the national accounts, and balance-of-payments statements. Though substantial in the past ($7.3 billion from 1953 to 1978), assistance has been equivalent to only five percent of budgeted defense expenditures in recent years.

While it is difficult to calculate the size of Korea's public sector or compare it with public sectors of other middle-income countries, something can be said of the pattern of the government's economic activities and of trends in revenues and expenditures. Infrastructure requirements during the early stages of development typically generate heavy government investment; demand for social expenditures increases government consumption at later stages. Government investment does not decline as a proportion of GNP in Korea, however, and government consumption remained a fairly steady 8 to 10 percent of GNP after 1953 before rising to 11 to 12 percent since the early 1980s. Revenues, in turn, typically rise more than proportionally with GNP as an economy develops. Growth of per capita income accounts only for absolute increase; the additional, relative increase is associated with other concomitants of development that increase tax capacity, such as growing monetization and expansion of foreign trade.[12] Korea's experience has been typical as revenue ratios increased from 14 to 16 percent during the early 1960s to 19 to 22 percent in the 1980s. The increase can be attributed partly to supply-side factors like monetization and reform of tax administration (since 1964), and partly to demand-side considerations like the high income-elasticity of demand for education and other publicly provided services.

Though revenue ratios and public-expenditure shares tend to rise with per capita income, they differ markedly among countries with the same per capita income. This suggests that the government's share in the economy is influenced by political preferences as well as by demand considerations or the government's revenue-raising capacity. The increase in expenditures (and therefore revenues) has been limited in Korea both by historical accident and by political preference. At the end of the Korean War the country inherited a swollen bureaucracy and a defense establishment that needed little expansion as the economy grew. Also, there has been a continued "pro-duction-first" philosophy that, like Japan's, has directed re-sources to increasing output rather than to social ends. This can be seen in Korea's recent government budgets, in which less than 10 percent of total outlays has been allocated to social-expenditure categories such as social security, welfare, housing, and community services.

What is unexpected in Korea is the large role of public enterprise in an otherwise free-enterprise economy. Jones and Sakong show that in 1972, for instance, public enterprises produced two-thirds of the country's electric, gas, and water supplies, 30 percent of transport and communications services, 15 percent of manufacturing, 30 percent of mining output, and an unusual 80 to 90 percent of financial services.[13] While many public enterprises originated in Japanese concerns whose own-ership was vested in the government after liberation, public-enterprise production is important (9 percent of domestic product in 1972, possibly more now) less because of inheritance than because of above-average growth in enterprise output during recent decades. The growth probably reflects increased demand for the sorts of goods and services suited to public production, a cost-efficient enterprise record rather than a history of drain on the public fisc as in many developing countries and a pragmatic rather than an ideological approach to issues of public *versus* private ownership.[14]

The Korean government may influence the economy more in other ways than by its fiscal activity or direct production, for the private sector accounts for roughly three-quarters of na-tional output and expenditure. Whether a government is active in economic affairs or not should depend on the priority accorded to economic goals, the regime's ability to control the bureaucracy, the ease or difficulty of governing the country, and possibly the earlier success achieved by assuming an active role. In each case the situation in Korea permits the govern-ment to exert great influence in economic matters, which perhaps explains why both the Park and Chun regimes played an active, even interventionist role in the economy.

One possible reason for the economic activism of Korean governments is that they have been led from the early 1960s until 1988 by authoritarian regimes, perhaps best described as military, bureaucratic-authoritarian regimes. They are "bureaucratic" because the military rules more as an institution than through the personal rule of a military strong man and "authoritarian" because obedience to government dictates is required of individuals.[15] There is no reason, however, why authoritarian regimes should be more active in economic affairs than democratic regimes except, perhaps, that without the same need for prior consultation and widespread agreement, they can act faster than their democratic counterparts. Rather, the activism of Korea's authoritarian regimes has probably resulted from their success, not their authoritarianism, because successful action should foster further action, whereas unsuccessful action would not. Another logical possibility, that authoritarian governments are successful because they are authoritarian, is contradicted by evidence that there is no correlation between economic success and type of regime, though countries with "authoritarian forms of government [tend to] perform either very well or very poorly."[16]

Other than success as a possible cause of activism, action is promoted by the factors that ease the tasks of government in Korea. One of these is the hierarchic and authoritarian Confucian tradition of family and political relationships. Though the Park and Chun regimes may not have received the Mandate of Heaven, they had at least the tacit support of the population. Consistent with this tradition has been a history of highly centralized government; regions and localities have never had much autonomy and do not now. Also, population, geography, and economic size are all favorable. Korea's land area (98,000 square kilometers) is compact, unlike that of Indonesia and the Philippines, while its smaller population (42 million) is easier to administer than the enormous population of countries like India and China. Market size (population times per capita income, now about $100 billion) is large enough to permit economies of scale. Though it may not be sufficient to support adequately a domestic aircraft industry, it is large enough to permit a much wider range of specialization than can be attained in small markets like Singapore's or Hong Kong's. Also, the population is unusually homogeneous; there are no linguistic or ethnic minorities with separatist tendencies or demands for special treatment. Furthermore, the threat of attack from the North has had a powerful unifying effect. Although the threat is sometimes used by the regime in a cynical fashion to stifle dissent, it also provides a sense of national economic purpose since economic strength is seen as a defense prerequisite. Finally, little evidence exists to indicate the social malaise associated with wide income disparities and multi-generational poverty. In fact, inequality of income distribution is unusually low and there seems to be a fairly high degree of social and economic mobility.[17]

Another reason for the government's active role in the economy, besides success with activism and the ease of governing, has been effective administration. It is effective because the state apparatus can be used to transmit and enforce the regime's policy directives either by compulsion or by administrative discretion. Gunnar Myrdal has characterized the "soft states" of South Asia as ones where "policies decided on are often not enforced" and where "the authorities...are reluctant to place obligations on people."[18] A "hard state" can be specified by contrast: one that is ready to place obligations on people and to enforce them if necessary. Korea is definitely a "hard state" in that the regime has been effective in obtaining compliance with government directives, either by direct command or by discretionary controls. The efficacy of direct command under an authoritarian regime is self-evident, but the success of discretionary controls deserves mention. Such controls work well in Korea because the leadership's commitment to economic development is passed down through the hierarchical command structure to the lowest administrative levels so that no official can afford to act in ways that obstruct development.[19]

Both types of control are widely used in Korea because the government has not hesitated to intervene in the economy, and because the approach to policy implementation has been highly pragmatic. If one type of intervention proves ineffective, another is tried.

A final reason for the government's economic activism has been the high priority attached to economic goals. Insofar as media coverage reflects public priorities, the unusual emphasis by the media on economic matters can be taken as evidence in point. The overall economic goal, typically the improvement of living standards for the population (mass welfare), is only one of several major regime goals in most countries, and Korea is no exception. Other possible goals such as the preservation of political power or the maintenance of national security are important too and may shape economic policies. These three are probably the major goals in Korea and are competitive as well as complementary, which explains why policies to achieve self-sufficiency in food production or to foster heavy industry may appear irrational to economists but make perfect sense to policy makers.[20] Since the early 1960s, the economic goal has perhaps been emphasized more in Korea than in most other developing countries because the economic failures of the Rhee government made economic improvement the overriding national objective and because good economic performance has been the main means of achieving legitimacy for new military regimes.

Evidence is plentiful that the Park and Chun regimes played active roles in economic affairs. (Roh regime interventionism cannot be assessed yet since Roh Tae Woo took office only in 1988.) For example, the list of items eligible for import, the terms of export financing, and tax-rate *maxima* are often changed. Besides the usual repertoire of monetary, fiscal, and commercial policy instruments, Korean governments have used other means to achieve economic ends, including direct market intervention. After the second oil shock and the disastrous harvest of 1980, for instance, the Chun regime used wage and price controls to curb inflation; both the Park and Chun regimes employed a "two-price" policy to increase farmers' incomes and reduce urban rice costs. Of particular interest, however, are planning and credit allocation. Planning, perhaps the leading symbol of government intervention, is of interest because the function of planning is controversial in Korea. Credit allocation is noteworthy because it is the major single instrument of government control.

The possible relation of planning to Korea's economic success has inspired a literature that comes close at one extreme to attributing accelerated growth to planning and, at the other, to viewing the plans mainly as a means for improving market functions. The plans themselves, which date back to the Rhee regime, have not always been adopted and vary widely according to the econometric sophistication with which they are constructed. Planning is probably more prescriptive than in Japan, for example, because the Korean government tends to intervene more in the economy than does the Japanese government, and because it has more power to allocate credit. Still, there is a large, market-oriented private sector that is not bound by the plans. Also, because actual growth has typically been well above plan targets, the plan itself, despite annual adjustments, tends to become increasingly irrelevant with time. In addition, the plans do not specify the means or policies that will be needed to reach plan targets, and it is evident that some targets are included without providing the means to achieve them, possibly because the planners must cater to political as well as economic imperatives.[21] Given such limitations, it is possible to adopt a minimalist position in assessing the function of Korea's plans; they serve to sustain market functions by reducing risk and uncertainty, minimizing information costs, and generating an expansionary psychology.[22] If plans do more than this—that is, if they have a role independent of improving market functions—then it may be to establish priorities and to ensure that public-sector activities are feasible and coordinated. To assert, however, that "public sector policies derived from the planning function were indispensable to the economic growth of the last 10–15 years [before 1977]" is to overstate the case.[23] Because other developing countries have employed planning without achieving Korea's economic success, what may be significant in Korea is not planning itself but the combination of planning and sophisticated policy implementation.[24]

Credit allocation and control of access to foreign exchange are perhaps the main means of achieving the government's economic goals in Korea. The typical enterprise is highly leveraged and therefore especially vulnerable to reduction or withdrawal of credit. Loanable funds are scarce, and lending rates are limited by statute so that the organized money market (that is, the banking system) cannot fully satisfy credit requirements. The government directs and supervises special purpose banks, such as the Korea Exchange Bank or the National Agricultural Cooperatives Federation, and controls commercial banks both through the Monetary Board, which supervises commercial bank activities, and until recently through stock ownership as the major shareholder in four of the five nation-wide commercial banks. Access to foreign credit is also controlled because foreign loans are guaranteed by the Exchange Bank. The unorganized money market (curb market) is the one credit source not controlled by the government.[25] Excess demand for credit can usually be satisfied in the curb market, but only at a cost of roughly three to six times going rates at banks. Since the government probably controls three-quarters to four-fifths of the supply and excess demand requires rationing, it is not surprising that credit is allocated in ways that are consistent with the government's economic goals to firms that promise to perform satisfactorily.[26] Allocation has favored export activity, heavy and chemical industry projects, the *chaebol*, or large conglomerate enterprises, and, more recently, skill-intensive industries like machinery and electronics.

Exports: Key to Korea's High-Growth Strategy

Export expansion has been the main theme of Korean economic policy since the mid-1960s. A wide range of incentives, particularly preferential loans, has been used to promote exports and, as indicated earlier, exports have responded by growing phenomenally.[27] The immediate reasons for new emphasis on exports were mainly negative, in that earlier import-substitution policies had failed and could not be continued, while exports would provide the foreign exchange needed to offset the expected decline in foreign assistance. There are also conventional economic reasons for export promotion, if only to offset the distortions created by foreign-exchange controls and the tariffs used to protect import-substitute industries. Positive reasons are provided by standard comparative-advantage arguments (in Korea's case, advantage in labor-intensive and possibly skill-intensive products) and the argument that competition in world markets makes output for export necessarily efficient. More recently, though, it has become apparent that export expansion has also been the key to Korea's high-growth strategy. Growth is maximized by allocating a very large proportion of total expenditure to investment, and Korea's investment ratios (investment+ GNP) of 25 to 35 percent in recent years have been among the world's highest. The investment is partly financed by foreign borrowing, which not only provides foreign exchange to pay for the imported equipment and other foreign goods and services needed for investment purposes but also makes up for insufficient domestic saving. Foreign borrowing (saving), in fact, financed about a third of investment until the early 1980s. Exports are important because they generate the foreign exchange needed to repay loans from foreign lenders. Continued export expansion is also important because it encourages foreign lenders to extend loans to Korean firms since expansion promises to generate the foreign exchange that will be needed to repay debts (which reached a peak of $47 billion in 1985) when they come due.

The three strategy alternatives that might, conceivably, have been adopted by the new Park government in the early 1960s included the continuation of earlier import-substitution policies, expansion of agricultural production for export, or reorientation of manufacturing from output for the domestic market to output for export. Import substitution usually follows a logical pattern in which the first or easy phase is devoted mainly to types of output for which there is an established market (that is, consumer goods) and that can be produced using simple, labor-intensive technology. Textiles, apparel, footwear, and processed foods are typical first-phase import substitutes. Korea had already entered the second phase of substitution by the early 1960s, however, a phase in which substitution shifts to intermediate goods or materials—such as cement and rubber products—that are produced by more complex, capital-intensive technology, often in large plants to benefit from economies of scale. Because these products were not well suited to existing factor endowments while domestic markets were too small to permit scale economies, production of second-phase products proved inefficient and the economy suffered from overcapacity and a decline in the rate of output growth. Continued emphasis on import substitution clearly offered little promise for renewing growth, and neither did agricultural exports. Though Korea had been a major source of rice for Japan during the colonial era, this market was now cut off. Also, high-value rice exports had been offset by low-value millet and barley imports (hence the term *starvation exports*), and the potential for expanding agricultural output, given Korea's limited supply of arable land, was distinctly limited. This left the export of labor-intensive manufactures, many of which were already being produced domestically, as the only feasible alternative. To bring this about required export-promotion measures, devaluation, and the other elements of a liberalization program that would encourage entrepreneurs to produce for export rather than substitute for imports. This was all accomplished, with United States backing, in the mid-1960s.[28]

An ample labor supply was not in itself sufficient to establish Korea's comparative advantage in labor-intensive manufactures. Labor had to be available, which it was since there was a surplus of underemployed workers who could be transferred to the new industries (without significant loss of output) from agriculture and the services.[29] Labor had to be cheap, which it was because there were no effective unions or other barriers to low wages, such as the high cost of wage goods. Labor also had to be productive since competitiveness depends on unit labor costs, a function of both wages and productivity. Productivity was fairly high because Korean entrepreneurs are adept at organizing production, while workers are relatively well educated, skilled, and hard working. Finally, the so-called strong factor hypothesis had to hold, so that what was produced by labor-intensive methods in Korea could not be undersold by employing capital-intensive methods elsewhere. Cross-national comparisons show that this hypothesis is, in fact, correct, and that what is produced by labor-intensive means in one country is produced by the same means elsewhere.[30] The hypothesis, incidentally, only requires similar ordering of industries by factor intensity; all production can be more labor-intensive in Korea than in capital-abundant economies like the United States. Figures for Korea's exports in 1972 and 1985 are given in table 7-2 and grouped according to whether they are products of L-industry (labor-intensive industry) or H-industry (capital-intensive industry) groups. Table 7-2 shows, not surprisingly, that Korea's export mix, particularly in earlier years, has been consistent with comparative advantage in labor-intensive manufactures.[31]

The main economic advantage of concentration in labor-intensive exports for a country like Korea is that products of cheap, abundant labor can be exchanged for capital-intensive

TABLE 7–2
Korea's Export Structure and Factor-Endowment Categories

	1972		1985	
	$ million	percent	$ million	percent
L - industries [a]	645	40	8,998	30
H - industries [b]	180	11	11,487	38
All commodities [c]	1,624	100	30,283	100

Note: L-industries or labor-intensive industries are those with particularly low value-added per worker, whereas H-industries or capital-intensive industries (both human and physical capital) are those with especially high value-added per worker.
[a] Includes textiles (SITC 65), travel goods (83), clothing (84) and footwear (85)
[b] Includes machinery and transport equipment (SITC 7) and instruments (86)
[c] Also includes exports of intermediate industries, or those which are neither very labor-intensive or capital-intensive

or natural resource-intensive products that are either expensive or impossible to produce locally. Evidence for this can be found in data for the 1960s, which show that Korea's imports were much more capital-intensive than its exports.[32] Another advantage is that export expansion provides productive employment for labor that would otherwise be underemployed. (Underemployment, not unemployment, is the most likely alternative to employment where, as in Korea, tightly knit families absorb the otherwise unemployed in family business and where self-employment rather than work for wages predominates). Several studies indicate that export expansion made a major contribution to employment during the 1960s, both in the export industries themselves, and indirectly in the industries that supply export producers.[33] Also, the growing importance of exports in Korea's output mix has undoubtedly increased overall economic efficiency. Exporters face worldwide competition and cannot hide behind tariff barriers as can producers for the domestic market. Subsidies provided by export-promotion measures, furthermore, have been too low to protect inefficient producers. Finally, exposure to new markets and the need to keep up with new technology should have diversified the economy's output and increased productive capacity more than if production was mainly devoted to supplying domestic markets.

Products that Korea exports are usually products that are already being produced for domestic markets. Though there are notable exceptions, such as the offshore assembly of electronic components for American firms, previous production experience is typically needed to reduce costs and raise quality. In the same way, production for domestic markets often substitutes for earlier imports. In fact, Akamatsu found that the sequence beginning with imports, then import substitution to supply domestic markets, and finally output for export described Japan's industrial development.[34] The same sequence, Akamatsu's "Wild-Flying Geese" pattern of growth, also fits much of Korea's industrial development. When import substitution becomes sufficiently competitive to generate exports, as in Akamatsu's sequence, the import substitution and export promotion strategies are not necessarily competitive. What Korea exports is explained, at least in part, by prior import substitution. Exports are also determined by changes in comparative advantage, both in Korea and elsewhere.

Heavy investment in education and in plant and equipment since the mid-1960s had substantially expanded Korea's capital stock by the early 1980s.[35] This expansion, marked by the growing importance of physical and human capital in Korea's factor endowments, was one reason for the shift away from L-intensive toward H-intensive exports shown in Table 7-2. Another reason is that, just as exports of labor-intensive products like plywood, textiles, and apparel from Korea, Taiwan, and other low-wage, newly industrialized countries reduced Japan's world-market share of labor-intensive manufactures, growing competition from China, the Philippines, and other even lower-wage countries has had the same effect on Korea's more labor-intensive exports in recent years. The Park regime's push to develop the heavy and chemical industries during the middle and late 1970s may have been partly designed to expand Korea's military capabilities, but it was also a response to this increase in competition from below. More recently, the Chun regime's industrial policy focused on expanding electronics, machinery, and other skill-intensive, high value-added types of production. Policy in both instances continues the shift in export composition from L-intensive to H-intensive products, and in each case the policy has been consistent with changes in Korea's comparative advantage.

Demand considerations, changes in relative prices, and exchange-rate manipulation have affected export expansion as well as the supply factors that determine comparative advantage. The *won* has been tied to the dollar, for example, and failure to devalue in the late 1970s reduced Korea's export competitiveness since domestic inflation was greater than inflation elsewhere. Devaluation was opposed because it would have contributed to inflation (via higher import prices) and increased the burden of servicing dollar-denominated foreign debt. However, sharp devaluation in 1980–1981 combined with a substantial drop in domestic inflation to raise Korea's real effective exchange rates (and export competitiveness) in subsequent years. Competitiveness increased through 1987, despite revaluation since the fall of 1985, mainly because the dollar was falling against the Japanese *yen* and thus lowering the prices of Korean exports in third markets where they compete with Japanese exports. Korea's real effective exchange rate has depreciated (that is, risen) more since 1981, in fact, than the rate for any of the other East Asian newly industrialized countries.[36] The consequent increase in export competitiveness, the fall in oil prices, the decline in world interest rates, and the appreciation of the *yen* have combined to raise exports, lower imports, and reverse Korea's trade and current-account deficits. The new surpluses, part of which have been used to reduce external debt starting in 1986, have also become a symbol of imbalance and a source of trade friction with the United States, Korea's major export market.[37]

Recent, Current, and Future Developments

Two features of the Korean economy—government intervention in economic affairs and a high-growth strategy based on export expansion—were examined here because they appear to be particularly significant for development. Their significance may diminish, however, if intervention miscarries or export growth slows. The excesses of President Park's heavy and chemical industries drive in the 1970s contributed, for example, to the crash of 1980 and subsequent calls by the Chun government to reduce intervention and restore market functions. Similarly, the worldwide recession of the early 1980s and growing protectionism in the United States and other major markets have inspired export pessimism and a search for ways to maintain growth without relying on continued export expansion. Most important, however, have been the revolutionary political changes in Korea, sparked by the riots that eventually led to direct elections and the inauguration of President Roh Tae Woo and an opposition party-dominated National Assembly in early 1988. The Roh regime has not yet been in office long enough to establish an economic record, but the political upheaval had a perceptible impact on the economy even before the elections. (The Chun government—which had not hesitated before to put down labor unrest—refused to intervene in the wave of strikes that swept Korea in the summer of 1987 because intervention would have hurt the electoral chances of Roh, Chun's designated successor.) Though goals and policy should continue to change under the new regime, it is still possible to assess recent developments and their implications for government intervention and export-led growth.

The Park regime, faced with a series of crises during the early 1970s—particularly the reduction of United States troop levels by the Nixon administration, growing protectionism after the breakdown of the fixed exchange-rate system, and import-carried inflation with the commodity boom of 1972–1973 and the first oil shock of 1973–1974—accelerated development of heavy industry with military potential, diversified trade (mainly by encouraging Middle East construction activity), and increased domestic food-grains production. These moves raised the level of intervention and, by increasing import substitution, signalled a retreat from earlier, more liberal export-expansion policies. Also, the Middle East construction boom generated skill shortages and wage escalation whose inflationary impact was magnified by overexpansion of the money supply to finance heavy industry and by consumer-goods shortages as investment in light industry was sacrificed to expand heavy industry. Inflation could have been curbed by devaluation and import liberalization, but it was countered by price controls so that an overvalued won and rising wage costs lowered export competitiveness. A stabilization program adopted in early 1979 to attack inflation was undone by a series of disasters—the second oil shock, harvest failures, the assassination of President Park and subsequent political disturbances—and not reinstated until 1981–1982.

The Chun regime not only reinstated the stabilization program but, as a new regime, was also able to criticize its predecessor's policies and establish its own program. The inflation and structural problems of the late 1970s, for example, were attributed to "excessive government intervention in the private sector" and increased complexity of the economy that reduced the efficiency of resource allocation under highly centralized decisionmaking.[38] An Economic Planning Board (EPB) summary of the Fifth Five-Year Plan (1982–1986) noted that the "major strategy adopted...is to change the overall management of the economy from one that makes extensive use of government controls to one which relies heavily on the operation of the market mechanism," while President Chun announced in his January 1982 state-of-the-nation address that "institutional reforms will be continued to strengthen the functioning of the market mechanism." Once stabilization had been achieved and inflation was no longer an immediate threat, the Chun government moved to implement reforms by denationalizing the banks, liberalizing imports, deregulating foreign investment, strengthening anti-monopoly regulations, and reducing farm price supports.[39] These measures, designed to undo structural problems inherited from the Park regime, have all served to reduce government intervention and increase reliance on the market mechanism. Despite such measures the pace of liberalization, restructuring, or adjustment (these three terms have been used as synonyms to describe the same process) has been glacial. Even at the end of the 1980s, financial liberalization was incomplete as there were still entry barriers and the government's Monetary Board still controlled deposit and loan rates. Similarly, though recent attempts to liberalize imports have raised the import-liberalization ratio from 69 percent in 1980 to 95 percent in 1988, commercial policy remains highly restrictive.[40] Since adjustment has been very limited in other respects as well, we are left with the question of why liberalization or the attempt to reduce government intervention has been so slow.

One possible reason is that no regime wants to yield power, as is required by reducing intervention. This is not very persuasive when the mounting costs and declining benefits of intervention are readily apparent and the Korean regime, unlike regimes in many countries, unquestionably controls the administration and policy implementation. Liberalization has been slow, more likely, because intervention has caused structural problems that are costly to solve and established attitudes and institutions that cannot readily be dismantled. Credit allocation, for example, has saddled Korea's banks with nonperforming loans so that the banks would probably go under if entry were freed and the banking industry opened to competition. Similarly, exports have been subsidized and imports restricted to generate and then conserve foreign exchange for high-priority uses. In order to liberalize, not only must posters in customs offices exhorting officials to "conserve foreign exchange for national prosperity" come down, but also the "strong moral prejudice against imports that the Korean government has diligently cultivated" would have to be reversed.[41] More generally, the industrial policy that has been at the heart of intervention would probably have to be abandoned. In targeting industries with export potential for development, credit subsidy, technology licensing, tariff protection, domestic-content requirements, and other forms of intervention have typically been employed to foster the infants. Though the Fifth Plan called for reduced government intervention, the Sixth Plan (1987–1991) does not. Instead, it focuses on industrial restructuring to develop industries with the best export potential—the auto, machinery, and electronics industries—and to promote the parts and accessories business and intra-industry trade.[42] Since restructuring is a form of industrial policy that requires intervention and the current five-year plan does not repeat earlier calls to strengthen markets, the outlook for continued liberalization is not promising.

Exports, as indicated earlier, have been the key to Korea's high-growth strategy. Export expansion has also been a major source of employment, a means of acquiring technical capabilities, and a force for economic efficiency since exports incorporate abundant resources, exporters must meet international competition, and export markets are large enough to permit economies of scale. Export expansion has been phenomenal; annual increases in 1953–1963, 1963–1973, and 1973–1987 averaged 10.4, 44.0, and 14.2 percent, respectively. Neverthe-less, a significant feature of the Sixth Plan is the "desire to reduce the country's heavy dependence of economic growth on international trade."[43] Rising protectionism, especially in the United States, is the reason for such export pessimism, and for elements of Sixth Plan restructuring (for example, promotion of the parts and accessories business and of intra-industry trade) that serve to divert protectionism and reduce trade friction.

Pessimism may be justified because Korea's exports are unusually protection-prone and because Korean exporters, especially in new industries, are heavily dependent on United States markets where protectionism has been rising. Korea's exports face particularly high tariff and non-tariff barriers because many of them (color TVs, steel, semiconductors) are sold in markets where earlier Japanese penetration triggered protectionist responses. Since restrictions aimed at Japan did not at first affect other countries' exports, they "provided an extraordinary window of opportunity for Korean entry."[44] However, as Korean exports expanded they too triggered protectionist responses. The problem has been most acute for new Korean products such as semiconductors and steel, where competitiveness depends upon scale economies. Korean mar-kets are too small for such economies, while Japanese markets have long been restricted to imports, as have European mar-kets; only the United States has markets that are large and open enough to provide scale economies.

A third of all Korean exports since 1970 have been sold in the United States, and half or more of Korea's new and more sophisticated exports. American reaction to rising trade deficits and what are perceived as mercantilist policies of other coun-tries has thus become a major threat to Korea's continued export expansion. The threat increased in 1985–1986 when public outcry in Korea over U.S. Section 301 cases on insurance and intellectual property rights and American attempts to open the cigarette and beef markets in Korea led to confrontation between the two countries. In particular, United States pres-sure on Korea to accelerate liberalization and expectations of reciprocity have encountered resistance in Korea, where trade issues have become politicized and import liberalization is regarded as unpatriotic because it hurts particular Korean interests.[44]

The recent political revolution and the replacement of an authoritarian by an elected regime should alter Korea's policy process and, consequently, the pace of Korea's development and possibly the tenor of economic relations between the United States and Korea. One reason is that democratic regimes have to cater to economic interest groups where authoritarian ones do not. In particular, opposition legislators can bid for support by favoring farmers and the other groups likely to suffer from liberalization. Another reason is that economic decisionmaking, which has been criticized in the past as over-hasty, should slow as policy makers who formerly could act independently now must first consult with interest groups and achieve consensus before implementing new policies.[46] Any observer can construct other, more apocalyptic visions of how political change might undo economic development, but three implications of Korea's democratization for the future now seem clear. One is that import liberalization and other elements of accommodation to Korea's overall or national economic interests are less certain to be achieved than before. Another is that the pace of development is likely to slow as the policy process is complicated by the demands of democracy. Finally, since no one foresaw Korea's recent political revolution or earlier economic successes, the future may well bring other, unanticipated events.

Notes

1. "Miracle economies," or simply "the Four," was the term used by Little in discussing Taiwan's growth in a comparative context. See Ian M.D. Little, "An Economic Reconnaissance," in *Economic Growth and Structural Change in Taiwan*, ed. Walter Galenson (Ithaca: Cornell University Press, 1979), 448–49.
2. See David I. Steinberg, "Development Lessons from the Korean Experience—A Review Article," *Journal of Asian Studies* 42 (November 1982): 91–104.
3. The issue of what constitutes worthwhile comparison is raised because South Korea's development is sometimes analyzed by comparing the economic situation before and after independence. We know that South Korea's agricultural production fell from 1940 to 1953, for example, but cannot explain this simply as a consequence of disruption during World War II and the Korean War because South Korea also lost rice markets with the dissolution of the Japanese Empire and the division of the peninsula into North and South Korea. The land, climate, and even the people may be the same, but analysis is confounded because the comparison involves otherwise totally dissimilar units.
4. *First* and *second restructuring* are terms used to denote the economic strategy of import-substituting industrialization adopted by most newly independent nations after World War II (the first restructuring) and the new, more market-oriented export-promotion strategy initiated by many developing countries during the 1960s (the second restructuring). See Benjamin I. Cohen and Gustav Ranis, "The Second Restructuring," Gustav Ranis, ed., *Government and Economic Development* (New Haven: Yale University Press, 1971), 43–69.
5. See Edward S. Mason *et. al.*, *The Economic and Social Modernization and Republic of Korea* (Cambridge, MA: Harvard University Council on East Asian Studies, 1980), Chapter 6.
6. Nor is Korea any more dependent than other peripheral states, as the term "dependent" has been used by *dependencia* theorists to describe exploitative economic relationships between center and peripheral states. A major element of this exploitation, for example, is the heavy penetration of foreign capital. Multinational corporations have a very small presence in Korea, while cumulated foreign direct investment of around $2.9 billion (end of 1986) has been insignificant relative to foreign borrowing (debt) of $44 billion. Heavy penetration of foreign capital may of course occur in forms other than direct investment or local activities of MNCs, and exploitation is not limited to heavy penetration of foreign capital but may be manifested in unequal exchange, "marginalization," or increasing inequality of income distribution, and so on. There is little if any evidence of these other features that necessarily distinguish center from periphery or explain the economic

backwardness of the periphery. See Sanjaya Lal, "Is 'Dependence' a Useful Concept in Analyzing Underdevelopment?" *World Development* 3 (December 1975): 799–810.

7. The shift from one economic phase to the next is much less precise than is implied by the single-year bounds used here. They are used, however, for the sake of convenience.

8. See Bela Balassa, "The Newly-Industrialized Countries after the Crisis," *World Bank Staff Working Paper* No. 437 (October 1980), 24–25; the author's "Response to External Shocks: The Experience of Four Countries in 1973–1980," *Economic Notes* No. 2 (1982): 137.

9. See the author's "The Dramatic Reversal of 1979-80: Contemporary Economic Development in Korea," *Journal of Northeast Asian Studies* (September 1982): 71–87.

10. The material in this section is taken in large part from the author's "The Korean Economy in the 1980s: The Roles of Government Restructuring, and Take-off," in Yoo Se-he, ed., *Political Leadership and Economic Development: Korea and China* (Seoul: Hanyang University, 1983), 139–162.

11. For example, industrialization failed in nineteenth-century China, it is argued, because the Ch'ing government's share of GNP was so low (an estimated one to two percent) that it did not have the resources needed to support industrialization. See Dwight Perkins, "Government as an Obstacle to Modernization: The Case of Nineteenth Century China," *Journal of Economic History* 27 (December 1967): 478–92.

12. Determinants of tax capacity are analyzed by Joergen R. Lotz and Elliott R. Morss in "A Theory of Tax-Level Determinants for Developing Countries," *Economic Development and Cultural Change* 18 (April 1970): 328–41.

13. Leroy Jones and Il Sakong, *Government, Business, and Entrepreneurship in Economic Development: The Case of Korea* (Cambridge, MA.: Harvard University Council on East Asian Studies, 1980), 150.

14. Ibid., 151–55. Issues of Korean public-enterprise pricing and efficiency are discussed in Gilbert T. Brown, *Korean Pricing Policy and Economic Development in the 1960s* (Baltimore: Johns Hopkins University Press, 1973).

15. Though the analogy is imperfect, the Park and Chun regimes were similar in significant ways to contemporary military regimes in Brazil and Argentina. See F. Cardoso, "Characterization of Authority Regimes," in David Collier, ed., *The New Authoritarianism in Latin America* (Princeton: Princeton University Press, 1979), 33–57.

16. G. William Dick, "Authoritarian *versus* Nonauthoritarian Approaches to Economic Development," *Journal of Political Economy* 82 (July-August 1974): 819. The presumed economic benefits of authoritarian regimes such as political stability, firm purpose of direction, and shielding of decisionmaking from popular demands or pressures of

economic interest groups, are probably offset by the greater individual participation, benefits of nonconformity, and increased effectiveness of criticism associated with democratic or more competitive regimes.

17. Low income inequality should follow from land reform in the late 1940s and 1950s, asset destruction during the Korean War and asset confiscation by the military government in 1961, and widespread generalization of education. A World Bank-Institute of Development Studies report shows an unusually low degree of income inequality in Korea, while an annex to the report (by Irma Adelman) suggests that the overall degree of income inequality has remained unchanged. See Hollis Chenery et al., Redistribution with Growth (London and New York: Oxford University Press, 1974). The validity of the evidence used to establish Korea's distribution has been questioned, however. See Bai Moo-ki, "Examining Adelman's View on Relative Income Quality in Korea: With Focus on Her Studies Outlined in the World Bank Report," (Korean Social Science Research Council-Korean National Commission for UNESCO) Social Science Journal 5 (1978): 85–99. The Fifth Five-Year Economic and Social Development Plan indicates that inequality has in fact increased from 1965 to 1980. See Government of the Republic of Korea, The Fifth-Five-Year Economic and Social Development Plan, Seoul, 1982 (English version), 9.

18. Gunnar Myrdal, Asian Drama: An Inquiry into the Poverty of Nations (New York: Twentieth Century Fund, 1968), vol. 1, 66, and vol 2, 895–900.

19. Jones and Sakong, Government Business, and Entrepreneurship, 139. This leaves the question of why the Rhee regime. Unlike the Park and Chun regimes, it was not effective in enforcing economic policies. One possible reason is that the regime was ineffective because it was not authoritarian. A more persuasive reason is that it was ineffective because President Rhee gave priority to political rather than to economic problems, and was therefore not committed to economic development, as were President Park and President Chun.

20. See B.R. Nayar, "Political Mainsprings of Economic Planning in New Nations," Comparative Politics 6 (April 1974): 341–66.

21. See the author's "Korea's Five-Year Plans," in Irma Adelman, ed., Practical Approaches to Development Planning: Korea's Second Five-Year Plan (Baltimore: The Johns Hopkins University Press, 1969), 40, 44–45.

22. See Youngil Lim, Government Policy and Private Enterprise: Korean Experience in Industrialization, Korea Research Monograph No. 6 (Berkeley, CA: Center for Korean Studies, Institute of East Asian Studies, University of California, 1981), 11–18.

23. L.L. Wade and B.S. Kim, Economic Development of South Korea, (New York: Praeger Books, 1978), 196.

24. For example, "the government developed effective plan procedures" and "it was…in the implementation of policy that the Park regime particularly distinguished itself from governments in most less-developed countries." See Mason et al., Economic and Social Modernization, 293.

25. Comprehensive descriptions of the organized and unorganized money markets are given by David C. Cole and Yuing Chul Park in *Financial Development in Korea: 1945–1978* (Cambridge, MA: Harvard University Council on East Asian Studies, 1983), chapters 3 and 4.

26. The extent to which the government controls the credit supply is necessarily conjectural. Curb-market activity is illegal so little is known about the volume of curb-market lending. See the author's *Economic Growth and Structure in the Republic of Korea* (New Haven: Yale University Press, 1977), 188–89.

27. Promotion measures are surveyed and effective exchange rates analyzed in Larry E. Westphal, "The Republic of Korea's Experience with Export-Led Industrial Development," *World Development* 6 (March 1978): 347–82.

28. Possible roles of American aid in restructuring are discussed by Ranis. See Gustav Ranis, "Why Foreign Aid?" *Ventures Magazine* (of the Yale University Graduate School) 8 (February 1968): 22–30. Effective subsidy rates for export and domestic sales are estimated in Charles Frank, Jr., Kwang Suk Kim, and Larry E. Westphal, *Foreign Trade Regimes and Economic Development: South Korea*, vol. 7 of a Special Conference Series on Foreign Trade Regimes and Economic Development (New York: National Bureau of Economic Research-Columbia University Press, 1975), 197–200.

29. Korea in the 1960s was, in short, the epitome of the sort of economy described by Arthur Lewis in "Economic Development with Unlimited Supplies of Labour," *Manchester School of Economic and Social Studies*, 22 (May 1954): 139–91.

30. See Hal B. Larry, *Imports of Manufactures from Less Developed Countries*, (New York: National Bureau of Economic Research-Columbia University Press, 1968), chapter 3.

31. Labor intensity is measured, by convention, according to value per worker. Where the value added is high, it is assumed that inputs other than raw materials or unskilled labor, such as physical capital or human capital (that is workers are paid more than unskilled wages), are high. The formulation here derives from Seev Hirsch, "Capital or Technology Confronting the Neo-Factor Proportions and Neo-Technology Accounts of International Trade," *Welwirschaftliches Archiv*, Band 110, Heft 4 (1974): 543–44.

32. Relative factor intensities of exports and imports depend upon whether imports are competitive or noncompetitive with goods produced in Korea, and on a number of assumptions that have to be made if noncompetitive imports (such as bananas) were replaced with domestic production. See Wontack Hong, "Capital Accumulation, Factor Substitution, and Changing Factor Intensity of Trade: The Case of Korea (1966–1972)," in Wontack Hong and Anne O. Krueger, eds., *Trade and Development in Korea* (Seoul: Korea Development Institute, 1975), 65–87.

33. See David C. Cole and Larry E. Westphal, "The Contribution of Exports to Employment in Korea," in Hong and Krueger, eds., *Trade Development in Korea*, 89–102.

34. Kaname Akamatsu, "A Historical Pattern of Economic Growth in Developing Countries," *The Developing Economies*, Preliminary Issue No. 1 (March-August 1962): 3–25.

35. The value of investment in human capital in 1960 was estimated by C.Y. Jung to be somewhat larger than that in physical capital, and to have grown more rapidly during the 1960s. A reference to Jung's estimates can be found in Youngil Lim, "Korea's Trade with Japan and the US: Issues and Implications," in *The Korean Economy: Issues of Development*, Korea Research Monograph Number 1 (Berkeley, CA: Institute of East Asian Studies, Center for Korean Studies of the University of California, 1980) 44–45.

36. "The extent of the depreciation in real terms between 1981 and the first quarter of 1987 was the largest for Korea (36 percent), followed by Singapore (31 percent), Hong Kong (19 percent), and Taiwan (13 percent)." See Bela Balassa and John Williamson, *Adjusting to Success: Balance of Payments Policy in the East Asian NICs* (Washington, D.C.: Institute for International Economics, June 1987), 18.

37. When Korea's overall trade surplus reached $7.7 billion in 1987, for example, the surplus with the United States was $9.6 billion. The surplus with the United States fell to $8.6 billion in 1988 and $4.7 billion in 1989.

38. John-seok Seo, "Fifth Five-Year Economic and Social Development Plan," *Monthly Review* (Korea Exchange Bank), 15 October 1981, 2.

39. Steps toward economic liberalization or "structural adjustment" are examined at some length in Vittorio Corbo and Sang-mok Suh, eds., *Structural Adjustment in a Newly Industrialized Country: Lessons from Korea* (Washington, D.C.: World Bank, 1987), unpublished manuscript.

40. On problems of financial liberalization, see Yung-chul Park, "Economic Stabilization and Liberalization in Korea, 1980–1984," in Bank of Korea, *Monetary Policy in a Changing Financial Environment* (Seoul: Bank of Korea, 1985), 75–139. On trade liberalization, see Soo-gil Young, "Korean Trade Policy and Its Implications for Korea-U.S. Cooperation," in *Korea's Economy* (Korea Economic Institute) 4 (May 1988): 3–15, and Richard Luedde-Neurath, *Import Controls and Export-Oriented Development: A Reassessment of the South Korean Case* (Boulder, CO: Westview Press, 1986). The import-liberalization ratio, quoted widely in the Korean press, is a misleading indication of liberalization, as any reasonably astute observer might realize. Why else, when the ratio has risen to over 90 percent in recent years, should there be mounting complaints about the restrictiveness of Korea's import regime? Luedde-Neurath shows, using the year 1982 as an example, that when the ratio published in Korean newspapers was 75 percent,

adjustment for imports subject to licensing, surveillance-type measures (on "sensitive" items requiring prior approval), special laws (on safety, health, and packaging), and for imports controlled by government agencies, the actual ratio was seven percent! (Ibid., 151–54).

41. Soo-gil Young, "Korean Trade Policy and Its Implications," 14.

42. See Lee Chong-hwan, "The Sixth Economic and Social Development Plan of Korea," *Monthly Review* (Korea Exchange Bank) 20 (December 1986): 3–26.

43. Ibid., 4.

44. Peter A. Petri, "Korea's Export Niche: Origins and Prospects," *World Development* 16 (January 1988): 61. Petri argues that the pattern of export development in Japan and Korea provides "a remarkable case study in the 'economics of following' " (Ibid., 48). Korean exports follow Japanese exports with a fifteen-year lag and, since the factors that explain exports (income and endowment levels) differ more between the two than for other country pairings, following has been deliberate. Small wonder that Korea has been perceived as a second Japan!

45. See Peter F. Allgeier, "Korean Trade Policy in the Next Decade Dealing with Reciprocity," *World Development* 16 (January 1988): 91–92.

46. "The government has been criticized both for quick policymaking and quick change in policies." (M. Shinohara, T. Yanagihara, and K.S. Kim, "The Japanese and Korean Experience in Managing Development," *World Bank Staff Working Paper No. 574* [Washington, D.C.: World Bank 1983], 69). See also Tony Michell, "Administrative Traditions and Economic Decision-Making in South Korea," *IDS Bulletin* 15 (April 1984): 32–37.

8

The Role of Science and Technology in South Korean Development

Richard P. Suttmeier

Introduction

AS WE APPROACH THE END OF THE TWENTIETH CENTURY, issues of science and technology in the domestic development of individual nations and in the international political economy are becoming both more pressing and more intriguing. Whether it be among the advanced nations of the OECD world, the NICs, the poorer countries of the third world, or those of the socialist "second world," a country's economic health, social development, and international competitiveness are all increasingly being linked to progress in science and technology.

Meanwhile, technical progress itself is rapidly changing the nature of industrial activity and the international movement and distribution of technical resources.[1] Thus, national development strategies face a moving target; the environment to which they are addressed is changing more rapidly than the pace of implementing national science and technology development policies. Only the fanciest of footwork will do.

The science and technology development experience of the Republic of Korea is an instructive case of these trends, and it is an interesting example of a "fancy footwork" strategy that shows considerable promise of succeeding. Korea's aggressive policies for science and technology are driven, like those of other NICs, by a desire to move upscale in the product cycle in the face of rising labor costs and increased competition in low-wage, low-technology production coming from the "proto-NICs." At the same time, nations of the OECD world with the advanced technology for higher value-added production are increasingly reluctant to transfer it, on conventional terms, for fear of increased competition from the NICs. The latter, accordingly, have all begun to attend to the development of domestic science and technology capabilities with renewed vigor.

Indigenous capabilities for original research and development thus are becoming central to the industrial restructuring which Korea and the other NICs are now experiencing. At the same time, the international dynamics of high value-added, high-technology industry are changing, and this fact poses a particularly challenging problem for Korean policy makers and business leaders. Is a development strategy inspired by Japan and based on assumptions about the product cycle a viable approach to the achievement of Korea's goal of becoming a fully "modern" nation by the end of the century? How does this strategy fit and compare with those of its East Asian neighbors? These are the kinds of questions usefully brought to an assessment of the Korean experience.

Background

A central issue found in post-World War II discussions of the role of science and technology in economic and social development has been the acquisition of "technical capabilities."[2] Swirling around this central theme have been a variety of debates about how this acquisition is best accomplished. These debates have often been crosscutting and multidimensional, involving issues of technology transfer from abroad *versus* indigenous research and development, and the relative importance of government actions and the behavior of firms.

For instance, what should be the role of government policy? Should it be to "push" technological innovation through the supply of technical knowledge in subsidized form to producers? Should the market be encouraged to work in the selection and acquisition of technology and, if so, how freely? Should a poor country commit scarce resources to the building of research and development institutions, or should its technical needs be satisfied by the transfer of technology from abroad? If the latter, will such transfers bring in their wake an enduring technological dependency which would compromise the nation's long-term economic sovereignty? Are there definable stages in the process of acquiring technological capabilities? If so, what are they, and can development policy be tailored to meet the "stage requirements" when necessary?

The Korean case pertains to many of these questions, and provides interesting answers to some of them. As we know, Korea did rely heavily on market forces and on the transfer of technology from abroad. Yet it also had an activist government devising authoritative policies and a legal framework for the promotion of science and technology. Of particular note were the early establishment of a major research and development center, the Korean Institute for Science and Technology (KIST) in 1966, and a specialized government ministry, the Ministry of Science and Technology (MOST) in 1967, well before economic conditions might have argued for such organizations. The impressive growth of science and technology activities which are catching international attention in the 1980s, thus, has its origins well over twenty years ago.

Korean experience seems to support the idea that a degree of planning for science and technology development in the early stages does pay off. It also suggests that it is possible to coordinate science and technology plans with economic and social plans, through a series of developmental stages, as well. As the Koreans see it, this synchronization of national objectives has taken the pattern shown in Table 8-1.

Foreign technology has clearly played an important role in Korean economic success and in the upgrading of the nation's technology. Yet, with the possible exception of Japan in an earlier period, the Korean case illustrates better than most the

TABLE 8–1
Phases in Coordination of Economic and Science
and Technology Development

Period	Industrialization	Science and Technology
1960s	1. Develop import substitute industries	1. Strengthen science and technology education
	2. Expand export-oriented light industries	2. Deepen scientific and technological infrastructure
	3. Support producer goods industries	3. Promote foreign technology import
1970s	1. Expand heavy and chemical industries	1. Expand technical training
	2. Shift emphasis from import to technology import	2. Improve institutional mechanism for adapting imported technology
	3. Strengthen export-oriented industry competitiveness	3. Promote research applicable to industrial needs
1980s	1. Transform industrial structure to one of comparative advantage	1. Develop and acquire top-level scientists and engineers
	2. Expand technology-intensive industry	2. Perform national research and development projects efficiently
	3. Encourage manpower development and improve productivity of industries.	3. Promote industry's technology development

Source: Ministry of Science and Technology (MOST), *Introduction to Science and Technology, Republic of Korea, 1988*, 16.

importance of modes of transfer and the need for active government action in providing the conditions to facilitate the assimilation of technology. Although direct foreign investment in Korea over the years has not been insignificant, as shown by Table 8-2, it is not thought to have led to much technology transfer.[3]

Technology transfer through licensing agreements is thought to have been a more effective means of technology transfer.[4] As Table 8-3 shows, Korea has used this mode of transfer extensively, especially since the mid-1970s.

The effectiveness of transfers via licensing agreements seems to have been strongly influenced by three major factors. First,

TABLE 8–2
Investment in Korea by United States, Japan, and Others
(In Millions of Dollars) 1962–1985.

	'62–'71	'71–'76	'77–'81	'82–'85	Total
Japan	41	377	214	738	1,371
	(43.8)	(66.7)	(36.5)	(52.4)	(51.5)
U.S.	34	68	208	461	771
	(35.4)	(12.0)	(35.4)	(32.8)	(29.0)
Others	20	120	165	208	513
	(20.8)	(21.3)	(28.1)	(14.8)	(19.4)
Total	96	565	587	1,407	2,655
	(100)	(100)	(100)	(100)	(100)

Note: ( ) -Ratio
Source: Ministry of Finance, cited in Park, *The National System*, 71.

Korean firms showed a zestful entrepreneurship in adapting foreign technologies to their production needs. Second, this process of adaptation would not have been possible without an indigenous research and development capability residing in government institutes and increasingly within industry. Third, government played an active role in approving license agreements. This role included a vigorous technology screening process involving numerous advisory committees with representatives drawn from industry, universities, and government laboratories. Government also played a strong role in guiding industry with regard to prices and restrictive clauses in the agreements.[5]

Studies of past technology transfer to Korea have also emphasized the critical role of informal technology transfer, and in some cases, these have been regarded as the most effective modes of transfer. Examples of such mechanisms have included:

- Overseas buyers of Korean output who impart technology in their product specifications
- Suppliers of equipment
- Koreans who return home after working in industry, research institutes, or universities abroad
- Recipients of training under turnkey plant sales[6]

TABLE 8–3
Korean Licensing Agreements for Technology Transfer (unit cases)

	62–66	67–71	72–76	77–81	82–85	Total	Ratio(%)
(By Sector)							
Food	2	6	7	30	84	129	3.7
Textile/Apparel	7	7	24	41	103	182	5.2
Chemical	7	76	93	222	266	664	18.8
Metal/Ceramic	2	39	54	139	131	365	10.3
Machinery/ Shipbuilding	6	59	126	447	470	1,108	31.4
Electric/ Electronic	8	80	101	263	386	838	23.7
Others	1	18	29	79	119	246	6.9
(By Country of Source)							
Japan	11	203	280	629	808 (397.7)	1,931	54.7
United States	13	61	90	301	358 (555.9)	823	23.3
Others	9	21	64	291	393 (386.3)	778	22.0
(total)							
Cases	33	285	434	1,221	1,559	3,532	
Royalty Payments ($ million)	1	16	97	452	774	1,339	

Note: ( ) -Royalty Payment
Source: Ministry of Science and Technology, 1986, Cited in Park, *The National System*, 73.

The Korean pattern thus seems to be one of attending to the development of human resources and of an institutional infrastructure for science and technology during the early stages, while relying on imported technology for most immediate production needs. Gradually, a link between imported technology and domestic research and development is forged, with continuing attention given to human resource development. In time, a full-blown national research and development policy emerges side by side with a continuing relationship with foreign suppliers of technology.

As we shall see below, technology transfer from abroad continues to be an important source of technology for Korea. However, as Korea moves into higher value-added production and thus begins to emerge as a competitor to the advanced countries, technologies from abroad are becoming less available on the terms used in the past or, in some cases, not available at all. Korea's current policy for science and technology development is thus both a response to an emerging technological protectionism and an effort to leapfrog through the product cycle to high-technology production.

Before examining that policy in detail, it is appropriate to reiterate that current efforts to develop science and technology build on infrastructure developed over a twenty-year period. These domestic science and technology assets not only provide a launching pad for the future, they also have played a key role in the selection and assimilation of technology that has been an important part of economic success in the past. Korea, like Japan, seems to demonstrate the importance of domestic research and development capabilities at a stage when there is still widespread importation of foreign technology. Thus, the primary purposes of private industrial research and development centers since their establishment in the 1970s were to, first, process "indomitable" foreign technologies into manageable forms so as to integrate them with the local production system as efficiently as possible; secondly, to imitate the foreign product design in order to locally produce these products with the least direct involvement of foreign technologies.[7]

Current Policy and Patterns of Development

Current science and technology policy in Korea both builds on the past and is also very much oriented towards the future. Like other countries, Korea has gone through a series of long-range planning exercises, the latest of which has resulted in a formal document entitled "The Long Range Plan for Science and Technology Towards the 2000s." Current policy thus is increasingly defined in terms of the long-term goals.

Korea's current strategy can be thought of as having nine main components.[8]

1. *Official Recognition.* Science and technology are given high priority in the promotion of the nation's socioeconomic

development. This includes high-level commitments to divert resources to science and technology and to encourage high-quality manpower development. The main organizational expression of this commitment has been the National Technology Promotion Conference. The conference, presided over by the Korean president, meets every three months and brings together some 250 leaders from government (including cabinet ministers), industry, and the research community. The conference does not make decisions but is instead a forum for exchanging information, building consensus, and expressing high-level support for science and technology.[9] In addition, there are plans for the establishment of a presidential science and technology advisory committee.

2. *High-Level Manpower.* Government and industry are to work together to expand the size and raise the quality of the science and technology manpower pool. In 1987, Korea had 54,000 scientists and engineers or thirteen per 10,000 people in the entire population. The government hopes to raise these numbers to 150,000 by 2001, or thirty scientists and engineers per 10,000. Of these, it is hoped that 15,000 will be "high-level," that is, capable of leading original research efforts.

3. *Research and Development Spending.* Expenditures for research and development in Korea have expanded rapidly during the 1980s, rising from $577 million in 1981 (0.9 percent of GNP) to $1.8 billion in 1986, or 1.99 percent of GNP. Current policy calls for continuing increases throughout the remainder of the century, with targets of 3 percent of GNP by 1991 and 5 percent by 2001. During the 1980s, government expenditures have been growing at about 15 percent per annum, while the rate of increase in the private sector has been approximately 60 percent per annum. The private sector's share has now become the dominant part of the overall national expenditure account, a point discussed further below.

4. *National Projects.* Since 1982, the government has singled out areas of strategic importance for designation as national projects. These are to get priority government funding, although the conduct of the projects is shared among government, industry, and university research facilities. As Table 8-4 indicates, industry's financial contributions to the national projects are not insignificant.

Criteria used in selecting national projects include technology intensiveness, international comparative advantage, conservation of energy and natural resources, and contributions to social development. Funding levels for national projects are increasing, as Table 8-4 indicates.

TABLE 8-4
Government and Industry Shares of Investment in National Research and Development Projects (In Millions of Dollars)

Year Sector	1982	1983	1984	1985	1986	1987	1988	Total
Government	18	28	26	35	58	64	82	311
Industry	8	17	13	19	53	58	51	218
Total	25	45	39	54	111	122	133	529

Source: MOST, *Introduction to Science and Technology*, 34.

5. *Sectoral Adjustment.* Whereas government research and development institutes had been taking the lead in Korean science and technology development since the 1960s, the more recent surge of activities in industry and universities has required that there be a redefinition of the roles of the three sectors.

In 1987, there were 968 research and development related institutions in Korea. Of these, 175 were public or governmental, 338 were at universities, while the remainder (455, increased to 503 by April 1988) were run by private industry. The growth of research and development in private industry has been remarkable, as Table 8-5 indicates. As recently as the early 1980s, the government's financial contribution to the nation's research and development effort was approximately twice that of the private sector's. By 1986, however, private industry had increased its expenditures to the point that its efforts had become three times those of government.

In adjusting sectoral responsibilities, the mission of government institutes is increasingly being seen to be the bridge between the universities, which are becoming the centers of basic research, and industry, which is concentrating on applications.

TABLE 8-5
Patterns of Korean Research and Development Investment by Sector
(In Millions of Dollars)

	1963	1970	1980	1986
R&D Investment	9.5	40.5	480	1,768
Government	9.2	31.0	325	460
Private	0.3	9.5	155	1,300
Proportion of GNP(%)	0.24	0.48	0.86	199
Ratio(Gov't:Private)	97:3	77:23	68:32	26:74

Source: MOST *Introduction to Science and Technology*, 35.

As part of this effort to promote intersectoral cooperation, the government is building an "Academic Research-Industry Cooperation Center" in the new Daeduk Science Town (discussed further below).

In addition, government institutes are to assume responsibility for high-cost, high-risk research which industry would be reluctant to undertake, and for generic technologies serving the needs of a variety of economic sectors (for which, again, industry would lack incentives).

6. *Incentives for Industry*. The government has had remarkable success in getting the private sector involved in research and development, as shown in Table 8-5. The fact that the greater share of the nation's research and development funding now comes from the private sector is a very rapid turnaround indeed. Not surprisingly, the number of research establishments in the private sector has increased as well, from some 52 large firms in 1980 to 503 in April 1988. In addition, there are now some 37 research consortia among small firms, whereas there were none in 1980.

Since the early 1970s, the government has sought to encourage research and development in private industry. It has done this by providing indirect incentives for the promotion of proprietary technology and direct and indirect support for research leading to more generic technologies. Large companies are encouraged to establish at least one research unit per company, and smaller firms are urged to enter research and development consortia.

A legal framework for these policies is provided by the 1972 Technology Development Promotion Law. The law allows for the setting aside of "technology development reserve funds" on a tax-exempt basis, and permits 10 percent of the costs of new research and development equipment and the costs of assimilating new technologies to be tax-exempt as well. Ninety percent of the initial investment in research and development and testing facilities is subject to special accelerated depreciation schedules. In addition, direct government grants are available to industry for work related to national projects, and long-term, low-interest loans are available for technology development projects. The special tax policies directed towards science and technology development are outlined in Table 8-6.

Special programs exist for small- and medium-size enterprises. Financial support is available to these through the Small and Medium Industry Bank. The Industrial Technology Center of the Korean Institute of Machinery and Metals (KIMM) has as part of its mission the provision of technical services to the small- and medium-size enterprise sector, and other government institutes are enjoined to provide technical guidance to the small- and medium-size enterprises as well. Firms in the sector have also been urged to pool research and development resources and form research associations, and by 1985, some 23 of these associations had been formed.

The package of programs to support the upgrading of technology and the expansion of industrial research and development also includes the establishment of special government corporations to provide venture capital for new entrepreneurial initiatives. Table 8-7 indicates that four of these are now in operation. Although their total capitalization is only slightly more than $100 million, they have been able to leverage loans and investments worth more than $580 million.

The rise of Korean industrial research is very much tied to the emergence and growth of the *chaebol* (industrial conglomerates), the strengthening of which the government encouraged during the 1970s. Industrial research and development, not surprisingly, is thus heavily concentrated in the *chaebol*. The ten largest conglomerates invested approximately half of the total private sector research and development expenditure in 1985, for instance.[10] Because of the sharp competition among

TABLE 8-6
Korean Tax Incentives for Research and Development

Incentives	Scope and Extent of Credit and Deduction
1. Tax deduction of technology and manpower development cost	Deducting 10 percent of technology and manpower development cost from individual or corporate income tax
2. Tax deduction of investment in R&D and accelerated depreciation	Either 8 percent (10 percent in the case of local products) deduction of R&D equipment cost from taxable income or depreciation of 90 percent of the cost in the first year
3. Inclusion of technology development reserve fund in loss	Technology reserve fund being permitted up to 1 percent of total turnover or 20 percent of the income (in high-technology industry either 15 percent of total turnover or 30 percent of income)
4. Tax deduction or accelerated depreciation of investment cost for commercialization	Either 6 percent of investment cost (10 percent in case of local equipment) or 50 percent depreciation in the first year
5. Special consumption tax reduction on new and high-tech products	Tentative taxation at low rate being applied to high-tech products for a certain period
6. Customs tax reduction on R&D equipment	65 to 70 percent tax deduction for R&D equipment imported by industrial research institutes
7. Local premises tax exemption for R&D facilities	Exemption of local tax on premises belonging to industrial research laboratories with more than 30 researchers
8. Special consumption tax exemption of samples for R&D purposes	
9. Tax deduction of technology income	Income from patent technology know-how (50 percent), engineering service (50 percent), etc.

Source: Ministry of Science and Technology, 1986, cited in Park, *The National System*, 54.

the *chaebol*, they have been positively oriented towards technological innovation, and thus welcomed the positive incentives to expand research and development provided by the government.

The largest number of research and development facilities is in the electronics and chemical industries, with the former

TABLE 8-7
Korean Science and Technology Finance Corporations

Organization (Year of Establishment)	Major Function	Capital as of '87 Loans and Investments Number of Cases
Korea Technology Development Corporation (KTDC) (1981)	Financial support for the development of new technologies, products and processes and for the improvement of existing technologies	$52.8 Mil $436.8 Mil 1,083 Cases
Korea Technology Advancement Corporation (K-TAC) (1974)	To link research organizations with businesses and entrepreneurs by translating research and development into practical applications	$6.13 Mil $5.52 Mil 25 Cases
Korea Development Investment Corporation (KDIC) (1982)	To foster and strengthen technology-intensive small and medium industries through equity investments and/or equity-type investment	$14.67 Mil $27.93 Mil 178 Cases
Korea Technology Finance Corporation (KTFC) (1984)	To invest in R&D and provide loans for R&D costs incurred either internally or through contracts with external research institutes for the initial commercialization of new technology and/or investments and arrangements related thereto	$111.2 Mil 345 Cases

Source: MOST, *Introduction to Science and Technology*, 39.

having the largest concentration of industrial research personnel. While having fewer institutes, the machinery industry nevertheless has the second-largest concentration of researchers, as Table 8-8 indicates.

Inspired by the Japanese experience, the Korean government since the late 1970s has been encouraging the formation of "research associations" for intra-industry cooperative research. The legal sanction for this encouragement is found in the 1977 Technology Development Promotion Act.

By 1985, some 27 associations had been formed. Most of these involve both a few large firms and a number of smaller

TABLE 8-8
Distribution of Korean Private R&D Facilities by Industry in 1985

Sector	Elec.	Mach.	Chem.	Food	Tex.	Others	Total
Number of Institutes	49	38	49	21	10	16	183
Number of researchers	3,834	2,606	1,542	548	324	372	9,226

Source: Ministry of Science and Technology, 1986, cited in Park, *The National System*, 65.

ones. The combined research and development expenditures of these associations in 1985 was $4 million, with about a third of the funding coming from government.[11] The great majority of the associations are industry-specific. Examples of recently organized associations include the Korea VTR Research Association (Samsung, Goldstar, Daewoo), the Korea Computer Research Association (Goldstar, Samsung, Hyundai, and seventeen other firms), and the Korea Telecommunications Research Association.[12] The largest number of associations is in the electronics industry, as Table 8-9 indicates.

TABLE 8-9
Research Associations in Korea by Industrial Sector

	Elec.	Auto.	Bio.	Soft.	Ener.	Total
1984	12	4	1	1	1	19
Number of firms	(76)	(16)	(16)	(8)	(120)	(236)
1985	16	4	1	1	1	23
Number of firms	(111)	(16)	(16)	(22)	(119)	(286)

Source: KIRI, 1966, cited in Park, *The National System*, 61.

The associations also involve the active participation of government. Government's role is not limited only to funding, however. In addition, government research institutes (and universities) are involved in collaborative research with the members of the associations. The government's research role is especially prominent in new fields of technology such as biotechnology, fiber optics, and advanced areas of electronics (including computers and semiconductors). Government is also involved in using the associations in the implementation of national projects. In 1985, for instance, 32 national projects were being carried out by associations. These involved expenditures of some $3 million; 60 percent of these funds were being supplied by the private sector.[13]

7. *International Cooperation.* The Korean government seems to have a keen sense of the growing internationalization of science and technology, and seeks to ensure a place for Korea in it. As a result, it has entered into some 59 science and technology cooperation agreements and has committed approximately $4 million to support the Korean side of 69 international joint research projects. More than most countries, Korea's efforts in international science and technology cooperation seem to be guided by a considered policy.

After years of being a recipient of foreign assistance, the Koreans now approach their international science and technology activities with a three-track policy. Dealings with the industrialized countries will be conducted on the basis of mutual sharing of benefits and costs. The Koreans would also like to expand science and technology relations with the developing world, and for this purpose they have set up a special budget line to allow the Korean side to assume the burden of the costs of cooperation, if necessary. Finally, Korea sees its interests served by its support of multilateral activities, including various UN activities in science and technology.

In cooperation with the OECD world, the Koreans are diversifying their contacts and have tailored programs to meet objectives appropriate for individual countries. With the United States, for instance, plans call for expanded cooperative research, and for the procurement of advanced equipment and technical training to help offset the trade imbalance. Cooperation in the industrial sphere includes the design and manufacture of sophisticated parts used in the automobile and aircraft industries. Cooperation with the United Kingdom will focus on information technology, that with France on oceanography and aviation, that with Germany on automation and robotics, and cooperation with Sweden will be centered on precision machinery.

In the last few years, Korea has also taken unilateral initiatives to revitalize and expand science and technology cooperation in the Asia-Pacific region. It volunteered to operate in Seoul the Coordinating Office of the Association for Science Cooperation in Asia (ASCA) and to host the tenth ASCA ministerial meeting during 1988. It has also proposed the establishment of a nongovernmental Pacific Science and Technology Cooperation Conference. Korea has also been quietly expanding its science and techology ties with China.

8. *Regional Distribution.* Although South Korea is a relatively small nation, and thus could be expected to diffuse science and technology achievements with comparative ease, the government has nevertheless adopted a policy of distributing science and technology activities at selected locations around the country.

The first of these centers is the Daeduk Science Town, located about 150 kilometers south of Seoul in Daejeon City, which has been under construction since 1974. Already nine government research institutes, five private institutes, and three universities have moved to the new location. According to plans, by 1991 Daeduk will have a population of 50,000 working in some forty institutes.

The regional distribution scheme also includes the development of other research and development centers. The Hongnung research and development complex and the genetic engineering center in the town of Suweon will make up the capital region center. In the southeast, there will be a special center for research on new materials in Pohang, Ulsan. The southwest is to have a center for fine chemistry and precision machinery located in the Hanam Industrial Region. Spatially, Daeduk appears as the hub of activities, with spokes extending outward to the other three regions.

9. *Civic Awareness.* The final component of the current policy is the creation of a climate of understanding supportive of science and technology in the general population. Working with industry, universities, and the mass media, the government is promoting a pro-science movement designed to aid the ordinary citizen in appreciating the benefits of science and technology in daily life, and to instill in the country's youth "a spirit of rationality, efficiency and creativeness."[14]

The Long-Range Plan

As noted above, current policy is increasingly linked to a plan for science and technology development for the remainder of the century. The latter is intended to ensure Korea's place in the high-tech world of the 21st century. In the fields chosen for emphasis and in the strategy to be followed, the Korean plan is, at least on the surface, similar to plans recently adopted by Taiwan, Singapore, and the People's Republic of China.[15]

The Korean plan calls for efforts in a variety of fields. These are grouped according to the following categories:

1. "Income-earners," or those which promise economic returns in the short run (microelectronics, information technology, automation, fine chemistry)
2. "Essential fields," which also have the potential for economic success in the medium term (new materials, biotechnology)
3. "Public good technologies" (health and environmental sciences)
4. "Pioneering fields," which also have the promise for short- to mid-range success (ocean, aeronautics, and space technologies)
5. "Common purpose fields" (basic research, metrology, systems engineering, project management technologies)[16]

The implementation of the long-range plan is expected to give special attention to distinctive Korean conditions. It thus postulates a mixed strategy calling for *specialization* in areas of Korean strength; the development of sophisticated forms of *cooperation* among the governmental, industrial, and academic sectors; increasing *internationalization* in order to benefit from foreign experience in areas of Korean weakness; followed by a strategy of *localization* designed to link research activities in various parts of the country in a nationwide research and development network. The enhancement of the autonomy of the private sector underlies the entire strategy of implementation.

High-Level Manpower

In spite of a skilled labor force and a reasonably well-educated population, the greatest obstacle to Korea's realizing its ambitions for science and technology is arguably a shortage of high-level manpower trained beyond the bachelor's level. Special programs have thus been established to address this need. The first of these is a distinctive institution, the Korean Institute of Technology, which provides tailored instruction to specially gifted children. KIT, located in Daeduk, is run by MOST in cooperation with the Korean Advanced Institute of Science and Technology (KAIST). It admits 540 students each year and maintains a faculty-student ratio of 1:10.

KAIST also contributes to the education of high-level manpower. Since its establishment in 1970, it has graduated 495 Ph.D.s and 4,753 holders of master's degrees. During the 1987-91 period, its planned output includes 1,055 Ph.D.s and 3,040 master's degrees. KAIST seeks cooperative ties with foreign universities for the expansion of its graduate programs.

Graduate education in universities, which had not been extensive, is now expanding rapidly. Whereas there were only 723 master's and doctorate recipients from engineering faculties in 1976, in 1987 there were 5,337.

Since the late 1960s, when special efforts were begun to attract Korean scientists and engineers abroad back to Korea, some 1,427 have returned. In addition, others have been recruited back on a temporary basis. Although the numbers are still not large, during the mid-1980s there were signs that the number of permanent returnees may be increasing as salaries and living and working conditions have improved in Korea. Whereas only sixty were repatriated in 1983, double that number returned in 1986.[17]

A final component of the strategy to upgrade the manpower pool is the expansion of government programs to send students abroad. A government scholarship program administered by the Korea Science and Engineering Foundation (KOSEF) is to be enlarged sufficiently to allow some 10,000 science and engineering students to receive post-doctoral training abroad in the 1986–2001 period.

Outposts

Korea, like Japan, Taiwan, and increasingly the People's Republic of China, has come to realize the importance of establishing technology "outposts" near dynamic centers of technological innovation. Since the early 1980s, Silicon Valley has been a location of choice. Though often requiring significant expenditures, Korean outposts there have clearly benefited their electronics industry. One of the larger operations, Samsung Semiconductor and Telecommunications, had some 213 full-time employees as of the end of 1986. A number of these were Korean-American researchers who were hired away from such companies as IBM, DEC, Bell Labs, Intel and Hewlett Packard.[18]

Prospects

On the face of it, Korea's strategy for science and technology development is most impressive.[19] Because of past planning and current policy innovations, Korea seems to be placed as well as any of the NICs to make the transition to a more knowledge-intensive economic system. It will be constrained somewhat by the availability of high-level manpower, but plans are in place to do something about this problem. Assuming that current political uncertainties can be managed, the prospects for science and technology development would appear to be promising.

Nevertheless, we should recognize that, however impressive its preparations for science and technology development, the need for Korea to confront a number of difficult but intriguing strategic choices continues. Increasingly, the pace of technological change itself, and its impact on the world economy, make the adequacy of domestic policies difficult to assess. In addition, we appear to be facing a series of new developments in the international political economy for which past experience may not be a reliable guide to the future. The technological and financial power of Japan is one such change. The movement toward further integration of the EEC in 1992 is another. The dramatic changes in the socialist countries and their entry into the international economy is a third.

One recent analysis of the implications of the new technological revolution for the international political economy points to a number of significant developments.

1. With technological change, labor costs have become an increasingly smaller percentage of total production costs. Forces for international industrial relocations in search of

inexpensive labor, according to product cycle logic, will thus be weakened.

2. New technologies seem to favor the concentration of research and development, design, production, and assembly in one location, ideally near major markets or "growth poles." An international network of low-cost suppliers of components is becoming less important to corporate strategies.

3. Because knowledge-intensive production requires ongoing inputs of technical knowledge, manufacturing locations will also be chosen with an eye towards the availability of scientists and engineers, a factor also unlikely to benefit most developing countries.

4. New technologies are unlikely to upset established international supplier relations, but current suppliers will be expected to move upscale technologically and in terms of quality production. The prospects of adding additional suppliers to the network are not good.[20]

If the above conclusions are correct, the prospective benefits from the new advances in technology for many developing countries are not bright. However, the implications for a country like Korea may be quite different. Those countries with an established science and technology capability seem to be ones who can benefit from the new technological revolution. Again, the Korean decision to build capability early would seem to indicate a great deal of foresight on the part of Korean policy makers in light of recent technological change.

The new technologies are also profoundly expensive to develop and often have product life cycles which are quite short.[21] The extremely high up-front research and product development costs are often daunting for even the largest of the world's corporations. We are thus beginning to see an increasing number of "strategic alliances" among large firms in different countries. These alliances bring together organizations with large concentrations of technical resources and typically involve two-way technology transfers. They often also leave room for low-cost research and development and other technical services which a country like Korea (and the other NICs and China) could provide.

These new features of the international technology frontier—the implications for location decisions resulting from new assumptions about manufacturing and the high costs involved in new product development—are likely to be powerful influences on the patterns of Korean science and technology development. However well conceived and implemented its science and technology development plans, Korea will always lack the human and material resources to emerge as an autonomous center of technological dynamism. It can, however, be an attractive partner in some form of strategic alliance. The question then is, with whom?

Korea seems to be approaching this question sensibly, with a strategy of diversification. It would clearly like to strengthen and deepen its technical ties with Japanese and United States firms, but ties with Europeans also seem increasingly attractive. The Europeans, like the Americans, are perceived to be more willing to transfer technology than the Japanese. However, unlike ties with the Americans, which increasingly link expanded technology transfer to the acceptance of United States government positions on export controls and intellectual property rights, relations with the Europeans may appear to hold somewhat less friction.

While technical relations with the firms and governments of the OECD world will continue to be at the center of Korean attention over the short to medium run, Korea's evolving relations with China also warrant monitoring. Although these relations have focused on trade and investment thus far, the possibilities for "strategic alliances" in research and development, and in science and technology cooperation more generally, should not be overlooked. China's large and capable research and development establishment dwarfs Korea's and could offer Korea access to technical manpower and (in some fields) to world-class research. Although the Chinese research establishment is increasingly oriented to commercial technologies, it lacks the managerial savvy possessed by the Koreans and needed to bring discoveries and inventions to commercial use. There is thus an appealing complementarity at the science and technology level paralleling the complementarity at the commercial level that has excited parties on both sides. Both the Chinese and the Koreans are quietly expanding contacts and gathering information about each other's science and technology capabilities.[22]

While it would be premature to assert that the center of the world's innovative activities in the 21st century will be found in East Asia, there can be no doubt that the East Asian region will be an important new player in international science and technology. The creation and accumulation of science and technology resources in Japan, China, and the NICs is remarkable. The prospects for Korea's science and technology development will be strongly influenced by the extent to which patterns of cooperation supersede conflict and competition in the evolution of this East Asian "techno-system."

Notes

1. See, for instance, Manuel Castells and Laura D'Andrea Tyson, "High-Technology Choices Ahead: Restructuring Interdependence," in John W. Sewell and Stuart K. Tucker, *Growth, Exports, & Jobs in a Changing World Economy* (Washington, D.C.: Overseas Development Council, 1988).
2. Two recent and useful contributions to these discussions are Carl J. Dahlman, Bruce Ross-Larson, and Larry E. Westphal, *Managing Technological Development: Lessons from the Newly Industrialized Countries,* Staff Working Paper # 17 (Washington, D.C.: The World Bank, 1985); and Aaron Segal, ed., *Learning by Doing: Science and Technology in the Developing World* (Boulder, CO: Westview Press, 1987).
3. Yong-Chan Park, *The National System of Innovation in Korea with an Introduction to the Semiconductor Industry* (masters dissertation, Graduate Programme in Science and Technology Policy Studies, University of Sussex, 1987), 72.
4. Ibid., 72 ff.
5. Ibid., 70 ff.
6. Ibid., 78 ff.
7. Ibid., 68.
8. Unless otherwise indicated, the discussion which follows is drawn principally from Ministry of Science and Technology (MOST), *Introduction to Science and Technology, Republic of Korea,* 1988, 17 ff.
9. Park, *The National System,* 38.
10. Ibid., 55.
11. Ibid., 61.
12. Ibid.
13. Ibid., 63.

14. For further discussion, see MOST, *Introduction to Science and Technology*, 50.
15. For the latter, see Richard P. Suttmeier, "Listening to China," *Issues in Science and Technology*, Fall 1988, 42–51.
16. MOST, *Introduction to Science and Technology*.
17. Ibid., 29.
18. Park, *The National System*, 118.
19. The following discussion has benefited from discussions with Professor Denis Simon of the Fletcher School, my co-investigator in a study of science and technology resources in the Pacific region sponsored by the National Science Foundation.
20. Castells and Tyson, *Growth, Exports, & Jobs*, 7–74.
21. See, for instance, Nathan Rosenberg, "Science, Technology and Economic Growth," paper presented at the 1987 Annual Meeting of the American Association for the Advancement of Science, Chicago, February 14, 1987.
22. Richard P. Suttmeier, "Chinese Efforts to Stimulate High-Technology: Implications for Korea," *The Korean Journal of International Studies* 19 (1988), 473–91.

9

Economic Development Strategy and Prospects for Reform in North Korea

Pong S. Lee

Introduction

IT IS WELL KNOWN THAT THE ECONOMY, polity, and society of North Korea are of the Soviet, indeed the Stalinist, type. The most remarkable aspect of the polity is Kim Il Sung's cult of personality and his nepotistic dictatorship, in which his son, Kim Jong Il, has been named his successor. To generalize, the ignorance of highly indoctrinated people permits, and the desire to be independent of Soviet and Chinese interference makes desirable, this sort of leadership.

In the mid-1950s, on the pretext of de-stalinization, certain North Korean communists tried to unseat Kim. Both the Soviets and the Chinese intervened, and the attempt failed. No doubt it was this experience, among others, that induced Kim to pursue his isolationist line. In fact, Kim was already leaning this way in 1955 when in a speech to a group of party workers he outlined his vision for an independent North Korea. Fundamental to that vision was a strong economy, able to grow without recourse to excessive levels of economic aid from China or the Soviet Union. Thus was born North Korea's national catchword, *juche*, which can be described as near-autarchy in economic terms.

Economic self-reliance for North Korea, a small country with limited resources and sharing common borders with both China and the Soviet Union, would be most difficult, if not impossible. Nevertheless, North Korea, through an inward-looking strategy and a highly centralized traditional Stalinist model, has achieved a rapid industrialization that, by most standards of developing economy, is quite respectable. As the economy developed and its structure became more complex the rate of growth began to slow down, primarily because the very advantages of the highly centralized command economy in turn become major impediments to further growth and modernization of the economy. The other problem for North Korea is South Korea, which through an open and outward-looking development strategy, began to take off in the mid-1960s, rapidly overtook the North in 1970s, and continues on today with its dynamic and impressive performance.

In recent years, a tide of political and economic reform has been sweeping over virtually all socialist countries, including China, Eastern Europe, and the Soviet Union. North Korea, despite its repeated claims of being an independent country of *juche*, cannot avoid the influences of its two major allies, China and the Soviet Union. More importantly, however, North Korea internally is in desperate need of fresh new approaches to its economic management. There are many signs that comprehensive economic reform is imperative for North Korea. Kim Il Sung, in his policy statement in December 1986, stated that "a new reality of economic development mandates improvements in economic leadership and enterprise management."[1] The revenue-to-state budget, the only official statistics published in series, declined from an average annual increase of 12 percent in the 1960s to 7 percent between 1980 and 1986. Even the rates of increase in gross industrial output value have not been made public in the 1980s, except for 1980 (17 percent) and 1982 (16.8 percent). Since 1984, in particular, appeals for improvement of economic management have sharply increased in number and urgency of tone. For example, in 1985 there were 45 articles on economics in *Kunroja* (Workers), an official publication of the Party Central Committee.[2]

The main purposes of this paper are, first, to review the North Korean economic strategies and, second, to examine and evaluate various North Korean economic reforms in recent years. One of the major problems in studying North Korea is the virtual absence of published economic statistics. For some unknown reason, all economic data—which were very rare to begin with—suddenly disappeared from official announcements beginning in 1964. Since then the only major sources of economic information have been Kim Il Sung's New Year's messages and the budget announcements by the finance minister each April. The data from even these two sources are largely qualitative and at times consist of misleading and fragmentary information. One exception, fortunately, is foreign trade statistics. These are available from most of North Korea's trade partners, including the Soviet Union, China, and other communist countries. Accordingly, we shall emphasize North Korea's trade, especially with the Soviet Union, China, and—beginning in the 1970s—with Japan. In section 2, the North Korean strategy of development and performance will be briefly reviewed. Section 3 will cover recent reform efforts, while an examination of future prospects for reform and concluding remarks will be made in section 4.

Development Strategy and Performance

The North Korean economy may be characterized as one of the most centralized planned economies remaining among communist countries. With the exception of small private plots (about 200 square meters each) and farmers' markets, virtually everything is socialized. The state not only owns and controls all means of production, but also decides what and how to produce and how to distribute the outputs. Of course, the prices of virtually all goods and services and the levels of wages are set by the government as well. Foreign trade is under the state monopoly and is carried out by the Foreign Trade Corporations, which are either parts of the Ministry of Foreign Trade or under some enterprises. In other words, the North Korean economy is one where no market force is permitted to function. With regard to incentives of workers and enterprise managers, North Korea places less emphasis on material incentives and more on moral incentives such as patriotism, revolutionary zeal, and loyalty to the leader. In most communist countries, there are two types of economic plans, intermediate plans of five or seven years and annual plans, which once adopted become law. North Korea seems to be taking the intermediate plan more seriously than do most other communist countries. This paper, therefore, will use the intermediate plan periods as benchmarks for reviewing North Korea's past economic performance. Table 9-1 indicates average annual growth rates of gross value of industrial output during different plan periods.

TABLE 9–1
Growth Of Gross Value of North Korean Industrial Output
Based on Official Announcements

		Average Annual Rate (%)
Three-Year Plan	1951–1956	41.7
Five-Year Plan	1957–1960	36.6
First Seven-Year Plan	1961–1970	12.8
Six-Year Plan	1971–1976	16.3
Year of Adjustment	1977	—
Second Seven-Year Plan	1978–1981	12.2
Years of Adjustment	1985–1986	—
Third Seven-Year Plan	1987–1993	10.0 (planned)

Post-Korean War to 1970

The three decades after the Korean War are encompassed by the periods of the three-year plan for postwar reconstruction (1954–1956), a five-year plan (1957–1960), and a seven-year plan, including a three-year extension (1961–1970). Despite the lack of comprehensive data, there are significant indications that the economy made major strides between 1954 and 1963. The rate of industrial growth was one of the highest among

TABLE 9–2
Average Annual Growth Rates in Selected Series

	1945–56 %	1957–60 %	1961–63 %
Gross Value of Social Products	28.7	23.0	11.1
National Income	30.0	21.0	10.8
Gross Value of Industrial Output	41.4	33.8	13.6
Gross Value of Agricultural Output	11.6	8.8	7.9

Source: Central Statistical Board. State Planning Commission of the DPRK, *Statistical Returns of National Economy of the DPRK, 1961* (Pyongyang: Foreign Language Publishing House. 1964).

communist countries. Table 9-2 shows the officially announced average annual growth rates in selected economic series between 1954 and 1970.

The unprecedented rates of growth during the period of the three-year plan for postwar reconstruction, 1954–1956, and the five-year plan of 1957–1960 represent not only the rapid reconstruction of North Korea's economy from the devastation of the war but also a substantial expansion of the economy. The speedy restoration of the war-damaged productive capacity and construction of diverse new facilities were possible primarily because of massive economic aid from communist countries led by the Soviet Union. The aid constituted about 31.4 percent of the state's budget revenue, in 1954, and it sharply declined, to 4.2 percent of the budget revenue, in 1958 when the Sino-Soviet split became apparent.

The 1960s, the seven-year plan period, were a time of continued Sino-Soviet estrangement when North Korea was walking a political tightrope between its two giant neighbors. This is reflected naturally in economic performance as well. As may be noted from Table 9-1, the rates of growth in almost all economic series rapidly deteriorated during the first half of the seven-year plan of 1961–1963. In fact, the year 1963 marked the beginning of the end of the unparalleled rate of growth in North Korea's economy, which reached its lowest point in 1966. Not surprisingly, beginning in 1964 all meaningful economic data suddenly disappeared from official publications. One expects the rate of expansion to slow down, naturally, from its phenomenal postwar high. North Korea's economic problems, however, appear to be more serious than what would normally be expected, judging from the fact that the original seven-year plan was extended in 1966 for three additional years, until 1970. Nevertheless, 12.8 percent annual average growth in gross value of industrial output in 1961–1970 is impressive when compared with other communist economies during the period.

Few reasons are known for the economic difficulties of this period. One cause of the problems hinted at by North Korean officials was the necessity to increase defense spending during this period. Another reason to which a number of writers attribute the difficulties is the ever-widening Sino-Soviet rift during this period. There are several events that may have necessitated North Korea's strengthening of its defense posture. One of these, no doubt, was the military revolution of May 1961 in South Korea, culminating in normalization of relations between South Korea and Japan in 1965.

In December 1962, the Party Central Committee of North Korea adopted the policy of the "four major military objectives." These were: (1) arming the entire people, (2) fortifying the country, (3) modernizing the military, and (4) making cadres of all military personnel. Implementing any of these objectives would have necessarily diverted scarce human and other resources from completing the seven-year plan that had started a year earlier. For example, arming the entire people would require lengthy military training of production workers, while the fortification of the country included building underground industrial and military facilities.

The initial seven-year plan, 1961–1967, was apparently drafted with the expectation that the normal flow of aid from both China and the Soviet Union would continue. After 1960, as the Sino-Soviet falling-out grew worse, North Korea tilted more toward the Chinese side of the dispute; and the Soviet Union allegedly retaliated by failing to deliver the industrial and farm machinery agreed upon in the first long-term trade agreement between two countries signed in 1960. These Soviet machines, of course, had been counted on to fulfill the seven-year plan. In 1963 North Korea had a quarrel with Khrushchev. One question—resembling an element of his simultaneous disaffection with Romania—was North Korea's excessive plans for heavy industry. Despite some long-term loans of about $150 million from China between 1961 and 1964, the lack of Soviet aid in the early 1960s may have been one of the major reasons for the failure of the seven-year plan and its subsequent extension for three years.

Kim Il Sung's desire to be economically independent of the Soviet Union and China notwithstanding, North Korea's dependence on trade and aid (in the form of a continued trade deficit) with the Soviets and Chinese is apparent.

In foreign trade, these were the decades when North Korea was trading exclusively with the communist-bloc countries. Throughout the period, over 80 percent of trade was conducted with communist countries, and trade with the Soviet Union alone constituted nearly 70 percent of it. We note the ups and downs of the North Korea-Soviet trade during this period in Table 9-3—a sudden decrease in trade volume starting in 1959 and then a noticeable rise in 1967.

The volume of North Korea-Soviet trade in 1959 fell to less than a quarter of that in 1958. In terms of commodities traded (not shown) North Korea's import of machinery and equipment dropped about 69 percent in 1959 and fell another 66 percent in 1960. On the other hand, a considerable increase in trade with China is noticeable, a 62 percent rise in 1958 and 28 percent in 1959. These increases in trade with China, however, were not sufficient to offset the drastic decrease in Soviet trade. Of course, China had serious problems of her own during this period, the economic fiasco of the Great Leap Forward and the withdrawal of Soviet aid and technicians from China. A striking feature of North Korea-China trade—unlike its trade with the Soviet Union—is that the trade balance has been consistently in deficit, strongly suggesting one form of China's economic aid to North Korea. For example, the total of North Korea's cumulative trade deficit with China was almost $150 million between 1960 and 1967; but it accumulated a $52 million surplus with the Soviet Union. A dramatic shift in North Korea's trade with her two allies can be seen over the three years, 1968 to 1970, the period of extension of the original seven-year plan.

TABLE 9–3
North Korean Visible Mirror Trade with China, Japan, and USSR,
1954–1979 (in millions of dollars)

		Year	Total	Exports	Imports	Balance
C h i n a	*Three-Year Plan*	1954	82.3	2.6	79.7	-77.1
		1955	76.1	3.5	72.6	-69.1
		1956	68.6	6.7	61.8	-55.1
	Five-Year Plan (completed a year early)	1957	56.0	19.5	36.5	-17.0
		1958	90.5	42.8	47.7	-4.9
		1959	115.8	45.0	70.9	-25.9
		1960	120.4	53.0	67.4	-14.4
	Seven-Year Plan (extended three years)	1961	116.9	53.1	63.8	-10.7
		1962	134.6	54.1	80.4	-26.3
		1963	151.4	64.3	87.1	-22.7
		1964	155.3	65.1	90.3	-25.2
		1965	180.3	83.3	97.0	-13.7
		1966	203.2	88.3	114.8	-26.3
		1967	176.6	83.0	93.6	-10.6
		1968	113.1	45.9	67.2	-21.3
		1969	92.1	44.9	47.2	-2.3
		1970	115.1	54.2	60.9	-6.7
U S S R	*Three-Year Plan*	1954	—	—	—	—
		1955	377.3	181.1	196.2	-15.1
		1956	466.8	227.6	239.2	-11.6
	Five-Year Plan (completed a year early)	1957	544.6	278.0	266.6	11.6
		1958	467.1	209.1	258.0	-48.9
		1959	125.7	51.6	74.1	-22.5
		1960	114.1	74.7	39.4	35.3
	Seven-Year Plan (extended three years)	1961	156.1	79.1	77.0	2.1
		1962	168.9	88.2	80.7	7.5
		1963	170.2	88.1	82.1	6.0
		1964	163.6	80.7	82.9	-2.2
		1965	178.1	88.3	89.8	-1.5
		1966	177.9	92.3	85.6	6.7
		1967	218.3	108.0	110.3	-2.3
		1968	293.1	120.9	172.2	-51.3
		1969	328.2	126.6	201.6	-75.0
		1970	373.2	143.2	230.0	-86.8

TABLE 9–3
North Korean Visible Mirror Trade with China, Japan, and USSR,
1954–1979 (in millions of dollars)

		Year	Total	Exports	Imports	Balance
J a p a n	Three-Year Plan	1954	—	—	—	—
		1955	—	—	—	—
		1956	1.6	0.5	1.1	0.6
	Five-Year Plan (completed a year early)	1957	4.1	2.0	2.1	-0.1
		1958	4.0	1.9	2.1	-0.2
		1959	3.6	0.8	2.8	-2.0
		1960	5.0	3.1	1.9	1.2
	Seven-Year Plan (extended three years)	1961	8.9	4.0	4.9	-0.9
		1962	9.4	4.6	4.8	-0.2
		1963	14.7	9.4	5.3	4.1
		1964	31.5	20.2	11.3	8.9
		1965	31.2	14.7	16.5	-1.8
		1966	27.7	22.7	5.0	17.7
		1967	36.0	29.6	6.4	23.2
		1968	54.7	34.0	20.7	13.3
		1969	56.4	32.2	24.2	8.0
		1970	57.7	34.4	23.3	11.1

Sources: For China: PRC State Statistical Bureau, *Statistical Yearbook of China 1981* (in Chinese). For Japan: *The Kita Chosen Kenkyu*, June 1979, no. 60, p. 77, and JETRO, *Kita Chosen no Keizai to Boeki no Dembo*, May 1983, pp. 89-90. For USSR: Trade Statistics Yearbook as cited, "Economic and Trade Relations between China and North Korea," in *China Newsletter*, 36; JETRO, p. 27; and JETRO, *Kita Chosen no Keizai to Boeki no Denbo*, May 1983, pp. 58-59.

Despite official claims to contrary, there allegedly remained a number of problems after the completion of the seven-year plan. These were: (1) a lag in coal production in spite of the heavy emphasis placed on it, (2) delay of transportation capacity buildup, especially in connecting the industrial complexes on the east and west coasts of North Korea, and (3) apparent labor shortages, as all of the labor force including women were already mobilized. The subsequent six-year plan, 1971–1976, clearly reflected the economic reality of North Korea in the 1960s.

Six-Year Plan, 1971–1976

The decade of the 1970s covers the period of the six-year plan, 1971–1976, and an early part of the second seven-year plan, 1978–1984. In fact, the period of the six-year plan marks the beginning of a new era in North Korea's economic development strategy. In terms of domestic economic structure or the system of economic management, virtually no changes were implemented. For a number of interesting reasons, however, North Korea underwent a major change in the course of her economic policy beginning around 1973.

After the disastrous experiences of the first seven-year plan, the six-year plan of 1971–1977 was launched with more realistic targets. For instance, the projected growth rate in national income and the gross industrial output value were 10.2 and 14 percent, respectively, compared with 15.2 and 18.1 in the earlier plan. Instead of new major construction, emphasis was placed on more conservative targets such as full utilization of existing productive capacities, use of domestic raw materials, and expansion of the energy and mining industries.

In September 1975, the thirtieth year since the liberation from Japan, North Korea announced the successful achievement of almost all targets which had been set for the six-year plan—a year and four months earlier than planned. The exceptions were steel and cement production. The announced rate of growth in the gross value of industrial output during the four-and-a-half-year period was 18.4 percent per year, a considerably higher rate than the planned 14 percent. Yet, there are no details on actual performance, even in such areas as mining and shipbuilding, on which great emphasis had been placed. An interesting aspect of the accelerated completion of the plan was the alleged contribution of the "three-revolution teams" dispatched to factories and enterprises beginning in 1973. The teams, according to the official version, were organized and led by Kim Jong Il, thus laying a groundwork for his eventual rise to power.

The price of the premature completion of the six-year plan appeared to be very high indeed, both internally and externally. Internally, not only had the remaining months of 1975 and the year 1976 to be devoted to catching up on the uncompleted parts of the plan, but 1977 was also designated as the "year of adjustment," strongly suggesting that the economy was in considerable disarray. Externally, the new policy of massive modernization resulted in a rapid accumulation of foreign debts, which we shall discuss later in some detail. In December 1977, the "year of adjustment," the second seven-year plan, for 1978–1984, was finally adopted.

Several events may have led North Korea to drastic policy changes in the early 1970s, when the East-West détente became a fact. That is, the Eastern European socialist countries also underwent a major policy reorientation and started to import advanced Western technologies. At the same time, several developed capitalist countries were actively competing for markets in the Soviet-bloc countries. China had been trading primarily with Japan and other noncommunist countries ever since the Sino-Soviet rift began, and the dramatic rapprochement with the United States occurred in 1972.

Some internal reasons provided additional incentives to North Korea to reassess its policy of economic dependence exclusively on the Soviet Union and China and pushed it to actively seek greater independence. First, of course, was the disappointing experience with both countries during the seven-year plan period of the 1960s, which had had to be extended for three additional years. Second, one of the crucial components of success in the six-year plan of 1971–1976 was to have been the technological revolution. Yet, without modernizing the existing productive capacity, which consisted mostly of outdated Soviet and East European machinery and equipment and domestic copies of them, the technological revolution would have been simply impossible. A third and perhaps more direct reason for North Korean independence was the pressure from South Korea. The South Korean economy had been rapidly developing for some time by 1971. The North Korean leadership may have realized the severity of their economic problems would not be eased unless some major changes in their policy were adopted. A fourth and perhaps a more immediate reason was the desire to complete the six-year plan more than a year earlier than the originally planned date of December 1976. The push for an earlier completion of the plan was apparently to make it coincide with the commemoration in autumn of 1975 of the thirtieth anniversary of the liberation of Korea from Japan and the establishment of the party. The consequences of the policy change were to cause North Korea to embark on a large-scale import of Western machinery, equipment, and other technologies in 1972 and 1973, retaining strong economic ties with China and the Soviet Union at the same time.

North Korea continued to rely on trade with China and the Soviet Union (see Table 9-4). During the six-year plan of 1971–1976, North Korea's total trade volume, imports and exports, with the Soviet Union was $2,748 million, and with China $2,052 million, compared to $1,137 million with Japan, its major noncommunist trading partner. During the same period, North Korea's trade deficit with the Soviet Union was $692 million, $455 million with China, and $365 million with Japan.

The bold new policy of North Korea which emerged in the early 1970s, to look toward the West for a massive infusion of machinery, equipment, and modern technology, produced problems that the North Korean leadership had not expected—rapidly mounting international hard-currency debts and subsequent problems of widespread delay of payment starting in the mid-1970s. The exact magnitude of North Korea's hard-currency debts to the West is not known, though various estimates converge around a billion dollars by the end of 1975.

A combination of variables adversely affected North Korea's balance of payments. One of the leading factors was the oil crisis of late 1973 and the ensuing worldwide "stagflation." After the crisis, the Soviet price for oil eventually increased considerably, though we do not know whether North Korea pays the CMEA price or the world price, which is always higher. On the other hand, the worldwide recession apparently caused a sharp decline in the prices of nonferrous metals and pig iron, the kingpins of North Korea's exports. An official explanation of the debt problem hinted at the shipping, rail, and other transportation bottlenecks that prevented North Korea from delivering her export products in time. It is quite conceivable that there was a lack of modern ports and other transportation capacities needed to accommodate a rapidly expanding international flow of commodities. There are other factors that may also have

TABLE 9-4
North Korean Visible Mirror Trade with the World, USSR, China and Japan
1971–1986 (in millions of dollars)

		Year	Total	Import	Export	Balance
J a p a n	Six-Year Plan	1971	59.0	28.9	30.1	1.2
		1972	131.8	93.4	38.3	- 55.1
		1973	172.5	100.2	72.3	- 27.8
		1974	360.7	251.9	108.8	-143.1
		1975	245.5	180.6	64.8	-115.8
		1976	167.7	96.1	71 6	- 24.4
	Year of Adjustment	1977	191.7	125.1	66 6	- 58.5
	Second Seven-Year Plan	1978	290.2	183.8	106.9	- 76.5
		1979	435.9	283.3	152.2	-131.8
		1980	554.4	374.3	180.0	-194.3
		1981	430.5	291.0	139.5	-151.5
		1982	465.2	313.2	152.0	-161.5
		1983	453.2	327.1	126.1	-200.9
		1984	400.0	254.7	145.2	-109.5
	Years of Adjustment	1985	426.4	247.1	179.3	-67.8
		1986	357.2	184.0	173.2	-10.7
		1987	455.5	213.7	241.7	28.0
		1988	563.5	238.9	324.6	85.8
C h i n a	Six-Year Plan	1971	116.7	94.3	72.4	-21.9
		1972	283.1	164.4	118.6	-45.8
		1973	336.0	217.6	118.4	-99.2
		1974	390.0	243.3	146.3	-97.0
		1975	481.9	284.1	197.8	-86.3
		1976	395.0	250.0	145.0	-105.0
	Year of Adjustment	1977	374.4	227.2	147.2	-80.0
	Second Seven-Year Plan	1978	454.3	230.1	223.6	-7.1
		1979	647.2	317.0	330.2	13.2
		1980	687.3	411.6	275.2	-135.9
		1981	540.4	329.9	210.5	-119.4
		1982	586.1	309.5	276.6	-32.9
		1983	531.8	300.7	231.1	-69.6
		1984	528.0	241.0	287.0	46.0

TABLE 9–4
North Korean Visible Mirror Trade with the World, USSR, China and Japan
1971–1986 (in millions of dollars)

		Year	Total	Import	Export	Balance
C h i n a	*Years of Adjustment*	1985	473.0	231.0	242.0	11.0
		1986	514.3	239.5	274.7	35.2
		1987	513.3	277.1	236.2	-40.9
		1988	579.1	345.4	233.7	-111.7
U S S R	*Six-Year Plan*	1971	502.6	366.3	135.8	-231.0
		1972	458.4	303.5	154.9	-148.6
		1973	480.6	301.3	179.3	-122.0
		1974	461.6	261.3	200.3	-61.0
		1975	468.5	258.8	209.7	-49.1
		1976	375.8	218.4	157.4	-61.0
	Year of Adjustment	1977	446.0	223.5	222.5	-1.0
	Second Seven-Year Plan	1978	552.5	257.9	294.6	36.7
		1979	749.8	358.9	390.9	32.0
		1980	880.4	443.1	437.3	-5.8
		1981	601.7	317.1	284.6	-32.5
		1982	774.3	362.1	412.2	50.1
		1983	667.8	298.3	369.5	71.2
		1984	909.2	442.9	466.3	23.5
	Years of Adjustment	1985	1,215.0	749.5	485.1	-300.4
		1986	1,620.0	1,078.6	542.2	-436.6
		1987	2,046.7	1,329.2	717.4	-611.8
		1988	2,617.2	1,735.6	881.5	-854.1
W o r l d	*Six-Year Plan*	1971	871.6	319.9	551.7	-231.8
		1972	1,058.1	408.4	649.7	-241.3
		1973	1,361.9	497.6	864.3	-366.7
		1974	2,004.6	718.5	1,286.1	-567.6
		1975	1,946.2	838.2	1,108.0	-269.8
		1976	1,468.0	593.9	874.1	-280.2
	Year of Adjustment	1977	1,592.3	784.8	807.5	-22.7
	Second Seven-Year Plan	1978	2,209.41	1,247.2	962.2	285.0
		1979	2,880.3	1,554.8	1,325.5	229.3
		1980	3,028.9	1,531.3	1,497.6	337.3
		1981	2,381.3	1,092.9	1,288.4	-195.6

TABLE 9-4
North Korean Visible Mirror Trade with the World, USSR, China and Japan
1971–1986 (in millions of dollars)

		Year	Total	Import	Export	Balance
W o r l d		1982	2,480.8	1,168.9	1,311.9	-143.1
		1983	2,205.3	1,006.8	1,198.5	-191.7
		1984	2,325.1	1,182.1	1,143.0	39.1
	Years of Adjustment	1985	2,325.3	961.3	1,364.0	-402.7
		1986	3,131.0	1,318.6	1,812.4	-493.8
		1987	3,664.3	2,260.2	1,404.1	-856.1
		1988	4,512.9	2,838.8	1,674.0	-1,164.8

Sources : for Japan, JETRO, *Kita Chosen no Keizai To Boeki no Tenbou*, 1987, 1988, and 1989. For China, *Zhong Guo Jing Ji Nian Jian*. 1987. JETRO, op. cit. For the Soviet Union, *Trade Statistics of USSR* (in Russian), each year. For World trade, UN Tapes, JETRO, op. cit., IMF, *Direction of Trade Statistics Year Book*.

aggravated the balance of payments problem—lack of experience in trade and finance with the West, and agricultural failure.

The basic and fundamental reason, however, seems to have been in North Korea's economy at the time. The economy was highly centralized and rigidly structured according to the ideology of *juche*, with tremendous emphasis on defense-oriented heavy industries. In other words, the North Korean economy was not structured to be competitive vis-à-vis noncommunist countries in the international market, either in consumer goods, which had been completely neglected in the past, or in the highly emphasized machinery and producer goods industry, except for nonferrous metals and metal products.

The first official North Korean announcement of the perceived need to trade with capitalist countries and to expand export capacity by upgrading quality as well as by gaining international confidence was made by Kim Il Sung at the Industrial Activists' Meeting on March 4, 1975.

> But from now on we must actively trade with emerging independent nations and capitalist countries. Under the circumstances when the economy is developing rapidly and new economic branches are

being created, we cannot satisfactorily meet all our needs if we depend only on socialist markets. Therefore, while continuing to rely on socialist markets, we must actively go out to capitalist markets to purchase materials and machinery we need....To carry out foreign trade well, we must decisively improve the quality of export goods. Since merchandise by nature is a thing produced not for one's own consumption but for sale to others, it should be of high quality. Of course, we must even make the products we turn out for domestic consumption neat and useful, but we must make export goods of a better quality.

Factories and enterprises turning out export goods should further improve the quality of products and pack them neatly. We must strive to win the reputation and confidence in the international market that our merchandise are very good. To carry out foreign trade successfully, it is important that we must put up the "confidence-first" principle.

While struggling to improve the quality of export goods with a correct view of foreign trade and factories, enterprises should thoroughly establish a system under which they fulfill their export plans ahead of schedule at the beginning of each month.

North Korean leaders continued to urge improvement of exports throughout the remaining 1970s. Although there was some shift of priority to the export goods, no major institutional changes took place during this period.

Second and Third Seven-Year Plans

In December 1977, the year of adjustment, the second seven-year plan was finally adopted, at the first meeting of the Sixth Supreme People's Assembly. The second seven-year plan in a sense is a reassessment of the major policy change initiated in 1972–1973. The new seven-year plan emphasized full utilization of existing productive capacity, which really was the original objective of the six-year plan before the policy shift in 1972–1973. The seven-year plan also listed self-reliance, modernization, and "scientification" of the economy as major goals. The targeted rate of growth in gross value of industry output during the plan period was 12.1 percent per year, the lowest in the postwar plans. Other targets and the final achievements announced are listed in Tables 9-5 and 9-6. Actual performance in industry during the first three years, 1978–1980, according to official publications exceeded the plan targets. This success was due, in part, to a series of "battles" carried out during these years, including the "Hundred Days' Battle" to commemorate the thirtieth anniversary of the North Korean liberation in September 1978. As has always been the case, the aftermath of forced acceleration of the plan apparently caused rather serious adverse effects in the economy by 1980. After 1981, there has been no publication of growth in gross industrial output, except for 1982—a sign of trouble. Table 9-7 shows two basic indices during the period. One can observe that the rate of increase in state revenue also significantly decreased in the 1980s, reaching a low of only four percent in 1986.

The economic problems of North Korea in the 1980s, it appears, stemmed not only from the fact that the leaders attempted a minimum change in domestic structure but also from the fact that they took a rather sudden and inexplicable turn in their economic direction, both domestic and external. The new direction was characterized by massive commemorative construction projects within the country, and expensive external campaigns directed toward the so-called nonaligned countries of the third world. Many programs were included which were clearly inconsistent with normal economic activities, including the successful completion of the second seven-year plan by 1984. In view of the fact that the new turn of events started with the Sixth Party Plenary Session in 1980, one wonders whether the change of direction was in some way connected to the fact that Kim Jong Il was there named to be his father's successor.

At the Sixth Party Plenary Session, North Korea announced ten major economic goals to be achieved by the end of the decade. These goals are much more ambitious than the targets of the second seven-year plan (as noted in Table 9-6). In 1981 North Korea launched "The Four Nature Recreation Projects," including 300,000 hectares of tideland reclamation, 200 hectares of new land development, the Nampo floodgate (lock), and the Taechon power generating station. Some massive beautification projects for the "Capital of the Revolution" started after the Party Plenum. These major efforts, however, officially billed as "great monumental construction projects," were oriented around celebration of Kim's seventieth birthday in April

Table 9–5
North Korea's Seven-Year Plans

	Second Seven-Year Plan		Third Seven-Year Plan
	Targets	Achievements	Targets
Gross value of social output	—	—	1.8 fold
Gross value of industrial output	2.2 fold	2.2 fold	1.9 fold
(Annual growth rate)	12.1	12.2	10.0
Producer goods	2.2 fold	2.2 fold	1.9 fold
Consumer goods	2.1 fold	2.1 fold	1.8 fold
Gross value of agricultural output	—	—	1.4 fold
National income	1.9 fold	1.8 fold	1.7 fold
Workers' real income	—	1.6 fold	1.6 fold
Farmers' real income	—	1.4 fold	1.7 fold
Rail freight transportation	1.7 fold	1.8 fold	1.6 fold
Automobile freight transport	4.0 fold	2.2 fold	2.6 fold
Investment in basic construction	—	1.5 fold	1.6 fold
Retail commodity flows	1.9 fold	1.9 fold	2.1 fold
Foreign trade volume	—	—	3.2 fold
Labor productivity in industry	1.7 fold	—	1.6 fold
Labor productivity in construction	1.6 fold	—	1.5 fold
Cost savings in industry per year (percentage)	3.7	—	3.4
Cost savings in construction per year (percentage)	5.1	—	4.6

Source: Premier Li Gun Mo's report on the third seven-year Plan presented at the second meeting of the Eighth Supreme People's Congress on April 21, 1987.

1982. These projects included a 170-meters-high "Tower of Juche Idea," a 60-meters-high "Arch of Triumph," and the expansion of a huge stadium, among others.

Though any of these projects may serve useful economic purposes, their cost must have been very high because a great amount of human and material resources would have had to be diverted from the immediate and normal processes of carrying out the annual plans and the second seven-year plan. In

TABLE 9–6
North Korea's Second Seven-Year Plan, Ten Major Goals,
and Third Seven-Year Plan

Categories	Second Seven-Year Plan			Third Seven-Year Plan
	Targets	Achievements		Targets
Electricity (billion KWH)	56–60	—	100	100
Coal (million ton)	70–80	70	120	120
Steel (million ton)	7.4–8.0	—	13	10
Nonferrous metals (million ton)	1	—	1.5	1.7
Chemical fertilizer (million ton)	5	4.7	7	7.2
Cement (million ton)	12–13	—	20	22
Textiles (100 million meter)	8	8	15	15
Grain (million ton)	10	—	15	15
Tideland reclamation (1,000 ha)	100	—	300	300
Marine Products (million ton)	3.5	3.5	5	11
Machinery	5 mil. ton	(2.3 fold)	—	(2.5 fold)
Chemical yarn (1,000 ton)	(1.8 fold)	(1.8 fold)	—	225
Local industry	(2.4 fold)	—	—	(2.5 fold)
Rice (million ton)		—	—	7
Livestock (1,000 ton)	800–900	—	—	1,700
Eggs (billion)	—	—	—	7
Fruit (million ton)	1.5	—	—	2
Housing construction (1,000 households)	200–300	—	—	150 a year
Doctors (per 10,000)	—	—	—	43

Source: Based on official announcements. Second and Third Seven-Year Plan figures are quoted from Teruo Komaki. "North Korea's Economy Today and Prospects," in *Kironi Tatsu Kita Chose* (North Korea at the crossroads), (Tokyo: Japan Institute of International Affairs, 1988), p. 66.

TABLE 9–7
Annual Growth Rates of North Korea's Industrial Output and State Revenue

		Gross value of industrial Output %	State revenue %
Six-Year Plan	(1971-76)	16.3	15.4
	1977	—	9.2
	1978	17.0	13.5
	1979	15.0	11.5
	1980	17.0	9.5
	1981	—	8.1
	1982	16.8	9.6
	1983	—	7.5
	1984	—	7.9
Second Seven-Year Plan	(1978-84)	12.2	—
	1985	—	4.3
	1986	—	4.0
	1987	—	6.3
	1988	—	5.1
Third Seven-Year Plan	(1987-93)	10.0 (Plan)	

Source: Various official announcements.

his 1982 New Year's message Kim urged that top priority be given to the "Four Nature Recreation Projects" and that all kinds of materials, machinery, and equipment be provided toward the goals. In view of other urgent economic needs, the opportunity cost of these grand projects, which usually require a long gestation period, must have been very high, indeed. There are some disquieting indications that the targets of the second seven-year plan may not have been achieved as the official announcements claimed. First, there are many projects whose results were not published. Those items for which the achievements were announced are almost identical to the elements of the original plan. Second, as the final year of the plan, 1984, approached, fewer references were made to achieving the plan targets. Instead, greater emphasis was placed on achieving the ten major economic goals. The results of the

Second Seven-Year Plan were not even mentioned in Kim's New Year's message, but on Kim Jong Il's birthday in February 1985. A comprehensive report was also made by the Premier Li Gun Mo two years later, in April of 1987, when he outlined the third seven-year plan.[3]

North Korea continued to trade with advanced capitalist countries. Japan, in spite of the well-known deficit problems, is still North Korea's major trading partner. In more recent years, Korean residents in Japan have played an increasingly prominent role in trade and economic cooperation with North Korea. During the second seven-year plan, North Korea's trade deficit with Japan accumulated more than a billion dollars (see Table 9-4). For China, the period coincided with the beginning of the reform movement initiated in December 1978. North Korea's trade deficit with China, nevertheless, amounted to $306 million during the period.

A major shift in trade relations with the Soviets occurred (see Table 9-4). Although North Korea's trade volume with the Soviet Union was larger than that with any other country, North Korea maintained a surplus of $175 million between 1978 and 1984. This surplus is evidence that North Korea began partial payment of past debts, imposing a considerable hardship on its economy. After the lengthy visit of Kim Il Sung in the Soviet Union and East Europe in 1984, however, there was a sudden and dramatic increase in North Korean imports from the Soviet Union and an unprecedented trade deficit was the result in 1985, 1986, 1987 and 1988. A major trade policy decision, announced in January 1984 at the third meeting of the Seventh Supreme People's Congress, was made to increase North Korea's trade volume with communist countries more than tenfold within the next five to six years. There may or may not have been any connection between the decision and the drastic changes in trade with the Soviets.

After completion of the second seven-year plan, two more years of adjustment, in 1985 and 1986, were needed before beginning the third seven-year plan, 1987–1993, which was finally adopted in April of 1987. The delay of two years was perhaps necessary in order to have time to carefully evaluate all the results of the second seven-year plan. Moreover, definite long-term commitments for economic cooperation from China and the Soviet Union were indispensable in finalizing the plan. A long-term accord for the period 1986–1990 was concluded in February 1986 with the Soviet Union. In September 1986 China also signed a cooperative agreement with North Korea covering 1987–1991.[4]

The main objectives of the third seven-year plan are: (1) to rapidly develop science and technology in order to promote a technological revolution in the economy, (2) to realize the ten major economic goals by improving productivity, and (3) to solve the problems of food, clothing, and shelter in order to improve the standard of living for the people. However, the primary content of the third seven-year plan emphasized attaining the ten major economic goals by 1993 instead of by the end of the 1980s as had originally been proposed (see tables 9-5 and 9-6). In general, targets are somewhat less ambitious than those of the second seven-year plan. For example, the planned rate of growth in gross value of industrial output decreased to 10 percent a year from 12.1 percent in the earlier seven-year plan. Nevertheless, in view of the deteriorating economic environment of North Korea, a successful completion of the third seven-year plan is highly doubtful unless, of course, North Korea is willing to implement the various desperately needed reform measures.

Economic Reform in the 1980s

For an inward-looking and rigidly planned economy like North Korea's, two closely interrelated aspects of economic reform are needed. One is a change in its basic structure, and the other is an open-door policy. Restructuring here refers to decentralization as well as some introduction of market forces in the economic decisionmaking process. The open-door policy here refers to measures of economic cooperation, especially with noncommunist countries. In view of recent events in China, a comprehensive economic reform clearly necessitates reform of the highly centralized political system itself.

North Korea initiated a major reorientation of her foreign trade policy in the early 1970s and attempted a bolder and more open policy in the 1980s. The more open policy thus far has achieved limited success, largely because of constraints imposed by the rigidity of North Korea's domestic economic

structure, which underwent only a minimal change. Our con-
jecture is that the North Korean leadership has been reluctant
to carry out the necessary domestic restructuring until now
primarily because such reform may be in direct conflict with
such major political goals as the smooth succession to power of
Kim Jong Il and achievement of the North Korean version of
unification with the South.

Reform in Economic Structure in the 1980s

North Korea's efforts to reform its domestic economic structure thus far have been limited to primarily organizational
changes in order to achieve "normalization of production at a
higher level." Although there have been some attempts to
increase the decision-making authority of enterprises, no efforts have been made to introduce market mechanisms into the
economy and allow enterprises to use them. In the 1980s, there
was a flood of government statements and articles in the party
newspapers and magazines emphasizing the need for reform.
Yet sifting through the documents, one finds proposals for few
domestic reforms as this paper has defined them. However,
three types of propositions that come close to reform have been
discussed. They are: (1) transfer of economic management to
the provinces, (2) integration of enterprises, and (3) State
Council Decision No. 20, which attempts, among other things,
to increase enterprise autonomy and to inject material incentives for some workers.

Transfer of Management to the Provinces.   In Kim Il Sung's
1982 New Year's message, he revealed that a comprehensive
reorganization of the industrial management system was
adopted in 1981. The new system, known to have been initiated
by Kim Jong Il, was the Provincial (municipal in the case of
"special cities") Economic Commission.[5] This was an organization directly under the State Council that was in charge of
managing all the economic affairs of the province. The commissioner had a rank comparable to that of a cabinet minister
and was appointed by the central government. Some of the factories and enterprises formerly under various cabinet ministries were transferred and placed under the jurisdiction of the
Prov- incial Economic Commission. The commission had

authority not only over the production of enterprises under its control, but also over their construction, the supplies of productive factors to them, the sales of their products, and even over their foreign trade.

This measure represented a reform in the sense that the control of some selected industries was transferred to the province where the factories are located and they were given greater autonomy than they had had under the ministry. Nevertheless, central control was very much retained by the commissioner, who was responsible to the State Council.[6] In May 1985, the Provincial Economic Commission became the Provincial Administrative and Economic Commission, whose new responsibility has not been made public. There is a possibility that the party's political administration is now merged with economic management, in which case any true reform will now be reversed. This suspicion is reinforced by the fact that in May 1985 the province party secretary also became the head of the province's people's committee.[7]

Integration of Enterprises. In July 1985, North Korea announced the upgrading of many enterprises to become integrated enterprises, each with greater autonomy. In fact, ten years earlier, in 1975, North Korea had converted several major enterprises into integrated form and gave expanded authority to them.[8] There are two types of integrated enterprises. One involves vertical integration of a key enterprise with others which have production and technical linkages with it. The other type involves a horizontal integration of several enterprises producing the same products and combines them with other complementary enterprises. By September 1986, the total number of integrated enterprises had reached 120; 61 were controlled by the central government, and the remaining 59 were placed under the management of the Provincial Administrative and Economic Commission.[9]

Based on the fragmentary information available, integrated enterprises appear to represent some degree of decentralization of decisionmaking, especially in the areas of production, sales, transportation, and material supplies. The managers of integrated enterprises during the upgrading of the mid-1970s reported directly to the cabinet minister instead of to the ministry bureau. After 1985, the authority to sign contracts for material supplies was transferred from the cabinet ministry to the integrated enterprises. The managers of integrated enterprises now have discretionary power to sell to other enterprises or even to export abroad a portion of their products in excess of the production quota. It is also said that the managers, within limits, have authority to send some employees abroad for the purpose of study or observation.[10]

State Council Decision No. 20. The decision of the State Council on April 22, 1986, which became law, is another attempt to increase the discretionary power of enterprises and to provide material incentives to laborers. All of the productive enterprises are using a so-called independent accounting system. These enterprises, "by improving management and by maintaining the balance between revenue and expenditure, must be able to meet expenditure with its own revenue and contribute a fixed profit to the state."[11] The new State Council Decision No. 20 increased the portion of excess profit that the enterprises can retain from 20 percent to up to 50 percent. "Excess profit" here refers to the profit beyond the mandatory sum that the enterprise must contribute to the state. According to Decision No. 20, those enterprises which earn foreign exchange can use up to 70 percent of what is gained to import machinery, equipment, and raw materials, with the approval of the appropriate state organizations.[12]

Decision No. 20, as a method of increasing material incentives for workers, introduced a variety of piecework wage rates. For example, for middle- or small-size enterprises, (smaller than class 4 enterprises), the maximum piece-rate wage was set at 130 percent of the basic wage. For larger enterprises, class 3 or above, the maximum limit for the piece-rate wage was eliminated. For an integrated mining enterprise, for example, a team of ten people used to form a unit which received piecework assignments. The size of the team is now decreased to four or five people; and, with the new piece-rate wage system, some workers earn income three or four times the basic wage. Decision No. 20 offered not only a carrot but also a stick; it eliminated the guarantee of basic wages to workers not performing the required work.[13]

There have been other measures to stimulate management autonomy in recent years in North Korea. For instance, some enterprises since 1985 have been allocated their planned production quota in value terms instead of in quantities. The composition of products representing the plan value was left to the discretion of the enterprise management. Banks no longer allocate circulating capital to enterprises as before. Now the banks provide loans to enterprises, charging differential rates of interest between the planned fund and the amount in excess of the plan.[14]

Following two speeches by Kim Jong Il on February 16 and August 3 of 1984, great emphasis has been placed on improving the people's standard of living. In consequence, the "light industry revolution" and the "service revolution" became North Korea's bywords. Nevertheless, there has been no major shift in North Korea's economic priorities in favor of light and consumer goods industries. Instead, the people were urged to set up workshops within enterprises, increase agricultural sidelines to produce more daily necessities, and distribute them through "August 3 consumer goods stores" set up throughout North Korea.[15] A statement revealing a glimpse of North Korean living standards was made by North Korean Premier Li Gun Mo. On April 21, 1987, at the second meeting of Eighth Supreme People's Congress, in reporting on the third seven-year plan (1987–1993), Li stated that

> by 1993, we will be able to solve problems of food, clothing and shelter for our people and to raise [our standard of living] to a new and a higher level. We, therefore, will be able to eat white rice with meat soup, wear silk clothes, and live in a tile-roofed house to gloriously materialize our people's desire of this century to live in happiness.[16]

An Economic Open-Door Policy

There are two benchmark periods as far as North Korea's open-door policy is concerned. The first was the early 1970s, when a dramatic reorientation of trade toward the West began. The second was in the 1980s, especially during 1984, when North Korea announced its plan for a joint-venture program. Attempts to expand trade with the West, as discussed earlier, resulted in a rapidly mounting hard-currency deficit in the 1970s. Since then, North Korea's external debts, especially hard-currency debts, have continued to increase, and problems of payment delay continued through the 1980s. This was the economic background which compelled North Korea to reassess her foreign economic policy in the 1980s, culminating in adoption of the Joint Venture Law in 1984.

Foreign Economic Policy in the 1980s. A sign of a new, open attitude was seen at the Sixth Party Plenary Session held October 10 to 14, 1980, when Western reporters were permitted to attend the meeting for the first time in North Korea, though with restrictions. The meeting, however, had a greater significance in confirming what everyone already knew—that is, that Kim Jong Il was going to be the successor to Kim Il Sung.

In foreign trade, North Korea appeared to have continuing problems of mounting deficits with advanced Western countries. The Soviet Union and China since the end of the six-year plan (1971–1976) no longer provide North Korea with aid disguised as trade deficits (see table 9-4). The major source of hard-currency surplus, Saudi Arabia, discontinued trade with North Korea after the outbreak of the Iran-Iraq war in 1981. Under these conditions, North Korea made a major trade policy decision in January 1984 at the third meeting of the Seventh Supreme People's Congress.

The content of the decision was somewhat new in the sense that it greatly emphasized trade with newly emerging developing countries and with other socialist countries. In fact, the new policy urged increasing trade volume with the socialist countries by more than ten times within the next five or six years. Dramatic increases in imports from the Soviet Union since 1985, after Kim's Soviet visit in 1984, may or may not be related to the January 1984 resolution. In spite of disappointing experiences with capitalist developed countries, the new resolution emphasized trade with friendly capitalist countries as well as with those with whom North Korea has no diplomatic relations, and it also urged technical exchange and economic cooperation with them. However, trade with capitalist developed countries still faced a major barrier, namely, the foreign debts that had not been settled in the nearly ten years since 1975. Attempts had to be made to attract direct investment, and a joint ventures law was thus adopted in September 1984.

Before the official announcement of the joint venture law, there had been a few joint operations in practice. For example, the British, possibly with American and Japanese involvement, had experimented with offshore oil drilling on the west coast of North Korea.[17] A North Korean official also mentioned that a North Korea-Poland Marine Transportation Company had been in operation before the law was adopted.[18]

The content of the North Korean joint venture law, despite official denial, was no doubt influenced by the Chinese experience. The essential parts are as follows: Projects are mainly to be in electronics, automation, mining, machine building, chemicals, food processing, clothing, construction, transportation, and tourism industries. The primary purposes of joint ventures are to introduce modern technology into North Korea, to improve product quality, and to contribute to expanding North Korean exports. No restriction on the amount or proportion of foreign capital for the projects was imposed, and the joint venture firm was to be managed under the direction of its board of trustees. Labor was to be hired and fired by the labor administration organization, though wage rates could be decided by the joint venture companies. There were to be no special economic zones.[19] Among the projects with noncommunist countries known thus far are the following:[20]

- *Yang Gak Do Hotel*: A well-publicized joint venture project was the construction of a modern 46-story hotel on the island of Yang Gak Do with a French construction company, Campenon Bernard. The hotel cost $12.8 million, shared equally between the French company and the North Korean government, and was to house all trade corporations as well as to serve foreign tourists. It was part of plan to build a prosperous but isolated foreign residence complex on the island in the Daedong River, which flows through Pyongyang. The project was to be completed by September 1987, but it has been rumored that the French firm had a number of disputes with North Korea.[21]
- *Kim Man Yu Hospital*: The Kim Man Yu medical facility was a joint venture with a Japanese hospital, which provided

modern medical technology and equipment while North Korea provided land and building. It was completed in April 1986 on 100,000 square meters; it is sixteen stores high, with 1,300 beds.

- *Rakwon (Paradise) Department Store*: Completed in February 1985, this project was jointly set up with a company owned by a Korean resident in Japan. There is a main store in Pyongyang with 31 branches throughout North Korea. It sells mostly Japanese products primarily to Japanese and foreigners in North Korea and accepts only foreign currency. High-quality Japanese consumer goods sold there will have some impact on most of the North Korean public, which seldom has had a chance even to see foreign consumer goods.[22]
- *Unsan Gold Mine*: This mine, initially started in 1896 by a United States mining company, is believed to contain deposits of up to 1,000 tons of gold. In April 1987, North Korea, jointly with Korean residents in Japan, decided to redevelop the mine and drastically increase its output. Mitsui is rumored to be willing to finance the project. The first eight ingots of about 100 kilograms arrived in Japan in July 1987.[23]

By October 1985, about ten projects had been agreed upon, with thirty more in the process of negotiation between North Korea and other countries. Among those confirmed were a metal tool factory in Nampo with Japan and a tire factory in Hamhung with Hong Kong. Other negotiations were going with such Western countries as Italy, for mineral exports; West Germany, for iron and steel; Sweden, for furniture; and France, for wine, beverages, and a satellite relay station.[24] So far, there has been no information as to the outcomes of those projects, which had been agreed upon or which were being negotiated.

Most other projects known to have been completed thus far have been done with Korean residents in Japan. Among them are a luggage factory, a supermarket, a tea room and restaurant mostly for foreigners, and other small-scale light industries. The list includes factories for bottles, clothing, food, candy, tissue paper, stainless sinks, and soy sauce. Recently the areas of joint venture have been expanded to include car batteries, engines, garments, construction materials, and chemical products. The joint ventures with Koreans in Japan by 1988 were said to number between eighteen and 44 projects.[25]

One gets the impression that North Korea is trying to rely primarily on pro-Pyongyang Korean residents in Japan in joint venture efforts. For example, a branch of the North Korean government, the Joint Venture Preparatory Committee, together with Joint Venture Research Group in Japan, formed a corporation, International Joint Venture Company, with $1.2 million capital. The head office is in Pyongyang, with a branch in Tokyo and other branch offices in Vienna, Wonsan, and Macao.[26] Another project, a conduit for bringing cash into North Korea, was set up in October 1987 with Koreans resident in Japan and North Korea's Rakwon Trading Company. They named the project the Rakwon Financial Joint Venture Company.[27]

In recent years, North Korea has changed its anti-tourism attitude and has become very much interested in attracting foreign visitors. Tour agencies in Hong Kong in 1985, in Great Britain in 1986, and in Japan in 1987 began to organize group tours to North Korea, sometimes including China in the package.[28]

As it has been only a few years since the new law was adopted, it is perhaps too early to make an assessment of North Korea's joint venture program. Nonetheless, in view of the initial fanfare, the results thus far must be very disappointing to North Korea. No doubt there are many complex and interrelated reasons for the lack of success. For example, North Korea's debts and inability to make agreed-upon payments poses a key barrier in attracting Western direct investment. The basic reason, however, for the failure to attract joint ventures must be the fact that North Korea retains one of the most rigid systems of economy, polity, and society. For instance, there exists an almost complete information blackout in North Korea. Foreigners know too little about the North Korean economy, enterprises, and business practices to have confidence in them. So far, there has been no change in politics and ideology and no indication of their future direction. In section 4 below, some conjectures are offered about North Korea's political goals and how they may be in conflict with desperately needed economic reform.

Conclusion

For external as well as internal reasons, comprehensive economic reform is imperative for North Korea. Reform attempts thus far have yielded little result, largely because of failure to implement a comprehensive domestic restructuring, an indispensable part of a successful open-door policy. The third seven-year plan, announced in April of 1987, does not show any signs of reform. Instead it retains very much the same command-type plan structure and a continued emphasis on heavy and producer goods industries. There is no reduced role for the party in economic decisionmaking, nor is there any emphasis on expanded trade with Western developed countries. The present political reality and the desires of the North Korean leadership to maintain the same political goals may present the major barriers to a comprehensive program of economic reform.

The most remarkable feature of the polity in North Korea is Kim Il Sung's cult of personality and his nepotistic dictatorship, his son, Kim Jong Il being designated his successor. The people are constantly reminded by the party that North Korea is "the socialist paradise on earth." In order to preserve the personality cult as practiced in North Korea, and in order for the people to believe in the notion of "the paradise," the party must continue to pursue two policies. One, the party must retain very tight control, directly or indirectly, over the people, over enterprises, and over all other units to guarantee their unconditional loyalty to the present leadership. Two, the party must continue to isolate the people from the outside world, in particular from those countries which may disprove the notion that North Korea is paradise on earth. On the other hand, in order for North Korea to achieve some of the goals emphasized in the 1980s—normalization of production at a higher level, technological revolution, more rational management of the economy and enterprises, and above all a higher standard of living for the people—it must carry out a comprehensive economic reform that includes decentralization of economic decisionmaking and an open-door policy with noncommunist countries.

The North Korean leadership is no doubt aware of the widely accepted notion that comprehensive economic reform necessarily requires a corresponding political reform. An example of the close interrelationship between economic and political reform can be seen in the recent Chinese experience.

At a symposium on the "Theory of Political Structural Reform" held in Beijing in late October of 1986, the majority of more than a hundred experts from various professions agreed that

> The current political reforms derive their motive power directly from the contradiction inherent in having an overcentralized political system and developing a commodity economy. With the development of the commodity economy and of the reforms, and economic policy-making power becomes decentralized. The economic changes demand corresponding political reforms and decentralization to wit:
> (1) Reform the highly centralized and directly controlled administrative management system....
> (2) Reform the highly centralized cadre system....
> (3) Reform the people's congress system....
> (4) Create an environment conducive to competition on an equal footing in order to encourage public participation in politics.[29]

The North Korean leadership, which has been carefully watching the developments in China, may regard the social and political by-products of the comprehensive reform attempts with great caution and perhaps with considerable dismay. As many Chinese conservatives lamented economic reform in China, North Korean leaders may view, for example, the decentralization of enterprises as a denial of the party's leadership, material incentives and the introduction of market mechanisms as a creeping tendency toward private ownership and therefore capitalism, and the open-door policy as a major source of bourgeois liberalism and spiritual pollution. The North Korean leadership's reluctance notwithstanding, pressure for reform is mounting from all directions. In addition to domestic economic problems, there are subtle pressures from two major allies, China and the Soviet Union. A new and much more accommodating attitude was revealed by the new leader, Roh Tae Woo, in South Korea in his July 1988, announcement. Already, North Korean coal is being imported directly into South Korea without going through Japan, as was the practice in the recent past. More than anything else, North Korea's leadership may have begun to recognize that the majority of

North Koreans, although never publicly admitting it, know in their hearts that they are not living in paradise.

In a tightly controlled society like North Korea what really is happening in the outside world must be whispered around by word-of-mouth. In the past, some top officials frequently traveled abroad. In last two or three years, North Korea began to send more scholars and students to China and East European countries for a period of two or more years. A large number of North Korean peasants are permitted to visit their relatives in the Yanbian region of China, where many Chinese Koreans have greatly increased their contacts with South Koreans.

For a number of reasons, the North Korean leadership cannot indefinitely postpone the reform by insisting North Korea is truly the socialist paradise on earth. On the other hand, the latest developments in China and Eastern Europe no doubt pose a major challenge and dilemma to the present leadership. China's economic and political reform efforts suffered a major setback after the Tiananmen incident of June, 1989, while the policies of *glasnost* and *perestroika* in the Soviet Union resulted in revolutionary changes in East European communist countries, including even the execution of Romania's Nikolae Ceausescu in December 1989. It is highly unlikely that North Korea will attempt any comprehensive economic and political reform in the near future because such reform will surely result in a drastic change in the present political structure. It is a dilemma for North Korea because the longer its leadership delays the urgently needed reform, the further North Korea will be isolated from even its former communist allies, and the serious economic problems that now confront North Korea will be further aggravated. Already Hungary and Poland have formal diplomatic relations with South Korea, whose economy continues its dynamic growth despite labor disputes and other problems.

Sooner or later, a strong wind of change will blow even in North Korea. This will be particularly true when the succession to power, of Kim Jong Il or anyone else, is completed, regardless of the circumstances surrounding the succession. A new leader who assumes power after a long dictatorial rule usually pursues a policy which is more popular and will visibly benefit the mass of people.

The long-run prognosis for the North Korean economy is good. At present, North Korea has a respectable industrial base compared to many developing countries, an endowment of substantial natural resources, and above all a population of hard-working Koreans whose productivity could be considerably improved provided they were offered proper material incentives instead of incessant battle cries to create so-called "moral" incentives.

Notes

1. Kim Il Sung, "For a Complete Victory of Socialism" (in Korean), speech at the first meeting of the Eighth Supreme People's Assembly (SPA), December 1986.
2. *Getskan Chosen Shiryo* (Monthly Korean affairs), May 1987, 38.
3. Teruo Komaki, "Kita Chosen Deizai no Genjo to Den bou: (North Korean economy's present and prospects), in *Kiron Tatsu Kita Chosen* (North Korea at the crossroads) (Tokyo: Japan Institute of International Affairs, 1988), 61.
4. Ibid., 69.
5. Japan External Trade Organization (JETRO), *Kita Chosen no Keizai to Boeki no Den bou* (Prospects of North Korean economy and trade), 1981–1982, hereafter referred to as Prospects.
6. Ko, Niten, "On Strengthening Self-Supporting Accounting System in Korean Socialist Economic Construction" (in *Getskan Chosen Shiryo* (Monthly Korean affairs), July 1987, 59–60.
7. Japan External Trade Organization (JETRO), *Prospects, 1985–1986*, 24.
8. Hyun Sung Il, "Development of Korea's Industrial Management System" (in Korean), *Tongil Ronchong* 5 (1985): 5.
9. Ko, "Self-Supporting Accounting System," 60–61.
10. Chosen Shiho, September 1, 1986, quoted by Dakeki Komura, "Aims of Third Seven-Year Plan in North Korea" (in Japanese), *Korea Hyoron*, July 1987, 28. See also *Rodong Sinmun*, September 10, 1987, cited in the Economists Intelligence Unit, *Quarterly Economic Review of China and North Korea*, Country Report No. 4, 1987, 29.
11. "Regulation on Self-Supporting Accounting System of National Enterprises," *Minju Chosun*, February 13 to May 1, 1985, Reprinted in Japanese in *Nicho Baeki*, September 15, 1985, 6.
12. Ko, "Self-Supporting Accounting System," 62.
13. *Chosen Shiho*, June 6, 1986, cited in Ko, "Self-Supporting Accounting System," 62.
14. Ibid., 61–62.
15. Komura, "Aims of Third Seven-Year Plan," 22–23.

16. Quoted from *Rodong Sinumn.* April 22, 1987, 5.
17. Hyun, "Development of North Korea's Industrial Management Systems," 162, quotes an article in *Petroleum Economists,* September 1979.
18. *Nicho Boeki,* October 15, 1984, 13.
19. Teruo Komaki, ed., *Chosen Hanto* (peninsulaKorean peninsula) (Tokyo: Institute of Developing Economies, 1986), 121; H.C. Yeon, *Pukhan Ui Kyong Je Jong Chaik Kwa Unyong* (North Korea's economic policy and operation), Seoul: Korea Development Institute, 1986, 74.
20. There have been many joint venture projects with the Soviet Union in recent years involving such products as aluminum, electric batteries, electric wires, and garments. See Economists Intelligence Unit, *Quarterly Economic Review of China and North Korea,* 1987, no. 2, no. 3; 1988, no. 1, no. 2, no. 3.
21. Komaki, *Chosen Hanto,* 124; Yeon, *Pukhan Ui Kyong Je Jong Chaik Kwa Unyong,* Kuni Akira, *Gendai Korea,* December 1985, 52.
22. Komaki, *Chosen Hanto,* 125; Yeon, *Pukhan Unyong,* 77.
23. Economists Intelligence Unit, *Quarterly Economic Review of China and North Korea,* 1987, no. 2, 46–47, and 1987, no. 4, 32.
24. *Nicho Boeki,* October 1, 1985; Yeon, *Pukan...Unyong,* 77.
25. *Gendai Korea,* May 1986, 16; July, 1986, 17; Economists Intelligence Unit, *Quarterly Economic Review on China and Korea,* 1988, no. 1, 39–40; no. 2, 39.
26. *Gendai Korea,* November 1986, 32.
27. Economists Intelligence Unit, *Quarterly Economic Review of China and Korea,* 1988, no. 1, 40. (Korea on November 26, 1988, announced a new Ministry of Joint Venture Industry.)
28. Ibid., December 1986, 57; Yeon, *Pukhan...Unyong,* 77.
29. *Beijing Review,* November 17, 1986, 14.

References

Books

1. Japan External Trade Organization (JETRO). *Kita Chosen no Keizai to Boeki no Denbou* (Prospects of Korean economy and trade. Annuals, Tokyo, 1982 to 1989.
2. Komaki, Teruo, ed. *Chosen Hanto* (Korean Peninsula). Tokyo: Institute of Developing Economies, 1986.
3. Okonogi, Masao, ed. *Kironi Tatsu Kita Chosen* (North Korea at the crossroads). Tokyo: Japan Institute of International Affairs, 1988. English translation of the same book is also available.
4. Yeon, H.C. *Pukhan Ui Kyong Je Jong Chaik Kwa Unyong* (North Korea's economic policy and operation). Seoul: Korea Development Institute, 1986.

Periodicals

1. Hyun, Sung Il. "Development of North Korea's Industrial Management System" (in Korean). *Tongil Ronchong*, vol. 5, 1985.
2. Ko, Niten. "On Strengthening Self-Supporting Accounting System in Korean Socialist Economic Construction" (in Japanese). *Getskan Chosen Shiryo* (Monthly Korean affairs), July 1987.
3. Komura, Dakeki. "Aims of Third Seven Year Plan in North Korea" (in Japanese). *Korea Hyoron*, July 1987.
4. Kuni, Akira. *Gendai Korea*, December 1985.

Others

1. *Beijing Review*, November 17, 1986.
2. *Chosen Shiho* (in Japanese) Tokyo, September 1, 1986.
3. Economist Intelligence Unit. *Quarterly Economic Review of China and North Korea, Country Report,*. no. 2, no. 3, no. 4, 1987; no. 1, no. 2, no. 3, no. 4, 1988.
4. *Gendai Korea* (in Japanese), May, 1986; July, 1986; November, 1986.
5. *Getskan Chosen Shiryo* (in Japanese), May 1987.
6. Kim Il Sung. "For a Complete Victory of Socialism" (in Korean), Speech at the first meeting of Eighth Supreme People's Assembly, December 1986.
7. *Minju Chosun* (in Korean), February 13 to May 1, 1985.
8. *Nicho Boeki* (in Japanese) September 15, 1985; October 1, 1985.
9. *Rodong Shinmun* (in Korean), September 10, 1987; April 22, 1987.

10

The Politics
of U.S.-Korean
Economic Relations

Young Whan Kihl

ECONOMIC NATIONALISM IS ON THE RISE both in the United States
and in the Republic of Korea as trade imbalances and disputes
between the two nations have escalated in recent years. Faced
with mounting trade frictions, the challenge to the Korean
government of President Roh Tae Woo and the United States
administration of President George Bush will be to sustain the
alliance structure intact while minimizing and containing the
political damage accruing from trade and economic conflict.[1]

Nationalism is historically a powerful force in world politics.
Not surprisingly, nationalism has found its expression in the
domestic political environment of the United States and Korean trade relations. The enactment of the Omnibus Trade and
Competitiveness Act of 1988, overriding presidential veto of an
earlier version, is an expression of the growing concern of the
U.S. Congress over the deteriorating American position in
world trade. The final version of the law, which President
Ronald Reagan signed, was watered down from the much
tougher initial "protectionist" legislation. But a "nationalistic"
sentiment in demands for a "free" and "fair" world trading

system fostered this historic legislation. The Seoul government's resistance to United States pressures for market-opening is often defended by nationalist elements in Korea. Radical student leaders in South Korea, for instance, have attempted to exploit the trade issue by inciting anti-American sentiment while promoting their own agenda for further democratization and politicization in South Korea.

Economic nationalism is often fueled by perceptions and fears as much as by facts. Emotionalized and distorted perceptions tend to cloud the economic issues. For this reason we must separate myths from facts regarding the politics of United States-Korea economic relations.

Image and Reality in Trade Conflict

Popular Images of South Korea in the United States

A prevailing perception in the United States is that South Korea is an "unfair" trade partner. This image has ben promoted and perpetuated by protectionist interest groups and is reinforced by the mass media. Lobbying activities by interest groups against foreign competition are defended on the grounds that foreigners are taking jobs away from American workers and are causing their standard of living to suffer and decline as a result.

United States industries are said to be losing the "competitive edge" to foreign companies because foreign production costs are supposedly unreasonably low and because their workers receive unduly low wages as compared with workers in the United States. These practices by foreign companies are therefore "unfair," and the United States must oppose the exploitative policies of these countries in allowing their workers to be deprived of their rightful higher wages.

This view of South Korea as an unfair trading partner is unfortunate, misleading, and also somewhat dangerous from the standpoint of the United States-Korea alliance. Like all misperceptions, it is a product of the tendency to simplify a reality that is often more complex. It depends on cliches and stereotypical views. Some of popular images of South Korea that are perpetuated in the media in the United States include the following: Korea is a "new" or "second" Japan whose

Mexico, Taiwan, and the United Kingdom, in that order (see Table 10-2).

Growing United States-Korea Trade Imbalance

As the United States trade deficit escalated in the 1980s, reaching a record of $173.7 billion in 1987, South Korea was held responsible for part of the United States' economic difficulties. The balance between the two countries since 1982 has been decidedly in favor of South Korea. The United States trade deficit with South Korea increased, for instance, from $162 million in 1982 to $9.6 billion in 1987 and $8.6 billion in 1988. As the United States trade deficit with Korea remains unacceptably high—an estimated $5–6 billion in 1989—it is precisely in order to stem the trend of increasing trade imbalance that the United States government has begun to exert pressure on Seoul. The United States criticizes Seoul authorities for not doing enough to open Korea's "protected" domestic markets and increase its import of American products.

TABLE 10–2
United States Leading Trade Partners (1987)

Country	Exports		Imports		Balance	
	billions	share of total	billions	share of total	billions	share of total
1. Canada	$59.80	(23.6)%	$71.50	(16.9)%	$-11.70	(6.8)%
2. Japan	28.20	(11.2)	88.10	(20.8)	-59.90	(35.0)
3. West Germany	11.70	(4.6)	28.00	(6.6)	-16.30	(9.5)
4. Mexico	14.60	(5.8)	20.50	(4.8)	-5.90	(3.4)
5. Taiwan	7.41	(2.9)	26.40	(6.2)	-18.99	(11.1)
6. United Kingdom	14.10	(5.6)	18.00	(4.2)	-3.90	(2.3)
7. Korea	8.10	(3.2)	18.00	(4.2)	-9.90	(5.8)
8. France	7.93	(3.1)	11.18	(2.6)	-3.25	(1.9)
9. Italy	5.53	(2.2)	11.70	(2.8)	-6.17	(3.6)
10. Hong Kong	3.98	(1.6)	10.50	(2.5)	-6.52	(3.8)
11. Others	91.55	(36.2)	120.22	(28.4)	-28.67	(16.8)
Total	$252.90	(100.0)%	$424.10	(100.0)%	$-171.20	(100.0)%

Source: U.S. Department of Commerce

In 1989 the United States-Korea trade disputes and negotiations revolved around both old and new issues. The American side charged that the Seoul government was too slow in implementing some of the trade agreements already entered into, such as protecting intellectual property rights. The United States side also demanded that progress be made in opening new economic sectors that are still protected. The agenda of new issues in bilateral trade negotiation in 1989 included

- Agriculture
- Service sector: banking, insurance, motion picture, advertising, civil aviation
- Foreign investment
- Protection of intellectual property rights
- Non-tariff barriers
- Co-production and technology transfer

United States pressure on South Korea to open its beef import market is the latest example of the mounting agricultural trade disputes. For reasons of domestic politics, in order not to alienate the farmers, the Seoul government has rejected the United States demand for opening South Korea's domestic market to imported beef. It hopes to adopt a policy of gradual increase in the volume and quota of imported beef for several years first, before heeding the American demand to liberalize its protected agricultural market completely. As the South Korean reluctance to acquiesce to United States demands became known, the United States brought its charges against South Korea to the GATT panel for violating the rule on free trade.

In short, the United States has grounds for demanding that South Korea abandon its policy of protecting its domestic markets and move to promote and sustain instead the liberal world trading system, of which South Korea has been a prominent beneficiary.

Policy Responses and Adjustment

United States Policy Responses in 1988

United States trade policy in 1988, on the eve of the November 1988 presidential election, was a curious mixture of the protectionist impulses of the U.S. Congress and the liberal trade stance of the Reagan administration. The variance between the positions of the two government branches was manifested by President Reagan's veto of the 1988 Omnibus Trade Bill, which the Congress succeeded in overriding, and of the 1988 Textile Trade Bill, on which the Congress failed to override a presidential veto. As the Reagan era drew to a close in 1988, United States trade policy was generally pursuing a mixture of pro-liberal and protectionist trade measures, invoking the Section 301 rule of the 1974 Trade Act, promoting United States exports and market access abroad, enacting comprehensive trade legislation in 1988, signing a free trade pact with Canada, and participating in the Uruguay Round of the GATT Multilateral Trade Negotiations (MTN).[4]

Of these, the trade legislation represents the protectionist approach of the United States Congress, while the other measures reflect the United States administration's continuing commitment to a liberal and free trade policy. The United States' export promotion and pursuit of market access abroad is a sound trade policy measure which, if successful, will strengthen the fabric of the liberal world trading environment itself.

On the basis of realistic trade policy considerations, the United States decided that General System of Preference (GSP) status should no longer be extended, as of January 1, 1989, to the East Asian NICs, including South Korea. Although this measure, when first announced in early 1988, was criticized by the NICs as trade protectionism in the United States, it is in fact a sound policy adjustment that reflects the change in the world trading environment. Since the GSP system was first put into effect in the United States in 1976, some 141 countries have benefited from this special duty-free treatment. However, the NICs, including South Korea, no longer need a "free ride" as they begin to graduate from the status of developing country economies.

Seoul's Reaction to United States Pressures

Seoul's response to United States pressure on the opening of South Korea's protected markets has been varied initially, combining delaying tactics with a posture of gradual concession. In accommodating to American demands, Seoul has proceeded with deliberate speed, moving step by step to open its domestic market to imports from the United States. Starting with yielding on the protection of intellectual property rights, Seoul has acted to liberalize the importation of various consumer goods and services and agricultural goods.

South Korea's nationalist intellectuals have been especially vocal in their criticism of the United States demands in several sectors, particulary increased sale of cigarettes, motion pictures, agricultural products, and opening of the banking and insurance industries. On the sale of American cigarettes, for instance, United States efforts have been equated with the British promotion of the sale of opium to China in the nineteenth century. Some Korean intellectuals have challenged the tobacco policy on moral grounds, insisting that the United States has adopted a double standard, encouraging the sale of cigarettes abroad for profit, while discouraging the smoking of cigarettes at home on health grounds.

Since the Sixth Republic was launched on February 25, 1988, the Roh Tae Woo government has adopted a progressive stance on market opening and liberalization of imports. On April 25, 1988, the government appointed a 25-member blue-ribbon Presidential Commission on Economic Restructuring, chaired by former Prime Minister Yoo Chang Soon. This commission has addressed the emerging challenges facing the Korean economy in the environment of growing protectionism and regionalism in the world community. An interim report of this commission indicates the need for far-reaching reform of South Korea's economic policy. Three problem areas in the South Korean economy are identified in this report: the needs to internationalize the economy, restructure industry, and improve social equity and the quality of life. The internationalization of the Korean economy, according to the commission, requires an outward-looking development strategy, opening of the domestic markets at an accelerated pace, and further development of international economic cooperation with advanced countries.[5]

The commission's final report, entitled "Realizing Korea's National Priorities for Economic Advance," admitted that "the country's substantial balance of payment surplus... [is] both threatening price stability and creating friction with trading partners." The commission recommended that "tariffs on manufactured goods should be significantly reduced and systems for the distribution of imported goods should be reformed to enhance the marketability of imported items." Although the import liberalization is recommended to apply to manufactured goods immediately, reform of agricultural markets, services, and capital markets will be subject to certain prior considerations: advance notice, restructuring of the affected industry, and compensatory assistance on impacted industries.[6]

As part of this new overall trade strategy, the Seoul government is pursuing a policy of diversifying its trade partnerships and patterns away from the traditionally heavy reliance on the United States and Japan, toward opening new trade with China, East European countries, and the Soviet Union.

Korean Challenges and United States Policy

Towards Realism in Economic Diplomacy

The rise of South Korea as an economic power also requires a policy adjustment on the part of the United States, especially by the Bush administration. Policy may benefit from rethinking and reassessment of the past assumptions of United States-Korea relations, which are now moving from asymmetry and Korean dependence to a relationship of greater symmetry and equality and promotion of cooperative endeavors into the decade of the 1990s.

The reality of the United States trade deficit and South Korea's current account surplus changed the nature of United States-Korean economic relations in the late 1980s. The United States' status as a dominant economic power is rapidly eroding with the rise of other world economic centers in the European Community, Japan, and the NICs. South Korea in 1987 was the twelfth largest trading nation in the free world, with a combined total of $88.3 billion in trade, surpassed only by the United States, Japan, the EC countries, Canada, Hong Kong, and Switzerland (see Table 10-3). South Korea's market share of the free world's trade in recent years has approached 1.5 percent of the total.

The major economic indicators in South Korea (see Table 10-4) also show that the real growth of its GNP was the largest in the world in recent years, with the annual growth rate of

TABLE 10–3
Largest Trading States (1987) In Billions of Dollars

Country	Total Trade	Exports	Imports	Balance
1. United States	674.5	250.4	424.1	-173.7
2. West Germany	522.5	294.2	228.3	65.9
3. Japan	382.0	231.2	150.8	80.4
4. France	307.0	148.5	158.5	-10.0
5. United Kingdom	285.7	131.2	154.5	-23.3
6. Italy	237.3	112.0	125.3	-13.3
7. Canada	190.8	98.1	92.7	5.4
8. Netherlands	184.6	93.2	91.4	1.8
9. Belgium-Luxembourg	167.3	84.1	83.2	0.9
10. Hong Kong	97.0	48.5	48.5	0
11. Switzerland	96.2	45.5	50.7	-5.2
12. Korea	88.3	47.3	41.0	6.3
13. Taiwan	84.9	53.3	31.6	21.7
14. Sweden	85.2	44.5	40.7	3.8
15. Spain	82.8	34.0	48.8	-14.8

Sources: International Financial Statistics, IMF, May 1988. *Direction of Trade Statistics*, IMF, various months.

12.9 percent in 1986, 12.8 percent in 1987, and 12.2 percent in 1988. Even if the projected rate of growth is smaller in the years beyond 1988, the total GNP is expected to almost double in four or five years, from $128 billion in 1987 to an estimated $226 billion in 1991. The GNP per capita likewise is projected to increase from $3,098 in 1987 to $5,100 in 1991.

The status of South Korea as a NIC will enable the people of South Korea to do more than in the past to actively participate and share responsibility for building the liberal world trade system from which the country has so greatly benefited.

Greater international cooperation and sharing of the burden for sustaining the security and stability of the world trading environment must be worked out by Korea in consultation with the United States as an ally and with other East Asian nations as trading partners. The exact formula and equitable ratio of security burden-sharing is obviously a subject that requires

TABLE 10–4
Major Economic Indicators of Korea (1985–1991)

Item	Unit	1985	1986	1987	1988	1991*
Gross National Product (GNP)	$bil.	89.7	102.7	128.4	169.2	226.0
Real growth rate	%	7.0	12.9	12.8	12.2	8.3
Per capita GNP	$	2,194	2,503	3,098	4,040	5,100
Current account balance	$bil.	-0.9	4.6	9.8	14.2	6.0
Ratio to GNP	(%)		(4.8)	(8.3)	(4.8)	(2.8)
Trade Balance**	$bil.	-0.02	4.2	7.6	5.0	3.0
Exports	$bil.	26.44	33.9	46.2	59.7	76.7
Imports	$bil.	26.46	29.7	38.5	48.1	73.3
Invisible trade balance	$bil.	-1.5	-0.6	1.0	1.0	—
Net unrequited transfers	$bil.	0.58	1.0	1.2	1.0	—
External debt/assets						
Outstanding debt	$bil.	46.8	44.5	35.5	31.1	23.0
Overseas assets	$bil.	11.2	11.8	13.4	15.5	23.0
Net foreign debt	$bil.	35.6	32.7	22.1	15.5	0.0
Inflation rate						
Wholesale prices	%	0.9	-2.2	2.7	2.7	—
Consumer prices	%	2.5	2.3	6.1	7.1	—
Investment ratio	%	30.5	29.1	29.2	30.2	34.0
Savings ratio	%	30.0	34.0	36.7	38.4	31.7
Unemployment	%	4.0	3.8	3.1	2.5	3.7

Source: Major Statistics of the Korean Economy (Seoul: ROK Economic Planning Board (EPB), May 1989), pp. 3,6,8,9
*The 1991 figures are targets set in the current Sixth Five-Year Economic and Social Development Plan (1987-1991).
**Trade figures for 1985-1987 are based on balance of payments. Trade projections for 1988 and 1991 are based on customs clearance.

further consultation and agreement between Seoul and Washington. But trade-security linkage in the liberal world trading system must not be overlooked; it should serve as the basis for policy consultation. Since South Korea, as well as Japan and Taiwan, enjoy a favorable current account balance with the

United States, some of the huge national savings must be used to support infrastructure-building for common defense and strengthening of liberal world trade.

In working out the details of burden-sharing the comparative national capability and performance of each country must be taken into account as the basis for allocating the cost (see Table 10-5).

Transcending Economic Nationalism

Economic nationalism is not bad *per se*, nor is it always destructive. A trade war ensuing from the practice of protectionism is obviously harmful to the promotion of greater international cooperation. But trade protectionism does not always follow from the rise of economic nationalism. So long as the sentiment is contained through enlightened public education on public policy, there is nothing inherently harmful in nationalism. The nationalist impulse could be harnessed and channelled into positive rather than negative efforts. Nationalism, in short, should not be exploited for private gains and partisan purposes.

The trade policies of the United States and Korea as allies must enlighten and guide their respective public opinions toward the constructive purposes of promoting mutual interests through free and liberal trade rather than seeking to further separate and sectional interests through trade protectionism and mercantilist practices.

The fact that many of the original protectionist provisions of the 1988 Omnibus Trade and Competitiveness Act were abandoned before the finalization of the law during the U.S. Congress's joint conference meetings is reassuring from the standpoint of strengthening free trade norms and institutions. The final text of the 1988 Trade Act is a watered-down version of the earlier protectionist legislation.

Although many of the United States' trade partners, including the European Community countries and Japan, announced that they reserve the right to bring to the GATT (General Agreement on Trade and Tariffs) meetings possible future grievances regarding injuries resulting from the new American trade law, the thrust of the new legislation is directed as much to the United States itself as to its trade partners. It urges

TABLE 10–5
Comparison of Major Economic Indicators (1987)

Country	Unit	Korea	Japan	Taiwan	United States
Area	thousand sq. miles	38.2	145.9	13.9	3,623.5
Population	mil.	42.1	122.0	19.5	241.5
Gross National Product (GNP)	$bil.	118.0	2,380.0	97.0	4,489.0
Growth rate	%		12.2	3.8	11.2
Per capita GNP	$	2,813	19,500	5,000	18,600
Current account balance	$bil.	9.8	86.7	21.1	-160.7
Trade balance	$bil.	7.6	96.5	11.7	-171.2
(Balance with US)	$bil.	(9.9)	(59.9)	(19.0)	
Total exports	$bil.	46.1	224.4	53.3	252.9
(Exports to US)	$bil.	(18.0)	(88.1)	(26.4)	
Total imports	$bil.	38.5	128.0	31.6	424.1
(Imports from US)	$bil.	(8.1)	(28.2)	(7.4)	
External assets	$bil.	-22.4	266.0	73.3	-435.4
Foreign debt	$bil.		35.5	N.A.	3.2
Foreign exchange reserves	$bil.	11.1	82.2	75.5	—
Consumer price increase	%	3.0	0.1	0.5	4.4
Wage increase	%	9.4	2.1	9.2	2.5
Currency appreciation	%	8.7	29.8	24.6	—
(5 mos. in 1988)	(%)	(8.1)	(-1.4)	(-0.2)	—
Investment ratio	%	29.3	32.3	38.7	12.8
Savings ratio	%	35.8	28.7	15.8	16.3

Sources: IMF, World Bank, Government publications.

improving the competitiveness of American industries and export promotion, rather than emphasizing punitive measures to protect United States industries from foreign competition.

In addition to the compensatory measures and assistance to United States industries, the new trade law also provides for government assistance in the readjustment and retraining of workers in the affected industries. Education rather than tariffs or barriers to trade seems to be the underlying philosophy of the new trade legislation. How the Bush administration will implement this legislation, however, will also make differences in terms of whether the 1988 Trade Act is helpful to United States trade interests or harmful to the cause of free trade.

The so-called "Super 301" rules for identifying unfair trading nations under the 1988 Trade Act were invoked by the Bush administration in May 1989. South Korea was not on the list of targeted countries (Japan, India, and Brazil) announced by U.S. Trade Representative Carla Hills. This exemption of South Korea from inclusion among "unfair" trading nations may not last beyond 1990–1991, however, unless further progress is made in South Korea's bilateral trade negotiations with the United States on liberalizing its protected market.

South Korea was not able, however, to escape designation by the U.S. Treasury Department as a country practicing currency exchange rate manipulation. This status was established for South Korea and Taiwan by the Bush administration in its report to the Congress in 1989, in accordance with provisions of the 1988 Trade Act. The Seoul government is obviously not happy with this development and is working hard trying to remove itself from the currency manipulator list.[7]

Conclusion

Promoting mutual interests through expanded trade while sustaining the alliance structure is the challenge facing the United States and South Korea in the decade of the 1990s. In their policy agenda the political leaders of both countries must abandon a narrow, self-justifying, zero-sum view of world trade. It is necessary to suppress protectionist impulses and promote a positive and variable-sum view of trade.

In sustaining economic cooperation between the two Pacific Rim nations, the leaders of the United States and Korea must be prepared to contain trade disputes lest they spill over into the political arena. A failure to limit the scope of trade problems in a timely fashion will unnecessarily politicize economic issues, thereby undermining the structure of the United States-Korea alliance.

As alliance partners, both countries must be flexible in their approach to resolving trade disputes and economic conflict. An economic agenda must be viewed from the broader political perspective of justifying the United States-Korean security alliance. This may entail the adoption of a flexible policy stance in regard to security-trade linkage. This may require willingness on the part of both nations to bear additional costs and sacrifices to maintain the alliance through increased burden-sharing.[8]

This negotiation strategy and the cross-linkage of issues would make bargaining and a quid pro quo approach to common problem-solving possible. Such a rational approach to the difficult problems associated with reducing the United States trade deficit with Korea is infinitely more enlightened and productive, allowing the avoidance of open confrontation and conflict growing out of a rising tide of economic nationalism across the Pacific Basin.

Notes

1. Recently, a number of pleas have been made by American observers to readjust United States perceptions of South Korea and to create a new policy toward Korea. Many of these studies attempt to place the policy debate on Korea on a more realistic and rational plane. See, for instance: *Korea at the Crossroads: Implications for American Policy* (New York: Council on Foreign Relations and the Asia Society, 1987; Selig S. Harrison, *The South Korean Political Crisis and American Policy Options* (Washington, D.C.: The Washington Institute Press, 1987); Ralph N. Clough, *Balancing Act: The Republic of Korea Approaches 1988*, FPI policy briefs (Washington D.C.: SAIS of the Johns Hopkins University, 1987). Also, see: Edward A. Olsen, *U.S. Policy and the Two Koreas* (San Francisco: World Affairs Council of Northern California, and Boulder, CO: Westview Press, 1988).

2. On these and other stereotypes of the Asian NICs, see various issues of economic journals and magazines such as *Business Week, Far Eastern Economic Review, Fortune,* and the newspaper coverage on the economic and trade relations with Asia.

3. *New York Times,* October 13, 1988.

4. *New York Times,* September 29, 1988.

5. "Korea's Presidential Commission on Economic Restructuring: Summary Interim Report," *FYI,* September 19, 1988 (Washington, D.C.: Korea Economic Institute, 1988).

6. *Realizing Korea's National Priorities for Economic Advance* (Seoul: Presidential Commission on Economic Restructuring, 1988), pp. 1–4.

7. *Korea's Exchange Rate Policy* (Seoul: Korea Foreign Trade Association, 1989).

8. As for my view on the U.S.-Korea security alliance in the 1990s, see Kihl, "Re-examining the United States Security Role in Korea: The Politics of Troop Reduction and Defense Burden Share." *Korea Journal,* vol. 30, no. 10 (October 1990), 44–52.

11

United States Assistance to Korea

A "Policy Dialogue" Retrospective

David I. Steinberg

Introduction

A GUIDING PRINCIPLE OF UNITED STATES foreign assistance policy
has been "policy dialogue," attempts by the United States to
encourage developing nations to adopt policies that, in the eyes
of the donor, will lead to greater productivity, growth, and
equity in those societies. Under the Reagan administration,
policy dialogue became one of the four cardinal *desiderata* on
which foreign assistance was determined, justified internally,
and presented to the Congress. The other three were: encouragement of the private sector, technology transfer, and institution building. Although at one level these concepts were used
as slogans to "sell" assistance internally (and each administration has had its share of them, used as sales and sloganeering
aids), they are all concepts that in some sense have been a part
of the foreign assistance program since the early years of its
existence in the 1950s and reflect needs, fads, and ideological
proclivities.

The present Foreign Assistance Act dates from 1961. Although amended many times, its most important change came in 1973, with the "new directions" that mandated assistance "directly" toward the benefit of the rural poor majority. Since it was passed, the law has been subject to a type of textual criticism usually reserved for sacred writings, meticulously interpreted and reinterpreted. In the act's earlier years, attention focused on rural smaller-scale activities, and even the training of (elite) technicians was sometimes avoided. Today, the administration interprets private sector activities as one of the most effective means to help the rural poor.

In 1988, there were at least three major efforts underway to redefine the purposes of foreign assistance, its content, and its foci, and to plan to rebuild a constituency for it in the Congress and with the public, for in both cases support had badly eroded or had even disappeared. Such efforts are, obviously, timed to affect a new administration. There are advocates of dealing with urban poverty, concentrating on the environment, treating AIDS, and even abolishing most administrative mechanisms and placing most development assistance under line agencies (such as agriculture and education).

These proposed new approaches are especially important as they reflect, as does policy dialogue, the diminished capacity of the United States alone, or even as a major provider of development assistance, to supply the magnitude of funds necessary for credible support to worldwide developmental efforts: Development assistance levels in current and constant dollars have dropped over the past ten years and today are a small proportion of military and security-related support. In effect, the United States assistance programs are large enough to be potentially effective when security issues are at stake (in Israel, Egypt, Pakistan, and parts of Central America, for example) and not for solely developmental efforts. As a further example, in spite of a security treaty, United States development support to Thailand is now less than two percent of all concessional aid and an infinitesimal percentage of all commercial and concessional flows combined.

Conceptually, as well as at the country level, the United States has often envisaged the change as a move from "retail" assistance (in project form) to "wholesale" support (policy assistance), where wider and more profound changes are thought to be possible at lower program and management costs. Today's financial stringency in foreign assistance is as much a matter of the reduced availability of administrative funds (and thus of staff positions in the field or in the United States) as it is the paucity of overall or program monies.

This paper examines some of the issues of present and planned assistance levels, sectors, and economic development negotiations in light of the United States' massive economic aid to the Republic of Korea and some of the negotiations that have taken place on policy issues during the period of United States aid. The paper's purpose is to glean from that earlier experience lessons that could be useful as applied to problems in other nations in the contemporary period. Although it is obvious that dangers exist in the casual application of any lessons across cultures and times, various continuities may exist that can serve, if not as a Virgilian guide for the descending circles of developmental hell, then as guideposts for the wary traveller in developmental lands.

The Hierarchy of Developmental Assistance and Conditionality

Various aspects of development assistance are loosely demarcated, even by the knowledgeable public. Such misnomers give rise to false expectations and spurious analyses of developmental efforts, past and present. The most blatant example of such thinking is the use of the term, "Marshall Plan" (or some variant thereof, such as a "mini-Marshall Plan") for assistance to such countries as the Philippines or in such areas as the Middle East or Africa. In popular parlance, the reference is to the magnitude of the assistance, but by implication it conveys the probability of its potential success.

In fact, the Marshall Plan applied to Europe following World War II was unique: It represents the apex of what has since become a hierarchy of types of economic assistance. It made available funds, in fields specified by the recipients not the donor, where financial and other institutions existed and were effective, where economic policies were in place, where infrastructure was developed, and where there was a plethora of trained personnel. It cannot with accuracy be applied to any other area or country, even today.

A hierarchy of levels of development assistance (from a donor perspective) has evolved over time that may inchoately be based on a diminishing set of confidences (which, because of their political implications, may never be articulated) that might be conceived as follows:

1. *The Marshall Plan*—where the donor has essential confidence in the economic policies, practices, and capacity of a state
2. *Sector or program lending*—where the donor has confidence in the policy potential and administrative capacity of a recipient nation in a specific field, such as agriculture
3. *Institution building*—where the donor has confidence in the actual or potential developmental role of an institution or organization within a sector
4. *Humanitarian or relief assistance*—where the need is acute and is unrelated to sustained developmental efficacy, or where general donor administrative confidence is weak or lacking

To be sure, other factors play roles. Aside from emergency relief support, this aid hierarchy reflects both the absorptive capacity of states (as viewed by donors) and the desire to avoid excessive "pipelines," where funds that have been authorized and committed remain unspent because of administrative bottlenecks. It also relates as well to the donor's concern for the timely obligation of larger amounts of money. Program, commodity, and sectoral loans are normally considered, as they have records for quicker disbursal as well as faster impact.

Related to such a hierarchy is the matter of "conditionality," the placing of strings on assistance to ensure its efficacy to promote the goals that the donor determines are in the recipient's best interests, to which the recipient agrees by choice or necessity. This phenomenon is spoken of in the donor trade as "leverage," the donor's use of funds or influence to affect recipient actions. At the apex of program hierarchy, the Marshall Plan, conditionality was not an issue, although it is at most other levels of assistance. United States conditionality normally diminishes down the hierarchy as trust increases; that is, it is more general and abstracted at higher levels, more detailed at lower levels.

The degree of conditionality is often effectively tied, positively or negatively, to nondevelopmental issues such as security concerns or broad political support (as in the case of Israel). In effect, developmental guidelines such as the sustainability of projects by host institutions are sometimes dis- carded for the sake of perceived and vast needs; money is pumped in too quickly and projects are beyond the local capacity of an administration to support if, or when, donor assistance ends. Many projects in Central America today, as in Vietnam in the past, could not be sustained by host governments if foreign support were withdrawn.

On the multilateral and the most financially intensive level, conditionality is most evident in the "structural adjustment" loans and goals promoted by the World Bank or the IMF in those nations where massive economic problems require profound and widespread policy reforms, often involving such matters as money supply, exchange and interest rates, and subsidies. (This occurred in Korea in 1980, following Park Chung Hee's assassination, with inflation brought on by the massive and overly rapid expenditures in heavy and defense industries in the 1970s, the second oil crisis, and the collapse of rice production in 1980.)

But conditionality exists at other levels in varying degrees: in sector or program lending, in institution building, and in more specific areas, such as in Title III food assistance, in which the United States forgives agricultural commodity loans in return for policy reforms in agriculture and food production.

Conditionality was a strong element in Korean-American economic relations and negotiations through much of the period (until 1975) in which foreign aid was provided to Korea, as we will note below; but it was, as in other countries, made more complex by a series of competing conditions in other fields, which vitiated some economic effects. Leverage could be applied in economic development programs or projects, but the leverage generated came from other arenas; in Korea, security issues and the United States' proverbial "seal of approval" (the issue of political legitimacy in that period) always gave the United States some leverage. In more recent times, the threat of United States protectionist policies has become important to Koreans, as about 40 percent of Korean exports are destined for the American market.

If policy dialogue implies planned reform or changes, it also implies (if it is to be dialogue and not direction) that such discussion be carried out under conditions of mutual trust in a peer relationship. There are, however, issues of how much trust or negotiating equality has been, or can be, present when support is massive and the international stakes are perceived to be high.

This hierarchical construct has evolved only after considerable experience, of which that in Korea was a critical and early, if unarticulated, element. The record of Korea's negotiations with the United States on economic assistance may provide insights into this process of policy dialogue.

Korean-American Economic Relations

There is no question but that Korea's economic success, probably the most profound of any modern nation considering its history, the devastation wrought by the Korean War, and its lack of natural endowments, is the envy of much of the developing world, the concern (in terms of its exports and, even more, its export and technological potential) of the developed societies, and for many a model to be emulated. It is often explained (at least in the United States) as an American success story because of the massive economic assistance that was provided (about $6 billion out of a total of some $13 billion, including military support), first to aid recovery from the Korean War and later as more focused developmental efforts. The importance of American assistance is the subject of considerable academic dispute; some argue that indeed United States aid was critical in the war years and immediately thereafter but was marginal later,[1] while others believe that the essential criteria for success were inherently Korean;[2] and the most popularly held United States official view is that indeed American assistance was both successful and in large (but unknown) part responsible.

This basic issue will not be settled with authority until many more documents are declassified in both nations. United States economic relations with Korea have been at the same time in different fields close and distant, acerbic and friendly, collaborative and competitive.

This relational dichotomy has existed over different times (very distant, for example, for almost two years following the military coup of 1961, but close in certain areas thereafter) and in various fields: For example, United States-Korean relations have been close in matters of security as a general rule, but the security relationship influenced the economic assistance roles when there were serious disputes. There were always trade-offs between security and economic needs: the Koreans effectively used the security requirements to mitigate what they regarded as antagonistic American demands for specific policy changes, including in later years trade openings, but also in regard to requests for political liberalization. Indeed, sometimes the Koreans were able to use the statements of the American military to imply support for Korean political or economic desires.

More recently, disputes on trade issues were exacerbated by the problem of negotiating styles. As befitted a centralized, bureaucratic state, Korea negotiated from the top with a unity of purpose that accurately mirrored its political density; one authority made coordinated decisions that were effectively implemented, and the Koreans preferred to negotiate all outstanding trade issues at one time. The Americans, on the other hand, responded to internal United States political pressures one at a time (today steel or tobacco; yesterday, textiles, and so on), and the pluralism of American society was evident in the competing priorities among various United States departments (State versus Agriculture versus Commerce versus Defense) and between them and elements in the Congress.

That is not to say that overall, in any comparative assessment, United States-Korean relations were not good (we have had equally or more serious disputes with the British or the Canadians) but that tensions were inherent in the intensity of the relationship and the perceived and varying interdependency of the two nations, and these tensions gradually shifted from ones involving an aid donor and a recipient, to ones between powers who, if not equal, were at least economically competitive. The United States gives (or gave) various Korean regimes some political legitimacy, while on the United States side, Korea served internal American requirements; the

Reagan administration was intent on improving the relationship with Korea that had deteriorated in the Carter years. American administrations and politicians have attempted to use Korean protectionism, and thus the need for new market openings, for their own political advantage. Korean politicians have also appealed to their voters' nationalism by protesting such pressures.

Policy Dialogue in Korea

Policy dialogue in general terms has been described as follows:

> Exchanges occur between aid donors and recipients about the domestic policy framework, influencing the outcome of an aid transfer and the behavior of the economy as a whole....The popularity of the concept among donors, however, has grown as donor perceptions of generalized economic malaise in a range of countries has spread.[3]

Dialogue presumes a commonality of concerns, preferably a peer relationship, discussions over time, a common set of assumptions on which to base such dialogue, and a strong element of trust that exists or at least develops over the period of negotiation. Sometimes these relationships can be remarkably effective; the IMF negotiated major changes in an Asian nation's interest rates over the telephone with nothing in writing because of such trust.

In Korea, the United States was continuously engaged in discussions with the Koreans about policy. This is in sharp contrast to the Japanese, who have eschewed such discussions on policy in many nations, and in Korea as a matter of principle, given the heated antagonisms of the past. (It is remarkable that the United States can carry out such open discussions in the Philippines, a former colony—although not without some trauma—while Japan feels it cannot discuss policy in Korea.)

Such joint issues need not be only or even primarily economic. The political stability or security of the state might be the focus around which economic policy discussions take place. In Korea, the economic objectives of the United States and the Koreans under the First Republic (1948–1960) were fundamentally different. As the elections of 1960 approached, there was intense disillusionment in both the United States executive branch and the Congress with the economic performance of the Koreans. Agreement had been reached that foreign aid levels to Korea would have to drop, but the Koreans' primary objective was to keep those levels high for as long as possible; thus production, economic self-reliance, and sustained economic growth were secondary. The Americans, on the other hand, were more concerned about improving the Koreans' internal resource mobilization and thus getting them to shoulder a greater share of the defense burden. Thus the policy overlap on which dialogue could take place was relatively limited: it centered on the protection of South Korea from any possible invasion or incursion from the North.

Policy discussions on economic issues were carried on between Korea and the United States at two levels during the First Republic: by the president, and by a joint United States-Korean economic committee. Syngman Rhee, in order to ensure that his dictates were followed, insisted that all matters relating to such issues as relations with Japan, adjustment of the exchange rates, and money supply were to have his personal approval.

The economic committee was a high-level working group that tried to negotiate many aspects of specific policies, and it began to attempt economic planning. It was only at the end of the Rhee regime that the first plan was formulated, but that government ended before the plan could be put into effect; and the Second Republic of Chang Myon (1960–1961) was too short-lived to do any planning. Although the minutes of the economic committee meetings have not been made public, there seems little question that the relationships within it were often tense and the disagreements often profound. The negotiating group existed well into the 1960s; but immediately following the Park coup of May 1961, the meetings were suspended by the Koreans, who sought to do economic planning without reference to the Americans. An ill-conceived currency reform—which did not work—was promulgated in 1961 without the knowledge of the United States, and the first five-year plan under Park was written without normal Korean-American consultations.

It may be argued that as the Koreans gave up considerable sovereignty in military matters by having their troops controlled by Americans, first under the UN command and then under the Combined Forces Command, they less obviously gave up considerable economic autonomy by agreeing to this formalized joint economic committee. It should be noted, however, that in both military and economic spheres the Koreans acted unilaterally when they felt it was in their interest.

Conditionality was a second aspect of the relationship. On major questions of resource mobilization or economic stability, such as the size of the money supply, the United States threatened to withhold funds if targets were not achieved. These funds totalled three to four percent of the overall aid package. An official AID report in 1970 declared that "the program loan was introduced as a carrot, a marginal element of assistance, but one specifically aimed at stimulating better stabilization performance."[4] In a number of cases there were significant delays in providing funds because of these disagreements. Yet the situation was not clearcut, for "since our [United States] political objectives could not permit real damage to the Korean economy, and since funds were never unlimited, we had to use available funds for dual purposes: to withhold for punishment and then making [them] again available."[5] The United States government noted that failure to meet goals did not result in deobligation of funds; and thus temporarily withholding them was not effective in changing policies, and release of such funds was not always tied to the recipient's attaining such goals.[6] Thus, conditionality had limited meaning and effect.

It can be argued, however, that conditionality itself, and even the amounts of money involved, were not the primary issues; what may have been more important was the possibility of public disclosure of any disagreements. Insofar as each regime in Korea has used its relationship with the United States as an element in its formation of political legitimacy, a public disclosure of United States censure of a Korean government position could have been very damaging for that regime. A significant portion of the public in Korea questioned the political legitimacy of Syngman Rhee, Park Chung Hee, and Chun Doo Hwan, and they thus were vulnerable. Chang Myon's government was too weak to question United States advice in any major ways; and the Roh Tae Woo government, freely elected, is in a much more legitimate position at the same time that the American role has become no longer significant in direct intervention into the Korean economy. (The leverage the United States now has for the opening of Korean markets is only because about 40 percent of Korean exports go to the United States.)

The United States has used public cautioning or criticism of any Korean government with considerable (perhaps often too great) circumspection. Although in many cases private consultations have taken place in which the United States has been very critical of a regime's actions or planned actions, most often these negotiations or discussions have been closely held. In some cases, generic issues were sacrificed for ad hominem concerns (overall human rights pressures as opposed to saving Kim Dae Jung's life, for instance). At critical times, such as in June 1987, if the government had declared martial law (as it is said some wished it to do) and the United States had publicly objected (as the American public through the Congress probably would have demanded, given the extensive coverage of the rioting on American television), then the United States disapproval would have been tantamount to calling for a Korean revolution. As Korean nationalism grew and the Korean War receded from the consciousness of many younger Koreans, the issue of public pressure had more diverse overtones. In the later period, United States pressures calling for the opening of the Korean market to American imports (such as cigarettes and beef in the past two years) resulted more in anti-American sentiment than in loss of Korean regime legitimacy. In fact, the debates may have increased regime legitimacy insofar as the leaders stood up to American pressure. This was especially true on the cigarette issue, both because of health concerns and because smoking of foreign cigarettes earlier had been a crime. The United States was pictured as the "elder brother" (an analogy often used by Koreans in informal discussions of these and other examples of unbalanced bilateral relationships, but a concept that Americans do not fully appreciate) and is seen as misusing that relationship in attempts to coerce its "younger brother," Korea.

Within the "policy dialogue" (perhaps debate might be a more accurate term) context, training has played a critical role. It is evident that in evaluations of the United States' assistance programs in Korea and Thailand and in less formal evaluations in a number of other nations, the aspect of American assistance that has been considered to have had the most profound impact has been training. The training effort has been carried out under various auspices in different countries: the official United States program, the program of the national governments, training with private outside assistance, and programs that were self-financed. Under whatever auspices, those trainees who return have a profound impact on the development of the society. In some cases (as in Korea under Syngman Rhee), they may have had little immediate effect, but their presence has been important in the formation and execution of policies and programs ever since.

Policy dialogue is best carried out under conditions where at least some of the objectives are mutually understood and agreed upon, the constraints are clear, and the premises on which policies are to be based are shared. Disciplinary training in economic policy or in technical fields often provides such shared premises and forms the basis of eventual trust. Even at the height of their influence in Korea, for Americans to unilaterally push economic policies on the Koreans was in many cases counterproductive. What was more important was for educated, respected Koreans within the bureaucratic decision-making process to advocate such policies themselves with the backing, financial and/or moral, of foreign advisers. In fact, at the project level in Korea it was evident that many Koreans felt that policy and technical advisers were often there to reinforce the power or prestige of an institution to which they were attached, or of an individual, group, or faction in that institution or ministry, and/or to guarantee the provision of funds, training, or commodities.

In some cases for which there is good anecdotal evidence, foreign backing and foreign support were used by one element of the Korean government as pressure for policy reforms on another element. It is said, for example, that in the 1970s, Korea borrowed funds from the World Bank on an occasion when they really did not need such funds. By borrowing from the bank, the Ministry of Finance could claim that the conditions of the loan required them to make policy reforms (related to internal subsidies) that the Ministry of Finance wanted in any case to make, thus giving them leverage with another ministry.

As AID noted, "Economic ministries used the conditions precedent of the program loans [in the 1960s] to counteract inflationary programs or policies proposed by other ministries. The program loan provided Finance Ministry economists with an excuse for unpopular policies they wanted to carry through anyway."[7]

It becomes evident that policy dialogue, as direct negotiations between the United States and a foreign nation, is an overly simplistic framework, and indeed perhaps a conceptually limited means for arriving at the goal of economic reform.

It is also clear that all Korean governments in their dealings with the United States have used policy dialogue selectively for their own interests, an unsurprising conclusion but one often ignored in United States official circles. Thus, policies are accepted as a result of such dialogue when those policies are means by which the Koreans, for example, could achieve their already stated objectives. One such case is the now famous interest rate reforms of 1965, when internal resource mobilization was vastly expanded through an increase in local interest rates on savings. This was a major goal of the Koreans, and one where United States policy advice was markedly successful. On the other hand, when such policy dialogue was expanded to cover fundamental issues such as the internal distribution of power, the government was often reluctant to make such changes. This occurred when foreign advisers suggested reform of the agricultural cooperatives, reinstitution of local government, banking reform, and other efforts where power of the central administration would have been shared or diminished. When, however, the government felt it was in their own political and economic interest to make such changes, regardless of any foreign policy dialogue, then it would begin to do so, working at its own pace and within its own intellectual construct of authority. Policy dialogue is thus most effective when it is internally demanded. That is not to say that policy options may not be discussed but that the conditionality of assistance based on policy changes demands great sensitivity, which is usually not a paramount attribute of the donor community.

Lessons from the Korean Experience

The United States-Korean experience indicates that fundamental policy shifts in developing societies are unlikely unless the internal political and economic conditions allow the proposed changes to contribute to the goals of the state. That is, privatization, heightened technological capacity, decentralization, export orientation, and other policies often advocated by the United States (or other donors) as necessary to economic success are unlikely to be adopted unless they meet local needs and local concepts of how power is to be distributed. Park Chung Hee needed export promotion for his own political interests; the United States assisted that effort. In a world of heightened nationalism, it is increasingly unlikely that direct policy interventions or suggestions from foreigners will be fruitful. It is more appropriate that policy dialogue take place within the host government or institution with foreign donors playing a supportive but subsidiary role in the process.

Training remains an important contribution to policy dialogue, for it contributes to the conceptualization of the issues in an internal atmosphere that allows greater scope for intense debate and change than outside pressures would allow.

The success of Korean economic growth is not simply a product of policy changes, although they were important. Equally important was their effective implementation. Although foreign assistance can support the development of institutional links between planning and implementation (the formation of the Office of Rural Development, linking agricultural research and extension in Korea in the early period of Park Chung Hee, can be attributed to United States advisers), implementation itself is an indigenous product, possibly facilitated by external assistance, but effective only when locally applied. Korea developed one of the most powerful implementation devices in the modern world, where a traditional hierarchical system was supplemented by a military command structure, where rewards (psychic and financial) were provided and punishments threatened for non-performance, where productivity was encouraged and rent-seeking activities discouraged. It was an effective method of developmental support.

It should also be remembered that donors do not have a monopoly on sound policy advice; many important Korean policies or expenditures were done against foreign advice, or were of a type that donors would not have advocated. All donors were against the Seoul-Pusan highway, which was regarded as flamboyant, uneconomic waste, yet it proved to be highly successful. If the "new directions" of 1973 had been in place earlier, the United States would have tried to convince Korea to expand its rural sector, not its urban, industrial base, and would have objected to the high rate of subsidization of much of Korean rural and industrial development. Yet in both cases Korean policies proved to be highly efficacious.

The Korean experience demonstrates the likelihood that in those countries important to the United States in policy, political, and economic terms, policy dialogue will take place under conditions where negotiations will be strongly influenced by non-economic factors—and factors are very likely to be non-economic. If, however, this dialogue continues over long periods of time with a continuity of participants on both sides, commonalities of interests may be built up so that the results of the dialogue are felt to be indigenous, and they then would stand a better chance of implementation. There were important, talented, and well-trained individuals within the Ministry of Reconstruction in the Syngman Rhee period with whom American economists dealt effectively and with whom such trust and dialogue was established. The successful relationship, however, was often subverted at the top.

The conditions for policy dialogue are not often met, but a review of the United States' assistance to Korea indicates that there are means by which it can be improved. Administrative structures may need to be changed for bilateral donors such as the United States. Other changes will include ensuring greater understanding of the recipient country's internal political and social processes by United States personnel, longer assignments in-country, greater encouragement of broad contacts in the society, and thus less time performing routine administrative matters.

Policy dialogue is, by definition, a two-way street to progress, although often in the past it has been treated as a one-way thoroughfare to reforms.

Notes

1. Edward S. Mason, *et al., The Economic and Social Modernization of the Republic of Korea* (Cambridge, MA: Harvard University Press, 1980).
2. David I. Steinberg, *The Economic Development of Korea: Sui Generis or Generic?* (Washington, D.C.: Agency for International Development, 1982).
3. Robert Cassen, *et al., Does Aid Work?* (Oxford: Oxford University Press, 1986), 69.
4. Elizabeth Carter, "Korea," in *The Use of Program Loans to Influence Policy,* AID Evaluation Paper 1A, March 1970, confidential, since declassified (Washington, D.C.: Government Printing Office, 1970).
5. Ibid.
6. General Accounting Office, "U.S. Assistance for the Economic Development of the Republic of Korea" (Washington, D.C.: Government Printing Office, 26 July 1972), 31.
7. Carter, "Korea."

References

Elizabeth Carter. "Korea," in *The Use of Program Loans to Influence Policy.* AID Evaluation Paper 1A, March 1970, Confidential [since declassified] (Washington, D.C.)

Cassen, Robert, and associates. *Does Aid Work?* Oxford: Oxford University Press, 1986.

General Accounting Office. "U.S. Assistance for the Economic Development of the Republic of Korea." Washington, D.C., July 26, 1972.

Mason, Edward S., *et al. The Economic and Social Modernization of the Republic of Korea.* Cambridge, MA: Harvard University Press, 1980.

Steinberg, David I. *The Economic Development of Korea: Sui Generis or Generic?* Washington, D.C.: AID, 1982.

_____ *Foreign Aid and the Development of the Republic of Korea: The Effectiveness of Concessional Assistance.* Washington, D.C.: AID, 1985.

_____ *The Republic of Korea: Economic Transformation and Social Change.* Boulder, CO: Westview Press, 1988.

12

The Structure of United States-Korea Economic Relations

Getting to Yes in a New Era

Bertrand Renaud

An Era of Transition

ECONOMIC RELATIONS BETWEEN the United States and Korea have entered a major period of transition, and they are evolving in a greatly more interactive world economy. Major changes in both countries have caused shifts in economic relations that would be significant in their own right. In addition, given the large scale of trade between the two partners, the resolution of economic issues must also be seen in the context of four major dynamic forces in world economic relations: the rapid economic ascendence of northeast Asia led by Japan, a trend which has been accentuated by the currency realignments of the 1985 Plaza agreements; the new stages in European integration with the EEC targets of 1992; the festering problems of the third world debt; and the conspicuous if incomplete demise of the old centrally planned socialist economic model everywhere, including in China.

In the United States, the Reagan era ended with five major international or domestic economic disequilibria which must now be corrected. On the external side, the United States trade and current account deficit cannot be left undiminished. The countries with trade surpluses must move toward better balance. An adequate resolution of the third world debt would revive a significant component of United States external demand and stimulate world growth. Allied burden-sharing must improve both in terms of defense and development aid. On the domestic side, the reduction of the fiscal deficit is an equally urgent task. The United States domestic expansion since 1982 has been one of the longest periods of sustained growth on record, but it was bought at a very significant price. There is much concern because the eight-year United States expansion was possible only with a massive inflow of some $700 billion of capital from abroad, and the United States foreign debt may well climb to $1 trillion before leveling off in the early 1990s. Inevitably, current borrowing implies future transfers of income abroad. Avoiding a decline in the future American standard of living will require higher growth rates, that is, less consumer demand and more productive investments.

For its part, Korea has reached the point of transition toward becoming a fully industrialized society and now faces a long political and social agenda. After being held back much too long, Korea's political development is finally beginning to catch up with the economic achievements of three decades. Major political changes in 1988 were marked by the departure of former President Chun Doo Hwan and the minority election of President Roh Tae Woo in competition with a divided opposition. For the first time, the executive is controlled by one party and the National Assembly by the opposition. This sudden change has completely redefined the economic policy-making process in Korea from a technocratic to a political one. The 1988 Olympics, intended by Koreans as a well-controlled coming-out party, improved its world status. On the other hand, what has attracted considerable attention abroad has been the stunning reversal of Korea's external position from being that of the fourth largest debtor country in 1985 to that of holding a net creditor position by 1990. This dramatic turnaround came from very successful structural adjustment policies in 1982–1984, followed by extraordinary growth rates above 12 percent per year in 1986–1988, which in three quick years expanded the size of the economy by 45 percent.

Facing the challenge of its twin deficits, the budget deficit and the trade deficit, the United States government has found it easier to work on the international agenda first. At least in the short term, aggressive trade demands can become a political substitute for more painful domestic adjustments. Increasingly unilateral trade adjustment processes have been written into successive trade laws. American public opinion has also singled out East Asian countries as prime targets, without differentiating much among Japan and the four NICs.

Two paradoxes in the current trade negotiations between the United States and Korea deserve to be examined. First, even if Korea did more than meet the trade and macroeconomic demands of the United States, this would not solve the disequilibria faced by the United States given the relative size of the two countries. Second, each new opening of Korea has so far benefited other countries—particularly Japan—more than the United States. Lacking choices, Korea is most likely to acquiesce to the acceleration in trade opening demanded by the United States, even if it finds the domestic social costs very significant or premature. There are unclear net benefits to the United States from putting great public pressures on Korea during a delicate democratic transition, which is much more significant to United States interests than pure trade reforms with limited long-term impact. United States positions are often presented as coming from a benevolent reformer making demands that are good for Korea. During the current democratic transition, United States positions will increasingly face debate in an open, noisy, and boisterous Korean political marketplace. Highly publicized American pressures could politically undermine the efforts of Korean advocates of a further opening of the Korean economy, or encourage a separate Asian trade zone.

Will cooperation or conflict prevail? To explore the possible path of future relations we can look in turn at the position of each party and at the evolving processes of trade discussions— in particular, the growing role of bilateral negotiations. Starting with the United States side, what leads American analysts to conclude that Korea must contribute to the correction of the

major United States macroeconomic imbalances that have
emerged during the decade? Second, why are Koreans increasingly voicing concerns that United States demands placed on
Korea are the wrong demands in the wrong form, and might
destabilize a long-standing relationship? Third, given these two
contrasting stances, are the evolving United States trade resolution processes—including the new ones created in 1988 with
the Omnibus Trade Law—likely to lead to cooperative and
lasting settlements of differences, or will they increase frictions?
What are the actions that each country could take which would
be mutually beneficial?

The Dominant United States Preoccupation:
Ending the Twin Deficits

> Historically, most American economic (and other) policies have
> been determined on strictly domestic grounds. The external dimen-
> sion was ignored or the country tried to export its external prefer-
> ences to the rest of the world. With the increase in America's
> dependence on world markets and the decline in its ability to dictate
> global outcomes, that approach is no longer viable.
>
> C. Fred Bergsten, 1988

The United States Economic Agenda and Its
International Implications

It is now understood that the United States has become
increasingly dependent on international trade and financial
flows. No longer do closed-economy models make sense in
evaluating domestic policies, the way they did a mere decade
ago. This change is vividly demonstrated by the fact that for the
first time in almost eighty years, a new administration and a
new Congress have to manage a debtor economy. Moreover,
the United States is the world's largest debtor for the first time
in history.[1] Based on current policy conditions, most economic
analyses project that it will be difficult to bring the current
account deficit below $100 billion. In other words, unless
policies are changed, the United States will have to continue to
attract about $10 billion per month of net foreign capital.[2] Most
of this capital has come from Japan and the balance from
Europe. An insignificant amount is from Korea, which has so

far been a debtor country. The United States international debt could reach $1 trillion by the early 1990s. Clearly, the American economic policy agenda and the state of the world economy are intimately linked.

To achieve simultaneously the elimination of the trade deficit, the continuation of economic growth, and a greater degree of financial stability, economists typically see the United States agenda as a four-part program.[3] First, they advocate domestic macroeconomic policy changes to restructure aggregate final demand away from consumer demand and government expenditures into more investment. This increased investment should go into expanding export capacity, which has reached its limits following the recent export boom. Such United States macroeconomic policies should be complemented or coordinated with macroeconomic changes in the countries that have the main current account surpluses with the United States, principally Japan, Germany, Taiwan, and Korea. Second, countries with major current account surpluses should be asked to continue to expand their domestic demand so that their markets will keep growing and import more. Economists also see further exchange rate adjustments in surplus-trade countries as necessary to balance trade patterns. Third, on the domestic side, the experts would also like to see the development of a very aggressive trade policy to promote exports. This should dissipate the rising tide of protectionism within the United States and open new markets abroad. Finally, everyone would like to see a resumption of growth in developing countries through an effective resolution of the debt crisis.

A serious concern is that a failure to achieve domestic macroeconomic adjustments toward more investment and greater international competitiveness—in short, an export-led growth— would leave the United States trade deficit hovering at around $100 billion. This could then trigger a major domestic political push toward protectionism or/and a recession.[4]

There is little doubt that greater gains in international cooperation will depend on the ability of the United States to put its domestic macroeconomic house in order. The failure to raise savings rates at home and to sustain an export-led growth orientation has so far impaired United States ability to win the necessary cooperation from European and East Asian countries; but it is not clear by how much. Recriminations on all sides could escalate beyond what has been heard over the last few years. The persistence of the domestic deficit[5] and the inability to shift to a genuine export-led growth beyond the rapid United States export gains of 1986–1988 could convince surplus-producing countries that not much is being done on the American side to solve the problem. Export surpluses would not decline enough. Most countries with surplus balances would then ask even more insistently why they should bail the United States out of its problems when its internal policies are at fault. On the positive side it must be noted that Japan has been adjusting its macro-policies toward encouraging domestic demand, and similar trends have also emerged in Taiwan and Korea.[6] Will Congress and the executive branch succeed in jointly tackling the twin United States deficits, as is needed? Can muddling through on domestic policies suffice?[7]

The Current United States Trade Situation and the Place of Korea

To put the current American trade situation in perspective, the trade results for 1988 must be discussed briefly. First, the good news is that the United States merchandise trade deficit declined in 1988 for the first time since 1980. The deficit fell by a large margin, 22 percent, over 1987's. The annual merchandise trade deficit in 1988 was $118.7 billion. This good result can be attributed to the very rapid rate of growth of export activities in 1988, which increased by 27 percent in one year, reaching a level of $322.2 billion. The worrisome news is that the improvement seems to have stalled at a very high deficit level. According to the monthly trade series, the deficit was widening again toward the end of 1988, with monthly imports at $39.4 billion and exports at $29.2 billion, leaving a $10 billion gap.[8]

Why Korea is so high on the United States international agenda is readily apparent from the 1988 trade results reported in Table 12-1. This table gives the global United States results as well as individual results with twelve major trading partners. By now Korea is the seventh largest American export market. Looking at United States imports, Korea is sixth. When bilateral

TABLE 12–1
United States Merchandise Trade 1988 (In Millions of Dollars)

Country	U.S. Exports	U.S. Imports	U.S. Balance	Share of U.S. Exports %	Share of U.S. Imports %	Share of U.S. Deficit %
1 Canada	70,862	80,922	(10,059):	22.0	18.4	8.5
2 Japan	37,732	89,802	(52,070):	11.7	20.4	43.9
3 Mexico	20,643	23,277	(2,634):	6.4	5.3	2.2
4 United Kingdom	18,404	18,042	362:	5.7	4.1	-0.3
5 West Germany	14,331	26,503	(12,172):	4.4	6.0	10.3
6 Taiwan	12,131	24,804	(12,673):	3.8	5.6	10.7
7 South Korea	11,290	20,189	(8,900):	3.5	4.6	7.5
8 France	10,133	12,228	(2,095):	3.1	2.8	1.8
9 Hong Kong	5,691	10,243	(4,552):	1.8	2.3	3.8
10 Brazil	4,289	9,324	(5,035):	1.3	2.1	4.2
11 Saudi Arabia	3,799	5,594	(1,795):	1.2	1.3	1.5
12 Soviet Union	2,768	578	(2,190):	0.9	0.1	-1.8
Twelve countries	$212,073	$321,506	($109,433):	68.5	72.9	92.2
United States	$322,200	$440,900	($118,700):	100.0	100.0	100.0

Source: U.S. Department of Commerce

trade imbalances are considered, Korea is fifth. Korea has twice the population of Taiwan, but because Taiwan's national income is higher, United States trade relations with Korea are comparable in magnitude to those with Taiwan. To facilitate comparisons, Table 12-1 also gives the percentage share of each of the twelve countries in the United States totals.

Several other important facts emerge from the data. First, trade imbalances tend to concentrate in the four East Asian countries that sell 33 percent of United States merchandise imports but take only 20.8 percent of American merchandise exports. The Japanese 1988 trade surplus of $52 million has improved only modestly, by $5 billion, over 1987's. Overall, the twelve countries account for more than 90 percent of the United States trade deficit. Finally, geographical contiguity matters, and the three North American countries form a very large trading block. In particular, it is worth noting that even under its strained economic conditions, Mexico is the third largest market for American products. This fact is too often overlooked. Encouraging the resumption of third world economic growth is simply enlightened American self-interest in the case of Mexico.

Macroeconomic Policies Expected by the United States from the Group of Asian NICs

The four Asian NICs, Korea, Taiwan, Hong Kong and Singapore, have been running considerable global current account surpluses as well as large bilateral trade surpluses with the United States, as seen in Table 12-1. For economic reasons and political convenience, many analyses focus on Korea and Taiwan. Taiwan, with its 20 million people, is one of the largest holders of foreign currency reserves in the world.[9] In contrast to Taiwan, Korea was the fourth largest debtor country as recently as 1985. Until very recently, the public debate centered on the burden of debt, and Koreans hold rather unpleasant memories of the problems they faced with public and private foreign lenders in the early 1980s. Very successful, if painful, structural adjustment reforms made between 1981 and 1984 produced a positive current account surplus in 1985. This surplus has been used to reduce the external debt and does not reflect a mercantilist policy: together with the debt reduction, external policies have included a broadly based program of trade liberalization initiated early in 1986.[10]

From the United States viewpoint, sustained foreign growth should be encouraged as a high-priority area of coordinated macroeconomic adjustment between the United States and the rest of the world. Influential economists believe that running current account surpluses is inappropriate for Korea and Taiwan at their present income levels.[11] Sustaining a current surplus is tantamount to exporting domestic savings rather than investing in the expansion of the domestic economy and improving standards of living.[12] This point is not taken at face value in Korea for various reasons. Korea has so far been a large debtor country and that there are fears of economic shocks during future political transitions. Korea also does not want to face again the problem period of structural adjustment of the early 1980s and it needs to reduce its external debt. Moreover, how permanent is the current account surplus?.

Three actions are advocated for Korea and Taiwan by United States economists: "increased government stimulus of domestic demand (employing both tax-cuts and stepped-up spending on infrastructure), faster trade liberalization, and currency appreciation."[13] The essential objective of these three actions would be to substitute domestic demand as the main engine of growth for exports, which should be more restrained. Apart from the question of their continuing validity over time, such proposals run into the obvious problem of being objectionable to Asian countries as long as the United States does not give convincing evidence that it is successfully tackling its own twin deficit problems. Otherwise, reasonable policy suggestions worth evaluating look like asking other countries to rescue the United States from its failure to adjust its own internal policies.

The Specific Bilateral United States Agenda with Korea

The economic agenda between the United States and Korea has two main components: trade and the exchange rate. The bilateral dialogue itself has five major components at present: the opening of markets to agricultural products; telecommunications; the opening of the service industries (insurance, banking, brokerage services, legal services); the treatment of intellectual property rights and various types of patents; and the broader area of general trade practices (tariffs, export financing, non-price regulatory barriers). Clearly, this agenda is built around the areas where the United States has kept a strong competitive advantage and where balance of payments progress can be made. It is also a list that is being negotiated with all the other Asian countries as well as with those of Europe.

It is not possible to detail the trade situation in each of these areas of trade opening. A recurring finding is that United States pressures on Korea to open its markets have benefited other exporting countries and have not really changed the bilateral trade imbalances so far. In industrial goods, trade opening has heavily favored Japan, for a variety of reasons including close proximity, strong after-sale services, high-quality goods with low probability of defects, and a close study of Korean market conditions by Japanese firms. The opening of the automobile sector has helped European models.

The opening of Korea's agricultural sector is contentious for non-economic reasons. On purely economic grounds Korea would benefit from opening the agricultural sector further and should facilitate the movement of low-productivity farmers to other activities. Economists recognize this long-term need. However, the government faces the social problem of a rapidly aging, low-income, yet still relatively large farm population.[14] How to share the benefits of growth is an intensely debated issue in Korea today, and the government does not see how it can impose more burden on the segment of the population which is aging most rapidly and has benefited least from development. Starting United States agricultural trade negotiations with tobacco goods was not a very felicitous choice and gave Korean opponents of an agricultural trade opening a field day. They pointed out that the United States government was pressuring Koreans to smoke more American cigarettes while officially warning its own citizens about the hazards of smoking. The opening of beef trade had also created tensions which were exacerbated by the poor management of beef imports by the Korean government, which hurt Korean beef producers at the time. A substantive problem for United States beef exports is that Australian products are more competitive in price and matching in quality. Beef imports are now 30 percent of Korean consumption, but Australia has 19 percent and the United States only 7 percent.[15]

To fend off United States political pressures and build up some economic clout, various non-market techniques have been used by Korea to increase United States goodwill. Highly publicized large buying missions have been sent to the United States to purchase capital-intensive and other industrial goods. Immediately after the first current account surplus of $4.6 billion in 1986, Korea set aside $2.5 billion in foreign currency loans and an additional $500 million of commercial loans to encourage imports of capital goods, equipment, and raw materials from the United States. For instance, in the case of beef, in order to placate the United States, Korea bypassed competitive tendering among foreign suppliers in Seoul and sent direct buying missions to states like Nebraska. It also informed suppliers about the kind of cuts preferred in the Korean market due to very different culinary habits. This reverse marketing and export earmarking ensured a share of beef exports from United States farmers and mitigated pressures.

For several years now, the United States has been putting pressure on Korea to raise its exchange rate.[16] The broader question for the United States is whether the dollar rate against the main currencies has stabilized too soon to improve the trade situation. At the current exchange rate, trade imbalances will remain. A domestic structural adjustment is needed to shift aggregate demand away from consumer demand to investment. The dollar adjustment had already begun in February 1985, and the United States deficit with East Asia declined globally from $107 billion in 1987 to $92 billion in 1988. Some analysts believe that the dollar devaluation has given all the adjustment dividends that could be expected. Why push so hard for nominal exchange-rate adjustments on the Asian NICs since trade relation issues are global? Because pressures on Korea and Taiwan do not affect very much the flow of funds to the United States, and Korea's exchange rate is linked to the United States dollar.

The Korean Perspective:
The Transition toward an Advanced Economy

> I think that there is a problem with mainstream economic thinking in this country. It relies on the rest of the world taking the initiative to do the job.
>
> Soon Cho, 1987

> The Korean economy is very dynamic and quick to respond to policy actions, so that adjustment actions might easily overshoot the target.
>
> Mahn-Je Kim and
> Sung-Tae Ro, 1987

It would be misleading to discuss Korea's economic priorities without referring first to the new political conditions.[17] The political changes of 1988 have completely redefined the framework of economic policymaking in Korea, making the process a technocratic rather than a political one. The transition to a democratic political system has been unreservedly well received in the United States. Currently, the executive branch is controlled by the ruling party and the legislature is controlled by competing minority parties. This new situation contrasts greatly with the authoritarian structure of the previous republic. It also ensures that United States economic pressures will move from having been predominantly technical reviews to coming under very public scrutiny, and that any policy decision will take more time.

The Korean economic agenda now focuses on managing the transition to advanced economic status. The present official policies are regrouped under five main headings: maintaining economic and social stability, balancing development among different social classes and areas of the country, accelerating liberalization and internationalization, reducing government intervention, and promoting economic fairness and competition. Because political issues are the most important, it is fortunate that Korea has just been going through three outstanding years of economic growth, above 12 percent. In all likelihood, domestic political progress and international adjustments will be paid for with considerably lower growth rates in the near future.

The United States' arguments that the won was greatly undervalued had lost most of their validity by the end of 1988. Korea's real effective exchange rate has adjusted in a major way through the joint effects of large increases in wages in 1987 and 1988 and exchange rates adjustment of equally large proportion. Since the 1985 Plaza accords, the Korean won has appreciated against the dollar by 32 percent. In 1988 alone the appreciation rate was 16 percent. The won was expected to appreciate still further in 1989. Wages rose by 20 percent in 1988 and, since productivity increased by only 10 percent, labor costs in economic terms increased by 10 percent. In Japan during the same period they declined by 10.7 percent (wages rose by 1.9 percent and productivity by 12.6 percent). In Taiwan, labor costs rose by only 5.2 percent. Under pressures from Congress, the U.S. Treasury Department has continued to make strong demands on Korea.[18] The net gains to the United States from further won appreciation are unclear, given that many of the goods that Korea exports to the United States are not produced in the United States. What is happening is substitution of imports into the United States from other sources. The fact is that Korean exports have already been slowing down drastically. In the first half of 1989, exports fell in volume terms and increased very little in value terms. The trends are still pointing downwards as further won appreciation is anticipated.

Maintaining economic and social stability is foremost on the Korean agenda at this time. Korean decision makers now speak with great concern about "the three highs": the appreciating value of the won; the rising prices of materials, parts, and components; and rapidly rising labor costs. Inflationary pressures have been increasing since 1987. After a five-year period of price stability that was very favorable to income equality, consumer prices rose by 6.1 percent in 1987 and 7 percent in 1988. As just noted, the rapid appreciation of the won had already led to a decline in the volume of exports in early 1989. This won appreciation has affected small and medium firms and the more labor-intensive sectors like textiles and shoe manufacturing. These activities also tend to be geographically concentrated in the Pusan region. A high priority is the effective development of labor relations processes in Korea that will stabilize labor markets, calm social tensions, and limit the number of strikes, which have had a clearly negative impact on the economy.

In the long term, the restructuring of the agricultural sector is a very high priority goal from both equity and efficiency viewpoints. The future of the rural population is a major part of the industrial transition. Korea does not have a comparative advantage in agriculture. It is therefore desirable to facilitate the transfer of the labor force from low-productivity agriculture to other sectors. This would also increase the scale of farm units, which is quite small. What is making a rapid opening of agricultural trade contentious is the structure of the Korean farm sector. In spite of a very high rate of out-migration, 20 percent of the population is still living on agriculture, compared to 5.2 percent in Japan and 2 percent in the United States. This high proportion of farm labor is a serious brake on rapid liberalization. Much of the farm population is aging and can not be retrained for other employment. A total of 2.3 million farmers, or 5 percent of the entire Korean population, is over fifty years of age. They represent the majority of heads of farm households.

The bottleneck slowing down agricultural adjustment has been the inability of industrial and regional policies to raise the non-farm income of rural households so far. There is a great contrast between Japan and Korea in this area. In Japan and Taiwan, off-farm income is the dominant source of rural income; in Korea non-farm income is still a low 30 percent of rural income. For these reasons and due to the fact that most of the urban population still has close ties with rural areas, agricultural trade discussions are particularly sensitive. They are seen at present in Korea as much more than mere economic or commercial issues. Various Korean studies are in progress for the organization of an agricultural structural adjustment fund and other alternatives to smooth out the transition. One approach which has been rejected is attaching a surcharge on farm imports to finance welfare payments to old farmers. Such funding could be also seen as a restraint of trade.

The Drift toward Unilateral United States Actions in Economic Relations

Process Protectionism and Voluntary Restraints Agreements

The general trade policy of the United States as the dominant economy has traditionally been to support the multilateral trading system represented by the General Agreement on Tariffs and Trade (GATT). During this decade, inability to gain control over the budget deficit and the trade deficit has gradually built up American trade policy as a rallying point of political debates. Political pressures have been rising to protect domestic industries, recapture traditional markets, and develop new ones. United States trade laws have a very broad coverage. Some of their most important provisions are: the unfair practices law, which allows the United States to determine unilaterally whether trade agreements are being followed (Section 301); the escape clause, which can bar a specific good from general trading rules but which is rather strict in the demonstration of economic injury (Section 201); unfair import practice laws (Section 337); and dumping and countervailing duty laws. Traditionally, the various trade laws gave a great deal of latitude to the executive branch on whether trade actions should be taken and how.

Two trends were in evidence during the 1980s. First, there was a consistent drift toward increasing automaticity in the application of United States trade statutes. Each successive trade law was aimed at refining and specifying criteria for action in order to reduce the scope for discretion on the part of the executive. This trend was caused by the deteriorating United States trade position and by the reluctance of the Reagan administration to intervene with tariffs—partly on policy grounds, but mostly for political reasons.[19] The Reagan administration raised the level of protectionism, but when granting protection it preferred quotas to tariffs, partly from the fear that retaliation breeds retaliation—or worse, emulation. As a substitute for explicit decisions, a pattern of "process protectionism" has developed whereby protectionism is built into the administrative "process" of determining import relief.[20] Both on political and rhetorical grounds, voluntary restraint agreements (VRAs) have been preferred.[21] The technique of using VRAs has been criticized by economists because such arrangements generate windfalls for protected United States industries and current foreign exporters without public gains in return. Benefited industries were not asked to demonstrate efficiency gains; and in some cases like automobiles it has been shown that VRAs raised United States prices, greatly increased the profitability of firms but were accompanied by losses of jobs, going against the standard political rationale for protection.[22]

Multilateral vs. Bilateral Trade: Japanese Surpluses with Asia

Trying to resolve trade problems bilaterally with the smaller economies of Asia may seem pragmatic. However, such thinking is flawed given the increasing trade interactions within Asia and the dominant role that Japan plays. The pattern of Japanese trade surpluses with Asian countries that have their own trade surpluses with the United States is presented in Table 12-2. These countries are listed by size of their merchandise trade deficit with Japan in 1987. The pattern is rather striking:

TABLE 12–2
Japan: Merchandise Trade Statistics with Asia and the United States
(In Billions of Dollars)

	1987 Japan balance with country	1987 U.S. balance with country	1988 Japan balance with country	1988 U.S. balance with country*
Hong Kong	7.37	-6.51	-0.37	-3.97
Korea	5.17	-9.89	3.62	-4.83
Taiwan	4.86	-16.01	n.a.	n.a.
Singapore	3.98	-2.34	5.96	-2.37
Thailand	1.17	-0.84	2.41	-1.36
China	0.86	-3.41	-0.37	-4.21
India	0.43	-1.26	0.28	-1.16
Philippines	0.05	-0.88	-0.31	-0.95
Malaysia	-2.63	-1.16	-1.68	-1.66
Indonesia	-5.48	-2.95	-6.55	-2.43
United States	53058.00		47978.00	

Source: International Monetary Fund, *Directions of Trade Statistics*
* The annual U.S. trade figures are based on extrapolation of data for the first nine months of 1988.
** Note that Japan-based figures in this table differ from U.S. based figures due to pricing.

all the countries with which the United States has a large trade deficit had the very same problem with Japan. Many Japanese exports to Asia are intermediate capital goods and not final good exports. Through Korea trade, Japan is running both direct and indirect surpluses with the United States. This table also confirms that the Asian NICs are not little Japans: they need to be more open to imports in order to grow. The question is once again who among the United States, Japan, or other countries is the source of these imports? For 1988, the trade data for the entire year were not yet available for the United States.[23] On the basis of extrapolation from the first three quarters, rapid change is apparent. The Japanese surpluses have declined significantly with the J-curve impact of the high yen and the macroeconomic policies encouraging shifts to domestic demand, consumer goods, and urban infrastructure.

Based on these Asian trade figures, one can think of at least three drawbacks to a bilateral discussion on trade between the United States and Korea rather than multilateral discussions. First, there is the shadow of Japan and the surplus which it has been running with the rest of Asia, including Korea. Second, if bilateral talks become the dominant United States mode of interaction, all smaller Asian nations including Korea will have to take a back seat to the bilateral United States-Japan relationship. There is some apprehension in Asia over the vision of a future United States free-trade area with Japan on the model of the treaty with Canada. Third, Korea would be fully exposed to the unilateral processes of the 1988 Omnibus Trade law without alternative channels for negotiation and redress.

An unintended result could well be that bilateral or unilateral United States approaches will simply stimulate intra-Asian trade, and in particular trade between Japan and Korea. In 1988, Korea overtook West Germany as Japan's second-largest supplier of manufactured goods, just behind the United States. Korea's exports climbed to $4.15 billion, an increase of 72.2 percent, while West Germany's exports were $3.8 billion. In spite of the drastic dollar-*yen* realignment since 1985, the United States' share of Japan's manufactured imports as opposed to agricultural goods and raw materials has continued to decline. This market share fell from the dominant position of 35 percent in 1985 to a market share of 26 percent in 1988, opposite to the direction of the dollar-*yen* adjustment.

The Lack of an Adequate Institutional Framework for Negotiations

United States-Korea economic relations face something of a double institutional void. Globally, institutions for international coordination of economic policies have become less effective. United States attitudes toward international cooperation have fluctuated widely since the early 1970s, sometimes sharply within short periods of time.[24] In spite of its dominant role in the world economic system, the United States has not been consistently supportive of economic cooperation. During much of the Reagan era, trade policies were a mix of benign neglect and selective protectionism. At other times, United States unilateral actions have been more militant. Interestingly, alternations between active and passive (benign neglect) unilateralism and multilateralism have not been synchronized between monetary affairs and trade issues, each policy area going independently through its own phases.[25] Less effective international institutions are another important reason for the disequilibria that emerged during the 1980s.

The problem of inadequate multilateral mechanisms is compounded for Korea and the other smaller Asian economies that do not have a forum where they can discuss their problems with other industrial countries. In earlier years, Korea avoided direct United States pressures on exchange rates by channeling them through the International Monetary Fund. As part of its transition toward a full industrial country status, Korea also signed in 1988 Article 8 of the IMF statutes, which sets rules for financial transfers across countries. However, there is no obvious mechanism for the multilateral discussion of trade issues outside the worldwide scope of the GATT and its various groupings. Ideas of an organization for Pacific nations comparable to the OECD have been discussed. Korea's joining OECD and following its trade rules is a possible alternative, but it has yet to happen.

The 1988 Omnibus Trade and Competitiveness Act: An Important Turn

The most dramatic unilateral trade move by the United States so far is the enactment into law in August 1988 of the Omnibus Trade and Competitiveness Act. This new law has made significant changes to many of the most important United States trade provisions. Its consequences are unpredictable. In this new law, Congress raised automaticity to very high levels, including a very specific calendar imposed on the president to which specific actions are attached. In the area of telecommunications it has very serious mandatory features.

What raises the prospect of international storms is the section of the Omnibus Trade Act dubbed "Super 301." The new law shifts the grounds for unfair trade in "sectors" to *countries* as unfair traders. That determination is to be made unilaterally by the United States government. Under the 1988 law, the United States trade representative (USTR) must produce an annual report describing barriers to United States exports. On the basis of this report, the USTR must select every year at least one priority country with which it must begin negotiations. The act provides a negotiating period of eighteen months for the countries initially identified and twelve months for countries identified in later years. This period may be extended for two additional years. If within three years no progress has been made, mandatory retaliatory actions are prescribed. Once a country has been designated, many steps become automatic. What is of great concern to the Asian NICs is that a United States administration may find it convenient to designate smaller countries for fear of retaliation from large countries. The smaller the country selected, the more severe the consequences of sanctions; but domestic deficits, competitiveness, or productivity in the United States would not be changed much by such actions.

A New Bilateral Twist: "Export Protectionism"

The desire to produce quick results under the ominous pressures of the 1988 Omnibus Trade Act and its "Super 301" clause is very likely to increase occurrences of managed trade, which runs counter to traditional American free trade principles. Due to continuing United States pressures, a pattern of "voluntary export expansion," or VIEs, is emerging among Asian NICs, where countries like Korea and Taiwan may divert trade from less powerful partners to give it to United States exporters.[26] A new form of "export protectionism" is emerging in favor of the United States, but contrary to earlier United States free trade policies.

Conclusion: Fundamental United States Choices Control the United States-Korea Agenda

Recent trends in trade relations between the United States and Korea give cause for some concern. The process chosen by the United States to address macroeconomic and trade issues between the two countries leads to unnecessary frictions. The great majority of Korean economists agree that maintaining an outward-looking attitude on imports as well as exports is very much in Korea's long-term interest. This is exactly what the United States wants. Korean economists were being heard at home and usually accepted. However, the publicity and mandated unilateral pressures embedded in the 1988 Omnibus Trade Law complicate rather than ease negotiations, given the political transition that Korea is undergoing. This new process undermines the position of the Korean decision makers who hope to pursue Korea's trade liberalization agenda at a good pace. Now that Korea is moving away from an authoritarian to a competitive political environment, those who are seen to agree to United States demands will be promptly accused of selling Korea out. Movement will become more difficult.

Given the size of its domestic market and its political and military role in Northeast Asia, there is little doubt that the United States can apply considerable trade pressure on Korea. Bilateral discussions can be transformed into unilateral moves. However, another paradox is that pressuring Korea to open up faster according to a United States-specified agenda will not solve the twin-deficit problems in any major way. The main causes of the trade deficit are domestic: they are the Federal budget deficit and the inability or unwillingness to consume less and invest more in competitive export industries.

The present United States problem is a chronic problem of priorities, not a chronic problem of instability. The key question is whether the United States will make the right choices in the Bush era. Allowing for generous blame on European and Asian countries, the primary obstacle to United States economic adjustments will remain if the underlying macroeconomic policies of the new administration continue much the same as those of the previous administration. There is no doubt that United States trading partners utilize unfair trading practices. However, on a purely objective plane Congress also knows that unfair practices account for only a small part of the United States trade deficit and that the roots of the problem are internal. They include a budget deficit which stimulates demand, raises real interest rates, and crowds out investment; the slow reorientation of business; and the inadequate education level and skills of the work force. However, the structure of decisionmaking is such that the question on everyone's mind is how long it will take Congress to tackle the basic changes that would make America truly competitive.

A treacherous and narrow strait has been created by the new trade negotiation processes. The negotiators who must navigate through it can still succeed, but it would be better to chart another course. What is urgently needed is to shift bilateral economic discussions to multilateral institutions such as GATT, OECD, or even a new body better tailored to the Pacific region. As we have seen, focusing on bilateral trade balances is not a good approach. In addition, trade discussions should be moved as much as possible away from industry—or (worse) product-specific discussions to agreements on broadly based rules and timetables. Excessively narrow and bilateral agendas favor organized protectionist lobbies and imply greater foresight on the part of governments than they really have. Doubtless, the expanding "process protectionism," which aims to exhaust exporters through an endless sequence of legal proceedings will expand the "Gross Legal Product" of the United States; it will also do little to increase United States competitiveness or consumer welfare.

On the Korean side, the domestic market is expanding rapidly, but it will never be large enough to make Korea like Japan. Korea must remain a trading nation, and it would be helpful to encourage the rapid development of its latent anti-protection lobbies to sustain outward-looking policies. Korea's self-perceptions should also catch up with its increased importance in international relations. Raising the level of economic education of the Korean political bodies during the transition toward advanced economic status is also a high priority. A greater understanding of economic alternatives will lessen chances of damaging domestic competition among political parties over the wrong external choices. The continuing development of bilateral and multilateral private United States-Korea business groups—and at some stage in Korea, labor groups—to supplement government-to-government processes is also very desirable.

The vast majority of people on both sides of the economic debate care very much about the continuation of good relations between the United States and Korea. Many are also aware that underlying very similar democratic and economic goals, social value systems and preferences differ in the two countries. Once again, they wistfully think, as Winston Churchill once did, that eventually the United States will do the right thing—when it has exhausted every other alternative. They are mindful that the costs of doing the wrong things too long are self-reinforcing negative behavior and spillover effects to third parties from United States-Korea economic relations. A growing risk is that unilateral processes such as "Super 301" could trigger a chain reaction of retaliatory moves between the United States and its most important trade partners in Asia and Europe, thereby starting a worldwide recession. There are better ways of confronting basic trade issues.

Notes

1. For a convenient history of earlier international capital movements see World Bank, *World Development Report 1985: International Capital and Economic Development* (New York, London: Oxford University Press, 1985).
2. See Stephen Marris, *Deficits and the Dollar, The World Economy at Risk* (Washington, D.C.: Institute of International Economics, 1987) and C. Fred Bergsten, *America in the World Economy, A Strategy for the 1990s* (Washington, D.C.: Institute for International Economics, 1988).
3. See for instance Bergsten, *America in the World Economy*, especially chapters 1 and 9.
4. See William R. Cline, "Macroeconomic Influences on Trade Policy," *American Economic Review*, May 1989, 123–27.
5. In fiscal year 1989, which started in October 1988, the budget deficit was about $23 billion per month. First quarter receipts were $222 billion, and outlays were $290 billion. The fiscal gap widened in 1989 with the slowdown of the economy, especially with interest rates leading to higher debt payments. The total 1988 fiscal deficit was $155 billion. The government paid $34.98 billion in interest in December 1989, compared with $18.14 in November. First quarter fiscal 1989 total interest payments were $68.27 billion.
6. The shift to internal demand-led growth underlines the remarkable flexibility of the Korean economy. Following the 12 percent growth rates of 1986–1988, the economy experienced a considerable cooling off, with growth dropping below six percent. A gradual recovery is now in progress, with a large component of household consumption and domestic demand as the engine of recovery.
7. A recent commentary points to increasing bipartisan political consensus favoring a tougher, more activist trade policy. Concern is expressed about the problem of "raising expectations that can't be

fulfilled...[due to] America's internal problems—budget deficits, a flawed education system, inattention to quality...as a large part of thetrade deficit cause. Most analysts—[Representative Richard] Gephardt included—acknowledge that these macro-economic problems account for 80 percent of the explanation, with only 20 percent chargeable to 'unfair' trade practices. In fact, the Reagan administration's first trade reperesentative, William Brock, used to say that 'the nightmare I have is that Japan does everything we ask them to do to open its markets and they still run a huge surplus!" See Hobart Rowen,"An Outbreak of Solidarity on the Trade Front," *Washington Post*, April 30, 1989.

8. Note that another trade figure is more widely used. It is the United States trade balance that includes freight and insurance (c.i.f. pricing), which yields a more comprehensive deficit figure of $137.3 billion for 1988 against $170.3 billion for 1987.

9. Few indicators could better illustrate the disequilibria which prevail across the world economy than the fact that the United States non-gold reserves in the middle of 1988 amounted to $25.3 billion. They were less than half as large as those of Taiwan, whose economy is thirty times smaller. These United States reserves were also half of those of Japan and Germany, respectively, and of the same order of magnitude as those of France, Italy, Spain, and the United Kingdom. (See Bergsten, *America in the World Economy*, 112.)

10. The adjustment process included reducing the fiscal deficit from 4.7 percent of GNP in 1981 to less than 0.1 percent in 1986. It also required painful and very unpopular freezes of public salaries and of the grain purchase price for farmers. Private wages and compensations were also stabilized. These sacrifices were rewarded by Korea's ability to take advantage of the new international opportunities created by "the three lows": in interest rates, in oil prices, and in the value of the dollar, to which the won is closely related. The three consecutive years of outstanding but not quite expected real growth rates of about 12 percent resulted from this willingness to take a long-term view and to work toward it.

11. Taiwan's per capita income was about $6,000 and that of Korea was $3,700 at the end of 1988, based on current exchange rates.

12. Bela Balassa and John Williamson, *Adjusting to Success: Balance of Payments Policy in the East Asian NICs* (Washington, D.C.: Institute of International Economics, June 1987).

13. Bergsten, *America in the World Economy*, 107

14. This rapid aging of the farm population is due to the accelerating rate of departure from farming. In 1988, the farm population of Korea declined by 6.7 percent.

15. In early 1989 the average c.i.f. price of a ton of American beef in Korea was $4,450, compared to $2,600 for Australian beef. *Business Korea*, March 1989.

16. The rationale for exchange rate adjustments was developed by Balassa and Williamson in their 1987 study, *Adjusting to Success: Balance of Payments Policy in the East Asian NICs.*

17. Soon Cho became deputy prime minister of Korea in December 1988. His comments were made at the 1987 IIE-KDI Conference in Washington. See Thomas O. Bayard and Soo-Gil Young, *Economic Relations between the United States and Korea: Conflict or Cooperation?* (Washington, D.C.: Institute for International Economics, 1988), 35. The quotes from Kim and Ro are from the same conference, 63.

18. Even considering congressional pressures, it is very puzzling for several reasons to see 1989 public statements by the United States Treasury accusing the Korean government of manipulating their currency for trade advantage. First, the *won* has appreciated significantly, and there is always a lag between nominal exchange rates effects and shifts in trade balance. The so-called J-curve effect refers to the fact that it takes up to two years for business adjustments to gather momentum. Second, rapid wage increases do matter! Before expressing strong views, it would be proper to analyze movements in the Korean real effective exchange rates at least since 1986, when the trade surplus first emerged. Finally, given the explicitness of the Korean trade opening plans, it is legitimate to ask whether distinction need not be made among various Asian countries and historical periods. The trade and currency policies of Korea in the 1980s are not those of Japan in the 1970s and earlier decades.

19. See James Cassing and Arye L. Hillman, "Political Influence Motives and the Choice between Tariffs and Quotas," *Journal of International Economics*, November 1985, 279–90.

20. For a recent and very lucid review of "process protectionism" ending prior to the 1988 Omnibus Trade Act, see Jeffrey J. Schott, "United States Trade Policy: Implications for U.S.-Korean Relations," in Bayard and Young, *Economic Relations between the United States and Korea.*

21. See Gary Hufbauer, *Trade Protection in the United States: 31 Cases* (Washington, D.C.: Institute of International Economics, 1986), and Gary Hufbauer and Howard Rosen, *Trade Policy for Troubled Industries* (Washington, D.C.: Institute of International Economics, 1986).

22. Clifford M. Winston and Associates, *Blind Intersection? Policy and the Automobile Industry* (Washington, D.C.: Brookings Institution, 1987).

23. Note that this simple table focusing on net trade surpluses and deficits does not reveal the rapid increases in gross flows across the Asia region from year to year. Also, note that the nature of Hong Kong trade is changing significantly as it rapidly integrates with its hinterland, Guangdong province in China. Since the opening of China to trade, Hong Kong has been steadily reverting to its historical role as an *entrepot* and service base to mainland trade.

24. Questions have been raised whether structural defects in United States international decisionmaking can be remedied effectively. Martin

Feldstein, former chief of the Council of Economic Advisers, has argued that the United States is weak in its capacity to participate effectively in international coordination of macroeconomic policies. This weakness is constitutional because the executive branch cannot make binding commitments on fiscal policy while the Federal Reserve Board has independent authority over monetary policy. See Martin Feldstein, "Thinking about International Economic Coordination," *Journal of Economic Perspectives,* (Spring 1988): 3–13. Regarding trade, it is noteworthy that the United States trade representative does not have direct decision-making powers.

25. In addition, the nature of monetary coordination among central banks has been drastically altered by the enormous growth and international integration of capital markets. Reportedly, upward of $450 billion cross international borders every day. Such figures dwarf the financial resources at the disposal of central banks to intervene in financial markets. Fortunately, central bank operations can still have a strong impact at the margin, due to the way they affect expectations about public policies. The point here is that the quality of international economic policy coordination has to improve given the ability of capital markets to move large volumes of financial resources across countries very quickly.

26. In response to the pressures of the 1988 Omnibus Trade Law, Taiwan has announced a "Detailed Action Plan" to reduce its trade surplus with the United States and increase United States imports. The plan calls for a 10 percent reduction of the trade surplus with the United States every year and a reduction of the total trade surplus from 10 percent down to 4 percent by 1992. Typical methods would be, for instance, to restrict automobile imports from countries other than the United States or the EEC and for Taiwan to steer the business to countries with whom it has large surpluses.

References

Balassa, Bela and John Williamson. *Adjusting to Success: Balance of Payments Policy in the East Asian NICs.* Washington D.C.: Institute of International Economics, June 1987.

Bayard, Thomas O. and Soo-Gil Young. *Economic Relations Between the United States and Korea: Conflict or Cooperation?* Washington D.C.: Institute for International Economics, 1988.

Bergsten, C. Fred. *America in the World Economy. A Strategy for the 1990s.* Washington D.C.: Institute for International Economics, November 1988.

Cassing, James and Arye L. Hillman. "Political Influence Motives and the Choice between Tariffs and Quotas." *Journal of International Economics,*

November 1985, 279–290.

Cline, William R. "Macroeconomic Influences on Trade Policy." *American Economic Review,* May 1989, 123–127.

Feldstein, Martin. "Thinking about International Economic Coordination." *Journal of Economic Perspectives,* vol. 2, no. 2 (Spring 1988), 3–13.

International Economic Cooperation. Chicago: University of Chicago Press, 1987.

Hufbauer, Gary, Diane T. Berliner, and Kimberly Ann Elliot. *Trade Protection in the United States: 31 Cases.* Washington, D.C.: Institute of International Economics, 1986.

_____ and Howard Rosen. *Trade Policy for Troubled Industries.* Washington D.C.: Institute of International Economics, 1986.

Krugman, Paul. "Is Free Trade Pass?" *Economic Perspectives,* vol. 1, no. 2, Fall 1987, 131–144.

Marris, Stephen. *Deficits and the Dollar, The World Economy at Risk.* Washington, D.C., Institute of International Economics, Updated edition, 1987.

Winston, Clifford M. and associates. *Blind Intersection? Policy and the Automobile Industry.* Washington, D.C.: Brookings Institution, 1987.

World Bank. *World Development Report 1985: International Capital and Economic Development.* New York: Oxford University Press, 1985.

13

The Military Situation and Capabilities of North Korea

Maj. Gen. Jack E. Thomas, USAF (Ret.)

Introduction

THE UNITED STATES HAS EXPENDED BILLIONS OF DOLLARS over the past thirty-five years in direct reaction to the perceived military capabilities and intentions of North Korea.* American Far Eastern policy and military strategy over this period have been directly linked with the rival military capabilities and strategies of the two Koreas as they face each other across a two-and-a-half-mile-wide artificially designated demarcation line near the 38th parallel.

In terms of personnel strength, the armed forces of the Democratic People's Republic of Korea (DPRK) are the sixth largest in the world, exceeded only by the military of the Soviet

---

* The judgments expressed herein are those of the writer and do not reflect the views of the United States Air Force or the Department of Defense, except as presented in the section titled "Views of the U.S. Department of Defense."

Union, China, the United States, India, and Vietnam.[1] Yet the DPRK covers an area smaller than that of Mississippi, and its population of about 22 million is less than that of California.

The Republic of Korea (ROK) is the ninth-largest military force in the world, although the ROK is only slightly larger than Indiana in area and its population of about 43 million is only a bit larger than that of the combined New York-Pennsylvania-Ohio region.[2]

Korean history goes back many centuries, but it has been rarely free of some type of foreign domination. This national history is significant, however, because it gives today's two Koreas a sense of being one people and endows them with an urge toward unification.[3]

Though politically independent since 1945, the two Koreas have had to depend on foreign military support, first in order to survive and later in order to build their own military capabilities—capabilities focused solely and directly against each other. Communist-controlled since its inception, North Korea is today one of the most tightly closed societies in the world. Kim Il Sung is the only leader that North Korea has ever had. Even though the pugnacity of his public foreign policy positions has diminished somewhat recently, he continues to pursue the goals, objectives, and controls that he has laboriously constructed. To that end he has for several years built up the role of his son, Kim Jong Il, as his designated successor.

The cult of personality that has been created around Kim Il Sung is such that thus far his life and personality are inseparable from the history of North Korea.[4] Students of the DPRK and visitors to that country tend to be convinced that the people of North Korea implicitly believe what Kim Il Sung tells them and will do whatever he directs. He has long taught North Koreans that a satanic United States forced the South Koreans to attack the North in 1950 and still plans to conquer and destroy North Korea.[5] Ostensibly to prevent this, Kim Il Sung has militarized North Korea, and there has been no indication of popular protest against the personal and economic burdens which this imposes. That is one reason why it is important that the United States, the Republic of Korea, and American allies and friends understand what has occurred and is still going on in North Korea.

The reopening of discussions between representatives of the ROK and the DPRK in 1988, after a long break, raised hopes that their antagonism might have mellowed a bit, but definite results are still lacking. It is probably significant that South Korea is developing contacts with the Soviets and Eastern Europe. Kim Il Sung has recently indicated a desire for economic and technical links with capitalist countries; but this, too, is highly tentative.

The United States maintains more than 40,000 military personnel in South Korea, primarily out of concern over what Kim Il Sung may have in mind for unification of the two Koreas by armed force. Outside the DPRK it is widely believed that any aggression would be initiated by North Koreans; thus this paper focuses on North Korea—its military capabilities and limitations, the support it might expect from communist allies, and the manner in which Kim Il Sung (or his successor) might use military force against South Korea.

How real are the risks of war in the Korean peninsula? If war should come, how do the forces of North and South compare? Do recent changes in the DPRK military force structure suggest planning for military action other than conventional warfare? Are recent developments likely to have an impact on the need for continued United States military presence in South Korea?

The picture is murky and the evidence somewhat conflicting, but enough is available to warrant careful examination.

The Korean War, 1950–1953

Today's military problems in the Korean peninsula did not begin with the Korean War, but they cannot be understood except on the basis of the Korean War.[6]

The military face-off in Korea exists today because of concerns on the part of American leaders in 1945 of complete communist takeover of Korea by Soviet troops, and because of artificial splitting of the peninsula into two parts based on United States initiative.[7] Had the division of Korea not occurred, other problems undoubtedly would have arisen in this part of the world; but they would have been different from what we experience today.

Had the Soviet Union not originally acceded to the United States proposal that the peninsula be divided at the 38th

parallel, today's Korea might well be a Soviet-controlled country providing airfields and navy bases for Soviet forces facing
the People's Republic of China (PRC) and Japan. The Soviet
Union plucked Kim Il Sung virtually from nowhere and in-
stalled him as North Korea's leader. If he had not been amenable to Soviet wishes in his early days of power, they would have
found someone else.

The splitting of the peninsula may have improved the situation from a United States-only standpoint, but it is debatable
whether the improvement was worth the cost—including 33,643
American battle deaths and 103,284 Americans wounded in the
Korean War.[8] What is hardly debatable, however, is that the
strategic interests of the United States in the Far East have been
improved by a free South Korea, just as the existence of South
Korea also supports the geopolitical interests of both Japan and
the Peoples Republic of China. In light of how South Korea has
developed economically and industrially, and how it seems to
be developing democratically, freedom also has proved to be
highly advantageous to the South Koreans.

The die was cast in 1945, and considering Soviet policies as
the cold war got underway, the drastic postwar demobilization
of the United States, and Kim Il Sung's extravagant ambitions,
the Korean War in retrospect was almost inevitable.[9]

Though firefights had occurred from time to time along the
demarcation line, even so the major assault by North Korean
forces across the 38th parallel on June 25, 1950, had an impact
on the postwar world that few anticipated at the time.[10]

Millions of words have been written about the Korean War.
In a nutshell, the North Korean surprise onslaught virtually
destroyed South Korea's smaller army, but the United States
sent in from Japan enough troops, even though poorly prepared, to enable retention of a foothold on the south coast at
Pusan. The surprise United States Inchon landing, behind the
main thrust of the North Korean effort, killed the impetus of
the North Korean drive; and the weight of United States
reinforcements, shells, and air attacks forced the North Koreans out of the south. In pursuit, the Americans overran North
Korea and continued north toward the Yalu River, which
brought out Chinese communist troops, who, primarily by
disregarding their own severe manpower losses, pushed the

Americans back to the vicinity of the 38th parallel. All of this happened within the first six months of the war. A war of attrition followed for more than two years near the present demarcation line, until an armistice was finally signed on July 27, 1953. That armistice is still in effect since no peace treaty has ever been signed.[11]

At the start of the war, the United Nations Security Council, with the Soviet Union temporarily absent, declared North Korea the aggressor and approved a resolution calling for withdrawal of the North Korean forces. Shortly afterward, the council recommended that member nations go to the aid of South Korea. Before the conflict ended, sixteen nations had provided military forces of some kind.[12]

The North Korean government has never retracted its initial claim—which North Koreans apparently still believe—that South Korea initiated the war on direct orders from the United States in order to enable the Americans to move in and destroy North Korea. Since North Korea experienced huge casualties and massive physical destruction during the war, it has not been difficult to teach North Koreans to "hate" Americans.

The People's Republic of China saved North Korea from being completely overrun and perhaps disappearing as a nation, but that is not what North Koreans believe today. In the Pyongyang museum devoted to furthering the cult of Kim Il Sung the section devoted to the "Great Patriotic War" has one fuzzy photograph showing Chinese troops crossing a bridge. When questioned about it, the guide has replied, "Well, yes, we did have a little help from the Chinese, too."[13] Because of the manner in which the Chinese committed troops en masse, that "little help" led to huge casualties. The Chinese have not released any figures, but estimates of at least a half-million men appear reasonable.[14]

From the broadest viewpoint, the most important effect of the Korean War was the determination by America's political leadership that the post-World War II demobilization and the retention of only very limited active-duty American military strength was tempting the Soviet Union to accept the risks of general war arising from Soviet support to communist governments in limited war. Even though the Soviets did not actually commit their own troops to combat, American officials strongly believed that without direct and continuing support and encouragement from the Soviet Union, the North Koreans would not have launched an invasion of the South. The Korean War led the United States to rebuild military forces of a size and type that had not been contemplated until the Korean War established such a need.[15]

It is admittedly problematical whether the drive to maintain strong military forces would have been sustained in the United States without the USSR's continued aggressive modernization of its own forces and seeking of state-of-the-art military capabilities; but the Korean War was nevertheless the turning point for the United States military in the postwar years.

The basing of foreign troops in an independent country, particularly when that basing continues for decades, cannot but pose problems. Nevertheless, the presence of United States troops in South Korea has, overall, been less troublesome than might have been expected. Leaders in both South Korea and the United States have viewed the presence of American troops in South Korea as a necessary deterrent to renewed military action by the North Koreans. President Carter, during his 1976 election campaign, suggested that United States troops might be withdrawn; but strong resistance both within the United States and from American allies such as Japan led to this proposal's being quickly dropped.[16] Withdrawal of United States military forces still has its advocates,[17] and the United States media have publicized anti-American military views of Korean student demonstrators, but the United States government has given no indication of any current intention to withdraw its forces from Korea.[18]

Military Growth

The foundation for today's military capabilities in North Korea was laid shortly after the armistice was signed in July 1953. Rebuilding of the nearly devastated country had first priority, and it took several years for Kim Il Sung to consolidate his position as the nation's leader; but at the same time he was rebuilding the war-shattered military forces. The level of tension between North and South Korea which followed the armistice made it inevitable that both sides would reconstruct their forces and seek continuing support from their superpower sponsors.[19]

North Korea had substantial natural resources, and the Japanese occupation had laid the foundation for an industrial base, so during the 1950s and 1960s, with help from both China and the Soviet Union, a major effort was put into development of an industrial base to support a sizable military structure.

Support came from an intensive propaganda effort that sought to change the traditional family-oriented Korean culture. Kim Il Sung and his cohorts attempted to move a society from one in which father-son relationships are the key to one in which ruler-subject relationships predominate. A major element in the indoctrination of the younger generation of North Koreans has been the concept that their basic responsibility is to fight and die if necessary for the national father, Kim Il Sung.

The North Korean leadership remembered well the devastating power that the United States had directed against North Korea after the initial phases of the Korean War, and as it became clear that reunification would not come easily and that the issues involved were very complex, Kim was forced to plan for the long haul.

The Soviet Union had provided the primary equipment and supplies during the Korean war, but in the years immediately following the war Chinese influence and support became more prominent. In the early 1960s there was an almost open break with Moscow as Kim sided with the Chinese in the Sino-Soviet split. Soviet aid was restored in 1965, but the problems had emphasized that North Korea needed to develop its own internal capabilities to support its military forces.

This fit with Kim's widely publicized concept of *juche* (self-reliance). *Juche* means that in national defense matters North Korea must have its own strong, self-reliant, fully credible military capability. Support from other countries can be important in wartime, but only in an auxiliary role. Self-reliant military preparedness is the most important factor.[20]

One complicating—and expensive—factor in military development was Kim's early decision to put emphasis on subversion and guerrilla actions while he was also building up conventional capabilities. More than 500 incidents occurred in 1967 as guerrillas and commandos attempted to penetrate the demarcation zone (DMZ). In January 1968 a special assassination team got to within 500 yards of the presidential palace in Seoul. Later that year commandos from the North landed near Ulsan on the South Korean east coast and survived long enough to fight their way inland. In late 1968 the North Koreans hijacked the USS *Pueblo*, a signals intelligence collector, and in early 1969 shot down a United States EC-121 while it was on an electronic reconnaissance mission over international waters.

As the 1970s began, relations between the two Koreas verged on undeclared war, and Kim recognized that he had to change his tactics. Growing effectiveness of South Korean security services, improvement of its military, and increasing economic prosperity plus political solidity in the South apparently convinced Kim Il Sung that the irregular warfare effort was costing more than it was worth. The reopening of relations between the United States and the PRC changed the complexion of Kim's world. As a partial compensation, Kim's propaganda machine focused on spreading the word that Kim was a revolutionary hero of worldwide stature.[21]

Facing reality at the Korean Workers' Party (KWP) Fifth Congress of November 1970, Kim Il Sung told his people:

> The national defense capacity we now have has been achieved at a very substantial cost. Speaking frankly, our national defense expenditures as compared with the small size of the country have proved too great a burden.[22]

Even so, Kim emphasized to the congress that North Korea had to stand on its own but had to tailor its armed forces and its war preparations to meet its own specialized needs. He told his followers:

> If we try, instead, to mechanically copy and dogmatically bring in foreign weapons and military technical equipment allegedly to modernize the People's army, it may bring a serious loss to the national defense building. We must perfect the art of war in such a way to make up for the defects in the People's army, reinforce its weak links, and foster its strong points.

The die was clearly cast. North Korea would have to sacrifice other things in order to pay for a strong military force. The policy remains unchanged, and if there have been grumblings they have not reached the ears of foreigners.

How serious Kim Il Sung was about his military buildup intentions is clearly shown by Table 13-1, which compares the military personnel strengths of North Korea and South Korea over the past 26 years. A critical changeover point came in 1978–1979. South Korea's military strength was only about half that of North Korea at the start of the Korean War, but from shortly after the shooting ended until the late 1970s military forces in the South consistently included more personnel than those in the North. In 1978–1979, however, the estimated size of North Korean forces jumped by 120,000 to 160,000, while South Korean military personnel declined in number. In that year North Korean forces became the larger for the first time since the armistice.

The North Korean increase reported in 1978–1979 was entirely in the army, where estimated strength rose from 440,000 to 560,000–600,000 and the order of battle showed a jump of fifteen infantry divisions, from twenty to 35. The 35-division estimate held firm until 1984, but it dropped back to 25 or 26 as North Korea developed motorized infantry brigades, more armored brigades, and at least 80,000 personnel in its special purpose forces. Reassessments in 1989 increased the total from 26 to 31 active infantry divisions and 25 reserve infantry divisions (rather than two divisions and eighteen independent brigades).[23]

Statistics which relate to a society as tightly closed as is North Korea must always be viewed with recognition that some degree of estimation is involved. During a July 1980 conversation with Congressman Stephen J. Solarz, Kim Il Sung insisted that the actual North Korean troop strength was 350,000 to 400,000, rather than the 700,000 estimated by American intelligence, and that North Korea was not receiving military aid from any other country, but was largely dependent upon its own efforts.[24]

In today's world, the size and disposition of military forces, particularly of large units, are very difficult to conceal from intelligence collectors, and Kim Il Sung's disclaimer was not reflected in later estimates.[25] Despite Kim's denial of receiving foreign assistance, North Korea's military aircraft and much of its other major military equipment are still identified as Soviet-built. Some Chinese-type equipment is still in use.

TABLE 13–1
A Comparison of North Korea and South Korea
Estimated Military Personnel 1963–1989

	North Korea	South Korea
1989	1,040,000	650,000
1988	842,000	629,000
1987	838,000	629,000
1986	840,000	601,000
1985	838,000	598,000
1984	784,500	622,000
1983	784,500	622,000
1982	784,000	601,600
1981	782,000	601,600
1980	678,000	600,600
1979	632,000–672,000	619,000
1978	512,000	642,000
1977	500,000	635,000
1976	495,000	595,000
1975	467,000	625,000
1974	467,000	625,000
1973	470,000	633,000
1972	402,500	634,750
1971	401,000	634,250
1970	413,000	645,000
1969	384,500	620,000
1968	384,000	620,000
1967	368,000	612,000
1966	368,000	571,600
1965	353,000	604,000
1964	352,000	600,000
1963	310,000	627,000

Source: International Institute for Strategic Studies, *The Military Balance* (London, annual publications)

Strength estimates and order-of-battle figures published by the International Institute for Strategic Studies are used throughout this article because they are the best available on a unclassified basis. American intelligence organizations seldom publish unclassified specifics on North Korea's military, but in 1983 the CIA's *World Factbook* reported that DPRK military personnel totalled 784,000 (army 700,000; navy 33,000; and air force 51,000).[26] The totals that were published for 1983–1984 by the International Institute were identical to those of the CIA, except for an additional 500 men in the navy, thus raising the institute's grand total to 784,500.

North Korea has developed the formidable military forces it now possesses even though its population of 22.5 million is only about half that of the 43.3 million in South Korea. The North Korea pool of manpower fit for military service is about 3.5 million, less than half the 8.1 million in South Korea. The North Korean GNP is less than one-eighth that of South Korea ($20 billion compared with $171 billion). The per capita income of North Koreans is less than one-fourth what it is in South Korea ($910 as against $4,045).[27]

North Korea's strategic military doctrine has been described as *juche* (self-reliance), people's revolution (or liberation), and protracted guerrilla warfare,[28] but the military power that has been developed in recent years is, in terms of personnel strength and equipment, capable of strong offensive and defensive actions as well as guerrilla operations.

Composition of North Korean Military Forces

Any peacetime assessment of the wartime capabilities of a military force is fraught with uncertainties. This is particularly true in the case of North Korea because of its closed society, the tight security applied to matters in which Western societies are quite open, and the lack of data on which to judge such matters—the quality of training, the quality of leadership, the technical skills of enlisted personnel, the adequacy of logistical backup, and the like. The test of past combat performance cannot be applied because personnel now in uniform had no field experience in the Korean War.

Several factors can be identified as favorable for the North Korean forces.

The senior military leadership is a trusted element of the national power structure. Because of the manner in which North Korea was founded and its government established, the military were never a potential adversary of the political leadership.[29]

Since military service is respected as a public duty, North Korean forces should benefit from the longer required terms of service in the North than is the case in South Korea. The service tour for all arms is 30 to 36 months in South Korea, but North Korean required service is five to eight years in the army, five to ten years in the navy, or three to four years in the air force. Some experience is gained by North Korean military personnel sent abroad to serve in a training role. In 1987 it was estimated that over 1,500 were on such assignments. This included about 300 in Iran, 1,000 in Angola, and small contingents in nine other African countries. The current total is much smaller but is believed to include advisers in ten African countries, including 100 in Madagascar.

Even though enough information is not publicly available to allow judgments as to the fighting quality of North Korean forces, enough is published in the West to make it possible to examine the composition of North Korean military forces and to draw comparisons.[30]

Ground Forces

About 90 percent of all North Korean military personnel are in the ground forces. Currently, the estimated strength of the DPRK army is 930,000, up from 750,000 in 1988, and more than double its strength in the late 1970s. Statistically, this army is a formidable force.

Included are 31 infantry and motorized infantry divisions, fifteen armored brigades, twenty motorized infantry brigades, and four independent infantry brigades, plus special purpose forces of at least 80,000 personnel and a large artillery command.

The army is estimated to be equipped with some 3,200 medium battle tanks, 350 light tanks, 1,600 armored personnel carriers, over 7,000 artillery pieces and rocket launchers, and 8,000 air-defense guns, plus 54 Soviet FROG surface-to-surface missiles. They are also rumored to have fifteen B-type SCUD SSM's.

Several developments in the North Korean ground forces during the past decade are also worthy of note. More than 1,000 medium and 150 light tanks have been added to the estimated inventory. The number of artillery pieces has doubled. Further, the number of anti-aircraft guns has increased by about 3,000 tubes. Ten years ago the North Koreans had only nine FROG SSMs. Today that number is believed to be six times as large. Some modification is seen in the basic organizational structure, with more emphasis on smaller units. Two tank divisions and five independent tank regiments are gone. Instead, fifteen armored brigades are listed. Twenty motorized infantry brigades are now identified as against none ten years ago.

Perhaps the most significant recent development has been the North Korean special purpose forces. In the late 1960s, the estimated North Korean army structure included "special commando teams" with an estimated total strength of 15,000. In the early 1970s, references to these teams were dropped. But in the late 1970s, the army organization showed as active three reconnaissance brigades and five airborne battalions.

The 1980 order of battle indicated that the North Koreans had 22 special forces (commando) brigades. The next year the number of brigades was 26, including three amphibious commando brigades. In 1982, strength of the special forces was estimated at 100,000; and the structure included a corps headquarters and twenty brigades, with an airborne element as well as the three amphibious commando brigades.

The structure was relatively unchanged for the next several years. However, the estimated personnel strength in the special purpose forces dropped from 100,000 to 80,000 in 1985. It came back up in 1986, and in 1987 it was estimated to be 112,000. In 1988 the figure was placed at 80,000. Also in 1987, 35 light infantry battalions were added to the composition of the Special Purpose Corps. Its composition is now believed to include 25 brigades, including three commando, four reconnaissance, and one river-crossing regiment; plus three amphi- bious, three airborne, and 22 light infantry battalions.

This corps, which includes nearly 10 percent of the personnel in the ground forces, seems to have been developed for something other than a defense of North Korea or a conventional move against South Korea.

Naval Forces

The North Korean navy is small. Its 40,000 personnel make it less than one-twentieth the size of the army. The two fleets are completely divided, one on the east coast and the other on the west coast. The navy's vessels are a mixture from Soviet, Chinese, and Korean shipyards.

The navy has grown by 13,000 personnel in the past ten years. Over this period the most significant change in its composition has been the upgrading of the submarine force. Clearly, North Korea has been seeking to develop a wartime capability to use submarines against both United States naval power and supply ships on which South Korea would be dependent.

Keeping track of the changes in North Korea's submarine strength again illustrates the problem of acquiring unclassified information about a tightly closed society. In 1977 the navy was estimated to have ten submarines of the Soviet W-class and Chinese R-class. The following year the total was fifteen submarines (four Soviet W-class and eleven Chinese R-class). Another Chinese R-class was added to the total in 1980, and three more in 1981. In 1982, however, the nineteen submarines of the North Korean navy were identified as four Soviet W-class, four Chinese R-class, and eleven locally built from the Chinese design and identified as the Type 033/R class. Two more locally built submarines were added to the force in 1983, and one was dropped in 1985.

A new element was added in 1986 when five miniature submarines, characteristics unknown, were listed as "possible." The number was raised to seven in 1987 and then dropped from the listing in 1988. Currently, North Korea is considered to have 23 submarines, including the four old Soviet W-class and nineteen Chinese Type 031/Soviet Romeo class, but it is not clear how many may have been built in Korea.

Amphibious craft increased from 90 ten years ago to 99 in 1983, and the number is currently set at about 126.

North Korea has two frigates; but the bulk of its vessels are patrol and coastal combatants, including 4 corvettes, 99 missile craft, 173 torpedo craft, and 157 patrol craft. The primary recent expansion has been in missile craft—from 10 years ago to 18 in 1983 and 29 in 1989.

Two coastal defense sites for SAMLET missiles were first identified in 1980. In 1983 six sites were identified manned by two missile regiments. There has been no known further expansion.

The Air Force

By the early 1960s North Korea's air force was estimated to have about 500 combat aircraft and 30,000 personnel. Over the years it has grown to a current 650 combat aircraft, 115 armed helicopters, and 70,000 personnel.

Eight regiments of ground attack aircraft have a strength of about 290 aircraft, down from a total of 400, which had been about the same since the late 1960s. Retirement of older aircraft caused the reduction. Until the early 1970s, these regiments were all equipped with what were originally identified as Soviet MiG-15/17, then identified as the Chinese-built version of the MiG-15 and -17, the J-2 and J-4 (*J* standing for *Jianjiji* or "fighter"). The J-2 and J-4 are no longer in the North Korea air force, replaced by 100 Chinese J-5s.

In 1972 a regiment of Soviet Su-7 aircraft was introduced, and that regiment now consists of 20 Su-7 and 10 of the newer Su-25/Frogfoot, the counterpart of the U.S. Air Force A-10. In 1981, MiG-19/W-5 aircraft were introduced, and within two years there were 100 aircraft of this type, now identified as the Chinese-built versions, the J-6/Q-5 (the *Q* representing *Qiang-jiji*, "attack aircraft"). These model aircraft are about thirty years old. The current total is 100 J-L and 40 Q-5 aircraft.

The North Korean fighter-interceptor force of 290 aircraft is composed of 120 MiG-21/Fishbed, introduced in North Korea at least twenty years ago, 60 Chinese-built J-6 aircraft (a version of the Soviet MiG-19 that first flew in 1961), 46 MiG-23/Flogger (an aircraft that has been in the Soviet air force since 1970, but was introduced into the North Korean air force only in 1986), 40 Chinese J-7 and 24 MiG-29. Despite the introduction of the MiG-23 and MiG-29 aircraft, the total size of the DPRK interceptor force is little different in size from what it was a decade ago.

Since at least the mid-1960s, North Korea's bomber component has consisted of three regiments of the now quite old Il-28 light bombers, eighty aircraft in all.

Not until 1987 was North Korea identified as having any armed helicopters. The number is now estimated at 115, of which 60 are the United States-made Hughes 500 models, illegally sold to North Korea by a West German firm in the mid-1980s.

SA-2 Soviet surface-to-air missiles have been in the North Korean inventory since 1967, when fifty sites with four to six missiles each were estimated to be in the army structure, as is the case for SAMs in South Korea. From then until 1975, the number of sites ranged between thirty and sixty, with 180 to 300 launchers. In 1976, however, it was determined that the SAM force, then estimated to be three brigades with 250 SA-2s, belonged in the air force rather than in the army. Since 1980 the order of battle has indicated that there are 45 sites; but in 1985, the number of missiles was increased from 250 to 800, remaining at that figure until 1987. The estimated total of SA-2 missiles has since been markedly reduced with introduction of two regiments each of newer SA-3 and SA-5 missiles.

Comparison of North Korean and South Korean Military Forces

Since the military threat that North Korea is considered to pose to South Korea is a major cause of United States interest and involvement in Korean affairs, the comparative current military strengths of the two countries is an important factor for consideration.[31] The total uniformed strengths and how they evolved over the past 26 years already have been presented in Table 13-1, so the following comparisons deal as directly as possible with structure and major equipment in the ground, naval, and air force components. This is in no sense a net assessment, since, as has been previously noted, available information does not permit a meaningful assessment of relative fighting capabilities.[32]

Comparison of Ground Forces

Importance of the ground force element of their military strengths is emphasized in both countries—the army includes 90 percent of the military personnel in North Korea and 85 percent of the military personnel in South Korea. The North

TABLE 13–2
A Comparison of North Korean and South Korean Military Forces

	North Korea	South Korea
Senior headquarters	15 corps (8 all arms, 4 mechanized, 1 armored, 1 artillery, 1 infantry)	3 armies 7 corps
Infantry division	31	19
Mechanized divisions		2
Motorized infantry brigades	20	
Armored brigades	15	
Independent infantry brigades	4	1
Special purpose forces	25 brigades	7 brigades
Artillery corps	1	
Artillery brigades		2
Reserves	26 infantry divisions	1 army hq. 23 infantry divisions
Medium battle tanks	3,200	1,500
Light tanks	350	
Armored personnel carriers	1,600	1,555
Towed artillery pieces	1,900	4,000
Self-propelled artillery	2,800	Considerable number
Surface-to-surface missiles	54 FROG, 15 SCUD-B (rumored)	12 Honest John
Air defense guns	8,000	600
Surface-to-air missiles	(SAMs in air force)	200 Nike Hercules, 130 Stinger, 110 Hawk, 100 Javelin
Aviation		
Aircraft		10
Helicopters		603

Korean army is 380,000 troops larger than the South Korean force–930,000 to 550,000. North Korea puts much more emphasis on special forces and on the use of independent brigades than does South Korea, which has a force structure patterned largely on the United States model, including an aviation arm.

The contrast between the two armies and their major equipment is clear from a statistical comparison. Unit personnel strengths tend to be smaller in the North than in the South. A comparison of the individual characteristics of numerous kinds of major equipment fielded by the two countries is far beyond the scope of this article.

The extent to which both countries have militarized their societies is indicated be the size of their civilian reserve and paramilitary force. North Korea reportedly has 500,000 reserve army troops, 40,000 navy reserves, and 115,000 security troops. Up to 5 million persons have some reserve/militia commitment, including a worker-peasant Red Militia organized on a province-town-village basis under a corps-brigade-battalion-company-platoon structure. Equipment includes some mortars and air defense guns, but some units are unarmed.

On the other hand South Korea has about 4,500,000 reserves, and a paramilitary Civilian Defense Corps composed of 3,500,000 personnel.

Comparison of Naval/Marine Forces

The two navies have been developed for quite different purposes and under different concepts. North Korea puts its emphasis on submarines that can attack the shipping on which South Korea depends for its economy and military support; on missile and torpedo attack craft; and on amphibious craft that could put troops ashore in the South.

South Korea puts major reliance on destroyers (of which North Korea has none), on frigates, and on aircraft and helicopters for antisubmarine warfare. South Korea has a marine corps, for which there is no counterpart in the North. South Korea also has a small coast guard.

Differences between the two navies are illustrated below in Table 13-3.

Comparison of Air Forces

The composition of the South Korean air force reflects the American concept that higher quality can compensate for lower quantity. South Korea has about two-thirds as many combat aircraft as North Korea, no bombers, fewer ground attack aircraft, and only about one-fourth as many air defense interceptors. But the South Korean aircraft, all American types,

TABLE 13–3
A Comparison of North Korean and South Korean Naval Forces

	North Korea	South Korea
Personnel	40,000	60,000 (including 25,000 marines)
Submarines	23	3
Destroyers		11
Frigates	2	17
Patrol and coastal combatants	363	79
Corvettes	4	
Missile craft	29	11
Torpedo craft	173	
Patrol	157	68
Mine warfare	40	9
Amphibious craft	126	15
Support vessels		
Ocean tugs	2	2
Support tankers		3
Naval air (antisubmarine warfare)		
Aircraft		25
Armed helicopters		35
Marines		
Divisions		2
Brigades		1
Coast defense		
Surface-to-surface missiles	2 regiment SAMLET (6 sites)	
Guns	122/130/152mm	

though some are assembled in South Korea, tend to be newer and more sophisticated than those of the North.

North Korean equipment is mostly of Soviet origin, but the ground attack aircraft are identified as Chinese versions of Soviet models. The North Koreans also have 86 American-made Hughes-300/500 helicopters obtained through illegal channels, including sixty armed Hughes-500s.

In the ground attack role South Korea has two squadrons of

F-16s, and sixteen squadrons of F-5s. The F-16 total doubled to 48 aircraft in 1989. The North Koreans have eight regiments—one with Su-7 and Su-25 aircraft, three equipped with Chinese J-5, another three with Chinese J-6 and one with Chinese Q-5 aircraft.

As for fighter interceptors, South Korea has four squadrons with a total of 68 aircraft (34 F-4Ds and 34 F-4Es) and North Korea has ten regiments: one with 24 MiG 29, two with 46 MiG-23 and seven with 220 older aircraft (120 MiG-21, 60 J-6 and 40 J-7).

South Korea is actively seeking to acquire additional current United States aircraft.

A comparison of the two air forces is shown in Table 13-4.

TABLE 13-4
A Comparison of North Korean and South Korean Air Forces

	North Korea	South Korea
Personnel	70,000	40,000
Combat aircraft	650	447
Armed helicopters	115	
Bombers	80	
Fighter/ground attack	270	252
Fighter interceptors	290	68
Helicopters	137	17 (search and rescue)
Counterinsurgency		23
Reconnaissance		10
Fighters used for training	180	86
Surface-to-air missiles	SA-2, -3, and -5	

Potential for Surprise

The possibility of a surprise attack from the North has provided a focus for much military planning and for readiness measures in South Korea. Memories are still vivid of the speed with which Seoul was taken in the initial operations following the North Korean attack in June 1950. Seoul, only thirty miles from the demarcation line, is a far more important national center today than it was in 1950, since about one-fourth of the entire South Korean population is in Seoul and its environs.

North Korea accentuates these concerns in a number of ways. Deep tunnels have been dug—and discovered—crossing under the demarcation zone. The bulk of North Korea's army is located within a short distance from the border. Kim Il Sung takes a belligerent stance in enough of his statements to keep the South forever on edge. The logic of surprise is on his side.[33]

Military history clearly demonstrates that serious attempts to achieve surprise in the initiation of a war have seldom failed—at least initial major attacks have rarely been blocked.

Students of indications and warning phenomena emphasize that warning cannot be considered to have occurred until it has been accepted by the recipient officials and a response has been initiated. If indications of pending attack reported by intelligence organizations fail to elicit a response from the officials being warned, then warning has not really taken place. In most situations, reports that an attack is about to begin are difficult to accept by leaders of a nation at peace. The outbreak of war would mean that the policies that these officials have been pursuing have failed.

Continuing tension is reflected in the firefights that still occasionally flare across the demarcation zone. None of these has ever expanded to the point of sparking a conflagration. Conceivably this could happen unless senior officials on both sides are alert enough to bring things under control. The machinery for international negotiations at the field level is in place at Panmunjom, but the record of accomplishments there is not encouraging. No machinery is in place for direct contact at senior levels. Neither North nor South Korea has any official representation in the other's capital.

So long, however, as the United States has troops in South Korea, the state of relations between the United States and the Soviet Union is likely to be the best gauge for measuring whether firefights in the DMZ might develop into something serious and whether any indications of preparation for an attack should be viewed seriously.

There have been times in the past when Kim Il Sung sought to show his independence from Moscow by emphasizing his ties with Beijing, but in recent years North Korea has become more dependent on the Soviets, particularly for modern military equipment. Aggressive intent on the part of Kim Il Sung and his cohorts probably can be kept in rein by the Soviet Union's leadership if it chooses to do so.

Views of the U.S. Department of Defense

Policy assessments and intelligence reports of the Department of Defense on North Korea are for the most part classified, tightly held documents, but enough has been published openly in recent years to provide evidence of official positions on North Korean rapprochement and Soviet provision of advanced equipment to the Koreans.

Though it exceeded 60,000 in the early 1970s, American troop strength in South Korea was in the 40,000-range in the 1980s, the total fluctuating upward when troops were in-country temporarily for field exercises. To illustrate, in March 1982 40,055 United States military personnel were in South Korea, and in March 1988 the total was 47,992. This was within a thousand of total United States military strength then in Japan and nearly three times the total then in the Philippines.[34]

North Korea is keenly aware that the United States is supporting the modernization of South Korean forces because the figures are publicly available. In Fiscal Year 1981, for instance, the United States had Foreign Military Sales (FMS) agreements with South Korea aggregating $384,368,000, plus a Military Assistance Program (MAP) totalling $99,795,000, the largest total for any of the eighteen countries then in the MAP. By FY 1987, the MAP for South Korea had ended because of the country's economic development and prosperity, but FMS agreements still amounted to $165,764,000.[35] In 1981, the FMS agreement that the United States had with South Korea was the fifth largest country total among the 74 nations in the program. By 1987, the number of countries had increased to 96, and South Korea was in fifteenth place.

South Korea, however, is still expending large sums on its military modernization program. In September 1988 the Reagan administration advised the Congress that the United States was arranging to sell South Korea $238 million worth of jet aircraft (including twelve F-4Cs with electronic countermeasures equipment from the U.S. Air National Guard stocks), aircraft spare parts, and air-to-air missiles.[36]

Annually since 1982 the Defense Department has published an unclassified volume titled *Soviet Military Power*. Some criticize the document, noting that each issuance is timed to appear while Congress has the defense budget under consideration; but because it is issued by the Secretary of Defense it has an official status.

It was not until 1985 that any mention of North Korea appeared in *Soviet Military Power*, and then it was merely to report that "Soviet support to North Korea in the wake of the October 1983 Rangoon bombing" was one of the factors that had reinforced suspicions of Soviet intentions among Asian states.[37]

An overall improvement in Soviet-North Korean military relations occurred in 1985. Soviet and North Korean air units held their first-ever exchange visits to commemorate the fortieth anniversary of the end of World War II in Europe; and later in the year, to commemorate the fortieth anniversary of the liberation of Korea from Japan, there occurred the first port call by major Soviet naval combatants to Korea. A KARA-class guided missile cruiser and two KRIVAK-class guided missile frigates took part.

The 1986 edition of *Soviet Military Power* noted that a marked expansion in Soviet-North Korean relations had occurred following the visit to Moscow of President Kim Il Sung in May 1984. His visit resulted in an increased focus on Soviet military assistance in exchange for expanded Korean cooperation in intelligence collection. These developments were described as "the most dramatic change in Pyongyang's foreign policy since the early 1970s."[38]

What the Defense Department saw as the "most significant trend in the improving bilateral relationship" was delivery of 26 MiG-23 Flogger aircraft, with a total of 35 to 45 expected. The Floggers and a limited number of SA-3/60A surface-to-air missiles were viewed as reflecting the Soviet conclusion that North Korea was "seriously prepared to improve bilateral relations." The deliveries were seen as concrete evidence that Moscow had agreed to renew deliveries to North Korea of sophisticated new military equipment. In return, the Soviets received permission to overfly North Korea by TU-16/Badger reconnaissance aircraft, TU-95/Bear-D naval intelligence collectors, and TU-95/Bear-Gs on strike mission simulations.

The 1987 edition of *Soviet Military Power* reported a continuation and expansion of the improvement in Soviet-North Korean relations that had started in 1984 and was by 1986 viewed as "among the most significant recent developments in Soviet policy in Asia."[39]

By then North Korea had received the equivalent of at least one Flogger regiment and part of a second, plus SA-3 surface-to-air missiles; a rudimentary air-navy training exercise had been held, and Soviet intelligence overflights of Korea had expanded. In 1985 Soviet overflights had been limited to southbound flights, but in 1986 northbound flights from Cam Ran Bay in Vietnam overflew North Korea to the Soviet Union. During these two-way flights, Soviet bombers conducted reconnaissance and simulated missile strikes. Targets were "U.S. and South Korean forces, Okinawa, Japan and probably Chinese naval facilities."

Improved Soviet-North Korean relations were reflected in joint celebrations during 1986. Aircraft and naval visit exchanges marked July celebrations honoring the 25th anniversary of the Soviet-North Korean Mutual Assistance Treaty. The Kiev-class aircraft carrier *Minsk* led a Soviet Pacific Ocean Fleet squadron on a port call at Wonsan, and shortly afterward North Korean navy elements made an official visit to Vladivostok to honor Soviet Navy Day. An unprecedented joint naval exercise took place in October 1986 off the east coast of North Korea. In October, Kim Il Sung confirmed the expanding relationship between his country and the Soviet Union by an official visit to Moscow.

The 1988 edition of *Soviet Military Power* reported that Soviet ties to North Korea had improved markedly since 1984, noting in particular Kim Il Sung's visits to Moscow in May 1984 and October 1986, the delivery (starting in May 1985) of 46 MiG 23/Flogger aircraft to North Korea, and surface-to-air equipment enabling North Korea to deploy several SA-3/GOA battalions and to update older North Korean SA-2/Guideline systems.[40] New Soviet equipment reportedly provided North Korea in 1987 were ZSU-23/4 self-propelled anti-aircraft guns and the long-range SA-5/Gammon surface-to-air missile launcher. Frequency of overflights of North Korea by Soviet Tu-16/Badger bombers, Tu-95/Bear-D Naval reconnaissance aircraft and Tu-95/Bear-G strike aircraft declined in 1987 from the 1986 level, but continued.

As the Soviet leadership continued to use its oceangoing navy in support of its international policies, Soviet navy visits were again made to North Korea in 1987, and combined North Korean-Soviet exercises were conducted in both 1987 and 1986.[41]

North Korea is one of the highly militarized client states of the Soviet Union, and arms deliveries to North Korea help to make the Soviet Union the principal arms exporter to the third world. The 1987 deliveries by Moscow aggregated an estimated $21 billion, and the military material went to thirty nations.[42]

The treatment of North Korea in the 1989 edition of *Soviet Military Power* includes a brief estimate of the situation titled "North/South Korean Military Balance." It is quoted here as an expression of the current DOD position.

> The continuing threat posed to South Korea by the North Korean Army (NKA) is significant, and is of particular concern to the United States because of the aggressive and unpredictable nature of the government in Pyongyang. For nearly 40 years the United States' support for the Republic of Korea (ROK) has provided a counter to North Korean ambitions to reunify the peninsula by force of arms. North Korea continues inexorably to modernize its large military forces through reorganization and the addition of more modern equipment. The current overall balance of military forces on the peninsula continues to favor the North. The recent apparent increase in military cooperation between the Soviet Union and North Korea—including Soviet shipment of modern fighter aircraft and air defense systems is thus of special concern. Although Pyongyang faces severe economic constraints, it is difficult to forecast the extent to which economic factors will constrain the pace of military modernization. It appears that North Korean forces will likely continue to improve their firepower capabilities, as well as their mobility and logistics support. The Republic of Korea is also modernizing its forces with the objective of establishing a technological lead over the North in key areas of weaponry, thereby compensating for the North's considerable numerical superiority. The foundation of Seoul's military modernization rests on its dynamic and expanding economy, which is over four times the size of North Korea's and growing over three times as rapidly. Analysis indicates that US and

ROK forces are capable of blunting a North Korean attack and restoring the Republic of Korea's territorial integrity. Superior US and South Korean air power, in conjunction with US Army forces, would play key roles in turning back such an attack. The outlook for reducing tensions on the peninsula remains uncertain, although recent moves toward harmonizing contacts between the ROK and both the USSR and China, as well as other communist countries, are encouraging. In the long run, the strong economy of the South contrasted to the weak economy of the North, and the trends toward democracy in the South contrasted to totalitarianism and patriarchal succession in the North are encouraging.[43]

Conclusion

The well-meant but perhaps not well-thought-through 1945 United States proposal to divide the Japanese colony of Korea at the 38th parallel has created a military problem with no end in sight.[44]

The alternative would have been to accept Soviet occupation of the entire peninsula, and the world might then have seen the creation of the Pacific equivalent of Eastern Europe, including Soviet occupation forces.[45] This alternative could yet come to pass if North Korea should ever conquer South Korea by force of arms.

Would the Soviet Union today or in the future accept the loss of influence over an area now under tight communist control if North Korea were to reunite with the South under the political and economic system of the ROK? There is nothing to suggest that this would be any more acceptable to the Soviets than a Soviet-dominated Korean peninsula would be to the United States, Japan, and China.

Could a prosperous, capitalist, democratic South Korea join in some sort of confederation with a communist, militaristic, relatively poor North Korea, with each retaining the essentials of its existing political system? While it is unwise to consider any such development impossible, the proposition poses such complicated and unprecedented problems as to seem nearly impossible.

A military stalemate has developed over the past 35 years, and the question originally posed by Kim Il Sung's launching of the Korean War remains unanswered. Will the North Koreans ever resort to war to forcibly bring the South under communist control? The military forces marginally capable of such an invasion have been developed, but will they be used?[46]

If, as North Korean officials contend and their citizens reportedly believe, the expensive military buildup has been purely defensive in nature, meant to ward off a "satanic" United States eager to destroy the DPRK, then there is little really to worry about. It is almost inconceivable in today's world that the United States would deliberately support an invasion of the North, and it is most unlikely that South Korea would move without full assurance of support from the United States.

In the entire post-World War II period, the United States has never supported initiation of armed action to invade a country with which the Soviets had a mutual defense pact, as it has with North Korea.

An aggressive intent to conquer South Korea militarily is in Western minds the most logical explanation of the extensive continuing efforts that North Korea has made to create sizable military forces at great economic cost. The forces now operational could be used in either offensive or defensive operations, but some key elements—including the armored units, the amphibious forces, bomber aircraft, and surface-to-surface missiles—are essentially offensive in character.[47]

On the other hand, a leader and a cadre of supporting officials capable of rebuilding North Korea after the 1950–1953 war and of knitting together the kind of society that North Korea has developed, would also be intelligent enough to recognize that there is no real threat of military aggression from South Korea.[48] The presence of American forces in Korea is virtually a guarantee against offensive South Korean action, even if that government were so inclined, and North Korea has no other neighbors who might be considered a threat.

But the same American troops that, in a sense, protect the North from an attack initiated by the South, also provide a strong curb on the launching of any North Korean attack. There is no indication that the Soviet Union or China ever gave Kim Il Sung any prior assurance that if he launched an attack against the South, one or the other of them would provide the reinforcing military troops that would be required to contest United States forces coming to South Korea's rescue. Realistically, if a North Korean attack were to have any chance of success in today's world, major reinforcements from at least one of North Korea's communist neighbors would be required. This is as true today as it was in 1950.

But suppose that Kim Il Sung is really as crafty as he has been reputed to be. Would he launch a surprise attack intended to seize Seoul if the circumstances appeared to be just right and if he were assured of support from the USSR?

An attempt to quickly seize Seoul followed by an immediate request for an armistice and a negotiated peace probably has been considered, but was likely rejected as too risky a course on which to gamble. The memory must remain of how quickly the United States intervened in the 1950 war, even though it had no troops at risk when the North Koreans launched their attack. Since Kim Il Sung was in charge of the 1950 operation, he cannot have forgotten.

For any judgment, therefore, that North Korean forces, positioned as they are, might launch an attack out of the blue, one must look not at North Korea but to the two superpowers. The worldwide relationship between the Soviet Union and the United States is the key.[49]

So long as the United States continues to make it clear that the independence of South Korea is a major tenet in United States Far East policy, and so long as the United States continues to base its own forces alongside South Korean units, not only will the North Koreans be deterred but also the leaders of the Soviet Union will recognize the risks involved in any attempt on their part to push North Korea into launching a new war.[50]

If for any reason a future Soviet leadership were to want the United States tied up in a Far Eastern war so that the Soviet Union could be free to pursue its own goals by military actions elsewhere in the world, then the Soviets might view the destruction of North Korea as acceptable, as of a pawn in a larger game. In such a situation there would be pressure on North Korea to go to war. So long as the Soviet Union pursues the goals currently stated by Mikhail Gorbachev, economic reform and development, Soviet support for a war in Korea seems unlikely.[51]

But there are some risks. Democracy is still evolving in South Korea. Political maturity takes time to develop. Student demonstrations in 1988 attracted wide attention, and South Korea's political environment is one in which active, militant minorities can stimulate trouble. Disappointment at the rate of progress toward idealized goals can create unrest. These are conditions of which North Korea might seek to take advantage. Its armed forces include sizable unconventional warfare units, the size of which a recent analysis puts at 15 percent of the total North Korean ground forces.[52] The North Korean navy has amphibious vessels to land special purpose forces personnel. Also, the North now has, for the first time, a sizable number of modern, armed helicopters. North Koreans infiltrated the South in previous years, and this whole effort could be accelerated.

If North Korea were to stimulate a situation in South Korea in which unrest began to verge on revolt, then North Korean forces would be on hand to provide assistance. This scenario, staged within South Korea, would be one in which it would be most difficult to use United States troops. North Korean participation could be at least semiclandestine and geographically dispersed.

The likelihood of such a situation's developing in Korea can only be speculated upon, but it certainly is not imminent. Still, it can be assumed that the North Korean leaders are watching carefully and planning where and how they might insert armed personnel if favorable conditions should ever develop. Careful watch will be needed to make certain that political developments in South Korea do not set the stage for North Korea to use its special purpose forces to its advantage.

Notes

1. International Institute for Strategic Studies, *The Military Balance, 1989–1990*, (London: The Institute, 1989).
2. Ibid. (Iraq and Turkey are in seventh and eighth place, between North Korea and South Korea.)
3. U.S. Department of the Army, *North Korea: A Country Study*, Area Handbook Series, DA Pamphlet 550–81. (Washington, D.C.: U.S. Government Printing Office, 1981).
4. See G. I. Kim and B. C. Koh, *Journey to North Korea: Personal Perceptions* (Berkeley: University of California, Institute of East Asian Studies, 1983).
5. Li Yuk-sa, *Juche: The Speeches and Writings of Kim Il Sung* (New York: Grossman Publishers, 1972). See 221–24, 243–55, 268.
6. A large number of highly detailed histories of the Korean War have been published by various U.S. government organizations. The commercially published literature also is quite voluminous. Three recent interesting additions are:
   Clay Blair, *The Forgotten War: America in Korea 1950-1953* (New York: Times Books, 1987).
   Max Hastings, *The Korean War* (New York: Simon and Schuster, 1987).
   Russell Spur, *Enter the Dragon: China's Undeclared War against the U.S. in Korea, 1950-51* (New York: Newmarket Press, 1988).
7. At the Potsdam Conference in July 1945, following the end of World War II fighting in Europe, the United States had little interest in Korea since it was focusing on the problems of mounting an invasion of Japan. The Soviet army could take care of Korea. The American attitude changed markedly, however, with the dropping of the atomic bombs on August 6 and 9 and clear expectations of both the surrender of Japan and a virtually unopposed Soviet march through Manchuria. Suddenly the United States decided that its security interests called for keeping Korea out of Russian control. On August 10 in Washington, D.C., the State-War-Navy Coordinating Committee unilaterally decided that Korea should be divided at the 38th parallel, with the United States the occupying power in the South and the Soviet Union the occupier of the North. The Soviet leadership accepted the 38th parallel dividing line, even though its troops reached there several weeks before the first Americans landed in South Korea. No one even bothered to pretend that there was any need to seek any Korean with whom to consult; the Japanese occupation had been too thorough.

   The Three-Power Foreign Ministers' Conference in Moscow in December 1945 accepted the American proposal that a four-power "international trusteeship" should oversee Korea for five years, by which time it would become an independent unified state. The Soviets had already established a communist government in North Korea and may have assumed that they had little to lose by acceding to a trusteeship.

It soon became obvious that while the United States and its allies wanted an independent Korea, the Soviet Union had different ideas. Therefore, on October 1, 1946, the United States advised the Soviets that United States forces would stay in South Korea until the entire country was united and free. In 1947 the United Nations called for an election to be held in May 1948 to create a united Korean government. The Soviet Union declined to accept this; and the election, which chose the nationalist Syngman Rhee as president, was held without participation by North Koreans.

Not unsurprisingly, when Syngman Rhee declared the independence of the Republic of Korea (ROK) on August 15, 1948, claiming sovereignty over the entire peninsula, the communist government in the North followed suit and on September 9 announced that the Democratic People's Republic of Korea had sovereignty over all of Korea. A United Nations Commission on Korea was established in early 1949, and on June 29 of that year the United States withdrew the last of its occupying troops from South Korea.

8. U.S. Department of Defense, American Forces Information Service, *Defense 88* (Washington, D.C.: U.S. Government Printing Office, September/October 1988), 47.

9. See Hastings, *Korean War*, Chapter 1, "Origins of a Tragedy," 23–45.

10. Failure clearly to predict the outbreak of the Korean War is still listed as a basic mistake of United States intelligence. See: John Ranelagh, *The Agency: The Rise and Decline of the CIA* (New York: Simon and Schuster, 1986), 186–89.

11. Perhaps not surprisingly, an official South Korean history of the war refers only to "Communist forces" and makes no mention of North Korea. See Republic of Korea, Ministry of National Defense, *History of U.N. Forces in Korean War.* Six volumes, 1966–1977.

12. Other than the United States, which bore the brunt of the United Nations effort, the other nations involved were Australia, Belgium, Canada, Colombia, Ethiopia, France, Greece, Luxembourg, the Netherlands, New Zealand, the Philippines, South Africa, Thailand, Turkey, and the United Kingdom.

13. Spur, *Enter the Dragon*, 316. (See the final paragraph of the text.)

14. Hastings, *Korean War*, 329.

15. For direct impact on the United States Air Force see Robert F. Futrell, *The United States Air Force in Korea, 1950–1953*, rev. ed. (Washington, D.C.: Office of Air Force History, 1983), 708–11.

16 John F. Emerson and Harrison M. Holland, *The Eagle and the Rising Sun: America and Japan in the Twentieth Century*, a Stanford Portable Book (Menlo Park, CA.: Addison Wesley, 1988), 16–17, 155–61.

17. See Doug Randon, "It's Time to Reassess the U.S.-Korea Defense Treaty," *USA Today,* Society for the Advancement of Education, July 1988.

18. Speaking at the National Defense University Pacific Symposium in Washington, D.C., on February 25, 1988, Richard L. Armitage, assistant secretary of defense (international security affairs) said:
    > In 1981 the United States pledged that in the Northwest Pacific it would provide a nuclear umbrella, offensive projection forces as necessary, and a continued presence in the Republic of Korea...Instead of de-stabilizing the region by pulling our forces out of Korea, the U.S. continues to make an important difference...The ROK should take care that its host nation support represents a fair share of the burden; and we welcome progress in this area. But loose talk about abrogating our defense role in Korea is irresponsible and potentially harmful and does not represent the view of the U.S. government.
    >
    > In U.S. Department of Defense, *U.S. Security Role in East Asia,* Defense Issues, vol. 3, no. 11.

19. See Robert A. Scalapino and Jun-Kop Kim, ed., *North Korea Today, Strategic and Domestic Issues,* Center of Korean Studies, Korean Research Monograph 8 (Berkeley: University of California, Institute of East Asian Studies, 1983). See especially Sung-Joo Han, "North Korea's Security Policy and Military Strategy," 144–63, which divides North Korea's military development into postwar reconstruction, 1953–1961, and emphasis on self-reliance and defensive capabilities, 1970–1978. (In actuality, the primary buildup has occurred since 1978.)

20. Kim Il Sung, *On the Korean People's Struggle to Apply the Juche Ideas.* (Pyongyang: Foreign Languages Publishing House, 1983). Kim Chong-il, *Let Us Advance Under the Banner of Marxism-Leninism and the Juche Idea* (Pyongyang: Foreign Languages Publishing House, 1983). Tai Sung An, *North Korea in Transition,* (Westport, CN: Greenwood Press, 1983), Chapter 5, "The Policy Aspects of the Chuch'e Ideology: Foreign Relations and Military Affairs."

21. *Kim Il-sung: Legendary Hero for All Ages* (Pyongyang: Foreign Languages Publishing House, 1978). A compilation of articles by non-Korean authors—three from Japan, three from Latin America, and one each from Australia, Pakistan and Syria.

22. Pyongyang Radio Home Service, November 2, 1970, Quoted in *Conflict Studies No. 28, North Korea's Growth as a Subversive Centre* (London: Institute for the Study of Conflict, 1972).

23. International Institute For Strategic Studies, *The Military Balance 1989–1990* (London: The Institute, 1989), 151.

24. U.S. Congress, House Committee on Foreign Affairs, *The Korean Conundrum. A Conversation with Kim Il-sung,* Report of a Study Mission to South Korea, Japan, the People's Republic of China and North

Korea, July 12–21, 1980 (Washington, D.C.: U.S. Government Printing Office, 1980).

25. Norman D. Levin, *A Rand Note: Management and Decision-making in the North Korean Economy* (Santa Monica, CA: Rand Corporation, February 1982). The author concluded that there were not many factors likely to motivate North Korea to decrease its military efforts, and that recent (1981) trends pointed to, if anything, a motivation to increase or at least maintain these efforts.

26. Central Intelligence Agency, *The World Factbook 1983* (Washington, D.C.: U.S. Government Printing Office, 1983), 121. Since 1983, *The World Factbook* has not included specific military strength data on North Korea or South Korea.

27. Central Intelligence Agency, *The World Factbook 1989* (Washington, D.C.: U.S. Government Printing Office, 1989), 163–66.

28. Tae-Hwan Kwak, Wayne Patterson, and Edward K. Olsen, eds., *The Two Koreas in World Politics*, IFES Research Series No. 20 (Seoul: Kyungnam University, Institute for Far Eastern Studies, 1983). See Chapter 5, 103–27, "The Dynamics of North Korean Military Doctrine," by Yong Soon Yim.

29. Suck-ho Lee, *Party-Military Relations in North Korea: A Comparative Analysis* (Ann Arbor, MI: University Microfilms International, 1984). A 1983 Ph.D. dissertation at the George Washington University, Washington, D.C.

30. The information presented is based on *The Military Balance*, published annually by the International Institute for Strategic Studies.

31. All of the statistics in this section are taken from *The Military Balance, 1989–1990*, 164–67.

32. For a South Korean view see Jae Kyu Park, Byung Chul Koh, and Tae-Hwan Kwak, eds., *The Foreign Relations of North Korea* (Boulder, CO: Westview Press, and Seoul: Kyungham University Press, 1987). Chapter 5, 81–105, "North Korea's Military Capabilities," is by Jong-chun Baek, Professor of Military Science at the Korea Military Academy.

33. Alex R. Hybel, *The Logic of Surprise in International Conflict* (Lexington, ME: Lexington Books, 1986). Dr. Hybel sees only three possible strategies of surprise: (1) time, (2) target, and (3) intention. Kim Il Sung has stated his intention and the target is known; only the timing is unknown.

34. U.S. Department of Defense, *Defense 88* (Washington, D.C.: U.S. Government Printing Office, September/October 1988), 26; and *Defense 82*, September 1982, 26.

35. Ibid., *Defense 88*, 44–45; *Defense 82*, 44.

36. "U.S. Plans Deal with Arms for Seoul," *Washington Times*, September 23, 1988, A-2.

37. U.S. Department of Defense, *Soviet Military Power, 1985* (Washington, D.C.: U.S. Government Printing Office, 1985), 130.

38. *Soviet Military Power, 1986,* 140.
39. *Soviet Military Power, 1987,* 136.
40. *Soviet Military Power: An Assessment of the Threat, 1988,* 27-28.
41. Ibid., 83.
42. Ibid., 138.
43. *Soviet Military Power: Prospects for Change 1989,* 119.
44. This article is concerned only with military aspects of the Korean situation. For another approach see Tae-hwan Kwak, Chinghan Kim and Hwong Nack Kim, eds., *Korean Reunification: New Perspectives and Approaches* (Boulder, CO: Westview Press, and Seoul: Kyungnam University Press, 1984). "Twenty-one articles analyze unification strategies of both Koreas; examine U.S., Soviet, PRC and Japan's policies toward the two Koreas, and the role of the U.S. Several approaches to the unification issue are presented." For a different military analysis see Tai Sung-an, *North Korea, A Political Handbook* (Wilmington, DE: Scholarly Resources Inc., 1983). Section 7, "Military Establishment," 99–111, discusses a war scenario.
45. Norman D. Levin, *The Strategic Environment in East Asia and U.S.-Korea Security Relations in the 1980s* (Santa Monica, CA: Rand Corporation, March 1983), p.v. This Rand study identified five factors as relating to United States-Korean security problems:
    * The Great Power military balance, particularly the Soviet Far Eastern military buildup and Soviet policies toward the Korean peninsula
    * Evolution of the Sino-Soviet split and triangular U.S.-USSR-PRC relations
    * Character of the Japanese-American relationship and Japan's role
    * Evolution of the political, economic, and military situations in North and South Korea
    * The role the United States plays as the region evolves.
46. The Joint Staff of the U.S. Joint Chiefs of Staff stated in 1988:
    The Soviet-supported North Korean armed forces continue to prepare for a military unification of the Korean peninsula should circumstances prove favorable. Despite negative economic impacts, North Korea continues to modernize its armed forces. In particular, Flogger aircraft and SA-3 and SA-5 missiles and ZSU-23-4s will improve significantly the North Korean air defense capabilities.
    United States Military Posture for FY 1989, 24–25.
47. See Lawrence E. Grinter and Young Whan Kihl, eds., *East Asian Conflict Zones: Prospects for Regional Stability and De-escalation* (New York: St. Martin's Press, 1987). At 100-101, emerging trends working against North Korea's achieving its unification goal without war are listed as
    * The North's increasing dependence on the Soviets for military hardware and economic trade

- Decreasing intensity and frequency in DPRK-PRC policy consultations
- Failure of North Korea to normalize relations with the United States because of the North's continued bellicose anti-American stance
- Failure of North Korea to develop official ties with Japan
- Strengthening of South Korea's alliance relations with the United States despite growing trade frictions
- Growth in scope and intensity of ROK-Japan economic and diplomatic ties
- Expansion of ROK-PRC trade and informal ties, such as sports
- Increasing frequency in informal Soviet-ROK cross-contacts.

48. Kim Il Sung may not believe this. See House Committee on Foreign Affairs, *The Korean Conundrum*, 8. After being assured by Kim Il Sung that North Korea was committed to the peaceful reunification of Korea, U.S. Congressman Solarz asked why Kim continued to strengthen his military forces, infiltrate agents into the South, and dig tunnels under the DMZ. Kim's reply was:

> What you have said happened as a result of confrontation between North and South....If we said we had not sent spies and dug tunnels, you would never believe us, even if I said here that we will not invade the South, you would not believe me. If you said you would not invade us, I would not believe you....If we continue to suspect each other, there will be no end of it.

49. Zbigniew Brzezinski, *Game Plan: A Geostrategic Framework for the Conduct of the U.S.-Soviet Contest* (New York: Atlantic Monthly Press, 1986). The former national security advisor to President Carter sees East Asia as one of the three central strategic fronts. (Western Europe and the Middle East are the other two.) In his view the Korean peninsula is the strategic nexus in the superpower competition in East Asia.

50. South Korea's interest in a continuing United States presence is suggested by public comments of Deputy Secretary of Defense William H. Taft IV. Speaking to the World Affairs Council of Inland Southern California in San Bernardino, California, on September 28, 1988, he said that the Republic of Korea has proved receptive to our burden-sharing concerns. Despite the fact that Korea—in contrast to Japan and our NATO allies—is still very much a developing nation, it has indicated its intent to continue to increase its contribution toward the cost of maintaining the American forces stationed there. "Coping with the Challenges of Collective Security," *Defense Issues*, vol. 3, no. 52, 3.

51. Grinter and Kihl, *East Asian Conflict Zones*, 221–22, list four measures to de-escalate tensions in the Korean peninsula:
   1. United States-Soviet discussions aimed at restraining and then

perhaps halting delivery of advanced fighter aircraft and missiles to either side

2. Conventional arms reductions by both Koreas and reduction of North Korea's forward area advantage by a unilateral force pullback in return for an appropriate South Korean response, such as reduction in ROK forces north of Seoul

3. Collaboration among the United States, Soviet Union and China on the possibility of a nuclear-free zone in and around the Korean peninsula

4. Acceleration of inter-Korean negotiations and bargaining, the objective being a nonaggression pact or treaty.

—For a detailed analysis see Chapter 5, "The Korean Peninsula Conflict: Equilibrium or Deescalation," 97–122, written by Mr. Kihl.

52. Joseph S. Bermudez, Jr., *North Korean Special Forces* (Coulsdon, United Kingdom: Jane's Publishing Company, 1988). The "Summary" of Chapter 1, "Overview," of this 182-page analysis is as follows:

Since their inception the KPA's Special Purpose Forces have undergone many changes and are presently tasked with a wide variety of missions. The importance of these elite forces in the KPA's strategic thinking, however has remained constant. The DPRK leadership envisages a war of reunification taking place on two "fronts": the first front located along the DMZ engaging conventional troops and the second being the warfare waged behind ROK defenses by these skilled warriors. The fact that 15 percent of the total KPA ground forces comprise these highly trained troops is a testimony to their potential importance. It is this fact, coupled with their extensive "extra-peninsula" activities, that identifies the Special Purpose Forces as significant contributors to the overall military capability of the DPRK and a threat on the Korean Peninsula and beyond. (p. 12)

14

North Korea in Transition

Changing Approaches to Unification

Selig S. Harrison

NORTH KOREA'S PROPOSAL for a confederal form of unification of the Korean peninsula is not new. In contrast to the original formulation of the confederation concept in 1960, however, more recent North Korean declarations have indicated a possible readiness for compromise concerning both the nature of a confederal structure and the pace of the preparatory stages leading up to a confederation. While continuing to reject the de jure recognition of two Koreas, Pyongyang appears to be prepared to discuss a new approach to the unification issue that would acknowledge the reality of two Korean states within a confederal framework. President Kim Il Sung reflected this new flexibility in his September 8, 1988, fortieth anniversary report to the Central Committee of the Workers party. In place of past demands for immediate steps to establish a confederal government, Kim suggested the creation of a North-South "committee for peaceful reunification" to explore ways of moving toward a confederation.[1]

During my two visits to Pyongyang, in 1972 and 1987, and in other discussions with North Korean leaders, I have found a tortured process of reappraisal concerning the unification issue that is still in progress. This essay will begin by tracing the evolution of North Korean policy, through both the formal official record and my own discussions. I will then explore the principal factors that are compelling Pyongyang to modify its posture, emphasizing the North's new economic priorities, its changing perceptions of the South, and the importance of the unification issue as a legitimizing *raison d'être* for the Kim Il Sung regime. At the same time, I will underline the unresolved policy struggles between moderates and hard-liners in the communist leadership. By design, I will focus on the North and will not attempt to deal here with the South Korean side of the equation or the complex history of North-South relations.

I

The legitimacy of the communist regime depends to a great extent on the credibility of its commitment to pursue the goal of unification. Thus, as originally formulated, the confederation proposal was uncompromising, projecting an integrated political and economic system following unification. In my 1972 discussions, North Korean leaders treated the proposed confederation as a way station on the road to full unification, with "the people" deciding what system would exist in the South and a "Korean consensus" determining the duration of the confederation. In my interview with Kim Il Sung on June 23, 1972, he stated that the North envisages "creating a supreme national council with representatives of the governments of North and South Korea, primarily for the purpose of jointly consulting about questions concerning the national interest of Korea and coordinating them in a uniform way, while maintaining the present different political systems of North and South Korea as they are *for the time being* "(italics added).[2]

This formulation has been echoed in numerous statements by Kim and others. In an October 1977 interview in New York with Ho Dam, then vice-premier and foreign minister, I attempted to elicit his views concerning the possible duration of any confederal arrangements. Pointing out that two very different systems had developed since 1948, I asked whether it would be unreasonable to conclude that a confederation would have to last for a comparable period of 25 to thirty years before full unification could take place. "This would be a political process," Ho replied, "so it is very difficult to say how many years it would require. Foreigners tend to think of a confederation as formed of two separate states but we see it as something that would be created by one nation in the process of moving toward unification. Our common objective would be unification, and the sooner the better." Then he added, "We are a homogeneous nation, with a history of many centuries as one people. In this light, 30 years is a short period. But the main point is this: if the American troops go out of Korea, the period of solution will be greatly shortened."

Ho Dam emphasized that the confederal body or bodies would be composed of an equal number of representatives of the governments of the two sides. Such an approach, it should be noted, could well become a major focus of contention, given the population imbalance between the two Koreas; Seoul's election proposal, by contrast, would give the South dominant representation reflecting the differential in population (42.7 million in the South in 1988, 21.9 million in the North). According to Ho Dam, a "Supreme National Committee" could deal with "such questions as cultural and economic exchange and the reduction of our military forces. On international issues, also, we could discuss our differences and arrive at a common line."

In a 1974 speech, after enumerating the possibilities for North-South cooperation on internal issues, Ho added that "as to external questions, we might also discuss and decide on measures for proceeding together to the international arena and defending the interests of the whole nation, entering the United Nations under a single national title and jointly countering the aggressive threat of foreign countries, if there is any."[3] When I asked Ho about this point in 1977, he expressed confidence that the North and South would be able to agree on common policies and would need only one UN delegate. He did not, however, explicitly rule out the two-delegate, one-vote idea.

The coexistence of differing economic systems under a confederation was implicitly envisaged in the revised constitution promulgated in Pyongyang after the 1972 North-South talks.

Article 5 states that the Democratic People's Republic of Korea "strives to achieve the complete victory of socialism in the northern half" while seeking only to "drive out foreign forces on a nation-wide scale."[4]

In the North's confederation proposal the confederal government would have a combined army and a standing committee that would "supervise" the two "regional" regimes. As noted above, this would be a transitional stage on the road to full unification, with "the people" deciding when, whether, and how to change the structure. Predictably, Seoul has rejected this idea, contending that Pyongyang would merely use interchange under such a system to further subversion in the South. However, in August 1987, South Korean presidential candidate Kim Dae Jung proposed an alternative to the North's "confederal republic of Koryo." In Kim's "confederation *of* Korean republics" (italics added), North and South would continue to be sovereign states with separate armies but would create joint bodies to develop exchanges, trade, and foreign policy cooperation under a single flag.[5] Kim has long called for a "loose federal system" linking the North and the South. As early as 1973, he suggested a plan under which each would be free to "conduct in its own way its own foreign policy, military affairs and domestic politics" but would seek to "adopt a joint diplomacy toward all countries of the world." Kim saw this as the first stage in a gradual movement toward unification.[6]

When I objected to the North's proposal as unrealistic during my 1987 visit, Hwang Chang Yop, a secretary of the Central Committee of the Workers party in charge of its International Department, replied, "You will find us very flexible if we are all going in the same direction, toward confederation, rather than toward legitimizing two Koreas." Pyongyang is ready to discuss Kim Dae Jung's idea, he said, "or any other idea consistent with movement toward confederation, however gradual."

In the North's changing concept, Hwang explained, confederation is no longer a transitional phase but the "final stage" of unification, and integration of the two differing social and economic systems is not envisaged. In principle, a combined army would be a long-term objective, but "if we can improve relations between the two Koreas, then having two armies would be acceptable, especially if their size can be reduced."

Hwang and other officials spoke with a new note of realism concerning conditions in the South and explicitly ruled out the possibility of unifying Korea under communist rule. Asked whether the upsurge in opposition strength foreshadowed a shift to the left and an eventual communist revolution, Hwang replied that "such a thing is quite impossible, completely out of the question. Nearly forty years have passed since the Korean War, and we recognize that many changes have occurred in South Korea. The opposition parties are not geared to changing the social and economic system in the South. If they are successful, it would not be a revolution, unless you would regard a democratic regime less beholden to the United States as a revolution."

Dismissing my suggestions that the growing student and labor movements might push the opposition to the left, he responded impatiently that "there might be other forces, but they are not strong enough to lead the people, and they are not likely to become so. We must find a way for North and South to co-exist peacefully under different social and economic systems."

Hwang strongly implied that Pyongyang is prepared to go along with a process of creeping "cross-recognition" of the two Korean regimes by the major powers in the context of parallel movement toward a limited confederation.

"Cross-recognition" (American, Soviet, and Chinese recognition of both North and South) is the stated goal of American policy. It has been rejected by the North. But Hwang hinted at a compromise when asked whether he would like to see formal American diplomatic relations with Pyongyang or would prefer, instead, to have the United States wait until it could have relations with a confederal republic. He replied that a liaison office would be appropriate after the signing of a peace treaty, and that full relations "might well" be possible when and if the United States agreed to a withdrawal of its forces and "expressed a favorable attitude toward confederation, even if it is not actually achieved."

II

Asked about the future of Pyongyang's security links with Moscow and Beijing, Foreign Minister Kim Yong Nam said during my 1987 visit that "there is nothing immutable in our undertakings, just as we hope that there is nothing immutable in the present form of your relations with the South....We intend to strengthen and develop our relations with the United States in the days ahead." He said "We want balanced relations with the major powers. This is in our interest, and yours... Once we fought a war," he added, "but we cannot continuously maintain an abnormal relationship. The past is past."

Pyongyang emphasizes that it is ready to reduce its armed forces to 100,000 if Seoul will join in a mutual force reduction agreement linked to a parallel withdrawal of American conventional and nuclear forces. In July 1987, the North suggested that the force reductions and American withdrawals should take place within four years. A more detailed proposal in November 1988, outlined a three-year process in clearly defined stages. But Foreign Minister Kim said that the time frame is negotiable, and could even be ten years, with American air and naval forces remaining longer than ground forces. Similarly, on the key issue of verification, I found him anxious to show that the offer was not a mere propaganda salvo.

For example, the North's proposal gives the responsibility for verification to the Neutral Nations Supervisory Commission (Sweden, Switzerland, Poland, and Czechoslovakia) that has been stationed in the Demilitarized Zone since the 1954 armistice. When I questioned the workability of this proposal, Kim Yong Nam countered that NNSC verification teams would be effective if they were large, well equipped, and authorized to operate throughout North and South. He agreed that such teams might well require thousands of men, possibly including technical specialists from countries other than the four NNSC members.

South Korea has offered to discuss arms control with the North on a bilateral basis but insisted on "confidence-building" measures before any discussion of mutual force reductions. The North is seeking a peace treaty between North Korea and the United States that would formally terminate the Korean War. But the United States argues that a bilateral North-South dialogue should come first, focusing on a nonaggression pact and measures to ease North-South tensions. Washington rejects high-level diplomatic contacts with the North but initiated exploratory exchanges following the successful conclusion of the 1988 Seoul Olympics without disruption by Pyongyang. Twelve meetings between the political counselor of the American embassy in Beijing and his North Korean counterpart were held between December 1988, and October 1990, with few visible results. Formal negotiations on mutual force reductions and a peace treaty, according to the Bush administration, should be preceded by informal negotiations on confidence-building measures to defuse tensions along the 38th parallel.

To break the impasse, Kim Yong Nam suggested a compromise under which North-South talks on force reductions and North Korea-United States talks on a peace treaty would be held in parallel at the same time and place. Given such a compromise procedure, he said, negotiations on confidence-building measures could be held first. As an example, he mentioned a reciprocal suspension of military exercises by both sides. Recalling that North Korea unilaterally suspended its annual military exercises in 1986, he sharply attacked the United States and South Korea for conducting a bigger "Team Spirit" exercise than ever in 1987.

China is urging the United States to accept a compromise formula on arms control negotiations. Chinese officials in Beijing complain that Washington is insensitive to the policy struggles in Pyongyang between pragmatists and hard-liners, warning that the hard-liners might prevail if the United States continues to rebuff relatively flexible North Korean proposals put forward by the pragmatists. According to these officials, North Korea has already agreed that South Korean representatives could come to China for a Korea conference despite the fact that Beijing does not recognize Seoul.

III

My 1987 visit persuaded me that economic pressures are gradually forcing North Korea to pursue two closely related goals: a reduction of military spending through an accommodation with Seoul and Washington, and a rapid influx of advanced industrial technology.

Prime Minister Lee Gun Mo said that an arms reduction agreement would "relieve many of our economic problems by releasing manpower and funds needed for the civilian economy." The economic impact of large-scale demobilization would be "particularly helpful in an economy like ours, with a serious labor shortage," Lee said, pointing to the mining industry, where expansion is needed to step up hard-currency exports of gold, iron ore, and other mineral resources. Moreover, a reduction in defense expenditures would have "a broad impact permitting us to give much greater emphasis to light industries and consumer goods production so that we can improve the lives of our people."

The popular hunger for more and better consumer goods is unmistakable on visits to Pyongyang's six bustling department stores and a recently opened underground shopping arcade. Intent crowds push and shove, critically appraising housewares, clothing, foodstuffs, and appliances that were better and more varied in 1987 than on my first visit but still overpriced for most North Korean workers and poor in quality by international standards.

Surprisingly, under its 1984 Joint Venture Law, the regime has permitted the establishment of a new chain of department stores where North Koreans can readily see the contrast between the quality of their own consumer goods and imports from Japan, Western Europe, and in a few cases, even the United States. Operated by Korean entrepreneurs living in Japan, the Rakwon (Paradise) stores are designed to attract hard currency in the hands of North Korean diplomatic personnel and foreign aid technicians working in third world countries. Purchases in these stores are restricted to diplomats and members of a North Korean "new class" who possess, the "red won," a special form of currency with a red stamp convertible to hard currency. Significantly, however, access to these stores is not restricted. Hundreds of people were lined up at the entrance of the main Pyongyang store on several random occasions when I visited, and hundreds more were filing through the aisles examining Gucci purses, Paris dresses, Savile Row suits, and frozen foods from Tokyo.

The North's Joint Venture Law is patterned partly after a similar Chinese law but has more liberal provisions concerning taxes and the remittance of profits. Other key provisions giving Pyongyang residual management control are tougher than those of China and have soured most Western investors, especially in the militarily explosive atmosphere of the Korean peninsula. Out of fifty ventures underway in 1987, 44 were with Japan-based Korean partners known in Pyongyang as "Japanese Koreans," who are free to have their own cars and enjoy other privileges, including deluxe apartments, denied to North Korean citizens.

Co-production arrangements without equity participation are attracting some West European partners. Lebek, a West German manufacturer of women's apparel, has equipped a factory near Pyongyang and purchased 90,000 jackets in 1987 for $200,000. Frank Ziegler, a technical adviser sent to supervise quality control, said that "the workers have the same skills and diligence as those in South Korea, and in five or six years they will be able to make products just as good as those we now get from the South." Lebek would continue to expand production, he said, if transportation bottlenecks could be solved.

Prime Minister Lee, a technocrat with a background in industrial planning, acknowledged that Pyongyang's hard-currency debt problems have deterred potential Western collaborators. But he objected to "continual exaggeration" of the debt's size. The correct figure is "about $1 billion," he said, adding that "we will not default, and this problem will be resolved to the satisfaction of all parties. It is a matter of delay, not default, and the amount involved is small compared to many countries."

The North has targeted a three-fold increase in exports during the Seven-Year Economic Plan now beginning. But this poses a catch-22 problem, since a successful export program would require massive imports of technology, which would in turn require either hard-currency credits or a major influx of joint venture partners.

During the 1950s and 1960s, the North made significant economic strides with its forced-march strategy, establishing a broad-based industrial infrastructure. This was accomplished despite relatively limited access to foreign technology in the form of Soviet-bloc and Chinese help, together with a nationalistic insistence on minimizing foreign links of any kind. During the past decade, however, as its industrial plant has become increasingly obsolescent, production has begun to stagnate. The 1987 report of the United Nations Development Program, the only foreign aid agency operating in Pyongyang, warned that "further development of basic industrial subsectors is being constrained because of the growing need for advanced technologies, available only from abroad. The introduction of advanced technologies is essential for achieving improved productivity and product quality."

In contrast to the North's customary self-congratulatory propaganda, the Workers party theoretical journal *Kulloja* recently conceded that "we can only enhance the productivity and quality of consumer goods if we are able to modernize our equipment and facilities." While not directly acknowledging the need for imported equipment, the journal stressed that North Korean industries "must be brought into conformity with the scientific and technological trends of the world." New technology is also required, said *Kulloja*, to modernize railroads, power plants and other infrastructure facilities on which industrial expansion depends.

Significantly, while pursuing a China-style economic opening to the West, Pyongyang is resisting the decentralization of economic decisionmaking now taking place in China and may be moving in the opposite direction. Kim Il Sung reduced the autonomy enjoyed by cooperative farms in 1987, terming it "imperative" for the control of cooperative property to be turned over to the state "so that the class differences between workers and farmers will disappear." Free markets for farmers, once permitted weekly, can now operate only once a month. Similarly, the "enterprise autonomy" given to many industrial managers in China has so far been rejected in North Korea.

It is often argued that economic relations between North and South Korea could set the stage for progress toward unification by creating bonds of interdependence that would gradually break down distrust. In the North's perception, however, economic relations with the South would further harmony and unification only if they were conducted on an equitable basis. In this view, "vertical" economic relations producing dependence of one side on the other would freeze division. By contrast, "horizontal" interchange would promote a healthy type of interdependence that would draw North and South closer together.

Thus, the South's purchase of the North's raw materials for its industries would be ruled out, but raw materials could be exchanged for raw materials and agricultural products for agricultural products. The reciprocal development of raw materials in each other's territory, using the developer's own equipment, would also be acceptable (for example, iron mines in the North by the South and tungsten mines in the South by the North).

In the short run, the potential for North-South trade does not appear to be very great, given the "structural similarities of the two economies, attained through a costly duplication of industrial structures."[7] There are, however, certain complementarities in resource endowments, and the two Koreas could profit from diverting to each other some of the trade presently conducted with other nations.

In the long run, both South and North Korea could gain considerably if each specialized in accordance with relative cost-price factors. In addition to resource complementarities, each possesses a comparative advantage in certain manufacturing sectors. Moreover, as one study has noted, South Korean exports to the North would require less labor and capital than comparable goods produced in the North for domestic consumption.[8]

As for the specific commodities that might be traded, several studies indicate that the general pattern would be one of exchanging North Korean raw materials or semiprocessed products for more sophisticated manufactures from the South. The most promising North Korean exports to the South are iron ore, pig iron, steel, semiprocessed iron and steel products, zinc and copper alloys, coal, magnetite, and barite. To demonstrate the advantages to South Korea of importing these items from the North, one study notes that in 1970 the South was paying $125 per ton for pig-iron imports, while North Korea was selling pig iron to Japan at $70 per ton; similarly, the South Koreans were paying $326 per ton for zinc and $1,721 for copper, whereas the North was exporting those commodities at $294 and $1,526 per ton, respectively. Potential South Korean exports to the North include petroleum products (from plastics to synthetic textiles), chemical products, telecommunication equipment, electrical appliances, rubber products, tools, sewing machines, leather goods, clothing and footwear, chromium concentrates, elemental sulfur, edible fats, and food.[9]

In a 1977 study, Chung Wung Hwak, a South Korean scholar, proposed North-South discussions on five basic principles for economic cooperation before any trade is initiated between the two Koreas:

1. The exchange of advanced industrial know-how which the South and North have introduced into their respective economies
2. Mutually beneficial participation in economic development through a regional division of labor between North and South
3. The positive promotion of development projects all over the Korean peninsula, *using the abundant manpower resources of South Korea*
4. A triangular trade system toward the respective markets which the South and North have already secured
5. Increased interlocking transportation along the roads and sea-lanes which would be reopened between the South and North in the course of such exchanges, resulting in closer though limited linkage of the divided halves of the peninsula as well as bolstered maritime transportation along the east, south, and west coasts.[10]

Chung blamed the North for an overall approach toward the North-South talks that, in his view, dims the possibility of economic exchanges. But he pointed out that the North has proposed economic exchanges, including the possibility of direct passenger service between Seoul and Wonsan and between Chinuiju and Pusan. The North has also proposed the opening of the North Korean ports of Nampo, Chongjin, and Hungnam to the South, and the South's ports of Inchon, Mokpo, and Kunsan to the North.[11]

To be sure, any significant development of North-South trade would depend on a willingness of both states to circumscribe their independent approaches to industrialization and to undertake specialization in production based on economic considerations.[12]

At present, there is little evidence that either side is prepared to consider any significant sacrifice of independence in order to achieve economic gains.

IV

The underlying reason for the North's interest in a confederation—and its corresponding refusal to accept a two-Korea framework on the former German model—lies in the symbolism that a confederation would have for North Koreans, as a step toward eventual unification. Elsewhere I have elaborated on the significance of the unification ideal to Koreans in both North and South.[13] In the case of the North, Kim has based the legitimacy of his regime in large part on his carefully cultivated mystique as the nationalist leader who helped to deliver Korea from Japanese colonialism and United States imperialism and who alone personifies the hopes of all Koreans for national unification. To be sure, the ultimate sanctions on which his regime rests are those of an unusually rigid and monolithic totalitarianism; but Kim has skillfully used nationalism as a psychological reinforcement to sustain these sanctions over the years. One of the strongest impressions I gained in the North was that Kim and his colleagues could not abandon, or appear to abandon, the unification goal without seriously tarnishing their leadership image.

At the same time, Kim confronts the reality of a South in which communist-oriented forces are extremely weak and where the prospects for early political changes favorable to the growth of a communist movement appear remote. Shifts in the strategic environment make a militarily enforced unification more difficult to achieve than in 1950, and economic compulsions make a peaceful relationship with the South desirable. Thus, a confederal setup might be a satisfactory compromise for Kim, providing a hopeful symbol of progress toward national unity sufficient to satisfy his domestic political needs. For example, as already noted, Pyongyang envisages that a confederal setup would make it possible for Korea to have joint representation in the United Nations and other international bodies. To foreign observers, this might seem like an insubstantial, cosmetic change in the context of a de facto two-Korea situation where separate economic systems and military command structures continue to exist. But in North Korean eyes, this would have considerable psychological importance, as the first assertion of Korean national identity on the contemporary world stage and as a vindication of Kim Il Sung's policies.

In addition to economic pressures and the domestic political importance of the unification issue, there is still another critical reason why the confederation proposal should not be dismissed as a mere propaganda ploy. As previously indicated, Pyongyang believes that the process of political interaction within a confederal framework would work to its advantage. The North is confident that it could make good use of such a forum for stimulating desired political change in the South, without the need for direct interference or subversion. Thus, one can easily project what Kim might have had in mind when he alluded to "jointly consulting about questions concerning the national interest of Korea and coordinating them in a uniform way."

To take an obvious example, Pyongyang could argue in a confederal forum that Korea as a whole faces the threat of neocolonial exploitation by Japan. The North would thus win sympathy among those in the South who feel that Seoul has permitted excessive Japanese economic influence on overly generous terms. The South, for its part, could stress the dangers of excessive dependence on communist countries. But Pyongyang expects to get the better of such exchanges, given the sensitivity of relations with Japan in the aftermath of the colonial period. Pyongyang believes there is a basic difference between its own purchases from Japan, for nationally controlled state enterprises, and the economic and political inroads gained by Tokyo through private investment in the South. From the North's perspective, the South's economic growth has been achieved at the cost of multiplying foreign dependence, constituting a betrayal of long-term Korean interests. The North believes that it is no trick to "grow" by deliberately inviting such a heavy dependence. Nationalists in both the South and the North could find common ground on this issue, as well as on other issues involving Korean interests vis-à-vis external powers.

While the South appears to feel that time is on its side economically, the North believes that it would have an advantage politically if the economic and psychological props provided by United States and Japanese support could be dislodged. This conviction on the part of the North appears to explain why Pyongyang has placed so much emphasis on the withdrawal of

United States forces. The intent goes beyond the immediate utility of this issue as a nationalist propaganda symbol and beyond its direct relationship to the military power balance. To the extent that the United States reduces its support of the South, Pyongyang calculates, Seoul will face the same conflict between economic and military priorities long faced by the North. According to this thinking, the South will eventually be forced to adopt a more conciliatory posture. The North appears persuaded that even if Seoul does not soften its approach, the political impact of a complete United States withdrawal from the South would erode the government's support. In this view, a United States withdrawal would gradually strengthen political leaders in the South, such as Kim Dae Jung, who favor a more flexible approach to North-South contacts.

V

The readiness of North Korea for meaningful compromise on the terms of a confederation and other aspects of North-South relations is likely to hinge in critical measure on the course of a continuing ideological struggle between outward-looking moderates and technocrats such as Lee Gun Mo, Kim Yong Nam and Hwang Chang Yop, many of whom have traveled extensively abroad, and more doctrinaire hard-liners centered primarily in the armed forces and other security organs. This struggle, in turn, is likely to be governed significantly by the degree to which the United States, Japan, and South Korea respond positively to North Korean overtures for an accommodation. Flexible policies responsive to North Korean probes would strengthen the hand of the moderates, while more rigid policies, such as the rejection of Pyongyang's 1987 arms control proposal, would once again vindicate hard-liners who dismiss the possibility of an accommodation.

The ideological conflict in North Korea should not be viewed as a "power struggle." Power appears to be firmly held by Kim Il Sung and his son, Kim Jong Il, anointed as his heir apparent, who balance and adjudicate the claims of hawks and doves. In many respects, the present ferment in the North resembles the process of transition that began to take place in China more than a decade ago in the prelude to Mao's death. The gradual liberalization of American policy toward Beijing that began as early as 1969 helped to crystallize support within the Chinese Communist party for a more open relationship with the West and Japan that would facilitate the influx of technology and capital.[14] Similarly, the forces for change in North Korea would be strengthened by purposeful American, Japanese, and South Korean policies during the next decade designed to promote accommodation. Recent experience in China has reminded us, however, that economic reform and greater exposure to external influences inevitably bring political consequences. Just as China's opening to the outside world helped to stimulate North Korea's first cautious moves toward liberalization, so the tragedy of Tienanmen Square could well embolden hard-liners in Pyongyang who fear that outward-looking policies will undermine the control of the Workers party.

Notes

1. "President Kim Il Sung Delivers Report, 'Let Us Accomplish the Cause of Socialism and Communism under the Revolutionary Banner of Juche,'" Press Release No. 94, September 9, 1988, D.P.R.K. Permanent Observer Mission to the United Nations, New York.
2. *Washington Post*, June 26, 1972, 1.
3. Ho Dam made this statement in his address to the 63rd meeting of the Central Committee of the United Front for the Liberation of the Fatherland in Pyongyang on November 8, 1974. See the press release issued by the office of the Permanent Observer of the D.P.R.K. to the United Nations, November 19, 1974, 4.
4. "Socialist Constitution of the Democratic People's Republic of Korea," *Korea Today* (Pyongyang), July 1973, 24.
5. Selig Harrison, "North Korea Floats a Revolutionary Ideology: Pragmatism," *New York Times*, November 22, 1987.
6. Kim did not take this position publicly in Seoul, where he would have been vulnerable to prosecution under the Anti-Communist Law, but rather in an address to the Foreign Correspondents Club of Japan, March, 1973. Cited in Tokuma Utsonomiya, "The Relaxation of Tensions and Korean Unification," paper presented at the Conference of U.S. and Japanese Parliamentarians on Korean Problems, Washington, D.C., September 19–20, 1977, 12.
7. Lee Joong-koon, "North Korean Foreign Trade in Recent Years and the Prospects for North-South Trade in Korea," paper presented at the 26th annual meeting of the Association for Asian Studies, Boston, April 1–3, 1974, 27.
8. Lim Young-il, "South Korea's Foreign Trade: Possible Impacts of Trade with North Korea," paper presented at the 26th annual meeting of the Association for Asian Studies, Boston, April 1-3, 1974, especially 9–14, 24–25.
9. Lee Joong-Koon, "North Korean Foreign Trade," 28.
10. Chung Wun-hwak, "The Possibility of Economic Exchanges between South and North Korea," *Theses on South-North Dialogue*, Theme Papers at a Seminar Held on the Occasion of the Fifth Anniversary of Issuance of South-North Joint Communique (Seoul: South-North Coordinating Committee, July 4, 1977), 93.
11. Ibid., 77.
12. Lee Joong-Koon, "North Korean Foreign Trade," 28.
13. Selig S. Harrison, *The Widening Gulf: Asian Nationalism and American Policy* (New York: Free Press, 1978), 209–31.
14. Gordon Chang, *Friends and Enemies*, forthcoming, Stanford University Press, 1989.

References

Books

Burn, Ellen, and Jacques Hersh. *Socialist Korea: a Case Study in the Strategy of Economic Development.* New York: Monthly Review Press, 1976.

Bunge, Frederica M., ed. *North Korea: A Country Study.* A Handbook Series of the U.S. Department of the Army. Washington, D.C.: Government Printing Office, 1981.

Haas, Michael. *Korean Reunification: Alternative Pathways.* New York: Praeger Publishers, 1989.

Harrison, Selig S. *The Widening Gulf: Asian Nationalism and American Policy.* New York: Free Press, 1978.

Prospects for the Reunification of the Korean Peninsula. Hearing before the Subcommittee on Asian and Pacific Affairs of the Committee on Foreign Affairs, House of Representatives, Second Session, May 24, 1988.

Hwang, In K. *One Korea Via Permanent Neutrality: The Peaceful Management of Korean Unification.* Cambridge, MA: Schenkman Publishing Co., 1980.

Kim Ch'ang Sun. *Pukhan sibonyonsa* [Fifteen years of North Korea]. Seoul: Chimun'gak, 1963.

Kim C.I. Eugene, and B.C. Koh, eds. *Journey to North Korea: Personal Perceptions.* Berkeley: University of California, Institute of East Asian Studies, 1983.

Kim Hak Joon. *The Unification Policy of South and North Korea: A Comparative Study.* Seoul: National University Press, 1977.

Scalapino, Robert A., and Chong-Sik Lee. *Communism In Korea.* 2 vols. Berkeley and Los Angeles: University of California Press, 1972.

Suh Dae Sook. *The Korean Communist Movement, 1918–1948.* Princeton: Princeton University Press, 1967.

Young Sung Chul. *Korea and Two Regimes: Kim Il Sung and Park Chung Hee.* Cambridge, MA: Schenkman Publishing Co., 1981.

Young Whan Kihl. *Politics and Policies in Divided Korea: Regimes in Contest.* Boulder, CO: Westview Press, Inc., 1984.

Monographs and Documents

Chung Wung Hwak. "The Possibility of Economic Exchanges between South and North Korea." *Theses on South-North Dialogue,* Theme papers at a Seminar Held on the Occasion of the Fifth Anniversary of Issuance of South-North Joint Communique. Seoul: South-North Coordinating Committee, July 4, 1977.

Harrison, Selig S. *Dialogue With North Korea.* Report of a conference on "Tension Reduction in Korea" sponsored by the Carnegie Endowment for International Peace, Washington, May 30-31, 1989.

Lee Joong Koon. "North Korean Foreign Trade in Recent Years and the Prospects for North-South Trade in Korea." Paper presented at the 26th annual meeting of the Association for Asian Studies, Boston, April 1–3, 1974.

Lim Young Il. "South Korea's Foreign Trade: Possible Impacts of Trade with North Korea." Paper presented at the 26th annual meeting of the Association for Asian Studies, Boston, April 1–3, 1974.

White, Gordon. "North Korean Juche: The Political Economy of Self-Reliance." In Manfred Bienefeld and Martin Godfrey, eds., *The Struggle for Development: National Strategies in an International Context, 323–354.* New York: John Wiley & Sons, 1982.

Address by President Roh Tae Woo of the Republic of Korea at the Opening session of the 147th National Assembly, Seoul, September 11, 1989.

Proposal for Reunification by Kim Yong Nam, Vice-Chairman, Committee for the Peaceful Reunification of the Fatherland, Pyongyang, September 28, 1989.

Proposal for a Confederation of Korean Republics. Address by Kim Dae Jung on Independence Day before the Council for the Promotion of Democracy, Seoul, August 15, 1987.

Proposal for the Phased withdrawal of the U.S. Forces and Arms reduction between the North and the South for a durable peace on the Korean Peninsula. Communiqué on the Joint Meeting of the Central People's Committee, Standing Committee of the Supreme People's Assembly and Administration Council of the Democratic People's Republic of Korea, Pyongyang, November 7, 1988.

Special Declaration on National Unification by President Roh Tae Woo, Republic of Korea, July 7, 1988.

15

Korea-United States Security Relations

Accommodating Change in the 1990s

Kyongsoo Lho

Introduction

IN THE POSTWAR ERA, the United States has enjoyed a unique position in Asia: Throughout this period, America's strategic power enabled it to pursue its national interests within the region and also ensure stability and progress for its allies. Until recently, the American foreign policy task was made apparent, if not simplified, by the stark demands of the cold war. The feasible and practical prescription for meeting the Soviet (and Chinese) challenge was to draw lines of containment around their periphery, bolster the military and economic capabilities of anticommunist and pro-Western regimes, and seek to split the Russians from the Chinese. In the vital Northeast Asian region, this meant that the United States would revive Japan's industrial capacity and strengthen South Korea's military capability commensurate with the perceived threat from North Korea, while making certain that America's strategic capabilities remained intact as the ultimate guarantee of regional security.

The success of this early strategy has been resounding. Japan has emerged as an economic power of global importance, while South Korea has also become an economic powerhouse in its own right with its security preserved. The relationship between Beijing and Washington, in turn, constitutes a cornerstone of the contemporary regional order in Asia. The success of America's Asian strategy has not led to an intensification of conflict with the Soviet Union. Instead, as this remarkable decade draws to a close, we may be witnessing the final chapter in the cold war. Soviet-American relations are at an all-time high, generating positive movement in East-West relations well beyond that achieved at the previous high-water mark in the early 1970s. If détente then raised hopes for more normal relations between the superpowers, this "second detente" promises to be more far-reaching because both Moscow and Washington appear to be engaged in a serious process of genuine reconciliation. The muting of the bipolar confrontation has already had a salutary outcome for Europe: the recent INF accords constitute a signal step towards further reduction of tension between the NATO countries and Eastern Europe.

The impact of the East-West thaw has been visible in Asia as well, even if this has not as yet produced any major strategic agreements, as it has in Europe. The Soviet Union under Mikhail Gorbachev has embarked on a serious fence-mending initiative with its regional neighbors. Gorbachev's July 1986 Vladivostok speech and the Krasnoyarsk speech in September 1988 clearly reveal Moscow's intention to project a new image. These verbal overtures, of course, have not as yet been accompanied by material changes in Soviet policy. Nevertheless, they have provided valuable momentum for Moscow and have helped to improve the Soviet Union's image—something which more than a decade of military buildup under Leonid Brezhnev failed to do. It is quite possible, indeed probable, that significant shifts in Moscow's Asian policy will have to await a restoration of stability to the Soviet Union's European periphery. But there can be no question, once the current pressures in areas such as Estonia and Latvia are resolved, that Moscow will turn its full attention to the dynamic Asian-Pacific region.

The United States and its Asian allies thus have a precious window of time in which to reevaluate their current security strategy and to prepare for coming changes in the region. The existing framework of American regional policy centered on security ties to Japan and South Korea, while effective in addressing the challenges presented by bipolar politics, must now be reassessed in light of the changes in Soviet policy and also with respect to the significant changes that have occurred in Washington's relationship with its regional allies.

In the next decade, the need to reassess and readjust existing policy will be greatest in Korea. Adjusting to the changing strategic circumstances will be a complex, at times difficult, process. Bilateral security policy must also come to look beyond the simpler, short-term remedies and address the problem of clearly defining strategic goals. The long-term objective should be to formulate an effective American and allied strategy flexible enough to accommodate change yet firm in the face of challenge from adversaries.

The purpose of this paper is twofold: first, to assess the present condition of the United States-South Korean security partnership; and second, to examine some possible adjustments in the relationship with a view to accommodating change in both the internal and the external dimensions of the alliance. In a recent paper, a noted observer of the Korean situation remarked that the "Korean peninsula is a Cold War island in a post-Cold War sea."[1] If so, then the task before the South Korea-United States alliance is all the more pressing; without a clear and coordinated strategy aimed at easing tensions in Korea, both the United States and South Korea will be bound by the limitations imposed by the need to sustain a policy no longer suited to the present requirements.

The following discussion is not guided by a predetermined objective to either support or refute the case for America's "disengagement" from Korea.[2] Rather, it is undertaken with a view to ventilating as best possible the range of difficult, often cross-cutting, issues that must be considered in their full ramifications before any decision is taken to alter the existing arrangement. If there is a guiding theme to this paper, it is that the United States and Korea must now undertake a frank, thoroughgoing reassessment of the state of their relations and, with an eye to the future, arrive at an explicit understanding of the basis for continued alliance. Without an intelligible rationale for the relationship, both Seoul and Washington will suffer the consequences brought about by misunderstanding, mistrust, and mutual recrimination.

South Korea-United States Alliance Relations

Underpinning the security ties between the United States and Korea is the 1954 Mutual Defense Treaty (MDT).[3] The MDT, concluded in the aftermath of the Korean War (1950–53), capped a dramatic reversal in American policy toward South Korea. It overturned the United States' pre-1949 equivocation regarding the strategic importance of the Korean peninsula and formalized the bonds established during the war. The MDT was intended to reassure the fragile Seoul government and transmit a clear signal of United States resolve to defend Korea against any future aggression.

Notable as the MDT was, however, it was no less the cold war rivalry between the United States and the Soviet Union which ensured a stable relationship between Washington and Seoul. Until the 1970s, a shared perception of the threat posed by communism in Asia bound the two allies in close, if asymmetrical, partnership. The United States had a vested interest in keeping noncommunist Asia, and therefore Korea, out of the reach of the Soviet Union and China. Korea, in turn, accepted American protection and involvement in its domestic affairs with equanimity. If the two allies had not defined other substantive grounds for cooperation, common threat perceptions alone would have argued for a cooperative security arrangement.

The most visible aspect of the American commitment to Korea's defense has been the stationing of American combat forces in Korea. At the end of the Korean War, the United States had over 350,000 soldiers stationed in Korea. By 1957, this number was reduced to about 60,000 men, consisting of two infantry divisions (the Second and Seventh Divisions) and supporting air and naval elements, under the overall command of the Eighth Army headquartered in Seoul. In 1971, the Nixon administration withdrew the Seventh Division, leaving approximately 40,000 still stationed in Korea. In 1977, the Carter administration moved to further reduce the level of United States troops stationed in Korea. In line with its plan to withdraw all ground forces from Korea by 1982, the Carter administration in 1978 began a phased withdrawal of American troops starting with the pullout of one battalion of the Second Division.[4] But against a storm of protest in Seoul, criticism from Japan (which saw the withdrawals as dangerous to its own long-term security), and finally under pressure from the congressional opposition, the Carter administration announced in July 1979 its intention to suspend subsequent withdrawals. Since then, the issue of further troop withdrawals has remained on the back burner in bilateral security discussions. Indeed, in the past decade, the Reagan administration's focus on strengthening America's defense capability produced a conformity of security perceptions between Washington and Seoul unparalleled since the Korean War.

South Korea's security, however, has not been dependent on arms alone. Seoul's concerted diplomatic efforts in the international arena and steady political support from Washington have been indispensable elements contributing to South Korea's security and stability. South Korea's understanding of the political dimensions of security began to mature in the early 1970s. Beginning in 1973, South Korea abandoned its stridently anticommunist foreign policy and instituted in its place a flexible and pragmatic policy aimed at developing better relations with both friends and adversaries. The fruit of this readjusted policy was evident at the Summer Olympic Games in Seoul. China, the Soviet Union, and nearly all of the Eastern European countries participated in the Seoul Games. More importantly, a number of these countries have quietly expanded their material ties with South Korea. Unofficial trade between South Korea and China, for example, reportedly exceeded $2 billion in 1987. South Korea's trade with the Soviet Union, though smaller in volume, approached $500 million in the same year. In October 1988, Hungary became the first East-bloc nation to conclude diplomatic ties with South Korea. In bringing about this transformation, Washington has acted as an honest intermediary, providing Seoul with stable backing in its efforts to open channels to both Beijing and Moscow. Close diplomatic cooperation between the United States and South Korea has been the crucial factor behind the vast improvement in Korea's external security environment.

The past ten years have seen other important qualitative changes take place in the United States-Korea bilateral relationship. On the positive side, the glaring asymmetry of capabilities and interests that characterized relations in the earlier decades has become more balanced in recent times. While Korea remains a small power in relation to the United States in absolute terms, a greater awareness of mutual interdependence now conditions the dialogue between the two countries. Moreover, Korea has graduated from American economic as well as military aid and credits. Instead, South Korea now spends nearly six percent of its Gross National Product for its own defense and in support of American forces in Korea. Seoul has also become a donor of foreign economic assistance to the poorer countries, with a projected external aid budget of $650 million in the early 1990s.

During 1988, Korea underwent an unprecedented transformation in its domestic political life. As the most recent presidential and National Assembly elections symbolized, pluralistic democracy has finally begun to take root in Korea. The diffusion of political power, in the shape of President Roh Tae Woo's leadership of the executive branch and the opposition parties' stewardship of the legislative branch, provides an important step in ensuring against a return to the authoritarian past. There is still much that Korea has to learn about power-sharing and political compromise, but in the recent train of conciliatory gestures by the rival parties lies hope for an era of stable domestic politics. For the United States-Korea alliance, however, there are two important implications of democratic reform in Korea. The first is that the present and future Korean governments will be more self-confident and therefore more assertive in their dialogue with the United States. The second is that a more decentralized and responsive South Korean government will be weaker domestically in its ability to implement policy measures.

Domestic political and social progress have been assisted by economic advance. Korea's economic growth during the 1980s averaged almost 10 percent, with growth registering 12 percent in both 1986 and 1987. Korea's GNP reached $120 billion in the latter year, and per capita income approached $3,000.[5] South Korea's rapid economic growth has been accompanied by universal education, which has produced a 95 percent literacy rate; urbanization; industrialization; expanded opportunities for overseas travel; the rapid dissemination of information; and increasing social activism—all of which in their respective ways have contributed to raise overall political and social awareness.

The effect of South Korea's economic growth has been most visible in its external trade. In 1987, Seoul registered a trade account surplus of $7.7 billion on two-way trade of $85 billion. Current-account surplus was an even higher $9.8 billion.[6] Significantly, industrial products accounted for over 94 percent of the exports. More than 50 percent of this was concentrated in relatively sophisticated goods such as electronic and electrical goods, automobiles and components, machinery, ships, steel and other metals, and chemicals. With respect to bilateral trade with the United States, after having experienced deficits for much of the postwar period, Korea began to register significant trade surpluses in this decade. In 1986, for instance, the United States took $12.7 billion of Korea's exports, while the latter's import of American goods amounted to $6.5 billion, providing Seoul with a $6.2 billion surplus. The United States has now become the second most important trade partner for Korea; and Korea in turn is the seventh largest trading partner of the United States.[7] The United States has also become an important destination for Korean investments overseas. Blue-chip Korean multinationals such as Samsung, Lucky-Goldstar, and Hyundai, for example, have already embarked on long-term investment projects in various regions of the United States. As these developments in part reveal, economic interdependence is now a vital element in the bilateral relationship.

Another important change is Korea's strengthened defense capability. Korea's ability to pay for its own defense has already been noted. As a result of Seoul's sustained effort at force modernization, its military capability today is nearing that of North Korea. Korea can now supply a good part of its armaments requirements. Daewoo Heavy Industries, for instance, produces a wide range of infantry weapons ranging from automatic rifles, mortars, and grenade launchers to 20mm Vulcan air defense systems, which can be mounted on aircraft or naval vessels. Hyundai Heavy Industries, better known for

its giant oil tankers and offshore drilling platforms, also produces indigenously manufactured fast frigates as well as the
Korean versions of the M48A5 and the XM1 main battle tanks.
The Samsung and the Hanjin groups produce under license
F-5E fighter aircraft and Hughes 500-MD helicopters. The
Korea Explosives Group and the Poongsan Metal Company,
among others, produce most of the ammunition for these
weapons. A knowledgeable observer has estimated that Seoul
is capable of supplying "up to 70 percent of its arms and
equipment needs from domestic sources."[8]

Improvements have also come in the training and organization of South Korea's armed forces. The army, air, and naval
services each have their respective service academies that provide a steady output of well-trained officer personnel. They also
have comprehensive training facilities for the large number of
young men who enter national service each year. Effective
leadership is assured by a wide cross-section of senior officers
with combat experience gained in Vietnam. This capability is
routinely tested in annual military exercises and further aug-
mented by sending large numbers of able officers for advanced
education in civilian universities and research institutes both at
home and abroad.

Other factors have also impinged on the United States-Korea
relationship in this decade. Until the mid-1980s, nationalistic
sentiments did not play a big role in shaping attitudes, much
less policy, in either Seoul or Washington. On the Korean side,
nationalist sentiments, especially among the radical students
and others of the younger generation, are fed by perceived
injustices at the hands of American policy makers, who claim
to espouse the principles of democracy and social justice but
are accused of supporting a succession of repressive governments in Seoul. In the economic sphere, virtually everyone—
government officials, businessmen, the media, students, and
the general public—expresses grievances from Washington's
trade pressures and demands for Korea to open up its markets
to American products.

On the American side, criticism of the "unfair" trade advantage taken by Korea and of Korea's getting a "free ride" in
defense matters have become more pronounced in recent years.
At times, such criticism takes on exaggerated proportions.

During the preliminary stages of the recent American presidential election campaigns, for instance, Representative Richard Gephardt's comments on the "$48,000 Hyundai" caused a stir in the Korean news media. Others in the United States, addressing the issue of American troops in Korea, have gone so far as to suggest that withdrawing these troops from Korea would not only lead Seoul to make renewed efforts for its own defense but, "by raising the specter of a *more militaristic* South Korea, ...force Japan to modify its minimalist defense posture."[9] A rather troubling proposal indeed, and not least for the potentially immense complications such a development would present for the United States' security policy and for Asia's peace and stability. Can American critics of the existing regional security framework truly wish for such an outcome?

But nationalistic sentiments in both Korea and the United States stem from much more complex backgrounds than mere resentment of specific trade or security policies. In the United States, such emotions in part hark back to a simpler time when the responsibility of global leadership did not impose such seemingly heavy burdens on the American psyche or purse. In part, it is also a popular, if somewhat romantic, reaction against entangling commitments overseas without which the United States might rid itself of its foreign and related domestic problems.[10] In Korea, the current spate of nationalist feeling touches psychological and emotional chords of the frustrated populist reform movements of the mid- to late nineteenth century that sought, unsuccessfully, to strengthen Korea against foreign encroachment.[11] In its contemporary form, Korean nationalism is also partly a reaction to the politics of division on the Korean peninsula,[12] and a manifestation of the deep-rooted desire, across generational lines, to reunify the Korean nation. Mixed in with this is an element of Korea's new-found pride in its accomplishments against the odds, and the optimistic sense that Korea can continue to beat the odds. Yet, nationalism of the sort advocated by the radical students has only a limited audience among the naive.[13] The majority of South Koreans fully recognize that unbridled nationalism brought only woe in the previous century, and that domestic and external objectives today are better served by international cooperation and interdependence.

Changes in the External Security Environment

Together with changes in the internal dimensions of the alliance, developments in the global and regional security environment carry important implications for security in Korea. A remarkable aspect of superpower politics in this decade is that the frosty character of its beginning did not lead to a renewal of the cold war but, paradoxically, ushered in a resurgence of detente between the United States and the Soviet Union. In Europe, the INF accord to reduce intermediate-range nuclear weapons has proved a positive step toward improved East-West relations. In the Middle East, the cease-fire between Iran and Iraq holds forth the possibility of a return to greater stability in that volatile region. In Afghanistan, Soviet troops have withdrawn after nearly ten years of fighting. Moscow has also applied pressure on Vietnam to end its costly adventure in Kampuchea. The frigid Sino-Soviet relationship has also experienced a gradual thaw since the mid-1980s, a process which continues in the present.

Certainly, the ten years of economic reform in China, together with more recent efforts in the same direction by the Soviet Union, hold out tantalizing new possibilities for greater superpower cooperation. China's open-door economic policy, along with its pragmatic external strategy, have greatly enhanced prospects for continued regional stability.[14] Likewise, General Secretary Gorbachev's July 1986 policy speech at Vladivostok and his September 16, 1988, pronouncements at Krasnoyarsk, for all their limitations, can nevertheless be seen as signals of Moscow's intention to seek more productive relations with the Asian countries.[15] Indeed, the success of Soviet efforts at *perestroika* hinge in no small measure on fruitful economic development of the Soviet Far East—a challenging task unlikely to be met without regional economic cooperation.[16]

For the United States in this decade the Reagan administration's focus on defense and its willingness to invest in expanded military capabilities restored its confidence vis-à-vis the Soviet Union. Not insignificantly, optimism engendered by the success of the INF negotiations has in part spilled over to Asia and has allowed the United States to begin exploring possibilities for parallel confidence-building and risk-reduction measures

in the region. Consequently, while it still regards Soviet intentions in Asia with a wary eye, the United States has toned down
considerably its rhetoric against the Soviet threat to Asia's
security and stability. Overall, the diminution of bluster and
posturing by all three powers characterizes a generally peaceful
environment in Asia in this decade.

Against this encouraging background, uncertainty over
Japan's future global and regional posture, together with North
Korea's erratic and unpredictable behavior, remain sources of
concern for continued stability and peace in Northeast Asia.
Japan's future course is somewhat clouded. The post-1945 era
has witnessed Japan's remarkable growth into the world's
second-largest economic power and its transformation into a
peaceful nation. The postwar Japanese constitution, whose
legitimacy owed to the imprimatur of Douglas MacArthur and
the Showa emperor, ensured a benign Japanese external posture. In the aftermath of the Showa emperor's demise, which
now appears possible in the near future, the Japanese "Peace
Constitution" may well be open to reinterpretation.

Perhaps at an even more fundamental level, Japan has for
some time already engaged in a process of revising its historical
record. The controversy over Japan's revision of its history
texts has raised concerns in Seoul and Beijing and fueled
suspicions.[17] Japan's revisionism, of course, can be understood
as a natural extension of the Japanese desire to overcome its
militarist record. It is also the expected product of Japan's
justifiable pride in its postwar accomplishments. On the other
hand, however, to those countries such as Korea, China, and
Singapore, among others, who bore the brunt of Japanese
aggression in the first half of this century, the still festering
memories of that experience conjure up new, if sometimes
exaggerated, fears of an unrepentant and re-militarized Japan.

Concerns surrounding Japan's future course pale sharply
when the far more uncertain path charted by North Korea is
considered. Aside from its xenophobic behavior and the de-
pressingly totalitarian nature of the Kim Il Sung regime, we
know little in concrete terms about conditions in the northern
half of the Korean peninsula.[18] The North Korea riddle has
become even more puzzling in this decade. In contrast to
China, which has begun opening up to the outside world, and

also in contrast to the Soviet Union with its policy of *glasnost*, North Korea appears unable or unwilling to avail itself of the opportunities created by the newly relaxed mood in Asia.

Based on available information, Pyongyang's difficulties result from a multiplicity of causes ranging from a stagnant economy to internal political tension resulting from the still-unresolved issue of leadership succession. While Kim Il Sung's son, Kim Jong Il, seems secure for the moment as the chosen heir, past experience in other socialist regimes suggests that prospects for his longer-term political survival are not particularly good. [19] Internationally, Pyongyang finds itself far behind Seoul in the contest for international prestige and influence. Pyongyang's self-imposed isolation has become an increasing handicap. Seoul is ahead in the diplomatic contest, having gained recognition from 118 countries (to 101 for Pyongyang). But the real gap in international influence lies much more in Seoul's broad contacts outside of the formal government-to-government channels. This is amply evident, for example, in Seoul's extensive global business networks and in its extensive athletic, cultural, and scientific links with the international community.

Even in the face of its current troubles, however, Pyongyang has been able to maintain intact its formidable military capability. The International Institute of Strategic Studies (IISS) estimates North Korea's armed forces to number over 800,000 men out of a total population of about 19 million.[20] Military expenditures to maintain this force have been a significant drag on North Korea's economy. Furthermore, this drag will become intolerable in the future against the far greater, and still rapidly expanding, economic capability of Seoul: Pyongyang would probably have to spend a third or more of its GNP for defense simply to match Seoul's 6 percent outlays from its own GNP. North Korea's autarchic economy, the result of Pyongyang's quixotic *Juche* (self-reliant) ideology, is further saddled by sizable external debts owed to both Western and East-bloc creditors. In 1984, debts owed to Western financial institutions by North Korea were estimated at $2.3 billion by the *Economist*, while Soviet sources have recently indicated that loans owed to them have had to be to rescheduled for 35 years.[21] Thus mired in its ideological and economic strait jacket, North Korea remains unable to move forward, unable even to emulate its patrons, China and the Soviet Union. Pyongyang today is hostage to the fear of abandonment by its allies, to the fear of losing the strategic contest with Seoul, and to resentment borne of profound frustration. Pressure building on Pyongyang, however, should come as small comfort to those wishing stability in the region. Increasing isolation, the seige mentality, and discontent are an extremely potent recipe for disastrously miscalculated actions by North Korea.

Towards a New Security Strategy in Korea

Pyongyang's growing discomfiture should be particularly worrisome to the two principal actors involved in the delicate power game on the other side of the 38th parallel, South Korea and the United States. As we approach the next decade, Seoul and Washington should reflect on the success of past policy and from this find the confidence to introduce some concessionary steps toward North Korea. Such concessions need not stem from North Korean pressures or from exaggerated expectations of what Pyongyang might do in return. They should be made in the interests of engaging North Korea in a process, however protracted, that will tie it more closely to the emerging cooperative regional arrangement in Asia. A North Korea more interdependent economically and politically with the outside world is a far more predictable and much more constrained actor. At present, it has few interests in maintaining cordial relations with either the United States and South Korea or their allies. Both Seoul and Washington must therefore move to create new incentives and rewards to encourage cooperative behavior from Pyongyang.

The first steps towards a revised strategy of engagement must come from South Korea. In this regard, President Roh Tae Woo's recent series of proposals to the North, including his calls for unconditional talks with President Kim Il Sung, constitute an important departure in the right direction. Washington's timely relaxation of trade and travel restrictions against North Korea, rescinding the ban put into place after the November 1987 destruction of a South Korean airliner by North Korean agents, constitutes another. North Korea has yet to respond positively to South Korea's conciliatory stance.

Nevertheless, it would be in the interest of the South to persist in its efforts to open up channels of communication with the North. Pyongyang no doubt is deeply troubled by the experience of Chinese and Soviet reforms and the potential implications of similar reforms in North Korea. North Korea will therefore be even more cautious than either of its two patrons in embarking on a course of domestic reform and an easing of its isolation. Neither South Korea nor the United States should act in any way to encourage these fears but should be sensitive to Pyongyang's current internal and external difficulties.

In addition to making coordinated efforts to ameliorate Pyongyang's extreme isolation, it is time for Seoul and Washington to reassess the actual security threat from North Korea in light of the changes that have taken place in the past decade. To the extent that no serious damage is done to the existing structure of deterrence against any North Korean threat, Seoul and Washington should seek to accommodate certain North Korean demands. The single most important and long-standing North Korean precondition for improved North-South relations has been the withdrawal of United States forces from the Korean peninsula. In earlier years, this demand was rightly rejected, given the disproportionate military strength of the North and its belligerent attitude. Numerous border incidents instigated by the North, including the violent ax murders at Panmunjom in 1976, allowed little confidence in Pyongyang's claims to peaceful intentions. The overall balance of military and economic capabilities between the North and the South, moreover, was still in favor of the North until recently.

Today, however, the balance is tilting irrevocably in favor of the South. South Korea's economic strength dwarfs that of the North and, while the North still retains a numerical advantage in armaments, the South's military capability is now sufficient to deter attacks from the North. American troops in Korea provide an extra margin of security, but this contribution to overall deterrence derives less from actual combat capabilities (the forces, after all, are limited to one infantry division and air and logistics support) than from the firm political commitment that the United States makes to the defense of South Korea.[22]

It may be time now, or in the near future, to test North Korea. Once again, South Korea should seize the initiative by demonstrating its readiness to proceed with plans to reduce the number and role of American troops in Korea. South Korea must not appear to be the party reluctant to see changes take place. An armed peace has never been a satisfactory substitute for genuine peace and accommodation with the North, which can only be realized through imaginative statesmanship and, in the context of the North-South rivalry, a certain degree of risk for South Korea. If South Korea felt such risk-taking premature in the past, given both external pressures and domestic vulnerability, today it is in a much stronger position to contemplate a degree of relaxation vis-à-vis the North. Should it choose to begin rapprochement, its confidence can be bolstered by the fact that neither Beijing nor Moscow would be particularly eager to support Pyongyang's return to its past aggressive behavior, and also by the increased flexibility such a move would produce for Seoul's diplomacy toward China and the Soviet Union.

The United States can play an important role in this process. First, should Washington refrain from pressing South Korea on the issue of burden-sharing, military analysts would be freed to concentrate on the more important task of assessing which steps to take, and in what order, American units might be reduced. Needless to say, such reductions, prudently made, would in themselves generate budgetary savings for the United States.[23] The United States, in addition, could provide valuable assistance to South Korean planners by cooperating in the planning of force reductions, rather than merely planning to withdraw. Second, the United States should energetically extend its confidence-building and tension-reducing efforts vis-à-vis the Soviet Union to include the vitally important Northeast Asian region. If American leadership can bring progress in overcoming the intractable issues dividing Western from Eastern Europe, there is no reason why similar leadership cannot accomplish the same for Asia. American and Soviet cooperation on the Korean problem would provide a positive backdrop against which Seoul and Pyongyang could move to narrow their differences. Third, Washington should make every effort to avoid linking security issues to trade issues. While it is apparent that South Korea's recent trade surplus with the United States will remain an emotionally charged political issue between the two countries, the security question must at all costs be protected from becoming politicized. We already have from the Carter years the example of the issue of human rights which, despite its laudable moral purpose, was used to politicize the withdrawal plans made earlier and led to poor security decisions. Finally, if the United States remains constant in its political commitment to South Korea's security against external aggression, it will provide the extra degree of confidence for Seoul as it embarks on a broad process of peaceful engagement with the North.

As South Korea and the United States together approach the coming decade, the two allies must reaffirm their commitment to one another and recognize the importance of their political, economic, and security interdependence. In the crucial area of security, both must seek to reduce tensions on the Korean peninsula not by greater preparedness against aggression but by actively seeking, in the political and economic arenas, measures to lower the external threat. Seoul and Washington must now seek to engage Pyongyang in a process which will draw it irreversibly towards involvement in the emerging structure of political cooperation and economic interdependence in the Asia-Pacific region. Debates over the sharing of defense costs and the relocation of bases in Korea and discussions about alternative command arrangements have their use but, in the absence of clearly defined objectives that these changes are supposed to address, they are at best partial solutions and at worst irrelevant suggestions. The objective of the South Korea-United States alliance in the next decade should not be to outline a different configuration to the armed impasse in Korea. It should be a clear commitment to resolving the North-South conflict and to the engendering of a peaceful regional environment in which the two sides can move towards reunification.

Notes

1. Bruce Cumings, "Power and Plenty in Northeast Asia," *World Policy Journal*, Winter 1987/88, 102.
2. For a recent example of the "pro-disengagement" argument, see Doug Bandow, *Korea: The Case For Disengagement*, Policy Analysis No. 96, 8 December 1987, Washington, D.C.: Cato Institute.
3. The treaty was signed in October 1953. However, it was not ratified by the U.S. Congress until the following January.
4. On the Carter administration's withdrawal plans see: Larry Niksch, "U.S. Troop Withdrawals from Korea: Past Shortcomings and Future Prospect," *Asian Survey*, 21 (March 1981): 325–41.
5. Republic of Korea, Economic Planning Board (EPB), *Major Statistics on the Korean Economy*, Seoul, 1987.
6. Ibid.
7. Karl Moskowitz in his edited volume provides a good general overview of the current economic relationship. See, Karl Moskowitz, ed., *From Patron to Partner* (Lexington, MA: D.C. Heath, 1984).
8. Shim Jae Hoon, "Standing on Its Arms," *Far Eastern Economic Review*, 23 October 1981, 25–26. For a more comprehensive study of South Korea's arms manufacturing capability, see: Janne E. Nolan, *Military Industry in Taiwan and South Korea* (London: Macmillan, 1986); also, Richard M. Curasi, *Neither a Puppet nor a Pariah Be*, unpublished paper, U.S. Naval Postgraduate School, September 1979.
9. Melyn Krauss, "It's Time for U.S. Troops to Leave Korea," *Asian Wall Street Journal Weekly*, August 24, 1987, 13. Italics added.
10. This is no doubt an all too simple encapsulation of the insights into American history and foreign policy offered by Arthur M. Schlesinger, *The Cycles of American History* (Boston: Houghton Mifflin, 1986), and Stanley Hoffman, *Gulliver's Troubles: Or the Setting of American Foreign Policy* (New York: McGraw Hill, 1968).
11. For Korea's unsuccessful response to external challenge in the nineteenth century, see: Kim Key Hiuk, *The Last Phase of the East Asian World Order* (Berkeley: University of California Press, 1980).
12. A good study of the major issues at the center of student movements in this decade is offered by Kang Shin Chul et. al. eds. *80 Nyondae Haksaeng Undongsa* (A record of student movements in the 1980s) (Seoul: Hyongsongsa, 1988).
13. Ibid.
14. On China's reform policy, see: Harry Harding, "Reform in China: A Mid-Course Assessment," *Journal of Northeast Asian Studies* III (Summer 1984); also, Gail W. Lapidus and Jonathan Haslam, eds, *Reforming Socialist Systems: The Chinese and Soviet Experiences*, Conference Report, (Berkeley-Stanford Program on Soviet International Behavior, 1987), 16–14. On China's external policy: Michael Oksenberg, "China's

Confident Nationalism," *Foreign Affairs* 65 (1987), 501–23; Jonathan D. Pollack, "China's Changing Perceptions of East Asian Security and Development," *Orbis* 29 (Winter 1986), especially 771ff; and Carol Lee Hamrin, "China Reassesses the Superpowers," *Pacific Affairs*, Summer 1983.

15. See Gorbachev's reference to the "Asia-Pacific knot": Mikhail Gorbachev, *Perestroika: New Thinking for Our Country and the World* (New York: Harper and Row, 1987), 180–83.

16. Moscow's new appreciation of the Asian region was noted by Soviet economist Yevgeniy Kovrigin. See "Glasnost's Asian Frontier," *Far Eastern Economic Review*, August 4, 1988, 24–29.

17. In the latest installment of this long-running controversy, Mr. Kamei Shizuka, a prominent right-wing member of the Japanese Diet, together with 41 other similarly minded legislators, repeated their support of Mr. Okuno Seisuke, forced to resign from his post as education secretary for insisting that Japan did not have "aggressive intentions" in China and Korea in the 1930s. See Susan Chira's article, "Japan is Again Accused of Trying to Sanitize Its War Role," *International Herald Tribune*, October 6, 1988, 6.

18. Some recent works, however, have begun to shed a bit more light on the subject. See, Kim Ilpyong, *Communist Politics in North Korea* (New York: Praeger, 1975); Kihl Young Hwan, *Politics and Policies in Divided Korea—Regimes in Contest* (Boulder: Westview Press, 1984); Yang Sung Chul and Park Han Shik, eds., *Bukhan Kihaeng* (North Korea Travelogue) (Seoul: Han Eul Publishing Co., 1986), provides a glimpse of ordinary life in North Korea.

19. For instance, there is something of a parallel between Kim Jong Il's current position and that of Jiang Qing in the immediate period prior to Mao Zedong's death.

20. International Institute for Strategic Studies, *The Military Balance 1985–1986* (London: IISS, 1985), 127–28.

21. Jon Halliday, "The Economies of North and South Korea," in John Sullivan and Roberta Foss, eds., *Two Koreas—One Future?* (Lanham, MD: University Press of America, 1987.)

22. Kyongsoo Lho, "The Military Balance on the Korean Peninsula," *Asian Affairs* 19 (February 1988): 36–44.

23. This assumes that units withdrawn from Korea will not be redeployed to the continental United States, in which case savings would not necessarily result.

16

Contemporary Soviet-Korean Relations

Yuri I. Ognev

THE RELATIONS BETWEEN THE SOVIET UNION and the Korean People's Democratic Republic are characterized by close interaction as set forth in the Treaty of Friendship, Cooperation, and Mutual Assistance signed on July 6, 1961. The joint will of our two parties and peoples further increase political, economic, and cultural contacts as well as defense contacts declared in the treaty. The Soviet-North Korean treaty serves as a key instrument to guarantee peace and security in the Far East.

One of the major approaches for the socialist countries' collaboration on international issues is the balanced relationship in which each country's national interests correlate with the agreed political line. Genuinely equal and mutually advantageous cooperation and a pledge of noninterference became the normal course of our relations with the DPRK. The Soviet Union strictly adheres to these principles.

In the last few years cooperation between our two countries has progressed significantly. A fresh impetus to the process was given by the Soviet-Korean summit May 1984, when the party-and-state delegation led by Kim Il Sung, general secretary of the Korean Workers' Party (KWP) visited the Soviet Union.

In August 1985, the fortieth anniversary of Korea's liberation from Japanese oppression by the Soviet army was celebrated throughout the country. Taking part in the ceremony were the Soviet party-and-state delegation led by Geydar Aliyev, then a member of the Communist party's Political Bureau, first deputy chairman of the Soviet of Ministers; the military delegation headed by Marshal Vasily Petrov, first deputy minister of defense of the Soviet Union; delegations of other ministries and institutions; and veterans of the Korean liberation.

As planned by the agreements between Kim Il Sung and Soviet leaders, the two sides entered a more active exchange of top-level delegations. In April 1985, Kim Young Nam, member of the KWP Political Bureau, deputy premier of the Administrative Council and the Foreign Minister of the DPRK, paid a visit to the Soviet Union. Kang Seng Sang, of the KWP's Political Bureau, premier of the Administrative Council at the time, visited the Soviet Union in December 1985. In January 1986 Eduard Shevardnadze, Soviet foreign minister and member of the CPSU Political Bureau, visited North Korea.

In July 1986, the Soviet Union and the Democratic People's Republic of Korea commemorated the 25th anniversary of the signing of the Treaty of Friendship, Cooperation, and Mutual Assistance. The party-and-state delegation of the Soviet Union led by Yuri Solovyov, alternate member of the CPSU Political Bureau, first secretary of the Leningrad party committee, arrived in Pyongyang on the occasion of a jubilee, and the party-and-state delegation, headed by Kim Hwang, member of the KWP Political Bureau and secretary of the KWP Central Committee was received in Moscow.

A friendly visit of Kim Il Sung, general secretary of the LPK, and president of North Korea, and his talks with Mikhail Gorbachev were the most notable new signs of Soviet-North Korean relations. The two leaders once again affirmed the significance of the Treaty of Peace, Cooperation, and Mutual Assistance and expressed their preparedness to further promote and consolidate bilateral party and state relations in keeping with Marxist-Leninist and socialist internationalist principles.

The relations between the Soviet Union and the Democratic People's Republic of Korea encompass various aspects of life—policy and economy, culture and art, science and technology, sports, and border region ties.

An important form of the Communist party contacts is the joint participation of the representative Soviet Communist party and the KWP delegations in party congresses allowing the leaders to comprehensively assess the major achievements and problems of the countries and to discuss crucial international issues and those of bilateral relations. Broad party-level working visits coincide with the biannual program of party exchanges.

The Supreme Soviet of the Soviet Union and the Supreme People's Assembly of the DPRK maintain close contacts. In 1986, the two sides exchanged visits of the Supreme People's Assembly delegation led by Yang Hyung Sup, chairman of its standing committee, to the Soviet Union; and the delegation of the Supreme Soviet of the Soviet Union, headed by V. Dolgykch, alternate member of the CPSU Political Bureau and of the CPSU Central Committee, respectively, to the DPRK. The DPRK initiatives on settling the Korean problem have been repeatedly supported from the rostrum of the Supreme Soviet sessions.

Cooperation between the Soviet Union and the DPRK on foreign policy issues has markedly expanded in recent years. In August 1985 and April 1988, Kim Young Nam, member of the KWP Political Bureau, deputy premier of the Administrative Council, and the DPRK's foreign minister, paid an official visit to Moscow. In January 1986, Eduard Shevardnadze, Soviet foreign minister and member of the CPSU Political Bureau, visited Pyongyang. The regular Soviet-North Korean consultations of deputy foreign ministers began. Every two years the Ministries of Foreign Affairs coordinate an exchange agreement for consultative meetings on data exchange and international issues, including the situations in the Asia-Pacific Region and on the Korean peninsula. The current plan was signed in Moscow in January 1987 during the consultative meetings between deputy foreign ministers.[1]

The Soviet foreign policy towards consolidating world peace and the complete elimination of nuclear weapons by the end of the twentieth century has generated a supportive response in North Korea. Neither Soviet peace initiative was left without due consideration in Pyongyang. The legitimate striving of the

Korean people for peaceful settlement on the peninsula is fully approved of by the Soviet Union and is regarded as an integral part of global efforts aimed at peace and security.

The leadership and mass media of the DPRK spoke highly of the Soviet-American INF treaty, proclaiming it to be a major step towards nuclear disarmament and peaceful settlement of regional conflicts through negotiations.

North Korean peace proposals to resolve the situation on the Korean peninsula are closely linked with the large-scale peace program for the Far East and Asia enunciated in Vladivostok by Mikhail Gorbachev and pursued in external activities by the Soviet Union and other countries of the region. This subject is further elaborated by Mikhail Titarenko, director of the Institute of Far Eastern Studies, USSR Academy of Sciences, in his presentation at the conference.

As a top-priority measure that would contribute to favorable conditions for reunification, the government of the DPRK proposes to reduce tensions and secure a lasting peace on the Korean peninsula. The DPRK's current peace initiatives are aimed at achieving this goal. Such an approach towards the Korean problem is reasonable and constructive, and our position was expressed by Mikhail Gorbachev in Vladivostok when he said that there were no serious reasons to avoid the dialogue proposed by the DPRK.

The following initiatives of the DPRK deserve, to our minds, the utmost support:

- A proposal (put forward in 1984) to replace the armistice agreement with a peace treaty and to sign a non-aggression declaration between the North and the South
- The unilateral North Korean commitment not to conduct large-scale military exercises on its territory with an appeal to Washington and Seoul to follow suit
- Proposals (put forward in June 1986) for a top-level military and political conference between the North and the South in order to discuss such tension-reduction measures as cutting the armed forces on both sides, reducing the arms race, turning the demilitarized zone into a zone of peace, and renouncing large-scale military exercises

- A new peace initiative of July 23, 1987, to reduce the military forces of North and South Korea to the level of 100,000 troops on each side in 1988–1991, with simultaneous stage-by-stage withdrawal of the United States troops and their nuclear forces from South Korea, as well as the decision of the North Koreans to unilaterally reduce their army by 100,000 troops by the end of 1987

The proposal of the DPRK to turn the Korean peninsula into a nuclear-free zone, enunciated in the government declaration of June 23, 1986, is especially timely and important.

The North Korean peace proposals, if accomplished through a special agreement among the United States, South Korea, and North Korea, would promote a considerable easing of tensions on the peninsula and a healthier political climate in East Asia. All the countries concerned could join such an agreement. Nevertheless, so far the United States and South Korea have been silent over the DPRK's initiatives. Such a stand is unrealistic. The situation in the Asia-Pacific region is a complex one, where the three neighboring nuclear powers are within immediate reach of each other and there are crisis situations in Korea and Indochina, where large-scale military conflicts have already occurred.

Settlement on the Korean peninsula would be only the first step towards a normalized situation in the Asia-Pacific region, and therefore it is given primacy in developing practical measures to safeguard Asian security. But at the same time, the general situation in the region, the correlation of forces of war and peace, and the choice of basic principles of relations among the countries concerned have a direct impact on realization of the proposals of the DPRK.

Korea cannot stand aloof from the system of international relations, irrespective of their form; it cannot remain isolated. Local conflicts are fraught with danger of a world disaster. In this aspect the Korean problem stands far beyond national concerns and is one of the major problems related to global peace and security.

The Korean problem cannot be narrowed to its military aspect alone although the need to reduce the level of military confrontation and to achieve peaceful settlement of the Korean division remains a centerpiece and top priority of foreign relations. Understandably, the large-scale United States-South Korean joint military exercises known as Team Spirit sharply aggravate tensions in the region. Saber-rattling on the Korean peninsula must be put to an end, as proposed by the DPRK.

The Soviet Union advocates a constructive inter-Korean dialogue aimed at settlement on democratic principles, without any interference from outside, in an atmosphere of mutual trust and confidence. That is why the Soviet Union has enthusiastically responded to South Korea's proposal to convene a meeting of parliamentary members from the North and the South and has approved other proposals for further constructive dialogue and contacts between the two Koreas.

The different positions of the Soviet Union and the United States in handling the Korean issue become crystal clear with full consideration of the United States military presence in South Korea. On this fact hangs the responsibility of the two superpowers for resolution of the Korean problem. Among all the states concerned, the United States, due to its military presence, remains the power most involved in Korean affairs. Positive steps are required mainly on the American part, since the United States, 35 years after the cease-fire and armistice agreement, is still formally at war with the DPRK.

In recent years economic relations between the Soviet Union and the DPRK have been improving considerably. In December 1985, two intergovernmental agreements were signed, on economic/technological cooperation and on nuclear power station construction in the DPRK. At the same time, a protocol on the results of Soviet-North Korean trade and economic cooperation in 1986–1990 was signed.[2] In December 1986 the two sides signed an intergovernmental agreement on cooperation in the field of light industry for the period 1987–1990 and until the year 2000.[3]

In May and June 1987, a regular Soviet-Korean consultative meeting on the problems of economics and science and technology took place. Both sides agreed to enhance joint efforts in working out a large-scale program on economic cooperation until the year 2000, to actively develop new forms of economic ties and direct industrial, scientific-industrial, and scientific-technical contacts. A number of intergovernmental agreements concerning this issue were signed.[4] In the DPRK by the mid-1980s 66 projects (38 of them industrial enterprises) were rehabilitated, built up, or reconstructed with Soviet economic and technical aid. In the near future seventeen more enterprises and projects will be built or reconstructed.[5] These will be mainly large factories forming the industrial core of DPRK's economy. In 1982, the share of Soviet-aided industrial plants in gross output of energy processing was 68 percent, steel 33 percent, iron 11 percent, rolled metal 38 percent, oil 50 percent, textiles 20 percent, chemical fertilizer 14 percent, iron-ore extraction 42 percent.[6]

With the help of Soviet specialists, a thermal hydraulic power station was constructed in Pyongyang (with a capacity of 700,000 kh by the beginning of the 1980s). The most powerful thermal hydraulic power station in Asia was set up in Pukchang (1.6 million kh). The construction of another thermal power plant is currently under way in Chongjin. From 1977 to 1984, the total energy processing capacities of the DPRK have doubled.

Cheap electric power has stimulated aluminum industry development in Pukchang, and a Soviet-aided aluminum producing plant has been constructed.[7]

The Soviet Union has contributed to the development of a new branch of machine-building in the DPRK—ball bearing production. Equipped with up-to-date Soviet machinery, the plant produces ten million ball bearings of 200 standard types —from gigantic to miniature.[8] Many other examples of Soviet-DPRK cooperation can be listed.

Soviet assistance in all branches of the DPRK's economy is not limited to transfers of equipment, machinery, and technology. The most highly qualified experts are designated to work in the DPRK.

The Soviet Union is the DPRK's major trade partner. The commerce is supervised by five-year plan agreements with protocols on commodity supplies specified annually. In 1985, the foreign trade total between the Soviet Union and the DPRK increased 1.8-fold against the 1980 figure and 3.2-fold against 1970's.[9]

Foreign trade with the Soviet Union meets most of the DPRK's needs in fuel, raw materials, and semi-finished and consumer goods. Machine-building commodities remain the chief export item; diverse equipment for enterprises constructed with Soviet aid constitutes the largest share (57 percent).

Although the DPRK's share in Soviet imports does not exceed 5 percent, the Soviet need for a number of import goods is satisfied to a considerable extent. For instance, in 1981–1982 the DPRK's share in meeting Soviet needs amounted to 71.2 percent in magnesium powder; 75.3 percent in cement; 75 percent in calcium chloride; 15.8 percent in cast iron; 4.8 percent in metal rolled stock; 46.1 percent in sports footwear.[10]

Trade between the Soviet Union and the DPRK is mutually beneficial.

Border trade that provides additional opportunities to explore local resources on mutually beneficial terms, to reduce transport expenditures, and so on plays an important role in economic relations of the countries.

The prospects for Soviet-Korean economic relations are related to the crucial aims of both countries today and the most significant goals for the future.

The cultural ties among the Soviet Union, the DPRK, and other socialist countries expand on a broad, planned basis. The most widely practiced forms of cultural cooperation for the last decade have included cultural and artistic exchanges; scientific and sport exchanges; exchanges of fiction, periodicals, and science literature; sponsoring of cinema shows, concerts, radio-television programs, exhibitions, and so on.

TABLE 16–1
USSR - DPRK Foreign Trade
(in million rubles)

Date	Total	Export	Import
1960	102.7	35.5	67.2
1970	329.3	207.0	122.3
1975	338.2	186.8	151.4
1980	572.1	287.9	250.3
1984	714.3	347.2	367.1
1985	1051.2	648.4	402.8

Source: *SSSR i Koreya* (Moscow, 1988), p. 339.

Business ties and contacts and Soviet-DPRK cooperation in training and education have brought fruitful results. At present several hundred citizens from the DPRK are being educated in Soviet higher schools. In 1984, for instance, about 400 students, trainees, and postgraduates from North Korea came to study in the Soviet Union. Soviet students and trainees are studying the Korean language in Pyongyang and the Russian journal, *Sovietskaya zhenschina*, (1985, No. 1), was translated into the Korean language by the Russian students and published in Pyongyang.

Higher education institutions in the two countries maintain direct and regular contacts. Thus, Moscow State University and Kim Il Sung University, Leningrad Polytechnical Institute and Kim Chaek Polytechnical Institute in Pyongyang, and the rail transport institutes in Moscow and Pyongyang closely cooperate. The agreements between them provide the basis for student and postgraduate exchanges, the invitation of lecturing professors and teachers, joint research efforts, the setting up of authors' groups to compile textbooks, and so on.

The North Korean and Soviet academies of sciences have stepped up contacts since the 1980s and started a five-year plan for bilateral scientific cooperation for 1986. In October 1985, a plan for academic scientific cooperation for 1986–1990 was signed, and in April 1986, the two academies concluded a long-term agreement and signed a plan for scientific cooperation (for 1986–1990) that facilitates scholarly exchanges for research, lecturing, and consultative work. Specific areas of academic cooperation among the respective institutes have been established.

The two sides maintain regular exchanges of literature on natural and social sciences (monographs, collected works, bulletins, and periodicals) between the libraries of their academies. Extensive ties have been established between the All-Union Institute of Science-Technical Information and the All-Union Committee of Scientific-Technical Societies on the one side and the Association of Science and Technology of the DPRK on the other.

Worthy of special note are the close and long-standing contacts of the professional health services workers. In December 1986 in Pyongyang the current plan of cooperation in the field of medical science and health services was signed between the Soviet Union and the DPRK Ministries of Health for the period of 1982–1990.[11]

Links between the public organizations like friendship societies, trade unions, youth organizations, peace committees, and Asia-Africa solidarity committees present an important part of Soviet-Korean relations. Soviet and North Korean youth organizations were engaged in serious preparatory work for the XIII World Youth Festival scheduled to take place in Pyongyang in 1989.

The friendship societies of our two countries actively collaborate. National celebrations and memorial festivities are held under regular biannual plans. The representatives and activists of the friendship societies meet annually. They address meetings and gatherings. Friendly ties are established between friendship society departments in a number of towns in both countries and at industrial enterprises. The month of solidarity with the Korean people's struggle for the foreign military withdrawal from South Korea and for peaceful democratic reunification of the country sponsored by the Soviet-Korean Friendship Society has become a traditional event in the Soviet Union.

The editorial boards of newspapers such as *Pravda, Izvestiya, Nodong Sinmun,* and *Minchu Choson* continuously cooperate and exchange delegations; the Tass news agency, APN, and CTAK have their own correspondents working respectively in Pyongyang and Moscow. In July 1986, a correspondent of Soviet radio and television entered upon his duties in Pyongyang.

Sports contacts are developing under the multilateral plan of sports exchanges among socialist countries and bilateral working plans within the framework of the long-term agreement of 1978 on further strengthening of cooperation in physical culture and sports between the Sports Committees of the USSR and the DPRK. The plans incorporate mutual sport team tours, joint training and friendly games, participation in international tournaments held in the USSR and the DPRK, exchange of technical achievements in sport, and invitation of experts and coaches.

The achievements and experience of Korean specialists in table tennis, judo, competitive gymnastics, archery, gliding, and heavy weightlifting arouse great interest among Soviet athletes. DPRK athletes would like to learn from Soviet experience in hockey, figure skating, gymnastics, and swimming.

The Soviet Union and other socialist countries have continuously opposed discriminatory measures against North Korean sports organizations by some sponsors of international tournaments when the official team names of the GDR and the DPRK were replaced respectively by "East Germany" and "North Korea," as practiced by certain organizing committees for a long time. Supported by socialist countries and progressive public circles, the 68th session of the IOC decided that the DPRK could participate in the Olympic Games under its legitimate name, the Democratic People's Republic of Korea. The Olympic Games in Moscow (1980) were the third Olympics for the DPRK's athletes. The weightlifter Ho Bong Won became a silver medal winner in the 1980 Olympiad.

Neither the DPRK nor the Soviet Union took part in the Los Angeles Olympic Games (1984).

DPRK athletes were a success at the Goodwill Games and Sports Forum in July 1986 held in Moscow under the slogan, "Peace and Friendship," where they won a gold and five bronze medals. Regrettably, their participation in the 1988 Olympics proved to be a rather complicated matter.

I would like to stress that the hard-working and well-disciplined Korean people, devoted to the great cause of their country's reunification, are most respected in the Soviet Union. We wish the Korean people every success in the buildup and improvement of their economy, culture, and well-being. We wish them prosperity and peace on the soil of Korea.

Notes

1. *Pravda,* January 9, 1987.
2. *Pravda,* December 28, 1986.
3. *Pravda,* December 19, 1986.
4. *Pravda,* June 4, 1987.
5. *Pravda,* May 17, 1987.
6. *Economicheskaya gazeta* 33 (1983).
7. *SSSR i Koreya* (USSR and Korea) (Moscow: *NAUKA,* USSR Academy of Sciences Publishing House, 1988), 334.
8. *Izvestiya,* July 6, 1983.
9. *SSSR i Koreya,* 340.
10. *Koreyskaya Narodno-Demokraticheskaya Respublika* (Korean People's Democratic Republic) (Moscow: USSR Academy of Sciences Publishing House, 1985).
11. *NodongSinmun,* December 8, 1986.

17

The Korean Peninsula Situation in the Eyes of the Chinese Media

(1978–1988)

Yang Li-wen

KOREA AND CHINA ARE NEIGHBORING COUNTRIES joined by common mountain ranges and rivers. There have been close relations between the two countries since ancient times, together with a traditional friendship between the Korean and Chinese people. However, after World War II, Korea was artificially divided and disparate governments were established in the north and the south. For more than forty years, this problem of division has remained unresolved, and it has brought great suffering to the Korean people and become a factor in the tensions in Northeast Asia and the world.

For a long time in the Chinese press and academic circles attention has been given to the situation on the Korean peninsula. Many changes have taken place in the internal situation of China and in international circumstances since 1978, when China began to carry out its policies of reform and openness.

During the period from 1978 to 1988, the Chinese media released much news about the Korean situation and made many comments on it, which will be briefly summarized in this paper.

The Continued Development of Friendship between China and North Korea, 1978–1988

China and North Korea have remained friendly in view of their common borders, similar socialist system, and historic military cooperation in the Korean War. But during China's Cultural Revolution (1966–1976), relations between China and North Korea cooled markedly as a result of the influence of the ultra-left diplomatic line pursued by Lin Biao and the Gang of Four.[1] Toward the end of the Cultural Revolution, however, Chinese diplomatic policies were greatly revised, allowing the friendship between China and Korea to be resumed. Since 1978, that relationship has been greatly strengthened by exchange visits of the leaders of the two countries. During the last ten years, almost all of the Chinese leaders, including Deng Xiaoping, Hua Guofeng, Hu Yaobang, Li Xiannian, Peng Zhen, Deng Yinchao, Zhao Ziyang, Li Peng, and Yang Shangkun (respectively, the general party secretary, the premier or vice-premier, the chairman of the Standing Committee of the National People's Congress, and the state chairman of China) visited North Korea. Korean leaders Kim Il Sung, Kim Jong Il, and others also visited China many times. The Chinese media released detailed reports of each of these exchange visits, and the leading Chinese newspaper, the *People's Daily*, carried many editorials and articles describing these visits as "calling on relatives," and declaring that they "continuously strengthened and developed the fraternal friendship between the Chinese and Korean people established in the long common struggles."[2]

Recently, when Chinese State Chairman Yang Shangkun returned to Beijing after visiting Pyongyang, the *People's Daily* carried yet another editorial, "Joyfully Seeing the Chinese-Korean Friendship: Passing on from Generation to Generation," which pointed out that "this visit fully demonstrated the fraternal close relation between the Chinese and Korean parties, governments and peoples; and it also showed that our party and government paid great attention to the development of the traditional friendship between China and Korea."[3]

One important expression of the friendship is that every September 9 (the national day of the Democratic People's Republic of Korea), October 25 (the memorial day of the Chinese People's Volunteers' going to the Korean War), and July 11 (the memorial day of the signing of the Treaty of Friendship and Cooperation between the People's Republic of China and the Democratic People's Republic of Korea), China sends messages of congratulation to Korea while government delegations join in celebratory meetings and memorial activities. Important Chinese newspapers and journals, including the *People's Daily*, often carry editorials and articles expressing congratulations, usually making the following points: (1) the establishment of the Democratic People's Republic of Korea is an epoch-making historic event; (2) splendid achievements have been made by the Korean people in defending their independence and constructing socialism under the leadership of the Korean Labor party and Comrade Kim Il Sung; (3) the program of independently and peacefully uniting the Korean peninsula put forward by the government of the Democratic People's Republic of Korea and Kim Il Sung is supported by China; (4) the friendship between the Chinese and Korean people will hopefully continue from generation to generation.[4]

From time to time, Chinese newspapers and journals publish some articles recalling how the Chinese and Korean people fought side by side in the Korean War and what mutual lessons have been learned and close cooperation achieved between the Chinese and Korean people in their respective socialist construction since then. In the last ten years, China and North Korea have made many economic accomplishments together, as well as cultural and academic exchanges. The People's Daily paints a lively picture of the close cooperation between the two countries as follows:

> Today, the Fenman Hydropower Station jointly operated by the two countries is transmitting electricity day and night in order to play a great role in giving impetus to the social construction and the living standard improvement of the two countries. Shanghai in China and Xianxing in Korea support each other by launching the friendship-city activities. The famous Korean rainbow trout has multiplied in our country's waters, and the Gang Bamboo of China

has also been cultivated in the Korean mountains and plains. The Chinese engineers and technicians who assist the Korean people in constructing their country are now fighting side by side with their Korean comrades at every construction site in order to capture every "stronghold" in construction. The Korean comrades take good care of the Chinese engineers and technicians so that they have good conditions for their work and life.[5]

In the field of diplomatic activities, the Chinese media generally supported the positions of the government of the Democratic People's Republic of Korea, and they often reported and reprinted news and articles from the Korean Central News Agency and the newspaper *Labour News*. At the same time, the Chinese media has treated circumspectly the Western media's criticisms of North Korea, such as Western speculations that North Korea has been involved in terrorist activities (for example, the explosion at Rangoon in October 1983, the September 1986 incident at Kimpo Airport in Seoul, and the explosion of a South Korean airliner in South Asia in 1988). The Chinese media brushed aside all these charges for lack of evidence but always approves the contributions of North Korea in relaxing tensions between North and South Korea and in promoting national reconciliation and unity. For example, when there was serious political unrest in South Korea in the summer of 1987, North Korea took no action to intensify the situation and certainly did not seize the opportunity to invade South Korea. In fact, North Korea had put forward many reasonable disarmament proposals and has promoted the peaceful unification of the country. All of this shows that North Korea has taken the whole peninsula's interests into account and has chosen genuinely practical actions to relax tensions while promoting national unity.

The Increase in Contacts and Exchanges between China and South Korea in Recent Years

For historical reasons, there are still no official diplomatic relations between China and South Korea, and thus no official contact or exchange occurred for many years. This situation has visibly changed recently so that direct exchanges are on the increase. News coverage by the Chinese media has also expanded sharply.

In May 1983 a CAAC airliner with 105 passengers and crew aboard en route from Shengyang to Shanghai was hijacked to South Korea by six armed thugs. In dealing with this incident the Chinese Foreign Affairs Ministry directly contacted the South Korean administration; ultimately the head of CAAC flew to Seoul to consult with South Korean representatives. Subsequently, the Chinese passengers and crew were returned to Shanghai from Seoul. Afterwards, Sheng Tu held a press conference and said that the South Korean administration had dealt cooperatively with this hijacking, and he expressed gratitude on behalf of the CAAC for the help of the South Korean authorities. The leading Chinese newspapers, including the *People's Daily*, released much news about the incident.[6] Generally speaking, it was admirable that the South Korean government took into account the situation on both sides of the Taiwan Straits in dealing with the affair.

In September of the same year, a South Korean airliner en route from New York to Seoul was shot down by the USSR because it had strayed into Soviet airspace. This incident evoked strong reactions worldwide, including in China. The Xinhua News Agency, the *People's Daily*, and other newspapers and journals in China widely reported the event. The *People's Daily* published an article portraying this incident as "a serious one in international civil aviation." The Chinese permanent representative to the United Nations, Lin Qing, expressed in a meeting the Chinese shock and pity that a Soviet fighter had shot down a South Korean airliner and killed 296 passengers and crew (including many Chinese living in Taiwan and Hong Kong). Obviously, the Chinese media was in agreement with international public opinion regarding this tragedy.

The political unrest in South Korea during the last ten years of military dictatorship is a product of Korean popular dissent, which has been constantly mobilized by the opposition to launch political attacks on the government. The Chinese media, including the Xinhua News Agency, newspapers, and radio and television stations, have paid careful attention to developments in South Korean politics, fully reporting and commenting on them. For example, the Chinese media called the ruthless suppression of the Kwangju demonstrations a "massacre" made by Chun Doo Hwan's fascist military government and said it was "a savage fascist act of persecuting the South Korean people."[7]

Moreover, in 1987 a large-scale struggle against dictatorship and for democracy and unification erupted in South Korea around the so-called "presidential campaign" and "constitutional revision." It was the largest mass demonstration since the fall of Syngman Rhee. Not only students and workers took part in the opposition, but people at all levels of Korean society. The Chinese media analyzed the tactics of the Chun Doo Hwan-Roh Tae Woo group and asserted that they "in fact, wanted to maintain a Chun Doo Hwan government without Chun Doo Hwan in order to survive its military dictatorship in South Korea."[8] The Chinese media also covered several leaders of the South Korean opposition. Among them, Kim Dae Jung was acclaimed "a famous democrat of South Korea who untiringly fought against the fascist rule of the South Korean administration, advocated democracy and supported peaceful unity of his own country."[9] Owing to this, the Chinese media closely followed Kim's house arrest and imprisonment. They considered it a pity that Kim Dae Jung and Kim Young Sam split with each other and let Roh Tae Woo profit from it to be elected president.

When the South Korean political situation changed greatly and was in crisis regarding maintaining the military dictatorship or going to greater democracy, Roh Tae Woo replaced Chun Doo Hwan as host of Chong Wa Tae. After taking up the presidency, Roh Tae Woo tried to establish a new image in order to separate himself from Chun Doo Hwan, and a new period of South Korean politics began. "The South Korean political situation will be further improved if it proceeds along its established course rather than revert to its past.... Such a South Korea will be a positive and useful factor in peace and stability of the Korean Peninsula and Northeast Asia as well as a factor in Korea's independent and peaceful unification."[10]

Compared with the political situation, South Korea's economy is visibly progressing. The spectacularly rapid growth of the South Korean economy in the last twenty years has exceeded that of even Japan. The South Korean GNP increased 51 times and per capita income 32 times in the same time, and such rapid progress seemed to be a kind of miracle. South Korea's foreign trade also developed rapidly, and the volume of exports in 1986 was 630 times that of 1962—another unprecedented economic feat.

While concentrating on its own economic development, China has paid great attention to South Korea's economic achievements. In Chinese academic circles, especially economics, numerous articles have been published analyzing the possible causes of South Korean economic development. Chinese authors hold that "this growth was possible under three conditions, that is, opportunities, policies and sacrifices."[11] They have concluded that

> South Korean industrialization and economic achievements were certainly neither so-called "miracles" nor the accomplishments of an especially outstanding regime, but strategies and policies necessarily pursued under special historical circumstances and an inevitable result of specific internal and external factors. The pattern of South Korean economic development would likely not be the best one for the developing countries. This development is to a large extent, a result of long-standing economic and political policies carried out by the United States and Japan.[12]

Therefore, behind the South Korean economic achievements there exist some crises, the first of which is a political one. For a long time, the political situation in South Korea has been uneasy and has often triggered economic crises. According to Hu Tianming and Shen Hilin, "whether the 'democrats' or the 'military' will be in power, political unrest in South Korea is unlikely to be put down in the near future. With the decline of the power and political influence of the United States, the political unrest in South Korea will inevitably be intensified."[13] Moreover, social crisis will re-emerge because of the increasing social problems in South Korea. In recent years, there have been many workers' strikes, student demonstrations, and continued peasant impoverishment, all of which were seen as caused by the wide gap between the rich and the poor. These social contradictions will not be eliminated in the short run, so that the media's outlook is not optimistic for South Korea's joining the ranks of the economic or creditor powers.

In spite of this, China clearly can make use of some of South Korea's experiences in economic development, for example by (1) seizing the opportunity to use changed international circumstances—for example, the contradictions between the United States and Japan in the field of foreign trade—to penetrate American markets; (2) paying greater attention to the development of heavy and chemical industries in order to create conditions for high-level technology; (3) developing education to train and advance talented people; (4) diversifying the industrial structure in order to develop quick openings into the world economy.

In recent years, with China's reforms and open door policy, especially the designation of coastal areas for economic development, China has greatly increased its trade with South Korea, and some corporations and personal investors operate increasingly in China in nonofficial ways.

China's Efforts to Promote the Independent and Peaceful Unity of Korea

The Korean peninsula is one of the "hot spots" in the world and is sometimes called the "Asian Balkans." Korea has been divided for 42 years, during which time armies of several hundred thousand have confronted one other along the 250 kilometers of the Demilitarized Zone, itself a potential trigger of unrest in East Asia. The 60 million people of Korea desire reunification so that family and social divisions can be ended as quickly as possible. China, as Korea's neighbor, certainly hopes that the Korean problem can be solved by the Korean people themselves and that the Korean peninsula will remain peaceful and stable indefinitely. China has made consistent efforts to promote independent and peaceful unity in Korea, and the Chinese media have published many articles about Korean reunification.

The Chinese government has broadly supported the series of reasonable proposals put forward by the government of the Democratic People's Republic of Korea and Chairman Kim Il Sung. As early as 1972, Kim advanced three principles for uniting Korea, namely, "being master of our own fate, peaceful unifying of the country and national unity." In 1973, he also put forward five guiding policies for realizing the three principles, including the resolution of the confrontation and tension between North and South Korea, the expansion of many kinds of cooperation and exchange between the two sides, and the temporary maintenance of different social systems of both sides. In October 1980, Kim suggested further that Korea be united through the establishment of a Democratic Federal Republic of Korea, and in January 1984, Pyongyang proposed tripartite talks including North and South Korea and the United States in order to create the new conditions for independently and peacefully uniting Korea. In addition, North Korea took many steps to improve its relations with South Korea. For example, in 1984, when a flood occurred in South Korea, North Korea sent disaster relief through the International Red Cross. Initiatives such as this will play a positive role in breaking the deadlock on the Korean peninsula.

In these years, relations between North and South Korea were alternatively warm and cold. The Chinese media supported relations with North and South Korea and talks between the two sides and expressed concern and disappointment during periods of cool relations. According to Chinese authors, the major cause of coolness and confrontation was the South Korean government and the United States. In South Korea, the population and the opposition politicians constantly organized democratic movements against the long-standing military dictatorship. In response, the South Korean government, on the one hand, relentlessly suppressed the progressive opposition, while on the other hand the authorities created a war atmosphere, diverting people's attention with the nonexistent threat of North Korea's invading the South. This is the reason that North-South relations tended to be relaxed in 1984–1985, while tension was heightened in 1986 when the democratic movement emerged in South Korea.

Moreover, the United States should be held responsible for the tension on the Korean peninsula from beginning to end. The United States has controlled South Korean policy for a long time in order to maintain its strategic dominance in East Asia. American forces have been stationed in South Korea for a long time, and frequent military maneuvers interfere in the internal situation of Korea, putting the South Korean administration at the American beck and call. It is necessary to point out that Japan not only supported the United States policy in South Korea but even tried to create a tripartite military alliance among the United States, Japan and South Korea. All of this, in fact, has intensified the confrontation and division between North and South Korea. It should also be pointed out that the Soviet Union became involved in the Korean peninsula after 1985. In recent years, adding to its economic aid to North Korea, the Soviet Union has helped to build a nuclear power station and has provided new weapons such as long-range missiles. The Soviet navy and air force frequently pass in and out of North Korea. The strengthening of Soviet influence in North Korea has to some extent caused the misgivings of the United States and South Korea, and thus the Soviets have intensified the complex nature of the Korean peninsula situation.

Though expressing concern about the situation in Korea, the Chinese media was also optimistic about Korean prospects. For "wholly speaking, the tension is only a temporary phase of historic development, while talks and unity accord with the will of the people and the general trends of events."[14] The reasons are as follows:

1. National unity and family reunification is the common wish of 60 million Korean people. Because of the past chaos caused by war, divided families in Korea constitute a large portion of its whole population, more than 10 million persons.

2. The two sides can not destroy each other, and the relaxation of tensions and the development of exchange and cooperation accord with the people's interests.

3. The international situation concerning the Korean peninsula has greatly changed, as the United States, Japan, China, and the Soviet Union have established diplomatic relations with each other. They are steadily strengthening their friendly and cooperative relations. Moreover, the evolution of the Korean problem has thus far prevented any one power from using the problem to achieve its aims. These powers should face this reality and respect the Korean national will.

The United States and Its Korean Policy

It is well known that the stationing of 43,000 United States troops in South Korea is a serious obstacle to solving the

Korean problem. For many years, in spite of international public opinion and the desires of the Korean people, the United States has refused to withdraw its forces from South Korea and has sent Korea sophisticated weapons and new fighters and held increasingly large-scale "united maneuvers" with South Korean troops.

In the past ten years, great changes have taken place in Sino-American relations. In January 1979, China and the United States established official diplomatic relations, and during and after the Carter administration substantial cooperation and exchanges were initiated between China and the United States. Correspondingly, the Chinese media greatly changed its views about the United States.

The Chinese media has tended to argue that the United States should change its Korean policies, especially as follows:

1. The United States should withdraw its troops from South Korea as soon as possible. Early in 1975, the thirtieth session of the United Nations General Assembly passed a resolution calling for foreign troops to withdraw from South Korea and disbanding the headquarters of the United Nations forces. A United States troop withdrawal from South Korea is not only the desire of the North Korean people but also the will of the South Korean people, firmly supported by the Chinese people and the people of the third world. After normalization of Sino-American relations, there emerged a belief that China "tacitly approved" or even "welcomed" United States troops remaining in South Korea as a counterpoise to the Soviet Union. This is a serious distortion of China's Korean policy and quite contrary to fact.

2. The United States should discontinue the perpetuation of two Koreas and try to resolve the Korean division. Occasionally the United States has advocated the powers alternately recognizing North and South Korea and in the meantime, having North and South Korea joining the United Nations. In the world political scene, "two Koreas" is a requirement for American perpetual dominance of South Korea. Maintaining the status quo in the Korean peninsula is in fact preventing the solution of the Korean

problem, for it keeps the Korean peninsula unstable.

3. The United States should see the Korean problem from all strategic angles. A unified nation under the "Korean Democratic Federation" would carry out independent, neutral, and non-aligned policies so that no one power could profit from interfering in the confrontation between North and South. The unification of Korea would make significant contributions to Asian and world peace, and the United States could totally break away from Korean affairs, which is in fact more in accord with its own interests.

4. Through concrete steps, the United States should accept the tripartite talks proposal advanced by Pyongyang so that the United States can contribute to the early peaceful resolution of the Korean problem. This suggestion was originally put forward by President Carter in Seoul in July 1979.

The Chinese people sincerely hope that the 60 million Korean people can end the suffering of national division as soon as possible. We also hope the Korean peninsula as well as the whole Asian-Pacific region can achieve permanent stability.

Notes

1. Zhang Ming-yang, "The Extreme Left Diplomatic Line of Lin Biao and Gang of Four," *Fudan University Journal*, no. 2, 1980, 81.
2. Zhou Bi-zhong, "On Friendship Carry Forward the Cause of the Older Generation and Break New Ground," *People's Daily*, October 6, 1986, 7.
3. Editorial, *People's Daily*, September 13, 1988, 1.
4. Editorial, *People's Daily*, September 9, 1988.
5. Zhou, "On Friendship Carry Forward the Cause of the Older Generation and Break New Ground."
6. *People's Daily*, May 17, 1983, 4.
7. *People's Daily*, July 29, 1980, 4.
8. Tao Bing-wei and Yu Shao-hua, "The Political Situation in South Korea during the Turning Point," *International Relation Studies*, no. 4, 1987, 15.
9. *People's Daily*, July 29, 1980, 4.
10. Tao and Yu, "The Political Situation in South Korea," 19, 20.
11. Hu Tian-ming and Shen Yi-lin, "The Development of Industry and Technique in South Korea," *Economy of Asia and Pacific*, no. 5, 1987.
12. Hu Tian-ming and Shen Yi-lin, "The Evaluation of Government's Achievements in Seven Years and Prospects of Economic Development in South Korea," *World Economy and Politics*, no. 7, 1988, 53.
13. Ibid.
14. Wu Ji-nan, "The Wind and Rain in Korean Peninsula," *International Prospects* (Shanghai), no. 2, 1987, 3.

18

United States-Japan-South Korea Relations

Toward the 1990s

Edward A. Olsen

THIS PAPER HAS TWO OVERLAPPING PURPOSES: to assess the state of contemporary United States and Japanese relations with the Republic of Korea (ROK) and to evaluate the ways in which diplomatic, economic, and political spinoffs of the 1988 Seoul Olympics may influence those relations. Most American (and South Korean) foreign affairs specialists are familiar with the main strategic, political, and economic themes in United States-Korea relations. Moreover, there are readily available contemporary studies of the bilateral relationship.[1] Many more studies of United States-Japan relations are available.[2] Consequently, those facets of the topic will be presented in a brief fashion, allowing a focus on the Japan factor in the trilateral relationship. This factor tends to be poorly understood by Americans as we concentrate on the two bilateral legs of United States ties in Northeast Asia. After analyzing that factor, the Olympics' impact on the changing international milieu of Northeast Asia will be assessed.

ted States-South Korea Relations

relations with South Korea have a much shorter
ᴘᴜ̇ᴛᴏ̇ᴩ   United States-Japan ties. Though the United
States and South Korea celebrated a much ballyhooed centennial of United States-Korea diplomatic relations in 1982,[3] that
was an artificial occasion because there was a major interrup-
tion in the hundred years caused by Japan's colonization of
Korea. For nearly half that century the United States had
recognized Japan as the authority in Korea. Making matters
worse, the United States did not merely acquiesce in Korea's
subjugation by Japan but was an active diplomatic player in that
bitter experience, consciously writing off Korea as part of
Japan's zone of imperial interest in exchange for Tokyo's
acknowledgment of American imperial claims in the Philippines. Consequently, Korean memories of indirect American
complicity in their country's subjugation were strong. American moral support for the Korean independence cause during
the colonial era assuaged those memories somewhat. The
United States' post-World War II role as victor over Japan and
liberator of Korea took much of the edge off the bitter legacy,
but a substantial degree of ambiguity was quickly reintroduced.
Although the United States is remembered as a liberator of
Korea, it also bears the stigma of being one of the two powers
whose cold war differences produced Korea's division.

Out of that division grew the two modern Korean states.
South Korea owes its existence to the United States. Without
American backing in the late 1940s, the Republic of Korea
would not have been created. Similarly, without American
support when South Korea was attacked by North Korea in
1950, the ROK would not have survived. Virtually all South
Koreans appreciate those United States roles, but they also
simultaneously understand that neither of those functions would
have been necessary had Korea not been cut in half by the superpowers. So, South Korean gratitude—while real—remains tem-
pered by a large amount of cynicism. It is difficult for Koreans
to be truly grateful to a country which bears some responsibility
for causing the problems that it subsequently helped resolve. The
difficulty is particularly acute among younger Koreans who did
not live through the formative stages of South Korea's creation.

In the more than forty years in which the United States has had relations with South Korea, that country has been utterly transformed. Most older South Koreans recognize and appreciate the contributions the United States made to that process of change. Many of them, plus virtually all of South Korea's younger generation, are nationalists who also correctly emphasize the role that the Korean people had in their own national development. One of the characteristics of South Korean politics that has been poorly understood by Americans from the outset is nationalism. This has always caused mutual misunderstandings. True of the Rhee, Park, and Chun eras, when those leaders' and their opponents' policies sometimes clashed with United States objectives, the tensions have grown markedly in the late 1980s as South Koreans are feeling their nationalist oats.

United States-South Korean relations, as of 1990, remain fundamentally sound, but are notable for rising tensions in economics, security, and politics. Many American journalists have remarked on the surge in anti-Americanism they detected during the Olympics.[4] Though not without foundation, the United States' reaction seems to have been excessive. Anti-American sentiments pre-date the Olympics by several years and are likely to remain a fixture of United States-Korean relations indefinitely. Actually, "anti-Americanism" should be seen as pro-Koreanism. It represents an external projection of Korean pride in the Republic of Korea's accomplishments and a desire that Americans show more respect for those achievements. To the extent these feelings manifest xenophobic tendencies in Korean culture they can be dangerous, but on balance they are a healthy consequence of Korean self-confidence.

So, when South Koreans are confronted by American demands that the Republic of Korea bend to United States trade pressures, yield to United States strategic goals, and (depending on which Korean views are being addressed) either accelerate political liberalization or accommodate to a gradual process of reform, they increasingly dig in their heels. South Koreans of all political stripes want their views on trade, finance, defense burden-sharing, the Combined Forces Command, regional diplomacy, and assorted other issues to be listened to with a new degree of seriousness. For South Korea, the age of its client-state subservience to the United States is over, and the willingness of South Koreans to stand up to Americans is evidence of that change.

Unfortunately, Americans have been slow to recognize these evolutionary shifts. Equally unfortunately, South Korean nationalistic hubris has made it difficult for the Republic of Korea to come to terms with the ways in which United States national interests are diverging from past expressions of bilateral common interests. American demands on South Korea are not precipitating frictions simply because South Koreans are more willing to say "no," but because those demands have changed in ways that reflect new American needs to be tougher minded when dealing with allies on trade and defense issues. In sum, therefore, contemporary United States-South Korean relations are most notable for the ways in which they are changing. Bilateral ties are moving rapidly into a new and more balanced era.

United States-Japan Relations

Though United States-Korean relations are changing, those changes are not likely to influence the entire world. The shifts that have occurred, and continue to unfold daily, in United States-Japan relations are likely to have precisely that impact. The United States-Japan bond is, as former Ambassador Mike Mansfield frequently and correctly says, the most important bilateral tie the United States has, bar none. This is not, nor has it ever been, a comfortable reality for Koreans. Throughout its history of dealing with Asia, the United States always has placed more emphasis on Japan than on Korea. Sometimes Americans were simply indifferent to Korea. More frequently, however, Americans have been sensitive to Korean concerns but have been compelled by the pursuit of larger United States interests to accord Japan primacy in the hierarchy of its relations with Asia. Despite the enormous growth in the importance of United States-Korea relations, this remains true today and is unlikely to change.

What makes Japan so important to the United States? Historically it was the potential, and then the reality, of its capabilities as a geopolitical rival and an armed adversary. In the postwar period, Japan's potential remained too significant to allow Japan to fall under Soviet control. Had that happened, the cold war probably would have been very different. Japan was one of the key venues of that ideological and economic struggle. It was essential to United States interests that Japan be in the Western camp. With American support Japan's political, economic, and military systems regained their health and evolved into a truly vital link in the Western network of alliances led by the United States.

During the 1950s, '60s, and '70s Japan grew rapidly into one of the cornerstones of the Western system. Certainly it was *the* cornerstone in Asia as far as most American leaders were concerned. No other country was a serious rival for that role. Throughout the 1980s Japan's role in the international system continued to expand rapidly. It has grown so quickly and so spectacularly that some Americans now speculate about the prospects for Japan supplanting the United States in a leadership role.[5] It is against that background that one must note the importance of United States-Japan ties and the problems on the United States' agenda with Japan.

United States-Korea trade and defense problems are important, but they are of essentially bilateral significance. On the other hand, the United States' enormous trade deficit with Japan, the issues of finance, banking, and investment, and the questions of who pays for and who does what in the defense of Pacific security are of crucial global importance. Their impact will be felt in the superpower balance, in Europe, and throughout Asia. They clearly will have enormous influence on United States policy toward Korea. Neither South Koreans nor North Koreans like this situation. Both are irritated by the United States' preoccupation with Japan. Like it or not, however, it is an unavoidable reality of contemporary international affairs. As important, it is a reality that is likely to remain a constant or perhaps grow. There is very little prospect of Japan's diminishing in importance to the United States or of its being eclipsed in American eyes by any other state in Asia.

Japan-South Korea Relations

The Korea issue is far more complex for Japan than for the United States. No other major power is so disliked by Koreans. This is primarily because of the colonial era, but it also is because of Japanese treatment of the ethnic Korean minority in Japan. As strong as North Korean animosity toward the

United States and South Korea may be, it pales and finds virtually common cause when the two Koreas complain about Japan. Recent examples of this tendency include denunciations from both Koreas in Japan's textbook revision controversy, its alien-fingerprinting uproar, and its resurgent nationalism. While some Korean enmity toward Japan stems from contemporary developments, they are salt in deep national wounds. For many Koreans, the harsh Japanese colonization of Korea and the ruthless sixteenth-century invasions of Hideyoshi are as active a memory as yesterday's perception of another Japanese insult. It is no overstatement to say that being anti-Japanese is almost ingrained in the Korean national character. Much of this trait is learned, and could be unlearned, but this is a difficult proposition, made more so by Japanese attitudes.

Japanese are even more ethnocentric, culturalist, and racist than Koreans, who also possess a full measure of each quality. Though Japanese mythical divine origins are recognized as such by modern Japanese, they still value the myth. More important, there are some Japanese who treat the myth as truth, and many more—probably a majority—who relish its allegorical qualities. Thus, a deep-seated aspect of the Japanese nation's identity is its feeling of being a uniquely chosen people. All other peoples rank somewhere below them.

This causes immense problems in Japan-Korea relations, because Koreans correctly see Korea as one of the basic cultures from which the Japanese nation evolved. Those roots also include a large dose of Chinese and a smaller dose of Southeast Asian culture, but a substantial portion of Japan's roots are either primitive Korean or derive from Sinified Korean culture. In essence Koreans believe that if one digs deep into Japan's derivative culture, one will discover major imports from Korea.[6] Except among some scholars and very liberal Japanese, total acceptance of those views is cultural heresy in Japan. The conflict in Japanese and Korean egos is magnified by popular Japanese perceptions of Koreans as inferior people who fell victim to colonial pressures, were somehow related to Japan's untouchable caste, could often be found in disreputable occupations in Japan, were argumentative and unruly, and produced two dictatorships to rule over them.

The Japanese attitude toward Korea has improved substantially because of South Korea's great material successes. This is especially true among younger Japanese. This small positive trend could grow in the 1990s if Seoul's political liberalization and the successful Olympics present the Republic of Korea in a positive light to the world, gain South Korea added respect from a variety of Westerners, and expose many more Japanese to Korea for a firsthand experience. In short, despite Japanese obtuseness about their uniqueness, it is possible that South Korea's image could improve. Unfortunately for overall Japan-Korea relations, North Korea's image is not likely to change as quickly. Nor is Japan's image of Koreans likely to change unless leaders in both Seoul and Pyongyang stop cultivating anti-Japanese sentiments for foreign policy purposes, to deflect attention from their own domestic mistakes and excesses. Japan is a handy scapegoat for both Koreas. Against such attitudes, Japan's relations with both Koreas leave much to be desired; it is amazing that they are no worse than they are.

Before examining Tokyo's relations with Seoul, it is necessary to differentiate Tokyo's official posture toward the divided Korean nation from the feelings of the Japanese masses toward each Korea. Japan must deal with its two closest neighbors and ethnic cousins, one a trade competitor, the other a potential military threat. For many Japanese this necessity is fervently unwanted. Until the Roh Tae Woo government moves toward genuine pluralism and democracy materialized,[7] many Japanese adopted a "plague on both your houses" attitude. They did not see much difference between the two Koreas. Both were seen as repressive dictatorships and hotbeds of militarism. They were considered troublesome whiners who would not let the pre-1945 period become history. Japanese perceptions of South Korean politics have improved since serious reforms were initiated there beginning in mid-1987, but South Korean dissidents' allegations that Seoul's human rights performance remains dismal cause many Japanese to be skeptical about South Korea. On balance, both Koreas are viewed as problems for the United States, the Soviet Union, and China that Japan should not address. In short, many Japanese would like their government to abstain in Korean affairs as much as possible.

Knowing this to be impossible, and facing pressure from the

United States to improve relations with South Korea so Washington will not be tagged with two allies barely talking to each other, Japan has gradually altered its relations over the past three decades. Tokyo conducted arduous negotiations with Seoul that normalized relations in 1965. Since then Japan-South Korea economic relations have blossomed. As of 1988, Japan-ROK economic relations are truly major ($21.5 billion in 1987), and South Korea is an up-and-coming competitor. Ironically, some of Japan's elder statesmen, lamenting what they see as a reduced Japanese work ethic among their younger generation, point to South Korea's work ethic as an example to admire. Business leaders in both countries are compatible and have good working relationships. The same is true of many of Seoul's political leaders and Japan's long-ruling Liberal Democratic party. They, too, frequently have remarkable rapport. Despite the mutual animosity between South Korea and Japan at the popular level, their leaders get on remarkably well. Interpersonally they often develop greater mutual empathy than is true for either United States-Korea or United States-Japan leadership interaction.

Despite that, popular animosities usually interfere and prevent smooth relations. In South Korea's case, this most frequently translates into criticism of Japan for economic "imperialism." The United States also is criticized by Korean radicals as an "imperialist" out to colonize Korea, but the allegations against Japan strike a special chord because of the history of the Greater East Asian Co-Prosperity Sphere. Many Koreans and Americans detect echoes of that sphere of influence in contemporary Japan's economic clout throughout the Pacific region. Other South Korean fears center on the dangers of Japanese cultural influences becoming pervasive via the media, music, television, and film. Since far more Koreans understand and read Japanese than vice versa, and there is a love/hate/envy of Japanese fashions and mores, this fear is not without foundation.

Much less credible, but as prevalent, is an unrealistic South Korean fear of revived Japanese militarism. No one can fault South Koreans for their bitter memories of Japanese militarism, or for expressing warnings that it could happen again. That is not, however, what South Korean critics normally do. Seeking out snippets of evidence that Japanese militarism is preparing to pounce on Asia again, they interpret the existence of nonmilitaristic Self Defense Forces to suit their purposes and advance evidence to prove their illusory case that Japan still harbors expansionist hopes. Examination of contemporary Japan undermines those allegations. There is no logical reason, economically or militarily, for today's Japan to revert to expansionism. Short of a major deterioration in international affairs, especially in ties with the United States, Japan has no reason to change course. Equally important, even if Japan did reverse course, how would it expand? The 1980s and 1990s are not the 1930s. There are no vacuums for Japan to fill. Japan would have to run a gauntlet of militarily powerful states, including the superpowers. Were irrationality to prevail in Japan, Tokyo would pursue expansionism in the virtual certainty that it would be suicidal.

South Korean worries are exacerbated by United States pressures on Japan to strengthen its self-defense capabilities. Seoul, too, encourages this development, but within clear constraints. South Korea is afraid that Japanese responses to United States pressures could get out of control. Seoul's reservations about Japan's ultra-cautious response to the 1990 Persian Gulf crisis illustrates its fears verge on paranoia. It also fears that some Americans and Japanese will connive, at South Korea's expense, to make Japan a surrogate for the United States in Northeast Asia. South Korean anxiety about Japan's ambitions in Korea strike an overwhelming majority of Japanese as paranoid, since they want as little to do with Korea as possible, do not care whether Koreans are influenced by Japanese tastes, and are stridently antimilitaristic and reluctant even to defend themselves, much less any other country. Korea is almost certainly the last place on earth where most contemporary Japanese desire to see their country militarily involved. South Korean accusations and fear of revived Japanese militarism aimed at Korea strike most Japanese as patently absurd, especially coming from a nation many Japanese believe is itself run by militaristic fascists.

Japan-South Korea relations at the government-to-government level, though strained by popular frictions and misunderstandings that contaminate the emotions of each country's policy makers and bureaucrats, were significantly improved in the wake of the 1983–1984 exchange of state visits by President Chun Doo Hwan and Prime Minister Yasuhiro Nakasone. Those symbolic occasions, including a semi-apology by Emperor Hirohito for past Japanese offenses to the Koreans, were a watershed in official relations. The more extensive apology offered by Emperor Akihito in 1990 further helped set an improved tone. However, the watershed was gradual and the new-found official bilateral goodwill could easily be reversed by a few highly negative developments. Both Tokyo and Seoul seem to be doing what they can, with only weak popular support, to prevent relapses to harsher times. Washington supports these trends.

United States reaction to the difficulties Seoul and Tokyo have in pulling their nations closer together has been profoundly cautious and tolerant. Anxious for its two allies to stop squabbling, Washington has strongly urged each side to get along better with the other. However, the United States has studiously avoided rushing a reconciliation that might precipitate new frictions between Japan and South Korea. It does not want to do anything that South Koreans or Japanese might construe as negative. In short, Washington does not want to get caught in the middle of their conflicts.

Washington has chosen to avoid that fate by perpetuating separate bilateral strategic, economic, and political ties—acting as a linchpin holding the threesome together in a cohesive relationship. While Washington applauds South Korea-Japan economic cooperation and sporadic political consultation, it also seconds Seoul and Tokyo's decisions not to become more closely tied strategically. Adopting this posture, Washington has stayed out of the briar patch of animosities only by becoming the buffer or crutch on which South Korea and Japan rely.

The logic of this policy is more than a little perverse, but the strategy persists. Moreover, because Seoul, Tokyo, and Washington all support it, it has been successful, causing United States leaders to be content with the state of Korea-Japan relations and the progress Seoul and Tokyo are making in enhancing harmony. Washington has been particularly sensitive to South Korean and Japanese fears that it is manipulating them into a close, triangular military pact, an intention routinely disavowed by senior United States officials. Frequent

North Korean allegations of a budding trilateral imperialist cabal aimed at it notwithstanding, the United States *can* be said to be fostering a loose alignment among the United States, Japan, and South Korea. Of course, a "loose alignment" arrangement would also characterize United States relations with the People's Republic of China, so it is easy to see why North Korea might be agitated by limited United States efforts to get its other allies to view the world in a similar manner.

If the United States is relatively content with the status of South Korea-Japan relations, it seems far less happy with the nature of Japan-North Korea relations. Neither Seoul nor Washington trusts Tokyo's position vis-à-vis Pyongyang. Japan's overall tilt toward South Korea is obvious. That is where its economic interests are heavier, its political bonds are stronger, and its geopolitical sympathies lie. Against that background, Seoul and Washington show consternation over Tokyo's determination to maintain a veneer of equidistance in its relations with South Korea and North Korea. The United States and the Republic of Korea would be more comfortable if Japan would line up more clearly on their side of the spectrum. However, Tokyo does not, and for years has kept its options vis-à-vis North Korea far more open than the United States, the Republic of Korea, or any other pro-Western country. Gradually, Seoul has displayed more tolerance for Japan's open-mindedness. South Korea has given the green light to Tokyo and Washington to improve their ties with Pyongyang. Japan has responded more affirmatively than the United States, culminating in a dramatic improvement in Japan-North Korea relations during late 1990, which may yield diplomatic recognition. In retrospect it may be argued that Japan's more progressive stance regarding North Korea over the years stimulated the shifts in South Korea's foreign policy toward a more flexible position. When viewed in the context of Seoul's new openness to China, the Soviet Union, and other socialist states, the parallels with Tokyo's "omni-directional diplomacy" are striking.

Tokyo's reasons for maintaining this slightly ambiguous posture are not hard to discern. Foremost is the domestic support for a hands-off, equidistance approach. There are many Japanese, harsh critics of South Korea, who do not want their government siding with the United States and the Republic of

Korea against a "threat" they do not perceive to be real, even after the North Korean attack on KAL 858, which aroused some Japanese animosity toward North Korea. So, despite Tokyo's tacit recognition of its strong relationship with Seoul, it cannot afford to be too explicit about what it is doing. Moreover, Tokyo sees a pragmatic utility in access to North Korea. If China and the Soviet Union can exert restraint on Pyongyang's potential recklessness, Tokyo does not see why it, too, should not try to exert its trade-oriented influence.

Despite North Korea's dismal trade record and defaults on debts, Tokyo still encourages Japanese firms to cultivate economic ties with the DPRK. This strategy was set back by Tokyo's cooperation with Washington and Seoul in restrictions against North Korea after the 1987 Korean Air Lines bombing, but these punitive policies were not as rigid in Japan as they were in the United States and Korea. Though Japan's willingness to be flexible regarding North Korea is a prudent policy that serves larger Western interests by giving the Kim regime a non-Soviet and non-Chinese alternative and serves Japan's interest in helping to reduce North Korean animosity, this posture was suspect in Seoul and Washington. Japanese overtures to North Korea struck many South Korean and United States officials as appeasement, undercutting the solidarity of the United States-based alliance network in Northeast Asia, and enabling North Korea to strengthen itself. Fortunately, this atmosphere has mellowed in ways that allow Seoul to see the wisdom in Tokyo's past policy.

Despite anxiety in Seoul and Washington over unreliable Japan-North Korea relations—which was so strong at one time that the United States reportedly did not consult with Japan about its South Korea-sanctioned plan for the United States to revive "smile diplomacy" and make other overtures toward North Korea[8]—Tokyo-Pyongyang ties have not been solid. North Korea is far more critical of Japan's policies than is South Korea. It routinely accuses the Japanese of imperialist conspiracies, subjugating South Koreans through its economic policies, and being unreconstructed militarists. One of its weirdest accusations concerned a Japan-South Korea hope to build a seabed tunnel, which Pyongyang visualized as an invasion route.[9] The irony of a notorious tunnel digger's being alarmed by the prospect of a legitimate tunnel seems never to have dawned on the Kim regime. Pyongyang also is far more troublesome in the way it manipulates the pro-North Korean ethnic minority in Japan than Seoul is in its use of the pro-South Korean minority. Furthermore, few Japanese admire the Kim dictatorship, and most recognize that its brand of Stalinism is abhorrent in many countries.

Why then has Tokyo persisted in cultivating North Korea? Is it because of domestic pressures and desires to be innovative regarding tension-reduction in Korea? This is possible but unlikely, even though it would be more compatible with the purposes of the Roh government. It is far more likely that Japan is guided by a desire to keep Korea divided and the status quo intact. Throughout the post-Korean War period Japan has portrayed itself as the epitome of evenhandedness vis-à-vis Korea. Despite a well-rounded set of relationships with Seoul, encompassing economic, diplomatic, political, and a smattering of strategic ties, Tokyo pointedly stresses its openness in dealing with Pyongyang. Japan-North Korea relations have been rocky at times, but at least they exist informally—unlike United States-North Korea "relations." To Tokyo and the Japanese public, their posture places Japan in a far more progressive stance than that of the United States. From the perspective of the Japanese it is the United States which is the laggard regarding improved relations with North Korea and between the two Koreas.

What accounts for this Japanese view? Clearly, it could be valid. However, it is not. Examining the reasons the United States adheres doggedly to its status-quo-ism in Korea, one almost always comes upon a connection to Japan. Despite appearances, Japan today is not interested in seeing Korea reunited as one nation in one state. There are several reasons for Japan's decided lack of enthusiasm about the reunification of Korea. Part of its attitude stems from its ties to South Korea and its stake, particularly its economic stake, in the Republic of Korea's separate existence. Another Japanese motive derives from Tokyo's very real fear that unification may come about as a result of North Korean conquest of the South. Should that occur, Japan might lose its economic influence in Korea and have to confront the prospect of countless anticommunist Korean refugees fleeing to the nearest reasonably hospitable shore, thereby aggravating Japan's already tense relations with its Korean ethnic minority and complicating Tokyo's ties with the new Korean regime. It might also risk being drawn directly into the war as a combatant. That could happen as a by-product of the presence of American bases, which could make Japan a target of North Korean retaliation, or as a result of the United States' failing to repel North Korea at an acceptable cost to the American public, thereby obliging Tokyo to enter the fray.

These reasons might be enough to foster Japanese reluctance to urge unification. Certainly they contribute to Japan's very strong pressures on the United States to be consistent in its support of the status quo. At times Japan seems to be acting on South Korea's behalf, as when it lobbies for firm American resolve in the United States' commitment to the Republic of Korea. Clearly, Seoul periodically requests such advocacy from Japan. The most graphic and successful episode of proxy lobbying was Japan's persistent pressure against the Carter administration's troop cutback proposals. However, Japan never would have undertaken any such diplomatic intervention advocating Seoul's cause if that intervention had not also served Japan's national interests in very explicit ways.

A divided Korea, with the United States being committed to the security of the Republic of Korea, offers Japan concrete advantages compared to those provided by a unified Korea, regardless of how unification might occur. To understand these advantages, one has only to imagine what a unified Korea might mean for Japan. A unified communist Korea would pose obvious strategic dangers. Japan probably could live with such a neighbor, but not comfortably and not cheaply. Tokyo would have to prepare for further Korean aggression without the advantage of American and South Korean forces as a buffer. Those preparations would be costly and compel Tokyo to make fundamental decisions about its defense policy which Korea's division now postpones.

A unified noncommunist Korea also could pose security problems for Japan. Though South Koreans may ridicule such views, many Japanese are unconvinced that the Republic of Korea is intrinsically peaceful. Given the vivid legacy of anti-Japanese sentiment, which is alive and well in both Korean societies, reunification of Korea under either Pyongyang or

Seoul would be seen by many Japanese as a threatening prospect. Such a state would possess experienced armed forces in excess of one million personnel, ample arms, the economic-technological base to sustain such forces, and—for the first time in modern history—the capability of inflicting vengeance on Japan for past actions if the opportunity ever presented itself. This is the stuff of which Japanese nightmares are made.

Even if a unified Korean state remained peaceful toward Japan—a doubtful prospect from the Japanese view—it still would pose significant economic problems. Under the leadership of either Korean government, but particularly under Seoul's experienced direction, a unified Korea would soon be a far more formidable economic competitor than either Korean state is today. Given the sometimes apoplectic apprehension Japanese business circles now express about South Korean economic prowess beating the Japanese at their own game, Japan is reluctant to foster a unified Korean economic competitor of any political stripe.

Keeping Korea divided also is good international politics for Japan. Like the Soviet Union and the People's Republic of China in the past, but unlike the United States, Japan enjoys considerable political leverage by playing off the needs, hopes, and aspirations of the two Korean states as each tries to use Japan to get the edge on its Korean antagonist. This balancing act by Japan and the two Koreas is Machiavellian in its subtlety and goes largely unnoticed by Americans, who tend to see Korean issues in black and white. This American disposition gives Japan leverage to use against all three concerned states, whether or not those states understand they are being manipulated.

Lastly, keeping Korea divided is far easier for Japan than the alternative. Tokyo enjoys its low diplomatic and political profile everywhere. It is good business, good politics, and good strategy. The last thing contemporary Japan wants is to take an overt stand on controversial issues anywhere, at any time. The very last controversy Japan needs is to take a firm stand on Korea. The Japanese are well aware of vitriolic Korean attitudes toward Japan. They are reminded often enough that they cannot forget. Consequently, it is easier for Japan to let the Korean people ferment in their divided state, casting aspersions on each other rather than shelving their ideological differences and turning their united attention to Japan. In this divide-and-manipulate variation of the ancient divide-and-conquer dictum, Japan's lack of enthusiasm for reunification, conveyed to and accepted by the United States, keeps Korean anti-Japanese sentiment at a manageable level.

Washington's reaction to Japan's *realpolitik* toughmindedness is remarkably benign. Americans are rarely candid about their own aspirations to perpetuate the status quo, even if it means the division of Korea is permanent, so it should be no surprise that little is said about similar Japanese attitudes. Both of the two Koreas occasionally criticize the major powers backing the rival Korea for perpetuating the status quo by their obstinacy. Of course, each Korea also regularly accuses the other of obstinacy that prolongs Korea's division. However, neither Korea is any more willing than the major powers to openly admit the unadmittable: everyone concerned long wanted to keep the status quo from unraveling because it was safer for all than the uncertainties inherent in any alternative. It was safer to pursue reduced tensions based on reinforcing the division of Korea than it is to risk a fundamental rearrangement of the Korean puzzle.

The unification of Korea remains a much-spoken-of long-term goal, but one that remains elusive. To be sure, all parties concerned express their strong support for Korea's unification. In both Korean states it is a political shibboleth. All leaders in Seoul and Pyongyang strenuously commit themselves to "unification," as though it were a panacea. Notwithstanding such views, there is strong reason to be cynical. Unfortunately, there are few signs yet that the leadership elites in either Seoul or Pyongyang are prepared to make the sorts of real concessions—sharing power—that might signal meaningful progress toward unification. In Washington, Tokyo, Moscow, and Beijing there is just as much timidity about such concessions. Despite the major improvements in ROK-USSR ties in the late 1980s that produced diplomatic relations in September 1990, unification remains a troubling issue for all the major powers concerned. All four say they are wholeheartedly committed to unification and cast aspersions on the sincerity of the backers of the "other" Korea, but sincerity seems in short supply on all governmental sides of the issue of Korean unification. Overt expressions of official support should not be taken at face value. All of the four major powers are manipulative regarding Korea and its division. This is no less true of the Soviet Union and China than of the United States and Japan. All of them are ready to support positions which seem to help unification, but in reality there always have been conditions in the positions they support which make it impossible to achieve. These are de facto catch-22s.[10]

Expressing this view should not be interpreted as sanctioning the division of Korea. The Korean people—on both sides of the dividing line—are the real losers in these arrangements. It is for their sake that unification must be pursued. One should not, however, be sanguine about the prospects for unification until a significant change of heart occurs in both Seoul and Pyongyang, and among the four powers, that would allow genuine concessions and compromise. In the meantime the two Koreas and the four major powers should be given due credit for their efforts at tension reduction, increased communication, and lowered economic barriers. They contribute to a more stable and safer environment in Northeast Asia. Eventually, over the long term, they might even point the way toward levels of confidence and trust which could become the basis for unification. Until the political and security milieu in Korea changes dramatically, however, these steps are better understood in terms of risk avoidance. This is precisely what is meant by keeping the status quo from unraveling. Change is occurring, but all sides want to control the processes of change so tightly that these shifts—impressive though they may appear—are unlikely to lead to unification any time soon.

United States-Japan Relations: A Comparison

A basic difference between United States and Japanese perceptions of the two Korean states and their interactions stems from our radically different histories. The United States' experience with Korea has been far shorter and less complicated than Japan's. Japan is a near neighbor that has often intervened harshly in Korean affairs. A long-standing, large, downtrodden, and politically divided Korean minority exists in an otherwise homogeneous Japan. And Japan harbors a pronounced disdain for Koreans and is distrusted by both Korean states. In contrast, the United States welcomes its often prosperous and rapidly growing Korean minority into a nation of minorities.[11] More important, the United States is a clear factor for the two Koreas—a strong supporter of one and a feared adversary of the other. Though the United States looms very large for both Korean states, causing for different reasons anxiety in both Koreas, neither Seoul nor Pyongyang distrusts the United States in the profound ways each distrusts Japan.

The United States and Japan support Seoul's negotiating position versus North Korea as a pragmatic approach to the difficult issues at hand, but the United States' support is more overt than Japan's. Tokyo retains elements of its ostensibly evenhanded approach to the two Koreas, which leads it to behave more ambiguously toward Seoul's positions. In large part this appears to be a reflection of the Japanese public's cautious attitudes toward inter-Korean affairs. While Japanese society and its government no longer stress a "plague on both your houses" style of objectivity, Japan still tries to maintain a greater level of impartiality and distance than the United States does. Washington firmly supports Seoul, and United States public and media opinion is strongly supportive of a positive policy toward a steadfast ally and thriving protege.

Both the United States and Japan are openly supporters of a peaceful unification of Korea. In part, they are able to take such a position because they do not think it will happen anytime soon. Neither Japan nor the United States is entirely enamored of the prospective realities of a unified Korea. Both countries would benefit from a lasting peace in Korea, Japan most directly in terms of its regional security interests and the United States most directly in terms of reducing the burdens and costs the United States now bears worldwide. Because of these factors, both Japan and the United States no doubt would outwardly rejoice should unification ever occur, but there almost certainly is significant concern about the problems a unified Korea could pose.

A communist unified Korea obviously is least desired by the United States and Japan. However, even a noncommunist unified Korea could cause serious problems for the United States and Japan. The United States might lose its bases in Korea, adversely affecting its capacity to maintain the American "nuclear umbrella" in Asia and perhaps jeopardizing the United

States' ability to assure closure of the maritime "choke point" between Japan and Korea. The United States also could ultimately face a Korea that would be a more formidable competitor because of enhanced economies of scale and reduced military expenditures. As noted above, Japan fears this prospect even more acutely than does the United States.

Were Koreans no longer preoccupied with each other, confronted by international threats, or inhibited by constraints imposed by the United States and the Soviet Union, Tokyo might have ample reason to fear Koreans' turning their combined attention to Japan. Though this may seem far-fetched to Americans who view Japan and South Korea in much the same light and hope to create a trilateral community of interests, it is not unthinkable to Japanese, who are well aware of lingering Korean hostilities toward, envy of, and desire to catch up with Japan. On balance, therefore, the United States and Japan are ambivalent about Korean unification, though for somewhat different reasons. Consequently, both seem comforted by the unlikelihood of imminent unification.

Neither Japan nor the United States seems to take the other's rhetoric supporting unification very seriously. Each sees it, and other pronouncements on Korean affairs, as part of the diplomatic price that must be paid to keep their overall Korea policies on an even keel. This is especially important for Japan, which recognizes the great value of the United States' strategic posture on the Korean peninsula and will do all it can to perpetuate the advantageous aspects of the status quo for as long as possible. Official American reactions to Japanese attitudes and policies toward Korea are generally sympathetic to Tokyo's reluctance to get involved, much less to go out on a limb on Korea's behalf by taking any initiatives which would depart significantly from past and present hypercautious policies. Since Seoul heartily seconds Washington's wishes to acquiesce to a low Japanese profile and reinforces Tokyo's pronounced unwillingness to elevate that profile, there is no sign of a major policy shift in either Tokyo or Washington.

On the other hand, if one examines the changing natures of United States-South Korea and Japan-South Korea economic relations, there is no way to camouflage the marked increase in tensions that troubles both relationships. Each supporter of the Republic of Korea now sees it as an increasingly important economic challenge as well as a valued partner. Though these separate bilateral problems could be solved with joint resolve, that level of will is not evident. Moreover, United States-Japan economic frictions are less easily handled, and those tensions promise to continue to spill over into United States-Korea ties. In short, both Japan and the United States are experiencing the rapid maturation of their relations with the Republic of Korea. If not managed prudently, to the benefit of all parties, it is easy to imagine the sorts of disruptive influences that could spin off from trade issues onto other facets of diplomatic and security relations.[12]

Since such developments might play right into the hands of North Korea, they should not be permitted to evolve gratuitously in negative directions. That Pyongyang might be able to take advantage of divisive tendencies means that Seoul, Tokyo, and Washington cannot safely engage in primarily ad hoc damage control, lacking a coherent plan to rectify the problems. All three should try to work out their differences so that they do not jeopardize the foundations of northeast Asian harmony. Such a resolution of problems, if it is to be equitable, must entail a degree of fairness and candor that does not currently exist. If that could be achieved, it would help rationalize the levels of support the United States and Japan provide for the Republic of Korea in general and specifically in regard to Seoul's diplomatic contest with Pyongyang. Though this would not necessarily facilitate success for Seoul in that contest, should Seoul prevail it would make the potential outcome less worrisome for Tokyo and Washington because South Korea would already have become a more thoroughly integrated partner of the United States and Japan.

The key question at this juncture is, will the successful 1988 Seoul Olympics and the changed diplomatic atmosphere it helped produce alter any of this? A dramatic change seems doubtful in direct terms. Despite the symbolism of the Olympics for South Korea's place in the world, it is unlikely to have a pronounced impact on United States-South Korea relations, which are wedded to geopolitical fundamentals that are inherently slow to change. However, the indirect effect of the Seoul

Olympics on the United States and Japan could contribute to profound changes, an Olympian era for South Korea.

Stemming from the publicity surrounding the Olympics, South Korea's newly perceived stature has enhanced—and perhaps exaggerated—foreigners' image of its economic prowess. This is likely to exacerbate already existing strains in the United States-South Korea and Japan-South Korea trade relationships which—in turn—could provide North Korea an opportunity to take advantage of those tensions. Another post-Olympics possibility relates to the degree to which Seoul used the Olympics as a forum for displaying the Republic of Korea's flexibility toward communist regimes. As President Roh Tae Woo openly hoped, the Olympics reinforced improved South Korean-Chinese and South Korean-Soviet contacts. That atmosphere ultimately yielded formal ROK-USSR diplomatic ties and the exchange of ROK-PRC official trade offices during late 1990. South Korea's relations with a transformed Eastern Europe also improved dramatically. Unfortunately, these positive shifts also reinforced anti-American sentiments in South Korea because of the ways in which Americans were perceived by Koreans during the Olympics. On balance, however, these shifts may create a precedent for reciprocally improved United States-North Korea and Japan-North Korea contacts.

In addition, since North Korean athletes participated in the 1988 Calgary Winter Olympics (with the North Korean flag flying near the American flag), and North Korea did not seek to impede the Seoul games, Pyongyang has displayed an ability to act reasonably. This sign of improved behavior cleared the way for improved North Korean contacts with the United States and Japan. Conversely, had North Korea caused disruption of the Summer Olympics, carrying out the threat implied in the 1987 KAL bombing, it would have severely set back the already limited prospects for improved relations with the North Koreans. Fortunately, none of the fears expressed about North Korea materialized. Nor was harsh South Korean political repression necessary to keep order during the games. In those terms the Olympics produced an aura of good feelings about Korea. Some fears remained that a post-Olympics political crackdown, once the glare of international publicity had been reduced, could reverse all those gains. That would, of course, have damaged the prospects for harmonious United States and Japanese relations with South Korea.

On balance, the chances for significant changes in United States-Korea or Japan-Korea relations have been enhanced by Olympic atmospherics, but those relationships have not been reshaped directly by the Olympics. Other events—notably domestic political events in the United States, United States-Japanese economic tensions, changes in the superpower balance, shifts in Sino-Soviet relations, Soviet politico-economic overtures in the Pacific, the end of the superpower cold war, and Seoul's innovative foreign policy initiatives—are doing more to reshape the context of Korean affairs. The positive political texture of the Olympics may subtly influence those broader events, but only at the margins. Consequently, the Seoul Olympics should not be considered a watershed in Korean affairs for Americans or Japanese, although it may yet prove to have been the initial portion of a watershed for inter-Korean relations.

Notes

1. The author contributed to that growing literature through his *U.S. Policy and the Two Koreas* (San Francisco: Northern California World Affairs Council, 1988), distributed by Westview Press. See also, Claude A. Buss, *The United States and the Republic of Korea; Background for Policy* (Stanford: Hoover Institution Press, 1982); Gerald L. Curtis and Han Sung-joo, eds., *The U.S.-South Korean Alliance; Evolving Patterns in Security Relations* (Lexington, MA: Lexington Books, 1983). *Korea at the Crossroads: Implications for American Policy* (New York: Council on Foreign Relations/The Asia Society, 1987); Karl Moskowitz, ed., *From Patron to Partner: The Development of U.S.-Korean Business and Trade Relations* (Lexington, MA: Lexington Books, 1984); Nam Joo-hong, *America's Commitment to South Korea; The First Decade of the Nixon Doctrine* (London: LSE Monographs in International Studies, 1986); and John Sullivan and Roberta Foss, eds., *Two Koreas—One Future?* (Lanham, MD: University Press of America/American Friends Service Committee, 1987).
2. For examples of survey assessments, see Stephen D. Cohen, *Uneasy Partnership; Competition and Conflict in U.S.-Japanese Trade Relations* (Cambridge, MA: Ballinger Publishing Co., 1985); Hiroshi Kitamura, Ryohei Murata, and Hisahiko Okazaki, *Between Friends* (Tokyo: Weatherhill, 1985); and Harrison Holland, *Managing Diplomacy: The United States and Japan* (Stanford: Hoover Institution Press, 1985). For a useful comparative study, see Chong-shik Lee, *Japan and Korea: The Political Dimension* (Stanford: Hoover Institution Press, 1985).
3. Commemorative studies include: Cho Soon-sung, Kwak Tae-hwan, John Chay, and Shannon McCune, eds., *U.S.-Korean Relations, 1882–1982* (Seoul: Kyungnam University Press, 1982); Han Sung-joo, ed., *After One Hundred Years: Continuity and Change in Korean-American Relations* (Seoul: Asiatic Research Center, Korea University, 1982); Koo Young-nok and Suh Dae-sook, eds., *Korea and the United States: A Century of Cooperation* (Honolulu: University of Hawaii Press, 1984); and Ronald A. Morse, ed., *A Century of United States-Korean Relations: Proceedings of a Conference at the Wilson Center, June 17–19, 1982* (Washington, D.C.: University Press of America, Inc., 1983).
4. See *Washington Post*, September 27, 1988, A12 and A17, and September 30, 1988, A18- A19; *Christian Science Monitor*, September 30, 1988, 7–8; and *Far Eastern Economic Review*, October 13, 1988, 74–76.
5. See, especially, Clyde V. Prestowitz, *Trading Places; How We Allowed Japan to Take the Lead* (New York: Basic Books, 1988).
6. For a clear statement of that Korea-centric viewpoint, see Jon Carter Covell, *Japan's Hidden History* (Seoul: Hollym Publishers, 1984).
7. For analyses of Roh's views, see *Far Eastern Economic Review*, October 20, 1988, 39; *Christian Science Monitor*, October 18, 1988, 9; and

Washington Post, October 20, 1988, 1 and A36.

8. *Far Eastern Economic Review,* April 23, 1987, 31.

9. *FBIS,* June 4, 1987, C1.

10. The author explored this issue more thoroughly in "Does Anyone Really Want Korean Reunification," *Asian Wall Street Journal Weekly,* May 16, 1983, 14, and "The Catch-22s of Korean Unification," *Asian Wall Street Journal,* June 1–2, 1984, commentary and analysis page.

11. Though it may be impolitic at a Washington Institute conference sponsored by the Reverend Moon's organization, it is important to note another parallel in United States-South Korean and Japan-South Korean relations. In both the United States and Japan there are similar suspicions about one sub-group in the Korean minority— namely the Moon organization's influence in conservative political activities in each society. Rumors and anxiety are rife in both countries that their influence (for example, through the *Washington Times* in Washington or through prominent figures in the ruling Liberal Democratic party of Japan) is excessive. The precise nature of the Moon organization's links to the South Korean government remains murky, the focus of speculation and the cause of suspicions. Without accusing anyone of McCarthyite tactics, it is important that concerned citizens, officials, and representatives of the Moon organizations in all three countries pay careful attention to these rumors, clarify misperceptions, and be sensitive to the appearance of undue influence which could be disruptive to future relations between South Korea and the United States and/or Japan whenever the latter two are governed by a more liberal political element.

12. The author addresses them in his *U.S. Policy and the Two Koreas.*

19

American Public Opinion on South Korea

Continuity and Change, 1968–1988

W. Wayne Shannon

Introduction

OUR PURPOSE IN THIS CHAPTER is to discuss American public opinion bearing on South Korea over the last twenty or so years. To do that I will review and interpret a sizable body of polling data.[1] This is a useful kind of exercise, often more productive than rushing out to do a new survey. As far as I can tell, there has been no previous effort of this sort specifically focused on understanding American attitudes toward South Korea. The only systematic writing on this subject seems to be that of William Watts of Potomac Associates, and this is entirely based on surveys done for Potomac by the Gallup Organization.[2] As we shall see, there are certain limitations inherent in trying to understand public opinion by relying on data collected by one firm and interpreted by one analyst. Modern polling, even on such a specialized subject as the one before us, produces a wealth of data. Questions are asked over time on many aspects of a subject in many different ways by many different firms. We get our best picture of American attitudes toward South Korea (or any other subject) by a "data-extensive" approach—consulting as many surveys as possible over a period of some years.[3] That is what we will do here.

The approach I take here is straightforward—to search out all questions asked about South Korea during the period we are interested in, to sort them into coherent categories by subject, and to *interpret* them as pieces of a picture Americans have of United States relations with this one nation in the larger context of our interests on the world stage. The key element in this or any other secondary analysis of survey data is to puzzle out what respondents are saying when they answer questions that are most often put to them in a rigid format not of their own making, on subjects not of their own choosing. In this exercise my own judgment admittedly plays a strong role. The data do not speak for themselves. Often, the answers to survey questions must be seen as artifacts of the way questions are asked. They cannot be taken literally. Many of the questions asked about South Korea show that we have never fully assimilated what Walter Lippmann tried to teach us long ago—that a public is not a seminar or a policy-making entity.[4] Ordinary Americans do not and cannot spend much time pondering United States-South Korean relations, and they surely do not mandate American foreign policy. These are matters they leave to elites. The public, we must remember, is answering as best it can questions that pollsters ask at a particular time for news media or other research sponsors. Answers to these questions are not equally valid. Questions, for example, that expect Americans to possess detailed factual knowledge about South Korea or to pass judgment on the details of strategic or trade policies produce answers of little or no value. I will argue that we should expect from the public only what a reasonable theory of democracy requires—very general attitudes and values toward South Korea. Public opinion at most establishes broad boundaries inside which proximate policy makers are free to act. Poorly interpreted, survey data may contribute to misunderstandings when they are read by a general audience. This, I will show, is the case with some of the questions on Korea.

In this kind of analysis we have no ability to choose subjects or to ask particular questions as we might wish to do in a new study; we are prisoners, as it were, of past decisions by survey firms and research sponsors over which we have no control. Fortunately, many different subjects have been addressed in the Korea questions in the Roper Center archive—Americans' knowledge about and interest in Korea, their general attitudes toward the country, their sense of American strategic interests there, and their attitudes about such matters as Koreagate, human rights, and trade arrangements. We will take them up one by one in this order.

What Americans Know about Korea

Quite a few questions have been asked in recent years to gauge Americans' understanding of "the facts" about Korea—its geography, the nature of the North and South Korean governments, the economics of the two Koreas, South Korea's trade relationship with the United States, the nature and amount of aid South Korea receives from the United States, Americans' ability to classify the government of South Korea in various ways, and the like. Nearly all of these are Gallup questions sponsored by Potomac Associates. The answers to these questions tell us, for example, that about two-thirds of Americans know that Korea is geographically a peninsula sharing a common boundary with the People's Republic of China. The rest do not seem to remember their geography lessons very well. About the same number know that North Korea is a communist state. Not much more than a bare majority of Americans seem to know for sure that South Korea is not communist. There was clearly not much public knowledge of the relative economic advancement of North and South Korea when questions were asked on this matter in 1978 and 1979. Only a small minority of the American public seemed then to be able to identify correctly the level of foreign trade between South Korea and the United States. The public registered considerable uncertainty when asked to classify the South Korean government as "communist," "military authoritarian," "civilian authoritarian," "mixed," or "democratic." Finally, the public seemed to "fail" abysmally the true-false test administered by Gallup/Potomac in 1980 on the facts of American aid to South Korea. (See following page.)

	% of Adults		% of College Educated	
	True	False	True	False
The United States provides major economic assistance and aid to South Korea	81	15	88	11

What shall we take these data to mean? William Watts has found the answer to the geography question "not entirely reassuring."[5] He has pronounced the "ignorance" of Americans on South Korean-United States trade relations "remarkable."[6] Even worse, he has written, is the public's mistaken perception that South Korea in 1980 remained "a major aid recipient" of the United States.[7] In sum, he has concluded that these survey findings reveal "a considerable amount of ignorance and misunderstanding about Korea."[8] To be sure, Watts points out that similar levels of ignorance or misunderstanding" exist about other Asian countries, but the tone of his interpretation is that there is a problem here about which something should be done. Somehow, Americans must be made better informed about South Korea!

The trouble with these questions and with Watts' interpretation is that they expect from the public something that it cannot possibly provide. They violate Lippmann's dictum that society is not a seminar. Polling on any and all subjects has produced similar findings whenever such questions have been asked. Would Americans have done better had they been asked any of the following about their own country? What states border Ohio? Who are their two United States Senators? Who is the governor of New York? What is the Ninth Amendment of the American Constitution? What is the size of the American federal budget deficit? We know from some fifty years of polling that they would not. Such questions always make the public look "ignorant." Elmo Roper said many years ago that his experience in polling convinced him that "a great many of us make two mistakes in our judgment of the common man. We overestimate the amount of information he has; we underestimate his intelligence."[9] We see here that these mistakes are still being made. In fact, there is no persuasive evidence that Americans know less than they should about South Korea relative to other countries. Nor would any number of civics lessons or public relations campaigns make them better informed. Questions that assume the public needs to be able to perform like quiz kids yield little useful information. Some of the Gallup/ Potomac "facts about Korea" questions are complex enough to stump all but a few Korea specialists. Moreover, the 1980 economic aid question is in effect a "trick question" of the sort that generations of college students have learned to hate. The public cannot be expected to make a distinction between economic and military aid unless such a distinction is made in the question wording. The public at large and the college-educated (who even more strongly say that Korea receives United States aid) are both probably reasoning that the United States maintains a substantial military presence in South Korea and that this costs a good deal of money and constitutes a form of aid. Common sense should tell us that a question wording that "fools" 88 percent of the college-educated is not a good one.

Americans probably know as much about Korea as they know about other countries. They cannot be expected to know more than they do. The picture they have is not a detailed one. Another Gallup/Potomac question asked in 1978 suggests that Americans' knowledge is mainly derived from the electronic media. (Asked to pick the one or two most important sources of information, 66 percent say television and radio; 51 percent, newspapers, magazines and books.) We know also that the American public's interest in Korea is relatively low. In July 1985, the Roper Organization included "relations between North and South Korea" in a long list of items on which the public was asked to say whether it was "following fairly closely,

Following Fairly Closely (partial list)	
Which prices are going up or down	75%
The energy crisis	69
Job layoffs and unemployment	66
Talk of a possible depression	53
Possible candidates for next president	39
President Ford and his administration	38
Economic problems of New York City	18
Relations between North & South Korea	16
The political situation in India	12

or just casually, or not paying much attention to." The results of this exercise are hardly surprising.

Of course, the public is not singling out Korea for a special kind of inattention. There is simply not much interest in any foreign country. Information about other nations and interest in what is happening abroad are always low, and that is how it must be, given the nature of democratic publics. There is surely no reason to conclude that the levels of information Americans have about Korea constitute a special problem. The real problem lies in the questions and the way they have been interpreted.

American Attitudes toward Korea

Several efforts have been made in recent years to measure how Americans feel about other countries—their "affect" toward them (whether they like them or dislike them) and whether they are trusted or distrusted as allies. Although the firms asking questions of this sort include different countries on their lists, South Korea is generally included. Since such lists cannot, practically speaking, be all that long, this in itself tells us something important; the elites designing the questions regard South Korea as a sufficiently important actor on the international stage to warrant collecting information about American attitudes toward the country. These, I will argue, are the best available data bearing on Americans' attitudes toward Korea. They are couched in very general terms, they ask about something that the public can understand, and they permit comparison of American attitudes toward Korea and several other nations.

Three distinct approaches to measuring Americans' feelings toward Korea and other nations are summarized in table 19-1. The Gallup Organization used a "thermometer scale" in 1978, 1982, and 1986 to gauge "warm feeling"/"cold feeling" toward a long list of countries for the Chicago Council on Foreign Relations. "Temperatures" on this scale ranged in 1986 from a high of 77 (Canada) to a low of 22 (Iran). On this measure Korea falls in the middle range with a reading of 50 degrees. Gallup in 1980 and 1985 under the sponsorship of Potomac Associates utilized a ten-point "scalometer" ranging from + 5 to -5 to measure the public's "like" or "dislike" of other countries. Most of the many countries included in this question get positive and negative ratings near the middle of the scale. Only one nation,

TABLE 19–1
American's Attitudes toward South Korea and Seven Other Nations
in the 1980s on Three Separate Measurements

Gallup "Thermometer," Mean Rating 1986[a]		Gallup Percentage "Favorable"/ "Unfavorable" Attitude 1985[b]		Yankelovich, Skelly and White, Percentage "Definitely Trust as Ally," 1983 [c]	
Canada	77	Canada	96/1	Canada	95
West Germany	62	Japan	84/12	West Germany	73
Japan	61	West Germany	84/13	Japan	66
Israel	59	Israel	77/19	Taiwan	53
China	53	China	71/25	Israel	44
Taiwan	52	Taiwan	68/27	South Korea	43
South Korea	50	South Korea	62/33	China	34
Saudi Arabia	50	Saudi Arabia	61/35	Saudi Arabia	30

[a] "I'd like you to rate...countries on this feeling thermometer. If you feel neutral toward a country, give it a temperature of 50 degrees. If you have a warm feeling toward a country, give it a temperature of higher than 50 degrees. If you have a cool feeling toward a country, give it a temperature lower than 50 degrees."
[b] "Favorable" means a score of plus 1 to plus 5 and "unfavorable" a score from minus 1 to minus 5 on a "scalometer" card running from plus 5 to minus 5. "You notice that the 10 boxes on this card go from the highest position of plus 5—or something you like very much—all the way down to the lowest position of minus 5—or something you dislike very much. Please tell me how far up the scale or how far down the scale you rate the following nations."
[c] "I'm going to read you a list of countries. For each one I would like to know if you feel it is a country the United States can definitely trust as an ally, or a country that we definitely can't trust as an ally."

Canada, gets highly favorable ratings of + 4 or + 5 from more than half of the respondents. These data are reported in Table 19-1 as a ratio of the percentages of favorable (+ 5 to + 1) to unfavorable (-1 to -5) responses. South Korea falls again in the middle ranges between the extremes of Canada (96/1) and the Soviet Union (23/74). These rankings for Korea and other nations are highly stable in two askings over a period of five years. All changes in readings are small and are much more likely to reflect sampling errors than changing public sentiment. Yankelovich, Skelly and White has used a different question designed to measure the public's sense of which nations they can "definitely trust as an ally" or "definitely can't trust as an ally."

Here the percentages of those choosing "definitely trust" runs from a high of 95 (Canada) to a low of 23 (Lebanon). The percentage of those saying they "definitely trust" South Korea is 43. Again, answers to this question are highly stable in the two askings in 1981 and 1982.

One of the virtues of the three studies summarized in Table 19-1 is that they permit the comparison of attitudes toward the same eight nations. Each study actually asked about a different group of nations, but these eight are included in each one. Their rank order is strikingly similar regardless of question wording whenever such questions have been asked in recent years. Canada consistently ranks highest, Saudi Arabia lowest, and South Korea is toward the bottom of the list. What do these data tell us about Americans' attitudes toward South Korea? We must first of all recognize that the list is an exclusive one. South Korea's relatively low rank in this kind of company should not be cause for concern. Again, it is worth pointing out that these particular nations are asked about so often because Americans have had some kind of special relationship with them. These three series of questions and many others like them produce very consistent and stable findings. Americans feel closest to and trust most the "family" of English-speaking nations; Mexico, our southern neighbor; and a few others with whom history has given us special bonds, especially those growing out of the aftermath of World War II. Feelings of extreme "warmth" are limited pretty much to "the family," while "favorable" attitudes and "trust" are distributed somewhat more widely, mainly as a function of perceptions of shared purposes on the world stage. Korea is clearly included in the second grouping. In the select company of nations in Table 19-1, it ranks toward the bottom. In longer lists its rank generally improves. It would be unwise to interpret public response to these questions as meaning much more than this.

There are many other data on Americans' feelings toward Korea, but they do not add much to this interpretation. For example, the Roper Organization has asked the public to classify South Korea and several other nations as "close allies," "friends," "neutrals," "mainly unfriendly," or "enemies" on at least three occasions since 1980. The percentages for South Korea are as follows:

	1985	1984	1982
Close ally or friend	41	43	33

This question produces answers very similar to the Yankelovich results in Table 19-1. When Gallup/Potomac has asked a straight prose question on attitudes toward South Korea (rather than using the "scalometer"), the ratios of favorable to unfavorable responses have been close to those derived from the "scalometer" in Table 19-1 (52/28 in 1978 and 58/27 in 1979).

Is there more than this to be learned through polling about American attitudes toward Korea? My answer is that there is simply not that much more valid public opinion to be found on the subject. Attempts to push the effort so as to provide more detail will only create pseudo-opinion. The public will answer the questions, but they will be playing a largely meaningless game. Efforts in this direction by Potomac Associates should be received with considerable caution. Understandably, the firm has been interested in providing details to an audience especially interested in Asian and, sometimes, specifically Korean affairs. Nevertheless, some of the questions on which fairly serious interpretations have been based push the subject well past the levels of detail that the public can reasonably be expected to handle. Potomac, for example, has asked the public to associate long lists of words and phrases ("crowding," "industrialization," "crime," "underdevelopment," "political unrest") with Korea and a long list of other Asian nations. The Potomac surveys have also asked the public to say whether they perceive Koreans and the other Asian peoples as "hardworking-lazy," "imitative-creative," "peaceful-warlike," "straightforward-deceitful," "individualistic-group oriented," "competitive-noncompetitive," and so on.[10] William Watts' interpretations of these data as they bear on South Korea suggest an "image problem" of considerable magnitude.[11] What are we to make of the answers that such questions produce? Watts notes, for example, that some 8 percent fewer Americans thought South Korea had poorer sanitation in 1985 than in 1980.[12] Before we make too much of this we should also note that some 7 percent more Americans associated Thailand with temples in the second of the two surveys and that some 7 percent thought the Philippines had developed more crime.[13] Are these really meaningful attitudes, and have they really changed over five years? South Koreans, it appears, are seen in 1985 as less "hardworking" than Chinese by some 14 percent of respondents, but they are seen as more "hardworking" by some 4 percent than they were in 1980. South Koreans are supposedly seen in 1985 as much less "creative" than Chinese (a 25 percent difference), but 4 percent more creative than they were in 1980. Such "findings" must be viewed with considerable skepticism. These are images seen through a glass so darkly that we must doubt that they mean anything at all. Moreover, it is simply not credible to argue that such small percentage differences from survey to survey capture changing public attitudes of any consequence.

We will do our best in trying to understand Americans' feelings of closeness and trust toward Korea and other nations to focus on questions like those in Table 19-1. Public attitudes on this level are basic ones that have developed over many years out of historical events of great magnitude that have shaped Americans' understanding of their friends and adversaries on the world stage. Such attitudes are characterized by impressive stability. Barring fundamental changes in a nation's behavior (say, on the order of those in Iran after the fall of the shah), there is very little evidence that public attitudes change much in the short run. Americans' feelings toward South Korea are of this sort. They are very stable. They were shaped by events of the late 1940s, the Korean War, and the subsequent United States-South Korean military alliance. They have not changed much over the last twenty years. In all of this, the public has more responded supportively to elite leadership in policy formulation than mandated anything on the basis of its own changing perceptions of South Korea. The interpretive thrust of the Potomac Associates studies gets this wrong. The picture there is of an American public, highly attentive to internal South Korean affairs, that makes very nuanced judgments on the basis of changing perceptions of economic development, regime changes, corruption, the Koreagate scandal, and the like. The public, as we shall see, has basic value preferences about these things, but there is no reason to suppose they have much to do with shifting South Korea's place in the rank order of friendly nations we saw in Table 19-1. I also doubt that basic American attitudes toward South Korea have much to do with stereotypes derived from "M*A*S*H" or with negative feelings toward the Unification Church.[14] In a very general sense, the American public has seen South Korea as "on our side" since the unfortunate division of the Korean peninsula in the aftermath of World War II. Ordinary Americans do not think about Korea in more detailed or nuanced terms. Questions that assume they do will not yield much useful information. We see here, again, how little there is to be learned by asking the public questions better suited to elites.

The American Commitment to South Korea's Security

American strategic policy toward Korea is the basic concern that drives both American and South Korean elites' interest in polling the American public. To get at the many questions that have been asked in surveys on this topic in a systematic way, I have divided them into several subcategories—Americans' sense of the nature of our interest in Korea, willingness to maintain troops and military equipment there, willingness to actually use them to fight a war, and finally, whether our commitment to South Korea should be conditioned on such factors as internal democratization and respect for human rights.

Two different question wordings have been used to measure public opinion on United States interests in Korea and other nations. The Gallup Organization has asked whether the United States has a "vital interest in certain areas of the world" in three different surveys conducted for the Chicago Council on Foreign Relations in 1978, 1982, and 1986. Because these surveys also posed the same question to a panel of leaders, they are particularly valuable in that they permit comparisons of public and elite opinions at different points in time. Gallup has asked for Potomac Associates a question about how important "it is for the United States to try to get along well" with several countries. Both series of surveys are unusually helpful in that they allow us to look at opinions about Korea in comparison with those about other countries over a period of several years. The Council on Foreign Relations series is summarized in Table 19-2.

It is worth pointing out again that South Korea is in pretty impressive company here. Mainly these particular nations are on the list because an organization that is part of the American foreign policy elite deems them important in one way or

TABLE 19–2

Perception of United States Vital Interests in South Korea and Other Selected Nations: Public Leadership Views in Three Gallup Surveys for the Chicago Council on Foreign Relations[a]

	1986		1982		1978	
	Public	Leaders	Public	Leaders	Public	Leaders
Britain	83	94	80	97	66	94
Canada	78	96	82	95	69	95
Japan	78	98	82	97	78	99
West Germany	77	98	76	98	69	98
Saudi Arabia	77	88	77	93	80	55
Israel	76	86	75	92	78	91
Egypt	61	n.a.	66	90	75	91
China	61	89	64	87	70	70
South Africa	54	63	38	54	63	42
South Korea	58	80	43	66	61	95
Iran	50	n.a.	51	60	67	92
Brazil	45	63	45	80	n.a.	n.a.
India	36	55	30	57	n.a.	n.a.

[a] Percentages are for those answering "Yes" to the following question: "Many people believe that the United States has a vital interest in certain areas of the world and not in other areas. That is, certain countries of the world are important to the United States for political, economic or security reasons. I am going to read you a list of countries. For each, tell me whether you feel the United States does or does not have a vital interest in that country."

another to American economic, political, or military interests throughout the world. South Korea ranked ninth among these thirteen nations in 1986. This placement should certainly not be interpreted as representing a low level of public perception of vital interests. Compared to public perceptions of most other nations, the Korea percentages show an unusual pattern of movement over the three surveys. The percentages of those recognizing vital interests in Korea move from 61 in 1978 to 43 in 1982, then back up to 58 in 1986. Not surprisingly, the leadership panel consistently affirms a stronger United States interest in South Korea. The same pattern of movement is apparent, but the percentages are much higher. Over the three surveys, elite affirmation of a vital United States interest in Korea never falls below two-thirds of the respondents. It is not clear why both public and elite opinion on United States interests in Korea dropped so sharply between 1978 and 1982. Elite opinions may reflect concerns about the Korean regime change in this period, the economic burden of our commitment there during a severe recession, or both. The public at large would not likely be influenced by the changes in Korean politics, but may, indeed, have been influenced by the recession. At any rate, by 1986 the public perceptions of vital interests had returned to the 1978 level and elite perceptions, although some 15 percent lower than in 1978, stood at a very high level—80 percent.

Table 19-3 contains a summary of the percentages of the public answering in the Gallup/Potomac studies that it is "very important" to "try to get along with" Korea and several other countries. This question seems designed to get at something quite similar to "vital interest," but it produces somewhat different results. The rank order to South Korea and the five other nations included in both questions is very similar; but, except for Canada, the percentages of those answering "very important to get along" are always significantly lower than of those affirming "vital interest" at roughly the same time (1978 and 1985/86). We see here the importance of comparing different question wordings. Support for United States alliance with South Korea seems higher in the Chicago Council on Foreign relations studies than in those by Potomac Associates, but of course it cannot be so. This effect is an artifact of question wording. Looking at both studies, we should conclude that public support for close United States relations with South Korea is relatively high (higher than that for all but a few other nations) and that it probably is not very different from what it was in 1978. The Chicago Council Studies provide strong evidence that elite support for United States commitments to South Korea is significantly higher than that of the general public. Elite support seems to have eroded somewhat from 1978 to 1986, but in the latter year it was still very high, at about 80 percent. There is also a sound basis for concluding that neither the public or elites have altered their perceptions of South Korea's relative importance to United States interests

TABLE 19–3
Another Measure of United States Interests: Public Attitudes on the Importance of "Getting Along" with South Korea and Other Nations in Three Gallup Surveys for Potomac Associates[a]

	1985	1979	1978
Canada	77	76	64
Japan	68	58	49
West Germany	58	54	46
China	55	57	43
Saudi Arabia	49	63	51
Israel	44	57	43
Brazil	29	34	26
South Korea	28	35	26
Taiwan	24	44	33
India	22	33	23
New Zealand	21	n.a.	n.a.
Indonesia	14	n.a.	n.a.

[a] Percentages are for those answering "very important" to the following question: "When it comes to pursuing our interests all around the world, how important do you think it is for the United States to try to get along well with each of the following countries—very important, fairly important, not so important or not important at all?"

from 1978 to the present. Its position is always lower than a few others, but that should not be interpreted as cause for concern.

What have Americans thought about our actual military presence, in Korea and elsewhere? The best data on this question are those from Gallup/Potomac surveys conducted in 1974, 1978, and 1985, in which very similar questions were used to ask whether American forces in Europe, Asia, and Korea, specifically, should be "increased, kept at the present level, reduced, or ended altogether." The percentages answering "increased" or "kept at the present level" are as follows:

	1985	1978	1974
Europe	73	68	55
Asia	70	64	59
South Korea	60	55	59

Majorities are supportive of maintaining at least the current level of United States troops in Europe, Asia, and South Korea in each of the three surveys. Support for the American military presence in Europe and Asia as a whole appears to rise significantly from the end of the Vietnam era to the middle years of the Reagan presidency. For reasons that are not clear, support for troops in South Korea, specifically, appears to decline somewhat in 1978, then return to about the 1974 level by 1985. It could be that the Carter administration's consideration of troop withdrawals from Korea had some effect on the public in 1978. At any rate, support for a continuing United States military presence in Korea appears to be as high in the mid-eighties as in 1974, with about 60 percent saying it should continue, at least at the current level.

It would be unwise to suppose that the public has meaningful answers to questions about military commitments of a more specific kind. The size of our actual military presence in South Korea has varied substantially since the end of the Korean War. The public cannot be expected to know such details as the actual number of troops stationed there before and after the Nixon administration's withdrawal of a division in 1981. The answers to several questions asked to determine public opinion on the Carter administration's proposal in the late 1970s to withdraw all United States ground combat troops over a period of years certainly illustrate the hazards of supposing a mass public has well-formed ideas on such details of strategic policy. Consider the following questions asked from 1975 to 1979:

(Roper, July 1975)	The United States has 40,000 troops in South Korea and has a treaty to use United States troops in defense of South Korea if needed. There is increasing talk of North Korea invading South Korea. Do you think we should stand by our commitment to South Korea in order to maintain our credibility and alliances, or that we should reduce our commitments to South Korea in order to avoid United States involvement in another war?	
	Stand by commitment	43%
	Reduce commitment	45%
	Don't know	12%

(Harris, June 1977)	Let me read you some recent foreign policy stands President Carter has taken. For each tell me if you favor or oppose that stand. His plan is to withdraw all 40,000 United States troops from South Korea in 4 or 5 years.	
	Favor	53%
	Oppose	28%
	No opinion	19%
(Gallup, June 1977, asked of the 78% who say they heard/read about the proposal)	In general, do you favor or oppose this proposal (to withdraw United States troops from South Korea during the next few years)?	
	Favor	40%
	Oppose	38%
	No opinion	22%
(Gallup/Potomac, April, 1978)	As you may know, President Carter has announced his intention to withdraw the remaining ground forces from South Korea over the next five years or so, while keeping United States Naval and Air Forces there. Do you think we should go ahead and withdraw our ground troops, or do you think we need to keep some of our ground troops there?	
	Should withdraw	35%
	Should keep some troops there	52%
	Don't know	13%
(NBC News/Associated Press, March, 1978)	Do you favor or oppose the gradual withdrawal of American ground troops from South Korea?	
	Favor	61%
	Oppose	27%
	Not sure	12%
(Gallup/Potomac, April 1978)	And what about South Korea? Should the commitment of American forces there be increased, kept at the present level, reduced, or ended altogether?	
	Increased	6%
	Kept at present level	49%
	Reduced	17%
	Ended altogether	17%
	Don't know	11%

(Gallup/Potomac, September, 1979)	And what about South Korea? Should the commitment of American forces there be increased, kept at the present level, reduced, or ended altogether?	
	Increased	9%
	Kept at present level	49%
	Reduced	16%
	Ended altogether	17%
	Don't know	9%
(Gallup/Potomac, September, 1979)	As you may know, President Carter originally said he would withdraw United States troops from South Korea. He has now decided there will be no further withdrawals until there is a better military balance of power between North Korea and South Korea or until there has been a significant reduction in tensions between North Korea and South Korea. Just your opinion, do you approve or disapprove of President Carter's decision, or doesn't it make much difference to you?	
	Approve	48%
	Disapprove	26%
	No difference	16%
	Don't know	11%

Were we to look only at one firm's findings at one point in time, we might conclude that the public was clearly for or against withdrawal of the troops. When we look at all available surveys, we see that the picture becomes more complex and ambiguous. Indeed, there are "opinions" here to support virtually every position on the subject. William Watts reported in *Japan, Korea and China* that 52 percent of the public opposed the Carter plan in 1978. Indeed, that is what the Gallup/ Potomac survey found. NBC News/Associated Press, however, at almost the same point in time found only 28 percent opposed to it. What is going on here? The answer is not all that mysterious. Where opinions are not well formed and the public is being asked about something remote from its personal experience, factors such as question wording, question order, response categories, and such can make a world of difference in survey results. Public opinion on the Carter plan was just not clear. No experienced reader of surveys should have taken it as either clearly supporting or opposing the president's position.

Yet a further complication arises when we consider the distinction between maintaining troops abroad and actually using them to fight a war. The Chicago Council on Foreign Relations studies in 1978, 1982, and 1986, Roper Organization questions asked on several occasions, and the Gallup/Potomac surveys help to throw light on this distinction. The Chicago Council and Roper questions are virtually identical. They ask about the kinds of "circumstances that might justify using United States troops in other parts of the world," supplying respondents with a number of "if" questions such as "if North Korea invaded South Korea" or "if the Soviets invaded Western Europe." The Gallup/Potomac question is slightly different, asking "if the United States should come to the defense of South Korea with military force if it is attacked by North Korea." The percentages of the public stating willingness to fight to defend South Korea against North Korea in years for which data are available are as follows:

	'86	'85	'84	'83	'82	'81	'80	'78
Chicago Council	24				22			21
Roper		23		27		20		
Gallup/Potomac		41	36				38	32

Aside from what appears to be a tendency of the Potomac wording to produce somewhat higher percentages, the findings are reasonably consistent. No more than a third of the public has expressed willingness to actually fight to defend South Korea, and there is no significant shift in sentiment over the period from 1978 to 1986. What shall we take this to mean?

First, I caution, these questions ask the public for just about the most demanding commitment that could be imagined— willingness to actually fight a war. These are unusually good data sets in that they permit comparisons between willingness to defend South Korea and several other nations over several years. When we look at the whole picture it becomes apparent that there are few "ifs" that Americans find sufficient cause for war. Majorities are consistently willing in the last ten years to defend Western Europe and Japan from a Soviet attack; but little else, it seems, justifies fighting a war. Should we take these answers literally? I think we should not. The public is saying in large part that it strongly dislikes the idea of war. Under real circumstances (not hypothetical "ifs") and subject to leadership by elites, the public may have a different answer. The Chicago Council studies show that elites are almost always more willing to commit American troops to war than the public is. In the case of Korea, they have been two to three times more willing to say we should fight to defend the South against an invasion from the North. In 1986, when only 24 percent of Americans took such a position, no less than 64 percent of the leadership panel supported it. Here, also, question wording can make a substantial difference, as the following Harris question illustrates:

(Harris, May, 1975)	The United States has 36,000 troops and a rmen in South Korea. If North Korea invaded South, we have a firm commitment to defend South Korea with our military forces. If South Korea were invaded by North Korea, would you favor or oppose the United States using troops, air power and naval power to defend South Korea?	
	Favor	43%
	Oppose	37%
	Not sure	30%

Here, 43 percent (an unusually large group) support the use of troops. It is hard to believe that prefacing the question with a statement identifying a "firm commitment" to South Korea's defense is not producing a positive effect. A year earlier a straight Harris asking of the "if North Korea invaded" wording with no such preface found only 25 percent willing to commit troops to defend South Korea.

At any rate, we should exercise caution in interpreting questions that in effect ask the public if it is "prepared to fight." In general, it is likely that a literal interpretation underestimates American willingness to use force, if necessary, throughout the world. Again, we should not expect the public to be actual policy makers. Decisions to commit American troops to war are fortunately not made in national town meetings. For better or worse, if the president decides such a course of action is necessary, experience strongly suggests that Congress and the public will support his decision, at least in the short run. If we really want to understand whether the United States is prepared to use force in Korea (or anywhere else for that matter), we would do better to understand the thinking of policy-making elites than that of the public. Public opinion does not direct such decisionmaking. As Lippmann argued it is inescapably an "executive" function.[15]

Even retrospective questions on the use of force should be interpreted with extreme caution, and we should never rely very heavily on a single survey taken at one point in time. This is easily illustrated by the example of retrospective views of the Korean War. Consider the following questions:

(Harris, December 1974)	Here's a list of international events that the United States has been involved in in recent history. For each please tell me whether you think it was a proud moment in American history, a dark moment, or neither a proud moment nor a dark moment. The United States role in the Korea War.
	Proud moment 22%
	Dark moment 41%
	Neither 27%
	Not sure 10%
(Roper, June 1975)	I'll name some major events in our history. I'd like to know for each whether you think this country did what was the right thing or the wrong thing...or something in between?....Fighting the Korean War.
	Right thing 29%
	Wrong thing 36%
	Somewhere in between 22%
	Don't know 13%
(Roper, August, 1984)	I'll name some major events in our history. I'd like to know for each whether you think this country did what was the right thing or the wrong thing...or something in between?....Fighting the Korean War.
	Right thing 31%
	Wrong thing 35%
	Somewhere in between 22%
	Don't know 13%

(Market Opinion Research/Americans Talk Security, September, 1988)	I'm going to read you some cases where the United States has used its military power since World War II. For each one, please tell me if you feel we should or should not have used our military the way we did. American participation with other nations in the Korean War.	
	Should have	60%
	Should not have	26%
	Don't know	14%
	Refused/No answer	1%

If we looked only at the recent Americans Talk Security question we would conclude that Americans, looking back, strongly support our use of troops in Korea. The Harris question in 1975 suggests just the opposite. Is the public remembering differently in 1975 and 1988? Was the public "spooked" by Vietnam in 1975? That is, of course, possible. However, the Roper questions in 1975 and 1984 both show pluralities of 36 and 35 percent opposing our participation in the Korean War. What can we conclude from these data? Not much, I would argue. The question wordings are different, feelings are ambivalent and the event is remote. Here, as in many other such cases, the opinions measured are so "soft" that we should give them little credence.

One other class of questions bearing on American attitudes toward the United States commitment to South Korea's security remains to be discussed. These in one way or another ask if the commitment should be tied to or made conditional upon various kinds of satisfactory performance on the part of the South Korean government. Depending largely on what is in the news, these questions ask the public if we should tie our security commitment to insistence that human rights be observed, an end to corruption, cooperation in investigating Koreagate and so on. For example:

(Harris, July, 1975)	"...South Korea is a dictatorship and takes away the rights of its political opposition, and it is wrong for us to support such a government."	
	Agree	42%
	Disagree	32%
	Not sure	26%

(Harris, July, 1975)	... "South Korea is a corrupt government and we should not be keeping corrupt governments in power."	
	Agree	40%
	Disagree	27%
	Not sure	33%
(Yankelovich, Skelly and White, March, 1977)	President Carter says that he is trying to bring more morality to our country's foreign policy.... Do you personally feel that President Carter should or should not continue to aid countries (like South Korea) because they are essential to our defense—even if they suppress human rights in that country?	
	Should	29%
	Should not	50%
	Not sure	21%
(Gallup/Potomac, September, 1979)	Would you favor making the United States security commitment to South Korea conditional upon an improvement in the human rights situation there?	
	Favor	49%
	Oppose	26%
	Don't know	25%

Such questions, as far as I can see, nearly always elicit public approval for the "tie-in" that is proposed. The public does not make a distinction between hard United States interests on the one hand and moral concerns about human rights violations and corruption on the other. In this sense Americans are exceptionally idealistic. Clearly, all such questions asked about South Korea show that Americans strongly value human rights, democracy, and government free from corruption, and, as William Watts has repeatedly argued, that they would like to see an improved record on the part of the South Korean government on each count. Yet, as we have seen, Americans have approved alliances with quite a few nations that could by no stretch of the imagination be regarded as free, democratic, or without corruption. We should not interpret the answers to these questions literally. It is simply unrealistic to expect the public to insist on specific changes in South Korean politics as a condition of continued strategic alliance with the United

States. The American public truthfully answers polling questions of this sort by saying that it wants democracy and civil liberties in South Korea, but it does not literally mean that it will cease to support the American military commitment there if they are not fully realized. We must remember again that elites make strategic decisions and that the public mandates nothing of a specific nature in this area.

Questions of the Moment

Korea questions in American polls other than those sponsored by elites in both countries who are especially interested in Korean-American relations are largely driven by journalistic interest in stories that seem newsworthy at the moment. In truth, there are fewer than we might suppose. Given the prominence of Koreagate (in retrospect it is hard to remember why that story got so much play), it is somewhat surprising to find that not many questions were asked about it. It is just as well. The questions tell us only that the public regards efforts to influence policy toward Korea through bribes and favors to public officials as unethical and illegal. It would be remarkable if it were otherwise. Even on the subject of democratic processes and human rights, I have found relatively few questions other than those included in the Gallup/Potomac surveys. These pretty uniformly demonstrate considerable awareness on the part of the American public that the South Korean government has often been authoritarian and oppressive in its treatment of the opposition and student dissidents. As for the future, the public is uncertain, as the following question by Louis Harris in June 1988 shows:

Recently, in Sough Korea, President Roh Tae Woo took office after being elected by the people in an open election. Do you think democratization in South Korea will progress a great deal, somewhat, will it stay the same...or will it get worse?	
A great deal	4%
Somewhat	33%
Stay the same	33%
Get worse	14%
Not sure	16%

Those who think things will get better are outnumbered by those who expect things will stay the same or get worse. While the public is not possessed of detailed knowledge of South Korean politics, it has clearly formed a general impression over the years that South Korea's path to democracy has not been an easy one.

Quite a few questions have been asked by polls about United States-Korean trade relations in recent years. To my reading they do not add up to a coherent public opinion on this subject. Given the complexity of the matter it is not surprising that the public seems somewhat confused. In June 1988 Louis Harris found that 42 percent of Americans perceived South Korea as a "tough and serious competitor against the United States in trade and industry." In February 1988 Gallup/Newsweek reported that 42 percent thought Korean products as good as or better than American ones. In the same survey 39 percent saw South Korea's trade policies as "unfair." When questions have been asked about the desirability of erecting trade barriers, the public has given no clear answer. Here things stand, for the moment. Korea's growth and export market (along with those of other Asian nations) has caught Americans' attention and earned new respect. Yet, trade policies are seen as serious potential sources of conflict in the future. When Gallup/Newsweek asked the following question in the context of a battery of questions on trade problems in February 1988, it got a seemingly ominous answer:

	How likely do you think it is that the following nations will become enemies of the United States? Very likely or somewhat likely.	
	South Korea	53%
	Japan	39%
	China	54%

Again, we should not take this response literally. There is no perception of crisis in United States-Korean relations now. The public is saying in effect that it sees problems here which may grow worse—possibly bad enough in the future to disrupt our long-standing alliances with our Asian allies.

Lately, a few questions have been asked that link United

States military commitments to budgetary concerns. The question of how to pay for our extensive military programs and commitments to some sixty countries is a pressing one for the president and Congress, but it is not one on which there is a great deal to be learned by putting questions to the public. When questions ask if there should be increased "burden-sharing," the answer will surely be "yes," as the following questions illustrate:

(Mellman and Lazarus, October, 1987)	Do you favor or oppose requiring the Japanese, Koreans, and Europeans to pay for their own defense?	
	Favor	86%
	Oppose	8%
	Don't know	5%
(Gallup/Newsweek, February, 1988)	The United States currently helps pay the cost of defending some Asian countries such as Japan, South Korea, and the Philippines. Do these countries pay too much, too little or about the right amount of their own defense?	
	Too much	6%
	Too little	69%
	Right amount	12%
	Don't know	13%

Ask the questions this way and the answer comes back loud and clear! What the public is saying, however, should not be interpreted as lack of support for American military commitments. In very general terms it is saying that it thinks the United States has carried more than its share of the costs of protecting our allies since World War II, and that it is time to expect others to do more. This attitude applies not only to South Korea, but to all of our defense partners. The option of removing United States troops from Korea (and Europe) is specifically included in a long list of possible ways to raise revenues or cut expenditures to reduce the federal deficit in a Gallup/Times Mirror question in May 1988. Some 27 percent checked off this option. (Multiple responses were permitted.) However, higher percentages registered support for increasing taxes on those earning more than $80,000 per year by increasing tobacco taxes (61), raising alcohol taxes (65), eliminating the Strategic

Defense Initiative (31), and several other options. There is no reason, of course, to suppose that public opinion will mandate troop withdrawals or any other of these specific courses of action. The respondents are only expressing their rough preferences by checking items from a list. It may be that the Bush administration will consider anew whether we can afford to keep troops in Korea in an era of severe pressure on the military budget, but public opinion will not require a change of policy. That will be left to the president and Congress.

American Opinion on Korea: More Continuity than Change

The central theme running through this analysis of American public opinion polling on Korea is that we must always interpret the data in the context of a realistic understanding of what a democratic public can and cannot do. The surveys reviewed here tell us useful things about the public opinion context of United States-Korean relations, but they are also subject to serious misinterpretations. Above all else, we should not make too much of this subject; we should not try to find more opinion on Korea than is really there. When we ask ordinary Americans to provide factual answers on complex questions like trade relationships or the nature of the South Korean government, we push public polling far beyond its proper function. These are questions that only elites can answer. The same is true when we ask the public to decide detailed policy questions. This is simply not a worthwhile exercise. Foreign policy, especially, is an inherently elite subject. In this realm of activity the public's role cannot be reasonably expected to go beyond the articulation of basic values and very broad policy preferences.

American and South Korean policy makers work in a public opinion context. Part of what they need to know can be found in American surveys. The things we have seen here are important to know. Americans have no unusual knowledge deficit about Korea. They do not need to know more than they do to play their proper role in the policy-making process. They consistently show a comparatively favorable attitude toward South Korea on a basic level of "affect" or trust. This attitude is very stable. Americans in a very general way have supported

United States policy toward South Korea since the Korean War. When a president proposes changes in policy (as in the late 1970s), the public is unable to provide a clear answer that the change is right or wrong. Nevertheless, it articulates basic value concerns. It says, in effect, "We want peace and protection of United States interests and our allies against our adversaries; you provide the details." About this it is very consistent. Americans have supported maintaining troops in Korea as long as United States administrations have held that such an arrangement is necessary. And their seeming reluctance to say that they back using them again must be understood as a statement of values. They are saying in effect, "War is about the last thing in the world we want." But we should never forget that some 50,000 Americans died defending South Korea. Literal answers to survey questions are often not good guides to what people will do in the real world.

There is not, I would argue, much more real public opinion than this to be found on Korea. What there is is important, but only in the context in which the United States-Korean relationship is discussed at the elite level at which policies are made in both countries. In these circles new policies may well be in the making. That is not the subject of this paper. We should understand, however, that defining the exact terms of what the public sees as a continuing Korean/American partnership is not something that survey research can advance very much. We would do well in future polling efforts to keep this very clearly in mind.

Notes

1. All of the surveys used here are in the archive of the Roper Center for Public Opinion Research at the University of Connecticut. I want to thank Lois Timms-Ferrara of the Roper Center staff for her assistance in locating them.

2. William Watts, George R. Packard, Ralph N. Clough, and Robert B. Oxnam, *Japan, Korea and China: American Perceptions and Policies* (Lexington, MA and Toronto: Lexington, Heath, 1979), Chapter 5; William Watts, "The United States and Korea: Perception versus Reality," in Richard L. Sneider and William Watts, *The United States and Korea: New Directions for the 1980s* (Washington, D.C.: Potomac Associates, 1980); and William Watts, "The United States and Asia: Changing American Perceptions," mimeo, Potomac Associates, Washington, D.C., 1985.

3. See Everett Carll Ladd, "Looking for the Gestalt: The Secondary Analysis of Opinion Data in Policy Research," in *Polling on the Issues*, ed. Albert H. Cantril (Cabin John, Washington, D.C.: Seven Locks Press, 1980), 115–19.

4. Walter Lippmann, *Public Opinion* (New York: Macmillan, 1960; first publication 1922), and *The Phantom Public* (New York: Macmillan, 1930). Unfortunately, the latter is out of print.

5. Watts, "The United States and Korea," 65.

6. Ibid., 67.

7. Ibid., 68.

8. Ibid., 70.

9. Elmo Roper, "So the Blind Shall Not Lead," *Fortune*, February 1942, 102.

10. See Watts, "The United States and Korea: Perception *versus* Reality," 70–77, and Watts, "The United States and Asia: Changing American Perceptions," 15–22.

11. See especially Watts, "The United States and Korea: Perception *versus* Reality," passim.

12. Watts, "The United States and Asia: Changing American Perceptions," 18.

13. Ibid., 17.

14. Watts, "The United States and Korea: Perception *versus* Reality," 76.

15. Lippmann, *The Phantom Public*, 143–45.

20

Images of Korea

An Analysis of Factors Affecting American Attitudes

Eui Hang Shin and Daeshik Cho

Introduction

THE PURPOSE OF THIS STUDY is to investigate the relationship between an individual's background variables and American attitudes toward foreign nations. We will compare American public images of Korea and Japan. We will present the structure and the underlying dimensions of attitudes toward other nations in terms of the theory of cognitive structure, and then proceed to examine some of the social correlates of these images. More specifically, this paper will focus on the following questions:

1. Are there any significant relationships between an individual's images of other nations and his socioeconomic status (as measured by education and family income)?
2. Is there any relationship between the images held of foreign nations and other social and political characteristics of the population?

3. Do elites and masses of the populations have different images of the same nations?

The Structure and Dimensions of Images of Other Nations

An individual normally carries in his memory a collection of images of the world in its various aspects. These images are combinatorial constructs, analogous to visual experiences. They are interdependent to varying degrees. The structure of some images can be inferred or predicted from the structure of others, and changes in certain images can produce imbalances tending toward change in others. To the extent that images are highly interdependent, the "image" must be built up "as a result of all the past experiences of the possessor of the image," and defined as the totality of his subjective knowledge or of what he believes to be true.[1]

As an attitude object, a nation is a complex of the images of the persons who contemplate it.[2] In general, the images people hold of foreign nations can be analyzed into their cognitive, affective, and behavioral components. The first represents perceived knowledge of a nation in terms of vital national interest, the second a liking or disliking of a nation, and the third a set of actions or policies toward a nation that the person deems appropriate.[3] Even though the three components can be distinguished conceptually, it should be emphasized that the components are different dimensions of a highly integrated, single attitude. There is considerable evidence from psychological and cultural analyses of a tendency toward correspondence among these image components.

This tendency reflects at least two basic kinds of psychological processes: (a) tendencies toward cognitive balance, which involve differential perceptions and affect within the same person concerning the various nation-objects that he recognizes and (b) interpersonal differences in tendency to be favorably or unfavorably disposed toward all foreign nations.[4] The three dimensions of attitudes toward foreign nations that have been elaborated here are meaningful analytical frames of reference since the complexity of attitudes toward foreign nations cannot be described as unidimensional.

Social Correlates of Images of Other Nations

There are numerous factors which affect the formation of attitudes through various socialization processes. In the case of attitudes toward foreign nations, however, there is a great deal of evidence to suggest that the following social factors have significant impacts on attitude formation.

Socioeconomic Status

Evidence from previous studies of a variety of nations indicates that members of lower socioeconomic status groups are more likely to show greater hostility toward national outgroups. The results of the public opinion surveys by the Australian Gallup Poll suggest that lower-status people in Australia, Canada, Great Britain, and the United States are more likely to display hostility toward foreign nations and pessimism concerning the prospects for peaceful international relations than are middle- and upper-class respondents.[5] Similarly, Eysenck's findings indicate that lower-class members of three political parties in England tended to be more "toughminded" in their attitudes toward other nations than middle-class respondents, a label describing a generally aggressive orientation in the conduct of foreign affairs. The research conducted in Canada also indicates that low-status groups are more likely to have unfavorable attitudes toward Germany, Japan, France, and Italy.[6]

In a series of studies on socialization, it has been suggested that parents at different levels in the class structure have different values that they communicate in socializing their children. The major findings of Kohn and his associates indicate that parents in the working class tend to value respect for external authority and conformity to the rule, while parents in the middle- and upper-middle levels of the stratification structure tend to place greater value on autonomy and creativity.[7] Lipset, in his description of working-class authoritarianism, contends that the low status and low education which characterize the working class predispose such individuals to favor extremist, intolerant patterns of political and religious behavior.[8] Lower-class groups tended to be "tough-minded," prejudiced, xenophobic, and jingoistic toward various levels of outgroups.

Lipset's findings have been supported by many researchers.[9] These researchers argue that the development of a repressed antagonism toward authority is the source of the authoritarian's hostility towards outgroups. They have explained this propensity to support authoritarianism in terms of the authoritarian dispositions and personalities formed by family socialization characteristics of the working class.

The correlation between unfavorable or aggressive attitudes toward outgroups and the lack of sophistication/education which characterizes lower-class people has also been supported in other studies. Kephart found that those who know more about other people and races tend to have favorable attitudes about them.[10] Allport, summarizing some of the existing literature up to 1954, indicates that knowledge of other groups derived through free communication is, as a rule, correlated with lessened hostility and prejudice.[11]

Consequently, we may conclude that knowledge about one's own nation and other nations leads to increased international understanding and, through such understanding, to more constructive attitudes towards international affairs and foreign nations. Further, we may expect to find a positive correlation between nationalism and hostile attitudes toward outgroups, since idealizing attitudes toward one's own group are the other side of rejective attitudes toward outgroups. In some studies, a positive correlation was also found between hostile attitudes toward national outgroups and nationalistic attitudes.

One of the earliest studies of this kind was done by Adorno, Frankel-Brunswik, Levinson, and Sanford, who found a high positive correlation between patriotism and negative images toward minority groups.[12] In another study, Allport and Kramer found a high positive correlation between nationalism and various forms of anti-Semitism.[13] Thus, we may expect a positive association between socioeconomic status and attitudes toward national outgroups. Moreover, we can extend these arguments to the dimension of mass (general public sample in this study) versus elite (national leader sample in this study) distinction. Overall, socioeconomic status is expected to have a significant effect on opinions across the three dimensions.

Region

It has been frequently observed that there is more hostility toward racial minority groups in the South of the United States than in the North. Bardes and Oldendick found that Southerners are the most isolationist in their attitudes toward foreign affairs.[14] This reflects their general orientation toward opposing cooperative internationalism and a dislike of other nations. Wittkopf and Maggiotto found that regional location, education, and political philosophy are the most important factors discriminating among respondents' attitudes toward foreign affairs.[15] In this connection, region is expected to have a significant effect on two of the dimensions: affective and behavioral.

Political Philosophy

Not much research has been done that would clarify the relationship between political philosophy and attitudes toward foreign nations. However, there is strong evidence that political conservatism in general is related to the general predilection toward a hard-line attitude pattern, while political liberalism is closely related to a conciliatory orientation. McClosky's study suggests that conservatism is often associated with aggressiveness and cognitive rigidity, which could dispose the individual to a fuller acceptance of the hard-line pattern.[16] Bardes and Oldendick's study isolated some important differences between conservatives and liberals on attitudes toward foreign affairs in general.[17] Conservatives were more militaristic and isolationist, and were less in favor of negotiating differences with other nations. Thus, we may expect a strong impact of political philosophy on opinions for the cognitive and behavioral dimensions.

Hypothesis

Based upon the above arguments, the following hypotheses will be tested in this study:

1. The higher the socioeconomic status, the higher the perception of the United States' vital interest in Korea.
2. The higher the socioeconomic status, the more favorable the attitudes toward Korea.

3. Southerners will show less favorable attitudes toward Korea than those in other regions.
4. Liberals will be more likely to have favorable attitudes toward Korea than will conservatives.
5. The higher the socioeconomic status, the more likely will be the support of the United States military involvement in Korea.
6. Southerners will be more likely to oppose the United States military involvement in Korea than will those in other regions.
7. Liberals will be more likely to support the United States military involvement in Korea than conservatives will.
8. Elites will be more likely to perceive the United States' vital interests in Korea than will the masses.
9. Elites will be more likely to support the United States military involvement in Korea than the masses.

Data

The data to be analyzed here were produced from the survey "American Public Opinion and U.S. Foreign Policy" sponsored by the Chicago Council on Foreign Relations in 1982.[18] These national surveys cover the attitudes of both the general public and the national leaders toward a wide range of international affairs and foreign policy issues and provide the basis for exploring the determinants of American attitudes toward foreign nations.

The data come from a study consisting of two surveys conducted in the United States during the final month of 1982. Variables measure attitudes concerning international affairs and foreign policy. Issues include the relationships between domestic and foreign policy priorities, the United States' political involvement in the world, the United States' role in the world, and perceptions of the United States' vital interests (defined as what is important to the United States for political, economic, or security reasons) in a wide variety of the nations throughout the world.

The first part of the study is a public survey involving a stratified, weighted, systematic national sample of 1,546 respondents aged 18 and older. The second part is a leadership sample including 341 individuals representing Americans in leadership positions with the greatest influence upon and knowledge about international affairs and foreign policy. Individuals for the leadership sample were chosen from the national political and governmental world, including United States senators and congressmen, officials of the Department of State, officials with international responsibilities in other government departments, the business community, communications field, and education and foreign policy institutes. A smaller number of leaders was also drawn from national unions, churches, voluntary organizations, and ethnic organizations. Variables in the public sample include age, income, race, sex, media attention, religion, educational level, occupation, and political orientation of the respondent. However, these background variables are not included in the national leader sample.

Variables

Dependent Variables

Cognitive Dimension of Images. To measure the respondents' cognitive dimension of images of other nations, both the national leader and public surveys used the respondents' perceptions of the United States vital interests in 22 countries throughout the world. Since perceptions of United States' vital interests in certain foreign nations reflect the contents of the basic cognitive dimension toward these nations, it is a reasonable measurement of attitudes toward other nations. In the 1982 studies, respondents were asked: "Many people believe that the United States has a vital interest in certain areas of the world and not in other areas. That is, certain countries of the world are important to the United States for political, economic or security reasons. I am going to read a list of countries. For each, tell me whether you feel the United States does or does not have a vital interest in that country." The list of countries includes South Korea, Mexico, Poland, Japan, Taiwan, Canada, Nigeria, Great Britain, and the Soviet Union.

Affective Dimension of Images. Respondents in the public sample were asked to indicate their degree of favorability toward each in a list of 24 countries on a thermometer scale, ranging between 0 degree (very cold, or unfavorable) and 100 degrees (very warm, or favorable). A thermometer rating of 50 degrees was designated as neutral. For this study, the thermometer ratings were recoded into three following categories: 0 through 49= unfavorable, 50= neutral, 51 through 100= favorable. Unfortunately, this item is not included in the national leader survey.

Behavioral Dimension of Images.   In both surveys, respondents from the public and the national leaders samples were asked to answer whether they favored or opposed the use of United States troops in several situations. The hypothetical situations, for example, included, "if North Korea invades South Korea," and "if the Soviet Union invades China." These variables are the behavioral components of attitudes toward other countries. Unfortunately, the corresponding item on the behavioral dimension of images of Japan is not available.

Independent Variables

Socioeconomic Status.   In this paper, education and family income will be employed as indicators of socioeconomic status. The education variable is collapsed into three categories as in Knoke and Burke's procedures: (1) none through eighth grade; (2) high school graduate (ninth through twelfth grade); and (3) post-secondary. The annual income variable is collapsed into three categories: (1) under $10,000; (2) $10,000 – $19,999; and (3) $20,000 and up.

Region.   The region variable is collapsed into two categories: (1) the South, comprised of all states in the census South and border states as in Knoke and Burke's study;[19] (2) the non-South, including the rest of the United States.

Political Philosophy.   Political philosophy is dichotomized into "liberal" and "conservative."

Methodology.   For this research, log-linear analysis will be used to examine and test for statistical relationships using ECTA, FREQ, and GAUSS.[20] Using various models, we will examine first the effect of education and income on each dimension of images set forth earlier, since education and income are indicators of socioeconomic status. In the next stage, we will consider the effects of region and political philosophy on each dimension of the images.

A series of log-linear models is estimated to select the preferred model. The preferred model is the one that contains all significant parameter effects, improves the goodness of fit over any other model with fewer degrees of freedom, and shows an acceptable fit itself.

Findings

About 54 percent of the American public saw the United States as having vital interests in South Korea. With regard to the favorability rating of Korea, the data in the public sample indicated that the public has a slightly unfavorable feelings toward Korea (44 degrees). On the behavioral dimension, the data shows that a quarter of the respondents in the public sample would favor sending United States troops if North Korea invaded South Korea.

On the cognitive dimension, the factors to be considered here first are indicators of socioeconomic status (education and family income). Our aim is to ascertain whether and to what extent education and income separately or jointly affect the cognitive dimension of images of Korea. Since the likelihood ratio chi-square for the model of independence is 4.99 with 8 degrees of freedom, we fail to reject the hypothesis of no association between the variables. Thus, we conclude that there is no association between the factors and the response. That is, the response on the cognitive dimension of attitudes toward Korea is independent of the respondent's socioeconomic status. We note that the data do not support the first hypothesis.

Table 20-1 presents a series of models from which the preferred model of the effect of education and income on the affective dimension of images of Korea is selected. In this table, although the null hypothesis of independence is marginally acceptable, we need to investigate further alternative models which allow a departure from independence. In Table 20-1, the first four models consist of the standard three-way analysis. Among these four standard models we find that model 3, which hypothesizes that response and education are conditionally

TABLE 20-1
Logit Models of Education and Income Effect on Response of Affective Dimension of Images of Korea and Comparisons between Models

Models	df	L2	p
1 (EI) (R)	16	22.92	.116
2 (EI) (RI)	12	18.17	.111
3 (EI) (RE)*	12	9.62	> .5
4 (EI) (RI) (RE)*	8	5.95	> .5
5 (EI) UA*	15	22.25	> .1
6 (EI) UAi	15	20.22	> .1
7 (EI) (RE) *UAi	11	7.58	> .5
8 (EI) (RI) UAe	11	18.12	.05> p> .1
9 (EI) (R) UAe UAi	14	20.17	> .1
10 (EI) Le	14	14.08	> .1
11 (EI) Li	14	20.07	> .1
12 (EI) (RE) *Li	10	7.01	> .5
13 (EI) (RI) Le	10	9.62	> .5
14 (EI) (R) Li Le	12	11.53	> .5
15 (EI) (R) Li Le Lei	10	11.28	> .5

Notes: Significant at p= .05 level. Le refers to a linear effect of factor e (education). UA refers to Uniform Association model. All models fit (EI) (R).

Comparisons of L2 between Models	df	L2	p
M1 - M3	4	13.30	< .01
M2 - M4	4	12.22	< .01
M6 - M7	4	12.74	< .01
M1 - M10	2	8.84	< .025
M11 - M12	4	13.06	< .01

Odds and Odds Ratios Under the Preferred Model 10 (EI) Le

Edu	Inc	Odds		Odds Ratios	
		Neu:Unf	Fav:Unf	Neu:Unf	Fav:Unf
Low	Low	.6374	.5943	1	1
	Mid	.6384	.5938	1	1
	High	.6369	.5950	1	1
Mid	Low	.9617	.6366	1.5093	1.0714
	Mid	.9620	.6368	1.5069	1.0724
	High	.9617	.6367	1.5099	1.0701
Hi	Low	1.4520	.6825	2.2787	1.1486
	Mid	1.4517	.6820	2.2740	1.1485
	High	1.4516	.6820	2.2792	1.1462

independent given income, provides a satisfactory fit. However, we need to consider the linear specification since the data consist of ordered categories (model 10 through model 15). According to Duncan and McRae, the concept of linearity should be considered in the event that the categories are ordered and scaled.[21] The merits of linear specification are conceptual compactness and parsimony.

Another attractive series of models (model 5 through model 9) are to fit a model that allows a uniform association across all adjacent rows and columns of the table. The uniform association model, if it is acceptable, allows us to describe the association in the table more parsimoniously by referring to a single parameter.

The preferred model is chosen from among those that show acceptable fits and include parameters that show a significant improvement of fit over others in selecting the preferred model. If there are two or more such models, the highest-order model showing significant improvement over any other is selected, so more parsimonious relationships are estimated. Among the models in Table 20-1, model 10, which hypothesizes that there are linear education effects on the affective dimension of images of Korea, is selected as the preferred model. We find that the linear education effect on the affective dimension of American images of Korea is significant. However, income has no significant impact on the affective dimension. Selecting model 10 implies that the level of respondents' educational attainment influences the degree of favorability toward Korea.

Table 20-1 also presents logit parameters describing the effect of education on the affective dimension under the preferred model. According to the preferred model, we can explain the association between education and response with the concept of linearity. That is, odds on being neutral relative to unfavorable increase proportionally by a factor of 1.51, and odds on favorable to unfavorable also increase slightly, by a factor of 1.07, as we move across the categories of respondents' education from low to high. In other words, the table shows that the higher the respondent's educational attainment, the more favorable his attitude toward Korea.

On the affective dimension, the next factors to be considered are region and political philosophy. Since the likelihood ratio chi-square for the model of independence is 10.05 with 6 degrees of freedom, we fail to reject the hypothesis of no association between the variables. Thus, we conclude that there is no association between the factors and the response. That is, the response on opinions for the affective dimension of attitudes toward Korea is independent of the respondent's regional location and political philosophy. Hence, we note that the third and fourth hypotheses are not supported by the present data.

Some of the models presented in Table 20-2 estimate the effects of education and income on the behavioral dimension of images of Korea. Of the models in Table 20-2, model 3, which involves the main effect of income, is selected as the preferred model. Table 20-2 also presents logit parameters describing the effect of income on the behavioral dimension of image. According to this data, being in the middle level of the income group rather than in the lower level raises the odds on favoring the sending of United States troops to Korea by a factor of 2.22; and being in a higher level of income category relative to a lower one raises the odds on favoring sending United States troops by a factor of 2.41. In other words, those in higher income groups are more likely to favor sending United States troops to Korea as we move across the categories of respondent income from low to high. Thus, selecting model 3 indicates that the higher the respondents' income level, the more likely they are to support active United States military involvement in Korea. It also indicates that education has no effect on this attitude.

The models presented in Table 20-3 examine the effects of region and political philosophy on the behavioral dimension of American images of Korea. Among the models, model 3 is selected as the preferred one. Table 20-3 also presents logit parameters describing the effect of regional differences on attitudes under the preferred model. The regional effect parameter indicates that being in the non-South rather than in the South raises the odds on supporting the sending of United States troops to Korea by a factor of 1.50. In other words, Southerners tend to oppose active United States involvement in Korea more than those in the non-South.

TABLE 20-2
Models of Education and Income on Response of Behavioral Dimension of Attitudes toward Korea (1) and Comparisons of Models

Models	df	L^2	p
1 (EI) (R)	8	29.53	.000
2 (EI) (RE)	6	25.52	.000
3 (EI) (RI)*	6	3.02	> .5
4 (EI) (RI((RE)	4	2.30	> .5
5 (EI) Le	7	27.01	.000
6 (EI) Li*	7	9.44	> .1
7 (EI) (RI) Le	5	2.97	> .5
8 (EI) (RE) Li	5	8.23	> .1
9 (EI) (R) Li Le*	6	10.38	> .1

Comparisons of L^2 between Models	df	L^2	p
M1 - M3	2	26.51	< .01
M1 - M6	1	20.09	< .01
M1 - M9	2	20.15	< .01

Odds and Odds Ratios under the Preferred Model 3 (EI) (RI)

Edu	Inc	Odds Yes:No	Odds Ratios Income Low
Low	Low	.1509	1
Mid	.3392	2.2478	
High	.3636	2.4095	
Mid	Low	.1509	1
Mid	.3353	2.2220	
High	.3633	2.4076	
Hi	Low	.1508	1
Mid	.3353	2.2235	
High	.3633	2.4092	

Table 20-4 presents a list of models from which the preferred model of the effect of income and region on the attitudes toward sending United States troops to Korea is selected. The preferred model in this table is model 3, which hypothesizes that there is an effect of income, but not region, on the behavioral dimension. As in the previous table, higher income raises

TABLE 20-3
Models of State (Region) and Political Philsophy on Response of
Behavioral Dimensions of Images of Korea and Comparisons of Models

Models	df	L2	p
1 (SP) (R)	3	8.26	.040
2 (SP) (RP)	2	8.18	.017
3 (SP) (RS) *	2	2.25	.324
4 (SP) (RS) * (RP)	1	2.23	.135

Comparisons of L2 between Models	df	L2	p
M1 - M2	1	6.01	< .025
M2 - M4	1	6.95	.01> p> .005

Odds and Odds Ratios under the Preferred Mode 2 (SP) (RS)			
		Odds	Odds Ratios
Region	Political Philosophy	Yes:No	Non-South:South
Non-South	Conservatives	.3683	1.4953
	Liberal	.3683	1.4953
South	Conservatives	.2463	1
	Liberal	.2463	1

the odds on supporting the sending of troops. Also, it should be noted that the effect of region disappears when the effect of income is controlled.

Table 20-5 presents a series of models from which the preferred model of the effect of education and income on the cognitive dimension of images of Japan is selected. In Table 20-5, the first four models consist of the standard three-way analysis. Among these standard models, model 2, which hypothesizes that response and income are conditionally independent given education, provides a satisfactory fit. However, we need to consider the linear specification because the data consist of ordered categories. Some models with linear specification are illustrated in model 5 through model 10. For example, the hypothesis of model 5 is that there is a linear effect of income on response, and model 9 incorporates separate linear effects of education and income on response. The results of the hierarchical comparisons between those models select model 5 as preferred.

TABLE 20-4
Models of Income and State (Region) on Response of Behavioral
Dimensions of Images of Korea and Comparisons of Models

Models	df	L^2	p
1 (IS) (R)	5	26.75	.000
2 (IS) (R)	4	26.61	.000
3 (IS) (RI) *	3	1.21	> .5
4 (IS) (RS) (RI)	2	0.16	> .5

Comparisons of L^2 between Models	df	L^2	p
M1 - M3	2	25.54	< .005

Odds and Odds ratios under the Preferred Model (IS) (RI)			
		Odds	Odds Ratio
Income	Region	Yes:No	Income Low
Low	Non-South	.1539	1
	South	.1538	1
Med	Non-South	.3314	2.1533
	South	.3314	2.1547
High	Non-South	.3635	2.3619
	South	.3636	2.3641

Table 20-5 presents odds and odds ratios computed from the preferred model, according to which we can conclude that odds on perception of United States vital interests in Japan increase proportionally by a factor of 1.58 as we move across the categories of the respondent's income from low to high. Unlike the results concerning Korea, income status has an impact on the cognitive dimension of images of Japan. One of the reasons for this may be the difference in levels of information about the two countries.

Table 20-6 shows a list of models from which the preferred model of the effects of education and income on the affective dimension of images of Japan is selected. Among the models in Table 20-6, model 8, which hypothesizes that there are separate effects of education and income on the affective dimension of images of Japan, is preferred. The corresponding statistics under the uniform association model are also displayed in Table 20-6. We observe that income effect in this case can be

TABLE 20-5

Model of Education and Income on Response of Cognitive Dimension of Images of Japan and Comparisons of Models

Models	df	L^2	p
1 (EI) (R)	8	20.44	.009
2 (EI) (RI) *	6	4.23	> .5
3 (EI) (RE) (RI)	6	12.43	.053
4 (EI) (RE) (RI)	4	1.02	> .5
5 (EI) Li*	7	5.38	> .5
6 (EI) Le*	7	14.04	< .1
7 (EI) (RE) Li*	5	2.46	> .5
8 (EI) (RRI) Le	5	2.84	> .5
9 (EI) (R) Le Li	6	4.06	> .5
10 (EI) (R) Le Li Lei	5	3.79	> .5

Comparisons of L^2 between Models	df	L^2	p
M1 - M2	2	16.21	.000
M1 - M5	1	15.06	.000
M1 - M6	1	6.40	.025> p> .01
M3 - M7	1	9.98	< .005

Odds and Odds Ratios under the Preferred Model 5 (EI) Le

Edu	Inc	Odds Yes:No	Odds Ratios :Income Low
Low	Low	5.8602	1
	Mid	9.2421	1.5771
	High	14.5773	2.4875
Mid	Low	5.8617	1
	Mid	9.2507	1.5781
	High	14.5985	2.4905
Hi	Low	5.8517	1
	Mid	9.2507	1.5782
	High	14.5985	2.4905

described by a single uniform association parameter. In other words, the higher one's income level is, the more favorable the attitudes toward Japan. The uniform association parameter 1.10 allows a uniform association across all adjacent rows and columns of the table.

TABLE 20-6

Education and Income on Affective Dimension of Images of Japan and Comparisons of Models

Models	df	L²	p
1 (EI) (R)	16	57.61	.000
2 (EI) (RI)	12	38.76	.000
3 (EI) (RE) *	12	12.39	.399
4 (EI) (RE) (RI)	8	6.66	> .5
5 (EI) UAi	15	40.61	.000
6 (EI) UAe	15	25.79	.000
7 (EI) (RI) UAe	11	19.58	.05< p< .1
8 (EI) (RE) * AEi*	14	8.06	> .5
9 (EI) (R) (UAi UAe)*	11	21.36	.05< p< .1
10 (EI) (R) Le Li	12	19.49	.05< p< .1
11 (EI) (R) Li Le Lei	10	18.27	.05< p< .1

Comparisons of L² between Models	df	L²	p
M1 - M3	4	45.02	.000
M3 - M8	1	4.53	< .050
M5 - M8	4	32.55	.000
M1 - M9	2	36.25	.000

Odds and Odds Ratios under the Preferred Model 8 (EI) (RE) UAi

		Odds		Odds Ratios			
				:Income Low		Education Low	
Edu	Inc	Neu:Unf	Fav:Unf	Neu:Unf	Fav:Unf	Neu:Unf	Fav:Unf
Low	Low	.5649	.9906	1	1	1	1
	Mid	.6563	1.2072	1.1038	1.2187	1	1
	High	.7234	1.4681	1.2166	1.4820	1	1
Mid	Low	1.3230	1.4827	1	1	2.2205	1.4968
	Mid	1.4572	1.7889	1.1037	1.2115	2.2203	1.4819
	High	1.6084	2.2011	1.2182	1.4845	2.2234	1.4993
Hi	Low	1.1244	2.3677	1	1	1.8910	2.3902
	Mid	1.2048	2.8834	1.1038	1.2178	1.8906	2.3885
	High	1.3701	3.5139	1.2185	1.4841	1.8940	2.3935

Notes: $(1.1038)^2 m 1.2183$, $(1.1038)^4 = 1.4844$

With regard to education effect, we need four parameters to describe the structure of the associations in the table. The parameters describing the effect of education show that having a middle level of education rather than a lower one raises the odds on having neutral attitudes toward Japan by a factor of 2.22, and having a higher level of education rather than a lower one raises the odds on having neutral attitudes by a factor of 1.89. They also indicate that a middle level of education raises the odds on having favorable attitudes by a factor of 1.49, and a higher level of education raises the odds on having favorable attitudes by a factor of 2.39.

On the affective dimension, the next factors to be considered are region and political philosophy. Since the likelihood ratio chi-square for the model of independence is 7.22 with 6 degrees of freedom, we fail to reject the hypothesis of no association between the variables, and conclude that there is no association between the factors and response. That is, the response on opinions for the affective dimension of attitudes toward Japan is independent of the respondent's regional location and political philosophy.

Table 20-7 presents odds and odds ratios under the preferred model of the effect of the elite/mass difference in their perception of United States vital interest in Korea. The saturated model is selected as the preferred model. Observed odds are identified with the expected odds, since we selected the saturated model as the preferred one. According to the preferred model, being in the mass public sample raises the odds on having no perception of United States vital interests in Korea by a factor of 1.76. In other words, people in elite groups are more likely to perceive United States vital interests in Korea.

Table 20-7 also presents odds and odds ratios under the preferred model of the effect of the elite/mass distinction on the affective dimension of images of Korea. The saturated model is selected as the preferred model. As in the previous dimension, we can conclude that being in a mass public sample raises the odds on opposing sending United States troops to Korea by a factor of 3.37. Hence, we confirm the hypotheses concerning the elite/mass distinction on two dimensions of images toward Korea. They are reaffirmed by the effect of elite/mass differences on the cognitive dimension of images of Japan.

TABLE 20-7

**Effects of Elite/Mass Difference on Response of Cognitive (a)
and Behavioral (b) Dimension of Images of Korea;
Cognitive Dimension of Images of Japan (c)**

(a) Odds and Odds Ratios Under the Saturated Model				
	Odds			Odds Ratio
	Mass:Elite			
Elite/Mass	Yes	No	No:Yes	Mass:Elite
Elite	1	1	.4609	1
Mass	1.5	2.6509	.8289	1.7674

(b) Odds and Odds Ratios under the Saturated Model				
	Odds			Odds Ratio
	Mass:Elite			
Elite/Mass	Yes	No	No:Yes	Mass:Elite
Elite	1	1	.9942	1
Mass	1.0819	7.0059	3.3455	3.3650

(c) Odds and Odds Ratios under the Saturated Model				
	Odds			Odds Ratio
	Mass:Elite			
Elite/Mass	Yes	No	No:Yes	Mass:Elite
Elite	1	1	.1014	1
Mass	3.9033	12.5714	.0211	5.1041

Discussion

This paper has examined factors affecting American images of Korea. We defined images of foreign nations as having three dimensions and analyzed the relationships between each dimension of images and its social correlates.

The results of the analysis show that among the structural factors considered here, respondent's family income and education are shown to be important factors distinguishing the respondent's attitudes toward Korea. The results also indicate that the respondent's regional location and political philosophy have only indirect effect, if effects exist at all, and that differences in educational attainment and family income level generally account for the observed effects.

Examining the effect of education on the affective dimension of images toward Korea shows that this variable has a fairly strong impact on favorability toward Korea; those in higher education groups tend to have more favorable attitudes. Another indicator of socioeconomic status, income, has a fairly strong impact on the behavioral dimension of images; those in higher income groups are more inclined to support United States involvement in Korea.

One striking result is the discrepant findings between Korea and Japan on the cognitive dimension of images of the two countries. It may be reasonable to interpret this inconsistent finding in terms of the political, historical, and the cultural circumstances of those countries. Since perceptions of United States' vital interests in certain foreign countries constitute the contents of the basic cognitive dimension toward a country, it may not be surprising that the vital interest perception toward Japan ranked relatively higher than that toward Korea. Japan has been perceived as a country with which the United States has strong political, economic, and security ties. However, Korea has not been viewed as a country with as much importance to the United States as Japan. The lower perception given to Korea may reflect a mood of increased security-consciousness since the inauguration of President Ronald Reagan in 1980. During the late 1970s, the public grew increasingly insecure about the perceived growing military imbalance between the Soviet Union and the United States. This preoccupation with military security became a major obsession, especially following the events in Iran and Afghanistan at the end of 1979. As a result of the heightened tension between the two major powers, the United States and the Soviet Union, the American public's concern about countries peripheral to that conflict such as Korea may be relatively weaker.

Findings of the present study seem to support the argument that elites and masses have dissimilar belief systems in two of the dimensions of images toward other countries. That is, national leaders are found to be more likely to perceive a United States vital interest in Korea than are the general public, and they tend to favor active United States involvement in Korea.

Probably the most striking result of this analysis is that structural factors considered in this study have not been found to impact greatly on attitudes toward Korea, even though some of the factors showed significant effects on some of the dimensions of images. It is possible that we can interpret the results as confirming one school of opinion, asserting that most American people lack the information and cognitive capabilities necessary to achieve a coherent belief system on foreign policy issues.[22] However, the opposing view, which asserts the presence of a relatively well organized foreign policy belief system among American people, cannot be totally disconfirmed since some of our findings provide evidence that can be interpreted to be consistent with such a view.

We can interpret the results as due to the nature of the specific image-object nation, Korea. That is, the public generally do not see third world countries as vitally important to them; they do not show much interest in issues concerning those countries and consequently do not have the information necessary to achieve a meaningful structure of attitudes toward them. This possibility is partially supported by the difference in attitudes toward United States vital interests in Korea and in Japan; the respondent's income has a significant effect on the perception of vital interest toward Japan, while it does not show any impact on the same cognitive dimension of attitudes toward Korea.

Another possible explanation for the contradictory findings reported earlier is the greater specificity of the object country and more narrow focus of the items tapping the dimensions of images toward the object country. For Americans, at least up to the early 1980s, Korea has been viewed as a country under constant communist threat. On the other hand, the mass media in the United States either did not cover Korea or pictured it negatively, focusing on such problems as human rights issues. It is possible that the specific characteristics of the object nation could be a confounding factor with respect to some dimensions of American attitudes toward Korea. Overall, the analysis reported here shows that some of the factors do have significant influence on attitudes toward Korea, even though the effects are inconsistent.

Notes

1. Karl W. Deutch and Richard L. Meritt, "Effects of Events on National and International Image," in *International Behaviors: A Social and Psychological Analysis*, ed. H.C. Kelman (Ann Arbor, MI: University of Michigan Press, 1966), 132.
2. K.E. Boulding, "National Images and International Systems," *Journal of Conflict Resolution*, 3 (1959), 20.
3. Ibid.
4. William A. Scott, "Psychological and Social Correlates of International Images," in Kelman, *International Behaviors*, 71–75.
5. Ibid., 98–110.
6. H.J. Eysenck, "The Primary Social Attitudes as Related to Social Class and Political Party," *British Journal of Sociology*, 2 (1951):198–209; H.J. Eysenck, *The Psychology of Politics* (London: Routledge and Kegan Paul, 1954).
7. Melvin L. Kohn, *Class and Conformity: A Study in Values* (Homewood, IL: Dorsey Press, 1969); also, Melvin L. Kohn and Carmi Schooler, "The Reciprocal Effects of the Substantive Complexity of Work and Intellectual Flexibility: A Longitudinal Assessment," *American Journal of Sociology*, 84 (1978): 24–52.
8. Seymour M. Lipset, "Democracy and Working Class Authoritarianism," *American Sociological Review*, 24 (1959): 482–501.
9. Alex Inkeles, "Industrial Man: The Relation of Status to Experience, Perception, and Value," *American Journal of Sociology*, 66 (1960) 1–31; Herbert H. Hyman, "The Value Systems of Different Classes," in *Class, State, and Power*, eds. R. Bendix and S.M. Lipset (Glencoe, IL: Free Press, 1966), 488–99; Herbert H. Hyman and Charles R. Wright, *Education's Lasting Influence on Values* (Chicago: University of Chicago Press, 1979).
10. William M. Kephart, *Racial Factors and Urban Law Enforcement* (Philadelphia: University of Pennsylvania Press, 1957).
11. Gordon Allport, *The Nature of Prejudice* (Boston: Beacon, 1954).
12. T.W. Adorno et al., *The Authoritarian Personality* (New York: Harper, 1950).
13. Gordon Allport and Bernard M. Kramer, "Some Roots of Prejudice," *Journal of Psychology*, 22 (1946): 9–39.
14. Barbara Bardes and Robert Oldendick, "Beyond Internationalism: A Case for Mutiple Dimensions in the Structure of Foreign Policy Attitudes," *Social Science Quarterly*, 59 (1978): 496–507.
15. Eugene R. Wittkopf and Michael A. Maggiotto, "Elites and Masses: A Comparative Analysis of Attitudes toward America's World Role," *Journal of Politics*, 45 (1983): 304–307.
16. Herbert McClosky, "Conservatism and Personality," *American Political Science Review*, 52 (1958): 27–45.

17. Bardes and Oldendick, "Beyond Internationalism."
18. Chicago Council on Foreign Relations, *American Public Opinion and U.S. Foreign Policy* (Ann Arbor, MI: Inter-University Consortium for Political and Social Research, 1982).
19. David Knoke and Peter J. Burke, *Loglinear Models* (Beverly Hills, CA: Sage Publications, 1983).
20. Leo A. Goodman, "A General Model for the Analysis of Surveys," *American Journal of Sociology*, 77 (1972): 1035–1086; S.J. Haberman, *Analysis of Qualitative Data*, vol. 2, (New York: Academic Press, 1979); also, Lee E. Edlefsen and Samuel D. Jones, *GAUSS* (Kent, WA.: Aptech Systems, Inc., 1986).
21. James A. McRae, Jr., "Changes in Religious Communalism Desired by Protestants and Catholics," *Social Forces*, 63 (1983).
22. Lloyd Free and Hadley Cantril, *The Political Beliefs of Americans* (New York: Simon and Schuster, 1968); William Watts, George R. Packard, Ralph N. Clough, and Robert B. Oxnam, *Japan, Korea and China: American Perceptions and Policies* (Lexington, MA: Lexington, Heath, 1979); Richard L. Sneider and William Watts, *The United States and Korea: New Directions for the 80's* (Washington, D.C.: Potomac Associates, 1980).

21

Korean Perspectives on American Democracy

American Policy Changes, Anti-Americanism, and Policy Recommendations

Sung Moon Pae

Introduction

NO COUNTRY HAS PLAYED SO VITAL A ROLE as the United States in helping the Republic of Korea defend its territorial integrity and modernize itself at a rate unprecedented in the modern world. The United States defended South Korea during the Korean War. Since the mutual defense pact was signed in 1953, the United States has guaranteed South Korean security by stationing some 40,000 United States troops on Korean soil. The United States also provided South Korea with a total of $6.8 billion military and $5.7 billion economic aid from 1945 to 1976.

The strategic importance of South Korea and the consequent national security interest of the United States there should by no means be completely disregarded in the American commitment to the defense of South Korea. However, Koreans believe that the more profound, and indeed the principal motive of the United States in its commitment and sacrifice for South Korea has been to protect and promote democracy not only in the United States but also in other countries, including South Korea.

People in many countries still believe in this sense of mission and expect the United States to continue to foster democracy in their countries. When the United States does not fulfill their expectations, they tend to feel resentment and betrayal. The anti-Americanism of recent years in Korea may be attributed to economic and trade frictions[1] and issues involving the American military bases in Korea.[2] But my thesis is that the anti-Americanism in Korea is primarily due to the drift of American foreign policy regarding South Korea away from "open diplomacy" in the 1950s and the 1960s and "quiet diplomacy" in the 1970s to the policy of cooptation with the authoritarian Chun regime of South Korea during the 1980s. Korean students and intellectuals perceived that President Reagan's policy of cooptation forsook the American mission of supporting democratization in foreign countries and instead helped the Chun regime to exercise more repressive measures against Koreans seeking democratic expression.

After a review of American foreign policy in Korea, this paper will offer some policy recommendations to alleviate anti-Americanism in regard to the perceived American role to further promote democratization in South Korea.

American Idealism

Koreans as well as people of many foreign countries—democratic and nondemocratic—have long perceived that the United States of America has a moral responsibility to promote and protect democracy not only in the United States but also in the rest of the world.

The American mission is based on the political philosophy that only democracy can build world peace and allow the happiness of individual citizens in their respective countries.

For example, if a state's domestic politics is not characterized by democratic institutions and processes, then that state has a tendency to threaten world peace. States with undemocratic institutions and processes have almost invariably turned to aggression for power aggrandizement.

President Woodrow Wilson's famous war message on April 12, 1917, attributed the cause of World War I to lack of democracy in Germany and the subsequent lack of consultations with the German people by their leaders.

> We have no quarrel with the German people.... It was not upon their impulse that their government acted.... It was a war determined as wars used to be determined upon the old, unhappy days when peoples were nowhere consulted by their rulers and wars were provoked and waged in the interest of dynasties or of little groups of ambitious men who were accustomed to follow their fellow men as pawns or tools.[3]

Only fifteen years after World War I did three nondemocratic countries—Nazi Germany, fascist Italy, and militarist Japan—begin their assaults on the continents of Europe, Africa, and Asia. President Franklin Roosevelt also declared nondemocratic institutions and processes as the main cause of World War II. Only if democracy were firmly established everywhere, would the final curtain fall on the violent struggle for power in the international arena. Therefore, President Roosevelt justified the American involvement in World War II by the same responsibility of America to protect democracy in Europe and other continents.

> Every realist knows that the democratic way of life is at this moment being directly assailed in every part of the world—assailed either by arms, or by secret spreading of poisonous propaganda by those who seek to destroy unity and promote discord in nations that are still at peace.

> During sixteen long months this assail has blotted out the whole pattern of democratic life in an appalling number of independent nations, great and small. The assailants are still on the march, threatening other nations, great and small.[4]

In addition to contributing to world peace, democracy is seen as a political means by which citizens may enjoy life, liberty, the

454 Korean Challenges and American Policy

pursuit of happiness, and self-actualization under the guarantee of the same basic freedoms and rights—civil, political, economic, and social—as Americans enjoy. Aiding other countries to achieve this has been America's traditional role.[5] Democratization is at the core of American foreign policy, because it is central to what the United States is and represents. Democracy is not something Americans tack onto their foreign policy; it is their very purpose. Jeanne Kirkpatrick saw democratization in developing countries is a legitimate purpose of American foreign policy.

> In democracies the need for moral justification of political action is especially compelling—nowhere more so than in the United States. The fact that Americans do not share a common history, race, language, religion gives added centrality to American values, beliefs, and goals, making them the key element to our national identity. The American people are defined by the American creed. The vision of the public good which defines us is and always has been commitment to individual freedom and a conviction that government exists, above all, for the purpose of protecting individual rights. ("To protect these Rights," says the Declaration of Independence, "governments are instituted among men.") Government, in the American view, has no purpose greater than that of protecting and extending the rights of its citizens. For this reason, the definitive justification of government policy in the U.S. is to protect the rights—liberty, property, personal security—of citizens. Defending these rights or extending them to other peoples is the only legitimate purpose of American foreign policy.[6]

President Truman made it clear that the United States should help foreign peoples to resist attempted subjugation by armed minorities or by outside pressure and to freely choose the democratic way of life.[7]

Many presidents of the United States have explicitly endorsed the American commitment to democracy and human rights abroad. President Eisenhower stated in his address to the American Bar Association on August 24, 1955, that there would be no true peace as long as "we find injustice to many nations, repressions of human beings on a gigantic scale...with constructive effort paralyzed in many years by fear." President Kennedy, in his inaugural address, delivered a message to the world: "Let every nation know, whether it wish us well or ill, that we shall pay any price, bear any burden, meet any hardship, support our friends or oppose any foe to assure the survival and success of liberty."

In his inaugural address President Carter called the attention of the American people to the same moral mission, which has been passed on from the inception of the republic.

> Because we are free, we can never be indifferent to the fate of freedom elsewhere. Our moral sense dictates a clearcut preference for those societies which share with us an abiding respect for individual human rights. We do not seek to intimidate, but it is clear that a world which others can dominate with impunity would be inhospitable to decency and a threat to the well-being of all people.[8]

American sense of mission indeed has brought about exceptional accomplishments. Among them may be listed a few salient examples: the Marshall Plan, the Truman Doctrine, the Point Four programs, and the postwar rebuilding of democracy in West Germany and Japan. The United States also led the United Nations to enshrine democratic values in legal instruments and international agreements: The Universal Declaration of Human Rights in 1948; the International Convention of the Elimination of Racial Discrimination adopted on December 21, 1965; the International Covenant on Economic, Social and Cultural Rights and the International Covenant on Civil and Political Rights adopted on December 16, 1966; and the Helsinki Agreement signed by 35 countries assembled in 1975 to give solemn approval to a commitment to implement the principles of human rights.

Changes in the American Policy toward South Korea

Open Diplomacy (1950s–1960s)

The United States commitment to the defense of Korea and the subsequent military and economic assistance during the 1950s and 1960s were explained and justified less by Korea's strategic importance to the United States than by the traditional American responsibility to protect democracy.[9] In fact, the evaluation of the Joint Chiefs of Staff in 1947 was that from the standpoint of military security, the United States had little strategic interest in maintaining troops and military bases in

Korea.[10] Secretary of State Dean Acheson also expected that there would be no overt military aggression in East Asia. What might be expected instead was political subversion and penetration, but that could not be stopped by military means.[11] If military attacks were to come, the initial reliance had to be placed initially on the Asian people themselves to resist, and secondarily upon the commitment of the entire civilized world under the Charter of the United Nations rather than on American forces alone.[12] Therefore, on January 12, 1950, Acheson announced the exclusion of Korea from the American defensive perimeter in Asia.

Upon the invasion of North Korean communists, however, President Truman took the decisive action, first of all, of ordering American air and naval forces to support the retreating South Korean units and then deploying American ground troops. President Truman and his policy makers saw the North Korean invasion as the same aggression, the same threat to democracy, and the same danger to global order as the threats from dictatorships in the past.

> Communism was acting in Korea just as Hitler, Mussolini, and the Japanese had acted ten, fifteen, and twenty years earlier. I felt certain that if South Korea was allowed to fall, communist leaders would be emboldened to override nations closer to our own shores. If the communists were permitted to force their war into the Republic of Korea without opposition from the free world, no small nation would have the courage to resist threats and aggression by stronger communist neighbors. If this was allowed to go unchallenged it would mean the third World War, just as similar incidents had brought on the second World War.[13]

The American commitment resulted in the unexpectedly high human cost of 33,000 Americans killed in action, 103,000 wounded and an expenditure of $50 billion in direct costs. Upon the conclusion of the truce in 1953, the United States continued to commit itself to the defense of South Korea. The United States Senate, by a vote of 81 to 6, ratified the mutual defense pact with South Korea on January 27, 1954. The vote was far in excess of the required two-thirds majority. The announced purpose of the treaty was to guarantee the security of South Korea against further attack by the communists in

North Korea. Moreover, in response to the demand for mutual withdrawal of Chinese and American forces from North and South Korea, respectively, the United States made it clear that the American forces would stay in South Korea until "the conditions for a lasting settlement laid down by the United Nations General Assembly be fulfilled."[14]

The United States also provided South Korea with economic aid on the basis of "the economic theory of democracy."[15] That theory holds that democracy is viable under economic growth and prosperity. When people are made miserable and daily survival is constantly threatened, democracy is less likely to take a firm root. The more economically prosperous a country is, the more stable its democracy becomes. Hence, President Truman's request to Congress for economic aid to South Korea was justified by the same moral position, the promotion of democracy as the essential American foreign policy.

> Korea has become a testing ground in which the validity and practical value of the ideals and principles of democracy which the Republic is putting into practice are being matched against the practices of communism which has been imposed upon the people of North Korea. The survival and progress of the Republic toward a self-supporting, stable economy will have an immense and far reaching influence on the people of Asia. Such progress by the young Republic will encourage the people of southern and southeastern Asia and the islands of the Pacific to resist and reject the communist propaganda with which they are besieged. Moreover, the Korean Republic, by demonstrating the success and tenacity of democracy in resisting communism, will stand as a beacon to the people of northern Asia in resisting the control of the communist forces which have overrun them.[16]

The United States was equally involved in Korea in inflation control, tax adjustment, land reform, and rehabilitation of economic infrastructure—such as road building, bridge repairs, constructing schools and hospitals—by mobilizing American engineering, technical, and medical military units.

The military and economic aid in fact became only the intermediate goals in America's ultimate objective of democratization in Korea. When democratic institutions and processes were violated in Korea, the United States was willing to pursue "open diplomacy"—publicly criticizing and protesting to the

Korean government, warning of reconsideration of military and economic aid in case of repetition of repressive practices. In order to demonstrate how strongly the United States committed itself to its traditional role, let me identify a few salient examples of "open diplomacy," which the United States applied to Korea during the 1950s and 1960s.

In January 1950, under the auspices of the government party, the National Assembly amended the National Security Law primarily for the purpose of reelecting President Syngman Rhee. The revised law, however, was subject to intense criticism because of two notorious provisions. They were the establishment of re-education camps and an ex post facto provision regarding offenses. The right to appeal was eliminated in the first case, whereas in the latter offenses committed prior to the laws were included. Because of strong pressure from the United States, the Korean government was forced to remove these two provisions from the new law.

In February 1950, when the state of national emergency was still in effect, the Korean government arrested fifteen opposition members of the National Assembly, eliminated an opposition press, and purged the judicial branch of so-called leftist agents, including nine lawyers and prosecutors and six judges. The Korean government then faced open protests from Philip C. Jessup, United States ambassador-at-large, on his visit to Korea at that time.[17]

In March 1950 President Rhee expressed his intention to postpone until June the date of the general election scheduled for May and later suggested that the election should be held as late as November, after the constitution was amended. Disappointed by President Rhee's violation of the principle of regular elections, Secretary of State Dean Acheson issued a public statement emphasizing that both economic and military aid to Korea were based on the existence and growth of democratic institutions within the republic.[18] Because of such strong pressure from the United States, President Rhee reversed his previous decision "since the opinion seemed to be that the election should be held as scheduled in May."[19]

In May 1952 President Rhee's veto was overridden 96 to 3 in the National Assembly, forcing martial law to be lifted for open competition in the forthcoming presidential campaign.

Nevertheless, martial law was not lifted by the president, and 47 opposition assemblymen were detained on the grounds that they had violated the still-effective martial law. Although President Rhee insisted that the United Nations Commission for the Unification and Rehabilitation of Korea (UNCURK) had no right to meddle in Korea's internal affairs, UNCURK transmitted a message to President Rhee demanding that martial law in Pusan be lifted without delay and that the assemblymen still under arrest or otherwise detained be released.[20] President Rhee's removal of Korean troops from the front line to enforce martial law in Pusan caused him to receive an unwanted visit from General James A. Van Fleet, commander of the Eighth Army, and Alan E. Lightner, counselor of the United States embassy.[21] In that meeting, President Rhee promised not to again deploy Korean troops to support his political purposes.[22] President Truman took the unusual step of sending a personal note to President Rhee expressing "shock" at his feud with the National Assembly.[23] All these open diplomatic actions pressured President Rhee to seek and arrive at a compromise with the National Assembly in the constitutional amendments. The legislature was permitted the right to dissolve the cabinet, and President Rhee was allowed to replace the former legislative election of the president with a direct popular election.

On May 16, 1961, when the Chang Myon regime was overthrown by a military coup, the United States strongly opposed the military government. Right after the military junta announced that it had seized power from the prime minister, the United States embassy in Seoul issued a statement opposing the military government and expressing strong support instead for the freely elected and constitutionally established government of Prime Minister John M. Chang (Chang Myon). General Carter B. Magruder, commander-in-chief of the United Nations Command in Korea, took a step further, calling on all military personnel in his command—American and Korean—to support the only recognized government of the Republic of Korea, headed by Prime Minister Chang. He stated, "The chiefs of the Korean armed forces will use their authority and influence to see that control is immediately turned back to the lawful governmental authority and that order is restored in the armed forces."[24] The American government unequivocally supported the statement of General Magruder and the American embassy in Seoul. Washington flatly rejected a suggested meeting between President Kennedy and General Chang Do Young.

Only when President Yun Posun, as the *de jure* commander-in-chief of the Korean armed forces, refused to take any military action with American assistance against the coup forces did General Magruder realize that there would be no way to forcibly remove the junta from control of the government. A head-on military collision might have resulted in severe casualties of not only military personnel but also innocent civilians in Seoul. The junta, on the other hand, promised to restore political rule to conscientious civilians soon.

America's open diplomacy was evidenced again in March 1963 when General Park Chung Hee announced withdrawal of a referendum originally scheduled for summer of 1965 for the ratification of the constitutional amendments or the extension of military rule for four more years. The United States issued a strong protest and demanded that stable constitutional rule be restored in South Korea. On April 16, 1963, General Park gave in to American pressure and stated that he would work toward holding elections in 1963.

Quiet Diplomacy (the 1970s)

During the 1970s the United States shifted its foreign policy in South Korea from "open diplomacy" to "quiet diplomacy." Open diplomacy, which had been implemented during the 1950s and 1960s in Korea, was characterized by open, formal protests against the Korean government when it violated democratic institutions and processes, explicit warnings against possible repetition of undemocratic practices, and strong public demands for corrections and improvements. Open diplomacy was usually accompanied by use of economic and military aid as the leverage. As a client country, because of its need for economic survival and growth and the security imperative, Korea had no option but to comply with the demands of the patron country.

Quiet diplomacy, which was implemented in Korea during the 1970s, was characterized by persuasion and recommendations rather than public protests and demands. Persuasion and

recommendations were also more likely to be offered by informal rather than formal, and behind-the-scenes rather than
open, means. Quiet diplomacy could focus on more specific
concerns rather than broad, comprehensive ones. Warnings
and threats were less likely to be employed. Economic and
military aid could no longer be effectively utilized as leverage
once Korea achieved significant development. Therefore, the
effectiveness of using economic aid as a lever was shrinking as
it became an ever-decreasing fraction of the recipient country's
GNP. Moreover, loans began to replace economic aid as the
main source for investment. Also because of rapid economic
growth, military aid began to be replaced by military sales. If
military sales were not allowed, weapons from other exporting
countries could be actively sought. Economic growth and the
subsequent independence of Korea from foreign economic and
military aid were such that the United States began to abstain
from threatening decreased aid to its former client country.

As Table 21-1 indicates, American military assistance during
the 1950s and 1960s accounted for 99 to 100 percent of the
total amount of United States military aid and military sales.
But in 1974 military sales began to increase, reaching about 13
percent of the total and gradually increasing to 95.7 percent of
the sum in 1979. This suggests that United States military aid
was completely phased out and replaced by sale of weapons and
equipment. United States military aid, for example, accounted
for 18.91 percent of Korea's total GNP in 1953 but for only .02
percent in 1979. United States non-military government grants
and credits accounted for 12.98 percent of Korea's GNP in 1973
but only .37 percent in 1979. The total amount of United States
grants and credits—military and non-military—amounted to
31.9 percent of Korea's GNP in 1953 but only 0.6 percent in
1979. In short, America's economic and military grants and
credits during the 1970s declined to only 2.25 percent of Korea's
GNP on average and consequently could not be used to put any
significant pressure on Korea for its democratization.

Moreover, because of its increasing economic strength and
other local factors, Korea became more strategically important
to United States national interests. The collapse of South Vietnam and Cambodia, the potential for spillover onto the Korean

TABLE 21-1

**Major Elements of United States Leverage on the Korean Government:
[Military assistance (MA),Military sales (MS), Non-military government
grants and credits (NMGGC), Total military and Non-military government
grants and credits (TMNGGC)]**

	U.S. MA to ROK	U.S. MS to ROK	Sum of MS & MA	Ratio of MA to Sum	Ratio of MS to Sum	Ratio of MA to ROK's GNP	U.S. NMG GC	Its Ratio to ROK's GNP	Total U.S. TMN GGC	Its Ratio to ROK's GNP
Year	(a)	(b)	(c)	(a/c)	(b/c)	(d)	(e)		(a+ e)	(f)
1953	300.0	.0	300.0	100.0	.0	18.91	206	12.98	506.0	31.9
1954	250.0	.0	250.0	100.0	.0	14.16	169	9.75	419.0	23.7
1955	230.0	.0	230.0	100.0	.0	12.87	276	15.44	506.0	28.3
56	231.2	.0	231.2	100.0	.0	12.47	307	16.55	538.2	29.0
57	265.5	.0	265.5	100.0	.0	13.62	373	19.14	638.5	32.7
58	353.5	.0	353.5	100.0	.0	17.24	311	15.17	664.5	32.4
59	212.4	.0	212.4	100.0	.0	9.84	232	10.75	444.4	20.6
60	213.1	.0	213.1	100.0	.0	9.80	261	12.01	474.1	21.8
61	232.7	.0	232.7	100.0	.0	10.07	230	9.96	462.7	20.0
62	189.5	.1	189.6	99.9	.0	7.88	238	9.90	427.5	17.7
63	194.8	.2	195.0	99.8	.1	7.47	240	9.20	434.8	16.6
64	137.8	.2	138.0	99.8	.1	4.88	158	5.60	295.8	10.4
65	219.2	.3	219.5	99.8	.1	7.16	167	5.45	386.2	12.6
66	168.7	.3	169.0	99.8	.2	5.19	168	5.17	336.7	10.3
67	153.2	.4	153.6	99.7	.2	4.19	193	5.29	346.2	9.4
68	204.1	.5	204.6	99.7	.2	5.11	191	4.78	395.1	9.8
69	210.0	.5	210.5	99.7	.2	4.57	260	5.66	470.0	10.2
70	216.3	1.9	218.2	99.1	.9	2.93	198	2.68	414.3	5.6
71	140.5	.4	140.9	99.7	.3	1.74	194	2.41	334.5	4.1
72	164.3	.2	164.5	99.8	.2	1.33	221	1.79	385.3	3.1
73	96.4	.3	97.7	98.6	1.3	.65	214	1.44	310.4	2.0
74	91.6	13.3	104.9	87.3	12.7	.56	63	.38	154.6	.9

(Units: $million & percentage)

peninsula, the increase in Soviet naval forces based in Vladivostok and the subsequent threat to Japan brought the United States to see South Korea as now strategically important.

Former Secretary of State Cyrus R. Vance dramatized the American dilemma.

TABLE 21-1

Major Elements of United States Leverage on the Korean Government: [Military assistance (MA),Military sales (MS), Non-military government grants and credits (NMGGC), Total military and Non-military government grants and credits (TMNGGC)]

(Units: $million & percentage)

Year	U.S. MA to ROK	U.S. MS to ROK	Sum of MS & MA	Ratio of MA to Sum	Ratio of MS to Sum	Ratio of MA to ROK's GNP	U.S. NMG GC	Its Ratio to ROK's GNP	Total U.S. TMN GGC	Its Ratio to ROK's GNP
	(a)	(b)	(c)	(a/c)	(b/c)	(d)	(e)		(a–e)	(f)
75	136.6	57.5	194.1	70.3	29.6	.74	314	1.76	450.6	2.4
76	91.5	136.5	228.0	40.1	59.8	.33	344	1.27	435.5	1.6
77	15.3	177.8	193.1	7.9	92.1	.04	250	.72	265.3	.7
78	26.2	414.1	440.3	5.9	94.0	.05	698	1.47	724.2	1.5
79	17.6	395.0	412.6	4.2	95.7	.02	228	.37	245.6	.6
80	160.4	295.2	455.6	35.2	64.8	.27	101	.17	261.4	.4
81	107.7	295.5	403.2	26.7	73.3	.17	193	.31	300.7	.4
82	139.1	218.6	357.7	38.8	61.1	.21	337	.51	476.1	.7
83	.7	299.0	299.7	.2	99.8	.00	448	.60	448.7	.6
84	1.6	261.0	262.6	.6	99.4	.00	208	.26	209.6	.2

Source: For (a) and (b), *Statistical Abstract of the United States*, various years; U.S. Defense Security Assistance Agency, *Foreign Military Sales and Foreign Military Construction Sales*; Department of Defense, *Military Assistance Facts* (Washington, D.C.: U.S. Government Printing Office, various years); for (e), Department of Commerce, *Foreign Grants and Credits by the U.S. Government*, various years.

We know from our national experience that the drive for human freedom has tremendous force and vitality. It is universal. It is resilient. And, ultimately, it is irrepressible.

In a profound sense, then, our ideals and our interests coincide. For we have a stake in the stability that comes when people can express their hopes and build their futures freely.

Yet, certainly the pursuit of human rights must be managed in a practical way. We must constantly weigh how best to encourage progress while maintaining an ability to conduct business with governments—even unpopular ones—in countries where we have important security interests.[25]

Secretary of State George P. Shultz also highlighted the difficulty of combining a moral mission with realism in foreign affairs: "How to realize our moral mission without risking the national security interests and without exhausting the national power, how to pursue noble goals in a complex and imperfect world, which disturb the United States in promoting and protecting democracy."26

The answer for Secretaries Vance and Shultz was "quiet diplomacy." So long as a foreign country like South Korea is important to the United States national interest and yet economically strong and independent of the United States, quiet diplomacy may be the only option for the United States government to employ in promoting democratization.

Korea in the 1970s witnessed a series of violations of basic freedoms, human rights, and democratic procedures. On the inauguration of the Fourth Republic in 1972 after the amendment and ratification of the Yushin Constitution, President Park issued a series of nine executive decrees. They prohibited debate on the constitution or proposal of any amendment; restricted the press from reporting anything except government views; closed the *Dong-A*, the nation's largest newspaper, dismissing thirteen of its editors and reporters; and imposed a new censorship law that forbade criticism of President Park. Korean armed troops occupied the Seoul campus of Korea University and closed some twenty other universities in Seoul for 41 days.

Many who were involved in the National Council of Christian Churches, the National Council for Restoration of Democracy, the Urban Industrial Mission, and a host of other organizations primarily established for civil, political, and economic democracy in Korea were arrested and tortured.

Koreans seeking democratization urged the United States government to use open diplomacy on President Park. Protests were voiced by American scholars, journalists, congressmen, and senators. A delegation of United States congressmen led by Representatives Thomas P. O'Neill, Jr., and John B. Anderson said that "South Korea's image is being damaged by Park's political acts."27 Professor Edwin O. Reischauer urged the United States to rethink its policy because President Park "is making a mockery of democratic institutions and undermining loyalty of South Koreans."[28] Edwin Reischauer, John King Fairbank, and 35 others signed a petition and protested the "injustice and inhumanity of President Park."[29] Representative Donald M. Fraser called for "an end to American military aid to South Korea until Park's repression ceases."[30] A group of American missionaries staged silent demonstrations in the United States embassy compound in Seoul, "urging the United States to make stronger protest to the South Korean government over the hanging of 8 persons convicted of attempting to overthrow President Park's government."[31] A letter signed by 119 senators and representatives on April 4 and a letter of protest signed by 154 United States congressmen on October 28, 1976, expressed "profound distress over arbitrary action in jailing political critics." They contended that continued American military support for South Korea might "make the United States an accomplice to political repression by President Park."[32]

Secretary of State Henry Kissinger ironically stated that the United States should continue economic and military aid to South Korea although the United States did not approve of South Korea's repressive measures at home. His rationale was that South Korea's strategic position in Asian security was crucial to Japan, and Japan shared the United States view.[33]

Quiet diplomacy was clearly exhibited in the typical soft phrases in statements by the United States government—"carefully watch," "does not feel comfortable about," "expressed concerns about," "privately indicated," "deplored human rights violations," and "privately protested." For example, Assistant Secretary of State Robert Ingersoll, after reviewing the United States stance on human rights with South Korean Deputy Premier Tae Wan Son issued a statement: "The United States continues to watch South Korean developments carefully. The Korean government is aware of United States views on human rights."[34] In fact, the term "quiet diplomacy" was officially used for the first time in 1974 by Secretary Ingersoll and Acting Assistant Secretary of State Arthur W. Hummel, Jr. Both of them deplored human rights violations but stressed the military importance of South Korea.

Quiet diplomacy was further demonstrated by the United States ambassador, Richard Walker, who showed reservation, in promoting Korean democracy openly and explicitly while a nation-wide police round-up of dissidents made a mockery of President Carter's human rights issue as the central theme of United States foreign policy.

President Carter aimed to be an advocate and implementer of quiet diplomacy. He was "working quietly behind the scenes to soften Mr. Park's policies without bruising South Korea's growing pride and independent spirit."[35] Against strong opposition from Korean dissidents and human rights leaders, President Carter made a state visit Korea and toasted President Park at a state dinner. This was seen by the public on the one hand as a betrayal of Korean human rights leaders and fighters for democracy. On the other hand it was known Carter had quietly called on the South Korean government to release more than 100 political prisoners.[36]

Cooptation (1980s) and Anti-Americanism

One has to keep in mind that in the whole history of Korean-American relations there had been no significant level of anti-Americanism except for a few occasions of sporadic complaint during the 1970s when quiet diplomacy was being implemented. The reason for the lack of anti-Americanism expressed was the fact that, even though it was far short of the expectations of many Koreans, the quiet diplomacy of the United States still had influence on Korean government leaders, and their strong grips on the people were somehow relaxed.

However, at the beginning of the 1980s the United States shifted from "quiet diplomacy" to a policy of "cooptation" with the authoritarian Chun regime. The political rationale behind the Reagan administration's adoption of the policy of cooptation was evaluation of international relations from a perspective of realism. Authoritarianism may be evil, but totalitarian evil is worse than the authoritarian one. The lessons of modern history are loud and clear that the authoritarian form of government still has the potential to become democratic, as in the most recent cases of Spain, Portugal, Greece, Turkey, Brazil, Argentina, Uruguay, Peru, Ecuador, and the Philippines since 1974.[37] But once a society is dominated by a Marxist-Leninist party, Western-style democracy is irretrievable.

Democracy lives in the hearts of those who are socialized by the democratic political culture, not in legal documents on human rights and freedoms. American diplomacy alone, whether open or quiet, without concurrent socialization of democratic political culture in the hearts and minds of citizens in other countries will be unable to guarantee a viable democracy. There is no fast way to achieve democracy.[38] External forces, no matter how nobly motivated, cannot impose justice, human rights, or freedoms on other states.

The American moral mission itself was pursued inconsistently and in often contradictory ways. President Carter and his secretaries of state, for example, had ceaselessly scolded authoritarian governments of friendly countries and ignored hostile or neutral authoritarian and totalitarian countries. This inconsistency was characterized as hypocrisy by Senator Barry Goldwater.

> The American Administration is quick to yell "foul" when appraising human rights in places such as South Africa, Rhodesia and Latin America, but we hear little if anything about the gross repression and violation of human rights in countries like Communist China, Cuba, Uganda, Cambodia, and Vietnam. I, for one, am sick of this hypocrisy.[39]

Moreover, even among friendly authoritarian countries, those vital to the United States national interest like South Korea were immune from direct and open criticism, whereas those less important were more severely criticized and urged to improve their behavior in human rights.

The promotion of democracy and human rights in foreign countries may often seem unrealistic because of the limited power of the United States to call for absolutely moral policies. Therefore, President Reagan called attention to words of historian Charles Beard, who warned nearly forty years ago that

> the defect of a foreign policy based on what he called the selfless sacrifice required by an absolute morality was the ability to understand the limited nature of American power to relieve, restore, and maintain life beyond its own sphere of interest and control—recognition of the hard fact that the United States...did not possess the power...to assure the establishment of democratic and pacific government.[40]

The United States in the 1980s did not rule out quiet diplomacy completely. Once in a while human rights violations in Korea seemed extreme, and the Reagan administration quietly influenced the Chun administration. In fact, Senator Kennedy and thirteen members of Congress acknowledged that the Reagan administration had exerted diplomatic pressure to bring about reduction of the sentence of Kim Dae Jung from death in May 1980 to life imprisonment in January 1981 to twenty years in March 1983; amnesty granted to 197 of 419 political prisoners; and restoration of civil rights to 125 involved in the Kwangju uprising.[41]

But cooptation with the authoritarian South Korean government on the basis of realism became the dominant foreign policy of the United States in the 1980s. Thus, the American policy was represented by lack of protest—open or quiet—against General Chun for his deployment of Korean troops against senior generals without prior consultation with General John Wickham; a lack of demands—open or quiet—for the restoration of civilian government after the December 16, 1980, revolt; approval by General Wickham of Korean troop deployment to Kwangju; refusal of United States officials—the president, the secretary of state, and the American ambassador to Korea—to meet with Korean opposition leaders and the subsequent lack of endorsement for democracy. While claiming political neutrality toward both opposition and government sides, the United States welcomed President Chun to the White House four times over a relatively short period of time and welcomed even the government party's presidential candidate, Roh Tae Woo, to the White House in September 1987 prior to the December 1987 presidential election in Korea. On the other hand, opposition leaders have never been invited. In fact, the United States policy of cooptation of the authoritarian Korean government became a root cause of anti-Americanism among those who believed that the United States had a responsibility for democracy abroad.[42]

In contrast to their protest of the 1960 coup, United States officials refused to comment on the arrest of the martial law commander, Chung Soung Hwa, and several other senior generals on December 16, 1979. General Chun in fact ignored the Combined Forces Command, the main operational military command under General John A. Wickham of the United States Army, and moved the Ninth Division and other units in to take military control. The Carter administration expressed "deep concern" over the crisis in the South Korean military. At the time the *New York Times* indicated that the United States had privately protested the breach of military guidelines on deployment of forces. However, the form of the United States protest to the South Korean government over General Chun's actions was unknown.[43] Upon complaints about the lukewarm attitude, the United States responded, "There is nothing Americans can do about the breach of the Combined Forces Command's rules." Rather, United States officials were concerned over the "possible reaction from North Korea to an apparent rift in South Korea's martial law command."[44] That kind of response, in the view of Koreans, was a green light for military leaders to take power at any time in the future and guaranteed that the United States would remain silent and pay attention only to security matters.

The United States government explained that the Korean Special Forces, which were deployed to Kwangju in May 1980, had never been under General Wickham's command. Only after the general came to know that the forces had been involved did he and Ambassador William Gleysteen arrive at a concurrence permitting the transfer of the well-trained troops of the Republic of Korea's Twentieth Division to restore law and order in Kwangju. Therefore, the United States has explained, it was not responsible for the Kwangju incident.[45]

This may be an accurate statement. But it arouses some critical questions. Why could not this explanation be given when requested in 1980? Why did the explanation appear in the *New York Times* belatedly two years later, in 1982, not on a voluntary basis but as a response to Bruce M. Cumings' criticism of the United States involvement in the Kwangju incident? More than eight years after the incident the National Assembly of Korea organized an investigative committee and agreed to ask then-Ambassador Gleysteen and General Wickham to appear before the investigation hearing. Unfortunately, the United States government refused on July 28, 1988, to receive such a request on the grounds that both witnesses were no longer active United States government officials. A request for American civilians to appear before the Korean Legislative Committee would have to be arranged through formal channels between the two governments.[46]

The American policy of cooptation may be further exemplified by the negative attitudes of United States officials toward opposition leaders and students. General Wickham, for example, was reported to have stated that the Korean people were "like lemmings that follow anyone who becomes their leader and are not ready for democracy." It was contended that his remarks were helpful in General Chun's takeover of governmental power.[47] Richard L. Walker, former American ambas- sador to Korea, called college students in demonstrations "spoiled brats." Inundated by protests from many angry Koreans demanding a public apology for his humiliating remarks, Ambassador Walker grudgingly acknowledged, "I frankly admit that the term 'spoiled brats' was a major mistake."[48] His negative attitude was evidenced by repeated refusals to meet with Kim Dae Jung, Kim Young Sam, Moon Ik Hwan, and Cardinal Kim Soo Hwan. Angered by the offensive remarks, 42 leaders of the Korean Christian Action Organization issued a statement asking President Reagan to recall both General John A. Wickham and Ambassador Richard L. Walker.[49]

Koreans were further disappointed by President Reagan and his cabinet members. Secretary of State George P. Shultz, for example, visiting Seoul on his way home from the Tokyo summit, held a breakfast meeting for Korean leaders. But he did not invite the two most prominent critics of the South Korean government, Kim Dae Jung and Kim Young Sam, on the grounds that they were "not leaders of their party."[50] On his state visit to Korea, President Reagan acted as host at a reception for religious and cultural leaders. Among them several were opponents of President Chun. But none of the South Korean president's more outspoken critics were invited. A United States official stated, "The point here is to speak to a representative group but not upsetting or provocative to our hosts."[51]

The United States has often declared it is politically neutral between the Korean government and the opposition. Assistant Secretary of State Gaston Sigur urged that it would be "Korean efforts that nurture and achieve the open and more consensual political system that all Koreans desire." The United States should not favor either side or interfere in political debates in

Korea.[61] Nevertheless, the American preference for the Korean government and disfavor toward the opposition side seems clear.

During a time of intense confrontation in Korea between the government and opposition leaders on the issue of constitutional amendments to bring about popular election of the president and other democratic reforms, Lee Min Woo, president of the opposition New Korea Democratic party (NKDP), decided to make a four-day visit to the United States. His main objective was to secure support from the United States for the constitutional amendments establishing the Sixth Republic of Korea. He assumed that American officials would still believe in their responsibility to spread democracy abroad. There might be only a few on the staff of President Reagan who were favorable toward the Chun regime, but, he believed, the majority of the American policy makers would certainly endorse the desire of the Korean people for a direct popular election of their president. He also assumed that even those few pro-Chun officials would change their attitudes if they were informed of a ten-million-signature campaign in Korea and the readiness of the Korean people for democracy based on economic growth, high levels of literacy, education, and urbanization. However, he was not enthusiastically welcomed or strongly endorsed by American leaders.

Under the impact of the campaign to collect ten million signatures, the South Korean government began confining over 300 opposition party members, including 80 NKDP members. The government mobilized fifty busloads of police, several armored cars equipped with tear gas dispensers, hundreds of plainclothesmen, and several thousand riot policemen to stop collection of the signatures. American support of the Chun regime and the absence of overt support of popular moves for democratic change were justified by Secretary of State Shultz: "What we would like to see is the continuation of that movement in a stable, orderly way. The way to have change take place is a nonviolent way and violence is not tolerated as a part of the democratic way of changing things."[53]

Robert E. White, former American ambassador to El Salvador and president of the International Center for Development

Policy, deplored the Reagan administration's policy of cooptation. At a crucial time for South Korea, during the campaign for constitutional amendment, he saw the Reagan policy as timid and confused. "The fundamental error of the Reagan Administration in South Korea" was "to identify US power and prestige with the survival of a military regime dedicated to hanging onto power regardless of the people's will."[54]

A.M. Rosenthal, a former executive editor of the *New York Times* asserted that

> those of us who have been graced by being born into freedom, or have settled within its arms, have the obli-gation to support as best we can those who struggle for what we possess and cherish. The enemy is dictatorship, left or right. I believe that, where we have the power to change it, we should. Where we do not have the power, we should draw a moral and judgmental political line between us and tyrants, making this plain to oppressor and oppressed.[55]

He has observed that American foreign policy unfortunately often is seen to "stand behind one tyrant or another." He deplored the fact that "Americans who live and flourish under liberty—writers, intellectuals, politicians, journalists, and scientists—decide that freedom is really not all that important—for others." He admitted, "I find myself still puzzled and pained about why my own country so often does not act as it talks and why many of my countrymen who demand freedom for themselves don't give much of a damn about it for long" in other countries.[56]

The American policy of cooptation protected security interests and secured economic gains by opening Korea more widely to more American goods and services—banking and credit services, insurance, beef, tobacco, American-made large-size cars, contracts for nuclear power plants—in return for the continued support of the authoritarian government. What the Reagan administration might not have perceived accurately was the potential for greater cooperation between the United States and South Korea if and when the latter would establish a democratic government. Only under democracy could more Koreans become more creative, energetic, and active in pursuit of enterprise, trade, and security.

Because of the Reagan administration's deviation from the traditional American approach to promoting and protecting democracy in Korea, anti-Americanism began to emerge in the 1980s. Criticism was expressed not only by rhetoric but by violence, and American facilities in Korea were attacked.

Conclusion: Policy Recommendations

Bruce L. Valley stated that "few people can live a long healthy life in a spiritual vacuum" and that "no society can long survive without a sense of its own national mission."[57] The traditional American mission, recently tarnished by the policy of cooptation, needs to be restored and pursued. Charles W. Bray reminds us of the American national responsibility, inherited from the Founding Fathers and strengthened by civil rights leaders throughout American history.

> It was "liberty." We were to be free men and women above all. Our Declaration of Independence proclaimed that purpose. The Constitution was written to assure it. To be free was more important than to be comfortable; had it been otherwise, our forefathers would not have had to pledge their lives, their fortunes and their sacred honor to the cause. . . .[58]

The thesis that freedom is more important than comfort is witnessed in many developing countries, including South Korea. It is because of their seeking freedom, liberty, and democracy that thousands of Koreans have been put into jail, have lost their jobs, their college degrees, and a comfortable way of life. Hundreds of freedom-fighters in Korea have been physically and mentally tortured and are still suffering. American responsibility is needed now more than at any time in the past. The United States' mission to promote democracy should be pursued not only to dissipate anti-Americanism but also to ensure human freedoms—civil, political, economic, and social. To fulfill its responsibility the United States took an aggressive and energetic approach by its open diplomacy in Korea during the 1950s and 1960s. The increase in strategic importance of South Korea, its economic growth, and the subsequent decrease in dependency were such that during the 1970s the United States began to adopt a policy of quiet diplomacy. Although quiet diplomacy was not so strong and powerful as open diplomacy, it was still effective in influencing the Korean government.

However, since the beginning of the 1980s, the United States has shifted from a policy of quiet diplomacy to one of cooptation. Promotion and protection of democracy became no longer a direct concern of the United States. Opposition politicians and civil rights leaders in Korea were avoided by the American ambassador and other officials. The diplomatic agenda did not address deprivation of basic rights and practices of torture of the Korean government. Instead, the United States was concerned with security matters and the the lowering of Korean tariffs and other trade barriers. The American mission was in fact forgotten amid the immediate security and economic interests. The anti-Americanism prevalent in many foreign countries had long seemed strange to Koreans. Koreans of the 1980s, however, had to resolve a cognitive dissonance between their perception of the American responsibility and the actual policy of cooptation implemented against them in Korea. This anti-Americanism, which had been once inconceivable to Koreans seeking democracy, began to emerge in their hearts and minds.

Let me conclude this paper with a few policy recommendations for the United States to consider implementing.

First, the United States must fully and accurately—though belatedly—explain the American role in the Kwangju incident of 1980 in relation to the Combined Forces Command, on the basis of the 1978 agreement between the United States and Korea.[59] Lack of understanding of the existing command arrangements caused both Koreans and Americans to blindly accuse the United States of complicity. Silence can be no longer tolerated.

Second, during struggles of hundreds of thousands of Koreans—opposition politicians, intellectuals, college students, and ordinary middle-class people—for democratic reforms, leading American newspapers, media, and television continuously speculated on a possible military coup or military intervention in politics. Such speculation merely strengthened the position of the authoritarian government and frustrated those engaged in struggles for democratic reforms. Nevertheless, no explicit and open statement had been announced on the position of the United States government except that a personal letter from President Reagan had been delivered to President Chun. At the last minute, June 29, 1987, a position was announced. As long as the American commanding general is in charge of the Combined Forces in Korea, the United States must be explicit, public, and open in declaring that no Korean troops will be deployed for political purposes without the approval of the commanding general. The United States government must be equally committed to the principle that it will by no means endorse military intervention in politics in Korea. A special task force might be established within the Combined Forces Command responsible to oversee troop mobilization for political purposes.

Third, there is a long way to go before President Roh's June 29 democratic pledges are fully implemented. A large number of political prisoners have not yet been released. Open and/or quiet diplomacy rather than cooptation must be pursued in seeking their freedom. Similar to military and diplomatic matters on which the United States and the South Korean government have had an annual consultation, democratic reforms and the June 29 spirit could be studied and consulted about annually between the two governments—not for the purpose of intervention in South Korea's democratic politics but for recommendations.

Fourth, the United States can play a very important role in helping to inculcate and socialize democratic cultural norms, values, and behaviors among Koreans by means, for example, of showing the films of the American party conventions, campaigns, and elections. American politicians, officials, and scholars—active or retired—are recommended to accept invitations by their Korean counterparts to a series of lecture tours and discussions explaining and emphasizing democratic values such as majority rule, minority protection, civilian control of armed forces, peaceful transfer of power, open and fair competition, political neutrality of government employees in elections, and the importance of interest group politics.

Fifth, the American embassy in Seoul needs to pursue interaction with people in all walks of life in Korea—government officials, opposition parties, students, labor unions, and professionals—so as to become aware of different views and expectations for better understanding and recommendations.

America's most delicate, difficult, and yet important task after the 1988 Summer Olympics was to play a role as an objective, third-party intermediary between the opposition parties and the government. Opposition parties intended to investigate and fully expose wrongdoing of the Fifth Republic on such issues as the Kwangju incident and the alleged corruption of former President Chun and his immediate relatives. Since President Roh and many key members of the administration, the government party, and the military in the Sixth Republic are directly or indirectly related to the Chun administration, full exposure may cause deep humiliation and embarrassment to them. Legislative investigations should be designed primarily to prevent repetition of such wrongdoing in the future and to assure proper compensation without political retaliation to the victims. At the same time, a possible military uprising is a last resort in saving the democratic political system; to prevent this the American role must be wisely played.

Ensuring peaceful transfer of power within constitutional government is the paramount task of the United States in Korea. If this delicate, thorny issue is handled by Koreans themselves, they will be greatly respected and praised. Otherwise American diplomacy used to settle this monumental dispute between government and opposition parties in Korea will be deeply appreciated as a stepping stone for a more solid foundation of democracy in Korea in the future.

Notes

1. Economic and trade frictions involve such controversial issues as market access, intellectual property rights, operations of United States banks and insurance firms in Korea, the scope and extent of the application of the American general system of preference (GSP), the potential for invoking Section 301 of the 1988 Trade Act in order to retaliate against South Korea for its possible failure in meeting United States demands, and revaluation of the Korean currency against the United States dollar. For a detailed analysis of these issues see William H. Cooper, *South Korea and Taiwan: Expanding Trade with the United States*, Issue Brief (Washington, D.C.: Congressional Research Service, 1986); Council on Foreign Relations and Asia Society, *Korea at the Crossroads: Implications for American Policy* (New York: Council on Foreign Relations and the Asia Society, 1987); Larry A. Niksch, *Korea's Political Crisis: Policy Alert*, Congressional Research Service Report 85-523F (Washington, D.C.: Congressional Research Service, June 22, 1987); Bruce Stokes, "Korea: Relations Worsen," *National Journal*, April 5, 1986, 814-19; U.S. Congress, Joint Economic Committee, *The Korean Economy in Congressional Perspective*, 99th Congress, 2nd Session (Washington, D.C.: Government Printing Office, 1986).

2. Military issues include the command structure involving the United States and Korean Combined Forces, representation of South Korea in the armistice talks held thus far exclusively between the United States and North Korea, the size and type of United States forces stationed in Korea, and their military bases and nuclear weapons. For further information on these topics, see Council on Foreign Relations and the Asia Society, *Korea at the Crossroads*; Selig S. Harrison, *The South Korean Political Crisis and American Policy Options* (Washington, D.C.: Washington Institute Press, 1987); Doug Bandow, *Korea: A Case for Disengagement* (Washington, D.C.: Cato Institute, December 1987).

3. Woodrow Wilson, "War Message," 65th Congress 1st Session, Senate Document No. 5 (Washington, D.C.: Government Printing Office, 1971), 3-8.

4. *Congressional Record* 87 (January 6, 1941): 46.

5. Hans J. Morgenthau, *In Defense of the National Interest: A Critical Examination of American Foreign Policy* (Washington, D.C.: University Press of America, 1982), 10.

6. Jeanne Kirkpatrick, "Human Rights and American Foreign Policy," *Commentary*, November 1981.

7. Harry S. Truman, "The Truman Doctrine: Special Message to the Congress on Greece and Turkey, March 12, 1947," *Public Papers of the Presidents of the United States* (Washington, D.C.: Government Printing Office, 1947), 178-79.

8. Jimmy Carter, "Inaugural Address of President Jimmy Carter," *Vital*

Speeches of the Day, vol. 33, February 18, 1977, 258-59.

9. Strategic consideration of the Korean peninsula was by no means excluded in President Truman's decision to defend South Korea. For further information see Harry S. Truman, *Memoirs* (New York: New American Library, 1965).

10. Quoted in Merle Miller, *Plain Speaking: An Oral Biography of Harry Truman* (New York: Berkeley, Medallion, 1974), 286-87.

11. Dean Acheson, "Crisis in Asia—An Examination of U.S. Policy," *Department of State Bulletin* 22 (January 23, 1950), 116.

12. Ibid.

13. Harry S. Truman, *Memoirs: Years of Trial and Hope* (Garden City, NJ: Doubleday, 1956), 333.

14. *New York Times*, July 3, 1958.

15. For further information on the theory and its application to South Korea, see Sung M. Pae, *Testing Democratic Theories in Korea* (Lanham, MD: University Press of America, 1986), Chapter 3.

16. U.S. Congress, Senate Committee on Foreign Relations, 83rd Congress, 1st Session *The United States and the Korean Problem: Documents 1943-1953* (Washington, D.C.: Government Printing Office, 1953), 32.

17. Ibid., February 2, 1950.

18. Ibid., March 27, 1950.

19. Ibid., April 12, 1950

20. Ibid., May 30, 1952.

21. Ibid., May 28, 1952.

22. Ibid., June 3, 1952.

23. Ibid., June 4, 1952

24. Ibid., May 16 and May 25, 1961.

25. Cyrus R. Vance, "U.S. Foreign Policy: Constructive Change," *Vital Speeches of the Day*, vol. 46, (July 1, 1980), 569.

26. George Shultz, "Power and Diplomacy in the 1980s: Facing the Future," Ibid., vol. 50 (May 15, 1985), 450.

27. *New York Times*, May 18, 1974.

28. Ibid., June 14, 1974, and March 19, 1976.

29. Ibid., July 15, 1975.

30. Ibid., August 2, 1975.

31. Ibid., April 17, 1975.

32. Ibid., April 4, 1976, and October 28, 1976.

33. Ibid., July 25, 1974.

34. Ibid., July 17, 1974.

35. Ibid., April 20, 1977.

36. Ibid., July 2, 1977.

37. Samuel P. Huntington, "One Soul at a Time: Political Science and Political Reform," *American Political Science Review* (APSR) 82 (March 1988), 7.

38. For further information on the cultural requisites for democracy see Gabriel Almond and Sidney Verba, *The Civic Culture* (Boston: Little, Brown and Company, 1963).

39. Barry Goldwater, "Mankind's Slow Painful Path," *Vital Speeches of the Day*, vol. 44, (May 15, 1978), 455.

40. Ronald Reagan, "Foreign Affairs: The Need for Leadership," *Vital Speeches of the Day*, vol. 44, (May 1, 1978), 422.

41. *New York Times*, March 3, 1982.

42. Ibid., December 16, 1979.

43. Ibid.

44. Ibid.

45. Ibid., July 6, 1982.

46. *Korean Times*, July 28 and 30, 1988; *Choung Ahng Ilbo*, August 16, 1988.

47. *Los Angeles Times*, August 8, 1980.

48. Dae-Sook Suh, "South Korea in 1981: The First Years of the Fifth Republic," *Asian Survey*, January 1982, 97.

49. *New York Times*, April 25, 1982.

50. Ibid., May 8, 1986.

51. Ibid., November 12, 1983.

52. Ibid., April 3, 1986, and April 18, 1986.

53. Ibid., April 21, 1986.

54. Ibid., March 5, 1985.

55. A.M. Rosenthal, "Journey among Tyrants," *New York Times*, March 23, 1986, 23.

56. Ibid., 25.

57. Bruce L. Valley, "U.S., National Security and Citizens: To Be Reinvolved in Government, *Vital Speeches of the Day*, vol. 50, March 15, 1984, 328.

58. Charles W. Bray, III, "What Do We Value—How Do We Assess It: The Idea Was Liberty,"*Vital Speeches*, 42, No. 4, December 1, 1980, 119.

59. In wartime the United States commander has operational control over all forces assigned to him by the United States and Korea. In peacetime neither the United States nor Korea has the obligation to assign all its forces in Korea to the Combined Forces Command (CFC). Both nations reserve the right to withdraw units assigned to the command. In case of using units assigned to the CFC for domestic purposes, the United States commander shall not prevent Korea from pulling out the forces upon proper notification.

□ 22 □

The Soviet Approach to the Problems of Asian-Pacific Security

And Peaceful Settlement on the Korean Peninsula

Mikhail L. Titarenko

IN 1985, MIKHAIL S. GORBACHEV ELABORATED A PROGRAM of re-structuring, or *perestroika*, of relations among states in the Asian-Pacific region, a vast and rapidly developing part of the globe. With comprehensive study of the lessons of the past and of current realities, and with due consideration of the initiatives and proposals of other countries, including, naturally, those of the socialist countries of Asia, the Soviet leader set forth as top-priority matters the tasks of defusing conflict situations, curbing militarism, and developing international cooperation in the region. To prevent the transformation of the Asian-Pacific region, with its tremendous economic and military potential, into a source of dangerous regional and world contradictions is, in our view, a most important task required for the future. The time has come for all countries in the region to start reasonable and comprehensive interactions based on the search for acceptable ways to improve international relations. In this respect independent scholarly research could play a very important and constructive role.

While setting forth specific proposals, we proceed from the understanding that regional concerns, including the important problem of securing the lengthy eastern borders of the Soviet Union, cannot be solved by the arms race or higher levels of military confrontation. These problems can be solved only by political and economic means, on the basis of principles of peaceful co-existence and the elimination of suspicion and mistrust in interstate relations. While suggesting this, the Soviet Union, as President Gorbachev said, does not seek any benefits for itself or advantages at the cost of others.[1] Today we see some healthy and hopeful developments in the Asian-Pacific region, and we realistically credit the Soviet Union with contributing to these positive changes.

Since the Vladivostok meeting the Soviet Union has carried on negotiations with many countries in the region and top-level and summit talks with some of them. These free and open negotiations, in our view, were a definite contribution to the general *perestroika* of international relations on the basis of modern principles.

Among the positive developments affecting the Asian-Pacific situation, I would name the following:

- Soviet-Indian relations have become a continuous and constructive element with international significance. The New Dehli Declaration outlined principles for achievement of a nonviolent and nuclear-free world. The November 1988 visit of President Gorbachev to India gave a new impetus to the search for mutually acceptable ways of stabilizing the situation in Asia and the development of bilateral relations.
- Better relations with socialist countries, our main partners in foreign policy.
- President Gorbachev's visit to China in May 1989 had reestablished the most friendly relations between the Soviet Union and China after thirty years of strained relationship. Soviet-Chinese relations are reaching a new level of political interaction within the framework of full

independence and respect for each side's commitments to its respective partners. A Soviet-Chinese summit occurred in 1989.

- The Afghan example of settling conflict on the basis of national reconciliation has had a strong impact on Asian-Pacific developments. The Geneva agreements on Afghanistan promoted a search for ways to dismantle other regional conflicts.
- Due to the efforts of Indochina and ASEAN countries, the settlement of the Kampuchean situation is proceeding. The Soviet Union is prepared to contribute in the future to the speediest attainment of agreements on Kampuchea while believing that direct talks between China and Vietnam could play an important role in settling this matter and improving the general situation in Asia. Vietnam has agreed to withdraw its troops from Kampuchea and Prince Sihanonk is back in his homeland to establish a coalition government.
- The situation on the Korean peninsula, though it remains complicated, shows some signs of reduced tensions. The North and the South speak ever more loudly in favor of peaceful reunification and put forward important initiatives aimed at peaceful resolution of the conflict situation.
- The eight-year war between Iran and Iraq has ended.
- Soviet-ASEAN relations are becoming more constructive. We are willing to maintain mutually beneficial and equal relations with all the states of this subregion, whatever their size or social system.
- The peace-keeping role of the United Nations and its secretary general has been heightened in the settlement of conflict situations. The Soviet Union does its utmost to support the reputation and the role of this international organization.
- Willingness on the part of the Non-Aligned Movement (NAM) to take part in the settlement and prevention of regional conflicts has been increased. In our view, the NAM can play an independent positive role in this regard.
- The Soviet-Australian summit is viewed by the Soviet Union as a turning point in its relations with South Pacific states.

- The Soviet Union places importance on the role of Soviet-Japanese relations in the Asian-Pacific region. We are seeking possibilities for interaction with the Japanese in order to surpass the present stagnation in our relations with Japan. We are optimistic that with due political will, farsightedness, and mutual willingness, Soviet-Japanese relations will become more dynamic and be counted among well-balanced bilateral and regional interests. It must be candidly admitted, though, that the Soviet Union cannot be indifferent to any Japanese military buildup or preparation for sharing "the military burden" with the United States; neither are we indifferent to the fact that Japan rejects peaceful overtures of the Soviet Union and other countries like North Korea and China and discriminates and applies sanctions against socialist countries. This is a matter of concern not only for the Soviet Union but for other neighbors (China, Korea, Southeast Asia) of Japan as well.
- The Soviet Union is determined to reach understanding and, possibly, interaction with the United States in resolving the acute problems of the Asian-Pacific region. We recognize the current realities, with due consideration of the United States political and economic interest underlying its important role in regional affairs. The Soviet Union is an opponent of confrontational politics and an ardent advocate of full cooperation and peaceful co-existence.

Regrettably, the United States still voices various cold war policy, suspicions, and mistrust in respect to the peace initiatives proposed by the Soviet Union. We are willing to develop cooperation with the United States, but, as stressed by President Gorbachev, this should be cooperation on an equal footing, without any great-power maneuvering.

The architecture of the Soviet Union's foreign policy in the Asian-Pacific region rests upon the strong belief that reduction of tension, arms, and levels of military confrontation, as well as changes in military policy and the extension of economic cooperation and contacts in all possible fields, is the key to international improvement in the region, as elsewhere in the world.

The Soviet-American treaty on medium- and short-range

missiles, the INF treaty, has given an important impetus to real progress towards nuclear disarmament. It confirmed the reasonability and realism of the Soviet concept of stage-by-stage elimination of nuclear weapons by the end of the twentieth century set forth by President Gorbachev on January 15, 1986. Together with the Stockholm agreements and the Geneva accords on Afghanistan, this treaty was a manifestation of the new political thinking. The Soviet Union is prepared to continue the search for new means of progress in this direction.

Proceeding from the understanding that in our time, when nuclear arsenals threaten the existence of mankind and when no political problems can be solved through military means, the Soviet Union, acting on new political thinking, has proposed specific measures meant to stop nuclear proliferation and buildup and to start negotiations on reducing naval activity, especially that of nuclear-equipped vessels. The Soviet Union stands in favor of reducing conventional armed forces and weapons to the level of reasonable sufficiency, as well as channeling discussions on confidence-building measures and non-use of force in the region into practice. The Soviet program for the Asian-Pacific region seeks regional settlements also. In fact, the Soviet Union invites all states, including the United States, to cooperate in the interests of peace and security.

The Soviet leadership recently put forward some new proposals to promote the cause of Asian security in the Krasnoyarsk address by Mikhail Gorbachev on September 16, 1988.

First, the Soviet Union stated that it would not increase nuclear weapons in the Asian-Pacific region (which has in fact been the case for some time already) and invited the United States and other nuclear powers to follow suit.

Second, the Soviet Union invited consultations on non-buildup of naval forces in the region among major Asian-Pacific powers.

Third, the Soviet Union has proposed multilateral discussions on reduction of military confrontation along the borders of the Soviet Union, the People's Republic of China, Japan, and North and South Korea.

Fourth, the Soviet Union expressed its readiness to dismantle, on agreement with the government of Vietnam, the material and technical naval supply base at Cam Ran Bay, if the

United States will dismantle its military bases in the Philippines.

Fifth, the Soviet Union, in the interests of safe marine and air communications in the region, proposed to jointly develop measures to prevent incidents on the high seas and in the air space over it.

Sixth, in response to the United Nations recommendation the Soviet Union plans to hold an international conference on turning the Indian Ocean into a zone of peace before 1990.

Seventh, the Soviet Union is willing to discuss at any level and with any representatives, the issue of establishing a mechanism for negotiation of any proposals related to Asian-Pacific security, possibly beginning with discussions among the Soviet Union, the People's Republic of China, and the United States as permanent members of the United Nations Security Council.

The Soviet Union is aware of the rapidly increasing environmental pollution in the Asian-Pacific region and proposes to consider forms of regional cooperation in this field. (Special conferences of experts might be one of them.) Other important problems for the Asian-Pacific region also require joint discussions and consideration. In this respect the Krasnoyarsk speech suggested holding a meeting of foreign ministers of all interested countries and specified a Soviet approach to the problem of economic security and cooperation in the region. The Soviet Union has expressed its willingness to join the conference for Asian-Pacific economic cooperation in any capacity acceptable to its members and welcomed the session of this international organization in Osaka. We recognize the fact that we face considerable difficulties in developing foreign economic contacts with the Asian-Pacific countries. Still, we firmly believe that radical economic reform and political *perestroika* in the Soviet Union will produce large-scale and high-quality development of Siberia and the Soviet Far East, which in turn would enable us—of course, with the willingness of our neighbors and more remote states—to develop in this part of Asia mutually beneficial contacts in the spheres of economy, science, technology, and culture.

At present we are already developing appropriate measures taking into account the specifics of our Siberian and Far Eastern regions. For example, it is planned to allow control of direct external economic operations by local enterprises, organizations, and productive cooperatives. Special "zones of joint enterprise" are being established in the Soviet Far East, with most-favored treatment in customs, licensing, and taxes. The possibilities of Sino-Japanese-Soviet economic activities under mutually beneficial conditions are under discussion. The Soviet Union is prepared to negotiate Soviet-Chinese agricultural co-production and joint civil construction in the regions of Amuria and Chita as well as in the Maritime Provinces on the principles of mutuality.

We also believe that the general political improvement on the Korean peninsula opens up good opportunities for contacts with South Korea. In our view, South Korean trade and industrial corporations, with their financial-economic potential and experiences in foreign economic cooperation, could take a mutually beneficial part in the regional development program of Siberia and the Soviet Far East. It should be stressed, though, that we consider possible economic contacts with South Korea not only from the point of view of economic benefit, but also as measures contributing to reduction of tensions on the Korean peninsula and improvement of North-South relations. Progress in Soviet-South Korean contacts will to a considerable extent depend upon the situation on the Korean peninsula and the state of North-South relations.

We suggest that progress in economic cooperation would pave the way for foreign tourism and more extensive people-to-people contacts. The Soviet Union proposes to consider establishing a regional center (with national branches) for cultural communications, so as to contribute to better contacts among scholars, students, and the populations of the various countries.

The Soviet security policy is open for everyone. It does not have any "false bottom." It is supported by specific proposals and ideas aimed at reduction of tensions and arms levels, greater trust, and development of multilateral international contacts and cooperation. This Soviet strategy is fully extended to the Korean peninsula, where the Soviet Union has defense commitments to our ally the DPRK (North Korea), based on our treaty of friendship, cooperation, and mutual assistance of July 6, 1961. The treaty reflects the willingness of our two peoples to strengthen political, economic, and cultural ties as well as mutual defenses.

It is noteworthy that article 1 of the treaty binds the two contracting sides "to take part in all international actions meant to keep peace and security in the Far East and in the entire world" and to "render their contribution to this noble tasks."[2]

At the same time it is necessary to underscore that the current Soviet perspective on the Korean situation takes into account the fact that the conflict was born of the cold war and that confrontational inertia multiplies mistrust and suspicion, psychologically and politically, and tends to perpetuate tension. It is only within the framework of the new political thinking and nonstandard approaches that real progress on the Korean peninsula is attainable.

The Soviet Union is interested in peaceful development on the Korean peninsula and offers its utmost support for the peace initiatives of the DPRK and its constructive proposals on Korean settlement, the more so because they are organically linked with the large-scale Soviet program of peace for the Asian-Pacific region.

In the course of the Moscow summit between Mikhail Gorbachev and Kim Il Sung on October 24, 1986, it was noted that reduction of tensions and normalization on the Korean peninsula—as well as the speediest settlement of the Korean issue—was "an inseparable component for the system of security in the Far East and Asia." The Soviet side fully supports the efforts of the DPRK aimed at the withdrawal of United States forces and nuclear weapons from South Korea, turning the peninsula into a nuclear-free zone and allowing peaceful and democratic reunification without any outside interference.[3]

In his interview with an Indonesian newspaper on July 21, 1987, President Gorbachev stressed again that the Soviet Union "is in solidarity with the policy of DPRK aimed at peaceful reunification of the country and elimination of military tensions. We also understand the willingness of the South Korean population to be rid of foreign forces and military bases as well as nuclear weapons."[4]

The Soviet approach has been clearly expressed in the well-known Vladivostok speech by Mikhail Gorbachev. He said:

> There is a possibility not only for lessening dangerous tensions in the Korean Peninsula but also for starting to move along the road

of solving the national problem of the entire Korean people. As far as Korea's real interests are concerned, there are no sensible reasons for evading a serious dialogue proposed by the Democratic People's Republic of Korea.[5]

Soviet-Chinese normalization is a new and rather important factor that has a favorable impact on the Korean situation. Regrettably, though, this factor has not been properly addressed in academic research thus far. Soviet-Chinese confrontations of the past negatively affected the Korean situation as well as the economic development of the DPRK and raised the latter's concern with its own security. Soviet-Chinese normalization will create a new environment around Korea and become an important factor of stability and progress in the region. It should be stressed that Pyongyang has made an evaluation of the situation and is making more specific and confident efforts in promoting peace in the region.

The government of the DPRK has set itself the task of removing military confrontation from the peninsula and attaining the speediest national reunification. The DPRK leaders understand that realistically Korean reunification is not a simple matter. As Kim Il Sung has noted, there are many difficulties and obstacles on this road.[6] According to Kim, easing of tensions, safeguarding of stability on the Korean peninsula, and creation of favorable conditions for peaceful national reunification are preconditions to reunification. Such are the objectives of all peace initiatives of the government of the DPRK in the recent years.

The DPRK's willingness to achieve detente on the peninsula has been manifested in the unilateral decision not to conduct large-scale military exercises on its territory after February 1, 1986.[7] However, Washington and Seoul chose not to follow suit.

With a view to normalizing the situation on the peninsula, the DPRK proposed a number of new peace initiatives in 1986 and 1987. The DPRK proposed on June 23, 1986, the turning of the Korean peninsula into a nuclear-free peace zone. The statement containing this proposal declared that the DPRK had signed the treaty on nonproliferation of nuclear weapons and faithfully observed all the respective obligations. The government of the DPRK has called upon the United States not to transfer new types of nuclear weapons to South Korea and to withdraw, stage by stage, all nuclear weapons already stationed there. At the same time the DPRK has expressed its readiness not to deploy nuclear weapons on its territory and to start negotiations with Washington and Seoul concerning this matter. This sensible initiative also met with no response on the part of the United States or South Korea.

Other proposals of the DPRK contain concrete and important ideas related to Korean detente.

In November 1987 the leadership of the DPRK put forward a set of proposals that, if implemented, could bring about Korean reunification by 1995. Once again, Pyongyang proposed tripartite negotiations among the DPRK, the United States, and South Korea aimed at stage-by-stage withdrawal of United States forces from the South and reduction of the armed forces of the two Korean sides to 100,000 troops each by the end of 1991. It has also been proposed to pursue military and political negotiations aimed at cessation of major military exercises and joint exercises with foreign participation. Our North Korean friends recognize that the difficulties involved in settling the Korean issue are largely connected with the continued mistrust between the North and the South. At the same time, they understand that to remove this mistrust DPRK-ROK dialogue is not sufficient and it is necessary to hold negotiations with the American side as well. However, the United States persistently rejects any contacts with the DPRK. North Koreans believe that eliminating military and political confrontation is a vital task in settling the Korean problem since it would pave the way to broader contacts and dialogue in other fields, including interparliamentary ties, economic issues, Red Cross contacts, and ultimately an inter-Korean summit.

In 1988, South Korea took steps to improve relations with the North. The Special Declaration by President Roh Tae Woo of July 7, 1988, favored direct North-South trade, diplomatic contacts, and broad exchange of political, social, and religious figures, athletes, journalists, and so on. We welcome the president's intention to resolve the antagonism toward the DPRK, to come to terms with the North as a partner in possible and mutually beneficial negotiations, and to show a new, cooperative approach to inter-Korean relations. A contribution in this respect is the decision taken by the South Korean government to refer to North Korea as the "Democratic People's Republic of Korea" at international conferences and to respect its national flag and anthem. We consider as very meaningful the decision by the South Korean administration on July 19, 1988, to stop criticism of the DPRK and its leaders broadcast over the radiotransmitter located at the DMZ. It is early to say whether these measures will be consistently implemented. Regrettably, South Korea did not propose any new ideas related to the primary task of removing military and political confrontation; neither did it respond to the numerous peace initiatives of the DPRK aimed at easing of tensions and reduction of the level of military confrontation on the peninsula. It should be admitted, though, that the speech of President Roh Tae Woo at the United Nations General Assembly in the fall of 1988 contained a number of new elements showing serious consideration of the problem.

The fact that the South Korean National Assembly agreed to the DPRK proposal of an interparliamentary meeting to discuss and adopt the North-South declaration on non-aggression is welcomed by the Soviet Union. We see it as one of the possible ways to comprehensive peaceful settlement on the peninsula. If the inter-Korean agreement is reached, the Soviet Union could take part in guaranteeing such a peaceful pact. We are in favor of normalization between South and North Korea and are willing to contribute to it by all possible means.

As demonstrated by recent statements of President Roh Tae Woo, leading circles in Seoul also view the continued mutual mistrust between the North and the South as a major impediment to their dialogue. But Seoul suggests a reverse order for settling the issue: beginning with non-political contacts, to open relations with each other, to gain mutual trust, and only then to consider military and political matters. To me, the DPRK's proposals are more logical and more constructive, since removal of mistrust and development of broad contact between the North and the South would be impossible under conditions of military confrontation. Since each side feels deep mistrust about the intentions of its counterpart, primarily in security matters, suspicion must be removed at the very start of the process. The DPRK proposals outline a clear road in this direction: first to withdraw foreign forces and nuclear weapons from South Korea, then to reduce forces of the North and the South to the level of 100,000 troops each, and finally to sign an agreement on peace and nonaggression. What is needed first and foremost is to start negotiations on how to put the process into practice. The problem is in no way simple, but such a means of settlement could be more conducive to stability and security on the peninsula than what has been proposed by United States politicians—that is, the buildup of the military potential of the South to the level of military superiority over the North, and only after that to consider withdrawal of United States forces.

The traditional reliance on force of the United States policy coupled with the well-known peculiarities of the DPRK foreign policy approaches, still influenced by some traditions of national liberation struggle, produces the sharp aggravation of tensions and unpredictable complications for the whole of East Asia. That is why we believe that this region requires implementation of political initiatives with new thinking and consideration of the specific current situation on the peninsula.

The declaration signed by President Gorbachev and President Reagan after their Moscow summit (May 29 to June 1, 1988) notes that the leaders discussed, among other regional conflicts, the situation on the Korean peninsula. Having recognized the serious differences in assessing the causes for regional tensions and the means for resolving them, the two leaders agreed that these differences should not hamper constructive interaction between the Soviet Union and the United States. They confirmed the two sides' intention to continue Soviet-American discussions at all levels, to help the participants in regional conflicts to find peaceful solutions conducive to their independence, freedom, and security.[8]

It was in this spirit that the Soviet-American Symposium on Peace, Security and Cooperation in the Asian-Pacific region held in Alma Ata June 23 to 25, 1988, discussed the situation on the Korean peninsula.

The American side was represented by the delegation from the International Strategic Institute at Stanford headed by its Chairman, Professor John W. Lewis. We were pleased to note that on some issues our views coincided and that could be reflected in a joint document. Specifically, we agreed that the politically unstable and conflict-ridden situation on the Korean peninsula is partly but not exclusively because of the unresolved problems between the two parts of Korea. The international environment would be conducive to an international dialogue if the Soviet Union, the United States, and other major powers of the region could create more favorable conditions for resolving the Korean problem, understanding always that the principal aspects of the problem are internal and must be solved by the two Korean sides themselves.

The joint document on strengthening security and settlement on the Korean peninsula contains some confidence building measures and other proposals. In particular, the American participants recognized it was necessary to address the issue of nuclear weapons, apart from the levels of conventional armed forces deployed in the North and the South. In this context the document says that if an agreement to withdraw nuclear weapons were achieved, nuclear weapons in the future would not be stationed in either North or South Korea, and "all nuclear powers concerned with Korea should join in providing appropriate guarantees to this effect." The United States also agreed to include in the document the issue of limiting transfers of armaments into Korea and the indigenous production of weapons.

The joint document also says that "Korean reunification is an internal affair of the Korean nation"; the Soviet Union and the United States should pursue a joint course of action directed at eliminating the explosive situation in Korea by reducing the level of military and political confrontation there and by transforming the military truce into a stable peace. It also says that the United States and the Soviet Union should work to gain the support of other interested nations for such a course of action, and that a conference of foreign ministers of the governments concerned could consider the arrangements agreed to as a result of bilateral negotiations; such a conference could also consider long-term international guarantees of peace and stability in Korea. (See the Appendix: "On Strengthening Security and Developing Cooperation on the Korean Peninsula.")

The United States forces stationed in South Korea provide ample evidence of the difference between Soviet and American approaches to the Korean issue. This circumstance also determines the measure of responsibility of our two countries with respect to developments on the Korean peninsula.

The United States military presence in South Korea has been unchanged since the end of the Korean War in 1953. The United States is in command of South Korean armed forces and represents the South Korean side in the Military Commission for Armistice Agreements, while South Koreans are represented in an observer capacity.

Due to its position, Seoul is constrained to avoid discussion of military issues with the DPRK and to block the latter's calls for tripartite conferences (among the United States, the DPRK, and South Korea) to replace the armistice agreement with a peace treaty. The Korean settlement obviously depends more on the United States than on the Soviet Union. Nevertheless, our side has expressed the understanding that improvement and better understanding between the Soviet Union and the United States would contribute to stability and peace on the Korean peninsula and in the entire Asian-Pacific region.

The joint document on security and settlement on the Korean peninsula, in our view, reflects the willingness of Soviet and American participants at the Alma Ata symposium to draw these proposals to the attention of scholars and policy makers in the interested countries and to invite them to build upon the concepts embodied in the document so as to improve the situation on the Korean peninsula.

Easing of tensions and consolidation of peace on the Korean peninsula would no doubt depend upon the international situation as a whole and on the relations among the interested powers—the Soviet Union, the United States, China, and Japan. We see favorable developments in this context. The independent policy of the People's Republic of China assists in easing the tensions on the peninsula. Japanese political circles are also rather active in their willingness to mediate among the concerned powers and the two Korean leaders. As for Soviet-American relations, they are also showing some hopeful changes in many areas, including regional conflict settlements. We are deeply convinced that better Soviet-American relations and understanding would help to promote the Korean settlement and improve the situation in the region as a whole.

In our view, the above analysis suggests consideration of the following proposals:

1. The leaders of both parts of Korea should admit that their objective are to attain peaceful and democratic reunification of the two Koreas without any outside interference; to respect the socio-political and economic systems preferred by the people in each part of Korea; to attain firm international guarantees of peace and security under the auspices of the United Nations. They should also agree that neither side would try to interfere in the internal affairs or change the existing system of the other.

2. To overcome the accumulated mutual mistrust and suspicion, both sides would proclaim the universal principles of relations embodied in the United Nations charter, that is, principles of peaceful co-existence as a basis for relations between the North and the South of Korea. At the same time the Democratic People's Republic of Korea and the Republic of Korea, in the course of their bilateral summit conference, would elaborate and sign a nonaggression treaty.

3. All countries that are contiguous to the Korean peninsula or have their interests there would apply maximum effort to the creation of favorable international conditions conducive to development of contacts between the two parts of Korea as well as to reduction of tensions and levels of military confrontation.

4. The international community would support the proposals on mutual stage-by-stage reduction of armed forces of the DPRK and ROK to 100,000 troops, each while the United States forces and nuclear weapons would be fully withdrawn from South Korea. The peninsula would be turned into a nuclear-free zone under the United Nations, with strict international verification.

5. The Republic of Korea, the United States, and Japan, as well as other countries whose forces took part in the Korean War under the United Nations flag, would render economic assistance to modernize the DPRK's civil economy and develop mutually beneficial contacts with the DPRK

in the fields of trade, economy, science and technology, and so on.

6. With full respect for the interests and positions of both Korean sides, it would be possible to address such measures as considerable expansion of the demilitarized zone between the North and the South and a firm guaranteed pledge of both sides to refrain from military activities, including exercises, in the areas adjacent to the DMZ. Having considered the specific situation, the two sides could agree upon the width of such an area and establishment of special economic zones in this area and the adjacent territories, with favorable conditions for foreign investments and joint ventures.

Appendix

On Strengthening Security and Developing Cooperation on the Korean Peninsula

Joint proposals of the International Strategic Institute at Stanford University and the Institute of Far Eastern Studies, Academy of Sciences of the USSR

Introduction

In Asia and the Pacific the major issues, which in most respects differ markedly from place to place, tend to have one thing in common: Their settlement requires the support and cooperation of the United States and the Soviet Union and of other major Asian-Pacific powers. Success in settling individual conflict situations, painful though the process may be, almost certainly will lead to a healthier international environment in Asia and to more-constructive interaction among the major powers. In the case of such U.S.-Soviet cooperation, the experience could contribute to a new pattern of Soviet-American relations and, in some instances, to a new pattern of relations between the major socioeconomic systems in the Asian-Pacific region. Korea may be such an instance.

The Korean Peninsula is one of the areas of acute political instability and conflict in the Asian-Pacific region. This is partly but not exclusively because of the unsettled problems between the two parts of Korea. The international environment could be more conducive to an inter-Korean dialogue, to national reconciliation, and to reunification. Without interfering in the internal affairs of the Korean nation, the United States and the Soviet Union, and other major powers of the region, could create more-favorable conditions for settling the Korean problem, understanding always that the principal aspects of the problem are internal and must be solved by the two Korean states themselves.

The Soviet-American Dialogue

At the end of their Moscow summit meeting, May 29–June 1, 1988, President Reagan and General Secretary Gorbachev issued a statement, which said that the question of the Korean Peninsula was among the regional questions that they had discussed. In this context they spoke of "serious differences both in the assessments of the causes of regional tensions and in the means to overcome them." They agreed, however, that these differences need not be an obstacle to constructive interaction between the United States and the USSR. The two leaders "reaffirmed their intention to continue U.S.-Soviet discussions at all levels aimed at helping parties to regional conflicts find peaceful solutions which advance their independence, freedom, and security."

It was in this spirit that the Soviet-American Symposium on Peace, Security, and Cooperation in the Asian-Pacific Region, held at Alma Ata, June 23–25, 1988, discussed the situation on the Korean Peninsula. The participants in the symposium considered how the ideas that they had incorporated in the Program for Strengthening Security and Reducing the Risk of War in the Asian-Pacific Region could be applied and given greater specificity in the particular conditions existing on the Korean Peninsula. They recalled and stressed in their discussions their agreed conceptual approach to confidence-building measures: "Confidence-building measures should reduce the possibility of armed conflict and pave the way for a balanced reduction of offensive forces, particularly in zones of acute military confrontation...A program of confidence-building measures, in sum, should serve not only a serious security purpose but also, for those countries taking part in the program, a concrete political purpose, that of moving from a stance that may be starkly confrontational to a relationship that is more cooperative and open. Thus, a process of dialogue and accommodation may begin—a process that may impart more dynamism to bilateral relationships and that may lead in time to a positive evolution of political and economic as well as security relationships on a broad basis."*

The participants in the Soviet-American symposium expressed their view that the United States and the USSR may be in a position to take parallel, coordinated actions to resolve some international aspects of the Korean problem. This would promote a dialogue between the governments in Korea, representing, as they do, two different systems within a single nation. The Soviet and the American participants in the Alma Ata symposium considered that a new pattern of intersystem relations in and around Korea would promote peace and stability on the Peninsula and encourage steps toward reunification of Korea. They stressed, however, that Korean reunification is an internal affair of the Korean nation.

Joint Policies Aimed at Strengthening Security and Reducing the Risk of War on the Korean Peninsula

The application of the foregoing principles in the effort to put the discussion of confidence-building measures in the Asian-Pacific region on a practical footing suggests the following conclusions:

The United States and the USSR should pursue a joint course of action

---

* A Program for Strengthening Security and Reducing the Risk of War in the Asian-Pacific Region (Stanford, 1987), 3–4.

directed at eliminating the explosive situation in Korea by ending the political confrontation there, by reducing the level of military confrontation, and by transforming the military truce into a stable peace. They should strongly support the peaceful reunification of the Korean people by encouraging the two parts of the country to normalize their relations, establish contacts and ties, and move toward a gradual rapprochement. This process should include more-normal trade and cultural interaction with the international community on the part of both North and South. The United States and the USSR thus should support efforts by either Korean government that would begin a process of reducing tensions and normalizing conditions on the Peninsula; for, in the final analysis, the Koreans themselves must be responsible for creating the spirit and the mechanisms that can lead to the peaceful reunification of the Korean nation. The United States and the USSR should work to gain the support of other interested nations for such a course of action, specifically the People's Republic of China and Japan.

Short-Term Actions and the Process of Rapprochement

The United States and the Soviet Union should encourage a program for establishing confidence in Korea, while recognizing that such confidence-building measures are essentially matters for the North and South Koreans to propose, discuss, and decide. These actions could include measures as basic as making human contacts and also measures that are political in nature. The fundamental purpose would be establish the fact that there might be more concrete and substantial matters to discuss. The first steps, intended to lead to more comprehensive negotiations, could be the following:

- Periodic meetings with an open agenda between officials who are the equivalent of ministers for reunification in North and South Korea or other senior governmental officials
- Renunciation of the threat or use of force, as codified in the United Nations Charter, and a pledge of noninterference in each other's internal affairs
- Cooperation on the basis of respect, independence, and mutual benefit, including the effort to solve all their disputes and differences through peaceful means
- A commitment to establish special bilateral channels to permit the discussion and resolution of all differences
- An upgrading of telecommunication links between Seoul and Pyongyang

The list is intended only to suggest the nature of the first confidence-building steps that would encourage the process of rapprochement. The precise content, form, and conditions of such measures obviously must be determined by the North and the South in discussions together.

Measures Appropriate to a Risk-Reduction Regime

A program of short-term measures could be accompanies by, or at least lead directly and promptly to, the negotiation and implementation of measures that would deal with some of the sources of tension and reduce the risk of armed conflict on the Korean Peninsula. For this purpose, certain measures adapted from the program of confidence-building measures set forth in the Stockholm Document of September 1986 would be suitable as a basis for discussion between those states whose forces are deployed on the Korean Peninsula.* Naturally, the specifics of these measures would have to be adapted to circumstances existing in Korea.

If discussions ultimately lead to some agreed arrangements-bilateral or otherwise—these could be consolidated in a document that might affect or at least be relevant to several of the principal actors in Northeast Asia. A conference of foreign ministers of the governments concerned could approve, take cognizance of, or put into effect measures agreed to as a result of various types of negotiations. Such a conference also could consider long-term international guarantees of peace and stability in Korea.

Measures to Limit or Reduce Military Confrontation

The intensity of the military confrontation in Korea could be further reduced if certain other measures affecting the levels of armed forces and their weapons were adopted. The Demilitarized Zone (DMZ) on the Korean Peninsula offers special challenges and opportunities in terms of first steps toward reducing the military confrontation. A first item on the agenda for limiting and reducing levels of forces, therefore, should deal with the question of what can be done to make the DMZ and its environs less prone to tension and conflict.

The level of forces of the North and the South throughout the Korean Peninsula should be a subject of negotiation, as should the overall level of foreign armed forces in Korea. Experience in Europe suggests that ground combat units and certain types of equipment should be the elements to be specified in an arms reduction agreement. For example, tanks and artillery and the units to which such equipment is assigned might be the subject of negotiations. This, of course, is a complex matter, which would need to be studied quite carefully in terms of the types and levels of equipment to be included in any reductions.

Nuclear weapons also should be addressed. If an agreement to withdraw nuclear weapons were achieved, such an agreement would provide that

---

* See a Program for Strengthening Security and Reducing the Risk of War in the Asian-Pacific Region, 4–5.

nuclear weapons, in the future, would not be stationed in either North or South Korea. All nuclear powers concerned with Korea should join in providing appropriate guarantees to this effect.

In addition to limiting the levels and types of forces that would be the subject of an agreement, it would be necessary to limit the transfers of armaments into Korea and the levels and types of weapons that could be indigenouosly produced. For example, if it were possible to reach an accord on the numbers of tanks allowed on the Korean Peninsula, there would have to be an understanding among any future suppliers of such tanks that the limits would not be exceeded. If it were agreed to reduce or to some extent to eliminate specific types of equipment, defense industries that produce such equipment would be limited in output, converted to other types of production, or dismantled.

Long-Term Political Objectives

The proposals outlined in this paper are aimed at peaceful change leading to the resumption of normal and natural human and state relationships among all parts of Northeast Asia. The Korean Peninsula offers a prime example of a people culturally, linguistically, and ethnically united for centuries but now tragically divided into two hostile parts. A program of the type described in this report, if fully supported by the two Korean sides and the major powers of the region, could create the conditions necessary for purposeful discussion of longer-term political objectives, including reunification, and for the progressive solution of current political problems. Furthermore, the implementation in a carefully calculated sequence of steps of the measures set out in this document could serve the interests of each of the major powers. The reduction of tensions in Korea and the strengthening of peace and security there would make it easier to resolve other security problems in the area.

Such are the longer-term possibilities of even the most tentative beginnings of discussions regarding stability, security, and cooperation in Northeast Asia.

Moscow
June 29, 1988

Notes

1. See *Pravda,* June 4, 1988.
2. *Othnosheniya Sovetskogo Soyuza s narodnoi Koreei* (The Soviet Union's relations with the people's Korea). Moscow, 1981, 196–97.
3. *Pravda,* October 25, 1986.
4. *Pravda,* July 23, 1987.
5. See *Far Eastern Affairs,* 1987, 19.
6. Kim Il Sung, Interview with the editor-in-chief of *Sekai* magazine, Pyongyang, 1985, 31 (in Russian).
7. See *Rodong Shinmun,* January 12, 1986.
8. *Pravda,* June 2, 1988.

23

Prospects for Peace and Arms Control

General R.G. Stilwell, USA (Ret.)

THE INTERDEPENDENCE OF PEACE and arms control agreements implies that peace *can be* assured by conventions regulating armaments. The twentieth-century history of this troubled world demonstrates that this is a flawed premise. Arms are neutral, neither pro- nor anti-peace. Each nation, big or small, has the sovereign right to maintain such military capability as it deems prudent to safeguard its population and institutions, ensure the integrity of its land, its airspace, and its territorial seas—and, *in extremis*, to reinforce agencies charged with the maintenance of domestic law and order. Peaceful relations among nations are threatened—or shattered—when any nation's political agenda includes employment of its military forces—in direct violation of the UN charter—external to its boundaries in order to impose its will on a neighboring state. This is not to say that verifiable arms control agreements make no contribution to the state of equilibrium called peace. They can—and sometimes do. But they are of peripheral importance unless and until they are preceded or accompanied by compelling evidence that the parties have forsworn expansionist goals, are in strict compliance with the regimen of international law, and are full and open participants in world affairs.

The North Korean armed forces outgun those of South Korea in every dimension of military power. Yet this quantitative imbalance is not the principal source of concern in Seoul or Washington or Tokyo. It is, rather, the stance of those North Korean armed forces and the long-established national objectives that the stance reflects.

- North Korean combat power is concentrated immediately north (and, indeed, encroaches in the northern half) of the Military Demarcation Zone (DMZ); and it is postured not for defense but for offense. While I was in command of the forces responsible for the defense of South Korea, I reckoned we would be fortunate to have even twelve hours warning of large-scale attack.
- Compounding this situation are the extremes to which the North Korean regime has gone to instill aggressive attitudes in not only its armed forces but in the entire population of twenty million. That body politic is mobilized for war. The most closed and secretive society on the face of this earth has deprived its people of any and all external information sources and ensured, by control of all media, that truth is what the government promulgates as truth. For example, the truth is that the Republic of Korea and the United States invaded North Korea on June 25, 1950; the truth is that the United States and South Korean forces are still poised to overrun North Korea; the truth is that the XXIV Olympiad was not, in fact, held; the truth is that the North Koreans have a better standard of living than South Koreans; the truth is that the overwhelming majority of the forty million South Koreans would joyously opt for the North Korean political, social, and economic systems were forcible restraints removed. I recall a Danish shipping executive's telling me that the harbor-master, a Communist party member, in the northeast port of Chongjin lamented the total absence of any nongovernmental information and expressed his willingness to put his life and career on the line for just *one* Western novel, which he could smuggle off a ship, page by page.

- The North Korean regime has succeeded to a degree unparalleled in world history in imposing total thought control on an entire population, for a full generation, by a combination of control over every information outlet and total denial of foreign travel for its citizenry. It is a feat which would merit admiration were the implications not so insidious.
- Finally—and overarching all—is the incessantly reiterated determination of the Great Leader, Kim Il Sung, to reunify the Korean nation under his aegis, by any means fair or foul. The record is earnest of that intent: the commando raids of the 1960s, clandestine forays of elite special forces detachments which continue to this day; the assassination of President Park Chung Hee's wife; the tunnels, so laboriously constructed, running under the DMZ; the bombing in Rangoon which decimated the South Korean cabinet; the destruction, with frightful loss of life, of the Korean airliner over the Andaman Sea.

This, then, is the powder keg: an all-powerful Kim Il Sung obsessed with achieving reunification of the Korean people, on his terms, during his lifetime or, failing that, during that of his similarly motivated son and heir apparent; twenty million North Koreans so effectively brainwashed as to be incapable of dissent, and thus totally at his beck and call; and a formidable array of military power imbued with fanaticism and poised for surprise attack.

Given this posture, it is not surprising that Kim Il Sung has consistently rejected any phased approach to rapprochement and thus the alleviation of the tensions that have characterized the past four decades. He has instead demanded that the very first step be the establishment of a super government—the so-called "Democratic Confederated Republic of Koryo" (DCRK)—which would leave the two political social and economic structures in place but would promulgate foreign policy and be backed by a single army. I ask you, how can a single army be drawn from two populations, totally different ideologically, one from the other?

The conventional wisdom is that there is virtually no prospect for perceptible change in the internal and external policies

long as the Great Leader is at the helm. I
,꞊r challenging this widely-held view. Yet it would
..at even Kim Il Sung cannot remain totally immune to
..ꞓ pace and extent of developments afoot on the international
scene. One principal ally, the Soviet Union, has renounced the
tenets of Marxist-Leninism; and the People's Republic of China
is moving away from a command economy. Both allies have
relaxed barriers to egress for their own citizens as well as
ingress for foreign travelers; and improved Sino-Soviet relations have decreased North Korean leverage in playing one off
against the other. Moreover, both are drawing closer to South
Korea politically, economically and culturally. So, too, are the
erstwhile communist nations of Eastern Europe. Meanwhile,
South Korea has steadily enhanced its international reputation
through the successful hosting of the XXIV Olympiad, its
substantial forward progress in democratization and its continuing economic achievements. Certainly the sum total of
these developments should, at least slightly, affect the calculus
of Kim Il Sung and his lieutenants if—as one must assume—
they have the future interests of their nation at heart.

There are two concrete and doable steps that could be taken
right now. One is conditioning, one political; and both are
consistent with the long-range goal of eventually uniting a
homogeneous people with a 5,000-year history. The conditioning step—which is absolutely indispensable—is the essence of
President Roh's six-point plan. It would require a gradual
opening of North Korean borders to permit its citizens, on a
steadily increasing basis, to travel and gain some familiarity
with the world around them, for right now they are like aliens
in the rest of the world. China has found this liberalization
essential to its growth; so, too, has the Soviet Union. Family
visits are now being allowed between the Chinese mainland and
Taiwan. We have been witness to this for some twenty years
across the intra-German zoned boundary. It might even be
helpful if Kim Il Sung were to spend a week in the Big Apple!
He may be omnipotent; but he is abysmally ignorant of many
facts of international life. The average North Korean citizen
has an even more deficient view. Mikhail Gorbachev had some
encouraging words to say at the United Nations on the subject.
He said that preservation of a closed society was no longer

possible, that freedom of choice was a principle that should allow no exception, that nation-states must freely exchange ideas and maintain open dialogue if the world's problems were to be solved. The challenge to the Soviet Union is to convince North Korea that these principles must be accepted.

Concurrent with this basic preparatory step, it would be highly beneficial to proceed with phased implementation of several interrelated international actions, long proposed and still valid. These involve:

1. Endowing the Military Demarcation Line with juridical status as the internationally recognized common boundary of North and South Korea (as the Helsinki conference did for the interzonal German boundary)
2. Admission of North and South Korea to United Nations membership jointly
3. Abrogation of the 1953 Armistice Agreement and dissolution of the United Nations Command in Korea
4. Cross-recognition of Seoul and Pyongyang by the Soviet Union and China, and Japan and the United States, respectively

As was the case of the two Germanys, these steps are in no way prejudicial to ultimate reunification; and their merits are clear. Both states would enjoy the benefits and the obligations of United Nations membership, the integrity of their internationally recognized territorial limits would be implicitly guaranteed by the great powers, and both states would be free to pursue international competition as something other than a zero-sum game. Unless the two Koreas decided otherwise, there would be no requirement to abrogate or otherwise modify any of their existent treaty arrangements.

Arms control could also contribute to peninsular stability. One would logically start with a series of measures commonly called "confidence building."

I don't know about Pyongyang, but any steps to reduce the possibility of surprise attack would be warmly supported by Seoul. With only two kilometers of separation between the two Koreas and upwards of a million men in close confrontation, that danger is ever present. I would suggest that the two Koreas agree that except for mobile patrols of specified size, no military forces, installations, fortifications, or barriers be permitted within ten kilometers of their common boundary, and that all installations presently there be demolished and so verified by United Nations-appointed observers. The current Neutral Nations Supervisory Commission (composed of Polish, Czech, Swiss, and Swedish representatives), re-mandated as an agency of the Security Council, could perform that role. All of this would be in the context of initiation of legal cross-border movement—of mail, services, trade, and individual travelers.

Exchange of observers at military exercises, long proposed by the United States and the Republic of Korea, should be initiated. As mutual trust deepens between Pyongyang and Seoul, a very large number of practical, confidence-building measures can be instituted.

One can also consider force reductions. We struggled many years in Vienna, throughout the Mutual and Balanced Force Reductions negotiations, to find mutually agreeable and equitable bases for such reductions. The aim, of course, was to achieve a stable balance, which almost inevitably requires asymmetrical reduction.

The North Koreans would like us to believe that a year ago they unilaterally reduced by a hundred thousand men as a gesture of good will. This must have been done with mirrors— or, perhaps, by diverting that many soldiers, pro tem, from normal military duties to improving the road from Kaesong to Pyongyang as fraudulent evidence of a never-intended participation in the Olympic Games.

In my view, deep reductions in the armed strength of both North and South Korea would be facilitated by the maintenance of their separate treaty arrangements—to the extent that Seoul and Pyongyang continued to have confidence that treaty commitments would be honored on either side. If one accepts, as I do, that the immutable geographic location of the Korean peninsula makes neutrality absurd, then one must accept the corollary premise that no conflict on the peninsula can be totally isolated and that therefore any such conflict would inevitably involve a wider war. On the one hand, North Korea adjoins the Soviet Union; and on the other, South Korea is linked to the defense of Japan. It is therefore clear that stability in that region would be enhanced if neither North nor South

Korea had the capacity to invade its neighbor.

However, the concept of making the Korean peninsula a nuclear-free zone (as periodically advanced by Pyongyang) is devoid of reality and has propagandistic value only. As is true of Japan, the security of the Republic of Korea is linked to the deterrent strength of the United States nuclear umbrella. To ensure the effectiveness of that deterrent, Pyongyang must always have the perception that American nuclear weapons— wherever based—have the capability to engage targets on an aggressor's soil. On its part, the Soviet Union has an abundance of weapons which are also capable of being targeted against the Korean peninsula; and if one could conceive the incredible scenario of a mad South Korean president and equally mad United States president launching a devastating attack against North Korea, one would expect the Soviet Union to employ nuclear weapons if necessary to prevent the extinction of a communist ally. In short, one must always look at nuclear and conventional armaments and the control thereof not separately but in context. Both must be subordinated to the goal of ensuring stable and enduring political arrangements between nation-states.

In summary, my instincts tell me that the prospects for improving the uneasy peace on the Korean peninsula are better than they have been at any time since 1953. I recognize the danger of using occidental logic in assessing the probable thought processes of Asian communists. Nonetheless, the developments I referred to at the outset cannot but have had a real impact on the leadership in Pyongyang. So, the ball is now in Kim Il Sung's court, and we must hope that his next move is in the right direction.

24

Fine-Tuning in U.S. Policy Can Avert Wrenching Break With Korea

Stephen J. Solarz *

AS WE MOVE INTO THE 1990S, the time has come for a review of American policy toward the Korean peninsula. Indeed, the easing of restrictions on contact with North Korea announced by the State Department some time ago suggests that a reexamination of United States policy toward Pyongyang is already well under way.

The dramatic progress toward democracy that South Korea has achieved in the past several years suggests that our policy toward Seoul deserves a fresh look as well. Clearly the old mentor-pupil relationship between Washington and South Korea is no longer appropriate. A prudent accommodation by Washington of growing nationalist sensibilities in Seoul now

---

* Rep. Stephen J. Solarz is chairman of the Asian and Pacific Affairs subcommittee of the House Foreign Affairs Committee.

can avoid a much more wrenching break between our two countries in the future.

One indication of the need for change is the disturbing growth of anti-American sentiment in South Korea beyond a small group of radical students where it has festered for a number of years. Ironically, this new anti-Americanism has been facilitated by the growth of democracy, since it is now far easier to voice such sentiments than when the government tightly controlled political expression.

At the same time, we must avoid exaggerating the extent of anti-Americanism in Korean society. The overwhelming majority of Koreans remain friendly and sympathetic to the United States, for they recognize the important contribution we make to the preservation of peace and the promotion of prosperity in their country.

We now need to adjust our relations with Seoul in ways that will remove gratuitous frictions that only exacerbate these anti-American tendencies. If not dealt with appropriately and expeditiously, these manifestations of hostility toward the United States may create a real backlash here in America that could poison the relationship between our two countries. And a breakdown in this relationship would not only increase the prospects for another war but could have unfortunate economic consequences for both countries as well.

There are a number of steps we could constructively take to head off such a breach. Discussions are already under way, for instance, that could result in shifting command of the United Nations forces in South Korea to a South Korean general. For forty years, ever since the UN Security Council dispatched an international force to the Korean peninsula to defend South Korea from the aggression of its northern sister state, an American general has directed all UN troops in Korea. Today there are approximately 600,000 South Korean troops under UN command, compared to 43,000 American troops. Given this disparity, it is easy to understand why South Koreans resent having a foreigner in seemingly perpetual command of their armed forces. It should be possible to adjust the command relationships in ways that are responsive to Korean sensitivities without diminishing the credibility of the American defense commitment.

We also should press ahead in the current talks with South Korea about relocating U.S. Army headquarters out of Seoul into a less populated part of the country. For many South Koreans, the presence in the midst of some of Seoul's priciest real estate of the headquarters complex, complete with an extensive golf course for the use of American troops, is a running political and nationalistic sore. Given the opportunity to reclaim this land, Seoul should be willing to pick up much of the cost associated with the move.

In order to head off South Korea's nascent anti-nuclear movement before it grows to significant proportions, the United States could also remove any nuclear weapons that it may have in the country. Senior United States military officials privately concede that they can imagine no conceivable scenario in which they would use nuclear weapons in Korea. It stands to reason, then, that since these weapons perform no useful purpose, their removal would not diminish our defense posture. Yet it would enhance our political position.

Some of the student radicals, echoing pronouncements from Pyongyang, have gone a step further and called for the withdrawal of all American forces from the Korean peninsula. But such a step under existing circumstances would be ill advised and ill timed.

The Korean peninsula remains a potential flash point for the kind of confrontation that could lead to a global conflict. Today there are nearly 1.5 million men under arms on both sides of the 38th parallel. In the North, a militant communist ideology and a demonstrated willingness to employ brutal terrorist tactics provide the ingredients for continued instability.

So long as North Korea enjoys significant advantages in manpower and materiel, it would be a mistake to pull out American forces, particularly in the absence of any real progress toward the diminution of tensions on the peninsula.

It bears noting, moreover, that the vast majority of the South Korean people find reassuring the tangible commitment to their security our troops offer. They rightly recognize that a premature United States withdrawal could significantly diminish South Korea's capability to deter another act of aggression such as Pyongyang unleashed in 1950, thereby bringing on the very war they wish to avoid.

In view of the deeply rooted desire for reunification shared by virtually all Koreans, it is also essential that the United States continually reaffirm its commitment to the peaceful rejoining of the two Koreas. We must ensure that the Korean people see America's presence and American policies not as a portent of perpetual division, but as the surest means of preventing another war and establishing the conditions under which ultimate reunification can peacefully take place.

The relationship between the United States and South Korea has contributed to peace on the Korean peninsula and stability in the region for a third of a century. It is in our interests to maintain and even enhance it. But changes have taken place on the peninsula, and especially in South Korea, that ought to be reflected in our foreign policy. We do not need dramatic policy shifts, just the fine-tuning that will carry Korean-American relations on a smooth course into the 21st century.

25

The Two Koreas' Unification Policies and Neutralization of the Korean Peninsula

In Kwan Hwang

Introduction

THE PROBLEM OF THE CURRENT KOREAN IMPASSE in its reunification efforts is analogous to the dual key system which is used to control the launch of nuclear missiles; that is, nothing happens unless both operators agree to turn their keys simultaneously. The question of peaceful Korean reunification is, first and foremost, the responsibility and duty of the two Korean states. It will never happen unless both Koreas are ready and willing to cooperate with each other; it will never be a one-way street for either side, or a win-lose proposition. However, it might be that neither Pyongyang nor Seoul wants a unified Korea. They may be too committed to the past to start anew. The only way to find out is through serious talks. Failing that, only a dark future will remain. Psychologically and intellectually, it is not easy for the two Koreas to cooperate, but there is simply no other choice if their goal is peaceful reunification.

The logic is too simple to need an elaborate explanation: it takes two to reunify.

In addition, peaceful Korean reunification will not be achievable unless the four external powers involved (the United States, the Soviet Union, China, and Japan), all of which have security interests in the divided peninsula, can agree on a framework for unifying Korea without threatening their own security interests. In other words, reunification has to take place in such a way that its end-product, a reunited Korea, does not pose a threat to any of the four powers; otherwise the vulnerable power will oppose reunification. The Korean War already taught that lesson to us.

Viewed in this light, it becomes increasingly clear that a workable reunification formula must include procedures and outcomes that will be beneficial and fair not only to the two Koreas but also to the four external powers. Can we find such a broad formula? It is my considered judgment that the statecraft of permanent neutrality (neutralization), which has succeeded in preserving Swiss unity and independence since 1815 and Austrian statehood since 1955, some failures notwithstanding, would be the most likely alternative to a divided Korea. Neutrality could be used as a protective political umbrella for the two Koreas as well as benefiting the four external powers. Under such a plan each Korea could negotiate its reassociation without fear of being "eaten" by the other, and the four powers could disengage themselves from the peninsula without fear that the balance of power in the region was being tipped against any of them—but was in fact benefiting all of them, as a neutralized Korea would also neutralize their own conflicts. No external powers want war on the peninsula.

It is against this background that the following pages will review briefly the two Korea's unification policies and will propose a synthesis of the two and some points of departure for United States policy with regard to the question of Korean reunification. It is long overdue for the United States to begin a search for new strategies aimed at peaceful reunification. The focus of a policy recommendation for the United States will be on the feasibility of converting the removal of United States forces from South Korea into a stepping stone toward a neutralized and unified Korea. As a policy guide, two model draft treaties, one for the two Koreas and one for six powers (the four external powers along with the two Koreas) are presented in this paper to stimulate debate.

Two Koreas' Unification Policies

In reviewing the two sets of Korean unification proposals, we find a fundamental flaw in the process of their formulation. All of them except the joint communiqué of July 4, 1972, were made unilaterally, without consulting the other side in Pyong-yang or Seoul, and were sought to be imposed by one side upon the other for propaganda purposes. Thus, every unilateral unification initiative from one half of Korea has been perceived by the other half as a plot and was approached with a zero-sum game attitude. This absence of mutuality is one of the major reasons that there is no progress toward national unity. For instance, it is impossible to conclude the INF treaty between the Soviet Union and the United States unilaterally, without bilateral, negotiated agreements between them.

Today, each half of Korea is still searching for a strategy of victory over the other. Each side, claiming to be the sole legal government of the entire Korea, regards the other's existence as unnatural or illegal, historically unjustified, and a fiction or fraud promulgated by a foreign power. The resistance of one Korea to negotiation with the other as an equal seems rooted in the view that national reunification cannot be shared because reunification achieved by the other side is tantamount to the destruction of its own destiny. Therefore, each is prepared to wait indefinitely until a decisive moment arrives in its favor. Neither side can be expected to make a move to accept the other's unification policy unless and until it develops a plan that ensures its own advantage.

Furthermore, in both Koreas unification policies have been treated as a government monopoly in order to protect the interests of the ruling elites. Such proposals are not subject to scholarly critique or public discussion, let alone expressions of public opinion. The unification policies are largely public relations gimmicks, domestic or international, apparently intended to deceive and mislead the innocent and credulous. Each side is ready and willing to use the specter of subjugation by the other to distract from its own failures and weaknesses and to perpetuate its own separate identity. It is also the persistent fear of being "eaten" by the other side that forces both regimes away from substantive political compromise on the problem of unification itself. As a result, the relationship between the two governments has become symbiotic; each manipulates the fear of subjugation in order to justify and legitimate its own self-promoting, authoritarian, and often unpopular government. The history of past unification politics bears this out. It is no wonder, then, that until recently, nothing has been done to alleviate the suffering of the separated families, who are the real victims of the division of Korea.

In 1945, with the surrender of Japan, the Korean peninsula was divided along the 38th parallel by an agreement between the United States and the Soviet Union. North Korea came under Soviet military occupation and South Korea under American. Unable to reach agreement with the Soviets on unifying Korea, the United States submitted the problem to the UN General Assembly. In line with recommendations of a temporary commission set up by the General Assembly, the United States promoted elections in August 1948, which established a government in South Korea; a separate government was established in the North in September of the same year. The General Assembly recognized the Republic of Korea as the only legal Korean government on December 12, 1948, since the government of North Korea had refused to permit United Nations observers in the North during the election to establish a unified government. Both the United States and the Soviet Union withdrew their forces in 1949 in line with General Assembly recommendations. On June 25, 1950, however, North Korea attacked the South, apparently seeking to unify the peninsula by force. However, the United States was determined not to let that happen as the peninsula was thought to be too important to be consigned to the Soviet communist camp since it would tip the balance of power against United States security interests in the region, especially threatening Japan. When the United States, under the auspices of the United Nations, countered the North Korean attack and carried the war to the North Korea-China border, Chinese forces intervened in support of North Korea. Had the peninsula come to be controlled by the Americans it would have posed major security risks to the rich industrial areas in the northeast of China (Manchuria). When it came the Chinese turn to cross the 38th parallel and carry the war toward the South, the United States countered again, creating a stalemate. The war finally ended in truce in July 1953, and a Demilitarized Zone between the two Koreas more or less along the 38th parallel was established, which froze the political division of the peninsula into the Republic of Korea (South Korea) with its capital in Seoul and the People's Democratic Republic of Korea (North Korea) with its capital in Pyongyang.

The lesson we should have learned from that devastating war is that Korean unification will never be a one-sided affair: neither side can claim a monopoly on its terms. There must be a compromised, negotiated political settlement between the two Koreas with the support of external powers that have vested security interests in the peninsula. However, each Korea is still determined to deal with the unification problem unilaterally, on its own terms, anathematizing the other as the sole obstacle.

After the 1953 truce, both Korean regimes were preoccupied with rebuilding their own separate nations with foreign support—North Korea with contributions from the Soviet and Chinese communist bloc and South Korea with aid from the United States and other capitalist nations, pushing the idea of a negotiated solution further away. President Syngman Rhee's rhetoric, "March north to unify" and "Recover lost territory," continued in the South, but concrete efforts were hamstrung by the US-ROK Mutual Defense Treaty (October 1953), whereby the United States abandoned the unilateral extension of the southern regime into North Korea by military means. Meanwhile, smarting under the military failure to unify, Kim Il Sung tried to change his violent image by taking up the theme of peaceful unification. However, it was not until the fall of the Rhee government in 1960 that Kim Il Sung presented the idea of a North-South confederation as a means of achieving peaceful national reunification. On August 14, 1960—on the occasion of the fifteenth anniversary of Korean liberation from Japan—as an interim unification arrangement, Kim made the following package proposal:

  1. Free general elections should be held in the North and the South, on the basis of democratic principles, without any

foreign interference, for the purpose of peaceful unification of the country.

2. If this should not be acceptable to the South for fear of communist domination, the North would settle for a North-South Confederation, a provisional measure, in order to iron out different issues.

3. The confederacy is to be maintained by a Supreme National Committee composed of the representatives of the two governments and coordinating the cultural and economic development of the whole of Korea, while the two current political systems would remain intact.

4. If the South Korean authorities still cannot accept the confederation, a purely economic commission composed of business representatives of the two governments would be set up to "relieve the South Korean brothers and sisters from hunger and poverty," while setting aside political questions for the time being.

5. The mutual reduction of armed forces to a 100,000-man level or less would be achieved after the withdrawal of United States troops from the South.[1]

Taken at face value, this proposal seems reasonable enough to receive serious consideration as a building block for peaceful national reunification. In fact, the confederal concept found some positive reactions in South Korea and helped improve North Korea's hostile image, especially among the Third World community since North Korea also officially renounced its "liberation [of South Korea] by force" policy in the following month.[2] However, the confederal plan was rejected by the government in the South because it was a unilateral North Korean proposal announced at a time of South Korean political instability and economic chaos following the April (1960) student uprising. In order not to lose the propaganda edge, the new Chang Myon government proclaimed that it also would change the previous administration's military unification position, "March north to unify," to a peaceful one through UN-supervised free elections. On August 24, 1960, Foreign Minister Chung Yil Hyong of South Korea made the following statement:

The government holds that the unification of Korea shot achieved through UN-supervised free elections throughout Korea pursuant to the United Nations resolutions. Such reckless policy of trying to unify Korea by force as advocated by the Rhee Government should now be discarded.[3]

In the meantime, the credibility of the confederal scheme was eroded when the North, taking advantage of the South Korean student demands for a North-South unification conference, established the Committee for the Peaceful Reunification of the Fatherland on May 13, 1961.[4] This North Korean propaganda move exacerbated the South's political instability and led to the subsequent military coup in the South on May 16, 1961. The tide of North Korean propaganda for peaceful unification was stopped when the South Korean coup leaders established anticommunism as the most important national principle. To this North Korea responded by extracting military alliances from the Soviet Union (on July 1, 1961) and China (on July 11, 1961). Its unification policy was also changed from a "peaceful approach" to a more aggressive one—through promoting an internal communist revolution ("a national liberation war" coupled with overt provocations) in the South. This was the pattern of Pyongyang's unification strategy throughout the 1960s. The 1968 attempt to assassinate President Park Chung Hee (on January 21), the capture of the USS *Pueblo* off the coast of Wonsan (on January 23), and the shooting down over international waters of an American aircraft (on April 15, 1969) are cases in point.

As it turned out, the confederal proposal served only as a propaganda tool for North Korea and contributed no substantive progress toward unification. Despite the South Korean rejection, the North continued to play games with the idea because of its propaganda value at home and abroad. From the South Korean perspective it appeared to be camouflage for intent to achieve unilaterally a communized unification after the withdrawal of American troops. Such a background is hardly likely to promote mutual trust or to make the task of negotiated unification easier.

On August 14, 1970, ten years after the first confederation proposal made by Kim Il Sung, South Korean President Park proposed talks looking toward peaceful reunification.[5] On

April 12, 1971, at the Supreme People's Congress, North Korean Foreign Minister Ho Dam presented an eight-point proposal for such discussions, essentially a reiteration of Kim Il Sung's proposals to the Fifth Korean Workers' Party Congress in November 1970.[6] Ho's eight points included the following:

1. Withdrawal of all United States forces from South Korea
2. Reduction of armed forces of both North and South to 100,000 men each or less
3. Abolition or nullification of all treaties and agreements between the two Korean governments and foreign countries
4. Establishment of a unified central government to conduct general elections in the North and South
5. Immediate release of all political prisoners and granting of guarantees of total political freedom to all political parties, public organizations, and individuals in South Korea
6. Establishment of a confederation of North and South Korea as a transitional step toward unification
7. Promotion of trade and economic cooperation together with exchanges in other fields such as sports, arts, culture, education, and postal services
8. Holding of a political conference between North and South Korea attended by all political parties and public organizations to negotiate the above proposals[7]

It is to be noted here that the idea of confederation, which is broadly similar to the one introduced by Kim in 1960, reappeared for the second time in this program as a transition step toward national unification. However, as with the 1960 program, this proposal also lacked a concrete framework for unification able to guarantee the security of South Korea after the withdrawal of United States troops, such as neutralizing the entire Korean peninsula for an indefinite period of time. Without such a security framework, negotiations for unification were bound to be difficult and unproductive.

Nevertheless, South Korea responded to this proposal in the months that followed. On August 12, 1971, immediately following the news that President Nixon would go to China, Kim stated that North Korea would be willing to talk with all South Korean political parties, including the ruling Democratic

Republican party, and other social organizations in South Korea.[8]

The South Korean Red Cross proposed that a meeting be held with its North Korean counterpart to discuss the problem of locating divided families. The North Korean Red Cross responded favorably, proposing such a meeting in September at Panmunjom. Thus, for the first time since the division of the Korean peninsula, bilateral negotiations between the two Koreas' Red Cross representatives began on September 20, culminating in the publication of the historic North-South joint communiqué on July 4, 1972, which seemed to usher in a new era of hope and genuine dialogue between the two Korean governments. But hopes where soon dashed when the discussions were called off unilaterally by Pyongyang in August 1973, after several meetings, in protest against the repression of the South's democratic elements and against the South's assertion that United States troops stationed there were not an "outside" force within the terms of the North-South joint communiqué.

Prima facie, the joint communiqué represented a reasonable step toward reunification. It enunciated three general principles: unification should be achieved through independent Korean efforts without any external involvement or interference; it should be achieved through peaceful means, not through the use of force; and unity should be sought that would transcend (but not eliminate) differences in ideas, ideologies, and systems.[9] Pursuant to these principles, the two sides agreed not to slander or defame one another, and not to undertake armed provocations. They set up a "hot line" between the two capitals and inaugurated a Joint North-South Coordinating Committee to follow up on their agreements.

However, due to mutual suspicions and vituperations arising from the fear that one side might dictate its own unification terms to the other, nothing concrete has resulted from either the Red Cross talks or the political dialogue through the Joint North-South Coordinating Committee. The fears on both sides are understandable and inevitable since there was no overall structure that could guarantee the unification principles laid out in the joint communiqué.

In retrospect, it is not hard to see why the first historic breakthrough failed to produce any positive results toward national reconciliation. Each side used the communiqué as a device to disarm the other and to seek the maximum political or security advantage for itself. In the communiqué and in subsequent talks no common unification formula worked out jointly by the two sides was proposed; only competing, rival, and separate measures were introduced, for propaganda purposes. Thus, in 1974, Pyongyang demanded that the 1953 armistice agreement be converted into a permanent peace treaty with the United States, and Seoul offered a nonaggression pact between the two Koreas. Meanwhile, a number of other maneuvers and countermaneuvers followed, but not a single agreement on unification was reached between the two Koreas. There was no meeting of minds even on what constituted national unification. Unification was viewed only as a zero-sum game by both sides.

During this impasse in North-South dialogue, on June 23, 1973, Kim Il Sung for the third time presented the idea of confederation, in a speech at a mass rally welcoming the visit of Gustav Husak, general secretary of the Czechoslovak Communist party. By way of responding to Park Chung Hee's proposal on the same day for the simultaneous entry of North and South Korea into the United Nations as separate states, Kim countered that the two Koreas should join the UN as a single entity under the name of the "Confederal Republic of Koryo"—referring to the ancient Koryo kingdom (935–1392). Five points emphasized in the same proposal are as follows:

1. To eliminate military confrontation and ease tension between the two Koreas in order to improve present relations and accelerate peaceful reunification.
2. To promote many-sided collaboration and interchange between the two sides in the political, military, diplomatic, and economic and cultural fields in order to expedite unification.
3. To enable representatives of people in all walks of life on both sides to participate in the nationwide patriotic work of unification by convening a Great National Congress.
4. To institute a North-South confederation under the name of a single country—the Confederal Republic of Koryo— leaving the two existing systems in the North and South

as they are for the time being.

5. Not to enter the UN separately. If both Koreas want to enter the UN before reunification, they should enter as a single state under the name of the Confederal Republic of Koryo, at least after the confederation is set up.[10]

A new element in this proposal was that a confederal government was to be instituted with the two existing systems remaining in the North and South. However, no provision was included in the proposal for creating any organ or body to supervise or monitor the activities of the confederal government. Nor were there any details or clarifications as to the structure, composition, timing, or methods of organizing the confederation. The call to convene a Great National Congress to discuss and resolve reunification questions dates back to 1948—two years before the outbreak of the Korean War. In April 1948 at Pyongyang a joint political conference of North and South Korean leaders was held to consider the question of national unification, opposing the separate elections scheduled for May in the South under the United Nations Temporary Commission on Korea. On June 7, 1950, a few weeks before the war, North Korea called for a similar North-South conference to be held June 15 to 17 at either Kaesong or Haeju to discuss problems relating to unification. This proposal, however, ruled out the participation of "traitors" such as Syngman Rhee and other South Korean leaders who had denounced the North-South conference of April 1948. North Korea proposed again, on June 19, that national unification be achieved by first merging the legislatures of Pyongyang and Seoul into a single body and that a meeting for this purpose be held on June 21, either in Seoul or in Pyongyang.[11] These meetings never took place. Instead, North Korea undertook the sudden military invasion of the South a few days later, on June 25, 1950.

Against this background, it seems natural for South Korea to be suspicious of the idea of convening a Great National Congress and to see it as a sinister attempt to discredit the South Korean government's legitimacy as a partner with whom to negotiate. The Pyongyang government may also have calculated that such a congress would be less likely to be manipulated by the Seoul government and might put pressure on it in favor of the North Korean position. Eventually, the South rejected the idea, saying that it was against the spirit of the June 4 (1972) joint communiqué which had designated the Joint North-South Coordinating Committee as the principal point of contact between the two Korean authorities. The idea of the Confederal Republic of Koryo was also rejected by the Seoul government, which suspected that it would be used as a device by which North Korea might engineer "national liberation" in the South, or as a cover for another military invasion of South Korea. Advocating the confederation idea, the North continued to insist that "if South Korea wants unification, it has to give up its anti-Communist attitude and start collaborating with Communists. For this purpose, South Korea has to repeal the Anti-Communist Act and the National Security Act."[12] Such statements were hardly conducive to promoting mutual trust and national reconciliation, and they made the task of reunification more difficult.

Meanwhile, for the fourth time, in October 1980, the confederation formula for unification was proposed by Kim Il Sung in his report to the Sixth Congress of the Workers' Party (North Korean Communist party). He offered a broader and seemingly more comprehensive ten-point program under a new name—the "Democratic Confederal Republic of Koryo" (DCRK). Although many of the proposals were repetitions and modifications of ideas long advanced by Kim, two new elements were added: the transformation of the DCRK into a "Permanent Peace Zone and Nuclear-Free Zone," and its neutral or nonaligned foreign policy. In their essence, the ten DCRK principles are as follows:

1. To be independent (not a satellite of any other nation) and to conduct a nonaligned foreign policy
2. To be democratic and free to form political parties and social organizations; not to question the past records of any organization or individual; to conduct no political reprisals
3. To bring about economic cooperation and exchange between the two Koreas and to develop an independent national economy

4. To facilitate North-South exchange and cooperation in the spheres of science, culture, and education in order to create a uniform national culture
5. To reopen suspended transport and communications between the North and South and ensure free utilization of the means of transport and communications in all parts of the country
6. To guarantee a stable livelihood for the entire people by providing work for everyone
7. To eliminate military confrontation between the North and the South and establish a unified national army by reducing the military strength on both sides to 100,000–150,000 and by abolishing the Military Demarcation Line
8. To defend and protect the national rights and interests of all Koreans overseas
9. To coordinate foreign relations of the two governments by repealing all treaties and agreements with other countries detrimental to national amity, including military treaties concluded separately by the North and the South prior to reunification
10. To develop friendly relations with all countries of the world by adopting a neutral or nonaligned foreign policy and to create a permanent peace zone and nuclear-free zone in the Korean peninsula by prohibiting the presence of foreign troops and bases and by banning the manufacture, introduction, or use of nuclear weapons[13]

On the surface, this seems a reasonable, even laudable, program for national unification. As to the organizational aspect of the DCRK, it is to be constituted with the existing governmental systems in the two Koreas intact, by way of setting up a supreme national confederal assembly composed of an equal number of representatives from both sides and of a certain number of representatives of overseas nationals. This assembly together with its subcommittee, a confederal standing committee, is to conduct unified national affairs.

Furthermore, Pyongyang for the first time officially recognized the viability of a neutral Korea; in other words, the foreign policy of a unified Korea was to be conducted along the lines of neutrality and nonalignment. However, this neutrality principle would not help the process of unification, as it belonged to a post-unification foreign policy; this meant "unification first, neutrality later" and was putting the cart before the horse. A productive sequence will have to be "neutralization first, unification later," that is, neutralized unification—meaning unification has to be managed peacefully by the instrument of neutralization. In any case, the DCRK proposal did not get anywhere because of the actual or implied preconditions attached to it stating that peaceful unification was impossible without the "democratization" of the South, the removal of United States troops, and the revolutionary overthrow of the Seoul government. This proposal was, naturally, interpreted by the South as a subversive, hostile, and unrealistic approach to national unification. Thus, the DCRK plan did not improve the prospects for unification as it did not provide a framework of guaranteed equal security for both sides.

Meanwhile, in January 1982, the South announced its counterproposal, the "National Reconciliation and Democratic Unification" (NRDU). It called for a North-South Consultative Conference for National Reunification, where representatives of both sides would draft a unified constitution. Once the constitution was drawn up, both sides were to make it into law through a free, democratic referendum throughout the peninsula. Then a unified government would be formed with a unified legislature, selected through general elections under the provisions of the constitution. In the meantime, until such a goal could be realized, inter-Korean relations were to be conducted according to a provisional, interim agreement on basic relations between the two Koreas, according to the following seven points:

1. Respect for the principles of reciprocity and equality in mutual relations pending the time of unification
2. Renunciation of the use of force of arms or other violence in favor of solving disputes peacefully through dialogue
3. Recognition of each other's political order and social system, and noninterference in each other's internal affairs
4. Maintenance of the existing armistice system and discussion of measures to end the arms race and dissolve the state of military confrontation

5. Promotion of opening of the societies of the two sides through multifaceted exchanges and cooperation (to reunite dispersed families, trade, transportation, postal service, communications, sports, academic pursuits, education, culture, press, health, technology, environmental protection, etc.)

6. Respect for each other's bilateral and multilateral agreements concluded with third countries, and consultation in matters affecting the interests of the Korean nation pending the time of unification

7. Establishment of respective permanent liaison missions in Seoul and Pyongyang[14]

The name of the unified country, the basic domestic and foreign policy directions, the form of government, and the procedures for general elections were to be discussed and agreed upon in the North-South Consultative Conference. In support of this proposal and to facilitate national unity, the Seoul government, in February of the same year, put forward a twenty-point pilot proposal covering a host of joint programs. They are worth noting.

1. The connection and opening of a highway between Seoul and Pyongyang

2. The realization of postal exchanges and reunion of separated families

3. The designation and opening of the area north of Mt. Sorak and south of the Diamond Mountains as a tourist zone

4. The joint management of homeland visits by overseas Korean residents by way of Panmunjom

5. The opening of the harbors of Inchon and Chinnampo

6. The freedom to listen to each other's propaganda

7. The participation of North Korean delegations in the 1986 Asian Games and 1988 Olympiad

8. The free access to all foreigners wishing to visit the South and the North by way of Panmunjom

9. The creation of joint fishery zones

10. The organization of mutual goodwill visits from various circles, such as politicians, businessmen, youths and students, workers, writers and artists, and sportsmen

11. The guaranteeing of free press coverage by the journalists of the two sides in each other's territory
12. The undertaking of joint research on national history
13. The exchange of goodwill matches in various fields of sports and participation in international games as a single delegation
14. The trading of consumer products of daily necessity
15. The joint development and utilization of natural resources
16. The exchange of technicians and exhibitions of manufactured products
17. The creation of sports facilities inside the Demilitarized Zone for goodwill matches between the South and the North
18. The administration of a joint academic survey to study the ecological system of the fauna and flora inside the Demilitarized Zone
19. The complete removal of military facilities from within the Demilitarized Zone
20. The discussion of arms control measures between the South and the North[15]

At face value, the South's counterproposal seemed rational, comprehensive, and accommodating; and there was no question of actual or implied preconditions unacceptable to the North. However, Pyongyang rejected the South Korean package, denouncing it as divisive and doctrinaire. The North claimed that the projects amounted to no more than a fraction of the ideas Pyongyang had already laid down for collaboration and exchange between the two sides. In view of Pyongyang's dogmatic, hostile attitude toward the South, its rejection of the South Korean package was not surprising. Furthermore, the North may have rejected it for fear of losing the propaganda advantage for its DCRK proposal and must have felt that Seoul was playing a game of "one-upmanship" with its twenty projects vis-à-vis the DCRK's ten-point programs.

Meanwhile, on July 7, 1988, President Roh Woo unilaterally announced his six-point proposal in an effort to break the logjam, which called for exchange visits (including those of overseas Koreans), reuniting separated families, duty-free inter-Korean trade, Seoul's approval of its allies' trade (of a nonmilitary nature) with Pyongyang, desisting from adversary-confrontational diplomacy, and promoting better relations among Pyongyang, Washington, and Tokyo.[16] The North's reaction, however, was less than lukewarm, and Pyongyang countered that it would not take the new proposal seriously unless the United States withdrew its troops.[17] Thus, Seoul's latest unilateral approach met the same fate as before—a negative response from Pyongyang.

Even though there are fundamental differences in underlying motives and strategic objectives in the unification approaches —such as Pyongyang's "Unification first, peace later" insistence on a "once-and-for-all" outcome and Seoul's "Peace first, unification later" emphasis on a step-by-step, incremental process —there are also many common elements that the two Koreas can accept. What is now lacking is the political will to accommodate those elements in good faith on both sides and to negotiate a process for their synthesis that can lead to national unity without creating victor or vanquished on either side.

Synthesis of the Two Unification Policies: Neutralization of the Peninsula

The brief review of the two Korea's unification policies in the preceding pages leads to an inevitable conclusion that the differing approaches of the two Koreas to national reunification have more to do with regime self-preservation, largely centered on the question of legitimacy, than with any argument over the ultimate goal of unification itself. Herein lies the crux of the Korean unification problem. So long as each Korea wants to control the entire peninsula as a means of self-preservation, there will be little progress towards national unity. Instead there will be only endless empty and harmful competition and rivalry.

The danger is that as each side maneuvers for a position from which to achieve reunification on its own terms, there will be temptations to resort to force, should favorable opportunity arise. This is not a pleasant prospect. It is against this background that the idea of neutralizing the Korean peninsula is examined in order to reduce this danger and move the two Koreas towards unity.

The geostrategic position of the Korean peninsula alone explains much of the rationale for neutralizing. Since the late nineteenth century, Korea has been the scene of rivalry among the major Asian powers—China, Japan, and Russia—each of which considered Korea important to its own national security (or expansion). The Japanese won the contest and annexed Korea in 1910 as a colony and integral part of their empire. Japan's defeat in the Pacific war resurrected Korea's independence, but independence did not last long. As soon as the cold war set in, Korea became a battleground between two rival camps—this time centered on the Soviet Union and the United States—in the tradition of earlier international rivalries which had been largely responsible for the division of Korea, for the subsequent war between the two Koreas in 1950–1953, and for the present stalemate. There is an old Korean proverb, "When two whales fight, it is the shrimp in the middle who gets crushed." This old wisdom is a reminder that Koreans should not get sucked into the quarrels of their big neighbors, should not let their land be used as a battleground, and should remain aloof from (or neutral in) the conflict. Few parts of the world have been more often affected by geographical location than Korea, whose most fundamental characteristic is the extent to which it has tended to be an object of big-power rivalries. Today, it is the only area in the world where the security interest of four major powers (America, the Soviet Union, China, and Japan) intersect.

Under these circumstances, the unification of Korea will indeed have great impact in Asia and cannot be easy. However, simple logic and common sense dictate that common ground must be found where unification is mutually beneficial to not only the two Koreas but also to the four external powers. It is toward a discussion of such a factor, neutralization, that we now turn.

Regarding neutralized states, the 1968 Princeton study gave the following definition:

A neutralized state is one whose political independence and territorial integrity are guaranteed permanently by a collective agreement of great powers, subject to the conditions that the neutralized state will not take up arms against another state, except to defend itself, and will not assume treaty obligations which may compromise its neutralized status.... Neutralization is a special international status designed to restrict the intrusion of specified state actions in a specified area. The status of neutralization is often referred to as permanent neutrality to signify that it is valid in times of peace as well as war.[18]

On the category of potential candidates for neutralization, the same study observed: "Neutralization is relevant primarily to geographically definable areas in which two or more external actors have substantial and competitive interest";[19] and it is "potentially attractive only for relatively minor states, that by reason of strategic or symbolic political value, have become or threaten to become the focal points of contests for control or dominant influence between principal regional or global rivals."[20]

Thus, the goal of neutralization is to stabilize an unstable international situation or to prevent the status quo in an area from becoming seriously disturbed by means of coercion. From the viewpoint of the neutralized state, the merit of neutralization is to defend its security, as well as its political and territorial integrity. From the viewpoint of the guarantor states, who have a strong and competitive interest in the neutralized state, neutralization may restrain or prevent them from engaging in military actions among themselves. They thus find in it a protection for themselves.

Neutralization serves to stabilize international order by regulating interstate disputes by peaceful means based on the principles of accepted international law and diplomacy, and may help to prevent the international balance of power in the region of the neutralized state.[21] Neutrality is also useful in preventing outbreaks of violence in an area already subject to intrusion of the competitive political and military interests of outside powers, and in terminating overt hostilities supported by external interventions in which neither side can hope to gain a decisive advantage at the existing level of conflict and in which the principal parties fear the consequences of uncontrolled escalation.[22]

In the context of Korean reunification, neutralization offers the best mechanism, for it would allow the emergence of a united Korea in such a way that neither side could gain at the expense of the other. In other words, it would produce a win-win end-product for both sides. It might also serve as an intermediate stage in ameliorating the psychological and political conflicts which exist between the two parts of the divided nation in the process of their unification. Viewed from this perspective, neutralization may well be the only available and workable statecraft to support the peaceful unification of Korea as it can provide a protective environment for the two Koreas as well as for the four external powers.

The most urgent task is bringing the two Korean ruling elites together to accept the neutralization idea and to start genuine dialogue. This is also the most difficult problem, but a modest beginning can be made by establishing an informal, private "North-South Joint Research Commission on National Reunification" on a permanent basis in a third country. Such a commission would be composed of an equal number of scholars, researchers, and other qualified civilians (including overseas Koreans) from both sides. This advisory body would be useful as an intermediary to inform, assist, and guide the two groups of government officials in developing a joint unification policy based on mutual benefit and understanding. Since national reunification is a joint venture and responsibility, its policy must be jointly developed if it is to have any measure of success. Informal, unofficial dialogue would help to create a climate in which the two sides could confront their mutual concerns, play out various scenarios, experiment with possible gestures, and jointly look for ways of redefining areas of conflict so that they become amenable to compromises and resolution.

Interaction of this kind cannot take place in an official, bureaucratic context since government-sponsored public negotiations do not provide a suitable framework for such purposes. What is needed instead is an opportunity for preparatory discussions preceding official negotiations. These discussions could take place in a situation in which representatives of the two Koreas could interact unofficially and privately with minimal risk and without prior commitments. Such a milieu would be essential to finding a mutually beneficial way of achieving unification. Since the two Korean regimes must solve the question of national reunification together, the lack of inter-Korean dialogue is morally indefensible and intellectually unacceptable, regardless of which side is at fault. (If and when the two Korean states are ready to talk about the substance of unification, they could entertain the idea of concluding the basic treaty offered in Appendix A.[23])

Policy Recommendations for the United States

Though the primary responsibility for unification rests with the Koreans themselves, they may never be able to achieve it without the support of the external powers that have security interests in the peninsula. Of the four powers, the United States has been the most intimately involved and holds most of the keys. Since 1958, when Chinese troops withdrew from North Korea, America has been the only outside power maintaining its troops on Korean soil. Thus, a major issue in the future Korean unification will be how the United States undertakes its troop withdrawal. The most constructive way would be for the United States to set certain preconditions favorable to national unity such as neutralization of the peninsula or Austria, or some other framework of a one-Korea superstructure.

It is time for the United States to begin a search for new policies conducive to Korean reunification. There is a strong case to be made for initiating neutralization by the United States in connection with the removal of its troops. It would be necessary for the United States to negotiate in advance with the Soviet Union, China, and Japan to gain their participation in guaranteeing the status of a neutralized Korea. Since none of these powers wants a major conflict that might embroil them in the peninsula, it is reasonable to assume their cooperation with the United States in this endeavor. As one of the conditions for the withdrawal of United States forces, Ralph N. Clough, author of *Embattled Korea*, has recommended a four-power agreement to "respect the neutrality of the two Koreas and of an eventual confederation of Korea."[24] He also thought that these three powers would support a "unified neutral or neutralized state, free of nuclear weapons."[25]

The idea of a neutralized Korea is based on the rationale that, while the United States endorses Korean reunification as an ultimate goal, it will not press for a united Korea under South Korean hegemony, for that would be construed by the Soviet Union and China as a direct threat to their security interests. In other words, the United States would give priority to its relations with the Soviet Union and China over its concern for Korean unification. It would not support any unification formula dictated by the South as that would incur Soviet or Chinese disapproval and destabilize the balance of power in the region.

It is instructive to recall the American efforts made during the Korean War to neutralize the peninsula as a price for ending the conflict. The war broke out in June 1950 during the Truman administration, and an armistice was signed in July 1953 during the first year of the Eisenhower administration. Throughout the three years of the conflict, both American administrations strove to re-establish an independent, unified, and neutral Korea. In a series of memorandums prepared during the war by the Department of State, "demilitarization," "neutralization," "permanent neutralization of Korea," and "a unified, neutralized Korea" were frequently discussed, considered, and recommended as part of a plan to end the war and to reunify Korea.[26] For instance on June 15, 1953, when the conclusion of the armistice was imminent, the Department of State declared, "It is in the interest of the U.S. and should be the U.S. objective to secure a unified and neutralized Korea."[27] The unusual fact about the neutralization recommendation for Korea is that it had the approval of Secretary John Foster Dulles, who had been known for many years to oppose the principle of neutrality "as immoral and obsolete except under very exceptional circumstances."[28] In spite of his apparent distaste for the neutrality principle, the secretary seems to have been aware of the potential value of neutralizing Korea as an exceptional case, in the service of achieving both peace and unification. A month later, William F. Knowland, senator from California, also endorsed the idea. However, nothing came of it due to opposition from the Joint Chiefs of Staff and the government of Syngman Rhee, who wanted to take advantage of the war in order to unify the peninsula under his own control.

In such an atmosphere, it was no longer possible for the United States to pursue its initiative for a neutralized Korea. America was anxious to conclude the armistice, and it was getting more and more difficult to persuade the Rhee government to accept it. The United States-ROK defense treaty, therefore, was offered to pacify President Rhee in October 1953. Thus United States troops were reintroduced in the South and remain there today. In retrospect, the wartime United States strategy for a neutralized-unified Korea was brilliant foresight and a viable alternative.

It is prudent for the United States to revive this concept by making troop withdrawal contingent on a neutralized Korea. To do so, the United States would need a new strategy that shows balance and flexibility in dealing with North Korea, including establishing diplomatic and trade relations. The constant focus on the threat from the North serves no useful purpose and seems out of tune with reality. Even in the absence of reciprocity, steps toward the establishment of relations with the North need not be viewed narrowly as concessions to the communists but as having a potential benefit to United States interests.

Instead of sliding into a strategy aimed at building a coalition to confront an exaggerated North Korean threat, it is time for Washington to approach Pyongyang positively—with due attention paid to the Seoul government—since Pyongyang seems to be ready to talk with the United States. This was evident to an American researcher, Selig S. Harrison, when he visited North Korea from September 23 to October 2, 1987, and met with North Korean leaders such as Premier Lee Gun Mo, Foreign Minister Kim Young Nam and Hwang Chang Yop, secretary for foreign policy of the Workers party. Hwang was quoted as saying that the United States could set up a liaison office in Pyongyang after signing a peace treaty and establish a full diplomatic relationship when and if it agreed to withdraw its troops from the South. He expressed a favorable attitude toward confederation, while recognizing that it might be impossible to achieve.[29]

On the future of Pyongyang's security links with Moscow and Beijing, Foreign Minister Kim said:

> There is nothing immutable in our undertakings, just as we hope that there is nothing immutable in the present form of your relations with the South....We intend to strengthen and develop our relations with the United States in the days ahead....We want balanced relations with the major powers. This is in our interest, and yours. Once we fought a war but we cannot continuously maintain an abnormal relationship. The past is past.[30]

On the issue of reunification, Harrison found Pyongyang's formal stand on "federalism"—linking the two Koreas with their differing systems by a combined army and a standing committee that would supervise the two regional governments—to be a "transitional step on the road to full unification with the people deciding when, whether and how to change the structure." When Harrison criticized this stand as unrealistic, the North Korean leaders remarked: "You will find us very flexible. If we are all going in the same direction toward confederation rather than toward legitimizing two Koreas, Pyongyang is ready to discuss any other idea consistent with movement toward confederation, however gradual."[31]

A similar view was expressed by Politburo member Ho Dam in an interview with *Mainichi Shimbun,* a Japanese newspaper. He stated that Pyongyang strongly desires to improve relations with the United States and is willing to have direct dialogue with the Americans "anytime, anywhere at any level and on any agenda."[32] In addition, Kim Il Sung has repeatedly stated that the North has neither the intention nor the strength to attack the South. Even though those statements cannot be taken at face value as they are often contradictory and less than ingenuous, the United States must evaluate every opportunity for meeting North Korean leaders to test their true intentions and sincerity. No one should underestimate the difficulties Washington would encounter in any such endeavors, but it would be essential for the United States to have better relations with both parts of Korea in order to convert United States troop withdrawal into a mechanism of neutralization.

Washington may have lost a good opportunity for rapprochement with the North when it rejected tripartite talks among the North, the South, and itself. The proposal for the talks first became public in a joint statement on July 1, 1979, issued during the visit of former President Carter to Seoul. North Korea did not respond favorably until January 1984, when it officially agreed to holding such talks; but the United States, the original proponent of the conference, reneged on its own proposition, probably due to South Korea's objections.

A principal co-author of the division of Korea, the United States will only hinder and delay the unification process by maintaining its military presence in the South, and by refusing to talk to the North because of South Korean pressure. Although the Koreans themselves will determine their future unification, Washington has to play a key supporting role in bringing the two Koreas together. After having established a mini-detente with North Korea, Washington could sponsor six-party talks (United States, the Soviet Union, China, Japan, and the two Koreas) to prepare for a neutralized Korea. The issue of United States troop withdrawal could be incorporated or programmed into a treaty guaranteeing Korean neutrality. (A model treaty for the six powers is found in Appendix B.[33])

Conclusion

As the Korean War ended in a truce, not in the imposition of unconditional surrender, the competition for legitimacy by the two Koreas continues. Their entrenched positions of today may be compared to the situation of two scorpions in a bottle, each capable of killing the other, but only at risk of its own life. Peaceful reunification is unachievable without an inter-Korean consensus. This is the frustrating logic of unilateral reunification by either side.

In such circumstances the essential precondition for Korean reunification is that the two Koreas learn how to compromise and cooperate, but there has been little mutual adjustment or agreement toward this end between Pyongyang and Seoul. Part of the problem is psychological and arises from the atmosphere of mistrust and suspicion caused by the trauma of the Korean War and the absence of normal contact between the two since the war. Furthermore, each Korea strongly prefers its own legitimacy and expends its efforts to ensure its dominant status in a united Korea rather than seeking compromises or cooperative arrangements with the other side, considered illigitimate, untrustworthy, and possibly more powerful. It is, therefore, imperative for the two Koreas to find a reunification framework which can guarantee equal security and justice, and eliminate the fear of "being eaten" by the other in a united Korea. The idea of limiting the age of the members of an All-Korean Youth Commonwealth—a prototype of a unified Korea—to those who were born and will be born after January 1, 1950, stems from the conviction that the older generation, who had been exposed to the Korean War, would have much more difficulty in reconciling with each other than would the younger generation, who did not experience the brutality of the war and are therefore free of the haunting memories of fratricide. There is every reason to entrust the unification task to the future, younger generation, who will have different values, circumstances, and political leadership. The realization of a unified Korea will require new political thinking and rational behavior on the part of both halves of Korea. Above all, Koreans must leave behind the frustrating pursuit of victory in the unification process, whose first rule is cooperation, however unpalatable it may be.

Another basic requirement is the agreement of all the interested external powers to respect and guarantee Korea's unified status. Divided according to the two major opposing (ideologically and militarily) blocs, the Korean peninsula has been the zone of international rivalry and competition since World War II and is still linked directly to the security interests of the four external powers. Thus a united Korea has to be created in such a way that it does not pose a security threat to any other nation.

It is against the background of those two fundamental prerequisites (internal and external) for unification that the idea of neutralizing the Korean peninsula as a useful and successful instrumentality of diplomacy is proposed in this paper. As demonstrated, in neutralization lies a "win-win" settlement—a mutuality in which all sides profit in the long run. No one would lose anything very important by such an arrangement, for neutralization could not result in a disguised form of victory for one side at the expense of the other.

In fact, the neutralization framework provides an opportunity for the two rival Koreas to learn or cultivate the art of compromise and cooperation by renewing the spirit of pan-Korean nationalism. As unification is a shared goal and a joint responsibility, such a renewal process is vital and can serve as an antidote and play a therapeutic role in the poisoned relationship of almost half a century. It will also enable North and South to experiment, without fear of one side's being absorbed by the other. Unification proposals made in the past—such as North Korea's ten-point programs under its confederal plan and the South's seven basic interim principles along with its twenty-point pilot projects and President Roh's six-point declaration—or any other ideas which seem worthy will all be available to facilitate their national reassociation. As far as the four external powers are concerned, neutralization can liberate them from their competitive military and economic obligations to support their respective client state—thus improving the chances of their own detente.

With regard to the withdrawal of troops by the United States for reasons of its own or under internal Korean pressures, neutralization would serve as a face-saving device without leaving a vacuum for rival powers to fill. In other words, the United States can plan phased or conditional withdrawals honorably and without damage to its national interests under the international umbrella of the guarantee system provided in the neutralization framework. Thus properly handled, neutralization can become a creative instrument of great benefit to both the United States and Korea.

It is therefore desirable for the United States to give serious consideration to the possibilities of the neutralization arrangements suggested in the two model draft treaties. From the American point of view, Korean neutralization should be judged in the light of available alternatives. Sooner or later, as Korean nationalism and the urge for national reunification intensify, conditions will develop in Korea which will demand troop withdrawal. The recent anti-American demonstrations by students and their march to the DMZ to show their desire for unity are cases in point, notwithstanding their being the efforts of a radical minority. Furthermore, the presence of United States troops has often been blamed for perpetuating reactionaries and dictators in power and militating against the establishment of real democracy in South Korea.

Now is an optimal time for the United States to introduce the discussion of Korean neutralization as there are certain features in the current international setting that make such a proposal an attractive alternative. There exists at present a double-balance stalemate in the peninsula—a local balance between the two Koreas and a roughly quadrilateral balance among the external powers. Furthermore a new three-way detente is developing between the United States, the Soviet Union, and China. Under *perestroika* and *glasnost* at home, Mikhail Gorbachev appears to want to live in peace not only

542 Korean Challenges and American Policy

with the West but also with China and is allowing a larger measure of freedom for his people. He has signed the INF treaty with the United States and withdrawn Soviet troops from Afghanistan. The Reagan-Gorbachev "new era" which was proclaimed at the Moscow summit in May 1987 should be conducive to a local compromise in the Korean impasse. China is similarly inclined to seeking good relations with the United States in order to make its internal political and economic reforms successful, even agreeing to receive the American Peace Corps.[34] The essential point is that both Soviet and Chinese behavior toward the outside world is going through a transformation—which makes a peaceful world seem more realistic. For these reasons we may be optimistic enough to assume that those external powers would not oppose the idea of a neutral, unified Korea, which would not threaten their security interests in the region. Moreover, neutrality would decouple the Korean peninsula from international conflicts involving the superpowers.

As an alternative to the long-term continuation of the American military presence in Korea (which may be forced out in any case), the concept of neutralization merits serious consideration by the United States government. It would facilitate orderly, safe United States disengagement from Korea. It would be a misfortune of no small dimension to both Korea and America if the United States were to miss the opportunity of converting its troop withdrawal into the instrumentality of Korean reunification. Used as a bargaining chip in the neutralization process, United States troop withdrawal from South Korea could play a critical and constructive role in creating a peacefully reunited Korea. Last June, Kim Il Sung himself was quoted in saying that the United States troop withdrawal could pave the way for peaceful reunification and diminish the chances of another war in the peninsula.[35]

It will not be easy, and it surely cannot be done at one stroke if only because of the Pyongyang-Seoul confrontation and intransigence; but it can be approached step by step, segment by segment. The sooner the process starts, the better it will be for all of Korea and for the United States, which is perceived rightly or wrongly by an increasing number of Korean students and intellectuals as the sole obstacle to their desired reunification.

state in the north eastern periphery of Asia, without much potential to alter the existing balance of power, will still be a good candidate for neutralization as a means of reunification.

It may be argued that neutrality has lost its validity with the end of the Cold War and has become less useful as a conflict-management mechanism. However, one should be reminded that it was the system of balance of power (power politics), not the Cold War, that created the doctrine of neutrality. Power politics will continue in the post-Cold War era, and so will the doctrine of neutrality. No one can think of creating a new world order free of international conflicts or competitions in one form or another—the current crises in the Persian Gulf is a case in point. Since United States-Soviet relations have improved drastically with the end of the Cold War, it is about time for Washington to show superpower leadership in restoring Korean unity. It has always had the power to do so but has lacked the will. In the future, Koreans will judge the United States—the co-author of the Korean division—by how it responds to their aspiration for peaceful national reunification.

Appendix A

Basic Inter-Korean Treaty on Peaceful National Reunification

The High Contracting Parties of the Republic of Korea and the Democratic People's Republic of Korea, All Korean Youths Commonwealth—a prototype of a united Korea,

Recognizing the desire of their people to reunify peacefully the divided fatherland, considering that more than 35 years have passed since the end of the Korean War, which inflicted immeasurable suffering on their people, conscious of the fact that in both parties a new generation has meanwhile grown up to whom a secure and a peaceful future should be guaranteed, determined to restore the historic continuity of their people as one nation and intending to create lasting foundations for preserving their political independence and territorial integrity as well as for developing peaceful neighborly relations throughout the world in conformity with the purposes and principles embodied in the United Nations Charter, have agreed as follows:

Article 1

The Governments of the two Korean States recognize each other's Government and reaffirm inviolability of the existing territorial boundary, which was drawn by the Korean Armistice Agreement of July 27, 1953, until this Treaty goes into force. In order to promote, facilitate, and guarantee peaceful national reunification, the two Parties shall set up an All-Korean Confederal Assembly consisting of equal numbers between them.

Article 2

The two Parties pledge that they will respect each other's political and territorial integrity without restrictions. They shall develop normal good-neighbor relations with each other on the basis of equal rights and obligations. Accordingly, they shall, pursuant to Articles 1 and 2 of the Charter of the United Nations, settle all their disputes exclusively by peaceful means and refrain from any threat or use of force in their mutual relations, now and in the future.

Article 3

To further their common aim of national reunification, each Party shall, in its own territory, remove its citizens who were born or will be born after January 1, 1950, from their citizenship status in order to form a free,

Autonomous Community independent of itself and guided by the principle of permanent neutrality in external relations. Both States shall support, assist, and guarantee the Autonomous Communities in their respective territories to merge into a united, independent, and neutral state, which may be called "All-Korean Youths Commonwealth"—a prototype of a united Korea.

Article 4

The Governments of the two Koreas shall transfer the right of administering the Demilitarized Zone, including the 1,000 square kilometers in the vicinity of Panmunjom, whose existing boundary line was laid down by the Korean Armistice Agreement, to an Autonomous Community therein (the details of its formation will be agreed upon by the two Parties) and shall jointly build within the area an administrative center for the All-Korean Youths Commonwealth. The Demilitarized Zone shall be placed under the direct jurisdiction of its own Autonomous Community. The three Autonomous Communities, one each in the ROK, the DPRK and the DMZ, will be federated in the All-Korean Youths Commonwealth in due time.

Article 5

Each Contracting Party shall accord to its constituent members of the Commonwealth the same right of abode as to its own citizens, and shall accord to the other constituent members the privilege of extra-territoriality in accordance with the status agreement to be concluded between the two parties.

Article 6

The Governments of the two States shall gradually transfer their respective sovereign powers to the Commonwealth in accordance with an "Agreement on the transfer of Sovereign Powers," to be negotiated between the two. The transfer of powers shall be completed within 15 years after the conclusion of this Treaty. The sovereign powers of the two Governments will, as time passes, fade into the hands of the Commonwealth.

Article 7

The Contracting Parties agree that they will undertake to conclude a "Six-Power Treaty on International Guarantee for Peaceful Korean Reunification" with the four external powers (the United States, the Soviet Union, China, and Japan) that have vested security interests in the Korean Peninsula.

Supplementary Provisions

1. The present Treaty is subject to ratification in accordance with the due constitutional process of each Party and shall enter into force on the date of exchange of the instruments of ratification which shall take place at Panmunjom.
2. The present Treaty and other relevant agreements shall supercede the constitutions and other laws of both Parties. The previous international agreements concluded by the two respective Governments shall remain in effect as long as they do not conflict with this Treaty and other relevant agreements.
3. The present Treaty shall be amended only by a mutual agreement between the two Parties and shall never be abrogated unilaterally.
4. In order to negotiate and carry out the provisions of this present Treaty and other relevant decisions, an office of Permanent Representative of the two Governments shall immediately be established at Panmunjom.

Appendix B

Six-Power Treaty on International Guarantee for Peaceful Korean Reunification

The Governments of the United States, the Soviet Union, the People's Republic of China, Japan, the Republic of Korea and the Democratic People's Republic of Korea,

Convinced of the fact that Korean reunification is an urgent necessity for peace in the Korean Peninsula and East Asia, recognizing that a unified, independent, neutral Korea will contribute to the harmonious coexistence of all mankind in freedom, security, and justice,

Desiring to lend expression, in the form of a Treaty to guarantee peaceful Korean reunification in progressive stages, and to cooperate continuously with each other for the maintenance of the unified Korea's political independence and territorial integrity,

Have agreed to conclude the following Treaty:

Chapter I : General Provisions
Article 1

Objective

The aim of this Treaty is for the High Contracting Parties to guarantee peaceful Korean reunification by encouraging, persuading, inducing, and assisting the Republic of Korea, the Democratic People's Republic of Korea, and the All-Korean Youths Commonwealth to respect and faithfully carry out the provisions set forth in the "Basic Inter-Korean Treaty on Peaceful National Reunification" and other relevant agreements.

Article 2

Method

The method of carrying out the objective of Article 1 of this Treaty by the High Contracting Parties shall be guided solely by the purposes and principles laid down in the present Treaty and in the United Nations Charter.

Article 3

Guarantee of Neutrality and Non-Alignment of the All-Korean Youths Commonwealth.

The Parties to the present Treaty declare that they will respect, defend, and cooperate with each other to guarantee the neutrality and non-alignment of the All-Korean Youths Commonwealth.

Chapter II: Organization
Article 4

Machinery

With a view to the smooth and effective implementation of the objective set forth in Article 1, the High Contracting Parties shall establish a "Council on International Guarantee of Peaceful Korean Reunification," including the following:
1. **Subsidiary organs.**
   a. Board of Guarantors
   b. International Tribunal
   c. Secretariat
   d. Military Staff Committee
   e. Neutral Nations Peace Observation Commission
   f. Other organs deemed necessary by the Board of Guarantors

2. **Location.** The Headquarters of the Council shall be located in the vicinity of Panmunjom in the Demilitarized Zone. However, if the peace, security, and neutrality of the DMZ area housing the Council Headquarters are violated and the various Council organs cannot function, the site of the Council Headquarters shall be moved to any other area chosen by more than four members of the Board of Guarantors in order to continue to perform its functions.

3. **Time to commence official business**
   a. The Board of Guarantors: Within two months after the present Treaty has entered in to force.
   b. The Secretariat: Within three months.
   c. The Neutral Nations Peace-Observation Commission: Within three months.
   d. The International Tribunal: Within six months.
   e. The Military Staff Committee: As directed by the Board of Guarantors.

Article 5

The Board of Guarantors

1. **Composition.** The Board of Guarantors shall consist of six members (with ambassadorial rank) representing the Six Contracting Parties plus three members in individual capacity.
   a. The six members representing their respective states are from the United States, the Soviet Union, the People's Republic of China, Japan, the Republic of Korea, and the Democratic People's Republic of Korea.
   b. The three members in individual capacity shall consist of two members elected, by secret single ballot, in order of plurality, in the All-Korean Confederal Assembly plus one member elected by majority vote in the Conference of the All-Korean Youths Commonwealth.

2. **Term and status of the members of the Board in individual Capacity.**
   a. The Term of the three Board members in individual capacity shall be five years.
   b. During the tenure of their office, those three Board members in individual capacity shall perform their duties independently and only as their national conscience dictates, and shall not hold any other public office or membership in the political parties in either the Republic of Korea (ROK) or the Democratic Peoples Republic of Korea (DPRK) or the All-Korean Youths Commonwealth.
   c. When unable to carry out their duties due to death, sickness, or other unforeseen events, the three Board members in individual capacity shall be succeeded by those whom they respectively designate and deposit as their successors beforehand in secret register with the Secretariat. If they voluntarily resign, their successors will

be elected to serve out only the remainder of their predecessors' terms.

   d. In the territories of the States signatory to the present Treaty, the Board members in individual capacity shall enjoy the same diplomatic privileges and immunities as the six other members representing their states.

3. **Functions of the Board of Guarantors**

   a. In order to investigate violations of, and to ensure prompt, effective and faithful observation of, the Basic Inter-Korean Treaty on Peaceful National Reunification and other relevant agreements by the Republic of Korea (ROK) or the Democratic Peoples Republic of Korea (DPRK) or the All-Korean Youths Commonwealth, the Board of Guarantors shall take the following measures along with other actions as deemed necessary.

   b. When it is discovered or reported that the investigative works undertaken by the All-Korean Confederal Assembly or by the International Tribunal on violations of the Basic Inter-Korean Treaty on Peaceful National Reunification are obstructed or unduly interfered with, the Board of Guarantors shall set up directly and immediately a "Commission of Inquiry" in order to continue the activities of investigation effectively and therewith to present the evidence material for judgment, trial or redress.

   c. The ROK, the DPRK and the All-Korean Youths Commonwealth must permit and guarantee the Inquiry Commission free access to any part of their territories for investigative purposes. If they refuse to do so, the Board of Guarantors, without sanction from the International Tribunal, may pass resolutions mandating such compulsory measures as set forth in paragraph (e).

   d. The Board of Guarantors shall enforce the decisions of the International Tribunal if the decisions are not carried out by the parties concerned.

   e. When the ROK, the DPRK, or the All-Korean Youths Commonwealth refuse to honor the Board's mandatory resolutions, the Board, in order to ensure the implementation of the resolutions, can coerce them by such measures as follows:

      i. The Board of Guarantors may arrest, extradite, and expel those who have been impeached by the All-Korean Confederal Assembly for violation of the Basic Inter-Korean Treaty on Peaceful National Reunification and other relevant agreements, or those who have defied the judgment rendered by the All-Korean Confederal Assembly.

      ii. The Board may boycott or sever diplomatic, economic, and communication relations with the ROK, the DPRK or the All-Korean Youths Commonwealth, if they refuse to carry out the Board's decisions.

      iii. In order to enforce its decisions, the Board may deploy the security forces of the "All-Korean Youths Commonwealth" or the armed forces of the member States of the Board.

f. The Board shall adopt its own rules of procedure, including the method of selecting its chairman, and prescribe operational rules for the Secretariat, International Tribunal, Military Staff Committee, Neutral Nations Peace Observation Commission, and other organs deemed necessary by the Board.

g. The Board may initiate any other measures, rules, and actions which may be required for the achievement of the objective set forth in Article 1 of this Treaty.

4. **The Board's Operational Procedure**

a. All the decisions of the Board shall be made by a majority of its members with the exception of the mandatory measures described in parts 3-e-ii, iii in this Article, which shall require a two-thirds vote of its members.

b. The Board of Guarantors shall be so organized as to be able to function continuously. Each member of the Board shall, for this purpose, be represented at all times at the seat of its office.

c. If necessary, the Board may conduct its business at any other place besides the Capital City of the All-Korean Youths Commonwealth in the DMZ.

d. Pending the creation of the All-Korean Youths Commonwealth or when, due to the violation of independence and neutrality of its administration zone, the three Board members in individual capacity are unable to attend the Board Meeting, four consenting votes of the six State representatives in the Board will be sufficient to carry out the Board's decision.

Article 6

Operations Procedure for the International Tribunal

1. **Composition.** The International Tribunal shall consist of two justices from each High Contracting Party who have served as judges in their respective governments or have high scholarly reputations in international law. They shall be appointed by their own Governments.

2. **Status and term of office.**

a. The judges of the Tribunal shall serve for a term of six years. In case of resignation, a successor shall be appointed by his Government and serve six years, regardless of the remainder of his predecessor's term.

b. With respect to rendering their judgment, all the judges shall act in accordance with rules of law and according to their own consciences, independent of the wishes of their own Government and any other external influences.

c. Governments of the High Contracting Parties shall accord the judges the same status as Ambassadors, including diplomatic privileges and immunities.

3. **Function of the Tribunal.**
   a. The International Tribunal shall examine whether or not the constitutions, laws, executive decrees, or any other practices of law of the ROK, the DPRK or the All-Korean Youths Commonwealth are in conformity with the Basic Inter-Korean Treaty on Peaceful National Reunification and relevant agreements.
   b. The Tribunal may refer for redress certain cases brought before it by the ROK, the DPRK or the All-Korean Youths Commonwealth to the All-Korean Confederal Assembly or to the Board of Guarantors or, if necessary, the Tribunal itself may undertake investigations in those cases. It may request the ROK, the DPRK or the All-Korean Youths Commonwealth to produce evidence and send witnesses, in order to conduct thorough investigations on cases submitted to it. It may also demand from these three Governments free access to any area in their respective territories for the purpose of thorough investigations. They must guarantee the Tribunal's fair and unrestricted investigative activities.
   c. The Tribunal shall decide whether or not the Basic Inter-Korean Treaty on Peaceful National Reunification and other relevant agreements have been violated, and shall render, in case of violation thereof, judgments, compensations, redress, and punishments.
   d. The Tribunal has the final authority to interpret the Basic Inter-Korean Treaty on Peaceful National Reunification and other relevant agreements.

4. **Method of Judgment.**
   a. The judgment of the Tribunal shall be made by a majority of its members. The tie vote is considered a negative decision.
   b. The Tribunal shall render judgments in accordance with the following criteria:
      i. Purposes and principles of the Basic Inter-Korean Treaty on Peaceful National Reunification and other relevant agreements.
      ii. Agreements reached by the Permanent Representatives between the ROK and the DPRK (Supplementary Provision No. 4 of the Basic Treaty).
      iii. Generally recognized customary international law.
      iv. Precedents and authoritative legal theories and doctrines in international law.
      v. Resolutions passed by the All-Korean Confederal Assembly.
      vi. The Tribunal shall perform its function in conformity with the procedure and method arranged by the Board of Guarantors.

Article 7

Secretariat

1. **Composition.**
   a. The Secretariat shall comprise a Secretary-General and such staff as the Council requires.
   b. The Secretary-General shall be chosen by the Board of Guarantors from citizens of a third country outside of the Six High Contracting States, or from the members of the All- Korean Youths Commonwealth. He shall be the chief administrative officer of the Council on International Guarantee of Peaceful Korean Reunification.
   c. The Secretariat's staff shall be appointed by the Secretary-General according to the rules prescribed by the Board of Guarantors. The paramount consideration in the employment of the staff shall be the necessity of securing the highest standards of efficiency, competence, integrity, and fairness.
2. **Functions.**
   a. The Secretariat shall perform such administrative functions as deemed necessary by the Board of Guarantors for subsidiary organs of the Council.
   b. The Secretary-General shall supervise his staff in the performance of the functions of the Secretariat.

Article 8

The Military Staff Committee

1. **Composition.**
   a. The Military Staff Committee shall consist of six members (with the rank of general), one each from the High Contracting Parties.
   b. The two members, one each from the ROK and the DPRK, shall be replaced with one member from the All-Korean Youths Commonwealth after the two Korean Governments have transferred their sovereignty to the Commonwealth.
   c. Neither of the two members from the two Koreas may participate in the Committee deliberations which is considering sanctions against his own government.
2. **Functions.**
   a. The Military Staff Committee shall command the security forces of the All-Korean Youths Commonwealth in order to defend and protect the independence and neutrality thereof.
   b. It shall be responsible for directing the security forces of the Commonwealth to carry out the compulsory military measures sanctioned by the Directorate of Guarantors for the defense of the Commonwealth.
   c. To further the peaceful reunification of Korea, the Military Staff

Committee shall command the Allied Peace-Keeping forces, which will be composed of soldiers from the Six Contracting Parties, in order to assist the security forces of the commonwealth to defend its independence and territorial integrity.

Article 9

Neutral Nations Peace Observation Commission

1. **Composition**. It shall be composed of four senior officers (with the rank of general), one each from Switzerland, Czechoslovakia, Sweden, and Poland—the members of the current Neutral Nations Supervisory Commission established by the Korean Armistice Agreement—plus one officer from India.
2. **Functions**.
   a. It shall undertake services of public information and public relations with a view to preventing the territorial violation of the ROK, the DPRK, or the Commonwealth and for the purpose of guaranteeing mutual nonaggression among the three parts of Korea.
   b. It shall have full authority to observe, investigate, and verify whether or not the territories of the three parts of Korea have been violated by firing of arms or introducing weapons and armed personnel into the territories thereof.
   c. Upon receiving allegations and reports of violating the borders and mutual nonaggression, it shall undertake investigations immediately.
   d. It may recommend peaceful resolutions to the parties concerned or, if necessary, appeal to the International Tribunal.
   e. It shall report regularly to the Board of Guarantors on its work.

Chapter 3: Expenditures

Article 10

Sharing Administration Costs

The expenses needed for the operation of the Council on International Guarantee of Peaceful Korean Reunification, including all its subsidiary organs, shall be borne equally by the High Contracting Parties.

Article 11

Budget

The Board of Guarantors of the Council shall consider and approve the budget, and the Secretariat shall be responsible for its appropriation.

Chapter 4 : Miscellaneous Provisions

Article 12

Abrogation of the Korean Armistice Agreement

The High Contracting Parties agree that the Korean Armistice Agreement of July 27, 1953, concluded between the Commander-in-Chief of United Nations Command, on the one hand, and the Supreme Commander of the Korean People's Army and the Commander of the Chinese People's Volunteers, on the other hand, will be completely abrogated by a resolution of the Board of Guarantors of the Council within three years after the present Treaty has entered into force.

Article 13

Withdrawal of Foreign Troops

The High Contracting Parties, except the ROK and the DPRK, shall, in accordance with the directions which will be specified by the Board of Guarantors of the Council, withdraw all their troops and military personnel, military bases, and installations of any kind from the ROK and the DPRK within five years after the present Treaty has entered into force. They also agree that they will never again introduce their troops into any region of the Korean peninsula without a mandate or sanction from the Board of Guarantors of the Council.

Article 14

All the High Contracting Parties agree that they will abrogate all the military treaties and mutual military assistance agreements concluded either with the ROK or the DPRK within five years after the present Treaty has entered into force.

Article 15

Entry into Force

This Treaty shall be ratified by all the High Contracting Parties in accordance with their respective constitutional processes and shall enter into force when the instruments of ratification thereof have been deposited with the Secretariat of the United Nations and have been officially promulgated to the world.

Article 16

Amendments and the Date of Expiration

Amendments to this Treaty shall be made only by the unanimity of all the signatories. This Treaty shall remain in force for thirty years after the date of its promulgation.

Article 17

This Treaty is written in Korean, English, Russian, Chinese, and Japanese. All of the five texts are equally authentic. In case of conflicts of meaning and interpretation, the Korean version shall be followed.

In witness whereof, the undersigned plenipotentiaries have signed this Treaty,

Done at Panmunjom on (date) in six originals in five languages.

For the Republic of Korea

For the Democratic People's Republic of Korea

For the United States of America

For the Union of Soviet Socialist Republics

For the People's Republic of China

For Japan

Notes

1. Se-Jin Kim, ed., *Korean Unification: Source Materials with an Introduction* (Seoul: Research Center for Peace and Unification, 1976), 252–54.
2. Sang-Woo Rhee, "North Korea's Unification Strategy: Review of Military Strategy," in Young Hoon Kang and Yong Soom Yim, eds., *Politics of Korean Reunification* (Seoul: Research Center for Peace and Unification, 1978), 136.
3. Se-Jim Kim, *Korean Unification.*, 255.
4. Ibid., 271–72.
5. For the text, see ibid., 303–04.
6. For Kim's proposal see ibid., 311–14.
7. Ibid., 315–16.
8. This statement was made on August 6, 1971, in a speech honoring the visit of Norodom Sihanouk. B.C. Koh, "North Korea: A Breakthrough in the Quest for Unity," in *Asian Survey*, 13 (January 1973), 83. Prior to this statement Kim Il Sung and his spokesman had repeatedly claimed that the Park government in the South was a "fascist regime," totally repressive and controlling its people through sheer force. They had insisted that they would negotiate with anyone except Park— inviting an overthrow of the South Korean president.
9. Se-Jim Kim, *Korean Unification*, 319–20.
10. Ibid., 340–45.
11. Rimm-Sup Shinn, "North Korean Policy Toward South Korea," in Young C. Kim, ed., *Major Powers and Korea* (Silver Spring, MD: Research Institute on Korean Affairs, 1972), 87.
12. Se-Jin Kim, *Korean Unification.*, 190–91.
13. Kim Il Sung, *Report to the Sixth Congress of the Workers' Party of Korea on the Work of the Central Committee* (Pyongyang: Foreign Languages Publishing House, 1980), 59–81.
14. *South-North Dialogue in Korea*, No. 028 (Seoul: International Cultural Society of Korea, March 1982), 8–11.
15. Ibid., 70–72.
16. For the full text of Roh's declaration, see *Korea Times*, Chicago, July 7, 1988, 1.
17. Ibid., July 9, 1988, 1.
18. Cyril E. Black, Richard A. Folk, Klaus Knorr, and Oran R. Young, *Neutralization and World Politics* (Princeton: Princeton University Press, 1968), xi.
19. Ibid., 66.
20. Ibid., v–vi.
21. Ibid., xv.
22. Ibid., 67.
23. I am indebted to Professor Nack Joong Kim in Seoul, Korea, for drafting this model treaty and especially for the innovative idea of an

All Korea Youths Commonwealth as a prototype of a unified Korea.
24. "North-South Relations on the Korean Peninsula," Hearing before the Subcommittee on Asian and Pacific Affairs of the Committee on Foreign Affairs, House of Representatives, 98th Congress, Second Session, March 20, 1984, 8.
25. Ralph N. Clough, *Embattled Korea: The Rivalry for International Support* (Boulder, CO: Westview Press, 1987), 383.
26. U.S. Department of State, *Foreign Relations of the United States, 1952–1954*, vol. 15, Korea (Washington, D.C.: Government Printing Office, 1984), part 2, 1156ff.
27. Ibid., 1180-83.
28. John Foster Dulles, "The Cost of Peace," Department of State Bulletin, vol. 34 (June 18, 1956), 999–1000.
29. Selig S. Harrison, "Conversation in Pyongyang—North Korea Floats a Revolutionary Ideology: Realism," *New York Times*, November 22, 1987, E4.
30. Ibid.
31. Ibid.
32. *Korean Herald*, October 3, 1987, 1.
33. I have also collaborated with Professor Kim on this model draft treaty.
34. *Christian Science Monitor*, June 28, 1988, 6.
35. *Korea Times*, Chicago, June 25, 1988, 1.
36. For President Roh's UN Proposal see *Korea News Review*, October 22, 1988, 4–6.

Glossary

Personal and proper names are listed under their customary spellings in the United States literature, with the family name first. A comma after the family name indicates that it appeared last in common use. The standard romanizations, according to the McCune-Reischauer system, are given in parentheses if they are different from the customary spellings; alternative spellings are also indicated in parentheses.

Anti-Americanism: political views within a country seeking to end American influence in that country and reduce substantially the country's range of contacts and ties with the United States.

Body politic: the combination of governmental and private institutions and public opinion which influence and determine public policy.

Burden-sharing: the distribution of financial and other responsibilities related to the common defense between allies.

Chang Myon (John M. Chang): Prominent Catholic layman and opposition political leader in South Korea; prime minister, 1960–1961.

Cheju Island: Island and province about 80 miles south of the Korean peninsula; in revolt against the central government 1946–1949.

Cho Bong Am (Cho Pong-am): Korean nationalist leader, at one time a member of the Korean Communist party, named as Syngman Rhee's first minister of agriculture. In 1956 he won a large minority of the vote as the Progressive party candidate for president of South Korea. He was subsequently tried for treason and executed in 1959.

Choi Kyu Han (Ch'oe Kyu-ha): Career civil servant and diplomat who was named prime minister by Park Chung Hee; he became acting president upon the assassination of President Park. Subsequently elected president by the electoral college in his own right, he resigned in August 1980.

Chough Pyong Ok (Cho Pyong-ok): Conservative opposition leader, prominent among organizers of the Han'guk Democratic party, and head of the South Korean police under the United States military government. Minister of home affairs during the early days of the Korean War, Chough was arrested in 1952 for his role in the constitutional crisis that year. He was the Democratic party presidential candidate in 1960 but died during the campaign.

Chun Doo Hwan (Chon Tu-hwan): Career South Korean military officer who, as commander of the Defense Security Command (the military intelligence command), seized control of the armed forces following the assassination of President Park Chung Hee and subsequently took control of the government. He was elected president under the constitution of the Fourth Republic in August 1980 and elected again under the new constitution of the Fifth Republic in 1981 to a non-renewable seven-year term. Keeping his pledge to step down upon completion of his term, he became the first Korean chief of state to relinquish authority to a successor in accordance with law.

Combined Forces Command: the joint military command of the United States and South Korea.

Confederation: Webster's New International Dictionary defines a confederation as "a body of independent states more or less permanently joined together for joint action in matters, especially in foreign affairs, which affect them in common." However, in the "Confederal Republic of Koryo" proposed by North Korea, the North and South would not be independent states but rather "autonomous regions" that would be "supervised" by the confederal government.

Confucian: Pertaining to a philosophy and social structure which originated with Confucius, the great Chinese philosopher of the sixth century B.C., and was interpreted and systematized by subsequent thinkers—notably Mencius and Chu Hsi. The Confucian tradition, which guided Chinese politics and society for over 2000 years, spread to other nearby countries and influenced their political and social structure as well as their relations with China. A recognized set of writings, attributed to Confucius or his disciples or authenticated by them, constituted the "Confucian classics," which had to be learned by all intellectuals and candidates for official position.

Constituent assembly: A body established (usually by popular election of its members) to constitute a government.

"Cross-recognition": A concept advanced by the United States in which American recognition of North Korea would be contingent upon parallel recognition of the South by the Soviet Union and China.

Democratization: a process of political change leading from an authoritarian or dictatorial system to a system modeled on Western democratic systems.

Democratic party: English translation of *minjudang*, the name of the principal conservative opposition party from 1955 to 1961. The core of this party was the former Han'guk Democratic party, organized in 1945, which became the Democratic Nationalist party in 1949.

Democratic Republican party (*minju konghwadang*): Party organized in 1963 by Kim Jong Pil to mobilize support for Park Chung Hee in the elections which civilianized the military government. The party was disbanded in mid-1980, along with all other political parties, but re-emerged as the Korean Nationalist party and most recently, in 1988—again under Kim Jong Pil's leadership—as the New Democratic Republican party, with 35 seats in the National Assembly.

Dependency theory: a set of beliefs emphasizing American and other Western control over the economies of developing countries and the outside suppression of national economic aspirations.

Diet: English term for the Japanese national legislature, created by the Japanese constitution of 1889 as a two-house body somewhat similar to Parliament in Great Britain.

Direct popular election: Election in which individual voters cast ballots for individual candidates by name.

Electoral college: A group of persons elected for the purpose of choosing one or more officials. Those so elected may meet separately in several political units, such as provinces or states, to cast their ballots.

Eligible population: The number of people legally entitled to vote. For the 1948 South Korea elections, the minimum age was set at twenty years, disqualifying those who were younger; this rule has since remained in place. Convicted felons and incompetents have also been disqualified.

Guam Doctrine: Statement by President Nixon in 1969 of United States policy to support democratic nationalist struggles logistically, to the extent they proved themselves worthy, but without supplying United States troops.

Han'guk Democratic party (*han'guk minjudang*): A conservative nationalist party organized in 1945, prior to the establishment of the United States military government, to oppose the socialistically-oriented Preparatory Committee for Korean Independence that had emerged at the end of the Japanese occupation. Many of the Han'guk Democratic party leaders were senior officials of the United States military government. Although the party has gone through many transformations and changes of name, it has been the nucleus of the conservative opposition throughout the history of the Republic of Korea.

Huh Chung (Ho Chong): Senior Korean nationalist leader, initially a supporter of Syngman Rhee, briefly prime minister during the Korean War. Recalled to public life as mayor of Seoul in 1959, he then became foreign minister. As senior cabinet member, he became acting president when Rhee resigned and presided over an effective interim government which oversaw the transition to the Second Republic.

Independence Club: A reform group organized by Philip Jaisohn (So Chae-p'il), an early Korean modernizer who returned to Korea in 1895 from a medical career in the United States. The organization for, among other things, a constitutional monarchy and organization of a legislature to represent the people. It published Korea's first daily newspaper, *The Independent.* When the Independence Club began to lead popular demonstrations in support of its platform, the conservative forces at court disbanded it and imprisoned its leaders in 1897.

Indirect election: Election of officials by representatives of the people, such as an electoral college or a legislature.

Joint ventures: Economic enterprises, especially in manufacturing and commerce, in which private or government partners in the host country share in ownership and in some cases management on agreed terms with foreign collaborators in order to obtain investment capital, technology and export outlets.

Kim Dae Jung (Kim Tae-chung): Longtime opposition leader and National Assembly member from South Cholla Province in southwest Korea, whose rivalry with Kim Young Sam thus has regional as well as ideological and personal dimensions. Kim Dae Jung nearly won the presidential election of 1971 against Park Chung Hee; he was kidnapped from a Tokyo hotel room in 1973 and nearly dumped into the sea but was imprisoned instead for most subsequent years until 1983, when he was permitted to go to the United States for medical treatment. Returning to South Korea in 1985, he joined Kim Young Sam in organizing a new opposition party which scored surprising success in that year's legislative elections. The two men soon disagreed again, however; their New Korean Democratic party split, with Kim Dae Jung heading a new Reunification Democratic party, holding the second largest bloc of legislative seats.

Kim Jong Pil (Kim Chong-p'il): Military officer, forced to resign as lieutenant colonel in 1960 for demanding changes in army leadership, who became associated with General Park Chung Hee and is regarded as architect of the 1961 military *coup d'état.* Kim subsequently served as head of the Korean Central Intelligence Agency, as chairman of the Democratic Republic party, and—several years later—as prime minister under President Park. Barred from political activity for several years after 1980, he returned to politics and ran for president of South Korea in 1988 as the candidate of the New Democratic Republican party, which he now heads and represents in the National Assembly.

Kim Young Sam (Kim Yong-sam): Longtime conservative opposition leader and National Assembly member from South Kyongsang province, whose expulsion from the Assembly in 1979 for criticism of President Park's policies was one factor in the unrest that led to Park's assassination. Mr. Kim vied with the other major opposition leader, Kim Dae Jung, for primacy in 1980 until martial law was declared and again in the period prior to the presidential election of 1988. He now leads the Democratic Reunification party with the third-largest number of Assembly seats.

Korean Interim Legislative Assembly: A ninety-member body established in January 1947 through elections in 1946 for 45 members and appointment of another 45 by the United States military governor.

Korean War: A conflict begun by North Korea on June 25, 1950, with the support of the Soviet Union, in an attempt to reunify Korea under communist leadership. The attempt would have succeeded had it not been for a reversal of United States policy which brought the United States and fifteen other United Nations members' forces to the defense of South Korea. Following a North Korea defeat, UN forces moved into North Korea; Chinese forces then came to North Korea's aid, pushing the UN forces back. After two years of negotiation and bloody positional warfare, an armistice was declared on July 27, 1953, which has remained in effect ever since; the war has never officially ended.

Korean Provisional Government: An organization established by Korean nationalists following the forcible suppression by the Japanese of a nationwide independence demonstration on March 1, 1919. the Provisional Government operated in exile in Shanghai (later Chungking), China, until 1945, when its leaders were allowed to return to Korea as individuals; it thereupon ceased to exist as an organized group.

Kwangju uprising: A student revolt in the southwestern city of Kwangju, capital of South Cholla Province, in May 1980, to demand greater political freedom and protest martial law. Brutal suppression by South Korean army special forces led to a citizen revolt, which was put down by regular army troops. Total loss of life was officially put at 193 but is generally believed to have been considerably higher.

Lee, Ki Poong (Yi Ki-pung): United States-educated long-time associate of Syngman Rhee, chosen by Rhee to be leader of the government's Liberal party in 1954. Lee was mayor of Seoul, speaker of the National Assembly, unsuccessful candidate for vice-president in 1956, and vice-presidential candidate again in 1960. Following the fraudulent 1960 election, Lee perished with his entire family in an apparent suicide pact.

Local councils: Elective local legislative bodies at township, city, and provincial levels, with severely limited powers of legislation and taxation. Such councils existed under the Japanese colonial government from 1921 to 1945 and in South Korea from 1952 to 1961.

Mandate of Heaven: In the Confucian tradition, the right and responsibility to rule humankind and to maintain order and harmony among them as a part of the order of the larger universe. The Mandate was conferred by Heaven upon the Chinese emperor and passed on by inheritance to his descendants.

National Assembly: The English translation of *kukhoe*, the name of the South Korean national legislature (which has consisted of one house only, except in 1960–1961, when there was an upper House of Councilors).

Neither confirm nor deny policy: the American policy of not discussing whether nuclear weapons are aboard American ships and planes or located at U.S. military bases.

Park Chung Hee (Pak Chong-hui): Career South Korean military officer who as an army major-general led the military *coup d'état* on May 16, 1961, that overthrew the Second Republic of Chang Myon. Elected president after his retirement from the army, Park was reelected four times; he was assassinated in 1979.

Plurality: The largest number of votes obtained by any one candidate or party in an election. In elections involving more than two candidates or parties, a plurality may be less than a majority.

Political pluralism: an environment within a country in which people can organize freely with the aim of influencing public policies.

Polity: A group of people—typically, a nation—accepting a single political and social order and leadership.

Proportional representation: Form of election in which two or more political parties present slates of candidates for legislative seats representing an entire nation or district. The seats are then awarded to persons on the party slates in numbers proportional to the percentages of votes received by each of the parties.

Pusan: South Korea's second-largest city, a port in the southeast, and a major center of the so-called Yongnam or southeast region (comprising North and South Kyongsang Provinces)—home of many South Korean government leaders since 1961 and home also of opposition leader Kim Young Sam.

Referendum: A popular vote on an issue referred to the public on a political question such as the approval of a constitution, a law, or a bond issue or tax levy.

Rhee, Syngman (Yi Sung-man): Prominent Korean nationalist leader, relative of the Korean royal family, educated in American missionary schools in Korea and United States universities. Rhee was active in the reformist Independence Club movement of 1897, was imprisoned for several years as a result, and then became a spokesman for the Korean nationalist cause in the United States. He was briefly president of the Korean Provisional Government in exile in China when it was established in 1919, but spent most of his time working for the Korean cause in the United States and Europe until 1945, when he returned to his homeland in triumph and became South Korea's first president, 1948 to 1960. The political upheaval that year led to his exile to Hawaii, where he died.

Roh Tae Woo (No T'ae-u): President of the Republic of Korea (South Korea) elected December 1988 for non-renewable five-year term. Career military officer, classmate of former President Chun Doo Hwan; after retirement as major general in 1981, served in several cabinet posts under President Chun and was chairman of the government political party (Democratic Justice party) when nominated to the presidency in June 1988.

Sin Ik-hui (P.H. Shinicky): Nationalist leader associated with the Korean Provisional Government in exile. After returning to Korea following its liberation from Japan, Sin worked with Syngman Rhee for a time but in 1949 joined with the opposition Han'guk Democratic party to form the Democratic Nationalist party. He was speaker of the South Korean National Assembly, 1948–1954. As opposition presidential candidate in 1956, Sin drew widespread popular support but died during the campaign.

Special relationship: an extraordinarily close relationship between two nations, based on intimate historical experience and wide-ranging contemporary political, military, and economic bonds.

Student Revolution: A massive demonstration and uprising of Korean university and high-school students in April 1960 protesting the blatant irregularities of the 1960 presidential election. Initially peaceful, the demonstration was turned into a bloodbath when guards at the presidential residence fired point-blank into the massed students, killing nearly 200. With the mass popular support that resulted, the students forced the resignation of Syngman Rhee and a complete change of government.

United States Army Military Government in Korea (USAMGIK): Organization set up by the U.S. Army to administer the United States occupation zone of Korea until the establishment of a Korean government and deactivated upon inauguration of the Republic of Korea in 1948. It was commanded by a United States military governor, who was subordinate to the commanding general, U.S. Army XXIV Corps (Lieutenant General John R. Hodge).

"Vertical" and "horizontal" economic relations: North Korea believes that the "uniform development" of North and South would contribute to the achievement of unification. Thus, it opposes what it calls "vertical" economic relations based on the dependence of one side on the other (e.g., the South purchasing raw materials from the North for its industries, while the North relies on the South's manufactured products). In "horizontal" interchange, raw materials could be exchanged for raw materials, or each side, using its own equipment, could develop raw materials in the other's territory.

Yun, Bo Sun (Yun Po-son): Edinburgh-educated, aristocratic leading member of the Han'guk Democratic party. Minister of commerce in the late 1940s, Yun served several terms in the National Assembly. As leader of the "old faction" of the opposition Democratic party, Yun was elected president of the Second Republic by the National Assembly in 1960 and continued to serve in that capacity after the military coup d'état as a figleaf of the government's international legitimacy. He won a large majority of votes against Park Chung Hee in the presidential election of 1963.

Yushin: Literally, "renovation," the term applied to the sternly autocratic Fourth Republic of South Korea, 1972–1980, and to its constitution.

Contributors

Ilpyong J. Kim Professor of Political Science, University of Connecticut.

Gari Ledyard Professor, Department of East Asian Languages & Cultures, Columbia University

William H. Brinker Professor of History, Tennessee Technological University

John Merrill Bureau of Intelligence and Research, Department of State

Donald S. Macdonald Research Professor of Korean Studies, Georgetown University

Larry A. Niksch Specialist in Asian Affairs, Library of Congress

Paul W. Kuznets Professor of Economics, Indiana University

Pong S. Lee Professor, Department of Economics, State University of New York at Albany

Young Whan Kihl Professor of Political Science, Iowa State University

David I. Steinberg Consultant, Distinguished Professor of Korean Studies, School of Foreign Service, Georgetown University

Bertrand Renaud Housing Financial Adviser, The World Bank

Jack E. Thomas USAF (ret.) Former Assistant Chief of Staff, Intelligence, USAF

Selig S. Harrison Senior Associate, Carnegie Endowment of International Peace, Washington, D.C.

Kyongsoo Lho Assistant Professor of History, Fellow, CISAC, Stanford University

Yuri I. Ognev Senior Research Associate, Institute of Far Eastern Studies U.S.S.R. Academy of Sciences

Yang Li-wen Professor of History, Peking University

Edward A. Olsen Professor of Asian Studies, the Naval Post graduate School, Monterey, CA

W. Wayne Shannon Director of MPO Program, Professor of Political Science, University of Connecticut

Eui Hang Shin Professor of Sociology, University of South Carolina

Daeshik Cho Foreign Service officer with the Ministry of Foreign Affairs

Sung Moon Pae Chairman, Behavioral and Social Sciences, Bellevue College

Mikhail L. Titarenko Director, Institute of Far Eastern Studies, U.S.S.R. Academy of Sciences

R.G. Stilwell General UA Army, Retired, President: Stilwell Associates, Inc.

Stephen J. Solarz Congressman (D-Calif.), U.S. House of Representatives

In Kwan Hwang Director, Institute of International Studies, Bradley University

Hong Nack Kim Professor, Department of Political Science, West Virginia University

Index